ADVISORY EDITOR

Edwin S. Gaustad

Religion in

WOMAN AND TEMPERANCE

OR,

THE WORK AND WORKERS

OF

The Woman's Christian Temperance Union

By FRANCES E. WILLARD

ARNO PRESS

A NEW YORK TIMES COMPANY

New York • 1972

Reprint Edition 1972 by Arno Press Inc.

Reprinted from a copy in
The Wesleyan University Library

RELIGION IN AMERICA - Series II
ISBN for complete set: 0-405-04050-4
See last pages of this volume for titles.

Manufactured in the United States of America

Publisher's Note: Pagination was irregular
(skipped from pages 296 to 299) in all available
copies; text appears to be complete.

Library of Congress Cataloging in Publication Data

Willard, Frances Elizabeth, 1839-1898.
    Woman and temperance.

    (Religion in America, series II)
    1. Woman's Christian Temperance Union.
2. Temperance. I. Title.
HV5227.W6W5 1972   178'.1   74-38443
ISBN 0-405-04093-8

WOMAN AND TEMPERANCE

Frances E. Willard.

WOMAN AND TEMPERANCE:

OR,

THE WORK AND WORKERS

OF

THE WOMAN'S CHRISTIAN TEMPERANCE UNION.

BY FRANCES E. WILLARD.

PRESIDENT OF THE NATIONAL W. C. T. U.

"O WOMAN, GREAT IS THY FAITH! BE IT UNTO THEE EVEN AS THOU WILT."—*Words of Christ.*

PUBLISHED BY

PARK PUBLISHING CO.

HARTFORD, CONN.

J. S. GOODMAN & CO., CHICAGO, ILLS.; W. E. BLISS,
DES MOINES, IOWA; WALKER & DAIGNEAU
BATTLE CREEK, MICH.

In Loving and Loyal Recognition and Remembrance
THIS BOOK IS DEDICATED
TO THE MEMORY OF MY GENEROUS BENEFACTOR,
THE LATE JAMES JACKSON, OF PATERSON, N. J.,
AND TO HIS DAUGHTER AND MY TRUE FRIEND,
KATE A. JACKSON,
TO WHOSE MUNIFICENCE I OWE EVERY ADVANTAGE OF THE
YEARS I SPENT ABROAD.

PREFACE.

This book is a collection of " Field Notes," roughly jotted down by one whose rapid transit left no choice of style or method. It has been put together under difficulties, which, could they be known, would go far toward excusing its defects. The publisher's wish, to present some of the author's addresses and personal observations of the work, has antagonized her preference to devote these pages entirely to showing forth the deeds of her beloved coadjutors. Under these difficult conditions, the attempt to compromise has met the moderate success herein exhibited. Our work has grown so greatly that its would-be veracious chronicler is well nigh bewildered by the *embarras de richesse*, for the choice names omitted so far exceed in number those referred to that there is no satisfaction in the final result. My table is crowded with collected notes of our work and workers, which must be reserved until some future day. But there is this consolation : the women to whom I have written for " some account of their life and works " have not, as a general rule, replied at all, and when they have done so the words " too busy toiling to tell what has been wrought " have recurred so frequently that the names " conspicuous for their absence " belong to those who will account themselves most fortunate. But, with all its faults, this birds-eye view, giving some notion of about fifty leaders, among the two hundred and fifty worthy to be introduced, will have a certain value as a record of events, and will, let us hope, be useful as an exponent of the aims and

methods of a temperance society, concerning which John
B. Gough said, what we would not have dared to claim
ourselves, that " it is doing more for the temperance cause
to-day than all others combined."

F. E. W.

" REST COTTAGE," EVANSTON, ILL., March 7, 1883.

*** Some of the sketches that follow were written for
the *Independent, The Christian Union, Our Union, The
Signal,* etc., and have been transferred by editorial permission.

ILLUSTRATIONS

CONTENTS.

CHAPTER I.

FRANCES E. WILLARD.

CHAPTER II.

PRELIMINARY.

CHAPTER III.

"W. C. T. U."

CHAPTER IV.

"LET IT BE NOTED";

CHAPTER V.

THE FIRST CRUSADERS.

CHAPTER VI.

"MOTHER STEWART."

CHAPTER VII.

MRS. ABBY FISHER LEAVITT.

CHAPTER VIII.

MRS. MARY A. WOODBRIDGE.

CHAPTER IX.

"THE SOBER SECOND THOUGHT OF THE CRUSADE."

CHAPTER X.

THE WOMAN'S NATIONAL TEMPERANCE CONVENTION FOUNDED AT CLEVELAND, O.

CHAPTER XVIII.

W. C. T. U. WORK FOR THE HOME.

CHAPTER XIX.

THE W. C. T. U. IN SOCIETY.

CHAPTER XX.

THE W. C. T. U. IN THE GOVERNMENT.

CHAPTER XXI.

MRS. MARY A. LIVERMORE,

Our Chief Speaker, and President of the Massachusetts W. C. T. U.

CHAPTER XXII.

CAROLINE BROWN BUELL,

Corresponding Secretary National W. C. T. U.

CHAPTER XXIII.

MY FIRST HOME PROTECTION ADDRESS.

CHAPTER XXIV.

WOMEN'S BRIGHT WORDS.

CHAPTER XXV.

MRS. ZERELDA G. WALLACE, OF INDIANA.

CHAPTER XXVI.

"PERSONAL LIBERTY."

CHAPTER XXVII.

THE MODOCS OF THE LÀVA BEDS IN THE INDIAN TERRITORY.

CHAPTER XXVIII.

MRS. L. M. N. STEVENS OF MAINE.—MRS. F. A. BENT, WITH HER GOLDEN CORNET.

CHAPTER XXIX.

LIFE AND WORK OF JULIA COLMAN.

Superintendent of the Literature Department of the National W. C. T. U.

CHAPTER XXX.

OUR JOURNALISTS.

CONTENTS. **15**

CHAPTER XXXI.

OUR SOUTHERN ALLIES.

CHAPTER XXXII.

GLIMPSES OF THE WOMEN AT WORK.

CHAPTER XXXIII.

THE CANADIAN LEADERS.

CHAPTER XXXIV.

THE CHILDREN.

CHAPTER XXXV.

HOW TO ORGANIZE A W. C. T. U.

APPENDIX.

A CARD.

We, the undersigned, representing as we do the fifty thousand women belonging to our National W. C. T. U. all over these United States, desire to make a statement of facts.

When we found that the publishers of this book wished our National President, Miss Frances E. Willard, to be its author, we at once realized the delicate position in which she was placed as regarded her personal share in our work, and we determined to take that matter into our own hands. We felt that the story of the work would be utterly incomplete without the story of one of the chief workers, and we also felt that it must be told fully and truly from our standpoint or not at all. We therefore secured the services of our gifted Mary A. Lathbury to prepare this sketch, and are ourselves reponsible for it in every particular, Miss Willard not having seen its contents until it was in print. The book is altogether hers, but this chapter is ours and ours alone.

MRS. MARY A. WOODBRIDGE,	MRS. Z. G. WALLACE,
Rec. Secretary National W. C. T. U.	President Indiana W. C. T. U.
MRS. L. M. N. STEVENS,	MRS. MARY T. BURT,
Assistant Recording Secretary.	President New York W. C. T. U.
MISS ESTHER PUGH,	MRS. J. E. FOSTER,
Treasurer.	Superintendent of Legislative Dep't.
MRS. SALLIE F. CHAPIN,	MRS. T. B. CARSE,
Superintendent Southern Work.	Pres. W. T. P. Association, Chicago.

MRS. HANNAH WHITALL SMITH,
Superintendent Evangelistic Dep't.

FRANCES E. WILLARD,

OF ILLINOIS.

BY MARY A. LATHBURY,

Author of "Out of Darkness into Light," etc.

Ancestry and birth—Character of parents—Early life—Travel and life abroad—The "Human Question"—Elected President of Woman's College—The Teacher—Character and methods—Introduction to the public—Impressions of a journalist—Character and aims—Call to the temperance work—Earlier work—Gospel work—Journalism—Birth of "Home Protection"—The great petition—Elected to the presidency of the National W. C. T. U.—Work—Incidents—Southern tours—Character as a woman—As a leader of women—As a type.

"HE shall be like a tree," sang the Psalmist of the coming man, the highest type of the race. Why *all* men are not of New England elms, or California pines, may be accounted for, perhaps, but for the fact that there are so few "large" women in these days, who shall account? The tree that lifts its fearless face to heaven, spreads its arms to the four quarters of the earth, and sends its roots to feed from a hundred secret springs, was never grown in a box, nor cut by conventional pruning-knives. This mental and moral "largeness" is as distinctly the birthright of women as of men; but the former have, as a class, been dwarfed in the training. Some have risen to exceptional moral height, with little lateral increase, while others have put forth root or branch in the one direction open to free growth.

It is probable that Frances E. Willard came into her inheritance, in part, through fortunate parentage, for she

(19)

is sprung from that strong New England stock which, when transplanted into Western soil, often finds the best conditions of growth.

Major Simon Willard, who traced his line of descent to the time of the Conquest, came to America early in the seventeenth century. The ancestor of Senator Hoar and Major Willard, with a few others, founded Concord, Mass., the literary centre of New England. One of the Willards was president of Harvard University, and his son vice-president. One was pastor of the old South Church, and another the architect of Bunker Hill Monument. Miss Willard's grandfather (who was a grandson of Major Simon aforesaid) was pastor of one church, at Dublin, near Keene, N. H., forty years, and was a chaplain throughout the Revolutionary War. Mrs. Emma Willard, the distinguished educator of Troy, N. Y., is of the family, which through its generations, has thrown its activities largely into education, politics, and the pulpit. The family motto is " *Gaudet patentia duris*" (patience rejoices in hardships), and the family name, Willard, means " one who wills."

Miss Willard's mother was of excellent New England parentage. Her maiden name was Mary Thompson Hill, and she is closely related to the Clements, being a cousin of Rev. Dr. Jonathan Clement, of blessed memory in the Congregational annals of New England. Both parents were natives of Caledonia County, Vermont, removing early to Western New York, where their third daughter, Frances Elizabeth, was born, in Churchville, near Rochester. When she was three years of age the family removed to Oberlin, O., where for five years both parents devoted themselves to study (although both had been teachers), and then removed to Wisconsin. As " brain and brawn " were wisely used in the development of his large farm near Janesville, J. F. Willard soon became a leader in movements tending toward the development of the State. His farm was known to be the field of successful experiments, receiving premiums at the annual fairs, and he was appointed president of the State agricultural and horticultural societies. He was also prominent in politics for years, and a member of the State Legislature.

Mrs. Willard was a woman of grand ideas and aspirations, which were only to be wrought out indirectly through her children. As her daughter once said of her: "My mother held that nature's standard ought to be restored, and that the measure of each human being's endowment was the only reasonable measure of that human being's sphere. She had small patience with artificial diagrams placed before women by the dictum of society, in which the boundaries of their especial 'sphere' were marked out for them, and one of her favorite phrases was, 'Let a girl grow as a tree grows—according to its own sweet will.'"

"She looked at the mysteries of human progress from the angle of vision made by the eye of both the man and the woman, and foresaw that the mingling of justice and mercy in the great decisions that affect society would give deliverance from political corruption and governmental one-sidedness."

During the years between eight and eighteen the child Frances grew in the free air, with leagues of prairie around her, her only companions her brother and sister; her books few, including no novels; her teachers a wise and gifted mother, and a bright, talented governess— Miss Annie R. Burdick—to whom she was devotedly attached. Education—not described by text-books and departments—was her daily food and inspiration, and was brought to the children through a thousand avenues that only a mother, with the divine intuitive gift that

Froebel had, could have opened. There were "sermons in stones, books in the running brooks." The world's work was reproduced in miniature in the little household, that the children might learn to take part in it. They had a board of public works, an art club, and a news-paper, edited by Frances, who also wrote a novel of four hundred pages which has never seen the light. Poems were written—a home-republic was formed, and the children trod their little world with the free step and the abandon that helped them to conquer it in after life. One took in life too largely for her early strength, and died at nineteen, and another fell in the midst of the work he began as a boy-journalist. The other, with a strength that is almost miraculous, lives to fulfill the unique destiny she always saw before her—undefined, yet certain, when she was still a child.

At eighteen years of age, school-life, in the conventional sense, began. After a term at Milwaukee, in the college founded by Catherine Beecher, the family plan was changed, the farm sold, and Evanston, Ill., chosen as the home; for the parents still wisely held to the plan of combining home and school; and as a college could not come to the home, the home must go to the college. The father became a banker, of the well-known firm of Preston, Willard & Kean, Chicago. In this beautiful suburban town the pretty cottage was built, which to mother and daughter are now sacred as the father's last gift. He died in 1868. Here the daughters graduated, and Mary, the one sister, lovely and beloved, was called into larger life—and from this point Frances Willard began to take up life with a new earnestness.

The question that, as a little child, she had taken to her father—"I don't see Christ; I don't feel Him; *where is He?*"—became the one question to be settled beyond doubt. And the fact that the beatific vision she longed

to attain proved to be a revelation of " Christ in us "—
the life of her own spirit—is the secret of her present
relation to the moral issues upon which she has laid her
hand. Some years of teaching followed in Evanston,
Pittsburg, Pa., and Lima, N. Y. While teaching in the
Female College at Pittsburg, Pa., she wrote " Nineteen
Beautiful Years," a most interesting and touching memoir
of the gifted Mary. It was published in 1864 by the
Harpers, and is a little shrine holding much of the early
life of both sisters. In 1868–70, as the guest of her
friend, Miss Kate Jackson, she journeyed through Europe
and the East.

The rare opportunities of study in Paris, Berlin, and
Rome were thoroughly improved, and nearly every Euro-
pean capital was visited. In the " College de France " and
" Petit Sorbonne " they attended the lectures of Laboulaye
and Guizot the younger, Legouvé, Châsles, Franck the
historian, Chevalier the political economist, and a score
of lesser lights. In one of a series of delightful letters,
since published by her under the general title of "A School-
mistress Abroad," we come upon this characteristic bit,
after a ramble among the relics of French royalty :

" It is good not to have been born earlier than the nineteenth century ; and, for myself, I could have rested content until the twenty-fifth, by which date I believe our·
hopeful dawn of Reason, Liberty, and Worship will have
grown to noon-day. Oh ! native land—the world's hope,
the Gospel's triumph, the Millenium's dawn ' are all with
thee, are all with thee !' "

The ladies traveled in Palestine, Egypt, Greece, and
Asia Minor, looking into foreign mission stations on their
way, sailing from Italy, and returning by the Danube.
While absent Miss Willard wrote often for home papers—
the New York *Independent, Harper's Monthly, The Christian Union,* and Chicago journals. She gathered much

material for literary work, and the experience added breadth to her sight of character and countries. Witnessing the condition of women in the East and in the greater part of Europe, she was led to a problem which has had large answer in her later life : " What can be done to make the world a wider place for women ? "

The " human question," which she often affirms is much more to her than the " woman question," began to shape itself in her mind and weigh heavily upon her heart. Jean François Millet, brooding over the burdened peasantry, who were almost on the plane of the dumb clods of the fields in which they wrought, threw upon canvass the pathetic pictures which go far toward redeeming French art and awakening the French heart. It was the " human question " which possessed him. It was this question also, reaching out for solution to the circle nearest her—her own sex—that knit the brows and dropped a shadow into the clear eyes of our young traveler all the way from Paris to the Volga, and through the East.

From that time she has been a lover of women. She saw that woman's condition has kept back civilization, as the stream does not rise higher than the spring that feeds it ; and she coveted for her countrywomen the " best gifts," to hold and to impart.

In 1871 she was elected President of the Woman's College, at Evanston, (an institution with none but women among Trustees or Faculty,) and there developed her plan of " self-government " for the students, which was watched by many with extreme interest, and is now pursued with success by several educators. On the union of the College with the University, when it became impossible to carry out her plan of government, she resigned her position.

One of her pupils during this time (now the wife of a college President) writes thus of Miss Willard in a private letter to a friend, after a graphic account of her rare work in the class-room :

" In the most important part of her work as an educator—the development of character—I can speak from the most intimate knowledge. In this I doubt if she ever had a superior, and but for Arnold of Rugby, I should have said an equal. Her power over the girls who came under her influence was most extraordinary. It is an amusing fact that some people regarded it with a mixture of wonder and fear, as something a little allied to witchcraft—an inexplicable spell not founded in reason. But she never used her personal power of winning friends for the mere purpose of gaining the friends. She never seemed to do anything from policy, nor to think whether she was " popular " or not. She was always planning for our happiness and welfare, and would go to any amount of trouble to gratify us. Then she was always reasonable. She never insisted that a thing must be simply because she had said so, but was perfectly willing to see and acknowledge it if she herself was in the wrong. Her ideals of life and character were very high, and she succeeded in inspiring her girls with a great deal of her own enthusiasm. I never, at any other period of my life, lived under such a constant, keen sense of moral responsibility, nor with such a high ideal of what I could become, as during the years in which I so proudly called myself one of ' her girls.' "

Says another, now near her in the work of life :

" Were one to ask the salient features of her work as a teacher, the reply should be: the development of individual character along intellectual and moral lines ; the revelation to her pupils of their special powers and vocation as workers, her constantly recurring question being not only ' What are you going to be in the world ?' but ' What are you going to do ?' so that, after six months under

2

her tuition, each of her scholars had a definite idea of a life-work."

From a concise report of Miss Willard's method of self-government already published, we quote:

" Practically she opened school without rules, but when an error in conduct occurred she stated it (impersonally) in chapel, submitted a rule to cover the case, and put its adoption to vote among the young ladies; and she never failed in the unanimous adoption of the rule offered, even the guilty condemning their own acts. Thus her rules became a growth that shadowed all defects, with " the consent of the governed," and were seldom violated. She did not even call them rules, but ' regulations of the code of courtesy,' the point being that to obey them was merely the courtesy of each toward all. Pupils who kept the code through a half year entered a ' Roll of Honor Society.' This was the intellectual gymnasium of the college, and was made measurably responsible for the behavior of its members, being allowed certain privileges, such as attendance upon evening lectures, etc., without special permit, but strictly upon their honor as to points of propriety; and the young lady who preserved a blame-less record in this society during one year was advanced to the ' corps of the self-governed,' having no school moni-tor but the following pledge:

" 'I promise, by God's help, so to act in respect to my conduct and habits that, if every member of this college acted in the same way, the greatest good to the greatest number would be secured.'

" Miss Willard found this system to secure not only good order, but also respectful affection for teachers, and to develop in her pupils a womanly self-respect and dig-nity of character."

About two thousand pupils have been under her instruc-tion in the different colleges in which she taught.

There was apparently more of accident than design in Miss Willard's introduction to the public as a speaker. While in Palestine she had visions of a new crusade which the Christian women of her country might enter upon, and the development of a new chivalry—the chivalry of justice—which gives to woman a fair chance to be all that God designed her to be. She spoke of it in a women's missionary meeting in Chicago, after her return. The next day a Methodist layman of wealth called upon her, and after urging upon her the development and use of God's gift to her—the ability to stand before assemblies "in His name"—he proposed to gather an audience for her in one of the large city churches, if she would address it. She laid the matter before her mother (blessed be the mothers who have open vision!), who said: "By all means, my child, accept; enter every open door."

She did accept, and spoke to a large audience that received her with the utmost cordiality. Several city papers reported her words, so that within two weeks she had received scores of requests to speak from all parts of the northwest.

As it was soon after this that she entered upon her work in the Women's College at Evanston, she gave herself few opportunities to speak in public gatherings ; but notwithstanding this she was ranked by many, among them an editor of the New York *Independent*, as holding the "first place among women who speak."

From an article by James Clement Ambrose, whom we have already quoted, in *Potter's American Monthly* for May, 1882, we extract the following graceful tribute to Miss Willard :

"As a public speaker, I think Miss Willard is without a peer among women. With much of the Edward Everett in her language, there is more of the Wendell Phillips in her manner of delivery. She is wholly at home, but not

forward on the platform, with grace in bearing, ease and
moderation in gesture, and in her tones there are tears
when she wills. It is the voice books call ' magnetic '—a
spell is in it to please and carry away. It is musical and
mellow, never thin, and on an exceptionally distinct
articulation, winds away to remotest listeners as sound
from the silvery bells of the Sabbath. Altogether she
wears the emphasis of gentleness under profound conviction. She never impresses her hearers as a speaker on
exhibition, yet she has not despised the use of aids, but
early in her public work took counsel of a celebrated
elocutionist, and she attributes much of her ease in
speech to her mother as a model. In her seasons of
larger leisure she has been a wide reader of the thoughtful authors. To Arnold of Rugby, Frederic W. Robertson,
and John Stuart Mill, especially in his ' Subjection of
Women,' she concedes the greatest influence over her
mind. Among women, they whose writings have done
most to mould her are Elizabeth Barrett Browning,
Margaret Fuller, and Frances Power Cobbe."

In October, 1874, a voice that had been thrilling her
strangely wherever she heard a sound of it, came to her
with a personal appeal. It was from the Woman's
Christian Temperance Union, and the invitation to work
with them was gladly accepted. She saw, with the clear
intuition which is peculiar to her, that the little " root
out of dry ground" was His promise of that which was
to cover the land with a banyan-like growth. Said she,
later: " I was reared on a western prairie, and often have
helped to kindle the great fires for which the West used
to be famous. A match and a wisp of dry grass were all
we needed, and behold the magnificent spectacle of a
prairie on fire, sweeping across the landscape, swift as a
thousand untrained steeds, and no more to be captured
than a hurricane! Just so it is with the Crusade. . . . .

When God lets loose an idea upon this planet, we vainly set limits to its progress; and I believe that Gospel Temperance shall yet transform that inmost circle, the human heart, and in its widening sweep the circle of home, and then society, and then, pushing its argument to the extreme conclusion, it shall permeate the widest circle of them all, and that is, government."

So closely identified had she become with the womanhood of our country, that the question came very distinctly to her as a representative woman, " Who knoweth if thou be come into the kingdom for such a time as this?" The old feeling of being born to a work, a "destiny," had passed over from her own personality to the sex with which she is identified, as it is now passing over to the race, the "woman question" becoming the "human question."

There is much to be written from this point which cannot be brought within the limits of this sketch. It would be an unnecessary re-writing of the history of the Woman's Temperance Movement. This seed of the kingdom, after its wonderful planting in Ohio during the winter and spring of 1873–4, was beginning to bear fruit through the Middle and Western States. In August of that year, at Chautauqua, the "birthplace of grand ideas," the Women's Christian Temperance Union was born. A convention was called for November of· the same year, at Cleveland, Ohio, and the National W. C. T. U. was then organized, with Miss Willard as Corresponding Secretary. It was at this Convention that she offered the resolution which, springing from the inspirations and the aspirations of the hour, has proved to be, in its spirit, a glory and a defence : " Realizing that our cause is combated by mighty and relentless forces, we will go forward in the strength of Him who is the Prince of Peace, meeting argument with argument, misjudgment with patience, and all our

difficulties and dangers with prayer." Her work grew
with the growth of the Union, and that growth was
largely due to the tireless pen and voice and brain of its
Corresponding Secretary.

While holding this office there occurred two episodes—
apparent digressions—which did not, however, sever her
connection with the Temperance work. In 1876-7, on
invitation from Mr. Moody, she assisted him in the Gospel
work in Boston for several months. Her hope in undertaking this enterprise was that the Temperance work
might be united with the Gospel work, and brought with
it to the front. The meetings for women, filling Berkeley
and Park Street churches, and her words before the thousands gathered in the great Tabernacle, are memorable.

Says one who lives " in the Spirit " as few women do,
" I have never been so conscious of the presence of the
Divine power, the unction of the Holy One, in the minis-
try of the Word, as under the preaching of Miss Willard."

In this connection we are tempted to quote from a published statement recently made by Miss Willard:

" The deepest thought and desire of my life would have
been met, if my dear old Mother Church had permitted
me to be a minister. The wandering life of an evangelist
or a reformer comes nearest to, but cannot fill, the ideal
which I early cherished, but did not expect ever publicly
to confess. While I heartily sympathize with the progressive movement which will ere long make ecclesiastically
true our Master's words, ' There is neither male nor female
in Christ Jesus ' ; while I steadfastly believe that there is
no place too good for a woman to occupy, and nothing too
sacred for her to do, I am not willing to go on record as
a misanthropic complainer against the church which I
prefer above my chief joy."

The second episode was in 1878, when Miss Willard
undertook a forlorn hope — the chief-editorship of the

Chicago Post, a daily evening paper, from which position her only brother, Oliver A. Willard, had been suddenly stricken down. With the generous enthusiasm and faith in the right that is a part of her, she took up the work, assisted by her brother's widow, and bravely carried it to the result long foreseen by all who knew the financial incubus that had for years been wearing out its life. But her love was larger than her strength.

Oliver Willard was an only son and brother, the pride of the family, of which no member, perhaps, was more gifted, genial, and beloved. He had the best advantages of education, and made a brilliant record as speaker, writer, and editor. His last year was the brightest of his life, for he turned to God for strength as never before, although he had known much of what Christ can do for human hearts. He conducted a Bible-class of one hundred young men, and spoke in religious and temperance meetings with remarkable power. Few have made more convincing appeals to tempted men than he did. He died in the calmness of Christian faith, saying to his beloved wife, "All your prayers for me are answered." The wife, Mrs. Mary Bannister Willard, is a rarely gifted woman, with special talent and experience in journalism. She was the dearest school friend of Miss Willard, and they are now side by side in the work of the W. C. T. U., she being the editor of the organ of the National Union,— *Our Union-Signal*, published at Chicago.

Miss Willard is the originator of the Home Protection movement. It came to her like a revelation in the spring of the centennial year, on a Sabbath morning, in Columbus, the capital of the "Crusade State." As she then and there knelt before God, it was borne in upon her spirit that the ballot in woman's hand as a weapon of "home protection," ought to be "worked for and welcomed."

She has been, from the first, some years in advance of

the times ; but with the patience characteristic of faith and foresight, she has endeavored to " slow " her steps to the pace of the more cautious and hesitant among her co-laborers, that the unity of the spirit might be kept in the bond of peace. She does not believe in the " total depravity of inanimate things," and has no fear of a vote or a ballot-box, if they can be used by men or women as a means of defence against the influx of evil. She *does* believe in the Word, which says ; " *All* things are yours." Believing that whatsoever dwarfs woman dwarfs man, she has looked with strong desire toward the day when women shall be able to speak and act for the help of humanity of both sexes ; and from advocating, as she did in the beginning of the Home Protection movement, a limited suffrage for women — local option — that should help to control the sale of liquor in their own locality, she came in August, 1881, to earnestly urge upon a convention of temperance workers at Lake Bluff complete enfranchisement, and in that gathering of representative men and women from twelve States, all identified with the temperance reform, the following plank was almost unanimously placed in the platform of the National Home Protection party, then organized :

" A political party whose platform is based on constitutional and statutory prohibition of the manufacture and sale of alcoholic beverages in the State and the nation is a necessity : and in order to give those who suffer most from the drink curse a power to protect themselves, their homes, and their loved ones, the complete enfranchisement of women should be worked for and welcomed."

At the national convention of the W. C. T. U. in Washington, two months later, this advanced position was not formally endorsed, but every State union was declared free to labor for suffrage if it chose. In the South Miss Willard has made no public allusion to this branch of temperance work, though frankly stating her opinions whenever questioned on the subject. Recognizing the right of each State to select such methods as are adapted to its sentiment, she has desired the ladies of the South to make their own free choice, and this mooted question has not come up at all.

The growth of the idea is equally marvelous. It was first projected in the form of petition in Illinois in 1879, while Miss Willard was president of the State union. It promised nothing; it only petitioned; but there was so much of promise — more of prophecy — in the whole movement, that we already seem to see the cap-stone lifted to its place " with shoutings, crying ' Grace, grace unto it ! ' "

She and her indefatigable coadjutors wrought like bees all through Illinois, and the result was a petition over two hundred and fifteen yards long and containing 180,000 names (80,000 of them voters), one of the largest petitions ever sent to any legislative body. It was placed on the calendar of the House as the " Hinds bill " (named from the Senator who presented it). Most efficient among the thousands who aided in preparing the great petition was Miss Anna Gordon of Boston — Miss Willard's private secretary — whose quiet and persistent labors have accomplished so much to increase the efficiency of her chief in the last six years of their united toil.

The bill was laid in apparent death, but the spirit of it was by no means " laid." It is seen in almost every State in the Union, and it bore a banner at the polls in Iowa in the spring of '82, where Miss Willard had spoken in thirty towns, and Mrs. J. Ellen Foster had wrought like Judith of old. Later it was publicly wedded to the Independent Prohibition Party.

The cry " For God, and Home and Native Land," which Miss Willard sent out as wings to the young Home Protection idea, has since become the motto of the National

W. C. T. U., and is fast being wrought into the fibre of a national party.

In 1879 Miss Willard was elected to the presidency of the National Union, and since that time this body of workers has expressed in a marked degree in its deliberative councils, and in the work of State and local organizations, the spirit and wisdom of its leader. Says one of her fellow-workers: " In the temperance field she is the same as in the educational; constantly developing methods of work and individual workers, so that the Woman's Christian Temperance Union has brought out nearly forty distinct departments."

As an organizer Miss Willard has no equal among our women. Her office is not only to plan work, but to be the life and inspiration of the workers. And in order to be this she not only freely uses her pen (she and her secretary wrote ten thousand letters, aside from literary work, during 1881), but is almost constantly on the wing, going at the call of the cause to plant or encourage new organizations; to confer with workers in council; to speak, at the request of leading thinkers and workers, of the moral questions of the day from a woman's point of view, and always and everywhere to give enough of herself to others to quicken the currents of life and touch new springs of activity into motion.

At the close of the Hayes administration, when that representative of the best American womanhood, Lucy Webb Hayes, retired from the White House, the women of the country, led by Miss Willard, executed a plan for placing the portrait of Mrs. Hayes in the Presidential mansion. It was painted by Huntington, at one time President of the Academy of Design, New York, and afterward engraved by Barrie, of Philadelphia. After its unveiling at a great meeting at Lincoln Hall, it was presented by Miss Willard to President Garfield in the White House, and now hangs in the Green Parlor in a carved frame executed by the ladies of the Cincinnati Academy of Design.

Miss Willard's two trips through the south in 1880–81 and 1881–82 were important steps in the only true policy of " reconstruction." In the first she was accompanied through some of the States by Mrs. Georgia Hulse McLeod of Baltimore, a cultured southern lady, who assisted in the organization of societies. In Charleston she met Mrs. Sallie F. Chapin, a lady of large influence and ability, who has since become superintendent of the southern work. At this time she organized Women's Christian Temperance Unions in Maryland, Virginia, North and South Carolina, Georgia, Florida, Alabama, Mississippi, Arkansas, Tennessee, and Kentucky, and included in the trip the Indian Territory. The second trip included points in Arkansas, and thirty towns in Texas, Louisiana, Mississippi, and several other States.

At the present writing—the close of 1882—she begins a third southern and western tour, when, if successful in carrying out her plans, she will have presented the gospel of temperance to the important towns of each State and Territory of the Union, and the provinces of Canada.

" It is a hard life," sighs somebody, reading this sketch in the sheltering home, surrounded by love and luxury. But here the words of the Lord Jesus sound strangely prophetic: "There is no man that hath left house, or brethren, or sisters, or father, or mother, or wife, or children, or lands for my sake and the gospel's, but he shall receive an hundred fold *now in this time*—houses, and brethren, and sisters, and mothers, and children, and lands, with persecutions, and in the world to come eternal life." To illustrate this comes the recollection of a late letter of invitation to visit Miss Willard in one of the rarest homes in this or any land, in which the following passage occurs: " You may feel as free as the air, for as long as Frank is here it is *her* house, and *she* is to order all its goings out and comings in."

And this is one of the thousands of homes all over our country that are hers, and the people in them are her sisters, and brethren, and fathers, and mothers, in a sense that must grow more strong and blessed forever, because the relationship and the possession is founded in the heavens.

One who knows her life thoroughly as a woman, and as a leader of women, says:

" To no one more than to Miss Willard do those words of Christ belong, ' Whosoever of you will be the chiefest shall be servant of all, for even the Son of Man came not to be ministered unto, but to minister.' They are expressed in the spirit of her life and conduct as in that of no other woman I have ever known."

And as we glance at the marginal reading of " servant of all "—" *bond-servant* "—we are reminded that the increase of service that has come to her in these last years, and her consciousness of it, has laid upon her still stronger bonds to serve, and the bondage is—love.

There are many things from this point of view which those who are nearest her in the work of life, and in the sight of the eternal verities, would be glad to have here expressed for them, for her friends feel always that the woman is larger than her work, and their love for her is far greater than their admiration for what she has done. But a sense of what she would prefer forbids more than this meagre outline of her life and work. It must, however, be added that as an educator of women in the wider sense; as an emancipator from conventionalities, prejudices, narrowness; and as a representative, on a spiritual plane, of the new age upon which we are entering, she takes her place with the foremost women of our time.

The annual meeting of the National Women's Christian
Temperance Union for 1882, in Louisville, Ky,—held a few
months before the writing of this sketch—not only illustrated the results of the educating influence of a woman
upon women, but was in a remarkable degree a proof of
what may prevail in congress or conventicle if only the
Spirit of Christ rule the heart of the ruler. A citizen
thus comments upon it in the *Evening Post :*

"I was a much interested witness to the proceedings
of the Women's Christian Temperance Union on Wednesday, and was vividly struck with some of the differences
between it and male convocations of similar size and
scope. The suavity and dignity of the presiding officer,
Miss Willard, the mild and even affectionately respectful
manner of each sister to all the others, impressed me with
the peculiar fitness of women to preside over and conduct
the business of a large audience. There was no jarring and
grating about parliamentary ethics; no discord, no calling
to order, but business was done decently and in order,
and impressed me as being as far ahead of any male
assemblages which meet in our city as a prayer-meeting
is ahead of a corn-husking."

Says another who looked deeper : "God was there, and
we all knew it."

At the election of officers, when the tellers declared
that, without one dissenting vote, Frances E. Willard was
re-elected President of the National Union, by representatives from thirty States, a wave of joy broke over the
whole assembly. The great audience rose to its feet with
a single impulse, and by waving of handkerchiefs and the
singing of a doxology, expressed the feeling of the hour.

Loyalty to the woman, in or out of her work, is shared
alike by men and women, for the former are never antagonized by her in speech or spirit, and the latter know
that while she has great faith in men, she has greater

faith in men and women, or, as she has expressed it, the "going forth hand in hand, of the two halves of humanity." A profound belief in the second incarnation of Christ in the body of humanity accounts for the fact that with her the race interest overshadows the love of self or of her sex.

The "largeness" referred to at the opening of this paper belongs no more to her mental and moral nature than to the affectional, as all who know her "heart to heart" will testify. Nor will these testify alone. The young girl with gifts, and no money—the woman who has lost heart and hope—the young collegian struggling with his doubts—the poor fellow who is in the "last ditch"—even a stranger, perhaps—will, with scores of their class, speak with a glow of the power of her sympathy—the real interest which can never say to famishing souls or bodies, "Be ye warmed and filled," without adding money, time, or influence to place them in relation with a means of support and hope.

Miss Willard is distinctively a woman of the future. She is not a prophetess, but a prophecy, and one of the types of the larger and diviner womanhood which our land shall yet produce, and which all lands shall call the "fittest."

CHAPTER II.

PRELIMINARY.

The W. C. T. U. compared with other Societies—"Without a pattern and without a peer."

I SHALL try to sketch, in the most practical manner, a subject of transcendent interest and importance. More than any other society ever formed, the Woman's Christian Temperance Union is the exponent of what is best in this latter-day civilization. Its scope is the broadest, its aims the kindest, its history the most heroic. I yield to none in admiration of woman's splendid achievements in church work and in the Foreign Missionary Society, which was my first love as a philanthropist, but in both instances the denominational character of that work interferes with its unity and breadth. The same is true of woman's educational undertakings, glorious as they are. Her many-sided charities, in homes for the orpnaned and the indigent, hospitals for the sick and asylums for the old, are the admiration of all generous hearts, but these are local in their interest and result from the loving labors of isolated groups. The same is true of the women's prisons and industrial schools, which are now multiplying with such beneficent rapidity. Nor do I forget the sanitary work of women, which gleamed like a heavenly rainbow on the horrid front of war; but noble *men* shared the labor as they did the honor on that memorable field. Neither am I unmindful of the Woman's Christian Association, strongly intrenched in most of our great cities, and doing valiant battle for the Prince of

(39)

Peace; but it admits to its sacramental host only members of the churches known as " Evangelical." Far be it from me to seem indifferent to that electric intellectual movement from which have resulted the societies, literary and æsthetic, in which women have combined to study classic history, philosophy, and art; but these have no national unity; or to forget the " Woman's Congress," with its annual meeting and wide outlook, but lack of local auxiliaries; or the " Exchanges," where women, too poor or proud to bring their wares before the public, are helped to put money in their purse, but which lack cohesion; or the State and associated charities, where women do much of the work and men most of the superintendence. But when all is said, the Woman's Christian Temperance Union, local, State, and national, in the order of its growth, with its unique and heavenly origin, its steady march, its multiplied auxiliaries, its blessed out-reaching to the generous South and the far frontier, its broad sympathies and its abundant entrance ministered to all good and true women who are willing to clasp hands in one common effort to protect their homes and loved ones from the ravages of drink, is an organization without a pattern save that seen in heavenly vision upon the mount of faith, and without a peer among the sisterhoods that have grouped themselves around the cross of Christ.

In the fullness of time this mighty work has been given us. Preceding ages would not have understood the end in view and would have spurned the means, but the nineteenth century, standing on the shoulders of its predecessors, has a wider outlook and a keener vision. It has studied science and discovered that the tumult of the whirlwind is less powerful than the silence of the dew. It has ransacked history and learned that the banner and the sword were never yet the symbols of man's grandest

victories, and it begins at last to listen to the voice of
that inspired philosophy, which through all ages has been
gently saying: " The race is not always to the swift,
neither the battle to the strong."

Beyond the history of its origin but little can be written here concerning that spiritual prairie fire in the
West, immortalized by fifty days of prayer, persuasion,
and victory, and called " The Woman's Temperance
Crusade." Its documentary history has been already
furnished by Mrs. Wittemeyer; its spirit lives in the
organic form of the " W. C. T. U.," whose white ribboned
host is in the field to-day fighting *"for God and Home
and Native Land."*

CHAPTER III.

"W. C. T. U."

Its objects—Hygiene—The "Religion of the Body"—Dress, economy of time—Value of a trained intellect—The coming of Christ
into five circles: Heart; Home; Denominationalism; Society; Government—Home protection—"The Old Ship Zion, Hallelujah!"—
Motto: "Mary stood the cross beside."

THE W. C. T. U. stands as the exponent, not alone
of that return to physical sanity which will follow
the downfall of the drink habit, but of the reign of a
religion of the body which for the first time in history
shall correlate with Christ's wholesome, practical, yet
blessedly spiritual religion of the soul. "The kingdom
of heaven is within you"—shall have a new meaning to
the clear-eyed, steady-limbed Christians of the future,
from whose brain and blood the taint of alcohol and nico-
tine has been eliminated by ages of pure habits and noble
heredity. "The body is the temple of the Holy Ghost,"
will not then seem so mystical a statement, nor one indi-
cative of a temple so insalubrious as now. "He that destroyeth this temple, him shall God destroy," will be seen
to involve no element of vengeance, but instead to be the
declaration of such boundless love and pity for our race,
as would not suffer its deterioration to reach the point of
absolute failure and irremediable loss.

The women of this land have never had before such
training as is furnished by the topical studies of our
society, in the laws by which childhood shall set out upon
its endless journey with a priceless heritage of powers
laid up in store by the tender, sacred foresight of those

(42)

by whom the young immortal's being was invoked. The laws of health were never studied by so many mothers, or with such immediate results for good on their own lives and those of their children. The deformed waist and foot of the average fashionable American never seemed so hideous and wicked, nor the cumbrous dress of the period so unendurable as now, when from studying one "poison habit," our minds, by the inevitable laws of thought, reach out to wider researches and more varied deductions than we had dreamed at first. The economies of co-operative house-keeping never looked so attractive or so feasible as since the homemakers have learned something about the priceless worth of time and money for the purposes of a Christ-like benevolence. The value of a trained intellect never had such significance as since we have learned what an incalculable saving of words there is in a direct style, what value in the power of classification of fact, what boundless resources for illustrating and enforcing truth come as the sequel of a well-stored memory and a cultivated imagination. The puerility of mere talk for the sake of talk, the unworthiness of "idle words," and vacuous, purposeless gossip, the waste of long and aimless letter-writing, never looked so egregious as to the workers who find every day too short for the glorious and gracious deeds which lie waiting for them on every hand.

But to help forward the coming of Christ into all departments of life, is, in its last analysis, the purpose and aim of the W. C. T. U. For we believe this correlation of New Testament religion with philanthropy, and of the church with civilization, is the perpetual miracle which furnishes the only sufficient antidote to current skepticism. Higher toward the zenith climbs the Sun of Righteousness, making circle after circle of human endeavor and achievement warm and radiant with the healing of its beams. First of all, in our gospel temperance work, this heavenly light penetrated the gloom of the individual, tempted heart (that smallest circle, in which all others are involved), illumined its darkness, melted its hardness, made it a sweet and sunny place—a temple filled with the Holy Ghost.

Having thus come to the heart of the drinking man in the plenitude of his redeeming power, Christ entered the next wider circle, in which two human hearts unite to form a home, and here, by the revelation of her place in His kingdom, He lifted to an equal level with her husband the gentle companion who had supposed herself happy in being the favorite vassal of her liege lord. "There is neither male nor female in Christ Jesus;" this was the "open sesame," a declaration utterly opposed to all custom and tradition, but so steadily the light has shone, and so kindly has it made the heart of man, that without strife of tongues, or edict of sovereigns, it is coming now to pass that in proportion as any home is really Christian, the husband and the wife are peers in dignity and power. There are no homes on earth where woman is "revered, beloved," and individualized in character and work, so thoroughly as the fifty thousand in America where "her children arise up and call her blessed, her husband also, and he praiseth her" because of her part in the work of our W. C. T. U.

Beyond this sweet and sacred circle where two hearts grow to be one, where the mystery of birth and the hallowed face of child and mother work their perpetual charm, comes that outer court of home, that third great circle which we call society. Surely and steadily the light of Christ is coming there, through the loving temperance Pentecost, to replace the empty phrase of punctilio by earnest words of cheer and inspiration; to banish the unhealthful tyranny of fashion by enthroning wholesome

taste and common sense; to drive out questionable
amusements and introduce innocent and delightful
pastimes; to exorcise the evil spirit of gossip and domes-
ticate helpful and tolerant speech; nay, more, to banish
from the social board those false emblems of hospitality
and good will,—intoxicating drinks.

Sweep a wider circle still, and behold in that ecclesiastical invention called " denominationalism," Christ coming by the union of His handmaids in work for Him;
coming to put away the form outward and visible that He
may shed abroad the grace inward and spiritual; to close
the theological disquisition of the learned pundit, and
open the Bible of the humble saint; to draw away men's
thoughts from theories of right living, and centre them
upon right living itself; to usher in the priesthood of the
people, by pressing upon the conscience of each believer the
individual commission, " Go, disciple all nations," and
emphasizing the individual promise, " Lo, I am with thee
always."

But the modern temperance movement, born of Christ's
gospel and cradled at His altars, is rapidly filling one
more circle of influence, wide as the widest zone of
earthly weal or woe, and that is government. " The government shall be upon His shoulder." " Unto us a King
is given." " He shall reign whose right it is." " He
shall not fail, nor be discouraged until he hath set judgment in the earth." " For at the name of Jesus every
knee shall bow, and every tongue confess that Christ is
Lord to the glory of God the Father." " Thy kingdom come, thy will be done *on earth*." Christ shall
reign—not visibly, but invisibly; not in form, but in fact;
not in substance, but in essence, and the day draws nigh!
Then surely the traffic in intoxicating liquors as a drink
will no longer be protected by the statute book, the lawyer's plea, the affirmation of the witness, and decision of

the judge. And since the government is, after all, a circle that include all hearts, all homes, all churches, all societies, does it not seem as if intelligent loyalty to Christ the King would cause each heart that loves Him to feel in duty bound to use all the power it could gather to itself in helping choose the framers of these more righteous laws ? But let it be remembered that for every Christian man who has a voice in making and enforcing laws there are at least two Christian women who have no voice at all. Hence, under such circumstances as now exist, His militant army must ever be powerless to win those legislative battles which, more than any others, affect the happiness of aggregate humanity. But the light gleams already along the sunny hilltops of the nineteenth century of grace. Upon those who in largest numbers love Him who has filled their hearts with peace and their homes with blessing, slowly dawns the consciousness that they may—nay, better still, *they ought* to—ask for power to help forward the coming of their Lord in government —to throw the safeguard of their prohibition ballots around those who have left the shelter of their arms only to be entrapped by the saloons that bad men legalize and set along the streets.

" But some doubted."

This was in our earlier National Conventions. Almost none disputed the value of this added weapon in woman's hand,—indeed, all deemed it " sure to come." It was only the old, old question of expediency ; of " frightening away our sisters among the more conservative." But later on we asked these questions : Has the policy of silence caused a great rallying to our camp from the ranks of the conservative ? Do you know an instance in which it has augmented your working force ? Are not all the women upon whose help we can confidently count, favorable to the " *Do everything Policy*," as the only one

broad enough to meet our hydra-headed foe? Have not
the men of the liquor traffic said in platform, resolution,
and secret circular, "The ballot in woman's hand will be
the death-knell of our trade?"

And so to-day, while each State *is free to adopt or
disavow* the ballot as a home protection weapon, and
although the white-winged fleet of the W. C. T. U. in a
score of States crowds all sail for constitutional prohibition, to be followed up by "Home Protection," still though
"the silver sails are all out in the West," every ship in the
gleaming line is all the same a Gospel ship—an "*old
ship Zion—Hallelujah!*"

MOTTO FOR THE W. C. T. U.

"Jews were wrought to cruel madness,
Christians fled in fear and sadness,
　　Mary stood the cross beside.
At its foot her foot she planted,
By the dreadful scene undaunted,
　　Till the gentle sufferer died.

Poets oft have sung her story,
Painters wreathed her brow with glory,
　　Priests her name have deified.
But no worship, song, or glory,
Touches, like the simple story,
　　Mary stood the cross beside.

And, when under fierce oppression,
Goodness suffers like transgression,
　　Christ again is crucified.
If but love be there, true-hearted,
By no fear or terror parted,
　　Mary stands the cross beside."

CHAPTER IV.

"LET IT BE NOTED";

Or why the Author is not a Critic.

THE W. C. T. U. is a sort of mutual admiration society, or to put the matter more accurately, it is doing more than any other one influence to develop among women that *esprit du corps*, for lack of which they have been so sharply censured. Therefore, no apology is made for the good things hereinafter related, concerning those who have not yet attained obituary honors.

"I thought before you died I'd just tell you how much I have always loved and honored you." This sentence, from a letter recently received, has in it matter for reflection. It hints at one of the most unaccountable errors in our conduct of life's relationships. We speak our words of praise too late. We blow the trumpet of our approbation at the earnest worker's ear—but not until Death's finger has closed it up forever. We utter at the graveside the tender words that might have kept sensitive souls with us in a new lease of life. We build monuments with money that, if bestowed upon the living toiler, would have re-enforced the wasted energies and re-awakened the declining courage. Dear friends, these things ought not so to be. I can speak freely to you who have been far more generous with me than I deserve. Let us as Temperance women be more thoughtful—all of us hereafter—lest we sing with sad regret some day, above the wearied and unconscious forms of beloved workers fallen:

> "Strange we never heed the music,
> Till the sweet-voiced bird is flown."

It is believed that the sketches now to follow will forever release their author from the clutches of that style
of remorse! For the rest, while not oblivious to faults
in the leaders herein described, it has seemed best to
observe the rule of Coleridge in matters of criticism;
"Never look for defects; they will present themselves
unbidden." As to treating of said defects, the author
has been largely governed by the spirit of the motto found
on a sun dial at Naples: "*I count only the hours that are
serene.*"

3

CHAPTER V.

THE FIRST CRUSADERS.

Mrs. Judge Thompson of Hillsboro', Ohio—First Praying Band—
First Saloon Prayer-meeting—Mrs. George Carpenter of Washington Court House—Story of the great victories—Scene at a National W. C. T. U. Convention—Presentation of the Crusade Bed-
quilt.

DECEMBER TWENTY-THIRD, 1873.

THE date is memorable. Some day its anniversaries
will be ranked among our national festivals. True,
in Fredonia, New York, the protest of women against the
snares men legalize under the name of "saloons" and
"sample rooms" had begun, under the leadership of Mrs.
Judge Barker, eight days before. True, in Washington
Court House, Ohio, on the 24th, noble Mrs. Carpenter
led a heroic band to a far grander victory. But the first
eddy of that Whirlwind of the Lord, which in a few weeks
had swept over the great State of Ohio, and grown to the
huge proportions of the Woman's Temperance Crusade,
began in Hillsboro', Ohio, December 23, 1873. By common consent of her sisters in the united churches of the
village where almost her whole life had been spent, Mrs.
Eliza J. Thompson was chosen to lead the first band on
its first visit to a saloon. Never did character and circumstance conspire to form a central figure better suited
to the significant occasion. "The first Crusader," a gen-
tle-mannered lady of sixty years, had been from her
early days a member of Christ's church and always
prominent in charitable work, thus endearing herself to
the class whose antagonism her new departure would

(50)

MRS. E. J. THOMPSON.

naturally arouse. She is a wife, mother, and grand-mother, loving and beloved; with marks upon her face of the grief which renders sacred, which disarms criticism, and in this instance, has a significance too deep for tears. She is the only daughter of Governor Trimble, than whom Ohio never had a chief magistrate more true.

Nearly forty years before, she had accompanied that noble father when he went as a delegate to the earliest national temperance convention, which was so small that its opening meeting was held in the dining-room of a Saratoga hotel of that period. Going with him to the door of this dignified assembly, where the white cravats of the clergy were a feature of prominence, the timid Ohio girl whispered, " O, papa, I'm afraid to enter, those gentlemen may thing it an intrusion. I should be the only lady, don't you see?" Upon this the Governor re-plied, " My daughter should never be afraid, even if she is alone in a good cause," and taking her by the arm, he drew her into the convention. What a prophecy was the first entrance of a woman—and *this* woman—upon a tem-perance convention made up of men! Read its fulfillment in her now happy home, her lawyer husband's leadership of the home protection movement in Ohio, and in the procession of white-ribbon workers that belts the world to-day.

Kneeling hand in hand with this dear friend and leader, in the room where first the " Crusade Psalm " was read and prayer of consecration offered, my heart was newly laid upon the altar of our blessed cause. Upon the thousands of faithful temperance women all over the land, let me lovingly urge some special annual commemoration of the twenty-third of December, as a day in which all our hearts shall be warmed with new love, stirred to fresh zeal, and lifted into clearer faith.

It is worth while to preserve in her own language the

account of that strange "call" which came to Mrs. Thompson in 1873. She wrote it out for a near friend in the following words:

"On the evening of Dec. 22, 1873, Dio Lewis, a Boston physician and lyceum lecturer, delivered in Music Hall, Hillsboro, Ohio, a lecture on 'Our Girls.'

"He had been engaged by the Lecture Association some months before to fill one place in the winter course of lectures 'merely for the entertainment of the people.' But finding that he could remain another evening and still reach his next appointment (Washington C. H.), he consented to give another lecture on the evening of the 23d. At the suggestion of Judge Albert Matthews, an old-line temperance man and Democrat, a free lecture on Temperance became the order of the evening.

"I did not hear Dio Lewis lecture (although he was our guest), because of home cares that required my presence, but my son, a youth of sixteen, was there, and he came to me upon his return home and in a most excited manner related the thrilling incidents of the evening— how Dr. Lewis told of his own mother and several of her good Christian friends uniting in prayer with and for the liquor sellers of his native town until they gave up their soul-destroying business, and then said,—'Ladies, you might do the same thing in Hillsboro if you had the same faith,'—and, turning to the ministers and temperance men who were upon the platform, added, 'Suppose I ask the ladies of this audience to signify their opinions upon the subject?' They all bowed their consent, and fifty or more women stood up in token of approval. He then asked the gentlemen how many of them would stand as 'backers,' should the ladies undertake the work, and sixty or seventy arose. 'And now, mother,' said my boy, 'they have got you into business, for you are on a committee to do some work at the Presbyterian Church in the morning at nine o'clock, and then the ladies want you to go out with them to the saloons.'

" My husband, who had returned from Adams County court that evening and was feeling very tired, seemed asleep as he rested upon the couch, while my son in an undertone had given me all the above facts; but as the last sentence was uttered, he raised himself up upon his elbow and said, 'What tom-foolery is all that?' My son slipped out of the room quietly, and I betook myself to the task of consoling my husband with the promise that I should not be led into any foolish act by Dio Lewis or any association of human beings. But after he had relaxed into a milder mood, continuing to call the whole plan, as he understood it, 'tom-foolery,' I ventured to remind him that the men had been in the 'tom-foolery' business a long time, and suggested that it might be 'God's will' that the women should now take their part. (After this he fell asleep quietly, and I resumed my Bible reading.) Nothing further was said upon the subject that had created such interest the night before until after breakfast, when we gathered in the 'family room.' First, my son approached me and gently placing his hand upon my shoulder, in a very subdued tone said, 'Mother, are you not going over to the church, this morning?' As I hesitated, and doubtless showed in my countenance the burden upon my spirit, he emphatically said, 'But, my dear mother, you know you have to go.' Then my daughter, who was sitting on a stool by my side, leaning over in a most tender manner, and looking up in my face, said, 'Don't you think you will go?' All this time my husband had been walking the floor, uttering not a word. He stopped, and placing his hand upon the family Bible that lay upon my work-table, he said emphatically, 'Children, you know where your mother goes to settle all vexed questions. Let us leave her alone,' withdrawing as he spoke, and the dear children following him. I turned the key, and was in the act of kneeling before God and his 'holy word' to see what would be sent me, when I heard a gentle tap at my door. Upon opening it, I saw my dear daughter, with her little Bible open, and the tears coursing down her young cheeks, as she said, 'I opened to this, mother. It must be for you.' She immediately left the room, and I sat down to read the wonderful message of the great 'I Am' contained in the 146th Psalm.

"No longer doubting, I at once repaired to the Presbyterian church, where quite a large assembly of earnest people had gathered.

"I was at once unanimously chosen as the President (or leader); Mrs. Gen. McDowell, Vice-President; and Mrs. D. K. Finner, Secretary of the strange work that was to follow.

"Appeals were drawn up to druggists, saloon-keepers, and hotel proprietors. Then the Presbyterian minister (Dr. McSurely), who had up to this time occupied the chair, called upon the chairman-elect to come forward to the 'post of honor,' but your humble servant could not; her limbs refused to bear her. So Dr. McSurely remarked, as he looked around upon the gentlemen: 'Brethren, I see that the ladies will do nothing while we remain; let us adjourn, leaving this new work with God and the women.'

"As the last man closed the door after him, strength before unknown came to me, and without any hesitation or consultation I walked forward to the minister's table, took the large Bible, and, opening it, explained the incidents of the morning; then read and briefly (as my tears would allow) commented upon its new meaning to me. I then called upon Mrs. McDowell to lead in prayer, and such a prayer! It seemed as though the angel had brought down 'live coals' from off the altar and touched her lips—she who had never before heard her own voice in prayer!

"As we rose from our knees (for there were none sitting on that morning), I asked Mrs. Cowden (our M. E. minister's wife) to start the good old hymn 'Give to the winds thy fears' to a familiar tune,* and turning to the dear women, I said: 'As we all join in singing this hymn, let us form in line, two and two, the small women in front, leaving the tall ones to bring up the rear, and let us at once proceed to our sacred mission, trusting alone in the God of Jacob.' It was all done in less time than it takes to write it; every heart was throbbing, and every woman's countenance betrayed her solemn realization of the fact that she was "going about her Father's business."

As this band of "mysterious beings" first encountered the outside gaze, and as they passed from the door of the old church and reached the street beyond the large churchyard, they were singing these prophetic words:

> "Far, far above thy thought,
>   His counsel shall appear,
> When fully He the work hath wrought
>   That caused thy needless fear."

On they marched in solemn silence up Main street, first to Dr. Wm. Smith's drug store. After calling at all the drug stores, four in number, their pledge being signed by all save one, they encountered saloons and hotels with varied success, until by continuous, daily visitations, with persuasion, prayer, song, and Scripture readings, the drinking places of the town were reduced from thirteen to one drug store, one hotel, and two saloons, and they sold "very cautiously." Prayer meetings were held during the entire winter and spring every morning (except Sunday), and mass meetings in the evenings, at the M.

---

* The tune was "St. Thomas."

E. church one week and at the Presbyterian the next.
This is, in brief, the story for which you have asked."

Mrs. Thompson also gives this record of

THE FIRST SALOON PRAYER–MEETING.

" After visiting the drug stores, on the 24th of December, 1873, our ' band' slowly and timidly approached the
' first class saloon' of Robert Ward on High street, a
resort made famous by deeds the memory of which nerved
the heart and paled the cheek of some among the
' seventy' as they entered the ' open door' of the ' witty
Englishman,' as his patrons were wont to call the popular
Ward.   Doubtless he had learned of our approach, as he
not only propped the door open, but, with the most perfect
suavity of manner, held it until the ladies all passed in ;
then, closing it, walked to his accustomed stand behind
' the bar.'   Seizing the strange opportunity, the leader *
addressed him as follows : ' Well, Mr. Ward, this must
seem to you a strange audience.   I suppose, however,
that you understand the object of our visit.'   Robert by
this time began to perspire freely, and remarked that he
would ' like to have a talk with Dio Lewis.'   Mrs. T. said :
' Dr. Lewis has nothing to do with the subject of our
mission.   As you look upon some of the faces before you
and observe the furrows of sorrow, made deep by the
unholy business that you ply, you will find that it is no
wonder we are here.   We have come, not to threaten—
not even to upbraid—but in the name of our Heavenly
Friend and Saviour, and in His spirit to forgive, and to
commend you to His pardon, if you will but abandon a
business that is so damaging to our hearts and homes ! '

" The embarrassment and hesitation of the saloon-
keeper were at once improved upon.   The ' leader' said,
softly, as she looked around upon those earnest faces :

---

* Mrs. Thompson.

'Let us pray.' Instantly all, even the liquor seller himself, were upon their knees! Mrs. Dr. McSurely (wife of the Presbyterian minister) was asked to lead in prayer by Mrs. Thompson as they bowed together, but she declined. The 'spirit of utterance' then came upon the latter, and perhaps for the first time, in a saloon, 'the heavens were opened,' and, as a seal of God's approval upon the self-sacrificing work there inaugurated, the 'Spirit' came down and touched all hearts.

As they arose from prayer dear Mrs. Daggett (now in Heaven) broke forth in her sweet, pathetic notes, all joining with her,

> "There is a fountain filled with blood,
>   Drawn from Immanuel's veins;
> And sinners plunged beneath that flood,
>   Lose all their guilty stains."

The scene that followed was one fit for a painter or a poet, so beautifully was the spirit of our holy religion portrayed. Poor wives and mothers, who the day before would have crossed the street rather than walk by a place so identified with the woes and heart-aches of their "lost Eden," were now in tearful pathos pleading with this deluded "brother" to accept the world's Redeemer as his own. Surely "GOD IS LOVE."

*HISTORY OF THE WOMAN'S CRUSADE AT WASHINGTON COURT HOUSE, OHIO.

On the evening of December 24, 1873, the Lecture Association of Washington C. H. had in its course a lecture on "Our Girls," by Dio Lewis. During the evening he dwelt somewhat largely upon the havoc being made by tobacco and ardent spirits, and offered to suggest a

---

* Wishing to have these important historic facts at first hand, I have obtained this sketch from Mrs. Ustick, Secretary of the Praying Band at Washington C. H., Ohio. Mrs. George Carpenter, the central figure in this marvellous picture, is wife of the Presbyterian pastor there.

new plan for fighting the liquor traffic, which, he asserted, if carefully adhered to, would close every saloon in the place in one week's time.

The proposition was heartily accepted, and a meeting appointed for Christmas morning, at 10 o'clock, in the Presbyterian church. At the designated hour on Christmas morning a large congregation assembled in the Presbyterian church, eager to see the plan of Dr. Lewis inaugurated with all earnestness and prayer. "Awake! Awake! Put on thy strength, O Zion!" was sung by the choir; prayer by one of the pastors, and reading a Bible selection by Dr. Lewis, who at once proceeded to his work. He told the story of his mother's experience and efforts; his faith in woman's prayer, patience, and love, for the cure of intemperance, and his own unsuccessful attempts to organize the women in various cities for the past twenty-one years. For one hour argument, illustration, appeal, and demonstration followed in rapid succession, until at the conclusion of the address the entire audience were ready to heartily indorse the plan presented, and there was organized one of the grandest reformatory movements of the age—the movement now so well and fitly known as the Woman's Crusade.

On motion of Dr. Lewis, three secretaries were elected, and instructed to report the names of all the women present, as a committee of visitation, whose duty it should be to go in a body to each of the saloons, and personally appeal to the proprietors of the same to stop the business at once and seek other means of livelihood. This committee was to enlist for the war—that is, until the work was accomplished. Fifty-two women enrolled their names.

On motion of Dr. Lewis, a secretary was appointed to take the names of a number of men, to be called a "Committee of Responsibility," who should furnish pecuniary means needed in the prosecution of this work. Thirty-seven men gave their names as members of this committee.

MRS. GEO. CARPENTER.

On motion of Dr. Lewis, the chair appointed Mrs. Geo. Carpenter, Mrs. A. C. Hirst, Mrs. A. E. Pine, and Mrs. B. Ogle, as a committee to draw up an appeal to our citizens engaged in the liquor business. Closing appeals of stirring power were made by Dr. Lewis and Rev. A. C. Hirst, and after a vote of thanks to Dr. Lewis for his work among us the meeting adjourned, to convene in the Methodist Church and hear the reports of the committees appointed.

Temperance was the all-absorbing theme on that day, around every Christian's board and upon all the street corners. In the evening a prayer-meeting was held in the M. E. Church, at which time the Chairman of Committee on Appeal, Mrs. Geo. Carpenter, reported the following:

APPEAL.

" Knowing, as you do, the fearful effects of intoxicating drinks, we, the women of Washington, after earnest prayer and deliberation, have decided to appeal to you to desist from this ruinous traffic, that our husbands, brothers, and especially our sons, be no longer exposed to this terrible temptation, and that we may no longer see them led into those paths which go down to sin, and bring both body and soul to destruction. We appeal to the better instincts of your own hearts, in the name of desolated homes, blasted hopes, ruined lives, widowed hearts, for the honor of our community, for our happiness; for our good name, as a town; in the name of the God who will judge you, as well as ourselves; for the sake of your own souls, which are to be saved or lost, we beg—we implore you, to cleanse yourselves from this heinous sin, and place yourselves in the ranks of those who are striving to elevate and ennoble themselves and their fellow-men; and to this we ask you to pledge yourselves."

Which appeal was adopted, and has since been used

very generally—not only in Ohio, but in several other
States.

On Friday morning, December 26, 1873, the meeting
convened pursuant to adjournment, in the Methodist
Episcopal Church. The services were opened with singing and prayer, and reading of the Scriptures. One hundred copies of the Appeal to Liquor Sellers were ordered
to be printed and circulated throughout the community.
Mrs. J. L. Vandeman and Mrs. Judge McLean were appointed to lead the procession, Mrs. A. E. Pine to lead
the singing, Mrs. M. V. Ustick as Secretary, and Mrs.
Geo. Carpenter as Captain and Reader of the Appeal.

And now came the most interesting moment of this
meeting. More than forty of the best women in the
community were to go forth on their errands of mercy.
There was much trembling of hearts, much taking hold
on God, much crying, and supplication in prayer. Such
a scene was never witnessed in Washington C. H.

Down the central aisle of the church marched these
women to their work, while the men remained, continuing in prayer to God, that He would be with these women
as they should go from place to place, with Christian
song and prayer, to appeal, face to face, in their various
places of business, to those men who were at work selling
liquor—the tolling of the church bell keeping time to the
solemn march of the women as they wended their way to
the first drug store on the list.

(The number of places within the city limits where
intoxicating drinks were sold was fourteen—eleven
saloons and three drug-stores.) Here, as in every place,
they entered singing, every woman taking up the sacred
strain as she crossed the threshold. This was followed
by the reading of the appeal, and prayer; then earnest
pleading to desist from their soul-destroying traffic, and
to sign the dealer's pledge.

The novel procession created the wildest excitement on the streets, and was the subject of conversation to the exclusion of all others. The work of the ladies was thoroughly done. Not a den escaped. The procession entered by the front door, filling both the front and back rooms. Prayer, followed by Bible arguments, was the answer to the excuses of these men. Down into the cellar, everywhere, they went with the same eloquent plea: "We pray you to stop this!" "We mean you no hurt!" "We beg you to desist!" In tears the mothers, wives, and sisters pleaded for their cause.

Thus all the day they went from place to place, without stopping even for dinner or lunch till five o'clock, meeting with no marked success. But invariable courtesy was extended them ; not even their reiterated promise, "We will call again," seeming to offend.

No woman who has ever entered one of these dens of iniquity on such an errand, needs to be told of the heart-sickness that almost overcame them as they, for the first time, saw behind those painted windows or green blinds, and entered the little stifling "back-room," or found their way down winding steps into the damp, dark cellars, and realized that into such places many of those they loved best were slowly descending through the allurements of the brilliantly lighted drug-store, the fascinating billiard-table, or the enticing beer-gardens, with their syren attractions.

A crowded house at night to hear the report of the day's work betrayed the rapidly increasing interest in this mission.

Saturday morning, December 27th, after an hour of prayer, an increased number of women went forth again, leaving a number of men in the church, who continued in prayer all day long. Every few moments the tolling bell cheered the hearts of the Crusaders by pealing forth the knowledge that another supplication had ascended for their success; meanwhile notes of progress being sent by the secretary to the church from every place visited.

On this day the contest really began, and, at the first place, the doors were found locked. With hearts full of compassion, the women knelt in the snow upon the pavement, to plead for the Divine influence upon the heart of the liquor dealer, and there held their first street prayer-meeting.

At night the weary, but zealous workers reported at mass-meeting the various rebuffs, and the success in having two druggists sign the pledge not to sell, except upon the written prescription of a physician.

The Sabbath was devoted to union mass meetings, with direct reference to the work in hand; and on Monday the number of ladies had increased to nearly one hundred. That day, December 27th, is one long to be remembered in Washington as the day upon which occurred the first surrender ever made by a liquor-dealer, of his stock of liquors of every kind and variety, to the women, in answer to their prayers and entreaties, said stock being by them poured into the street. Nearly a thousand men, women, and children witnessed the mingling of beer, ale, wine, and whisky as they filled the gutters and were drank up by the earth, while bells were ringing, men and boys shouting, and women singing and praying to God, who had given the victory.

But, on the fourth day, the campaign reached its height; the town being filled with visitors from all parts of the country and adjoining villages. There was another public surrender and another pouring into the street of a larger stock of liquors than on the previous day, and more intense excitement and enthusiasm.

Mass meetings were held nightly with new victories reported constantly, until on Friday, January 2d, one week from the beginning of the work, at the public meeting held in the evening, the secretary's report announced every liquor dealer unconditionally surrendered : some having shipped their liquors back to wholesale dealers, others poured them in the gutters, and the druggists all signed the druggist's pledge.

Thus a campaign of prayer and song had, in eight days, closed eleven saloons, and pledged three drug-stores to sell only on prescription.

At first men had wondered, scoffed, and laughed, then criticized, respected, and yielded.

Morning prayer and evening mass-meetings continued daily, and the personal pledge was circulated till over one thousand signatures were obtained. Physicians were called upon to sign a pledge not to prescribe ardent spirits when any other substitute could be found, and in no case without a personal examination of the patient.

A property-holder's pledge was also circulated—pledging men not to rent or lease property to be used as saloons, nor to allow any dealings of the liquor traffic to be carried on upon any premises belonging to them. This pledge was generally signed by holders of real estate.

During this week came a plea for help from Hillsboro. In answer to that call, on Monday, January 12th, a committee consisting of Profs. Morehouse and Dean, and Mrs. Geo. Carpenter, Mrs. Judge McLean, Mrs. Judge Priddy, and Miss Anna Ustick, went to Hillsboro, spent the evening in attendance upon a mass-meeting there, and the next forenoon in prayer and conference with the workers, returning in time to attend the mass-meeting at home, bringing with them encouraging words.

By this time the new method of fighting whisky began to attract the attention of the press, and people in surrounding places ; and meetings were announced to be held in every village and school district in the county. Committees of ladies and gentlemen were sent out from Washington C. H., to assist in these meetings. Committees were also sent, by request, into all adjoining counties, the meetings being constantly kept up at home, and all the while gaining in interest. Early in the third week the discouraging intelligence came that a new man had taken out license to sell liquor in one of the deserted saloons, and that he was backed by a whisky house in Cincinnati to the amount of $5,000, to break down the movement. On Wednesday, the 14th, the whisky was unloaded at his room. About forty women were on the ground, and followed the liquor in, and remained, holding an uninterrupted prayer-meeting all day and until eleven o'clock at night.

The next day—bitterly cold—was spent in the same place and manner, without fire or chairs; two hours of that time the women being locked in, while the proprietor was off attending a trial. On the following day, the coldest of all the winter of 1874, the women were locked out, and stood on the street holding religious services all day long.

Next morning a tabernacle was built in the street, just in front of the house, and was occupied for the double purpose of *watching* and prayer, through the day; but before the night the sheriff closed the saloon, and the proprietor surrendered; thus ended the third week.

A short time after, on a dying bed, this four days' liquor dealer sent for some of these women, telling them that their songs and prayers had never ceased to ring in his ears, and urging them to pray again in his behalf; so he passed away.

About this time came word from Columbus that the Adair Liquor Law was in great danger of being repealed; consequently the following communication was sent to every known temperance organization throughout the State:

WASHINGTON C. H., Jan. 30, 1874.

To the Secretary of Women's Temperance League at ———:

DEAR SISTER:—By order of the entire board of our Temperance League, we send you an earnest request that you immediately appoint a committee of not less than six of the most earnest and effective workers, who shall be ready at an hour's notice to respond to the call embodied in the following resolution:

Resolved, That the secretary of this meeting be requested to correspond with the ladies in all places where the temperance movement is now, or may be progressing, asking the same to appoint a delegation to appear at Columbus, when called, if any action of the legislature, threatening the safety of the Adair Liquor Law, may be contemplated.

"Please notify us of your decision in the matter, forwarding us one name to whom we may telegraph if necessary."

[Signed by the Secretary.]

Responses poured in from all Leagues addressed, the word "Ready." But the law remained undisturbed that winter.

At this time the Cincinnati *Commercial* sent a reporter, Mr. J. H. Beadle, to investigate the rise of this movement, from whose graphic pen we quote the following, as a correct word-picture of the occurrence:

"I reached Washington C. H. at noon of January 20th, and seeking Mr. Beck's beer-garden found him in a state of terrible nervousness, as the ladies had spent the forenoon in front of this place. He evidently regarded me as a spy, but was much mollified when assured that I was only a journalist, and made a voluminous complaint in 'High Dutch' and low English:

"'I got no vitnesses. Dem vimens dey set ub a schob on me. But you don't bin a 'bitual drunkard, eh? No, you don't look like him. Vell, coom in. Vot you vant, beer or vine? I dells you, dem vimens is shust awful. Py shinks, dhey build a house right in der street, und stay mit a man all day, singin' und oder foolishness. But dhey don't get in here once agin, already.'

"In obedience to his invitation, I had entered by the side door—the front was locked and barred—to find four customers indulging in liquor, beer, and pigs' feet. One announced himself as an 'original Granger,' a second as a 'retired sailor,' while the others were non-committal.

They stated that two spies had just applied for admission —'men who would come in and drink, then go away and swear they were habitual drunkards under the Adair law' —and that accounted for Mr. Beck's suspicions of me.

"The Adair law I find everywhere to be the great horror of saloon-keepers. It allows any wife or child, or other relative directly interested, to prosecute for the sale of liquor to husband or father; and almost any one may prosecute for the sale of liquor to a 'habitual drunkard.'

"Whether such a law be just or constitutional, there is much dispute; but it is evident that it gives great opportunity for fraud and blackmailing. It is, however, just now the strong rock of defense of the Ohio temperance people; and it may be that by its enforcement some saloon-keepers have been driven out of the business who would have withstood the prayers of an archangel and all the tears that sorrowing pity ever shed.

"Mr. Beck kept open house nearly all that night; the sounds of revelry were plainly heard, and in the morning several drunken men came into town, one of whom tumbled down in a livery stable and went to sleep on a manure pile, from which he was carried to the lock-up. Matters were evidently coming to a crisis, and I went out early; but the ladies reached there in force just before me. I met Mr. Beck hurrying into town to consult his lawyer, or, as he phrased it, 'to see mein gounsel vhen I no got some right to my own broberty.'

"The main body of the ladies soon arrived, and took up a position with right center on the door-step, the wings extending each way beyond the corners of the house, and a rearward column along the walk to the gate. In ludicrous contrast the routed revelers, who had been scared out of the saloon, stood in a little knot fifty feet away, still gnawing at the pigs' feet they had held on to in

their hurried flight; while I took a convenient seat on
the fence. The ladies then sang:

'O do not be discouraged, for Jesus is your friend,
He will give you grace to conquer, and keep you to the end.'

"As the twenty or more clear, sweet voices mingled in
the enlivening chorus,

'I'm glad I'm in this army,' etc.,

the effect was inspiring. I felt all the enthusiasm of the
occasion; while the pigs'-feet party, if they did not feel
guilty, certainly looked so. The singing was followed by
a prayer from Mrs. Mills Gardner. She prayed for the
blessing of God on the temperance cause generally, and
in this place particularly; then for Mr. Beck, his family
and his friends, his house and all that loved him, and
closed with an eloquent plea for guidance in the difficult
and delicate task they had undertaken. In one respect
the prayer was unsurpassed: it was eminently fitting to
the place and occasion. As the concluding sentences
were being uttered, Mr. Beck and his 'gounsel' arrived.
The ladies paid no attention to either, but broke forth in
loud strains:

'Must Jesus bear the cross alone?
No, there's a cross for me,'

when the lawyer borrowed some of my paper, whispering
at the same time, 'I must take down their names. Guess
I shall have to prosecute some of them before we stop this
thing.'

"I should need the pen of an Irving and the pencil of
a Darley to give any adequate idea of the scene. On one
side a score of elegant ladies, singing with all the earnestness of impassioned natures; a few yards away a knot of
disturbed revelers, uncertain whether to stand or fly;
half-way between, the nervous Beck, bobbing around like
a case of fiddle-strings with a hundred pounds of lager-
beer fat hung on them, and on the fence by the ladies a

cold-blooded lawyer and an excited reporter, scribbling away as if their lives depended on it. The scene was painful from its very intensity.

"The song ended, the presiding lady called upon Mrs. Wendel, and again arose the voice of prayer, so clear, so sweet, so full of pleading tenderness, that it seemed she would, by the strength of womanly love, compel the very heavens to open and send down in answer a spark of divine grace that would turn the saloon-keeper from his purpose. The sky, which had been overcast all the morning, began to clear, the occasional drops of rain ceased to fall, and a gentle south wind made the air soft and balmy. It almost seemed that nature joined in the prayer. Again the ladies sang,

Are there no foes for me to face?'

with the camp-meeting chorus:

'O, how I love Jesus,
Because he first loved me.'

As the song concluded, the lawyer suddenly stepped forward and said: 'Now, ladies, I have a word to say before this performance goes further. Mr. Beck has employed me as his attorney. He can not speak good English, and I speak for him here. He is engaged in a legitimate business, and you are trespassers on his property and right. If this thing is carried any further you will be called to account in the court, and I can assure you that the court will sustain the man. He has talked with you all he desires to. He does not want to put you out forcibly, as that would be unmanly, and he does not wish to act rudely; but he tells you to go, and, as his attorney, I now warn you to desist from any further annoyance.'

"Again the ladies sang,

'My soul, be on thy guard,
Ten thousand foes arise,'

when Miss Annie Ustick followed with a fervent prayer
for the lawyer and his client; but they had fled the scene,
leaving the house locked up. After consultation the
ladies decided to leave Mr. Beck's premises and take a
position in the adjoining lot. They sent for the 'tabernacle,' a rude frame building they had used in front of
Slater's saloon. This they erected on an adjoining lot,
put up immense lights to illuminate the entrance to the
beer garden, and kept up a guard from early morn till
midnight."

For two weeks religious services were held in the
Tabernacle day and night, and the women were constantly on duty, at the end of which time an injunction
was granted Mr. Beck, and the Tabernacle was taken
down. Suits were then in progress against the two beer
sellers, under the Adair Law, and judgments were being
obtained in various amounts, the ladies appearing in force
in the court room during each trial, thus giving their
moral support to their suffering sisters.

On Friday, February 6th, another man opened a beer
saloon in a new locality. The ladies immediately visited
him by committees, and thus spent the day. Next day,
however, they took up their stand in front of his door,
continuing their services late into the evening, at which
time their force was increased by the entire congregation
at mass meeting, who chose to conclude their services in
unison with the watchers before the saloon.

Temperance was still the pulpit theme on the Sabbath,
and on Monday morning, February 9th, all the business
houses were closed from 8 to 9, to attend the business
men's prayer meeting. Large delegations were present
from adjoining villages at that early hour. At the meeting there came a messenger from this man stating that
he would give up his business, which announcement was
received with cheers. It was then decided that all who were

not enjoined from so doing should march out to Mr. Beck's beer garden, where the proprietor met them at the gate, and after a brief consultation with a committee appointed for that purpose, he publicly announced : " You comes so many I quits. I will never sell any more beer or whisky." Again the crowd gave vent to their feelings in cheers. Messengers were dispatched to the women who remained praying in the church, to join them. All the bells commenced ringing, and the procession, numbering 200 strong, started out to Sullivan's beer house, now the only remaining saloon in the township. Marching up Court Street the number increased, and, amid the most profound silence, the men and women pursued their journey. About half-way there the man in question was met and interviewed. He asked two days to consider, which were granted. The procession then returned, the bells all the time ringing out their chimes upon the crisp morning air. Meetings, morning and evening, continued with unabated interest, and at each came to us the cry from other points : " Come and help us."

On Wednesday morning, February 11th, at mass meeting in the Presbyterian Church, Mr. Sullivan came and publicly pledged himself to " quit, forever, the liquor business." A general rejoicing and thanksgiving followed this surrender of the " last man."

Thus, through most of the winter of 1874, no alcoholic drinks were publicly sold as a beverage.

As Dr. Dio Lewis had signified his intention of again visiting our village on Tuesday, February 17th, that day was appointed as one of general rejoicing and thanksgiving. Accordingly arrangements were made for a mass meeting to be held in Music Hall at 2 P. M. At 1.30 a thousand people were gathered at the depot awaiting the arrival of the train. Promptly at the hour, Dr. Lewis, accompanied by quite a corps of newspaper men, alighted from the car, and was greeted with music from the band and cheers from the vast concourse of people, who immediately proceeded to the hall, where the following brief words of welcome were addressed to him by Mrs. Geo. Carpenter:

" *Dr. Lewis:* In the name of the women of Washington, I welcome you. Eight weeks ago, when you first came among us, you found us a people of warm hearts, generous impulses, fully alive to the evils of intemperance, and needing only the magnetism of a master mind to rouse us to a determined resistance of its ravages. Yours was that mind. Dr. Lewis, your hand pointed out the way. You vitalized our latent activities, and roused us all, men and women together, and we have gone forth to the battle side by side, as God intended we should, ourselves perfect weakness, but God mighty in strength. He sent you here. He put the thought into your heart. He prepared our hearts to receive it. And now He has brought you among us again to gladden you with the fruition of hope long deferred—to see the seed sown years ago by your mother springing up, budding, and bearing fruit. Dr. Lewis, I welcome you to the hearts and homes of Washington."

Dr. Lewis replied substantially as follows :

Madame and Friends : I cannot make a speech on this occasion. I have always been on the frontier, always engaged in the battle of reform. And now to find something really accomplished—to find a town positively free from the curse of liquor-selling—it really seems as if there is nothing for me to do. I feel as one without working harness. But I will say this : none but God can ever know how much I owe to this town, nor how fortunate it was for me and for many others that I came here. I will not say that this is the only community in which the work could be begun. The heroism and self-sacrifice displayed in other places would make such a remark invidious," etc., etc.

After the response by Dr. Lewis, the remainder of the afternoon was spent in general speech-making. The evening was occupied in listening to a lecture by Dr. Lewis, and the day fitly closed by an informal reception given the orators of the occasion, at the home of one of the crusaders.

At the spring election for Mayor and City Council, Temperance was made the issue, and, from motives of policy, the Temperance men brought out conservative candidates. The other party did the same thing. The whisky party were successful, and, emboldened by that success, many of the former saloonists gradually reopened their business. Since that time five of these men have gone to render to God an account for their violated vows.

The summer was given up to the defeat of the license clause in the new Constitution, which was to come before the people on the 18th of August.

Mass Temperance picnics were a prominent feature of the season, and the untiring zeal of the workers was crowned with success on election day.

During the intervening years weekly Temperance League meetings have been kept up by the faithful few, while frequent Union mass meetings have been held, thus keeping the subject always before the people.

To-day the disgraceful and humiliating fact exists that there are more places where liquors are sold than before the crusade.

In the almost decade of years which has flitted by since these events occurred, the reformation started here has belted the world. In many of the lines of work, Fayette County is showing herself worthy of the spirit which could inaugurate so wonderful a movement. For while Dr. Dio Lewis inaugurated a similar movement in three

other places during the same winter before it was started
here, results proved that it would have been classed as
the idle vagary of a bewildered brain, but for the marvelous success which attended it first in Washington and
gave it a "local habitation and a name," which struck
fire there, and has been answered by flame upon every
hilltop in almost every State of our land.

Scene at a National W. C. T. U. Convention (1877).

PRESENTATION OF THE CRUSADE QUILT.

The afternoon of the last day of the Convention at Baltimore, in 1877, was the occasion of a most interesting and
enjoyable event. At three o'clock the "crusade quilt"
was presented to Mrs. E. J. Thompson, of Hillsboro, Ohio,—
Leader of the First Praying Band of the "Crusade."

The quilt contained a square of a different color for
each State represented, and had, in embroidery, upon
each square the device and motto of the several auxiliary
organizations. It was a beautiful evidence of woman's
skill and taste in needle handicraft, and, as it hung in
graceful folds from the gallery, was a banner of which no
body of men or women need have been ashamed.

At the suggestion of Mrs. Wittenmyer, all the crusaders
in the Convention — by which was meant every woman
who had gone into a saloon and prayed and remonstrated
with the keeper and with the drunkards—arose and
united in singing the hymn which "the band of seventy"
sang when they started the movement in the town of
Hillsboro, beginning:

> "Give to the winds thy fears,
> Hope and be undismayed."

The author of this book made the first speech of
presentation, which was thus reported in the Baltimore
papers:

What is there in the dry and humdrum subject of

4

temperance to give these inspirations? That work, my friends, has in it thrilling sentiment and a deep romance, as superior to the ordinary impulses of life as the poetry of action is greater than the poetry of words, by as much as the doing of one kind act excels the fine morality of a page of Shakespeare, by as much as one deed of self-sacrifice overshadows the sweet and tender sentiments of a Dickens or a Hawthorne! Two days before Christmas, 1873, down in the quiet town of Hillsboro, in the Buckeye State, the sweet-voiced, saintly-faced woman you see before you, dropped her knitting and arose to bring salvation to a manhood that was vitiated and depraved. Far away on every hand, like wild prairie fire, went the flame enkindled by this spark. The quiet school-teacher in Illinois, with her college full of girls, felt that here was scope for all her dreams. Women throughout this great and glorious land became aware that it was time for them to enter into business for themselves. I am reminded at this moment of how you started this mighty ball a-rolling. When you told your husband, he said to you, "It's all tomfoolery, Eliza," and you replied to him that the men had been monopolizing this tomfoolery so long that it was about time the women were taking a hand. I am reminded too, that these are bonds of sympathy so strong uniting the women of this Union that nothing but death can sever them. I am made to feel that it means much for God to let a moral idea loose upon this earth, and to believe as the sum and substance of philosophy that God designs that Christ shall reign within the homes and institutions of this country. We look to Hillsboro as to the Mecca of our crusade, and have nothing to regret as we go back to the time when women were praying on the sanded floors of dram shops, surrounded by the drunken and the curious. It must, indeed, be a women's convention that would make so curious a testimonial as a quilt.

This one contains the autographs of 3,000 women, and, among other curious things sewn in the centre-piece, a prophecy to be opened in the year 1976, and not before.

Within its folds are hidden all our hearts. The day will come when, beside the death-sentence of a woman who was burned as a witch in Massachusetts, beside the block from which a woman was sold as a slave in South Carolina, and besides the liquor license that was issued by the State of Illinois to ruin its young men, there will hang this beautiful quilt, to which young men and women will point with pride, and say, " There is the name of my great-grandmother, who took part in Ohio's great crusade."

Mrs. Lathrop, of Michigan, also spoke. She said the quilt was an evidence of woman's patience in matters of detail — a quality that had been valuable in temperance reform. She considered that the results of the Union's four years of labor were simply the results of answered prayer. One of these results was the tramp of thousands of children throughout the land toward maturity, some with feet incased in kid, and more with copper-tipped shoes, every one with a temperance pledge in the pocket, and the resolution in their hearts never to drink, nor to use tobacco, nor to swear. I am glad it was none of us *wild* Western women that started this movement. It was this quiet lady, whose sweet, low voice can scarce be heard in this assembly, that led, and it was in a Presbyterian church, the least radical of all, that it was planned. Miss Willard has spoken of the next Centennial. Let us hope to meet at the next Centennial on the hills of Paradise, and trust that we may then be able to look down upon a country redeemed from the curse of alcohol.

Mrs. Thompson spoke affectingly in response. She explained that when the quilt was made by the women of Ohio, from the ten-cent contributions of over 3,000 mothers and daughters, she had no idea it would ever become hers as a testimonial of the National W. C. T. U.

CHAPTER VI.

"MOTHER STEWART."*

Ancestry—A Teacher—A Good Samaritan in War Times—Defends a Drunkard's Wife in Court—Enters a Saloon in Disguise—A Leader in Two Crusades—Visits England—Goes South—Critique of *London Watchman.*

MRS. ELIZA D., known the world over as "Mother Stewart," is a native of Ohio, born in Piketon, April 25, 1816. On the maternal side she is a granddaughter of Col. John Guthery of Revolutionary fame, one of the earliest pioneers of the State, and founder of Piketon. Her father, James Daniel, a man of superior talent and courtly manners, was a native of Virginia. Left an orphan before she was twelve, she was very early thrown upon her own resources, and soon began to develop the characteristics which have won for her an enviable reputation among the representative women who have done their share in molding western character.

With few of the facilities afforded the youth of to-day, she acquired a sufficient education to teach, then, alternately teaching and attending first Marietta Seminary, then Granville, she reached a good position among the educators of her State.

In her sixteenth year she made a profession of religion, and united with the Methodist church.

She has been married twice; her second husband, Hiram Stewart, is still living, is a staunch advocate of the principles she teaches, and seconds his wife in all her labors.

---

* Contributed.

MOTHER STEWART.

Mother Stewart has known all the sorrow and bereavement, but none of the joys of motherhood—none of her children living. But she took to her great motherly heart two bright sons of her second husband, and with conscientious devotion educated and prepared them to take their places among men.

These brief glimpses give us an intimation of the way by which the Lord led her; and though often passing through the valley of tears and by Marah's bitter fountain, He never forsook, but made her meet for His use in the coming years.

When the war came, while husband and sons went to the front, she devoted her time to gathering and forwarding supplies to the sick and wounded soldiers, and aiding their families, finally going herself to the scene of action, where from the "boys in blue" she received the name she wears as a crown, and by which she loves to be called.

We may be sure that such a woman could neither be blind nor silent on the subject of the liquor curse. So we find her more than twenty years ago, by voice and pen, throwing her influence on the side of temperance. Incidents of this period are not without interest, marking her as an advanced thinker, and foreshadowing her work of later years.

But later, in January, 1872, having addressed a large audience in her own city, and obtained a pledge from the ladies to stand by the drunkards' wives in prosecuting saloon-keepers under the Adair law recently passed, she went, a few days after, into the court-room, where a test case was being tried, and was induced by the prosecuting attorney, Geo. Rawlins, Esq., to make the opening plea to the jury. A lady in the court-room, and winning her case against one of the best lawyers in the city, created quite a sensation. Henceforth the poor women, fancying that at last they had found a sympathizing and helpful friend, brought her their tales of sorrow, and besought her aid. Again, in October, 1873, a woman came and with streaming tears repeated the old, sad story.   Having little hope of success, Mother Stewart first thought to send her away, but finally taking her to the law firm of which her friend Rawlins was a partner, stated the case, and asked if they could do anything.   Mr. R. said he would take the case if Mrs. Stewart would help him, and without hesitation she consented to do so.   Now came the thought, " Only through prayer can we prevail against this liquor power."   She invited influential ladies of the different churches to come to the court-room, and when there exhorted them to continue in prayer, while, amid great enthusiasm, she won this case.

At this time appeared in the city paper her "Appeal to the Women of Springfield, from a Drunkard's Wife," which added not a little to the excitement.   People were slow to believe, so little had they thought on the subject, that even one woman in Springfield was suffering as this pitiful appeal indicated.   Next going to the ministers, she requested them to preach on the subject, suggesting as a text, " Am I my brother's keeper ?" to which they readily assented.   Then with a petition signed by over six hundred ladies, and accompanied by a large delegation, she visited the council chamber, and in a brief, telling speech besought the council to pass what was known as the " McConnelsville Ordinance," prohibiting the sale of liquors within the corporation.   The subject was new, but it was taken up by the city benevolent society, and a committee appointed to wait on the ministers and ask their co-operation in inaugurating mass-meetings.   The ministers pledged their hearty support, and the first meeting was held on December 2d.

But by this time calls were coming to Mother Stewart

to " Wake up the women ! " It seemed to be impressed on the minds of the people that somehow deliverance, or at least help, must come by the hand of woman. On this evening, having been invited to Osborn, Green Co., she addressed a meeting and organized the first Women's Union, Mrs. Lee being elected president and Mrs. Hargrave secretary.

Next, observing with what impunity the saloon-keepers plied their trade on Sunday, Mrs. Stewart might have been seen—if she could have been recognized under her effective disguise—entering a saloon on Sunday, buying and carrying away a glass of liquor, for which the saloon-keeper was duly prosecuted.

Soon after, Dr. Dio Lewis came West, presented his plan of saloon visitation first to the ladies of Hillsboro', who at once accepted it, then, other towns in rapid succession following, the excitement spread like a flame on the prairies.

Henceforth Mother Stewart was in constant demand, lecturing, organizing, leading out bands, and rallying the forces to the deepening conflict.

About this time, impressed that she had a message to deliver to our sisters across the seas, she was praying for an open door, when an invitation came from that enthusiastic worker, Mrs. Margaret Parker, of Dundee, Scotland, and others, to visit Great Britain. Here her welcome was so warm that her visit was an ovation throughout the kingdom. The English say few women ever visited their shores who received the attention paid to Mother Stewart, the Crusader. Throwing all her enthusiastic nature into her work, she attracted great throngs to her meetings, and infused a new spirit into the staunch workers over there. The London *Times*, and other leading journals, greatly aided her by the extended and flattering reports they gave.

The result of her meeting was the formation of the British Women's Temperance Association, which is wielding a blessed influence among all classes in that country. Once more turning her eyes towards our sisters of the sunny South she said, Why shall we not invite them to join our holy alliance? and was crying to her Heavenly Father, "Here am I, send me," when she was made Chairman of the Committee on Southern work by the National Convention that met at Indianapolis in 1879.

She at once entered upon her duties, visiting various points; introduced our gospel temperance work, everywhere receiving the proverbial Southern welcome and the cordial support of the ministers, as well as of the most eminent ladies of the South.

Though a veteran, Mother Stewart is still full of fire and enthusiasm, and able to do effective service in the cause she loves and to which she has devoted her life. Of her on the platform we quote from the London *Watchword:*

"Her voice is sweet, and though not loud, is clear, and sometimes penetrating. She goes straight to the point, speaking with all the artlessness, originality, and *verve* of one full of the subject and charged with a mighty mission, yet talking naturally, and expressing just such thoughts, narrating such facts, and making such appeals as occur at the moment, couched in racy but idiomatic Saxon.

"One's heart goes out to Mother Stewart, standing there, pleading for help in her righteous cause. If not large in frame, she has a spirit powerful enough to rouse and inoculate a vast legion of supporters; her eye flashes, her ardent feelings and aspirations heighten the color in her face; now and then the voice will falter just a little, to prove how womanly she is. And oh, how well—though it may be briefly—she pleads! Hearing and reading her speeches are very different. A report fails to convey the native raciness, the undefinable charm of her manner, though, in reading, our words seem to come back to us from over the sea, and we can trace how strongly the northern, Saxon elements of our language flourish in congenial soil, as we look at those sharp, short terms; terse, brief, and pungent."

As the gathering army presses forward, let us not forget the veterans of the earlier day!

CHAPTER VII.

MRS. ABBY FISHER LEAVITT.

"Leader of the Forty-three"—The shoemaker and little white shoes.

"THERE'S lots of human nature in folks." Did "Samivel Weller" say that, or was it the "Widow Bedott"? Both are philosophers.

A human being is like a huge church organ—with many pipes, and stops, and banks of keys. And the kind of music that you get depends upon the sort of player that you are. Some call out only discords, some strike the minor chords alone, others evoke the music of laughter or of joy, while others still compass the whole diapason "from grave to gay, from lively to severe," and are particularly skilled in bringing out the sweet and tremulous *vox humana.*

If Mrs. Leavitt has this rare last-mentioned gift; if she is one whom we all thoroughly and heartily love; if she makes us do what she likes, yet never domineers; if one minute she sets us laughing, the next calls an argosy of pocket-handkerchiefs into requisition; if she seems to us to be "made up of every creature's best," what is the explanation? Her history gives it so plainly that "he who runs may read." From this unique character-study there is much to learn.

This prominent figure of the Crusade owes much of her efficiency in that great movement, to her strong frame and firm health, equilibrium of brain and heart, and varied experience. This "human pippin," as I am fond of calling her, grew on a hardy New England stock, where vigorous sea breezes charged the air with vital salts; it mellowed

(88)

MRS. ABBY F. LEAVITT.

in the sunshine of the South, and got its final flavor in kindly Indiana valleys, and on the prairies of proud Iowa. Best of all, does Mrs. Leavitt's courage never falter and her devotion to the dear Temperance Gospel never flag? This is the explanation: Her life is set to the sweet music of her favorite hymn, which she was singing when arrested for praying on the streets of Cincinnati—"Rock of Ages, cleft for me."

Bangor was her birth-place and early home. There seems a justice more than poetic in the coincidence by which so many of our best workers have been placed by birth or education under the influence of that grand old prohibition school-master, the State of Maine. In 1854, at the age of nineteen, Miss Fisher graduated from the Young Ladies' High School of her native town. She went South as a teacher soon after leaving school, and succeeded admirably, remaining until the war broke out. In the autumn of 1861 she become Principal of a Grammar School in Evansville, Indiana, and remained there until 1866, when she married Samuel K. Leavitt, a lawyer of Evansville. Four years later Mr. Leavitt was ordained a minister of Christ, and was immediately called to the charge of the First Baptist Church of Keokuk, Iowa, where he enjoyed a pleasant and successful pastorate until 1872, when he was invited to the First Baptist Church of Cincinnati, where he and the "help" so "meet" for a Christian minister of his enlightened views concerning women in the church, are still laboring side by side. Ministers who mourn and lament "the deadness of the church," and then say in prayer-meetings, "The *brethren* will please occupy the time," would find in the genial pastorate of Mr. Leavitt many matters worthy their thought. Besides leading in plans for the promotion of home and foreign missionary work, teaching in Sunday-school, visiting the poor, and interesting herself

particularly in the young people of the church, Mrs.
Leavitt was State Secretary of the Baptist Women's
Foreign Missionary Society of Ohio, where her efforts
have resulted in a marked increase in contributions to
the work.

When the crusade burst upon the women of Ohio, she
recognized in it the hand and call of God, was among the
first to take her place in the ranks of workers, and, on the
principle of the "survival of the fittest," was at once promoted to the leadership of the "Praying Band." Day
after day for weeks, accompanied by a long procession of
noble Christian workers, she visited saloons, holding religious services within whenever permission was granted,
but outside, if it was refused, and always closing up the
day's work with an earnest Gospel meeting in the church
from which the bands had gone out in the morning. The
church would be filled to overflowing with crowds of men
and women who were hungry for salvation. At these
meetings hundreds signed the pledge, and asked the
prayers of Christians. On the 16th of May, 1874, while
engaged in this work, Mrs. Leavitt, with forty-two others, wives of clergymen and other leading citizens, was
arrested and taken to jail. It is a strange and thrilling
story, as she tells it, and none else could do it justice.
Suffice it that the mayor said the women shouldn't pray
upon the sidewalk's edge, though beer barrels and blowsy
drunkards are permitted to obstruct the passageway so
often in that city, swimming in "lager." Hardly believing the threat against them would be executed, they went
out as usual. Being denied admission to a saloon, they
knelt upon the pavement, and just as Mrs. Leavitt began
singing,

"Rock of ages, cleft for me,"

a burly policeman laid his hand on her shoulder, saying,
"You are my prisoner."

"Let me hide myself in thee,"

sang on the clear, untroubled voice, and they marched to jail, continuing the hymn. There they held a prayer-meeting, in the midst of which stood the mayor, unable to escape, while hard-faced men were weeping on every side. They were locked into a corridor, and Mrs. Leavitt talked through the grated doors with several of the prisoners. She found a woman who had been arrested because of drunkenness. "It is a curious conundrum," said Mrs. Leavitt, with that contagious smile lurking in the corner of her mouth, "that here's one woman locked up for getting drunk, and another equally locked up for trying to get people not to be drunk. Curious country this is, anyway ! "

After their arrest the ladies changed their plans of work, going to saloons in companies of two and three instead of by eighties and hundreds. Gospel temperance meetings were held in churches, jails, and hospitals, cottage prayer-meetings in neighborhoods, and constant efforts made to extend the work of carrying the bread of life to those whom some one has aptly called the " elbow heathen," who jostle us as we walk along the city pavement; "the great humanity that beats its life along the stony streets," and may justly bring up to the bar of God the accusation against its well-to-do neighbors, " No man cared for my soul."

When the Praying Band of Cincinnati was reorganized into the Woman's Christian Temperance Union, Mrs. Leavitt was chosen president, and has never lowered the white flag of temperance. The headquarters of the Union on Vine street are open every day for a Gospel meeting, often conducted by her, and hundreds of wayward boys, away from their homes and tempted on every side by rum shops, bless the day they first heard her kind and earnest voice, and knelt beside her while she commended their souls to God.

During the trying days of 1874, previous to the October election, when the rum power was using every endeavor to induce the people of Ohio to vote for a law licensing the traffic in and sale of intoxicating drinks, Mrs. Leavitt, with hosts of temperance women, spoke in halls, churches, tents, and groves against license.

When the result of the election was announced, and the State was saved from the disgrace of a license law, many men, good and true, thanked God for temperance women who were willing to lift up their voices " for God and home and native land."

Mrs. Leavitt was for years treasurer of the Woman's National Union, and her appeals for help, at once so witty and convincing, were among the " humors of the convention." She was the first woman elected by the first National Convention for president of the Woman's Christian Temperance Union, which position she at once declined.

Among the ablest and most constant friends of our national paper, Mrs. Leavitt should ever be remembered. For two years a member of its publishing committee, she has invested much time, thought, and prayer on its behalf. It is especially fitting that her friends (and the term includes everybody who has ever seen or heard of her) should have the pleasure of getting some hint, at least, about her from the engraving and this sketch. Somehow its preparation has been peculiarly a labor of love, and, unconsciously, my pen has been betrayed into a freedom of expression to be explained partly by the genial character of the subject, and partly by the tender regard of the writer. Garrulous as this presentation may appear, there has been under every word the grateful remembrance of this dear friend's faith, tranquil and pure as a June sky. In days never to be forgotten, this serene trust in Christ, this unalterable love for Him, and devotion to His cause, have been to one tired heart, at least, as " the shadow of a great rock in a weary land."

THE SHOEMAKER AND LITTLE WHITE SHOES.

Mrs. Leavitt has often told the following story from the platform:

" One morning during the Crusade, a drunkard's wife came to my door. She carried in her arms a baby six weeks old. Her pale, pinched face was sad to see, and she told me this sorrowful story: ' My husband is drinking himself to death ; he is lost to all human feeling; our rent is unpaid, and we are liable to be put out into the street; and there is no food in the house for me and the children. He has a good trade, but his earnings all go into the saloon on the corner near us ; he is becoming more and more brutal and abusive. We seem to be on the verge of ruin. How can I, feeble as I am, with a babe in my arms, earn bread for myself and children ? '

" Quick as thought the question came to me, and I asked it: ' Why not have that husband of yours converted ? '

" But she answered hopelessly, ' Oh, there's no hope of such a thing. He cares for nothing but strong drink.'

" ' I'll come and see him this afternoon,' said I.

" ' He'll insult you,' she replied.

" ' No matter,' said I ; ' my Saviour was insulted, and the servant is not above his Lord.'

" That very afternoon I called at the little tenement house. The husband was at work at his trade in a back room, and his little girl was sent to tell him that a lady wished to see him. The child, however, soon returned with the message, ' My pa says he won't see any one.'

" But I sent him a message proving that I was indeed in earnest. I said, ' Go back and tell your pa that a lady wishes to see him on very important business, and she must see him if she has to stay till after supper.'

"I knew very well that there was nothing in the house to eat. A moment afterward a poor, bloated, besotted wreck of a man stood before me.

"'What do you want?' he demanded as he came shuffling into the room.

"'Please be seated and look at this paper,' I answered, pointing to a vacant chair at the other end of the table where I was sitting, and handing a printed pledge to him.

"He read it slowly, and then, throwing it down upon the table, broke out violently :

"'Do you think I'm a fool? I drink when I please, and let it alone when I please. I'm not going to sign away my personal liberty.'

"'Do you think you can stop drinking?'

"'Yes, I could if I wanted to.'

"'On the contrary, I think you're a slave to the rum-shop down on the corner.'

"'No, I ain't, any such thing.'

"'I think, too, that you love the saloon-keeper's daughter better than you do your own little girl.'

"'No, I don't, either.'

"'Well, let us see about that. When I passed the saloon-keeper's house I saw his little girl coming down the steps, and she had on white shoes, and a white dress, and a blue sash. Your money helped to buy them. I come here, and your little girl, more beautiful than she, has on a faded, ragged dress, and her feet are bare.'

"'That's so, madam.'

"'And you love the saloon-keeper's wife better than you love your own wife.'

"'Never; no, never!'

"'When I passed the saloon-keeper's house, I saw his wife come out with the little girl, and she was dressed in silks and laces, and a carriage waited for her. Your money helped to buy the silks and laces, and the horses and the carriage. I come here and I find your wife in a faded calico gown, doing her own work; if she goes any where, she must walk.'

"'You speak the truth, madam.'

"'You love the saloon-keeper better than you love yourself. You say you can keep from drinking if you choose; but you helped the saloon-keeper to build himself a fine brick house, and you live in this poor, tumble-down old house yourself.'

"'I never saw it in that light before.' Then, holding out his hand, that shook like an aspen leaf, he continued, 'You speak the truth, madam—I am a slave. Do you see that hand? I've got a piece of work to finish, and I must have a mug of beer to steady my nerves, or I cannot do it; but to-morrow, if you'll call, I'll sign the pledge.'

"'That's a temptation of the devil; I did not ask you to sign the pledge. You are a slave, and cannot help it. But I do want to tell you this: *There is One who can break your chains and set you free.*'

"'I want to be free.'

"'Well, Christ can set you free, if you'll submit to Him, and let him break the chains of sin and appetite that bind you.'

"'It's been many a long year since I prayed.'

"'No matter; the sooner you begin the better for you.'

"He threw himself at once upon his knees, and while I prayed I heard him sobbing out the cry of his soul to God.

"His wife knelt beside me and followed me in earnest prayer. The words were simple and broken with sobs, but somehow they went straight up from her crushed heart to God, and the poor man began to cry in earnest for mercy.

"'O God! break these chains that are burning into my

soul! Pity me, and pity my wife and children, and break the chains that are dragging me down to hell. O God! be merciful to me a sinner.' And thus out of the depths he cried to God, and He heard him and had compassion upon him, and broke every chain and lifted every burden; and he arose a free, redeemed man.

"When he arose from his knees he said: 'Now I will sign the pledge, and keep it.'

"And he did. A family altar was established, the comforts of life were soon secured—for he had a good trade—and two weeks after this scene his little girl came into my husband's Sunday-school with *white shoes and white dress and blue sash on*, as a token that her father's money no longer went into the saloon-keeper's till.

"But what struck me most of all was that it took less than *two hours* of my time thus to be an ambassador for Christ in declaring the terms of heaven's great treaty whereby a soul was saved from death, a multitude of sins were covered, and a home restored to purity and peace.

MRS. MARY A. WOODBRIDGE.

CHAPTER VIII.

MRS. MARY A. WOODBRIDGE.

President of the Crusade State, and Recording Secretary of the National W. C. T. U.—A Nantucket Girl—Cousin of Maria Mitchell —Western education—Baptized into the Crusade—Speaks in fifty Presbyterian Churches—The author's glimpse of the Crusade—The Crusade in Calcutta—Margaret Parker.

[THE sketch drawn by Rev. A. M. Hills, the gifted pastor of my gifted friend is so excellent that I give it in full:]

"A brilliant writer has said: 'A radiant and sparkling woman, full of wit, reason, and fancy, is a whole crown of jewels. A poor, opaque copy of her is the most that one can render in a biographical sketch.' I feel the truth of this remark in attempting the task laid upon me —to give a word-picture of Mrs. Mary A. Woodbridge.

"Mary A. Brayton was born in Nantucket, Mass. Her father, Isaac Brayton, was for a score of years captain of a whaling vessel which cruised in the Pacific. But he was destined to rule over a wider domain than a ship's deck, and to command more men than a ship's crew. His townsmen, appreciating his rare qualifications of heart and mind, sent him to the Massachusetts Legislature in the days when Edward Everett was Governor, and when that body was composed of as able and distinguished members as ever sat in the Congressional halls of any State.

"Mr. Brayton afterward moved to Ohio, and was elected to the Legislature, where he won deserved distinction for his ability. He was the author of the bill by which the

(101)

public institutions of the State are still controlled. He was also afterward an associate upon the bench with Benjamin F. Wade.

"The mother of Mrs. Woodbridge was a sister of the great astronomer, William Mitchell, father of the famous Prof. Maria Mitchell, of Vassar College, and of Prof. Henry Mitchell, of Smithsonian Institute.

"It is not surprising that the daughter of such parents should have unusual intellectual powers. Mary early gave brilliant promise. When she was but six years of age, Horace Mann, the famous educator of Massachusetts, passed a day in Nantucket examining the public schools. To his great delight, the precocious little girl went through the multiplication table backward and forward up to the twenties. When she had finished, he laid his hand kindly on her head and said : ' Well, my child, if you persevere you will be a noted woman.' There can be no doubt in the minds of those who know her best that she was at once the pride and the torment of all her instructors.

"It must have been morally impossible for her to be a ' proper-nice ' child. She was too full of intense vitality, too mirthful, too keenly alive to the ridiculous, and too adept and merciless as a mimic, to be a model of good behavior to schoolmates. To outstrip her companions in intellectual feats in the school-room, and then to be their ringleader in semi-innocent mischief, must have been as natural to her as to breathe—a thing altogether to be expected.

" Mary was nine years of age when her father moved to Ravenna, O., from which time she studied either under private instructors or in an excellent private school in Hudson, O.

" She was converted at the age of fourteen, and married at seventeen a promising young merchant—Frederick

Wells Woodbridge. She was mother of three children when but little more than twenty. Such an early marriage and such a family would have been, with most women, the end of all study and intellectual achievement; but it was not so with her. She never lost her enthusiasm for books, nor her thirst for knowledge. She had too much energy of character and power of perseverance to be balked by difficulties. Her mind must have food, and she fed it, studying with her book on a rack before her, while her quick hands were engaged with household tasks. She took lessons in German and French, and recited in her own house while holding one of her babes on her knee and quieting another at her side. She was at that time presiding over a family of twelve, having the entire management of her domestic affairs and performing many of the commonest duties herself. For the first six years of her married life she lived at Ravenna; then the family moved to Newburgh, now a part of Cleveland, O., where for twenty years she lived the life of a cultured Christian matron, and an unusually brilliant member of society, yet otherwise undistinguished from the multitudes around her. Six years ago Mr. and Mrs. Woodbridge returned to Ravenna. She entered again upon the same uneventful, everyday life. Thus she might have lived to the end of her days unknown beyond her social circle, had she not been summoned from her seclusion by the stirring events of the next few months.

"The Crusade came—came with the suddenness and the power of Pentecost; bringing also, like it, a baptism of the Holy Ghost. In common with thousands of others of her Ohio sisters, she felt the movings of the Spirit. Her eyes were opened, to see in a new light the woes caused by intemperance. She went to her closet, and there, when alone with her God, heard the Divine voice asking, 'Whom shall I send?' She had the grace given her to lay herself upon the altar in consecration, with the prayer, 'Here am I; I will be or do whatever pleaseth Thee.'

"But she did not yet understand the vision nor realize that a live coal had touched her lips. She had been a professing Christian for thirty years, but had never spoken a word in public or offered an audible prayer. Soon she attended a great union meeting, which had come together in the excitement of the hour without any one having been appointed to preside when gathered. It was thought best that this should be done by a woman. Who should it be? One after another thought of her, and she was asked to take the place. She was utterly over-come with fear and a sense of inability, and pleaded to be excused. Her aged father came to her side and tenderly reminded her of her consecration vow, and then left her. Her pastor came a second time, when, with a struggle, she said to one standing by: 'Doctor, ask the audience to rise and sing 'Coronation'; I never can walk up the aisle with these people looking at me.' As they sang she went forward, trembling with weakness and praying every step, 'Lord, help me! Lord, help me!' She called upon a brother to pray, then she read a verse of Scripture, and began to say she knew not what. But God put His own message into her anointed lips. The depths of her woman's heart were moved. Self was forgotten in her message. She pleaded for the degraded victims of drink, for their heart-broken wives and mothers, for their suffer-ing and degraded children. Her words poured forth in tender and resistless eloquence, till the multitude were moved as one man. The strong were melted to tears. Christians wept and prayed together. A cool-headed judge arose and solemnly declared that he had never been in an audience so manifestly moved by the Holy Ghost.

"In that one sacred hour she was lifted by the providence of God into a new life. Her mission had come. Like St. Paul, she had had a revelation, and she has not since that time been disobedient to the heavenly vision. No single experience could well make a more marked change in a woman's life. It may be truly said of her that during the years since the crusade "she hath done what she could."

"At once the little country churches around began to call upon her, and she would speak to them on foreign missions, Sabbath-school work, or temperance, as the case might be. No opportunity to do work for Christ or humanity was slighted, and no occasion was ever too insignificant for her to give her best. And she still retains the same beautiful spirit. She drinks deeply the spirit of her Master, who would address either the multitudes on the mountain-side or the one wicked woman at the well. Though constantly pressed by urgent invitations to the great cities, she will, when opportunity permits, preach at the missions of her pastor in country school-houses in his absence.

" She now fills the offices of Recording Secretary to the Woman's National Christian Temperance Union, and President of the State organization of Ohio.

" Her husband is in closest and fullest sympathy with all her work, always assisting by every means her part, while performing his own share in the church or in the broad fields outside.

"As my thought in the near relation of pastor goes over her work, I am reminded that she has spoken in more than fifty Presbyterian churches during the last year from the pulpit; and she speaks from a text! Whisper this in the ear of that New York Presbytery which tried and solemnly warned one of its ablest members for admitting the saintly Miss Smiley into his pulpit. The fact is, even Presbyterian prejudice about women speaking in meeting melts away under the influence of the sweet womanliness, the dignity, the power, and the tender, Christ-like spirit of such an one.

"A few such as she would do much to—yea, will—bring her sex into their true liberty, and wipe out the prejudices created by a few unwomanly advocates of woman's rights who, a few years ago, engaged the attention of the public mind, but now, happily, have dropped out of sight.

" In addition to all this public effort, and official duties, Mrs. Woodbridge also edits weekly several columns of the *Commonwealth*, a temperance paper. As a temperance worker she is in the advance line, advocating prohibition and home protection.

"A statesman is he who can govern and create statesmen around him. A soul is great that can make others great. Measured by this standard, Mrs. Woodbridge is a great power for good. Many a woman comes under her influence for a day, and receives an uplifting inspiration which is never lost. As with cultured intellect and loving heart she pleads, like an anointed prophetess, for the souls of dying men and for the holiest interests of humanity in home and States, many another heart throbs with holier emotions and worthier ambitions than it has been wont to feel, and the God-given talents are brought out and laid in tearful yet joyous consecration on the altar of the Lord.

" It yet remains for me to write a word about her home-life. Many persons can coruscate in brilliant rhetoric before an audience, whose home and private life do not bear inspection. Mrs. W. does not belong to that class. Her home is beautiful, her hospitality most gracious, and all the affairs of the household move off with the orderliness and precision of machinery. Her home life is the fitting complement of that which is seen. Her family, until quite recently, has always been very large, because no one ever became an inmate of the household who did not prolong his stay. A clerk who came to stay a week tarried three years. Her father-in-law came to make a visit, and staid eleven years—till death. Her own father came to the home one week after Mr. and Mrs. W. were married, and he still abides with them. One other characteristic I must not fail to mention—a grace as rare as it is beautiful. Above any other person I ever knew she carries in her roomy heart the joys and the sorrows of others. The little tokens of remembrance which she sends to the sick and the feeble, and the comforting notes which go from her hand and heart to the sorrowing and troubled, are simply innumerable. To sum up her character—humility and power, grace and strength, courage and earnestness strive in her for the mastery. I cannot say which has it.

"Happy is the father, honored is the husband, blessed are the children, favored is the friend, and fortunate is the cause, that commands the advocacy of such a woman."

MY GLIMPSE OF THE CRUSADE.

Right here, under the wing of my beloved friend and associate, let me put in my only personal experience of the Crusade.

Never can I forget the day on which I met the great unwashed, untaught, ungospelled multitude for the first time. Need I say it was the Crusade that opened before me, as before ten thousand other women, this wide, "effectual door?" It was in Pittsburg, the summer after the Crusade. Greatly had I wished to have a part in it, but this one experience was my first and last of "going out with a band." A young teacher from the public schools, whose custom it was to give an hour twice each week to crusading, walked arm-in-arm with me. Two school-ma'ams together, we fell into the procession

5

behind the experienced campaigners. On Market street we entered a saloon, the proprietor of which, pointing to several men who were fighting in the next room, begged us to leave, and we did so at once, amid the curses of the bacchanalian group. Forming in line on the curbstone's edge in front of this saloon, we knelt, while an old lady, to whose son that place had proved the gate of death, offered a prayer full of tenderness and faith, asking God to open the eyes of those who, just behind that screen, were selling liquid fire and breathing curses on his name. We rose, and what a scene was there! The sidewalk was lined by men with faces written all over and inter-lined with the record of their sin and shame. Soiled with "the slime from the muddy banks of time," tattered, dishevelled, there was not a sneering look or a rude word or action from any one of them. Most of them had their hats off; many looked sorrowful; some were in tears; and standing there in the roar and tumult of that dingy street, with that strange crowd looking into our faces—with a heart stirred as never until now by human sin and shame, I joined in the sweet gospel song:

> "Jesus the water of life will give,
> Freely, freely, freely!"

Just such an epoch as that was in my life, has the Crusade proved to a mighty army of women all over this land. Does anybody think that, having learned the blessedness of carrying Christ's gospel to those who never come to church to hear the messages we are all commanded to "Go, tell," we shall ever lay down this work? Not until the genie of the Arabian Nights crowds himself back into the fabulous kettle whence he escaped by "expanding his pinions in nebulous bars"—not until then! To-day and every day they go forth on their beautiful errands—the "Protestant nuns," who a few years ago were among the "anxious and aimless" of our crowded population, or who belonged to trades and professions over-full—and with them go the women fresh from the sacred home-hearth and cradle-side, wearing the halo of these loving ministries. If you would find them, go not alone to the costly churches which now welcome their voices, while to those who are " at ease in Zion " they gently speak of the great, whitened harvest. But go to blacksmith shop and billiard hall, to public reading-room and depot waiting-room, to the North End in Boston, Water street, New York, the Bailey coffee houses of Philadelphia, the Friendly Inns of Cleveland, the Woman's Temperance Room of Cincinnati, and Lower Farwell Hall, Chicago, and you will find the glad tidings declared by the new " apostolic succession," dating from the Pentecost of the Crusade.

THE WOMAN'S CRUSADE IN CALCUTTA.

The Crusade wave spread fast and far. As its result we have the Woman's Christian Temperance Union of Great Britain and Canada, while in Australia and the Sandwich Islands there are local auxiliaries, and isolated societies in India and Japan. Mrs. Viele of Albany, and that lovely young missionary, Miss Susan B. Higgins of Boston (so " early crowned "), started a grand work in Yokohama. Rev. Joseph Cook, newly returned from his trip around the world, says they are watching women's work everywhere from the other side the globe with earnest hope. Mrs. May of Calcutta, secretary of the ladies' branch of " Bengal Temperance League," writes the following remarkable account.

" HOW WE BEGAN IT.

"It is now more than two years since we commenced our work in Calcutta, and as I review the past my heart is full of gratitude to God for the success he has seen fit to

vouchsafe us. It was suggested through reading about
'The Woman's Crusade in America,' and Dr. Thoburn,
of the American Methodist Episcopal Church, thought
that a similar work might be done in this city.

"Never shall I forget our first Sunday in Flag street.
This street is one of the lowest parts of Calcutta, and one
side of it is principally devoted to grog-shops and boarding-houses, which on Sunday afternoon are pretty well
filled with men more or less intoxicated. A little party
of four ladies left our carriage and asked for permission,
through a gentleman who that day accompanied us, to
sing in one of the grog-shops. The manager refused,
saying: 'If you are not gone I will throw water over
you; you are ruining our trade.' Denied an entrance,
we four women sang the Gospel at the door, and learning
that we must *ourselves* make the request, in every other
drinking-saloon we gained admission.

"On this first Sabbath we only sang, but ever after we
talked to the men pointedly, each addressing the little
group nearest, and usually making some remark suggested
by the hymn. After singing the one commencing with

> " 'Art thou weary, art thou languid,
>   Art thou sore distrest?
> "Come to me," saith One; and coming,
>   Be at rest,'

one fine, manly fellow responded, saying, 'I am weary.
I want to come to Jesus.' We directed him to the
Saviour. Before leaving, it is our rule as far as possible
to ask them to join in prayer, and while one of us leads
many bow with uncovered heads, and, may we not hope,
join in our supplications from the heart?

"As I was kneeling one sailor said, 'Don't be too long,
missus, for it is eight years since I knelt in prayer.' On
another occasion, while we were singing,

> " 'Joy, joy, joy! there is joy in Heaven with the angels,
>   Joy, joy, joy! for the prodigal's return,'

my attention was drawn to a young officer, who looked quite out of place there. He sang most heartily, while the tears flowed down his face. Then followed the confession of a mother's prayers and a father's counsel disregarded, and of twelve years' pleadings with God by his parents for the prodigal's return. He was induced by us to attend the service in the evening, and gave himself to Christ. His account of himself was : 'It was that hymn about the prodigal that broke my hard heart.' I have since learned that his father is an earnest minister in England.

"We take tracts in sixteen different languages, as sailors from every land are to be found in Calcutta. It touched our hearts to see the delight of a Greek one day on receiving a Testament in his own language. He *literally* danced with joy, and then sat down to read the precious book. It seemed so strange to hear him and his companions conversing in that strange language.

"Thus, from Sunday to Sunday, our work progresses. During the cold season as many as forty or fifty are induced to go to God's house, and many remain behind to be instructed in the way of salvation. But as a whole it is a work of faith, and results will only be known in the Great Day.

TAKING UP THE CROSS.

"One Sunday we found five sober men striving to induce their shipmates to leave the grog-shop. Failing in the attempt, they were leaving, ashamed of the bad company. After assuring them we knew they had not been drinking, we gave each a tract. One was entitled, 'I wish I could see my father again.' 'That's me,' said the man who took it. 'My father has died while I have been making the voyage here. He was a good father to me, and I do want to see him again.' We told him that if he would serve God here his wish would be realized. This little group of five listened most attentively while we entreated them to come to Jesus, explaining the sacrifices they will have to make in giving up old companions and bearing the sneers of ungodly friends, etc. They replied, 'We know all that, but we don't mind,' and on the spot they professed to receive Christ, and told us they would not care about the scoffs of their shipmates, but would kneel right down and pray to God to keep them from sin every morning and night. Nothing strikes us more than the childlike simplicity of the sailor. He just takes God at His word, and therefore 'receives' as well as 'asks.'

JUST IN TIME.

"At one saloon I felt an unaccountable prompting to go to the end, where a gentleman sat in such a position as to prevent our seeing his face. His manner and bearing seemed strangely out of place there, and he was so mortified to be found in a grog-shop by ladies that I felt half sorry that I had spoken ; but trusting in the One who had led us thither, I said : 'You seem to be depressed, and I am come to tell you of a Friend who will be with you always, even to the end of the world.' The word about God's love touched him, and he broke down and wept bitterly. It was some moments before he was sufficiently composed to speak ; his heart was too full. Then followed a sad story of deep distress, which, alas, was beyond our power to ameliorate. We took him home, and then he astonished us by saying : 'You saved my life to-day. I was bent on committing suicide. I felt as though no one cared for me, but the few kind words made me feel life was precious after all.'

MORE SUCCESSES.

"In the saloon an officer with two midshipmen arrested our attention. They expressed and looked great surprise at seeing ladies there. We explained to them our object, and invited them to our evening service. They came, and we had a conversation with them afterwards. The officer promised never to frequent such places again, and I have since learned that, although surrounded by temptations, he has kept his word, and more, he has become a total abstainer. After four months' absence from Calcutta the midshipman returned, and this time we met in God's house. Flag street was forsaken for the house of prayer.

"At one of the largest houses we met a man disposed to argue the point of the propriety of our singing hymns there. We told him this was our only opportunity of speaking to him. He talked much and loudly, but after we had prayed he became much more reasonable, and said: 'Tell me what time service begins, for I believe I shall go. I have the tract you gave me in my pocket.'

AN ANTIDOTE PROVIDED.

"Three sober men were sitting at another table. We said: 'What pleasure can it be to you to be here, where there is so much confusion and noise?' They replied: 'We have no other place to go.' I am thankful to be able to add that a gentleman has provided a "House of Rest,' a 'Seaman's Coffee and Reading-room,' where these poor men, whose life is full of toil and temptation, can spend their leisure time in peace, free from the snares and temptations which are spread for them at the grog-shops, and where they will be surrounded by good and holy influences. He has fitted it up beautifully, in home fashion, with matting and comfortable seats; there is a reading-room, spacious and airy, where are little tables, at which two or three can enjoy a quiet chat together, also two rooms adjoining for singing, Bible-classes, etc., but the attendance is voluntary. Tea, coffee, lemonade, and other refreshments are sold at a moderate

price. The whole place is very inviting, and brightly
lighted up with gas. Pray that the hearts of the men
who frequent this place may be illuminated by God's Holy
Spirit."

MRS. MARGARET ELEANOR PARKER,

President of the International Woman's Christian Temperance Union.

The position and character of our transatlantic cousin
combine to render her an attractive picture for our gallery.

Margaret E. Parker, of Dundee, Scotland, may be set
forth in a sentence as a modest gentlewoman with a life
devoted to noble purposes and philanthropic deeds. Born
of an old Tory or Conservative line, and reared with all
the prejudices of aristocratic birth, her generous heart
has over-leaped these barriers, and in the face of opposition which would have crushed a soul less brave, she has
become a philanthropist and a reformer.

Her beneficent activities began in that department of
church work where women have always been allowed an
"equal right" with men, viz.: that of paying off church
debts and raising funds for "church extension." Nothing succeeds like success, and as Mrs. Parker has never
been associated with a losing enterprise her name has
become the synonym for victory. Whether conducting a
charitable fair, circulating a temperance petition, organizing Mother Stewart's lecture campaign, or the British
Woman's Temperance Union, she is always gently confident, untiringly diligent, and sure to win.

"An orthodox of the orthodox," she worked for woman
suffrage side by side with the party of John Stuart Mill;
a wife, mother, and housekeeper of the New England
school, she addressed the British Social Science Congress
on the question of capital and labor; a modest, soft-
voiced woman from the home-hearth and the cradle-side,

MRS. MARGARET E. PARKER.

she marshaled " the bonnets of bonny Dundee," leading
a procession of sixty of her townswomen to the headquarters of the magistrate, where they presented a no-license
petition with nine thousand names of women — all this
in the days of our "Crusade," and under its blessed
inspiration. Mrs. Parker is a great admirer of our country, and this was not the first time she had taken up its
bright ideas. Indeed, our own John B. Gough counts
her among his most valued converts, for at one of his
lectures in Dundee, some twenty years ago, Mrs. Parker
and her husband first saw their duty, as Christian parents
and members of society, to become total abstainers.
Many of us have seen her " bring down the house " by
telling how, in their zeal, they banished not only wine
bottles, decanters, and glasses from their sideboard, but,
forgetting that they should continue to drink "Adam's
ale," sent away their tumblers also! Concerning her
appreciation of "Yankee Notions," Mrs. Parker once
wrote: "I have an American cook stove in my kitchen,
an American sewing-machine in my sitting-room, and all
the American books I can get in my library, and now I
must have your wide-awake American paper, the Boston
Woman's Journal."

Active as she had always been in reforms, the Crusade
movement stirred Margaret Parker's heart as nothing
else had ever done. The presentation of her temperance
petition to the authorities of Dundee struck the key-note
for the United Kingdom, aroused Christian women to a
sense of their responsibility, and led to the organization
of temperance unions in Dundee and many other towns.
The press having brought to her the name of Mother
Stewart of Ohio, as prominently connected with the Crusade, Mrs. Parker invited her to Scotland, and arranged
a temperance trip for her which greatly enlisted the public
interest, and from which resulted a meeting at Newcastle-

on-Tyne. Delegates from all parts of the Kingdom were present; women who had never heard their own voices on a platform before spoke with fluency and convincing earnestness, and proceeded, with all due observance of parliamentary forms, to organize the "British Women's Christian Temperance Union." Mrs. Parker was elected president of this new society, and was sent as a delegate to the Woman's International Temperance Convention which met in the Academy of Music, Philadelphia, in June of the Centennial year. There Mrs. Parker was unanimously elected President of the Woman's International Christian Temperance Union, the avowed object of which is "to spread a temperance Gospel to the ends of the earth." Twice, since the Crusade, Mrs. Parker has visited our country to study the spirit and methods of the Woman's Temperance work. A charming little book, entitled "Six Happy Weeks among the Americans," records her impression of the land she had so long desired to see. A reception was given her by Sorosis, and she was elected a member of that society and of the "Woman's Congress." Mrs. Parker is not an orator, but her refined manners and gentle presence, combined with her strong sense and ready wit, made her one of the favorite speakers at the great Chicago Convention called by the National Temperance Society, of which Mr. J. N. Stearns is Secretary. We very frequently hear the mis-application of our Lord's statement that "a prophet is not without honor save among his own kindred." We have no prophets nowadays, but observation teaches that people in general, and even the much-abused "women with a career," are apt to be honored and beloved by their own townsfolk if they deserve to be. Mrs. Parker's record illustrates this. Nowhere is her influence so great as in her own city. Twice she has been offered a place on the School Board of Dundee, which she has declined

only that she may give her time to the work of the local
Woman's Temperance Union, of which she has been
President since its organization, and to the duties of her
more distinguished but hardly more onerous office as
President of the International.

Naturally enough, we wish to know something of the
home life of a woman so prominent in public work — for
there is one test on which Society has a right to insist in
the name of its deeper right of self-preservation. If, by
taking on themselves the burdens of government, of philanthropy, of carrying the Gospel message, women are to
forget to light the hearth and trim the evening lamp; if
the voices of their little ones are to be drowned in the
applause of multitudes, then Home shall fall, "and when
Home falls, the world."

"To the word and to the testimony!" What does our
British sister teach us on this vital question?

She is the wife of Edward Parker, proprietor of an
extensive manufactory. She had six children — five sons,
one daughter — until her noble Harry was lately called
away. OUR UNION has contained nothing more tender and
beautiful than the account of this young man's death.
During the childhood of her sons and daughters, Mrs.
Parker gave herself up to their happiness and training, and
a more loving and harmonious family circle cannot be
found. Mr. Parker is a man of broad and generous soul,
who delights in his wife's ability and work, and heartily
enters into and fosters all her plans. Their elegant residence, "The Cliff," is beautiful for situation, "looking
off upon the German Ocean and old St. Andrew's of
classic memory." In the best sense it is a model Scotch
home. Here "the latch string is out," for all men and
women whose chief aim is to make the world a more
sunshiny place because they've lived in it. Here is
"society" in a true and royal sense, undreamed of by

the votaries of fashion and of pleasure. As Antoinette
Brown Blackwell aptly puts it, "After all, a mother's
child is but an incident in her life. Love it as she will,
it will grow up, and in a few years it is gone. But a life
work remains for a life *time!*" Thus, those who by their
gifts of brain and heart were formed to be in some sweet
sense mothers to those outside their homes, may bring to
the wider ministries of life's long afternoon the culture
of soul they acquired in the ministries of the cradle and
the fireside.

Mrs. Parker closed her annual address before the
British Woman's Temperance Union, at its meeting in
London, with these words, which may fitly put a period
to our hasty sketch:

A mighty conflict is before us. Shall we, standing here beside the
Cross, place ourselves in God's hands to do His work? I believe
many hearts here respond, "By Thy grace I will." I stand before
you to-day under the shadow of a great sorrow, coming as I do from
the grave of a dear son of seventeen years. He has left a bright record
of work done for the Master in the cause of temperance. His dying
words to me were, "Go on in your blessed work while it is day, for
the night cometh." And so say I to you — work while it is day, the
night cometh. Time is so short, eternity so great, and the ravages of
strong drink so fearful, that it behooves us to rise in the might and
the power with which God has endowed us, and in the name of the
perishing, and the God who cares for them, demand that the traffic in
strong drink shall cease.

At present Mrs. Parker is living in England with her
family, and working side by side with her successor as
President of the British Women's Temperance League,
Mrs. Margaret Lucas, sister of Hon. John Bright, M.P.

MRS. MARGARET LUCAS,

President of the Woman's Temperance League of Great Britain.

In this well-known lady we have a fitting illustration of
what may be wrought for the great outside world in the
serene hours of life's long afternoon by the wife and

MRS. MARGARET B. LUCAS.

mother whose meridian years were occupied with the cares and duties of her home. Of Quaker ancestry and training, the sister of John Bright, ablest and best beloved of British Commoners, with wealth, position, and an honored name, Mrs. Lucas brought to our ranks gifts many and rare. She had long been a Good Templar, having affiliated with that order of true-hearted men and women because of her deep sympathy with their aims and spirit. She visited the United States some years ago, but though cordial, how different the welcome she then received from what awaits her now could she be persuaded to "cross over." There is not a W. C. T. U. of all the three thousand that would not exhaust both resources and ingenuity to do her honor. Mrs. Lucas is sixty-three years of age, is well preserved, erect and vigorous. She has but one daughter, Mrs. Thomasson, wife of a member of Parliament, and one son, a deaf mute, who with his lovely family, lives near her. She was perfectly devoted to her children until they grew to maturity and were settled near her in their beautiful homes. Now they are so devoted to her, that although she is very desirous to make her American sisters a visit, they will not hear to her making another trans-Atlantic voyage. But she goes from one end to the other of the United Kingdom without harm or seeming fatigue, speaking and organizing branches of the flourishing society of which she is Presi dent. She is, like her distinguished brother, a very great friend of America, and it was by her kindness and that of Margaret Parker that our editor, Mrs. Mary B. Willard, was enabled to make researches so extended and valuable, into the varied and mighty temperance movement of Great Britain on the occasion of her recent visit.

Margaret Lucas at sixty-three, organizing the women of her country for work in the great cause ; Neal Dow at seventy-eight, campaigning for prohibition in Wisconsin ;

Rebecca Collins of New York at the same age, honorary president of the Metropolitan Union, Mother Hill of Newark at eighty, attending our conventions, and my own dear mother at seventy-three, president of the W. C. T. U. of Evanston, these, with hundreds of like examples speak well for the brain and brawn of the "teetotallers."

CHAPTER IX.

"THE SOBER SECOND THOUGHT OF THE CRUSADE."

Chautauqua, Summer of 1874—Poetic justice—Dr. Vincent—Mrs. Ingham's sketch—Mrs. E. H. Miller's circular.

ONCE more appears the poetic justice ever recurring in this unique movement of the W. C. T. U. Rev. Dr. John H. Vincent, the noble founder of that delightful sylvan University, is perhaps the most quietly uncompromising opponent of women's public work to be found among the enlightened tribes of men. And yet, right here, with his cordial endorsement, on the 15th of August, 1874, good and gifted women gathered fresh from the Crusade pentecost, and prayed and planned into permanent organic form the work which has since sent hundreds of temperance Esthers and Miriams to the platform and the polls. The history of these small beginnings is thus graphically told by Mrs. Mary B. Ingham of Cleveland, who can say truthfully concerning them, " all of which I saw and part of which I was."

THAT CHAUTAUQUA COMMITTEE MEETING.

" The handful of corn upon the tops of the mountains grew apace after its wonderful planting in Ohio during the winter and spring of 1873-4. The fruit thereof shook like Lebanon throughout the Middle and Western States, and in August of that year many of the seed-sowers had gathered upon the shore of Lake Chautauqua for a fortnight in the woods. In primitive fashion we dwelt in tents, or sat in the open air about the watch-fires kindled at the first National Sunday-school Assembly. Women

(121)

who had drawn near to God in saloon prayer-meetings felt their hearts aflame again as they recounted the wonders of the great uprising.

"It was at Chautauqua, the birthplace of grand ideas, that our union originated. It is time the story of its beginnings was written, and there is no more fitting place for its rehearsal than in this goodly presence—the city of Louisville, where South and North meet beneath the olive branch to rejoice over its achievements and consecrate anew its altars.

"One bright day a very few ladies were in conversation upon the subject that filled their hearts, inspiring the thought that the temperance cause needed the united effort of all the women of the country. The suggestion came from Mrs. Mattie McClellan Brown of Alliance, Ohio. Mrs. G. W. Manly, leader of the praying-band of Akron, accepted the idea, and it was said: 'Why not take steps right here toward its formation?' Upon further consultation it was decided to call a meeting of the ladies, notice of which was read from the platform of the auditorium by Rev. Dr. Vincent. Mrs. Jennie F. Willing of Illinois, a guest of the assembly, maintained that so important a movement should be controlled by women engaged in active Christian work. In order to arrange the preliminaries of the announced meeting Mrs. Willing invited Mrs. Brown, Mrs. Manly, Miss Emma Janes of Oakland, California, and Mrs. Ingham of Cleveland, to meet her in a new board shanty on Asbury avenue.

"The Woman's National Christian Temperance Union was born, not in a manger, but on a floor of straw in an apartment into which the daylight shone through holes and crevices. In a half hour's space every detail was prepared, including a proposed formation of a committee on organization, to take place that very afternoon succeeding the regular 3 o'clock session of the assembly. At the

MRS. W. A. INGHAM.

temperance prayer-meeting at 4 o'clock P.M., under the canvas tabernacle, were, perhaps, fifty earnest Christian women; of them were several from Ohio, Mrs. H. H. Otis of Buffalo, Mrs. Niles of Hornellsville, and Mrs. W. E. Knox of Elmira, N. Y. Mrs. Willing was leader of the prayer service, and acted as presiding officer of the business session convened afterward. At this conference women were chosen to represent various States, an adjournment being had to the following day.

"At the hour appointed, August 15, 1874, a large audience had gathered, Mrs. Jennie F. Willing in the chair, and Mrs. Emily Huntington Miller, secretary. As results of the deliberation, the committee on organization was formed, and the chairman and secretary of the Chautauqua meeting were authorized to issue a circular letter, asking the Woman's Temperance Leagues everywhere to hold conventions for the purpose of electing one woman from each Congressional district as delegate to an organizing convention to be held in Cleveland, Ohio, November 18, 19, and 20, 1874. The call duly appeared. The writer of this paper was nominated from Ohio, but withdrew her own name, substituting that of Mrs. Brown, who was known to have made the original suggestion.

"Vicissitudes have occurred during the eight years passed, but all tend, in our onward march to the forefront of battle, to bring nearer to that which overcoming faith and labor are sure to win—victory!

"Independent organizations, with large membership, have multiplied on both sides of the ocean until a score are in active operation as the outgrowth of the great awakening.

"More than all, better than all, the 'Rock of Ages' women are proving themselves worthy of the title, and are praying to-day even more earnestly than when with sublime faith they went out into the streets and saloons of Ohio, believing that ere long our Lord will say to us, ' O, woman, great is thy faith; be it unto thee even as thou wilt.' "

As a matter of history, Mrs. Miller's Chautauqua card is here subjoined:

WOMAN'S NATIONAL TEMPERANCE LEAGUE.

During the session of the National Sunday-school Assembly at Chautauqua Lake, several large and enthusiastic temperance meetings were held. Many of the most earnest workers in the woman's temperance movement from different parts of the Union and different denominations of Christians were present, and the conviction was general that a more favorable opportunity would not soon be presented for taking the preliminary steps towards organizing a national league, to make permanent the grand work of the last few months.

After much deliberation and prayer, a committee of organization was appointed, consisting of one lady from each State, to interest temperance workers in this effort. A national convention was appointed to be held in Cleveland, Ohio, during the month of November, the exact date to be fixed by the committee of organization. The chairman and secretary of the Chautauqua meeting were authorized to issue a circular letter, asking the Woman's Temperance Leagues to hold conventions for the purpose of electing one woman from each Congressional district as a delegate to the Cleveland convention.

It is hardly necessary to remind those who have worked so nobly in the grand temperance uprising, that in union and organization are its success and permanence, and the consequent redemption of this land from the curse of intemperance. In the name of our Master—in behalf of the thousands of women who suffer from this terrible evil— we call upon all to unite in an earnest, continued effort to hold the ground already won, and move onward together to a complete victory over the foes we fight.

The ladies already elected members of the committee of organization are: Mrs. Dr. Gause, Philadelphia; Mrs. E. J. Knowles, Newark, N. J.; Mrs. Mattie McClellan Brown, Alliance, Ohio; Mrs. Dr. Steele, Appleton, Wis.; Mrs. W. D. Barnett, Hiawatha, Kansas; Miss Auretta Hoyt, Indianapolis, Ind.; Mrs. Jennie F. Willing, Bloomington, Ill.; Mrs. Ingham Stanton, LeRoy, N. Y.; Mrs. Frances Crooks, Baltimore, Md.; Miss Emma Janes, Oakland, Cal.

JENNIE F. WILLING, *Chairman.*

EMILY HUNTINGTON MILLER,
  Secretary of the Chautauqua Meeting.

CHAPTER X.

THE WOMAN'S NATIONAL TEMPERANCE CONVENTION, FOUNDED AT CLEVELAND, O.

The First Woman's National Temperance Convention, Cleveland, Ohio—Red-Letter days—Officers—Resolutions, etc.—Representative Women—A brave beginning.

NOVEMBER 18th, 19th, 20th, 1874: red-letter days in the history of the Crusade.

Well, it began with prayer—I mean away back at Chautauqua Lake Sunday-school camp-meeting. "Honor to whom honor is due." And a Western pilgrim to Cleveland, the Mecca of the Crusade, may mildly mention that, in the capacity of "a chiel amang ye, takin' notes," she learned that Mrs. Mattie McClellan Brown, of Alliance, O., first thought out "this Convocation." Nay, better than that—the idea of it was put into her heart as an inspiration, while she knelt in prayer at Dr. Vincent's camp-meeting. She named this to a lady kneeling by her side, Mrs. Russell, of Chicago, and they at once brought it before the prayer-meeting in which it had been given to them, and all the people said, "Amen." Prominent and earnest women, encouraged by the best men, moved forward actively in getting this idea before the women of the country. Mrs. Jennie F. Willing and Emily Huntington Miller were appointed to send out the invitation; Mrs. Brown, the "prime mover," and Mrs. Mary B. Ingham, of Cleveland, a woman of marvelous energy, combined their efforts with those of the ladies above mentioned. Temperance women all over the land were delighted with the idea. State conventions were held and delegates appointed, and on the morning of November 18th we were " with one accord in one place," gathered up from Maine and Oregon, from Alabama and Iowa, from Massachusetts and Colorado, and many States between.

And we began with prayer. In the lecture-room of the Second Presbyterian church, an hour before the Convention was to open, we gathered for a

PRAYER-MEETING.

Sitting there, listening to the mild voices of that mild-faced throng, singing,

"Jesus, I my cross have taken,"

one could but feel that, as heaven looks down on things, this was the hopefulest of convocations since that one in Philadelphia in which they wrote of " life, liberty, and the pursuit of happiness."

When our prayer-meeting ended, and we went in rambling procession to the church, what a general hand-shaking there was, and " Where are you from?" and " Crusaders need no introduction," were words often repeated.

In the spacious auditorium of the Presbyterian church, the Convention was called to order by Mrs. Jennie F. Willing, of Bloomington, Ill. We were seated in delegations, according to our States and Congressional Districts, after the most approved method. We chose our committee on temporary organization, with one member from each State, which reported the following list of

OFFICERS OF THE CONVENTION.

President—Mrs. Jennie F. Willing, Illinois.

Vice-Presidents—Mrs. S. K. Leavitt, Ohio; Mrs. Ex-Governor Wallace, Indiana; Mrs. J. Backus, Vermont; Mrs. Matchett, Pennsylvania; Mrs. Professor Marcy,

Illinois; Mrs. Gifford, Massachusetts; Mrs. Dr. Steele, Wisconsin; Mrs. Mary T. Lathrop, Michigan; Mrs. Helen E. Brown, New York; Mrs. E. A. Wheeler, Iowa; Mrs. Otis Gibson, California; Miss Lizzie Boyd, West Virginia.

Secretaries—Miss Auretta Hoyt, Indiana; Mrs. Mary T. Burt, New York.

Treasurer—Mrs. Mary B. Ingham, Ohio.

These ladies were duly elected.

Mrs. Dr. McCabe, of Delaware, O., President of the State League, then made a most admirable address of welcome.

To this Mrs. Mary C. Johnson, of New York, responded in words fitting and beautiful.

Some discussion arose as to the rights of those who had not brought credentials, but the following resolution, offered by Mrs. Wittenmeyer, of Philadelphia, settled the question:

Resolved, That the several State delegates be allowed to add to their number from representatives from each State, to the number of Congressional Districts in that State.

This matter disposed of, the Convention addressed itself to business, of which there was no lack, the following list of committees indicating its general character:

Committee on Credentials—Miss Auretta Hoyt, Indianapolis, Ind.; Mrs. S. J. Steele, Appleton, Wis.; Mrs. H. N. K. Goff, Philadelphia, Pa.; Mrs. W. A. Ingham, Cleveland, O.; and Mrs. Joel Foster, Montpelier, Vt.

On Business—Mrs. Almira Brackett, Biddeford, Me.; Mrs. E. R. Backus, Springfield, Vt.; Mrs. E. A. Bowers, Clinton, Mass.; Mrs. E. A. Wheeler, Cedar Rapids, Ia.; Mrs. A. M. Noe, Indianapolis, Ind.; Mrs. Peter Stryker, Rome, N. Y.; Mrs. H. M. Wilkin, Paris, Ill.; Mrs. S. R. Leavitt, Cincinnati, O.; Miss Lizzie Boyd, Wheeling, W. Va.; Miss Emma Janes, Oakland, Cal.; Mrs. J. A. Brown,

Milwaukee, Wis.; Mrs. Mary T. Lathrop, Jackson, Mich.; Mrs. S. B. Chase, Great Bend, Pa.

On Circular Letter to Foreign Nations—Mrs. Lathrop, Michigan; Mrs. S. B. Chase, Pennsylvania; Miss Emma Janes, California.

On Resolutions—"Mother" Stewart, Ohio; Mrs. Governor Wallace, Indiana; Miss Willard, Illinois; Mrs. Butler, New York; Mrs. Collins, Pennsylvania; Mrs. Black, Pennsylvania; Mrs. Brown, Ohio; Mrs. Goff, Pennsylvania.

On Constitution—Mrs. J. Ellen Foster, Iowa; Mrs. L. M. Boise, Michigan; Mrs. Finch, Indiana; Mrs. Wittenmeyer, Pennsylvania; Mrs. Runyon, Ohio; Miss Boyd, West Virginia; Mrs Gifford, Massachusetts; Mrs. Kenyon, New York; Mrs. Brown, Wisconsin; Mrs. M. Davis, Vermont; Mrs. J. Dickey, Ill.

On Finance—Mrs. Dr. Leavitt, Cincinnati, O.; Mrs. Peter Stryker, Rome, N. Y.; Mrs. S. P. Robinson, Pennsylvania; Mrs. Foster, Iowa; Mrs. M. Valentine, Indiana.

On Memorial to Congress—Mrs. Annie Wittenmeyer, Philadelphia; Mrs. Governor Wallace, Indiana; Miss Frances E. Willard, Chicago.

On Constitution for National Temperance League—Mrs. M. M. Finch, Indiana; Mrs. Wittenmeyer, Pennsylvania; Mrs. Runyon, Ohio; Mrs. L. M. Boise, Michigan; Mrs. J. Dickey, Illinois; Mrs. S. A. Gifford, Massachusetts; Mrs. J. A. Brown, Wisconsin; Mrs. Dr. Kenyon, New York; Mrs. J. E. Foster, Iowa; Mrs. M. Davis, Vermont; Miss Lizzie Boyd, West Virginia.

On Address to the Young Women of America—Mrs. Mary T. Lathrop, of Michigan, Chairman.

On Letter to American Women—Mrs. Marcy, Illinois; Mrs. Johnson, New York; Mrs. Leavitt, Ohio.

On Juvenile Organizations—Mrs. E. J. Thompson, Ohio; Miss Willard, Illinois; Mrs. A. M. Noe, Indiana.

On Establishing a National Temperance Paper—Mrs. Annie Wittenmeyer, Pennsylvania; Mrs. S. J. Steele, Wisconsin; Mrs. S. K. Leavitt, Ohio; Mrs. S. A. Gifford, Massachusetts; Mrs. E. E. Marcy, Illinois; Miss Emma Janes, California; Mrs. M. C. Johnson, Brooklyn.

Passing by the discussions, which were sufficiently lively, but (as was stated by a delegate present, who had been so happy as to witness thirty conventions) not at all extreme, " considering," we will give a *résumé* of the results arrived at by this significant assembly.

1. Resolutions were adopted as follows, embodying a sufficiently exhaustive " confession of faith:"

WHEREAS, Much of the evil by which this country is cursed comes from the fact that the men in power whose duty it is to make and administer the laws are either themselves intemperate men or controlled largely by the liquor power; therefore,

1. *Resolved,* That the women of the United States, in this convention represented, do hereby express their unqualified disapprobation of the custom so prevalent in political parties of placing intemperate men in office.

2. *Resolved,* That we will appeal to the House of Representatives, by petition, for their concurrence with the Senate bill providing a commission of inquiry into the effects and results of the liquor traffic in this country.

3. *Resolved,* That we respectfully ask the President of the United States, Senators, Representatives in Congress, Governors of States, and all public men, with their wives and daughters, to give the temperance cause the strength of their conspicuous example by banishing all wines and other intoxicating liquors from their banquets and their private tables.

4. *Resolved,* That we will endeavor to secure the co-operation of great manufacturing firms in our effort to pledge their employees to total abstinence, and that we will ask these firms to consider the advantages to sobriety of paying their men on Monday rather than on Saturday evening.

5. *Resolved,* That we respectfully request the physicians to exercise extreme and conscientious care in administering intoxicating liquors as a beverage.

6. *Resolved,* That as the National Temperance Society, and Publishing House in New York—J. N. Stearns, Publishing Agent—pre-

sents the best variety of temperance literature in the world, consisting of books, tracts, *The National Temperance Advocate* and *The Youth's Temperance Banner*, we hereby recommend the ladies of America to encourage the dissemination of this literature in connection with their work.

7. *Resolved*, That all temperance organizations of our land be invited to co-operate with us in our efforts for the overthrow of intemperance.

8. *Resolved*, That all good temperance women, without regard to sect or nationality, are cordially invited to unite with us in our great battle against the wrong and for the right.

9. *Resolved*, That in the conflict of moral ideas, we look to the pulpit and the press as our strongest earthly allies, and that we will, by our influence as Christian women and by our prayers, strive to increase the interest in our cause already manifested by their powerful instrumentalities, gratefully recognized by us.

10. *Resolved*, That we will pray and labor for a general revival of religion throughout our land, knowing that only through the action of the Holy Spirit on the hearts of the Church and the world will they be warmed to a vital interest in the temperance cause.

11. *Resolved*, That recognizing the fact that our cause is and will be combatted by mighty, determined, and relentless forces, we will, trusting in Him who is the Prince of Peace, meet argument with argument, misjudgment with patience, denunciation with kindness, and all our difficulties and dangers with prayer.

A constitution was adopted as follows:

PREAMBLE.

We, the women of this Nation, conscious of the increasing evils and appalled at the tendencies and dangers of intemperance, believe it has become our duty, under the providence of God, to unite our efforts for its extinction.

CONSTITUTION.

1. This Association shall be known as the "Woman's National Christian Temperance Union."

2. The officers of the Union shall be a President, one Vice-President from each State, a Corresponding Secretary, Recording Secretary, and a Treasurer. Said officers shall constitute a Board of Managers, to control and provide for the general interests of the work.

3. Each State organization may become auxiliary to the Union by indorsing its Constitution.

4. Each Vice-President shall make to the Corresponding Secretary an annual report of the work in her State.

5. The Annual Meeting of the Union, at which time its officers shall be elected, shall be in November, the time and place to be fixed by the Board of Managers; said officers to be elected by ballot.

6. The Annual Meeting shall be composed of delegates chosen, one from each Congressional district, by the Auxiliary Woman's Temperance Unions.

7. Each State organization shall pay annually to the National Fund an amount equal to five cents per member of each Auxiliary Union.

8. This Constitution may be altered or amended at any Annual Meeting of the National Union, by a vote of two-thirds of the delegates present.

The following ladies were elected officers for the ensuing year of the Woman's National Christian Temperance Union:

President—Mrs. Annie Wittenmeyer, Philadelphia, Pa.

Vice-Presidents—Mrs. Mary A. Gaines, Saco, Me.; Mrs. Joel M. Haven, Rutland, Vt.; Mrs. S. A. Gifford, Mass.; Mrs. L. N. Kenyon, N. Y.; Mrs. S. B. Chase, Great Bend, Pa.; Mrs. E. J. Thompson, Hillsboro', Ohio; Mrs. Rev. S. Reed, Ann Arbor, Mich.; Mrs. E. E. Marcy, Evanston, Ill.; Mrs. S. J. Steele, Appleton, Wis.; Mrs. Z. G. Wallace, Indianapolis, Ind.; Mrs. M. J. Aldrich, Cedar Rapids, Iowa; Mrs. R. Thompson, San Francisco, Cal.

Corresponding Secretary—Miss Frances E. Willard, Chicago, Ill.

Recording Secretary—Mrs. Mary C. Johnson, Brooklyn, N. Y.

Treasurer—Mrs. W. A. Ingham, Cleveland, Ohio.

Thus much for the official decisions reached by the first National Convention of temperance workers who were women.

Aside from this, we had good talk and plenty of it, at which some hint is given elsewhere. Four mass-meetings were held during the Convention. Dr. J. M. Walden, of Cincinnati (Chief Knight of the new Crusade), presided at the first—a quite exceptional honor, no other member of the regnant sex being allowed to lift up his voice

6

throughout the whole Convention. Mrs. S. K. Leavitt, one of Ohio's strongest and best women, conducted the second; Mrs. Dr. Donaldson, of Toledo (whose mind seems as incisive as the blade which bore that name), was generalissimo of the third, and Miss Auretta Hoyt, of Indiana, as "genuine" as she is practical, carried on the fourth.

Crowded houses signalized these meetings, and Crusade hymns were pleasantly interspersed with the excellent music furnished by trained singers of Cleveland.

Some salient features of the Convention may be referred to in closing this shadowy outline of what was a picture full of life, color, and "tone." This was a representative gathering, not only numerically and geographically, but in respect to character and to achievement. We had a bright little lady lawyer, Mrs. Foster, all the way from Iowa, to be chief of our Committee on Constitution, and to set us right on legal points in general. We had a thorough-going lady physician, Mrs. Harriet French, of Philadelphia, who was competent to tell us of the relation of alcohol to medicine. We had three or four editors, any quantity of teachers, two college professors, Quaker ministers, looking out with dove-like eyes from their dove-colored bonnets; and besides these, three licensed preachers of the Methodist persuasion, besides business women not a few, and gray-haired matrons from scores of sacred homes, all up and down the land. Goethe's prophetic words, "The ever-feminine draweth on," received new confirmation when, at the close of our last mass-meeting, one of our ablest speakers, Mrs. Mary T. Lathrop, of Michigan, after a telling address, made a brief prayer, and then stretched out her hands and gave us the apostolic benediction. And this in the pulpit of a Presbyterian Church!

We bespeak for the work done by this Convention the

thoughtful study of every man and woman who may read these lines.

"Something practical" is what our people clamor for, and justly. Well, we have here a plan of organization that is meant to reach every village and hamlet in the Republic; a declaration of principles of which only Christ's religion could have been the animus; an appeal to the women of our country, another to the girls of America, and a third to lands beyond the sea; a memorial to Congress, and a deputation to carry it; a National Temperance Paper, "of the women for the women;" a centennial temperance celebration projected; and, finally, a financial plan, involving two cents a week for each member.

A BRAVE BEGINNING.

Surely, a generous, comprehensive plan for "new beginners" to devise.

Not least in value was the decision, deliberately reached, after a free discussion, to stand by the name as well as the faith of Him to whom woman owes all she has come to be. That name, "Woman's National *Christian* Temperance Union," has volumes in it which this gainsaying age may profitably ponder.

There is no harshness in the utterances of the Convention, as there was none in its spirit, but the earnest words of one of the ablest workers in the cause, fitly express the deep conviction which prevailed there:

"Woman is ordained to lead the vanguard of this great movement until the public is borne across the abysmal transition from the superstitious notion that 'alcohol is food' to the scientific fact that 'alcohol is poison;' from the pusillanimous concession that 'intemperance is a great evil' to the responsible conviction that the liquor traffic is a crime."

And while woman leads, her courage and her hope all come from Him who said, "Lo! I am with you alway."

CHAPTER XI.

PARLIAMENTARY USAGE *VERSUS* "RED TAPE."

Mrs. Plymouth Rock and Friend Rachel Halliday engage in a discussion.

TIME—Just after the National W. C. T. U. Convention.
PLACE—A Pullman car, eastward bound.
PERSONS—A New England delegate to the Woman's Temperance Convention and a Philadelphia "Friend," also a delegate.

MRS. PLYMOUTH ROCK—" Well, Cousin Rachel, I must say I've added largely to my stock of ideas at our Convention. I'm First Vice-President of the Union in Cobblestone, and I mean to have our business carried on, after this, in a parliamentary manner. By the way, do you remember the price of that book, 'Rules of Order, by Major Roberts?' (Consults her memorandum book.) O, here it is; seventy-five cents, and the publisher is S. C. Griggs, Chicago."

RACHEL HALLIDAY—" I tell thee, Martha, I believe thee is under a delusion. Thee says thee has added to thy stock of ideas, but I tell thee plainly thy stock of spirituality has not increased. This parliamentary code is grievously oppressive, to my mind."

MRS. P. R.—" I think I must plead guilty to the charge you make about my state of mind; but that's my own fault, and not to be set down against the thoughtful, deliberative assembly of which I'm proud to have been a quiet member. After all, I think religion is a very broad word, and to transact business for God and humanity may be quite as religious as to pray."

MRS. RACHEL—"'Diligent in business, fervent in spirit, serving the Lord,' is a favorite text with me, but thee sees it was borne in upon my mind that we had too much red tape—we magnified our office. Now I don't object to an order of business, nor even to 'moving and seconding,' for we have something like that in Friends' meeting, but when thee, my cousin Martha, who used to be content to sit by me in the meeting-house and commune with thy heart and be still, when thee popped up and said to the President, 'I rise to a question of privilege,' I tell thee I hung my head."

MRS. P. R.—(Briskly.) "And, indeed, I should like to know why? You ought to have been proud of me, for I don't believe there were a dozen women in the Convention who could have done it. Did you raise your diminished head in time to see how, by that move, I got the floor in time to explain my position on the Bible wine question, thus setting myself right with my home constituency?"

MRS. RACHEL—"Thee knows it is quite beyond me, the whole of it, and I'm very willing to remain in ignorance. But even with thy views thee surely wouldn't defend a Christian woman getting up as they did there and offering an 'amendment to an amendment?' I don't know when I've had such an exercise of the mind as I did over that."

MRS. P. R.—"In the first place, I should certainly defend a woman for '*getting up*' to offer what you mention, for it would be impolite to the president and inconvenient to the convention for her to speak when sitting down. In the second place, if there's one thing I'm glad I've found out about it's this particular point. Let's see, how did Mrs. Clerecut illustrate it to Hypatia and me? O, I remember: ' A motion made and seconded is the house; an amendment is the addition to the house; an amendment to an amendment is the wood-shed of the house; and you vote upon the wood-shed first.' "

MRS. RACHEL—(Loosing her drab bonnet-ribbons and gazing helplessly toward the ventilator.) " Martha, thee is going clean daft. If I did not remember thine ancient propensity to tease thy poor cousin, I would be seriously concerned for thee. Now check thy merriment and tell me truly what is the good of thy profane little book with its rules of order; of the endless committees, secretaries, rulings, reports, and so on ? They may do very well for the world's people, but I am persuaded that Christian women have no call to make use of such devices."

[At this juncture Mrs. Plymouth Rock takes off her gloves, rubs her energetic little hands, and, laying aside all defensive tactics, makes a lively onslaught upon the citadel of her cousin's prejudice. With index finger pointed straight at the placid features of her antagonist, she thus proceeds :]

" There's no use mincing matters, Rachel. You see things as you do, because of your bringing up. You're non-combative to that degree that old Apollyon and all his hosts couldn't ruffle your feathers a particle. But I'm not so. ' The Sword of the Lord *and of Gideon'* is the most musical sentence in the Old Testament, to ears like mine. And, with all due deference, I know more about this business than you do.   Haven't I seen in the Union at Factoryville, near Cobblestone, just because Mrs. Holdfast is persistent as gravitation, and wise in parliamentary usage as the chief justice, that she carries everything to suit herself, and our dear, meek women sit by as if demented ? You've got to take this world as it is, and not as it ought to be, and the facts are—for any quantity of women told me so at the convention—that in many a locality the woman who ' knows the ropes'—as men would say—moulds the policy of the Union, and the rest

are blown like thistle-down before the breeze. For there
seems to be a sort of mysticism in the minds of women
about this matter of parliamentary usage. And because
Mrs. Holdfast looks so alarmingly wise when she says,
'The chair rules that Mrs. Prettyman has the floor,'
poor, dear sister Prettyman forgets what she wanted to
say. Now the whole thing is easily learned, and some
women will most assuredly proceed to learn it, and for
my part I mean that in our Union all the members shall,
and then they won't be so easily cowed by one or two
master spirits."

MRS. RACHEL — (Neither silenced nor convinced.)
"But where's the utility of it, when one has learned it?
Answer me that thou, Martha, 'careful and troubled about
many things.'"

MRS. P. R.—"Well, take an example. There was a
delegate from the West who knew of a young lady who
would have added much strength to the committee on
young women's work, and whom she wanted to nominate
to a place on that committee. Up got some wide-awake
leader, and moved that the old committee on young
women's work be continued through the year, and in the
twinkle of an eye the motion was carried through. Meanwhile, this lady felt like a boat stranded high and dry,
and went off lamenting that the bright girl who would
have worked so well, and in whose appointment there
would have been such fitness, couldn't be 'put on,' and
she bitterly cried out, 'Too much red tape.' But, in fact,
there was too little. Rather, there was too much ignorance inside her own particular cranium. If she had
studied as our temperance women are surely going to
study, she would have found out this : That a body called
'a convention' can, like an individual body, change its
mind while it's alive, and it isn't dead till it's adjourned.
Any decision it comes to can be reversed—any action
can be nullified."

MRS. RACHEL—(Aside)—"Nullified! O my! What is she coming to?"

MRS. P. R.—" So that lady could, in any one of half a dozen ways, have called attention to her pet idea of adding this young woman to the committee—only she didn't know how. Some of us told her this, but she went off grumbling, ' When a thing's done, it's done, according to my way of thinking.' Ah, cousin, knowledge is power. Parliamentary rules are the result of centuries of experience in conducting the proceedings of deliberative bodies, while one person acts as the mouth-piece, keeps matters well in hand, and impartially gives to every delegate, according to certain prescribed regulations, a chance to bring forward her views, and to affect the decisions of many women of many minds."

MRS. RACHEL—" I see thee does really make a point about a few who know this rigmarole unduly influencing the rest, and concerning that dear woman who felt so set back about her plan for the young lady, but I see, too, thee does not even try to answer my chief objection— that all this takes out the freedom and spirituality from our meetings."

MRS. P. R.—(Taking her cousin's hand, and waxing eloquent.) "Now, I confess I want you on my side in this. For, if there is a Christian, you are one, and, like you, I would say, give ' rules of order' to the wind, if for their sake we must lose one bit of spiritual power. But ' order is heaven's first law.' ' Let everything be done decently, and in order,' is a sacred command. What cleanliness and neat arrangement are to a room, and what good manners are to an individual, just that, rules and regulations are to an assembly. I was talking about all this to Judge Fairmind, in whose home I was a guest through the convention. He said what delighted him most in our proceedings was the prompt application of parliamentary rules, the evident knowledge of them among a majority of delegates, and the good nature in their observance; also the way in which by means of them we got through such a great amount of business in those four days, and the ease with which we turned from the regular order of business to hymns of praise and words of prayer. He said it was to his mind a foretaste of the good time coming, when methods useful in themselves, but hitherto secular, shall be informed by the spirit which giveth life. Then, cousin, you cannot deny that the utmost Christian forbearance and gentleness characterized the deportment of every member, and ' rules' did not prevent frequent prayer even while a question was pending. Moreover, you never saw, and never will see, a lovelier sight than the election, so simple and unpremeditated, nominations all made in open meeting, and hymns, tears, and prayers coming in as freely as if no 'red tape' were in the world."

MRS. RACHEL—" There is much in what thee says, Martha; thee is an excellent woman after all,—most excellent. I cannot quite see as thee does, but I confess there is a method in thy madness, to say the least. But as for me, I am quite sure thee will never convert me over to a real and lively affection for thy little book of rules. Nevertheless I will follow thee part way—but not so far as ' an amendment to an amendment,' and thee will never, never hear thy cousin say 'I rise to a point of order,' or 'I call for the ayes and noes.' "

CHAPTER XII.

OUR MANY-SIDED WORK.

IT has been prophesied that the temperance reform, which has now marshaled into its ranks both men and women, gospel and law, shall one day bring about the enfranchisement of women as an instrument, and the brotherhood of races as a result of its triumph over humanity's worst foe. Be this as it may, one who surveys the field from various sides, and whose whole life is bound up with the battle, finds evidences multiplying constantly of the many-handed hold upon the people's life which this reform has gained.

A few of these straws upon the current, growing every day more strong and deep, may help the courage of some overburdened heart, for that there are so many ways of working is an inspiring feature of the situation.

For instance, a lady said to me in Denison, Texas: "I didn't go to your temperance meeting in the Opera House last night, but I staid at home and took care of five babies beside my own, so that their mothers could attend," and her eyes twinkled as she added, "Wasn't that real temperance work?"

Again: "Give me those notices. I can take them to a printer who will strike them off as his mite for the treasury;" thus gently whispers a young mother whose voice we never hear "speaking out in meeting," but whose heart is in our work.

A young girl writes: "Here are twenty-five letters, leaving me as many more to copy for you. *Be sure* to have something else ready for me to do when these are

(142)

finished. It isn't much that I can accomplish, but you
don't know the pleasure I have in putting even a tiny
thread into the great cable of work and prayer that is to
bridge the fiery sea."

Just here an energetic voice chimes in: " I don't speak
—thumbscrews wouldn't force a word from my lips—but
I know a pair oı temperance workers who never tire of
talking, and whom the people like to hear, whose glove-
buttons, dress-braids, and general mending would be in a
sorry plight if I didn't carry the needle-case and thimble
which they get so little time to use."

" Well, my talent doesn't lie in that direction," says a
quiet, motherly-faced lady, taking out her purse, and paying the street-car fares of her two guests, as she speaks,
" but God has given me a pleasant home, and I delight to
open its doors for our temperance apostles."

" I fear we are too likely to forget how many ways
there are of helping, and to think because we neither
speak, write, nor organize, our activities are unimportant,"
replies a lady from Ohio, temporarily sojourning in the
Eastern city where the scene of our conversation is laid.

She continues: " The beauty of our work is, that there
is in it a place for every willing head and hand and heart.
It was just so in the Crusade. I know women who went
just that they might count one in the procession. A dear
old grandmother who never missed going out with us
said, ' I don't amount to much ; I can only go along and
cry.' A servant-girl, an Irish Catholic, whose mistress
led our band, says, ' Sure, an' I can hold th' umbrelly
over yer head, mum, and keep the sun or the rain off
while you pray.' In that same band was a young lady
who had spent years in the Musical Conservatory at
Paris, but who sang through storm and shine, and when
her beautiful voice showed signs of failing, said, in reply
to the protests of her friends, ' I have no gift too good to

lay upon the altar of the woman's temperance crusade.'
Even our silent neighbors, the lower animals, came to our
help. Mrs. Hitt of Urbana, one of our grandest leaders,
had a great dog, which walked beside her with stately step
all through those wonderful days, and, by his presence,
added not a little to the interest of our long procession."

"Somehow, there's a homelikeness in everything that
women do; there must be in the very nature of the case,"
remarks guest number two, "and bringing this very
element out into religious work, and eventually into government, is to be one of the blessed results of this new
movement, as I look at it. Why, this home feature is the
ear-mark in everything that women say, and the trade-
mark on everything they do." (Draws a letter from her
pocket.) "For instance, here is a contribution to our
paper, with this note:

"'NOVEMBER 8.—Your request that I should contribute
to the next number of our paper was received last night,
while I was rocking my baby to sleep. It is now half-past
ten in the morning. I am *sans* cook, *sans* nurse, *sans*
everything save my own two hands; but I have managed
to get breakfast, wash the dishes, put my house in toler-
able order, comforted the three babies, swallowed a *license
victory* in our town, and here's the article, subject to the
editorial *guillotine*. Do not judge me severely, remembering all the facts, and that two of the little chicks have
been beside my desk, emulating their mother's quill-driv-
ing in a slightly distracting way. But woman's door of
opportunity for blessed work swings wide, and I, for one,
am bound to enter.'

"And here is another note, illustrating this same point.
The chairman of our committee on 'Out-door Gospel'
writes it—a woman gifted as she is gentle, and brave as
she is modest."

"Yes, women go at everything in such a homelike

fashion," muses guest number one, as the trio alight from the jingling cars, and wend their way to the delightful home where they are to find the rest they so much need. "Down in Maine, last summer, in a large meeting for ladies, to which, as a natural consequence, men gathered in great numbers, a noble temperance worker of that State arose and said: 'There is a woman beside me who wishes me to ask this question: What can I do, who have no talent, no money, and no influence, to help forward this reform?' It was not hard to answer. In the first place, *everybody counts one.* Everybody can pray, can set a good example, can join herself to a union of temperance women, if there is one, and if there isn't, can *stir about* until one shall be formed. It was a poor washerwoman, who came on Saturday evening to a distinguished pastor, saying: 'O, sir, I've heard of the woman's crusade; I've prayed that we might have it here, and I believe God tells me to ask you to do something about it'; and as she wept the good man's heart was stirred. Next day he announced a meeting for his church, the other pastors followed, a week later the town was in a blaze; a fortnight later not a saloon remained. A human being is a wonderful potency, and can accomplish prodigies. The trouble is, we underestimate our powers. Whoever comes along, shakes us by the shoulder and helps us to believe in ourselves, does us an immense service, almost the greatest. And the Woman's Temperance Unions of this land are revealing to hundreds of women their gifts, and to hundreds more their possibilities. 'The silent sisters,' who do not help with voice or pen, are yet as indispensable as any. They 'hold up the prophet's hands;' they furnish the grateful rest beside the wells of Elim; their sturdy good sense keeps the balance between real and ideal safely adjusted; they are the 'joy and song' of the talking fraternity, even as the latter are *their* pride and glory. Choice gifts indeed 'the silent sisters' bring into the common treasury. Largely from their wealth or industry we gather the sinews of war. To their social position, and the prestige of names they or their fathers or their husbands have made as towers of strength, we are indebted for the vantage-ground we hold in public estimation. Their homes are our shelter, their hearts our resting-places."

"O, blessed bond, the sweetest that my life has known; and marvelous, benignant age which welcomes all of us to new avenues of usefulness, and eloquent, persuasive voice which, in the ears of high and low, rich and poor, of ignorant and taught among us women, calls at this hour, '*The Master is come and calleth for thee!*'"

Just then the tea-bell rang, and guest number one awoke to the fact that in her enthusiasm she had well-nigh crossed the line that separates a colloquy from an oration.

CHAPTER XIII.

MRS. JANE FOWLER WILLING.

President of the First National Convention—An Earnest Life and Varied Work—Speaker—Organizer—Teacher—Author.

" THE life of aimless reverie must be replaced by the life of resolute aim "—so said a teacher once, addressing her girl pupils. If I had chosen to bring forward an illustration of the last half of the antithesis, I could not have done better than to name the gifted woman whose pen and brain picture I here present. Among the many sagacious observations of my father, which are recorded in memory's standard edition of " Household Words," is this: " If you've got *the victory in you*, you'll succeed in life; that's all. If it's in, it's in, and will come out, on the principle of a steam engine, a streak of lightning, or a gunpowder plot. But what's wanting—well, ' What's wanting can't be numbered.' "

This is homely as it was home-made philosophy, but all the same it hits the mark, and applies to the case in hand.

Look at this life a little :

Mrs. Willing was born in Burford, Canada West, January 22, 1834. When she was eight years old, her parents removed to Illinois, and she grew up in the surroundings of country life, and with such scanty schooling as the Prairie State could furnish in that early day. Even this was almost steadily interfered with by her own ill health, and was abbreviated by her marriage at the age of nineteen years. Few proverbs are truer than this,

(147)

that "blood will tell"—perhaps, however, "brains" is better for the initial word. Mrs. Willing's maternal grandfather, Rev. Henry Ryan, her mother, Mrs. Horatio Fowler, and her brother, Rev. Dr. Charles H. Fowler (recent editor of the N. Y. *Christian Advocate*), may be mentioned as three points in a family quadrilateral, which she herself completes, of characters altogether exceptional in mental vigor and in force of will. The mother was, in native strength of mind, fully the peer of her father and her children. Mrs. Willing sketched her mother's life in the Ladies' Repository, a few years since. Without teachers, she had mastered many of the school's hardest lessons in the sciences; without travel or society, she knew the world; in history she was a marvel of accuracy and research; and there was no great question touching human weal, either in times past or present, to which she had not given eager and intelligent attention. She lived lonely and unknown among our Illinois prairies, but she crowded behind that massive brow, which none who saw it can forget, more of aspiration and intellectual achievement than many who "ransack the ages, spoil the climes" in their pursuit of knowledge, hindered by no difficulties which wealth and opportunity can mitigate.

It counts for much to have had such a mother, and the stimulus of such a brother's endeavor and achievement.

But all who know the Rev. Dr. W. C. Willing will agree that, in the development of those intellectual gifts which his wife has employed in activities so helpful to the church of Christ, his influence has been only second to that of her own earnest and unflagging purpose.

For the sake of womankind in general, not less than from a sentiment of generous loyalty, we should be quick to recognize such knights of the new chivalry as he has proved himself to be. Instead of setting himself to stifle the aspirations of his wife toward learning, literary work,

MRS. JENNIE F. WILLING.

and public speaking, he has delighted in and steadily encouraged them. From the day when, as a girl of nineteen, she gave to him the sacred right to influence, almost controllingly, her aims and life, he has, like the strong, brave man he is, said to his wife, "I have no greater pleasure than in helping you up to the level of your best."

In spite of the fortunate circumstances mentioned, the problem of an education was not easy of solution for a young minister's wife, with home and church cares crowding upon her attention, in a western village, twenty years ago. The record, if it could be written, would be full of incentives to many a noble girl who reads these lines. I have heard Mrs. Willing tell of the book fastened against the window-sill and read to the rhythm of the flatiron, or kneaded into the brain while the hands were busy performing a work quite analogous upon the bread. Elihu Burritt, pounding iron and ideas at once, is a heroic figure. Why not equally heroic this quiet woman at her kitchen table with her books and thoughts?

Well, something is pretty sure to come of work like that. Later on we find our friend installed as Professor of the English Language and Literature in Illinois Wesleyan University at Bloomington, an institution of first grade. Largely through her influence a "Woman's Educational Association" was formed in connection with the University, and this organization has provided a home where cheap board is furnished for young women who are struggling to secure a higher education. We find her preparing essays, serials, sermons, and orations — all of them evincing vigor of thought, in clear-cut forms of expression, and abounding in classic, historic, and scientific allusions which could only come from a cultured intellect.

All the achievements of her pen and voice move along religious lines. For surely the philanthropies in which she has wrought so well are outgrowths of His Gospel, whose angel heralds announced the coming of " peace on earth, good will to men."

In 1869 she was elected one of the corresponding secretaries of the Woman's Foreign Missionary Society of the M. E. Church. This position she has filled ever since, having care of the four States lying about Chicago. Indeed she may be said to have created the position and the society in the States under her jurisdiction, for her patient, persistent work brought order out of chaos and changed apathy to enthusiasm. When the Crusade sounded its muster-drum, Mrs. Willing was among the first to enlist in the new army. She did excellent service in Bloomington, sandwiching temperance work between college recitations and speaking eloquently night after night. She presided at the preliminary meeting held at Chautauqua Lake S. S. Assembly in 1874, in which the first arrangements were made for calling a convention to organize our National W. C. T. U.; she issued the call for the Cleveland Convention, and presided over it in November of the same year. She was the first editor of our national paper, and was for years President of the W. C. T. U. of the State of Illinois.

Mrs. Willing is already well known, for, aside from her writings, she has delivered sermons and addresses in most of the chief pulpits of her denomination in all the large cities, both East and West. In 1873 she was licensed as a local preacher in the M. E. Church, and is usually occupied, on Sabbaths, preaching in the pulpits in or near Chicago. In no character has she appeared to better purpose than as a minister of the New Testament. Her revival meetings are scenes of especial power. She is also a somewhat voluminous writer, her latest book (published by D. Lothrop & Co., Boston) being a strong temperance story entitled " The Only Way Out." The others are " Through the Dark," " Diamond Dust," " Chaff and Wheat," and ' Rosario."

Like all strong souls, Mrs. Willing has for her motto "*plus ultra*"—more beyond. In car or steamer she is always busy with book or pencil, yet keenly observant of the lessons best learned from the changeful page of human life, and she stands to-day in the prime of her years and strength. With rare culture of manner and of utterance, with her clear brain, steady purpose, and consecrated heart, we may expect even more of her future than we have recorded of her past. As I think about her, the question asked of Queen Esther comes to my memory, and my affirmative reply will be echoed by all who share my information of her work :

" Who knoweth whether thou art come to the kingdom for such a time as this ?"

CHAPTER XIV.

MRS. EMILY HUNTINGTON MILLER.

Mrs. Emily Huntington Miller—Secretary Chautauqua preliminary
meeting—Author, Editor, Home-maker.

JUST after our October Convention, in 1877, I called
one morning, by order of our Publishing Company, at
a pretty cottage in my own home town of Evanston, the
"classic suburb" of Chicago. The door was opened by
dark-eyed Fred, known as "a regular mother's boy"
among the neighbors round about. It occurred to me, as
he uttered his smiling "Good morning," that I had not
seen him before since I watched him proudly acting as
escort to his mother when she started from our railroad
station for Chautauqua, to give her "Home Papers" before
the S. S. Assembly, a few months earlier. Fred's mother
was at her writing-table in the sunny cottage, with its
pretty book-cases, charming pictures, most of them illustrative of child-life, its bay-window full of vines, ferns,
and flowers, and, blending all, its cheery air of home.
Busy, as she always is, filling varied literary engagements, she readily promised to comply with the official
request, of which my friend and I were bearers, that she
should "write for *Our Union*." For Emily Huntington
Miller was Secretary of the meeting held at Chautauqua the
summer after the Crusade, which sent out the "call" for
a National Convention, whence resulted the society of
which our paper is the "official organ." Whoever has
read her stories—and what child has not?—knows that
she is a staunch temperance woman.

(154)

MRS. EMILY HUNTINGTON MILLER.

In those memorable winter days when the Crusade was everybody's theme, when, in the university at Evanston, hundreds of young men and women, newly aroused to interest in what they had considered a trite and hopeless subject, were debating, orating, and writing essays on temperance, the high-water mark of expression was not reached until Mrs. Miller gave a lecture on the "Home side of the Question."

Our friend was born in Brooklyn, in 1833, and is a daughter of Dr. Thomas Huntington, a good man and a righteous; and her mother was one of those women whose children rise up and call her blessed. Her grandfather, General Jed Huntington, of Revolutionary fame, was one of Washington's staff officers. Huntington, the great artist, is her cousin. She was educated at noble old Oberlin College, where she met among her fellow-students Mr. John E. Miller (brother of Lewis Miller, "of Chautauqua"), to whom she was married in 1859. This alliance is one of the number, happily increasing in these later days, in which the blending of two lives to form the beacon-light of home dims no ray of native brilliancy in the gentler of the two. Himself a man of educated tastes, at first a professor of ancient languages, and afterward a publisher and prominent S. S. worker, Mr. Miller never seems so thoroughly well pleased as when listening to an appreciative comment on his wife's achievements. They have had four children, of whom three—all of them boys—are growing up into the "whole-souled" sort of men who never sneer at "intellectual women."*

"The Little Corporal" was perhaps the most vigorous and attractive literary child of the great war. Alfred L. Sewell, of Evanston, a Chicago publisher, resolved to help the Sanitary Commission by getting the children all over

---

* The recent death of Mr. Miller removes one of the truest friends of the W. C. T. U.

the land to buy pictures of "Old Abe," the Wisconsin
War Eagle. So grandly did the boys and girls respond,
not only purchasing for themselves, but securing sales
among their friends, that a fabulous number of pictures
were disposed of, and thousands of dollars were poured
into the treasury of the Commission, under the auspices
of the magnificent Sanitary Fair, conducted by Mrs. Livermore and Mrs. Hoge. Mr. Sewell resolved to have a
paper through which to communicate with his army of
juvenile helpers, and founded *The Little Corporal*—the
brightest and best beloved child's paper ever seen, except
that noble *Youth's Companion*, down to the epoch of *St.
Nicholas* and *Wide Awake*.

In the first number of this paper, Emily Huntington
Miller (already known to a large circle of readers through
her contributions to various newspapers and magazines)
began a juvenile series. This was the chief feature of
The Corporal at the beginning, and from then until the
time when, as one of Chicago's misfortunes resulting from
the great fire, the paper was merged into the glowing
splendors of *St. Nicholas*, Mrs. Miller's pen was always
busy brightening its pages. Indeed the best part of her
life, thus far, has been put into her favorite paper. For
ten years she was associated with it editorially; at first
as Mr. Sewell's associate, and afterwards taking the entire
supervision. Aside from this work, Mrs. Miller has contributed, with more or less regularity, both poetry and
prose to many papers and magazines of the best class, and
has written several juvenile books, Nelson & Phillips,
of New York, having published six of these, "The Royal
Road to Fortune" and "The Kirkwood Library." S. C.
Griggs & Co., of Chicago, published "What Tommy Did,"
an illustrated story, which is having a large sale; and E.
P. Dutton & Co., of New York, have brought out her
latest story, "Captain Fritz." Mrs. Miller's "Home
Papers," given at Chautauqua, are now in press.

Besides her literary work, Mrs. Miller has prepared and given, with great acceptance, lectures on temperance, also on missionary and educational subjects. She is prominently connected with the Woman's Foreign Missionary Society of the M. E. Church, and is a Trustee of the Northwestern University at Evanston.

All objections to an exceptional career for women (and especially for women who have husbands, children, and homes), find conspicuous refutation in the fragile yet indomitable, modest yet independent, loving and beloved, yet brave and business-like little woman whom I have here the honor to introduce. On one thing she particularly prides herself, viz.: her ability to make bread and darn stockings with any woman living. But her husband's especial pride was in the sweet poems that he often wrote down fresh from her own lips, and the manly, wholesome characters, the

> "Creatures not too bright or good
> For human nature's daily food,"

which she embodies in her story books.

Talk of the "chivalry" of ancient days! Go to, ye mediæval ages, and learn what that word means. Behold the Christian light of this nineteenth century, in which we have the spectacle, not of lances tilted to defend "my lady's" beauty, by swaggering knights who could not write their names, but of the noblest men in the world's foremost race, placing upon the brows of those most dear to them, above the wreath of Venus, the helmet of Minerva, and leading into broader paths of opportunity and knowledge the fair divinities who preside over their homes.

CHAPTER XV.

MRS. ANNIE WITTENMYER.

First President of the W. C. T. U.—War Record—Church Work— Philanthropy.

A NEW YORK journalist thus describes the varied enterprises which have been helped forward to success by the gifts and energy of this indefatigable Christian worker:

"Mrs. Wittenmyer's maiden name was Turner. She was born in Ohio, but her early home was Kentucky. Her grandfather was a graduate of Princeton College, and an officer in the war of 1812. Her father was a native of the State of Maryland, her mother of Kentucky, so that she inherits the warm, fervid temperament of the South, united with the cool, calculating reason of the North. She attended, for several years, a seminary in Ohio, where her education was carried much farther than was usual for young ladies at that time. She was married in her twenty-first year, and enjoyed many years of happy married life. She was very prominent in the Church in consequence of religious zeal and enthusiasm, and also for her great activity in all charitable enterprises. At the beginning of the late war, Mrs. Wittenmyer was appointed by the Legislature, Sanitary Agent for the State of Iowa. Secretary Stanton, of the War Department, gave passes for herself and supplies through the army lines, and a letter of instruction to army officers to coöperate in her enterprise for the relief of the soldiers. In this worthy endeavor she continued throughout

(160)

MRS. ANNIE WITTENMYER.

the entire war, changing her relation to it, however, by resigning her position as Sanitary Agent for Iowa to enter the service of the Christian Commission. Here she had the oversight of two hundred ladies, and she developed in this work her plan of special diet kitchens, to the great advantage of the health of our soldiers. The first kitchen was opened at Nashville, Tenn. In it was prepared food for eighteen hundred of the worst cases of sick and wounded soldiers. These kitchens were superintended by the ladies under her direction. In this work she had the assistance of the Surgeon-General, Assistant Surgeon, and all the army officers, both military and medical. General Grant was a personal friend, and did all in his power to facilitate her efforts.

" By invitation of the Surgeon-General, she met the Medical Commission appointed to review the special diet cooking of the army. The work of this commission led to a thorough change in the hospital cooking of the army, which was lifted to a grade of hygienic perfection far above anything before known in military affairs, and from which it is not likely to fall again to the old standard. It is simple justice to add, what is a matter of history in the United States Christian Commission, that these improvements in the diet kitchens of the army were the means of saving thousands of valuable lives, and of restoring noble men to health and usefulness.

"About the close of the war Mrs. Wittenmyer set in motion the idea of a ' Home for Soldiers' Orphans,' and became herself the founder of the institution bearing this name in Iowa. It is not generally known that this enterprise originated with the brave woman who had cared for the husbands and fathers through the perils of camp and hospital life. When the fact that such an institution was to be opened in Iowa was generally known, hundreds of soldiers' orphans became the wards of the State. By
7

request of the Board of Managers of the Iowa Home, she went to Washington City, and obtained from Secretary Stanton (other departments coöperating), the beautiful barracks at Davenport, which cost the Government forty-six thousand dollars, and hospital supplies amounting to five or six thousand more, subject to the approval of Congress, which was afterwards obtained. The institution thus founded and equipped, has accommodated over five hundred children at one time, and it still maintains in a flourishing condition under the care of the State.

"Mrs. Wittenmyer next conceived the idea that the vast amount of talent and energy brought into activity by the philanthropies of the war should be maintained on a Christian basis in the Church. Bishop Simpson, always ready to aid in any movement promising greater usefulness for women, entered heartily into the plan, and the Methodist Church established a Home Missionary Society of women, organized for the express purpose of ministering to the temporal and spiritual needs of strangers and the poor. This organization was made a General Conference Society at the session of 1871, and Mrs. Wittenmyer was elected its Corresponding Secretary. During the year 1876, over fifty thousand families were visited under its auspices.

"At the commencement of this new work Mrs. Wittenmyer removed to Philadelphia and founded her paper known as *The Christian Woman*, an individual enterprise which proved exceptionally successful. More recently she established a juvenile paper called *The Christian Child*. In addition to this large publishing work, she carried forward all the enterprises of the society above described and known as ' The Ladies' and Pastors' Christian Union,' traveling in its interest thousands of miles, and speaking in every State from Maine to California.

"When, as an outgrowth of the Crusade, the temperance

women met in their first national convention, after Mrs. Leavitt ('Leader of the 43') had declined the presidency to which she had been chosen, Mrs. Wittenmyer was elected to that post. She wrought earnestly for the society in all its earlier years. Twenty-three States were organized as auxiliary to the National Union, and a paper founded as its organ. Mrs. Wittenmyer also labored tirelessly in the lecture field, speaking sometimes six evenings in the week, besides traveling hundreds of miles. She attended all the large conventions, of which forty-six were held in 1875. At the second annual meeting of the National Woman's Christian Temperance Union, held in Cincinnati, November, 1875, she presided with marked ability, and was re-elected president for the Centennial year by a unanimous vote of the delegates.

" One of the most notable acts which characterized her administration was the presentation to Congress (in February, 1875) of a huge petition on behalf of our local, State, and National unions, asking for the prohibition of the liquor traffic, on which occasion a 'hearing' was granted by the Congressional judiciary committee. Another act even more important was the sending of a letter of inquiry to the International Medical Association, which met in Philadelphia in the summer of the Centennial year. This led to another hearing before a committee of celebrated physicians of Europe and our own country, and resulted in the well-known 'Resolutions,' expressive of the most important medical opinion against intoxicants on record, when we consider the representative character of those who gave it. Still another official act was the holding of the first 'Woman's National Camp-Meeting' at Ocean Grove, which, conducted wholly and addressed largely by women, commanded the earnest attention of the thousands present to the close, and was equally remarkable for spiritual and intellectual power.

We believe the first woman's camp-meeting on record was held in Iowa the previous year, and it was quite in keeping that one whose public work began in that noble young State should have conducted the first east of the Alleghanies.

"At the annual meeting in Newark, 1876, Mrs. W. was elected a third time to the chief office in the gift of the temperance women of America, and by a unanimous vote.

"It was a pleasant sight to see Mrs. W. in her cheery Philadelphia home, with her efficient secretary, Miss Merchant, and her exemplary son, Charlie, around her, all of them blithe and busy as so many bees. In addition to the care of her two papers and the duties of her office as president, this ceaseless worker has written several books, among them a 'History of the Woman's Temperance Crusade.' For three years past she has been chiefly engaged in Pennsylvania, doing excellent service in the great cause of constitutional prohibition.

"Mrs. Wittenmyer is devoted to the advancement of her sex in usefulness and opportunity. First, last, and always she is 'a *woman's* woman.' Her editorials 'cry and spare not' against the tyranny of prejudice and custom. She tilts a free lance, and deals blows worthy of a more stalwart arm. 'The See Trial' ('none so blind as those who *won't* see') was the occasion of several cogent arguments from her pen, to prove that women 'have a right to preach or speak in the pulpit,' and she once added to the larger of the two editions of her paper a department headed 'Pulpit of *The Christian Woman*,' in which a 'sermon' appeared monthly from the pen of some member of the rapidly-growing sisterhood of evangelists.

"The Crusade spirit abides with Mrs. Wittenmyer; the gospel work is her delight, and her hymn of 'Victory,'

written for the convention at Newark, embodies her
declaration of faith as a temperance reformer. The first
verse of this hymn forms a fitting close to this sketch:

> " The Lord is our refuge and strength,
>   His promises never can fail;
>   We've learned the sweet lesson at length,
>   His grace over sin can prevail.

> " In the sweet by and by,
>   We'll conquer the demon of rum;
>   In the sweet by and by
>   The kingdom of heaven will come."

CHAPTER XVI.

MRS. MARY T. BURT.

Second Corresponding Secretary of National W. C. T. U.—An Episcopalian—Editor of "Our Union"—President of New York State W. C. T. U.

[This gifted woman was one of the secretaries of our first National Convention, and has since borne a part so prominent in the work that a sketch of her comes in appropriately here.]

MARY TOWNE BURT, the daughter of a gentleman of English birth who was educated for the Episcopal ministry, is claimed as a daughter of the Queen City— Cincinnati. Her father died when she was four years of age, on his return voyage from his native shores, which he had visited on business. Upon the widowed mother then devolved the trust of rearing the children, of whom there were three—a daughter older than Mary (now Mrs. Pomeroy, a member of the W. C. T. U. of Chicago), and a son younger. No stronger proof of this mother's fitness for and fidelity to her trust is needed than the fact that they arise and call her blessed, and her affectionate testimony to their ever-watchful tenderness for her comfort. She removed to Auburn, N. Y., when Mary was twelve. Until sixteen the young girl, all unconscious of the powers within, yet a faithful student, attended the public schools of Auburn. She then became a pupil of Professor M. L. Browne, at the Auburn Young Ladies' Institute. Here her talents made her an especial favorite, and Professor Browne offered her every facility if she would

(168)

MRS. MARY T. BURT.

remain with him, but this was not practicable. Her home at this time was with her uncle, John T. Baker, who, with his wife, regarded the young girl, now just on the threshold of womanhood, with warm affection.

Four years after leaving school she married Edward Burt, son of one of Auburn's oldest and most honored residents. Soon after this she was confirmed a member of the Protestant Episcopal Church by the venerable Bishop Coxe.

For a long time she was much withdrawn from society by frail health, and learned in the solitude of her chamber and under the loving hand of her Father the lessons which can only be learned thus, but which polish and perfect heart and mind. Her husband's health also failing, in 1872 they spent three delightful months at Nassau, and, beside the present enjoyment, reaped lasting benefit in strength and vigor.

When the Crusade swept over the land, it aroused Mrs. Burt, as it did the thousands. She engaged the Opera House and delivered a lecture on temperance, March 24, 1874, before a most cultured and refined audience, Professor Browne, her former instructor, presiding. Temperance was no new thought to her; her father and mother were both strong advocates, and the principles had been instilled into her earliest training. Her mother (now residing with her) gives her fullest sympathy to all her present work. In Auburn a W. C. T. U. was organized and Mrs. Burt elected President, which position she held two years. When the women were called to a national council in Cleveland, O., in the autumn of 1874, Mrs. Burt was made one of the Secretaries, thus coming to the front in the National Union at its inception. During the winter of 1875, Mr. and Mrs. Burt removed to Brooklyn, and in the fall of 1876, at the Newark Convention, she was made a member of the publishing committee of *Our Union*, and elected its publisher. In thus taking charge of an enterprise very dear to her, her success proved her abundant qualification for the arduous service. The paper had been started; was almost an experiment; had no capital but the love and faith of the W. C. T. U., and was largely in debt. She took hold of her new task with energy and vigor, enlarged and improved the paper in many ways, pushed its interests with the intensity of personal love; and during the subsequent year its subscription list was nearly doubled. Her work on our paper can best speak for itself to the thousands who know its results. The next year Mrs. Burt assumed the position of managing editor, and here still further endeared herself to the constituency of our W. C. T. U. At the same time they were becoming better acquainted with her personally, for she had been elected Corresponding Secretary at the Chicago Convention, the duties of which position she filled during two years.

Severe afflictions have been hers, the loss of a gifted and only brother being among them. But with a winsome patience she has borne every cross, endearing herself greatly to our sisterhood of workers by her attractive manners and sincerity of spirit. Cautious in counsel, and gifted in utterance, Mrs. Burt is a rare favorite in State and nation. She is President of the State W. C. T. U. of New York, and actively engaged in building up the work at large, as well as in her Brooklyn home.

DEFINITENESS OF RESULTS TO BE EXPECTED.

Does any definite, permanent result ever come of this restless agitation, this endless series of meetings, these perpetual prayers, these hundreds of Bands of Hope, the tons of Temperance tracts, in short, this ferment extending from one end of our country to the other?

We answer boldly, Yes! A result is coming, more definite, more permanent, more clearly within measurable limits, than could be hoped for in any other moral reform now in progress. And we believe that the responsibility for this work, and the credit of its final assured success, depends mainly upon the women of America as they shall be led onward by their sisters of the National W. C. T. U.

Whatever of supposed enjoyment comes from pleasures which are outside the moral law, falls mainly to the share of the men, while the dreadful penalties must be borne mainly by the women; and most of all by the good and innocent women. The drinking man has a temporary respite from care and sorrow in the cup, which is unshared by the wife and daughter who are starving or pining at home. The disgrace and penalty of social transgressions are comparatively unshared by the man in the world's estimation. Not only the finer moral nature of woman, but even her self-interest also, are both involved in sobriety and chastity.

To the women of America, therefore, we look for the complete reformation of the drinking habits of our country; and happily we do not look in vain.

An illustration is often better than an argument, and we give one of many in the history of the town of Millville, N. J., a place of about ten thousand inhabitants, calling attention to the painful past of its history, its comfortable present. and its hopeful future, in connection with the work of the Woman's Christian Temperance Union there.

Its principal interests are the manufacture of glass, and an iron foundry. A generation ago it was conspicuous for its immorality, resulting from the almost universal use of liquor. The whisky flasks were carried even into the workshops and freely used there. The writer remembers when it was not always considered safe, during times of agitation on the wages question, for the Philadelphia proprietors to visit their own factories. Many of the men were brutal, their wives wretched, their children ragged.

The churches had done all they could to stem the ever increasing tide of evil, but seemed powerless beyond a certain point. Temperance societies of men alone made noble efforts, but the evil remained unchecked.

At last the women were roused. The future of their brothers, their husbands, their sons, and of their daughters also, from whom they longed to avert the suffering many of themselves had borne, was all at stake. Enthusiastically, yet wisely and prudently, they used their influence for the abolition of the seductive snares spread for those they loved. They talked, they prayed, they worked, and gradually public sentiment changed, until the question of whether or not the liquor traffic should be licensed in Millville became the principal issue in all the local elections.

The women could not vote, but they could influence the voters, and they did it faithfully and vigorously. At one time, when the strength of the two parties was nearly balanced, and in the town council a butcher held the deciding vote as to licensing, the women went to him and told him if he should cast his vote in favor of license, they would never again purchase any meat of him. In consequence of their remonstrances he withheld his vote, and the licenses were refused.

Another year the three hotels of the town announced that they could not afford to keep open if they were not allowed to sell liquor, and they all joined to refuse accommodation to travelers. This was met by a spirited lady who had the largest house in the town, and who opened her comfortable home to travelers, thus showing the hotels that they were not indispensable. Two were turned into boarding-houses, and the third is now a well-ordered Temperance hotel.

The women held meetings, paid private visits, distributed literature, brought attractive lecturers to the town, and worked in every way, both publicly and privately, to abolish the evil traffic. And for ten years now there has not been a single licensed place in Millville to tempt its inhabitants to drink, nor a single man whose business it was to draw young men from their homes, and to enrich themselves at the cost of the demoralization of their fellow-men and the misery of their neighbors' families.

Instead of three taverns, the town now has three music stores. Instead of thousands of dollars squandered in the fiery stimulants for the men, six thousand dollars are now annually spent in cottage organs for their homes. The drunkards' wives who used to cower and suffer, now rejoice. The daughters are sent to school; the children are well fed and well clothed; and it would be hard to find anywhere a more prosperous or happier manufacturing community.

The question of license or no license was for many years stoutly contested at the polls, but the influence of the women has finally triumphed, and the question has ceased even to come up before the nominating conventions, so nearly unanimous has become the sentiment of the people. Even those who once were addicted to drink are thankful now to have a temptation which they are too weak to resist removed from them, and join in the prohibition vote.

With the removal of the drinking places of resort, however, a need arose of a place of innocent recreation for the many young workmen who were boarding, and consequently had no comfortable place in which to spend their evenings. The W. C. T. U. met this want partly by securing a pleasant room where the boys of the town were entertained nightly with books and music and pleasant company. This proved so successful that a larger enterprise was set on foot, and within the last year there has been erected, at an expense of nearly twenty-five thousand dollars, mainly supplied by the workmen of the town, the Millville Mechanics' Institute, a substantial, elegant structure, fifty by sixty feet. It contains a large gymnasium, used for the present as a skating rink; baths, which are patronized by hundreds; an elegantly furnished library and reading-room, opened in the afternoons to ladies, and drawing several hundred young men in the evenings weekly; a newspaper and amusement room, where about three hundred men every evening read the papers and play innocent games of skill; a large auditorium, holding about seven hundred seats, which by the constitution of the Institute is given free of charge to the W. C. T. U. forever; and several class rooms which are in constant use for adult evening classes, some of whom are for the first time learning to read. Two acres of ground, fronting on the beautiful Maurice river, are appropriated to tennis, croquet, base ball, and other out-door games.

From a definite past involving much of sorrow and degradation, Millville has advanced to a definite present of comparative virtue and elevation, and looks forward to a definite future of still greater development in virtue and intelligence.

CHAPTER XVII.

WOMAN'S CHRISTIAN TEMPERANCE UNION WORK FOR THE INDIVIDUAL.

Gospel Temperance, or the Light of Christ shining in the circle of one heart—"The Lord looseth the prisoners"—A reformed man's speech —Woman's Christian Temperance Union work in the Church universal—Its wholly unsectarian character—"Let her not take a text" —Our Evangelists—Mrs. S. M. I. Henry—"The Name"—Mrs. Hannah Whitall Smith—"How to prepare Bible Readings"—Mrs. Mary T. Lathrop—Miss Jennie Smith—The Indian Chief Petosky—The first temperance Camp-meeting—Alcohol at the Communion Table— How one woman helped—That fossil prayer-meeting—Woman's Christian Temperance Union Training School—"The Master is come and calleth for thee."

"THE Lord looseth the prisoners." This was the first message of the Woman's Temperance Crusade. The Bible was read in ten thousand haunts of sin; "the Rock of Ages women," as saloon-keepers began to call them, pointed the men enslaved by drink to the Gospel declaration: "If the Son shall make you free, you shall be free indeed." Never before had this message of hope been carried straight from the church to the dram-shop and its deluded votaries. The church-bells had said "Come," to souls possessed of sin, but now their daily chimes said "Go," to saints enlightened by the Holy Spirit. The mountain had not come to Mahomet, and at last Mahomet went to the mountain. "How can we reach the masses?" had long been the question. "By going where they are," was now the answer—not in empty words and paralytic theories, but vital, glowing deeds. To get the flask out of a man's side pocket was not enough: the New Testament

(176)

must be placed there in its stead. The pledge was good, but men must have, as a drinking man has said, "The Lord behind the pledge." Attendance at church increased one hundred per cent. during the fifty days of that Crusade which routed the liquor traffic, "horse, foot, and dragoons," out of two hundred and fifty towns and villages. "What must we do to be saved from our sin?" "Sirs, we would see Jesus?" were questions which pastors' hearts had ached to hear. Thank God! on every side they heard them now!

In general terms, the invitation of the women who went to saloons and returned to the church, followed by hundreds of penitent drunkards, was this: "Brother: You are not a sinner above all the Galileans, though down on you has tumbled the tower of public disgrace and shame. It is true you have that very inconvenient sort of sin that cannot be covered away out of sight. It advertises you by the breath which poisons all the air about you; it advertises you by the zig-zag steps you make along the street, so that he who runs may read; it advertises you by the trademark of the drink demon stamped upon your cheek, so that even little children know. But what if the demon of envy, malice, or pride; of ambition, greed, or appetite in other forms should set his mark upon the faces of us all — would any cheek be fair? Nay, verily; not one, except as Christ has lifted us above the level of the self that was, into the victory over sin. And so, because He has thus helped us, we have come to tell thee, brother. We have brought with us the Declaration of Independence—our total abstinence pledge—and we ask thy name. But we would not single thee out, like a specimen in a museum to be labeled and certified and set up to be gazed upon; we would not treat thee like a black sheep in this great, good-natured flock. No, not at all! You take the pledge—we'll take it too; you wear the badge of ribbon, blue or red—we'll wear it

too, and we will make that pledge and badge, not on your
part the confession of past degradation, but on the part of
all of us the kindly bond of a present brotherhood and
sisterhood."

Going to the drinking class in such a spirit, what wonder that, though we had been told " their hearts were
hard," we found they could be cleft in twain by the
sledge-hammer blow of the kind word and helpful deed.
It is one thing to reach down, but quite another and a
better to extend what Elihu Burritt used to call " the
horizontal palm." The women had no theory about "the
removal of the appetite for drink," any more than for
other miracles of grace. Nobody has ever claimed that
the lions failed to attack Daniel in the den because their
teeth had been extracted, nor did the Crusaders stop to
query whether a diseased stomach was miraculously
restored—and if they had, it is quite likely they would
not have claimed any such physiological miracle. But
the fact remained that men who had been drinking forty
years left off their cups and have never touched them
since. " The expulsive power of a new affection," Horace
Bushnell would have called it, and perhaps with truth.
The *rationale* is not so vital as the result. Peter did not
find the waves turned to a solid path for his feet, and yet
he walked upon them safely just so long as he looked
into Christ's face. It is just so with the soul. Faith
forms the *nexus* with God's power, and faith alone. It
is absolute truth in spiritual dynamics that " *Prayer
will cause a man to cease from sinning, even as sin will
cause a man to cease from prayer.*"

Glorious were the trophies of the Crusade along the
line of faith and prayer. Many and delightful are the
books in which their memory is embalmed. Heroic are
the figures that make up the reformed men's group.
Francis Murphy, the typical Irishman, stands there, a

royal and brotherly heart, saved " by the kind touch of a Christian's hand," and going forth to his glorious mission on both sides of the sea, " with malice toward none and charity for all." Hundreds of thousands have risen up from the ashes of dead hopes to clasp that strong hand as Brother Murphy cried in earnest tones: "Come and sign the pledge, while we sing ' I hear Thy gentle voice that calls me, Lord, to Thee.' " Dr. Henry A. Reynolds, the Harvard graduate and gallant Knight of the Red Ribbon, stands there, proudly confessing, "I attribute my salvation from a drunkard's grave to the Woman's Temperance Crusade of Bangor," and with his gentle wife journeys both east and west, organizing Reform Clubs dedicated to his manly motto, " Dare to do Right," and rallying the manhood of Michigan behind him, five hundred thousand strong. J. K. Osgood, founder of the first reform club, is a dignified, pathetic figure in this group, and in every State we count as the most loyal friends of woman's work the men who themselves have borne, and labored, and had patience, not only in the mighty work of personal reform, but in the Christ-like effort to help others into " the victory that overcometh, even our faith." Some sketches of this Gospel temperance work, by which the heart-circle is filled with light, will now be given.

A REFORMED MAN'S SPEECH—A VOICE FROM THE RANKS.

We live in an age in which a suspicion, at least, has lodged itself in the average mind, that the secret of a happy life is somehow mixed up with the practice of "going about doing good." True, it has taken many generations for the "enthusiasm of humanity," that blessed wave the flow of which began at the foot of Calvary's cross, to rise so high that it threatens to submerge all other ideals of the good supreme. But, none the less,

"it's coming up the heights of time," and in the sparkle
of its foaming crest,

"This poor old world is getting brighter."

Almost every minister, evangelist, and "without leave or
license" preacher of the time, from Dr. John Hall and
Dwight L. Moody down to the humblest itinerant crusader, has for the burden of a speech to which the common
people listen gladly, this notion, stated in incomparable
language by the Master: "It is more blessed to give than
to receive!" It is good for us to hear "that same" from
the ranks of those who, in the Master's day, were called
"the publicans and sinners." Theirs is a different point of
view, and science teaches that a fresh angle of vision often
helps to greater vividness of sight. Journeying about
through the New England States in the interest of our
dear "National," I have listened to scores of admirable
speeches for "the cause." Among them all, however,
none has impressed me quite so much as the following,
by a REFORMED MAN at Old Orchard Beach, where we had
one of the grandest temperance camp-meetings on record.
He was a "rough-and-ready" sort of fellow, this premium
orator of mine; short, stout, and ruddy-faced, with sign-
post gestures, steady, earnest voice, and the "chopping,"
Yankee style of articulation. He didn't mince matters a
bit, but when he was called came sturdily forward, and
talked on this fashion:

"I shan't speak mor'n three minutes. Can tell all I
know inside o' that. Yonder sets Dr. Reynolds of Bangor, who goes about and gets up reformed men's clubs.
I want you all to look at him. Wal, I picked up a paper
on my work-bench, and I read one o' that man's temperance speeches. Nothin' so dreadful remarkable in it, to
be sure, but I tell ye, with me, it just happened to *strike in.*
I'm but an unlearned fellow, as you see — a carpenter by

trade—a drunkard, too, by trade, for twenty years. Wal,
now, will you believe it ? I've lived in a nice town here in
Maine all that time, and I'm a white man and a Yankee
to boot, and in all these twenty years never a minister
or a Christian of any sort ever came near enough to me
to tell me I was goin' to hell. Never one of 'em, man,
woman, or child, ever opened their heads to me about my
sins or my soul. They preached well and they prayed
well, and they sang first-rate, up at the meetin'-house.
Sometimes I used to hear 'em as I went by to where I
got my liquor. But I never went to meetin' in all them
years. Ye see, I didn't want to go, and I hadn't decent
enough clothes anyway, and, besides, nobody ever asked
me ; but I wasn't such a hard fellow after all, for, as I
tell you, this little speech of the doctor over there—God
bless him!—telling how he had reformed, and how bad
he wanted everybody else to do the same—it just whirled
me right round on my heels, and I've been walkin' away
from the beer mug ever since.

"Now jist a word of what you good folks call exhortin'.
There's lots o' men like me that ye could save by only
half tryin'. Why didn't ye never come to my house all
them years ? now, *why didn't ye ?* That's a big question !
I aint a blamin' nobody. The ministers they've got their
hands full a studyin' their sermons ; bnt why didn't some
o' the high privates come, or the reg'lar rank and file ?
Now, I tell you, that's the doctrine. Go for us fellows !
That's the way the Master did. Don't it speak somewhere in the Good Book about ' My people perishin' for
lack o' knowledge ?'

"Why, now I'm reformed, it seems to me I can't do
enough to bring other men to the comfort that's in my life
and my home. I go miles and miles, after my day's
work, when I hear of a poor drunkard, such as I used to
be. And if it's so much to me jest to be temperate, what

must it be to be all made over new, as you Christians tell
about? "Mercy on us! I shouldn't think you'd taken a
bit o' rest from carryin' the glad tidings to us poor
wretches, who hain't really had half a chance o' our lives
from the start.

"But it's all so new to me, you know, that mebbe I'm
too fast. I don't mean no offense, and I do remember
that Christ said, '*go*, go, go, unto all the world,' and I'm
sure that means into the back alleys and down among the
dirty little houses in your own village, as well as away
over to the Chinese.

"I've about made up my mind we've got to depend on
them that was first at the sepulchre and last at the cross
to do this business. Ladies, won't you take hold and
help? Won't you seek out the fellows that don't go to
church? Speak a kind word to their wives, and set down
with 'em in their houses, and jest tell 'em about this
Jesus you love so much, and who went about doin' good;
for if you do, I tell you—and I'm one o' the fellows,
you'll save 'em every time, just as true as twelve inches
makes a foot. Now, I'm a carpenter, remember, and I
know when I've hit the nail on the head, even if I don't
know much else."

W. C. T. U. WORK IN THE CHURCH UNIVERSAL.

After the heart and home circles have the light of
Christ through Gospel Temperance, the work of the W.
C. T. U. widens to its best evolution in the religious
homes of the people, collectively known as "the Church."
Going out on the street to pray signified a good deal
when one comes to think about it. First of all, it meant
going outside denominational fences. The Crusaders felt
that "unity of the Spirit" was the one thing needed, nor
feared to join hands with any who had the Bible and
the temperance pledge for the two articles in their "Con-

fession of Faith," who rallied to the tune of "Rock of Ages," and had for their watchword "Not willing that any should perish." Of this blessed fact the illustrations from that wonderful epoch are well nigh numberless. We give but one:

In front of a saloon that had refused them entrance, knelt a crusading group. Their leader was the most prominent Methodist lady of the community. Her head was crowned with the glory of gray hairs; her hands were clasped, her sweet and gentle voice was lifted up in prayer. Around her knelt the flower of all the churches of that city—Congregationalists, Baptists, Presbyterians —many of whom had never worked outside their own denominations until now. At the close, an Episcopal lady offered the Lord's prayer, in which joined Unitarians, Swedenborgians, and Universalists; and when they had finished, a dear old lady in the dove-colored garb of the Friends' Society was moved to pray, while all the time below them on the curbstone's edge knelt Bridget with her beads and her Ave Marie.

"LET HER NOT TAKE A TEXT."

I have wondered sometimes whether "our ministerial brethren" draw the line between our ministrations and their own, on a technicality or on a principle. Once upon a time, in a country village where it was the excellent practice for three evangelical ministers to join in a temperance service one Sunday night in the month, it happened that two of the ministers were to be absent upon the regular evening. The remaining one had preached the previous month, and was not ready with another sermon on that topic. So he sent to a lady temperance speaker, sojourning in the place, an invitation to occupy the pulpit, saying, however, that he "should not expect her to take a text." She accepted the invitation and filled up the allotted time to the entire satisfaction of the minister, as she afterwards learned. She then apologized for not sending any definite rejoinder to his message, saying that she presumed it would be all right, as she had taken " not one but forty texts." No one seemed to think she had passed the bounds of decorum in explaining the bearing of many Bible passages upon the subject of temperance. But if she had taken *one* and explained its bearing, or made it a " point of *departure*," as is often the case when our brethren " take a text," who could have answered for the consequences ? Since then I have often seen the same distinction made, but I have sought in vain for the principle involved. I hear women giving Scripture readings with great acceptability, involving comments on a large scale, using a much wider and more difficult range of thought than is commonly given to a sermon with one text, and I am more perplexed than ever. Can any one inform me ? What makes the difference ? Where is the line ? How *many* texts must we take in order to keep within our proper " sphere ? "

OUR TEMPERANCE EVANGELIST, MRS. S. M. I. HENRY, OF ILLINOIS.

Under the sway of a Christian civilization the tendency is toward individuality of character, and, as a natural sequence, of vocation also. Hence this is the age of specialists and experts. "This one thing I do," must be the motto of that man or woman who would condense into a year, results once thought sufficient for a life-time. Perhaps no field of labor illustrates this practical truth more clearly than our well-beloved " W. C. T. U." Since we emerged from the nebulous period, and sought specific work, through superintendencies, national, state, and local, the change has been as from a picture in Berlin wools to a clear-cut steel engraving. Among those who,

MRS. S. M. I. HENRY.

while their gifts would have made them successful in almost any field, showed their wisdom by the careful cultivation of one, Mrs. Henry, for years our Superintendent of the National Department of Evangelistic work, stands prominent.

Long before either of us had asked concerning the blessed cause of Temperance, "Is all this anything to me?" I had read with great interest the poems of Sarepta M. Irish, in the *Ladies' Repository.* The same love for humanity and loyalty to its best Friend, that characterized her earliest lines, shines forth in her Temperance addresses, books, poems, and daily life.

Sarepta M. Irish, afterward Mrs. Henry, was born in Albion, Erie County, Pennsylvania, November 4, 1839, of New England stock. Her father was an architect before he was a preacher. He was sent out to N. W. Illinois as a missionary in 1840, in the days when Indians and wild deer roamed the prairies. His daughter retains a distinct recollection of both. The former used to come often to the little parsonage, stack their arms at the gate, and enter. She has now a wampum garter that a chief took off and tied about her neck because she kissed his pappoose when she was a tiny child.

Her great grandfather, on the mother's side, was a surgeon in the Revolutionary War; her grandfather a captain of militia in the war of 1812. Her father's family were Quakers.

She learned to read from her Bible—a little calf-bound copy that her grandmother gave her when a very little child. Her father taught her himself until she was nineteen. She had hardly ever attended school until she went to Rock River Seminary, at Mount Morris, Illinois, under the kind reign of President Harlow. During the first term she was called home to see her father die. This was an irreparable loss to her, for they were more to each

other than can be expressed; he seemed her life. He
had been an invalid for eight years, and she was his constant companion, reading and writing for him. She even
used to do her thinking aloud to him. He was a remarkable man, drawing young people to him even when confined to his room, and winning them to all things pure
and true by his real love for them, and by the genuine
greatness of his own noble nature. I think none ever
forgot him who knew him. Sarepta was fond of literary
pursuits from childhood, and her mother, with a patience
which would surprise us in any *but* a mother, humored all
her poetic fancies, so that her life until her marriage was
like a dream, knowing no care, feeling no responsibility.
Mrs. Henry says:

"I do not remember when I was converted. I was given
to God honestly by my parents, and taught that I belonged to Him, and that an obligation of Christian living,
binding as a contract, rested upon me. The time came
when I chafed under this yoke, and when there was great
danger of wreck to my soul on the shoals of skepticism,
and had not my father been the judicious man he was, I
should doubtless have gone down. But he was a wise
man; he never dogmatically stated anything to me, but
placing himself at my side, in the work of seeking truth,
so directed my mind in its processes that I came out on
the bright side of an undimmed faith that shines like a
great sun in a cloudless heaven to-day and always; no
mists having ever been able to hide its beauty from my
eyes."

Her school life was spent at Mount Morris, Illinois,
where began an acquaintance with many choice men and
women who helped her future. Rev. Dr. John H. Vincent was her pastor, brother, and friend, and with his
wife took her, when a fatherless and almost heart-broken
child, under their tender care, and made it possible for

her to rally and go on after her bitter bereavement. Her boarding-place was in the home of Rev. B. H. Cartwright. A portion of every day was spent with him and his wife in their study, and a tie was formed then that has but strengthened with the years.

She had nothing but the promise of God, back of her pen, as the means of an education, and the Lord and her friends know much better than she does how she got along. She was paid very liberally for her pen work, however, and so spent two years at school. She had many convictions that she ought to enter the foreign missionary field, and had there been the agencies at work then that are now so successful, she would doubtless have done this. Our friend was married to James W. Henry of New York, March 1, 1861, four days after Lincoln was inaugurated, and just on the eve of the civil war. Her husband was a scholar and a man of deep and tender nature, a poet of no mean order, a teacher by profession, but the principle involved in the war was deep as his life, and he enlisted when the first call was made for men. He was not, however, mustered in at first, because he was a trifle under regulation height, so they went East, to his home, and settled down on a farm, where the years that the war allowed to them were spent. Here was born, in June, their daughter Mary, who has been so much to her dear mother all these years. It was during the first year of her life, and while she was cradled in her mother's arms, that Mrs. Henry's first book—" Victoria "—was written. That poem grew with her first beautiful year, but was not published until Mr. Henry was a soldier. He enlisted again in October, 1864, in the 185th New York Regiment, Company E. Her oldest son, Alfred, was born the 4th of the next April, just ten days before Lincoln was assassinated. The husband came home an invalid in July, 1865, having been in every battle and on every long march of the closing campaign conducted by the 5th Corps. He lived over four years, bravely battling disease, but was finally conquered and went to his rest in the cemetery of his native valley. Arthur, the youngest son, was nearly three years old when his father died. Mrs. Henry was left absolutely helpless to all appearances, but she had her faith and the word of God, and she went to work to rear her children for God and her country. It would take a volume to tell the story of the faithfulness of our Heavenly Father to this helpless group—the mother and her babes. Mrs. H. taught for the next three years; for the first two and a half in the village where she had lived, but later on returned to her Illinois home. She began teaching in Rockford, under Professor Barbour, in the public school, and was trying to get her children settled in a little home where she could have them with her, when, in answer to her cry to God, a wonderful deliverance came to her in a time of great need, the details of which would transcend the limits of this sketch. As a result she was settled sweetly at home in a cosy little place where, at her study table, she worked out the problem of daily bread with her pen, writing the "After Truth" series, for which she was paid a fair price down. The Crusade found her at this study-table, and she was called out of the quiet she had always known before. She was a most timid woman. No one ever expected her to do anything in public, but under the pressure of a conviction that had to be answered, she made the call for the Christian women to come together, and became the mouthpiece of a W. C. T. U., March 27, 1873.

She made her first public address in the State Street Baptist Church, Rockford, during the Crusade, to an audience that overflowed into the street, and with as little embarrassment as she has ever since experienced. She was very conservative and always looked to the time

when she would return to literary work; but as the years
pass it becomes more and more evident that it was a life-
work to which she was then called.   A Reform Club was
organized the year after she began her work.   " Pledge
and Cross " tells the story of its redemption.   She gave
five full years to active temperance work in Rockford, one
year of Gospel work in Michigan, and has been three years
in the field in Illinois.   In July of 1879, Mrs. Henry removed to my own town of Evanston, to educate her
children in our university.   Mary is a sophomore, and
has been her mother's housekeeper all these years ; but
for her Mrs. H. could not have done her work.   Alfred is
also in the course of the Northwestern University, and
Arthur has begun his studies there.   The boys have made
it possible for their mother to do her work by faithfully
keeping her words in their hearts during her absence, and
their promise to be loyal to mother, sister, and God.

Mrs. Henry was one of our most effective speakers at
the capitol of Illinois when we presented the great " Home
Protection Petition."   She made the memorable plea from
the point of view of a widow with fatherless children,
and asked the same power to protect them from the
dram-shops which their father would have possessed had
he not given his life for his country.   Her lecture on
" What is the Boy Worth ? " is a masterly presentation
of the most vital question of the hour, and has been given
with telling effect in scores of towns and cities.   The new
book, " Roy, or The Voice of his Home," is one of Mrs.
Henry's best, and our young folks will be delighted with it
and its still happier sequel, " Mabel's Work."   " Pledge and
Cross " has had the largest sale of any book of its kind,
and conveys the very essence of the Gospel Temperance
Crusade.   All are published by J. N. Stearns, 58 Reade
street, New York, and ought to be read aloud in every
local union.   The Temperance Training Institute is a

8

happy invention of Mrs. Henry, by which normal Sunday-School methods are applied to the elucidation of our work, and the spiritual side is strongly emphasized. Dr. Vincent has invited Mrs. Henry to prepare a series of Biblical Temperance Lessons for the *Sunday-School Teacher*, which will be a mighty power in the Church. Mrs. Henry is also superintendent of our National Training School for Temperance Workers.

THE NAME.

BY MRS. S. M. I. HENRY.

God's name is Love.
He wrote his name in stars; and from the shining throng,
And from the heavens, there rolled a swelling tide of song.
The earth, which from the Hand Divine to motion sprung,
And quivering 'mid the hosts of heaven, in floods of glory hung,
Had not an eye to read the Name; for praises, had no tongue.

God's name is Love.
He wrote his name again in every changing hue,
And set it high upon the clouds, a promise great as true.
Men saw the ensign, but forgot the wondrous name it bore;
The earth beneath the archway swept, forgetful as before,
And yet God kept the hues, and wrote that one Name o'er and o'er.

God's name is Love.
He wrote it yet again 'all o'er the meadows fair,
In grass, and rose, and lily-bells, that man might read it there.
His sweetest, tenderest, dearest name he beaded with the dew,
And called the winds to publish it each breaking morn anew.
Man saw and heard, but in his heart the Name he never knew.

God's name is Love.
And when each chosen sign of earth, or sea, or sky
Had been employed to fix and hold man's restless eye,
From out his heart of love God drew a wondrous plan,
By which to seize the wandering gaze, and touch the heart of man.
He wrote his name in blood, on Calvary's rugged hill,
And heaven was veiled, and all the earth with awe grew still.
The dead stepped from their graves to see and read the wondrous sign,
And man, with heart grown tender, owned the Signature Divine.

MRS. HANNAH WHITALL SMITH.

MRS. HANNAH WHITALL SMITH, NATIONAL SUPERINTENDENT
OF EVANGELISTIC WORK.

There is no nest so likely to fledge philanthropists as a
Quaker home. Beyond any other religious society have
" Friends" nourished every reform based upon the eleventh commandment and the sermon on the mount. The
gospel temperance movement in this land has no leader
more trusty and tried than Hannah Whitall Smith, a
" Friend indeed," by ancestry and for many years by
membership. In all our meetings, the dove-like plumage,
peaceful face, and sweet " thee and thou" utterance, tell
us that in the army which, with the sword of the Spirit,
fights the rum power, even the women of the " Quaker
church" will take up arms.

The father of our beloved " Hannah" was known, in
his day, as " the best-loved merchant of Philadelphia."
His gifted son-in-law has characterized him thus: " He
was a bright, cheery, joyous, yet Cromwellian soldier,
clapped by mistake under the broad-brim of a Quaker;
but this extinguisher was never able to hide his gladsome
piety. And the daughter is her father over again."

Her mother was a portly Quaker matron, not unlike
Elizabeth Fry in appearance—one of the purest Quaker
types, and the soul of everything beautiful and good.

Hannah has two sisters and one brother—the latter at
the head of the great firm of Whitall, Tatum & Co., who
operate at Millville, N. J., the largest white glass factory
in the world—employing two thousand hands. This firm
is so loyal to the temperance reform that no orders are
accepted by them from men whose bottles or glasses are
to be used to contain intoxicating drinks. Their relations
to their employees involve no conflict between capital and
labor. An elegant " Mechanics' Institute," with library,
reading-rooms, bath-rooms, etc. (the whole costing twenty-
five thousand dollars), has been built by their operatives.

The large audience hall is to be perpetually at the service
of the Millville W. C. T. U., free of cost. What wonder
that workmen with such noble ambitions have dropped
the ballots that have closed out the saloons of the city.
Indeed, the work of the W. C. T. U. at Millville, under
the leadership of Mrs. Mickle, has borne such fruit that
our society has no friends more loyal than we find among
the well-known firm referred to, in which the husband of
our own H. W. S. is a partner.

Mrs. Smith has two sisters, who partake largely of
the gifts which have made her such a leader. Mrs. Dr.
James Carey Thomas, of Baltimore, leads our forces in
that city and in the State of Maryland, and Mrs. Nicholson
is one of the rare spirits made " perfect through suffering"—ill health alone compelling her to leave the ranks
of active service, where, in the dawn of the W. C. T. U.,
she wrought so well.

Mrs. Smith received her education in the Friends'
schools of Philadelphia, supplementing it by travels at
home and abroad, and by the steady devotion of a lifetime to whatever is purest and best in literature and
friendship. No home in this land has a wider or more
delightful hospitality; no " table talk " is more stimulating to whatever things are " lovely and of good report "
than in this household, where the gifted parents and highly-
endowed children exchange ideas with poets, orators, and
travelers, or study with untiring zest the heavenly ways
of God toward man. There is no fear of the " next
thing," because it is the next and not the last. There is
no looking back, after the puerile fashion of Lot's wife,
but, with earnest gaze forward and upward, this family
group moves forward, blessing and blessed. " Keep your
top eye open," is the mother's constant motto for her children; and the high-minded boy and girl at college, and
the lovely young daughter at home, are of the noblest

type of cultured "young Americans." Charming "Mariechen" writes me from Smith College :

"You ask me Mother's traits. She seems to me perfectly unselfish, and she carries this into the smallest details. For instance, if there is any choice of seats at the
fire, or dishes at the table, she always prefers everybody
before herself. Sometimes I think Mother is too careless
of herself; and yet I feel more and more each year that
the strong, unconscious influence of her self-forgetfulness
leads us as no formal teaching could. She never preaches
' in the bosom of the domestic circle.' We can never get
her to repeat her sermons and Bible talks to us. ' What
did thee talk about ? ' we ask. '*Goodness*—my child!' is
her invariable reply.

" She has always treated her children like reasonable
human beings, never in all her life giving one of us an
arbitrary ' Yes ' or ' No,' but always showing us the
principles behind. She always gives us a chance to make
our own decisions, counting self-discipline worth all the
rules in the world. We think she leaves us free to decide for ourselves and we pride ourselves on our freedom,
but all the while the steady influence of her steadfast life,
exerted almost unconsciously to us, constrains us to love
the right. Mother never condescends to us, but treats our
little affairs as if they were of the deepest importance.
We are her friends as well as her children. She does not
talk down to us from a height, but lifts us up beside her.
Indeed there is perfect confidence between us. She isn't
too curious though, or interfering. That's not her way.
Some mothers worry their daughters dreadfully—by in-
sisting on reading all their letters, for instance. But our
mother never acts that way. Confidences are never
dragged from us, and as a consequence, we *love* to tell her
everything. I suppose I ought to hint tenderly at her
faults, but really I can't seem to think of any, unless, per-

haps, she trusts us too much, admires us more than we merit, and makes us have too good a time."

One day Mrs. Smith went to this bright eldest daughter and said, " I want thee to read this tract of mine and tell me what thee thinks," whereupon Mariechen answered, " O mother, I don't need to read thy tracts to know that they are good—*thee lives them.*" There isn't much flavor of "Mrs. Jellaby" in such a testimony! Indeed it is the crowning glory of the W. C. T. U. that the patroness of "Boorioboola Gha" Mission has never yet cast in her lot with us. Says one who knows her life better than any other: " Hannah is no *doctrinaire.* She is the most practical woman I ever saw. Why her genius for housekeeping is something wonderful. From year's end to year's end there isn't a screw loose in this establishment. Were you ever in one that went more as if it ran on wheels ? I don't believe a more contented, obedient, grateful company of servants, nor a service more eagerly rendered, can anywhere be found. But it isn't strange that with such a magnificent and abiding concept of the Fatherhood and Motherhood of God she should, by her grip on that great principle, find herself ' seated in heavenly places in Christ Jesus,' and so be a pervasive harmonizer in her own home, as everywhere. I never met a person less affected by either praise or blame, or sustained at a more uniform elevation above life's pettiness and frailties." Truly may it be said of the woman whose views of Christian experience have influenced more lives than those of any other since Madame Guyon, "Her children arise up and call her blessed—her husband also, and he praiseth her." " The Christian's Secret of a Happy Life," which has been translated into Russian by a Countess, into German by a daughter of the historian Niebuhr, and into many other foreign languages, and which to-day is moulding character into conformity with

Christ wherever the English tongue is spoken, was first lived out in this quiet Philadelphia home. " I learned my theology in the nursery with my children " is the frequent observation of her whom the world knows as " H. W. S." " The story of Frank, or Record of a Happy Life," has been translated into eight languages and had a wider circulation than any religious biography of our day, unless we except " The Dairyman's Daughter." The meetings addressed by Mrs. Smith at Brighton and Oxford, in 1875, each gathered up seven thousand persons from all Europe—men and women of the noblest aims of culture, anxious only to know the way of God more perfectly. Mrs. Smith was a guest in many patrician homes, and was welcomed to Broadlands, formerly the seat of Lord Palmerston, as the trusted friend of his successors, Lord and Lady Mount Temple, and their circle, but who would dream of the honors she has shared, by any allusion she has ever made ? Other women with a tithe of her achievements count themselves famous and are occupied with their " career," but worldly *prestige* has few charms for one who has found such anchorage in God as holds Hannah Smith's life-barque firm.

An English paper reports her meetings at Brighton, thus: "So great is the demand to hear Mrs. Smith that she is obliged to deliver her exposition in the Corn Exchange, and then immediately afterward in the Dome, and as each of these gigantic buildings will hold more than 3,000 persons, her congregation is larger than Mr. Spurgeon's. Punctually to the moment, like Mr. Moody, she steps to the front of the platform, dressed in Quaker simplicity, and then speaks for fifty minutes by the clock, without hesitating for a moment. Her freshness, her profound spiritual insight, are as remarkable as her surprising fluency." The correspondent of another English paper, who listened more critically, declares that "for

fluency of utterance and vigor of expression, she is unquestionably one of the most wonderful of all the female
orators it has been my fortune to hear, and by all she is
recognized as the leading spirit of the Convention. Mrs.
Smith has little of the feminine in her style of oratory.
Both as to their form and expression her addresses are
the most vigorous and masculine of any that are to be
heard at these gatherings. Decision marks every sentence
she utters. The pathetic element is almost wholly absent.
As an expositor of the Bible she is trenchant and often
powerful."

From *Times of Refreshing:*

"However worn the subject may be, it becomes fresh
and new as Mrs. Smith groups rapidly and clearly her
texts, and pours out in the homeliest language a stream
of vigorous thought. Avoiding all vexed questions, all
dark uncertainties, the fruits of her devout study of the
Scriptures become at the feast as the already drawn
water turned into wine—sweet, healing, and leading to
an atmosphere of soul-rest hitherto unconceived of by
many. If we might characterize in one phrase the substance and result of her teaching, it would be The Sunshine of True Faith.

"The personality and work of Christ, the authority of
Scripture, the simplicity of faith, the absurdity of unbe-
lief, the baptism of the Spirit, and the infinite love of God
to us—these subjects form the staple of her addresses.
Her grasp and vigorous use of the types and analogies of
the Old Testament Scripture form most useful features
of her teaching.

"The effect of Mrs. Smith's addresses was greatly
increased by her strong but restful voice, which rang
through the grove more distinctly than that of any
speaker present. The clear-cut articulation of her simple sentences relieves the hearer of all effort in following

the subject. Consecrated talent and careful research, aided by a fine physique of unusual vigor, fit this lady for her special vocation. A frank *naiveté* of manner adds to the brilliant charm which wins the heart, while it irresistibly convinces the intellect. Curiously, the clergymen, notwithstanding any scruples as to the preaching of women, are always found the most diligent attenders of her meetings."

With calls coming to her from almost every State and both sides of the sea, this loyal wife and mother, who so dearly loves to preach "the unsearchable riches of Christ," remains contentedly at home to cheer and cherish those who need her most, going, perhaps, to some obscure suburban church near by to speak on Sabbath evening, and faithfully attending Friends' meeting and Sabbath School. At her writing table she spends several hours each day preparing articles, bible leaflets, letters of consolation and help ; and carrying on, by the aid of her secretary and the printed circulars constantly sent out, her new duties as our superintendent of evangelistic work. Every few weeks she gives a " hobby party," one of her own happy inventions, as a mode of sociability, and greatly enjoyed by her children. Notes are sent to thirty or forty friends, inviting them to meet certain philanthropists, scientists, or religionists, as the case may be, who are distinguished by the cultivation of their specialty, and each will metaphorically pace his favorite equine up and down before the gathered circle, hoping to secure the prize of their preference and adhesion. The truth of God, of nature, of humanity—these are always the ends sought. Good cheer for heart and soul, as well as weary hand and brain, these are always to be had in the beautiful Germantown home, the " House Beautiful," as one of our leaders calls it. What a procession it would be if all those whom that broad roof and motherly heart have sheltered should form in line! To my own knowledge, not less than a score of Christian workers have there found solace within the last few weeks, not as mere visitors, but as those welcomed to their own "ingle side."

The development of women as evangelists is the dearest wish and purpose of H. W. S., and she hopes ere long to found a training school for this specific work. "Greater must be the company of them that publish the glad tidings;" this is the key note of her present work. The noble Saxon word "lady," means "giver of bread;" ere long it shall acquire a heavenlier significance, "lady, giver of the Bread of Life." Our temperance hymn, "Rescue the Perishing," can have no narrower significance. "But Mrs. Smith is always so cheerful—can she have known much sorrow?" This inconsiderate speech has been made so often in my hearing that I intrude upon the sacred privacy of what would be unutterable grief to a less sunlit heart. Three graves of lovely children are in the family burial ground. The eldest born lies there —a heavenly-minded girl. "Frank," the Princeton collegian, with his bright promise and rare Christian character—the world knows about him. Within three years Mrs. Smith's noble father and tender mother have passed onward, and her choicest blossom, the child most like herself, the pride of her home, little Ray, died but two years ago. Besides all these bereavements, there have been other sorrows harder to bear—misconceptions, injustice, bitterness worse than death. But, to the praise of that dear Name above all other names, let it be said this Christian heart knows, proves, illustrates, always and in all life's changeful discipline, the victory that overcometh, even faith. No sentence is so familiar to her friends, from those dear smiling lips that open but to speak brave and tender words, as this: "I cannot be unhappy—*for always I have God.*"

The true heart which has interpreted New Testament ideals of Christian experience to millions of inquiring readers ought surely to be heard as a witness on her own behalf. Hence this letter is given just as it came from her hand, in reply to my inquiry :

MY DEAR FRANK:—Thee asks for the story of my religious life, and I am very willing to send it to thee, because there is nothing in it peculiar to myself alone, but its secret is one open to every other human soul. And this secret is simply that of entire surrender and perfect trust, to the best I know, on whatever plane my soul has found itself.

I have gone through many "experiences," I have had many differing "views," I have embraced and outgrown many "dogmas." But through all and in all my one attitude of soul has had to be just this of consecration to the best light I had, and of faith in the best God I knew. And out of all or in all, whether they have proved to be truth or error, I have found that my Divine Master to whom I had surrendered myself, has been able to give me food convenient for me, and has made all things, even my mistakes, work together for my eternal good. When I have made mistakes, and they have been many, they have all come from a want of one or other of these two things, either want of obedience or want of faith. When I have been helped and blessed, it has all come through these two channels of consecration and trust. At every moment these have been necessary on my part; and at every moment when these have been active, God has never failed to respond with his wondrous grace.

I was brought up very guardedly in the Society of Friends by devoted parents, and was always, as we say, "religiously inclined." But not understanding this simple way of surrender and trust, I spent many weary years in legal striving, resorting in vain to every expedient my soul could devise for gaining the favor of the God who was, I thought, angry with me, and had turned His back upon me. At the age of twenty-six I suddenly discovered that all the while this very God had been loving me, and that He was my Saviour and my Friend, and only wanted me to give myself up to Him and trust Him. I saw that Jesus had died for me because He loved me, and that all my sins had been taken away by Him. And I heard and obeyed His divine call, "Come unto Me all ye that are weary and heavy laden, and I will give you rest." Up to my light I surrendered myself to this Almighty Saviour, and up to my strength I trusted Him, and began to obey Him.

There followed on this at first great joy and a wonderful victory over sin. But failing to keep in the continued attitude of obedience and trust, not understanding, in fact, the vital necessity of keeping there, I very soon began to slip back to the old level of conflict and failure, and found myself at last living in the seventh of Romans, with the sorrowful experience of finding a law within me that "when I would do good evil was present with me," so that the "good that I would, I did not; while the evil that I would not, that I did." This seemed all wrong to me, and contrary to the Scriptural idea of the Christian life, and I tried in many ways to remedy it, but all in vain. The same legal strivings to which I had resorted when seeking the forgiveness of my sins were again renewed, only now on a different plane; and for nine years I struggled to gain the victory over sin by my own efforts, just as I had before struggled by my own efforts to gain reconciliation with God.

During all this time I never doubted the fact of my being an heir of God, and a joint heir with Christ, but this assurance only seemed to add to my burden; for to believe one's self to be a child, and yet to be unable to act like a child, could not but be a source of bitter sorrow.

At last, in the year 1867, the Heavenly Father threw into my company some dear Christians who knew a better way. They taught me that I was the clay and God was the Potter, and that He alone could make me into a vessel unto His honor. They showed me that if I would surrender myself up to His workmanship and would trust Him to do the work, He would accomplish for me all that I had been so wearily and so vainly trying to do for myself. Again I saw, as I had seen at first, that surrender and trust were the imperative conditions of my spiritual life. It was made clear to me that they were the two wings of the soul, without both of which it could not rise, and again I consecrated and trusted up to the fullest measure of light that was given me. I chose Christ to be my Master and Owner and Potter and Keeper forever, and, having chosen Him, I trusted Him and obeyed Him.

This is all there was about it as far as I was concerned, and this is all there ever has been about it since on my side. As a dear little girl said one day, I have had nothing to do but "just to mind." But on His side what has there not been? What heights and depths of love, what infinite tendernesses of care, what wise lovingness of discipline, what grandeur of keeping, what wonders of revealing, what strength in weakness, what comfort in sorrow, what light in darkness, what deliverance from bondage, what uplifting from anxiety, what easing of burdens; in short, what a God and Saviour!

No wonder that as the years have gone on this life of yielding, trusting, and obeying, which at first was hard, has become the very delight of my heart; and that to say, "Thy will be done," seems to me now the sweetest song of the soul.

Moreover, as the result of this attitude of heart towards God, there has come in the very nature of things an acquaintance with Him. We soon learn to know the Master whom we trust and follow. And because we know Him we cannot but love Him, for who could know Him, ever so little, and not love Him best of all!

> "Who that one moment has the least descried Him,
>   Faintly and dimly, hidden and afar,
> Doth not despise all excellence beside Him,
>   Pleasures and powers that are not and that are?
> Aye, amid all men hold himself thereafter,
>   Smit with a solemn and a sweet surprise;
> Dumb to their scorn, and turning on their laughter
>   Only the dominance of earnest eyes."

More and more I realize that I am nothing, but that He is all and in all. *I* have no wisdom, nor goodness, nor strength, but *He* is everything that is glorious, and good, and loving, and true, and just; and He is mine and I am His, and therefore all must be well. All my needs, and all my perplexities, and all my sorrow are met and answered *by the fact of God.* Not what He does, not what He gives, not what He says, but simply and only what He is. Not anything from Him, nor anything for Him, but He Himself, the God who is revealed to us in the face of Jesus Christ, *He* is the one universal answer and solvent of every need. His ways or His plans I might misunderstand, but goodness of character I cannot mistake, and it is His character that is my impregnable fortress of refuge and of rest. "God is" gives perfect peace in everything.

This has been my life's lesson, to learn to "know God." I have advanced only a very little way as yet in this knowledge; but all that has come to me has come along this one pathway of surrender, trust, and obedience, and by no other. And as I abide steadfastly in these, I believe grander outlooks will be continually given me, and I shall find it more and more true as our Saviour said, that "this *is* life eternal, to know the only true God, and Jesus Christ whom Thou hast sent."

This pathway lies open to all, and everyone who walks in it will know. My coming into the temperance work was after this fashion: At the time of the Crusade I was in England, engaged in religious work. My American friends sent me over the newspapers containing the accounts of the marvelous pentecostal baptism on the Christian women of our land. My soul was stirred within me. I recognized my Master's voice calling me to a consecration of myself to the same work, and as I sat before an English open fire in the drawing-room of our London house, I joined that Crusade. In my heart I said, "Those women are my sisters, and their work is my work, from this time forward until my life ends." It was as real a transaction as was ever made, though no outward act was performed and no audible word was said. As soon as I returned to America I put my name on the pledge roll of the nearest W. C. T. U., and joined the ranks of the workers. And from that time to this the fire has burned with ever-increasing fervor. To-day the National W. C. T. U. of America seems to me one of the grandest instrumentalities for the Lord's work that this world has ever known, blessing equally both the workers and those for whom we labor.

"HOW TO PREPARE BIBLE READINGS."

[Practical Suggestions sent out to the W. C. T. U. by Mrs. Smith.]

For your study of the Bible you require four things:

I.   A Bible, with references, if possible.

II.   A complete "Analytical Concordance." [You can now get a a very good copy for 25 cts.]

III.   A blank-book that can be ruled in columns.

IV.   An undisturbed desk or table, where you can keep the above three things, with pen and ink, always ready. Having provided these few necessary things, proceed as follows:

I.   Commit yourself, in a few words, to God, asking for light and guidance, and expecting to receive them.

II.   Choose a subject appropriate to the occasion.

III.   Find in the Concordance all the words referring to this subject, and select from among the texts given such as seem to you best to elucidate it, noting them down under their appropriate headings in your blank-book.

IV.   Read over these selected texts carefully, and make a list of the most striking on a separate piece of paper, putting them in the order that will best develop the lesson. Begin this list with a familiar text, and gradually progress to those not so well known, letting each successive text develop the subject a little more clearly than the last. Close the list, if possible, with some practical instance from Bible history, or some typical illustration.

V.   Having thus prepared your list, open your Bible at the first text, and on the margin beside it write the reference to the second text on your list. Turn to this second one and write beside it the reference to the third. Turn to the third and write beside it the reference to the fourth. And so on through the whole list.

VI.   On a blank page at the end of your Bible write down an index of all the subjects you have thus studied, with a reference at each to the first text on your list concerning that subject. If you have no blank leaves at the end of your Bible, gum the edge of a half sheet of note paper and fasten it in.

MRS. MARY T. LATHROP.

VII. If you prefer it you may write a list of all your chain of texts on the margin beside the first text, so as to have them all before you at once to choose from.

VIII. By this plan you will have a complete chain of texts on any given subject running all through your Bible itself, each verse referring you to the next one you wish to read, without having the trouble of loose slips of paper to embarrass you. Also, having once studied out a subject, you have it all ready for any future use; and by turning to your index list, you can at a moment's notice open your Bible at the foundation text, and can then turn to one text after another through the whole course of your lesson, without hesitation or embarrassment.

MRS. MARY TORRANCE LATHRAP OF MICHIGAN.[*]

When God plans a great moral reform movement that will lift society out of the ruts of indifference and stagnation to the level of righteous intent and heroic action, He always prepares beforehand the workers for His work.

The Woman's Temperance Crusade was one of those remarkable, providential uplifts that brought together at the feet of the Master many of His chosen and trained workers. It was the coming of "the hour for the women and the women for the hour" in a great social reform movement.

In the brilliant galaxy of women that has added luster to the Woman's National Christian Temperance Union, which is a direct outgrowth of the Crusade, Mrs. Lathrap is a star of the first magnitude. When the Lord called the women of the nation to temperance work, through the Crusade, she was ready to answer out of an uttermost consecration: "Here am I, Lord; send me."

She came to the first temperance convention of women, a prepared worker, and took rank at once as one of the most forceful and eloquent advocates of the cause.

Her broad and varied experience in connection with the "Ladies' and Pastors' Christian Union," and the "Woman's Foreign Missionary Society," had made her familiar with the needs of humanity, and given her a wide outlook in the direction of social reforms.

---

* By Mrs. Wittenmyer.

But the secret of her remarkable power was in her entire devotion to God and duty, and the deep undertone of her religious life, "that like a billow in mid-ocean never breaks upon the beach" of human discontent.

Mary Lathrap, *née* Torrance, was born on a farm in Central Michigan, April 25th, 1838, only twelve miles from the city of Jackson, where she now resides.

Her childhood was spent amid the hardships of pioneer life, for at that early period there were no railroads west of Detroit, and the vast resources of the State were undeveloped.

She was educated at Marshall, Mich., where she lived during her girlhood days. And, although her education had only the finish of the common schools, yet she had superior teachers, who directed her in an after-course of reading and study, which took her far beyond the ordinary school course. At fourteen she began to write for the county paper, under the *nom de plume* of " Lena."

Strangely enough, her first public speech was a temperance poem. She has since written very many beautiful things. One of her temperance poems, " The Dead March," has been republished in most of the newspapers of the country, and is frequently used by elocutionists in their public readings.

She was converted at the early age of ten years. The light flashed suddenly into her soul as she walked home from the Presbyterian Church where the family statedly worshiped. Her conversion was clear and strong ; and, child as she was, the deep convictions of that hour and the solemn witnessing of the Spirit to her covenant with God were so vivid, that she has been held through all these years faithful to her vows. She desired to unite with the Church, but she was thought to be too young to be brought into the fold at once. She was too timid to try again, and so was harmed by the delay, and was not received into the Church till she was nearly eighteen. But she had a good strong Scotch-Irish Presbyterian mother, who held her to the white line, and who, though left alone to rear her family, maintained a strict, godly rule over her children, who now "rise up to call her blessed." In her old age the mother, with work well done, sits in sweet content· beside Mrs. Lathrap's hearthstone, calmly and joyfully awaiting the messenger who shall bear her away to her mansion and her crown.

Mary Torrance taught in the public schools of Detroit from 1862 till 1865, when she was married to Carnett C. Lathrap, then assistant surgeon in the Ninth Michigan Cavalry.

Dr. Lathrap, who is a genial, whole-souled gentleman, has always had a reverent faith in his wife's special call to Christian work, and has in every way possible helped her in it, even at the sacrifice of his own comfort. They have not been blessed with children, but a young girl, Dr. Lathrap's niece, is a member of the family, to whom they are both devotedly attached.

Soon after her conversion, Mary Torrance had the most profound exercise of mind on the subject of preaching the Gospel; and, although but a child, and brought up in a Presbyterian Church, where the voice of a woman had never been heard, yet her convictions were so strong that life seemed to her a failure unless she could do the one thing that to her was all-important—preach the Gospel.

Two years after her marriage she removed with her husband to Jackson, and, as Dr. Lathrap was a member of the Methodist Church, she united with that church by letter, where they still maintain their membership.

Through all these years the call to preach Christ's Gospel has never left her. Day and night, even in her most careless moments, it has sounded down into the depths of her innermost soul. Her gifts and graces were so remarkable, that the Quarterly Conference of the Methodist Church granted her a license to preach. During the last eight years she has held a local preacher's license, which has been renewed from year to year till last year, which was not done, owing to a derangement in the District Conference plan. But the anointing that comes from above still abides. Her preaching is with power and the demonstration of the Holy Ghost. Bishop Simpson, after listening to one of her sermons, came forward and said, reverently, "God has certainly called and anointed our sister to preach His Gospel."

The deep earnestness of her soul is manifest in every word she utters. The truths she brings to others have taken deep root in the subsoil of her own soul, and are couched in such clear, ringing, eloquent words, that the attention of the most careless listener is at once riveted. There is no effort at oratory, no clap-trap of wit or words to win applause, for she is as free from ambition as a little child. But I have often seen her hold the earnest attention of six or seven thousand people, many of them standing, for over an hour, by her clear logic, original thought, and her deep earnestness in putting the Truth. When she speaks on temperance or preaches the Word, her silver trumpet gives no uncertain sound, for she hears a voice ever behind her saying, "Take heed what ye speak." And the power of this voice is intensified by the unusual individuality of her soul. In the presence of duty she stands alone with God, as though there was not another being in the universe. This soul-consciousness of God makes her unusually true and truthful to the very core of her being. As a friend, she is frank, honest, generous, and ardent. She does not change friends with every new moon, but, while she constantly makes new friendships, her fidelity is unwavering

to old friends right through the years, unless she finds
them untrue in moral character. As a speaker on the
temperance question, she has been so popular in Michigan
that her time has been greatly taken up in work in that
State.

She is President of the State W. C. T. U., and earnestly engaged with the workers of Michigan in efforts to
secure prohibition by constitutional amendment. As one
of the secretaries of the " Ladies' and Pastors' Christian
Union," a home missionary society, she has, during the
last ten years, addressed a very large number of the
annual conferences. She has also done a large amount
of work for the "Woman's Foreign Missionary Society."
After she was licensed she preached her first six sermons
by invitation of the pastor in the Congregational Church
of her own town. The church was crowded, and the
impression was profound. Since then, as an evangelist,
she has labored in many churches with great success.
Often in her revival meetings her intense interest for the
salvation of souls brings her into fellowship with the
Master to such an extent that for the time she would willingly die to save souls.

Naturally she is witty and light-hearted, and has a keen
sense of the ridiculous, but grace has so tempered her
spirit that her wit and joyousness of life is without levity
or uncharitableness.

She has always felt a deep interest in the welfare and
elevation of her own sex. And at the State Convention
of the Women's Christian Temperance Union in 1878, at
Grand Rapids, Mich., she read a paper which stirred the
audience on the question of working for the reformation
of fallen women, as I have never seen an audience stirred
before or since. A resolution looking to immediate action
was at once passed unanimously, and a petition to the
Legislature prepared for circulation. Twelve hundred

extra copies of the speech were circulated, and Mrs. Lathrap, Mrs. Dr. Morse Stewart of Detroit, and Mrs. Church of Greenville, appointed as a committee to take charge of the matter. Mrs. Lathrap and others went to Lansing and got a bill through the Legislature appropriating $30,000 for such an institution as they desired. It is to be located at Adrian. The land has been secured, and before another year goes by it will be opened for inmates.

Ladies have been appointed by the Governor of Michigan to serve with the men charged with this responsibility. Mrs. Lathrap's consecrated voice, which is so strong to plead with the erring and to plead for the fallen, has won for Michigan what is needed for every State—a girls' reform school. In all Mrs. Lathrap's labors in this country and Canada, everywhere she gathers in the multitudes and makes them feel the power of truth. Her words are hooks that hold, and are remembered and bring forth fruit through the years, and doubtless, when the angels gather in the harvest, she will have many sheaves to lay at the Master's feet.

MISS JENNIE SMITH, OUR RAILROAD EVANGELIST. *

At the time of the Crusade, Jennie Smith, our valued Railroad Evangelist, was a helpless invalid, having been confined to her couch for many years without once being able to put her foot to the floor. Her soul was stirred within her like all the rest by the great awakening of God that swept so many Christian women into the ranks of the temperance reformers, but she could do very little to help.

In 1878, however, the Lord gave her a wonderful deliverance. She had been taken to a homeopathic hospital in Philadelphia in the hope of benefit from a new treatment, and had been relieved of some very distressing symptoms.

---

* By "H. W. S."

But she still continued a helpless invalid, utterly unable to be even lifted up in bed.   She says, concerning it: .

"All my hopes were shattered, not because my physician had given up the case, but because I thought I saw plainly that the treatment was continued more to gratify me than from confidence in its success, and especially I was forced to believe that my back was worse instead of better. I found I could not say, 'Thy will be done,' to suffer on. I felt compelled to overcome this feeling, and on the night of April 22, 1878, I passed through the severest struggle of my life. The question came before me as to whether I would be willing to be a helpless and suffering invalid all my life if by this means I could more effectually reach the souls around me. During my illness I had traveled on a wheeled couch a great deal, and when on railroads had of course been obliged to go as baggage. This had brought me into intimate association with the railroad employees, and their uniform and chivalrous kindness to me in my helplessness had won my heart. As I passed through the struggle on this never-to-be-forgotten night, there came before me as in a vision all the railroad employees in the nation, a mighty multitude of hungry souls, and I said in the very depths of my being, 'Yes, Lord, I am willing to suffer forever, if I may only help these men who handle my couch on the railroads.' This gave victory, and I felt myself to be more swallowed up in the will of God than ever, and to desire only an incoming of Divine power to do the work that seemed laid upon me. The next evening I summoned to my bedside a few sympathizing friends, and told them I felt an assurance that if they would unite with me in waiting on the Lord, He would bestow the needed power."

After a most solemn consecration of body, soul, and spirit to Him for His use either in sickness or health, the little circle prayed and waited, realizing very vividly the

Divine presence in their midst. Between eleven and twelve Jennie felt a shock of life go through her from head to foot, and immediately lifted herself up in bed *for the first time in sixteen years.* She then said, " I believe the Lord would have me rise up and walk," and her physician helped her to her feet. She walked a few steps, and kneeled in thanksgiving, and then retired to rest with a heart full of praises. From that moment her restoration to strength and health was very rapid, so that in a short time she was entirely well, and was able to undergo more exertion and fatigue than most of her friends around her.

She at once began to use her renewed and consecrated powers in the work of the Lord for the uplift of humanity, and the call she had heard on that memorable night to help the railroad men was never out of her mind. But she could not see any way of carrying it out, and could only wait and trust. In the fall of 1881 she attended the National Woman's Christian Temperance Union Convention held in Washington, and there told out the desires of her heart. And our women, hearing the divine call in her longings, inserted in the grand, broad platform of our National Woman's Christian Temperance Union a plank in the shape of a department called " Work among Railroad Employees," and she was made its superintendent. This gave her a backing, and a door was soon opened for her through the Woman's Christian Temperance Union of Baltimore on the line of the Baltimore & Ohio Railroad, where she has worked with wonderful success for several months. A rich harvest has already been gathered as the result of her labors, over one thousand souls having been brought into the kingdom of Christ from among the railroad men and their families. A marvelous change has been wrought in the whole *morale* of the shops and depots belonging to the company, as well as along the line. As

MISS LUCIA E. F. KIMBALL.

one man said, "We hardly know ourselves on this road any more. Where we used to meet each other with oaths and blasphemy, we now hear the greeting, 'God bless you, brother. Praise the Lord for his goodness to-day.'" Drinking has been almost abolished along the line as far as the work has extended; "Railroad Temperance Unions" have been formed, and all the converts have been pledged to total abstinence and the temperance cause.

In many other fields of work Jennie Smith has been blessed and owned by the Lord of the harvest, and has brought in rich sheaves. But nowhere is she so happy and so much at home as among her "Railroad boys." And nowhere does she receive a more loyal respect and devotion than from them.

The work is still going on, and she is hoping and praying that other workers may be raised up to join her in this long-neglected, but most needy field.

MISS LUCIA E. F. KIMBALL,

Superintendent National Sunday-School Department,

AND MRS. T. B. CARSE,

Founder of *The Signal.*

In the spring of 1874 the tidal wave of the Crusade struck Chicago—that city of mighty antitheses. Three thousand dram shops; three hundred churches; Dwight L. Moody, the evangelist; Mike McDonald, the gambler; Philip Bliss, the greatest gospel singer of our age, and Majors Whittle and Cole, the lay preachers, offset by socialists the most incendiary, and infidels the most profane; the Washingtonian and Martha Washington Homes, and the "Rehoboth" for women inebriates, offset by that moral "Burnt District," known as the "Black Hole," —these are a few among unnumbered contrasts that reveal the hot contest between Christ and the devil in the most marvelous city of modern times. A thrilling volume might be written on the efflorescence of woman's philanthropy in Chicago. There is no depth of misery and shame into which the sweet leaves of its healing have not brought cleansing and light. The day seems all too short for the tender ministries to which the gentler members of Christ's church have gone forth in that city which, with all its faults, is so liberal and appreciative of the work of women. But I must not suffer the warm sympathy I feel for that noble army of workers to beguile me from the present duty of delineating two among the hundreds of devoted women whom I know and love, in the city where my philanthropic work. begun. One morning, as I was preparing the usual Friday "Chapel Talk" for my dear college girls, in the sunny home parlor at Evanston, Mrs. Charles H. Case of Chicago—half an hour distant by rail —called to invite me to speak at a temperance meeting in her own church, Union Park Congregational, Rev. Dr. Helmer, pastor. "The tidal wave," referred to in the opening sentence of this chapter, was at its height. In ten days canvass by the temperance ladies, fourteen thousand names had been secured to a petition to the Common Council asking for the enforcement of law against the dram shops, which request, presented by the best women in the city (led by Mrs. Rev. Moses Smith), had been summarily disregarded, and the ladies rudely hissed at by a whisky mob. Great audiences assembled at noontide to discuss the situation. Pastors gave their influence in favor of the women's movement, and a W. C. T. U. was already organized. Out of my quiet, bookish life, where I had only been stirred sufficiently by the great events daily reported in my brother's paper, to get my rhetorical classes at work, debating the questions of total abstinence and prohibition, this invitation beckoned me, and the next Sabbath night, before an immense audience in the elegant city church, I tried to speak.

Two ladies, among the many I met there, especially impressed me. Indeed, Mrs. Case had said: "We have two members in our church who can become mighty for God and temperance, if they consecrate themselves, as I believe they will, to this new work." One was Mrs. T. B. Carse, a name beloved wherever known by all right-minded people, for her work's sake. She is now president of her district and of the Central W. C. T. U. of Chicago, a society which has reached out wider, stronger arms of help and blessing than any other in the United States. It has maintained a daily gospel meeting for eight consecutive years, in which thousands have been brought to temperance and Christ. It founded the "Rehoboth," a name given by Mrs. Carse to the refuge for inebriate women who are taken there from the police court, and if they pass their novitiate, are graduated into the beautiful "Martha Washington Home" outside the city, and thence into the church and back to a reputable life. It has placed four matrons at the four police stations, and induced the city government to help maintain them there. It sends special missionaries (like Mrs. Skelton and Mrs. Obenauer), to the wards where foreigners are congregated, to speak to them in "their own tongue wherein they were born;" also supports a temperance missionary among the colored people. It keeps open headquarters the year around, where men come to sign the pledge, and whence temperance literature is circulated throughout the city and the northwest. It maintains meetings in various parts of the city, and in the breezy enthusiasm of its work is a reminder of the primitive church whose practical Christianity it so grandly illustrates. It carries on a lecture course—the chief one of our great city—attending to all the details of so huge an enterprise, furnishing elevating recreation to the people and putting money in its purse for the benignant uses of the temperance reform.

9

And at the head of those glorious women who have stood shoulder to shoulder in this glorious work, is Mrs. T. B. Carse, whose good fortune it is to have a lovely home and time at her command, and whose noble boys, David and John, beloved by all of us, are the joy of their mother's heart, and illustrate that discriminating remark of a great man, " Commend me to a Christian widow's sons as models of good bringing up."

But as the "Founder of *The Signal,*" Mrs. Carse will longest be remembered. I shall never forget the look of exaltation with which she came to me at Old Orchard Beach some years ago, and said: "I had a vision last night of the paper we must have at the West to represent our broad, progressive work;" and then, with her beaming countenance and earnest words, she laid her plan before me, adding impressively: "I have prayed much about this, and it is to be." Those who know her magnificent energy, tireless perseverance, and winning manners, will not wonder that Mrs. Carse raised thousands of dollars requisite for this enterprise from our generous Chicago merchants, Robert D. Fowler, Chicago's temperance- Mæcenus, and his earnest-hearted wife, contributing, with true English liberality, beyond others. So we had a weekly paper, with wider space and fresher news, and later on *Our Union* (whose presence in the home, Mary T. Lathrap happily called " analogous to that of a refined Christian lady,") merged its destiny with that of its wide awake sister of the west. So much for nine years' work of one brave temperance woman.

MISS KIMBALL

spoke on the evening of my own timid debut in the Congregational Church at Union Park. Of fine bearing, pleasant voice, and clear enunciation, filling that great auditorium without apparent effort, I recognized at once in her gifts and earnestness peculiar fitness for the oncoming

work. Why should it not be so? Miss Kimball was
born and reared in Maine, of parents noble in the truest
sense, who in their childhood, seventy years ago, took a
firm stand, amid much contradiction, for total abstinence.
No shadow of intemperance ever darkened their home
or that of their children. Indeed, it is a noteworthy
fact that fully ninety per cent. of our temperance women
are not such because of any personal experience or sorrow,
but, on the contrary, have had life-long immunity from
this greatest scourge of home. What a libel it is upon
human nature, touched by God's grace, when the dreary
commonplace is uttered concerning any of our workers,
"Well, I suppose she has suffered, and so she takes an
interest in this movement." Was that the reason why
our Master "took an interest" in poor, dazed, bereft
humanity, or did God "so *love* the world" as to send the
Sinless One for our redemption?

Foremost in every reform that tended toward the uplifting of the race, the father of my gifted friend, often when
standing almost alone, was wont to utter this golden sentence—often on her lips in her references to him: "*I
must do what I ought; God will take care of the rest.*"

In a letter recently received, Miss Kimball says: "You
know how utterly opposed I am to being written up, and
I trust you will bear this in mind." Being made aware
that something would be stated—her prominent position
in our counsels making this inevitable—she wrote: "If
anything must be said, I do want my parents to have
credit for any effort to do good that I may have put forth,"
and later: "To my mother I owe what no words can
express." A beautiful book, "In Memoriam of our
Mother," has been written by Miss Kimball for circulation
only among the family friends, but the reading of which
is like breaking an alabaster box of ointment, so fragrant
of all rare, sweet virtues is the life disclosed.

Miss Kimball is a graduate of Mt. Holyoke Seminary, that school upon which Mary Lyon's memory rests like the halo of a saint, where the essence of New England character and culture is as balmy and penetrating as the perfume of trailing arbutus on its hillsides, and whence have gone forth more consecrated young lives on embassies for Christ more distant, adventurous, and widely varied than from any other one spot upon the globe.

To any person of intelligence "a Holyoke graduate" stands upon blessed vantage ground in any work for Christ. The trained intellect might be found elsewhere, but its combination with trained sensibilities, conscience, and will,—with self-control and dedication to duty as an ultimate principle of action, have nowhere, in my judgment, been so grandly illustrated or so strongly accentuated as at "South Hadley."

Miss Kimball was for several years a teacher in Chicago, but, like many another, resigned her position and left a vacancy in the overcrowded ranks, that she might join the newly recruited "Army of the White Ribbon." She at once, as might have been expected from her training, dedicated herself to a specialty. Here again the preparation of the heart is seen. No institution of its kind ever gave the place to Bible teaching which Mary Lyon insisted on at Holyoke. Five times did she study the cover off her own leather-bound copy of the Holy Word, and I remember the sweet awe that came to my heart, when I rose to speak in the "Chapel" where she had stood so often to talk and pray with "her girls," as I remembered how she used to come to a duty so sacred straight from the "silent hour" with that beloved Bible under her arm. Naturally, then, a generation later, we have in Lucia Kimball, a pupil of this Bible-studying seminary, one fitted by long training to make the introduction of Sunday-school temperance teaching her special work. It was her thought to have this branch of Christian instruction systematically carried on by putting into the International Series the Quarterly Temperance Lesson, on the principle that thus only would it be regularly taught, and for the reason that the universally confessed curse of Christian civilization is intemperance. The largest Sunday-school petition ever known was the one circulated by her for this object, presented at the great Atlanta Sunday-school Convention in 1878, and at that time acceded to. Subsequently, however, the Quarterly Lesson was thrown out by the International Committee at its Saratoga session, notwithstanding a petition again set on foot by Miss Kimball containing names of ministers and Sunday-school superintendents, no others being invited to sign. But our friend works right on, visiting Sunday-school leaders, petitioning lesson publishers, and speaking in her earnest, polished way to audiences from Maine to Great Salt Lake.

Miss Kimball is an attractive writer, as her two books, "Faith Hayne" (a temperance story) and "More than Conquerors" (biographies of saintly women), abundantly testify. She is invited to do literary work enough to keep even her busy brain fully employed, and writes for some of our leading religious weeklies, but allows nothing to interfere with the beautiful mission for childhood's weal and home's protection, to which her rare and cultivated powers are dedicated. She delights in her mission, hints at no hardships, advertises no sacrifice, but works right joyously and bravely on.

THE INDIAN CHIEF PETOSKEY AND THE PLEDGE.

A rare incident occurred at the second camp-meeting in Petoskey, Mich. It was at the close of the last of three meetings held on the day allotted to the subject of temperance. An Irish lady, beautiful and cultured, who had given her time and talents to the temperance work, was inviting all who would to sign the pledge and permit her to tie on the red ribbon. The night was one of extreme beauty; the harvest moon shed its silvery light upon those assembled beneath the shelter of God's own canopy, who had come up there, amid the stillness of the forest, to worship Him. The air was echoing the last strains of "Ho! my comrades," and the atmosphere was laden with prayers, when through the centre aisle an aged chief was led by two of his tribe. One hundred and four summers had he seen, and still time had left gently her touch upon him. He walked with the step of dignity which marks so peculiarly the Indian, and, in touching musical cadence, he said: "I am Petoskey, chief of the Indian people. I want to take the pledge from the white lady,* and let her fingers tie the red ribbon on old Petoskey's coat." It was a scene fit for a painter, as there, amid such sacred surroundings, the white lady descended the platform and with a beaming face told of hope and an anchorage beyond. With a voice full of tears, she said: "My dear brother, far away from beyond the blue Atlantic I have come, from my home in the Emerald Isle, where one I loved lies sleeping, to take you by the hand, and to call you, chief of the Indian tribe, 'my brother.' I welcome you as you clasp hands with us, workers in this sacred cause of temperance, a cause which means not alone patriotism and nationality, but, blessed be God, it means religion. I shall go on my way stronger as I remember that up here in the wilds of Northern Michigan our numbers are strengthened by Petoskey's signature." Pointing upward the old man said, in his native tongue: "I'll meet you beyond that sky, where we shall need no more moon or sun, for He will be the light thereof." And so Petoskey signed our temperance pledge.

---

* This was Mrs. Kate McGowan, an Irish lady, gifted and beautiful, whose one year of blessed service and whose tragic death are known to Western workers.

THE FIRST TEMPERANCE CAMP-MEETING.

The first temperance camp-meeting ever held convened at Old Orchard Beach camp-ground, September 8, 1874. It was a witty and blessed invention of Francis Murphy. The attendance from the first was large, but on succeeding days a vast and enthusiastic multitude greeted those who had come from many States with their rich experience of work in the great cause.

Following the opening exercises, a business meeting was held at the stand, to which the ladies were invited—doubtless the first instance of their participation in the "cabinet councils" of such an enterprise. Mrs. Hartt, of the Woman's Temperance Union, Brooklyn, N. Y., was asked to pray, and her appeal to God for guidance, and for the constant presence and inspiration of the Holy Spirit, met an earnest response from all those workers, of so many different "ways of thinking" in religious things. Francis Murphy's exclamation after the prayer: "Let us trust—let us just trust—O let us come together in God's name," was prophetic of the spirit that predominated in the meeting from its first hour.

The first evening meeting was, like those which followed it, delightful. It was just "sitting together in heavenly places in Christ Jesus." Dear old "Camp-meeting John Allen" opened the meeting by repeating, with his face all aglow with pleasure, and with his own inimitable tone and gesture, the whole of Paul's Epistle to Timothy. He seems to have the Bible "all by heart." Experiences and prayer filled up the hour that followed. It may be interesting to group here a few notes of testimonies in the social meetings:

MR. —— testified that "the appetite for liquor which he had indulged during twenty-five years was, upon his conversion to Christ, instantly taken away."

MR. J. K. OSGOOD (founder of the first reform club)

said : "Temperance and Christianity must go hand in hand together—we can never separate them."

CAPT. STURDEVANT : "I am glad to go into the gutter to bring men out, give them the pledge, get them upon the total abstinence platform, and into the arms of the Lord Jesus Christ. No drunkard shall ever have a cold shoulder from me, unless it is made cold by taking off my coat that I might put it upon him."

An old gentleman, living near by, told this "pointed" anecdote :

"Father Hart was a good old man, a preacher here in Maine in the old times. A retired sea-captain was the only temperance man in the town where Father Hart lived. He tried to get his dear old pastor to sign the total abstinence pledge, but he refused, saying, 'I don't care much about drink—you all know that; but I don't like this idea of signing away my liberty.' Soon after, he called at the grocery, and the man who kept it, and who was a notorious drinker and rumseller, came up very cordial-like and said, 'The Lord bless you, father Hart, I'm glad to see you ; I hear you've got grit enough not to sign the pledge, and I bless the Lord for it;' and as he spoke he came up, half tipsy, and leaned on Father Hart's shoulder. The old dominie jumped up, saying, 'Bless my soul! What have I done ? Give me a pledge—quick—somebody! I'll not consent to be a post for a drunkard to lean against.' "

REV. DR. CARRUTHERS of Portland, said : "The best possible method of getting rid of any sin whatever is not to do it. The best possible cure for intemperance is—temperance. Moderation in drinking is very likely to go on to excess in drinking. I spent many years in Russia, a country overrun with drunkenness through the direct influence of the government itself, which monopolizes the entire liquor traffic—every cork bearing the imperial stamp of the State.

"A great Russian statesman went to the Empress Catharine and urged her to have the traffic stopped. 'But,' argued she, 'it yields the largest part of our revenue.' 'Yes,' he replied, 'but in encouraging your people to drink, you are cutting down the tree with one hand while you gather its fruit with the other.' The Empress did not heed this warning of her wise counsellor. Seventy years have passed, and Russia is now, through all her vast territory, a nation of drunkards."

Rev. I. Luce: "I haven't much faith in the temperance of political parties. I haven't much hope of a man if he stands and alone in his own strength only. I have faith in a man if his hands cling to those of Christ."

A Brooklyn lady gave this experience: "I was told that a rumseller wished to see two or three Christian ladies, begging that they would come quietly and privately to his saloon. Then it flashed over me: 'Now if I were anxious about myself spiritually, should I want a procession of women to file in, and severally and collectively take my case in hand? No, I should be like this man—I should want a very few only, and that they should come quickly, privately.' And so I thought, 'Why, that we can do, any of us, at any time, in the spirit of our Master;' and from that day saloon-visiting was divested of its terrors. Nearly a thousand have been visited by our ladies in Brooklyn, and the work is only just begun. And we have never been treated rudely. These men are courteous to us and willing to listen to what we have to say, and I could tell you what would greatly encourage your hearts, had I time to speak of the results of our efforts. I could tell you of men who are Christians to-day who were saloon-keepers six months ago; of young men whom we have found in these places, who have signed the pledge, and are now standing nobly by us as we go on in this work to which God has called us."

MRS. MARY E. HARTT, OF BROOKLYN W. C. T. U.

A reformed man introduced Mrs. H. as "the Grace
Darling of the Crusaders," who were rescuing the drunkard from his wreck of shame and woe. She said she
"came only as a Christian woman from her home, not as
a Temperance lecturer." She told a touching incident
on this wise: After one of the saloon prayer-meetings
held in Brooklyn last spring, a woman came to her, saying that as she left the meeting she overheard two rough
men talking. One said: "Jim, come on now and get a
drink." "No," was the answer, "I shan't drink to-night.
I can't forget the way that lady who led the meeting
spoke about our mothers. I'm going to go home. I
won't drink to-night." Said Mrs. Hartt: "I've never seen
Jim, I never shall here; but I've presented him to God
in prayer many and many a time, and I expect that poor
Jim and I shall meet in Heaven." She continued:
"Dear sisters, men and methods have failed in this work.
They have not been equal to the great emergency. But
God has, in these last days, taught us as never before the
power of prayer, and I believe that by this means He will
exterminate this curse of intemperance from our land.
Let me say to each one here: *Consecrate yourself to this
work of God.* If you feel that you have not the power,
go to your closet upon your knees before God; and if you
will take it, He will surely bestow the power richly upon
your soul." There was a dash of drollery in one of Mrs.
Hartt's sentences, which it will do no harm to quote. In
the first part of her excellent exhortation she said: "*My
sisters, begin now, and don't come trailing in afterward,
when this thing has become popular.*"

HOW ONE WOMAN HELPED.—COMMUNION WINE.

While numbers of us have been descanting on the evils
of using fermented wine at the communion table, one lady

of my acquaintance has been quietly at work proving her faith by works. She is a member of our W. C. T. U., and recounts the matter to me in this fashion :

" I have always felt sure our Bible wasn't on the wine-drinking side of the argument, and equally sure that the Church ought not to be there either.

" More than that, I haven't believed that the Church desired or meant to be on the wrong side. I was confident the majority of communicants would prefer an unfermented wine, if well made and fit for use on an occasion so sacred.

" Some time ago our Church decided not to use fermented wine, but somehow a sort of logwood decoction got into the chalices, which was entirely out of place and harmful to our cause. Some of the deacons said : ' We can't have such a mixture as this—it will not answer ; ' and they were right. The matter troubled me. At last I said to my husband : ' I can't go out much to the temperance meetings or take an active part in the work of the Woman's Union, but I can prepare wine enough for our church of eight hundred members, for all the communions of this year, and I'll do so.' It was no easy undertaking. It kept me in my kitchen, wide-awake and on the alert, for several days ; but I've got the wine all bottled up, and the people are well pleased with it." Let some lady in each church go and do likewise, and she will have helped our many-sided cause in a noble, efficient way.

RECIPE FOR UNFERMENTED WINE.

" Take twenty pounds Concord grapes (Ohio grapes preferred), and add two quarts of water. After crushing the grapes, put them into a porcelain kettle ; when at a boiling heat the juices separate from the pulp and skins. Then strain through a tin sieve or cullender, using a little

more water. Add six pounds granulated sugar. After
the sugar is all dissolved, strain through a thick cloth.
Then heat hot and pour immediately into stone bottles,
and seal tightly while hot. The abóve will make three
gallons.

"If properly strained, it will be clear and of a bright
color. The quality of the grapes will make a great difference in the quality and quantity of juice. Some judgment
will be necessary as to the quantity of water added. The
above quantity will make three gallons of wine, and if
properly put up in perfect bottles and well sealed will
keep any length of time; but all air must be kept from it
till wanted for use. Bottles that will hold the quantity
needed for each communion would be best. Two gallons
will serve eight hundred communicants."

The foregoing is furnished by the lady whose unobtrusive but valuable " temperance work " I have chroni-
cled, in the earnest and prayerful hope that it may serve
the cause she loves.

"THAT FOSSIL PRAYER-MEETING."

She was paying a visit to the home of her birth; one of
our gentlest and most gifted workers. In a distant part
of the country she had joined us, and, in the warm, vivid
atmosphere of the Woman's Christian Temperance Union,
her dormant talents had budded and blossomed out into
lovely words and deeds "for God and home and native
land."

So well had she wrought, that her name was beloved
by a large constituency of the most earnest and intelligent soldiers of Christ, both east and west. Dutifully
she went to prayer-meeting in the " Sleepy Hollow " village of her "auld lang syne." It belonged to one of
those churches whence the edict has gone forth, "Let no
one speak but the holy men." Two-thirds of those who

faithfully maintained this meeting and "held up the hands" of this pastor were holy women; but they had been strictly taught to "keep silence in the churches."

In Sabbath-school their ministrations were the delight of the young and the strength of the organization; but then Sabbath-school was held in the chapel. At the literary society and sociable the women were the life of the occasion, and their nimble tongues were in constant requisition to "make the occasion pleasant and successful"; but the prayer-meeting was a place quite too sacred and decorous for their participation, though, very likely, if the excellent deacons had been asked, "Why is this thus?" they would have found no better answer than that "regulation phrase" of the conservative mind from the days of the Sanhedrim and Pharisees of Christ's era down to the barbarous races of our own time: "It is our custom."

A few minutes at the opening of this fossil prayer-meeting were redeemed by a carefully prepared dissertation from the pastor on some topic previously announced. Then came a hymn of painfully attenuated continuosity; then came what a naughty youth once called "That Prayer," enunciated at weekly intervals for the last half century, by Deacon Dutiful; and then followed that pause (every reader is familiar with it), dull, dismal, dun-colored, settling like salt-marsh fog over the assembly and piercing to the joints and marrow by reason of its borean frigidity. The Quaker's pause, in their meetings of devotion, is, at least, placid; is often comforting, and always calm; but the pause of the Fossil Prayer-Meeting is awesome, if not actually uncanny. A hymn is absolutely the only way out, and is welcomed with an eagerness that half takes away one's breath. Then follow other oft-time prayers, until from three to five have been not "offered," but sedulously solicited, interspersed with "remarks" not unfamiliar as to their wording, and still less so as to their scope, all well separated by repetitions, pauses, and singings, and so on to the end. Now it did not occur to these devout and well-intentioned prayer-meeting killers, that our earnest-hearted friend might possibly have said a word to edification; or, if it did, their scruples preserved them from any such unseemly "branching out." It did not occur to them that the great, warm-hearted temperance movement, best known as "Christian," had in it matter of infinite pith and moment to the interests of that very "fossil remain" of which they formed a part. Did they ever observe the lack of growth in that meeting, the absence of young people (except certain saintly-faced and silent maidens) and the dislike of Sunday-school scholars to attend?

Why must these things be? Is the wine of God's spirit being indeed poured into new vessels? Are Christ's gleaners flocking to fresh fields because the old are spoiled by drouth? And is this process to go on in certain grand and estimable denominations until the prayer-meeting yields to the inevitable law of non-survival of the unfittest, and over its vacant courts are written the words which come into my mind whenever I attend such a specimen as I have here described: "Behold your house is left unto you desolate."

W. C. T. U. TRAINING SCHOOL.

The training school for temperance workers is a new feature of our W. C. T. U. The general outline of study to be pursued is the following, prepared by the committee in charge:

1. The origin, history, aims, and methods of the temperance reform to be systematically taught in a series of studies to be determined, and lectures to be given by a faculty appointed by the Woman's National Christian Temperance Union; the studies to extend through

one year and be pursued at home, the lectures to be given in the summer at some leading Christian resort.

2. Written examinations to be held there, on the entire course, and certificates given in accordance with the results.

3. A model W. C. T. U., with young ladies' and children's branches, to be organized, officered by officers of the Training School, and made, so far as possible, to illustrate the methods taught.

4. The faculty of the school to be chosen by the Executive Committee of the Woman's National Christian Temperance Union, and authorized to select and employ such specialists in physiology, hygiene, medicine, and different branches of philanthropic, legal, and political work, as will in their judgment conduce most to the success of the object in view, viz.: sending out into our local, State, and National work the largest possible number of women, especially trained in our system and methods.

A "school of the prophetesses" (or evangelists), intended as a help to women engaged in Gospel work, will also be held every summer, in connection with this training school.

THE MASTER IS COME.

Dear Sisters :

Our Lord is a most uncomfortable master when he is but one of many. "Some for self and some for Thee," is an offering pitiable indeed. It involves a miserable life, as all half-hearted life must always be, entailing in worldly enjoyment anxiety, and in religious duty irksomeness. "How much of my hold upon the world can I retain?" This is the constantly recurring question of those who take Christ as *a* master only. In this spirit the young convert asks: "Can I not dance, if very careful when and where?" "Can I not have a game of cards, if only church members make up the party?" "*A* master?" The Christian who takes Christ as such is like the timid bather who steps into the edge of the wave, where sand and gravel frictionize him, and floating is impossible; when if he would launch out into the sea, the swell of its great billows would bear him up. Those who, in childlike faith, have chosen Christ as *the* Master, are always beckoning gleefully to loiterers near the shore, calling out in blessed reassurance, "It is better farther on!"

Let us remember that, whether for weal or woe, we all have masters. Our forms of speech afford unconscious. and hence all the more convincing, proof of this. "The Goddess of Fashion," "Bacchus, God of Wine," "Mammon," all these expressions grow out of the instinct of worship and obedience to something higher than ourselves. "Be ye not many masters," is the dictate of worldly prudence not less than of the heavenly philosophy of him who adds the blessed reason, "For one is your master, even Christ." So let us seek a clear idea of who our master is and why he is so, for unity of purpose must characterize every life which is to manifest development that is natural and genuine. If iron-filings are to fall into line, the magnet must first be held near them. The heart that is not polarized will never turn toward Christ, but turning, his attraction will grow stronger with every throb of that steadfast heart. We want our lives to have unity and to be full of benignant strength, and there is One who can make them so, as all have proved who have tried Him. He was as much made to be our Master as light was made for our eyes, air for our lungs, love for our hearts.

The process by which Christ becomes our Master is analogous to that by which any master is chosen by pupils intelligent and earnest. We must take his ways in the place of our own. We must make his words ours, his maxims our laws, his slightest will our cherished wish. In brief, we must consecrate our thought, affection, purpose, to our Master. In proportion as students in a school do this, they make swift progress in the branches taught. A music-master requires the pupil's unresisting hand to be laid upon the key-board in thorough abandon-

ment to the master's will. Utterly flexible to his command it must become before he can impart to it the
secret of his skill, and you must put yourself wholly
under his tuition—he cannot teach you till you do. So,
in a strict sense, the hand is consecrated. Then comes
faith in him to whom this consecration has been made,
and just how to distinguish the latter from the former
act is difficult, since by the laws of mind the consecration
is impossible, except on a basis of faith in him to whom
its powers are yielded. Thrice happy are they who, welcoming with glad obedience the Mastership of Him who
gave Himself for us, can say with honest hearts, "For
me to live is Christ." O, how that simplifies a life; how
it chastens and makes holy!

The Master is *come*. For what? First of all, to give
you personal security and individual peace. Some persons pause all their lives long to ponder this wonderful
fact. *He is come.* No longer down the dim ages does
humanity gaze with wistful eyes, longing "until the day
dawn and the shadows flee away." Nay, "It is finished."
He is come in the full provision for making us at one
with God. In the open Bible is the constantly recurring
invitation, to the "peace that floweth like a river, making
life's desert places bloom and smile."

But, blest with all spiritual blessings in Christ Jesus,
let us not forget that the Master is also come in the marvelous opportunity of this "the Gospel age." To Christian women this coming is most of all significant. We
have all along been amateurs in doing good, but we are
learning, in the blessed latter dispensation of these days,
that to do good is the business of life—is just what Christians are for, not as their secondary business, but as their
first—before riches, before knowledge, before honor, all
these falling into line after those other occupations with
which the Master was so busy when He trod the ways of

men. This business of being such people and doing such things as shall help make those about us more like what they ought to be, grows daily in the comprehension of all thoughtful disciples of our Lord. We are learning more and more about the blessedness of the Benignant Life; understanding more perfectly the truth that not in the acquisition of a language, not in the mastery of a piano key-board, not in acquaintance with current literature lies the secret of the happiest life, but that to guard the ninety and nine which went not astray, to train their tender steps to love the safe, sure path, and then to go out after the hundredth who has wandered

"Away on the mountains, bleak and bare,
Away from the tender shepherd's care,"

in this lies the sweetest of human joys.

A grand old word is that Saxon word "lady," meaning "giver of bread." But "the Master is come" in the deeper insight which leads us to revise this definition in accordance with the latest researches, so that it reads, "lady, giver of the Bread of Life." In the sweet evangelism of home, some are bestowing their best energies— and this world has no employment that is more sacred— while daily increasing numbers are giving their leisure hours in the larger home of Christian philanthropy, where society becomes the foster parent of thousands worse than motherless. Let us work from, rather than toward the cross. "Saved to start with," (as a sweet girl phrased it once,) let us strike out into the desert from the sweet oasis of our "rest of faith," bearing the waters of life to those who, on the barren sands, cheated by the mirage of wordly pleasure and parched by the soul's insatiable thirst, stretch towards us their feverish hands for help and succor.

CHAPTER XVIII.

W. C. T. U. WORK FOR THE HOME.

"Combination view" — Church — Saloon — School-house — Home — Mother and boy—Philosophy of our plan of work—Doctor, Editor, Minister, Teacher must all stand by the Christian mother—Society the cup-bearer to Bacchus—The sovereign citizen—Education of the saloon—The arrest of thought—Mrs. Mary H. Hunt, National Superintendent of Scientific Department.

IN the evolution of the W. C. T. U., the light of Christ having illumined the tempted human heart, comes next to the next larger circle made up of two united hearts. Lord Erskine said that "twelve honest men inside a jury box, were the best results of civilization." But we may say more truly that the bright, consummate blossom of our Christian civilization is what Whittier pictures as "the dear home faces whereupon the fitful firelight paled and shone," as those bound by the tender tie of kindred and affection gather around their family altar and their fireside hearth. This Home, then, is the shrine for whose high sake all that is good and pure on earth exists. It is the fairest garden in the wide field of endeavor and achievement, the place where we are best beloved that we are anywhere, and in it dwell those who love us best that they love anybody. Yet, from the curse of the drink habit and the liquor traffic, home is like the shorn lamb, to which no wind is tempered. Gaze on the " combination view " which life's real stage presents, and compare its actual pathos, its strange romance, with that mimicry we rightly name " the play."

For life is the only drama worthy of our study. Upon

(235)

its real stage behold a "combination view." Study home's environment. Think of a Christian mother's tragic fight to save her boy and discover whence is the origin and what is the philosophy of our simple "plan of work" in the W. C. T. U.

Behold on one corner of the street a church, stately and beautiful, its tall spire pointing like a finger up toward God, and leading your heart thither. Behold upon the other corner of that same street a school-house, with its widely welcoming door inviting boys and girls to enter and drink at the pure fountain of knowledge. But between these two, behold an institution equally American, equally guaranteed by our laws, more than equally fostered by our politics, more than equally patronized by our people. The youngest child that reads these lines knows what I mean, for this third institution, so cozily sandwiched in with church on one side and school-house on the other, has a sanded floor, and curtains half way, a screen across the front so that you do not see what is going on inside, and fumes coming out of it which, if you are pure and cleanly in your habits of life, incline you to pass by upon the other side. But there is another feature of this "combination view." Indeed, if there were not this book would have no being, because the sacred theme of woman's temperance work would not have been. Just across the way from the dram-shop stands the *Home.* What does the Woman's *Christian* Temperance Union propose doing to rear defences round the place, even as the hills are round about Jerusalem ?

First, it has made a study of the situation. It has found that among the little children who come to Sunday-school and sit on the front seat with their feet far from the floor there are just as many boys as girls, with faces just as innocent and sweet. But it has found that in the intermediate classes of the Sunday-school there is a deplorable weeding out of the boys; that in the Bible-class young men are conspicuous for their absence, and that on communion Sabbath two-thirds of those who partake of the emblems of Christ's sacrifice are women.

But in the homes of our fortunate membership (for ninety per cent. of our workers never knew the drink-curse there), are fathers and husbands, sons, brothers, and lovers too noble and true for us to accept the cynical explanation that "girls naturally take to good ways and boys to evil ones." Our women believe that special efforts should be made to help the mother in her unequal warfare with the dram-shop for the preservation of her boy. It is plainly perceived by them that something is wrong in the popular division of responsibility by which, although the father may be a moderate drinker, the failure of the boy to grow up good and pure is adjudged to be his mother's fault. Hence their studies of the science of heredity and cognate subjects and their careful circulation of scientific treatises, with a view to opening the dull eyes of the public to the changeless law of God that "whatsoever a man soweth that shall he also reap." But this is not enough, for girls, equally with their brothers inheriting the taste for stimulants, seldom develop it; hence in the environment we must seek for farther explanation. How many of us can think of homes where a noble Christian mother taught total abstinence to her boys and girls alike, enforcing pure precepts by a spotless example, from which the boys, though often by nature more amenable to gospel truth than their sisters, have gradually sunk away into the slavery of the drink habit. And so the W. C. T. U. has arranged its careful, systematic plan of work with strict reference to the child in the midst who is also in the market-place, where they are bidding for him—the men who keep saloons. For they must constantly recruit their patronage from the ranks of our youth, or it will ultimately fail. This is a matter of business with them, and of business only. As one of them said to our own Mrs. Hunt of Boston, "Just so long as there is eight cents profit on a ten-cent drink, so long I shall stick to my trade." What then can such a man do to render his success absolutely certain save precisely what he does, viz.: carefully study the natural and innocent tastes of boys and of young men—their taste for amusement, fondness of variety, and love of young company—that he may lead them into his trap with games, songs, stories, object lessons, literature, all mingled skillfully with the bewilderment of tobacco and alcoholic drinks?

The W. C. T. U. naturally asks the question, What are the little foxes that spoil the vines, with their beautiful, tender grapes? What are the errors in a boy's training, and the failures of this church and school near by to take sides with the mother in the fight to save her son? Alas, perhaps the dear lady herself has never studied hygiene, or the laws of physical life, especially the relation of food to the appetite for stimulants. Let us then begin just there with the scientific gospel of whole wheat flour, a diet largely farinaceous, simplicity in dress, abundant ventilation, and generous exercise.

But these great, moulding forces of society—how can we secure their allegiance to our plan of rescue for that boy? How shall they be intelligently arrayed in solid phalanx so that the sum total of society's benignant force, at least, shall come up to the help of the Lord, the mother and the boy against the mighty hosts of the saloon?

"Benignant forces, did you say? Why, they are on your side already," replies the untrained well-wisher who "doesn't belong."

Are they, indeed? Let us investigate. Here is the boy, with his mother, in the fortress of home. Into that stronghold comes the family physician, "revered, beloved." How often he prescribes, not "for external application only," the alcoholic stimulants against which the boy has been so sedulously warned. Into that stronghold comes the newspaper year after year, with its plea for the "superior manliness" of moderate drinking. Into that stronghold come men of kind heart and good business standing, whom the boy has seen going day after day to the saloon just opposite. Out of that stronghold goes the boy to Sunday-school, and though he may be taught many good things and true, may grow familiar with the wanderings of the Israelites, able to enumerate the sacred mountains, or tell the story of the cross, he is not taught the Pauline doctrine of total abstinence for others' sake; he does not study about the Rechabites, the Nazarites, the Hebrew children, Sampson, John the Baptist—total abstainers all, and spoken of with highest praise for this high virtue. He is not shown the daily application of that deep principle, "The body is the temple of the Holy Ghost; he that destroyeth this temple him shall God destroy"—not in vengeance, but as the sequence of a law full of benignity. Perhaps if questioned as to this neglect, the Sunday-school teacher (noble and well-intentioned though he be) will answer, as indeed I have often heard him: "It might be well to teach these things, but then we have so much to do. You see, there is the lesson to be said, and the golden text, the general questions, the singing, giving out of books, besides the foreign missionary exercises, and we really can't find time." This familiar explanation always reminds me of what my little sister, who detested mathematics, said one day as she came running in from school and flung her slate and book upon the table as she called out triumphantly: "Mother, I'm quite too busy going to school to study 'rithmetic!"

Perhaps, indeed, some of our good friends in Sunday-school are as "far back" as a worthy old gentleman in

Illinois who was asked by the W. C. T. U. to introduce a quarterly biblical temperance lesson into his class, and to whom, on his replying that there were no suitable passages, the ladies read the story of the sons of Jonidab, whereupon this veteran teacher exclaimed : " Well, I've belonged to the church nigh on to forty years, and I didn't know there was any such a piece in the Bible! "

The boy sits in the old family pew at church and seldom hears a temperance sermon, though there is no prohibition argument stronger than " Every plant that my Heavenly Father hath not planted shall be rooted up," and no total abstinence text for childhood like " Keep thyself pure." The boy sees the pastor set out upon the sacramental table intoxicating wine, and offer it as the symbol of the Life by which we live. He knows that his mother would not suffer that cup to stand on her own table, or its contents to pass her lips at home. He knows how good and noble is this minister, and mightily indeed would mother's total abstinence teachings be bolstered up if pastor and Sunday-school teacher but confirmed them. They never do, however, in their official capacity at least, and, though the lips are silent, the hard young head grows skeptical concerning mother's notions, and concludes: " They're well enough for girls, but for a boy it's different, you know! " He goes over to the public school, and finds there a well-intentioned woman who would gladly aid and abet his mother's plans for his physical salvation ; but one thing she lacketh, and that is just what doctor, editor, preacher, and Sunday-school teacher lacked before her. What is it ?

THE ARREST OF THOUGHT.

Gladly would she instruct him in the laws of physiology, chemistry, and hygiene, as opposed to the drink and the tobacco habits, but it simply does not occur to her even as it did not, in former days at least, to the other worthies I have named.

" Evil is wrought for want of thought more than for want of heart."

Suppose that in this day of science-worship the school should echo the mother's total abstinence teachings; suppose that with the majesty of law and dignity of learning, the State should require and the teacher inculcate lessons like these? Then indeed it would be "manly" to let strong drink alone; then it would be steadily wrought into the warp and woof of boyish character and habit to "abstain from fleshly lusts that war against the soul."

But the boy goes out into society, and perhaps the hand of beauty or of fashion presses into his the cup that cheers and then inebriates; perhaps the "nearer one still and the dearer one yet than all other" persuades him for a love sweeter just then than mother's, to pledge her health in wine. Perhaps some man of influence who takes a social glass merely to close a bargain, to conciliate an opponent, to win a vote, or simply to comply with an elegant custom, asks "mother's boy" to treat. And thus what ought to be the benignant force of that larger home we call society, fails in the imminent and deadly breach of temptation to be "a power not of herself that makes for righteousness" in the anxious mother's well-beloved son.

But all the way toward manhood that dram shop, so social, so seductive, has been just across the street. Indeed the boy has run the gauntlet of scores and hundreds of such places, and not unscathed, as he went out into life to take his chances with the rest. He has found out that in municipal council room, legislative hall, and national congress, the so-called guardians of the public weal have been the guardians of the liquor traffic. He has found that the government of the nation his mother taught him to love next to his home and God, throws its protecting aegis around the dram shop rather than the home.

Dear friends who read these lines, written in sorrow, not in anger, seeing these things are so, what manner of persons ought we to be who compose the W. C. T. U. ? Heaven be thanked that our "plan of work," developed in nine years of prayer, study, and experience, is simply this: to bring about the arrest of thought in the intellect and conscience of husband, father, physician, editor, pastor, teachers, fashionable leaders, and official law-makers, so that perceiving their relation to the mother's anxiety and the boy's temptation, they may discharge their duty.

But we do not forget that all homes have not a Christian mother to be the priestess of their altar fires. Alas, some women are intemperate, and many women need missionary work done in their own hearts; many children are orphaned or worse than motherless. Hence, for home's sake, we have special lines of work radiating thither as a centre, even as all roads once led to Rome. The Bands of Hope, the Reading Rooms and Friendly Inns, Police Station, Rescue work for Women, and many other branches will be mentioned in their appropriate place. But be it understood, once and forever, that it is for home's sweet sake we toil, striving to rear high the defences around that sacred citadel of health, happiness, and relig-ion, and knowing if they are not reared, then home shall fall, and when home falls—the world!

MRS. MARY HANCHETT HUNT,

Superintendent of the department for introducing the study of scientific temperance into our schools and colleges, is a native of Canaan, Connecticut. The Taughtonia Mountains, in their course through western Massachusetts, with the beautiful Housatonic winding through their valleys, give to that region the rugged and picturesque scenery for which it is famous. Their rocky

MRS. MARY H. HUNT.

peaks and wooded hills reach over into northern Connecticut, and there in the town of Canaan, one Fourth of July morning, a little girl was born whose quick brain and true heart were destined to do more for America's real independence than most statesmen of our day have either dreamed or realized. Her father, Ephraim Hanchett, and his brothers were iron manufacturers, bringing their ore from the Salisbury mines, first discovered and opened by their great-great-grandfather. This far-away ancestor, fresh from his Welsh home and training, saw the ore cropping out from these rough rocks, bought the mountain side from the Indians for a song, built his forge on the stream hard by, and here, in this primitive fashion, were the beginnings of the famous Salisbury iron works. He was thrifty and industrious, accumulated what was a fortune in those days, and dying, left it to his only son. This son died in middle life, leaving a large family of boys. Only Ephraim (grandfather of our Mary) remained near the old home in Canaan. His wife (Mary's paternal grandmother) was a woman of strong Christian character, who reared her boys, Ephraim, Isaac, and John, to fear God, and abhor strong drink. When the great thought of the Temperance Reform came to Rev. Dr. Lyman Beecher, in his parish on Litchfield hills, seeking the co-operation of his brother ministers in his county, he came to Canaan ; securing the hearty sympathy and help of "Parson Cowles," of the Congregational Church. Meetings were called, the people gathered to hear Beecher's burning words, and to begin the mighty battle against intemperance that is raging still. Then and there was organized the Litchfield County Temperance Society, with Rev. Dr. Lyman Beecher for President, and Ephraim Hanchett, Jr., father of our scientific temperance apostle, one of its Vice-Presidents—his mother's training had been prophetic of this new office, which found him, a young man, with that sustained enthusiasm of humanity and already markedly developed Christian character, that made him, by all the forces of his nature, a life-long friend and ardent supporter of both the temperance and anti-slavery causes.

But it was only distilled liquors they fought against at first. Every family had its cider barrel. The decanter from which they had been wont to treat their minister and other friends was put away, but a pitcher of cider was set in its place. Had the Mary Hunt of to-day been present in good Lyman Beecher's meetings, and had not the prevailing prejudice frowned upon the woman who should dare to rise and utter her convictions, they would soon have learned that since alcohol is the favorite ingredient in cider, as well as in rum, and since the appetite for alcohol, as for all other poisons, insensibly grows by what it feeds on, all beverages containing it are dangerous and should be included in the pledge.

Upon her mother's side Mrs. Hunt is descended from a long line of Puritan ancestry, dating back to " Rev. Peter Thacher, a distinguished minister of the gospel in Sarum, England, in the sixteenth century." An ancient memoir, still extant, says : " He was a man of talents, and possessed a liberal and independent mind ; he dissented from the established church, and being, in consequence, harrassed by the spiritual courts, resolved to turn his back on royal and ecclesiastical folly and persecution and emigrate to New England for the enjoyment of religious freedom." The death of his wife altered his determination. There is still in existence a letter which he wrote to the bishop of the diocese, in which he firmly declines reading certain directions of the vicar-general, which he said were " against his conscience and would tend to disturb the order of worship." " Many of this family, with puritanical zeal and courage, opposed the prelatic power,"

says this old record.   His son, Thomas Thacher, then in
his early minority, turned from the University of Cam-
bridge (England), disgusted with the prevailing ecclesiastical tyranny to which he must have been subjected,
and, with his father's brother, Rev. Anthony Thacher,
of the celebrated St. Edmund's Church, Salisbury,
England, sailed for this country, landing in Ipswich,
Mass., June 4, 1635.   Completing his preparation for the
ministry under the tuition of Rev. C. Chauncy, in Plymouth, young Thomas Thacher was ordained pastor of
the Congregational Church in Weymouth, Mass., January
2, 1644.

When the Old South Church was founded in Boston he
was installed its first pastor February 10, 1670, and continued in that station until his death.   Thacher's Island,
in Boston harbor, received its name from the fact that
Rev. Anthony Thacher and wife were thrown upon its
shores, the sole survivors of a shipwreck, in which his
cousin, Rev. Anthony Avery, and family, who came with
them from England, were lost.   Whittier's beautiful
poem, " Swan Song of Parson Avery," has immortalized
this scene.   Most of the male descendants of these Thachers, like their ancestry in England, were ministers, filling, in their respective generations, some of the most
influential pulpits in eastern Massachusetts.   Among
them, the Old South, the New North, the New South, and
the Brattle Street,—Congregational churches in Boston,—
and many churches of the same order in the suburban
towns.   Upon their scholarly and noble lives New England annals dwell at length.

" When Peter Thacher, fourth generation from Rev.
Peter—of Sarum, England—was ordained pastor of the
Congregational Church in Attleboro', Mass., November
30, 1748, he was—according to family tradition—the
fourteenth oldest son, in succession, employed in the

work of the gospel ministry." An old lady of Milton, Mass., recollected hearing sermons from Thachers of five generations in direct succession.

On the commencement of the controversy between the American colonies and our English ancestry, these men, in their various generations, are recorded as " opposing with noble zeal and courage, the various stages of British encroachments on colonial rights, from their pulpits and the press of those days." The early New England pulpit shaped, not only the future history of that section, but directly and indirectly that of the nation. James Thacher, M.D.—sixth generation from the first Rev. Anthony—was a surgeon in the Revolutionary army. When eighty years old, he closes an historical paper in the *New England Magazine* of July, 1834, with these significant words : " For seven years and a half I was in the service of our country in the great rebellion of 1775, and participated in the glorious consummation of Independence. . . . I have a recollection of days fraught with wondrous things and wondrous results. I have seen our precious liberties and freedom wrested from the hands of the oppressors, by the immense sacrifice of lives, of treasures, of perils, and of sufferings. How many have I seen at the hour of death exclaiming : '*I die for my country!*' I now see the fair heritage of our fathers in imminent danger of being sacrificed at the shrine of a *reckless, sordid spirit of party interest.* I have seen public offices courting competent men to fill them, and I have seen them filled by men, who, with a religious conscientiousness, acquitted themselves of duty. But this seems already to be antiquated morality ; for I now see unworthy, incompetent men, seeking and laying claim to public offices, as a reward for desecration and unfaithfulness. My fellow-citizens, I have seen *the days that tried men's souls.* I claim the privilege of age to

forewarn you, that, unless you view your elective franchise in a light more precious than heretofore, ere long
you will have no office to bestow ; all will be anarchy,
confusion, ruin, and despair.   O ! how great would be my
consolation, could my benediction avail for the meliora-
tion of my beloved country's welfare !"

PLYMOUTH, June, 1834.

Rev. Peter Thacher, D.D., pastor of a Congregationalist church in Malden, Mass. (fifth generation), was
chosen by that town a member of the convention, called
in 1780, to form a Constitution for the Commonwealth of
Massachusetts.   "Few were more active or influential"
in that important work.

From such a maternal ancestry Mrs. Hunt is descended,
—the ninth in the generations since the Rev. Anthony
and Thomas Thacher came to this country.   What wonder, then, that this same gift of intellect, of Christian
sensitiveness, of humane and patriotic zeal, of choice
and fluent speech, should crop out in a feminine descendant, under the influence of these more tolerant days!
Surely, the fact is a salient illustration of her favorite
subject of heredity.

The little girl Mary, on Canaan Hill, was bright and
frolicsome, committed from the first to the sunny side of
every circumstance, and brim full of a harmless fun, that
was held in check by a quickened conscience ; for there
was born in her heart, when she was less than nine years
old, the love for and faith in the God of her fathers
which has been the controlling inspiration of her life.
This early experience toned, but by no means shaded,
her natural, happy girlhood.

Says one who shared her life as a child :

"In our long daily walks across the fields to the little
brown school-house, her busy brain and hands were
always finding treasures. She spied and bore off the

first pussy-willows leaning over the brook we crossed on stepping-stones, and brought home in her apron to her disgusted mother some little grasshoppers, the fruits of her research into a sheltered nook, when the March sun had coaxed them from their hiding-place, as proof that the long, dreary winter was gone. The principal value of a tree in her eyes then was the good seats on the limbs, the higher up the better. She did not stop to analyze her delight in the beautiful landscape about her home. The squirrels and the birds were her friends, but books were then her trial. She learned easily, but the monotonous lessons were irksome. She was too full of fun to apply herself to study, so, of course, was often in disgrace with her teachers. The teachers complained, the parents reproved, but it availed little. One summer day, after a serious talk with mother about a certain arithmetic lesson for the next morning, Mary asked permission to climb into her favorite locust tree and sit there, promising that she would " get it then." The picture of that fun-loving girl, perched high in the leafy locust branches, with book and slate, studying a little, and watching the birds more, is one long to be remembered. But her play-days were almost over. At fifteen she came to realize that life had problems for her solving, needing honest preparation. Conscience and ambition were roused. A change came over the spirit of her dreams. The intellect of this nature-loving child began to assert itself. She heard voices calling: 'Face the other way.' The dog's-eared, worn school-books which had been her trial she now took up in quite another spirit. With a determined will and earnest purpose she studied to learn. Her teachers were surprised and delighted at her progress. In one year of hard study she had gone over the work of two. At sixteen, with some misgivings, she engaged to teach a country school, and surprised herself and friends by her power of waking the love of study even in the dullest and most wayward of her pupils. The turbulent, lawless children, who had been, the term before, the terror of the neighborhood, were now well-behaved, studious boys and girls."

A year of teaching was followed by study at Amenia Seminary, N. Y., where Rev. Gilbert Haven, afterwards Bishop Haven, was president. A little later on, we find her a student at Patapsco Institute, near Baltimore, where Mrs. Almira Lincoln Phelps presided as principal. For the influence of these eminent educators, at that formative period of her life, Mrs. Hunt is very grateful. She graduated with honor from Patapsco, and was at once chosen as a teacher in this same institution. As a student, the natural sciences were her specialty, and in this department she taught with a success foreshadowing our coming superintendent of scientific instruction.

When extending the invitation to become one of the faculty, Mrs. Phelps said to her, " I have always designed to keep you here. Added to other qualities, you carry your own sunshine with you, and are always true." But she did not keep her long, for in the autumn of the following year she was married to Mr. Leander B. Hunt, of East Douglass, Mass. In the coming years, hers was the home-life of the wife and mother, of the lady in society, dispensing hospitality with a liberal hand, and a helper in benevolent, Sunday-school, and church work.

The two younger of her three children died in infancy, but she had two step-children, who bear witness to her fidelity in words of love that could not be more tender were they writing of their own mother.

In the autumn of 1865, Mr. and Mrs. Hunt removed to Hyde Park, then a Boston suburb, just springing out of the wilderness. The Congregational church was but a handful of people, worshiping in a hall. The novelty of the situation and the need of work fired her enthusiasm, and, with a company of devoted ladies, she toiled hard to build up the church and to help crystallize the new society on a religious basis.

She was quickly recognized as a leader, and, before she realized it, was organizing and helping set in motion forces that have shaped the character of this enterprising place.

In the misfortunes that attended the family about this time the strength and heroism of Mrs. Hunt's character was exhibited. She had been active as a Christian since her childhood, but now she learned those more advanced lessons of the faith in God which trusts unfalteringly *in the dark*, and the real consecration that lays all on the altar of a Heavenly Father's *unexplained* will. Thus does God fashion with sunshine and storm and the pruner's knife His chosen fruit-bearing vines.

A member of the church of her fathers (the Congregationalist), she had been brought up to believe "a woman should keep silence in the churches." Her first departure from this ancient custom was at the earnest request, almost command, of her pastor, Rev. P. B. Davis, that she should relate to the Friday night church prayer-meeting, as she had to him privately, something of her spiritual experiences. From that time, in response to the solicitations of Christian friends, her voice was often heard in the prayer-meetings of her church—and her first lessons taken for the larger utterance waiting her.

To the education and training of her only surviving child, Alfred E. Hunt, she devoted herself until he graduated from the Mass. Institute of Technology in Boston, in 1876, and went out to make a man's place for himself in the world.

Home cares were lessened. She had lost her relish for general society. Always a student, even in her busiest years, the Bible grew more and more to supplant other books, and now she turned to its study with a zeal that increased with her leisure to gratify it, little herself dreaming whereunto it would lead her. As she studied, "a great hunger," as she says, "came into her heart to do more for the Master." She supposed this would be met with perhaps new additions to the large Bible class of ladies, who recall her teaching with enthusiasm; or another burdened soul to comfort; or another poor family to look after.

The Woman's Temperance Crusade, five years before, swept over the country, reaching the East, gathering into its ranks of workers many noble women, but not yet the Leader of our Educational Department.

With much timidity and shrinking, in response to appeals, she had given a few Bible Readings in the mission churches of Punkapaug, Milton, and Clarendon Hills near her home. That the people listened when she spoke encouraged her.

And now accidentally, or providentially, her thoughts were turned to the physiological or scientific side of the Temperance question. These impressions were intensified by listening to Rev. Joseph Cook's lectures on "Alcohol and the Brain." With absorbing interest she began to read on this phase of a hitherto, to her, trite and common-place topic. On every page she saw fresh evidence in natural law of the relation of the Temperance Cause to the uplifting or downfall of the race, and to the answer to the prayer "Thy kingdom come." The ancestral fires were glowing in her spirit, and when a friend who had heard her Bible Readings urged her to give, in a distant country town, a Temperance talk, she did not dare say "No."

On the Easter Sabbath night of 1879, in the town hall in Leominster, Mass., she gave her first Temperance

address. When, a few week's later, the Mass. W. C. T. U.
appointed her a vice-president of the State Society, she
was ready to do with her might what she could. The
unpopularity of a cause to which convictions and conscience were committed was no barrier to this descendant
of the Puritans. In the solitude of her home, over no
personal experiences, but the scientific works of Drs. Richardson, Lees, Story, Hargreaves, Carpenter, and others,
she had been converted to no ephemeral interest in the
Temperance work—so clearly to her vision her Master's
cause. The rapidly developing gift of public speech had
found its mission, and quickly attracted attention.

In less than six months from the first "arrest of
thought" on this subject which had so fired her enthusiasm, she was speaking three and four times a week in its
interests, under the auspices of the Mass. State W. C. T.
U.—shrinking and trembling at her own temerity, yet
longing to utter the alarm she felt for the future of a race
poisoning itself, soul and body, with alcohol. The following autumn, at the repeated solicitations of the Boston W.
C. T. Union, she accepted a position which made her their
advocate for this reform in the churches of the city where
so many of her maternal ancestry had preached the Gospel of Grace and Freedom. With so little previous platform experience, this was a severe test of her faith in the
promise, "Go, and I will be with thy mouth." The
result proved the genuineness of the call. Pulpits from
which no woman had ever spoken before were opened to
her, and before the year closed the work and worker
received the hearty indorsement of the most eminent
men as well as the public of that cultured city.

It was an early conviction with Mrs. Hunt that the
success of the Temperance reform depends upon the universal education of the successive generations of the
people as to the real nature and physiological effects of

alcoholic beverages. To accomplish this, in this country, she now devoted her life. She quickly saw that the public school system of America must be the vehicle, and that suitable text-books must be prepared. Dr. Richardson's Lesson Book on Temperance, just published, was too advanced for the common schools—the Alma Mater of the masses. An extended correspondence and consultation with friends of the cause, of longer experience, led her to invite Miss Coleman to write "Alcohol and Hygiene," a book now used in many intermediate schools in this country. At the close of her year's engagement in Boston, the books being ready, the National Woman's Christian Temperance Union, at their annual meeting in that city, in 1880, created the Department for the Introduction of Scientific Temperance Instruction in Schools and Colleges, and made Mrs. Mary H. Hunt its Superintendent, sending her out commissioned to make real her vision of hope. Cordial hearings were granted her by popular and scholarly audiences in different States, as she unfolded the plan of educating all classes in childhood and youth to abhor strong drink, by teaching them, as a regular branch of study in the schools from text books, graded from the comprehension of the primary to the higher students, what Alcohol is and what it does to the living body of the drinker as well as the character. People had said before, " The Temperance Reform must begin with the children." This was a showing *how* to " begin" effectively. " It is just the thing to do," " I wonder this has not been done before," enthusiastic hearers said. As the work developed, it became evident that other than moral arguments were needed with Boards of Education with beer and whisky-drinking constituents. Said a polite chairman of a Board of Education, " We must teach what the law requires man." " Now if the law of the State only required this about Alcohol taught, we could do it." "And the law of the State *shall* ere long require you," mentally rejoined our earnest-hearted Superintendent, who began at once planning and working to that end, and the Michigan Legislature enacted the following law in 1883:

CHAPTER III.

"SEC. 15. The district board shall specify the studies to be pursued in the schools of the district: *Provided always,* That provision shall be made for instructing all pupils in every school in physiology and hygiene, with special reference to the effects of alcoholic drinks, stimulants, and narcotics generally upon the human system. . . . No certificate shall be granted any person to teach in the schools of Michigan who shall not pass a satisfactory examination, after September first, 1884, in physiology and hygiene with particular reference to the effects of alcoholic drinks, stimulants, and narcotics upon the human system."

Vermont passed a similar law in November, 1882. To few is it given, to work so broadly for the future as our leader of the educational forces, with her noble band of State Superintendents of her Department, is doing.

Perhaps no woman in our great national society has risen so rapidly to eminence as Mrs. Hunt. The bent of her mind is scientific, and she brought special preparation to her work, having, as a student, excelled in the natural sciences and made a careful study of the best and latest researches in England and France, as well as here, concerning the effect of alcoholic stimulants upon the tissues of the body and the temper of the soul.

CHAPTER XIX.

THE W. C. T. U. IN SOCIETY.

The Light of Christ in the circle of society—The hostess of the White House—Sketch of Mrs. Lucy Webb Hayes—Memorial portrait—Lincoln Hall meeting—"The Two Bridges"—Mrs. Foster's address—Presentation at Executive Mansion—President Garfield's reply—"Through the Eye to the Heart"—Lucy Hayes Tea Parties, Impressions of the Garfields—Society work of young women—Mrs. Frances J. Barnes of New York—Miss Anna Gordon—Y. W. C. T. U. of Michigan University—Wellesley College—Kitchen garden—Miss McClees—Sensible girls—"The W. C. T. U. will receive"—Nobler Themes—"All for Temperance"—Miss Esther Pugh, Treasurer of National W. C. T. U.

THE next evolution of the **W. C. T. U.** is into the domain of Mrs. Grundy. This ought to be congenial soil for the growth of every kind of helpful thought. Society should be, and will certainly become in the restitution now going forward, a larger home for all who dwell there. The social sentiments, under that mild sway which Christian hearts confess, are those which most ennoble human nature, because widest in scope and most general in endowment. When the Golden Rule shall be wrought into deeds within the social realm; when in that charmed circle " all men's weal shall be each man's care," then will the strong be glad to bear the burdens of the weak, and total abstinence will be " the fashion." But the key note of social observances is set high up in the octave of society. When Dr. Guthrie, of Scotland, turned his wine glass right side up at a banquet (and that means up side down,) it changed " the custom " of thousands in the bonnie land of cakes and ale. When

(255)

Lady McDonald, of Canada, banished alcoholics from her dinner table, and Sir and Lady Leonard Tilley gave to seven hundred guests an evening entertainment, elegant in its appointments as befitted their high station, yet without wine; when the good Queen of England said, " Every person at my table shall obey his conscience," thus rebuking those who sneered at the total abstainers— then the light shone into a wider circle of influence for the W. C. T. U. Significant indeed is the fact that the grandest as well as earliest pioneer in the highest rank of American social life was a daughter of Ohio, and an earnest friend of the Women's Temperance Crusade.

MRS. PRESIDENT HAYES,

The Hostess of the White House.

Probably there is no woman in the United States who has been more earnestly prayed for or so much beloved by the W. C. T. U. as Mrs. Rutherford B. Hayes. A plain, straight forward account of her life and character is here attempted, from sources the most trustworthy.

Dr. Webb, the father of Mrs. Hayes, died when she was an infant, but any account of her which makes no reference to her mother is like the play of " Hamlet " with Hamlet left out. When her daughter was about ten years old, Mrs. Webb determined that she would remove from Chillicothe to Delaware, Ohio, with her two sons and her little girl, the youngest of the family. The Ohio Wesleyan University had been recently established there, and was the magnet which attracted this sagacious mother. Subsequently she took rooms in the College, and here for two years Lucy recited with her brothers. Mrs. Webb was of the best blood in the land, as many think, for she was of New England ancestry. Her convictions of right and her loyalty to duty had the three-fold intensity of inheritance, education, and personal experience. The Bible was,

MRS. LUCY WEBB HAYES.

with her, judge, jury, and advocate, on all questions concerning practical every-day life. Three letters lie before me from those who were personally acquainted with Mrs. Webb. This is their testimony:

"She was a woman of solid worth, rare common sense, and symmetrical Christian character. I am sure if the course of Mrs. Hayes is such as to command the respect of the true-hearted people of our land, she inherits the ability to make it so largely as a legacy from her mother."

Another letter, from an altogether different quarter, employs precisely the same phrase as the first:

"The mother of Mrs. Hayes was a lady of rare common sense, in which the daughter strongly resembles her."

A third has this:

"There is one trait in the character of Mrs. Hayes which I should like to emphasize for the sake of any who may read your sketch. She absolutely *will not talk* '*gossip.*' Even in the intimate confidences of daily intercourse, she is as guarded as in the presence of the multitude. The executive mansion has for its mistress one who is a living exemplification of Christ's Golden Rule. Except in very rare instances, when some act of oppression to the poor or the defenceless outrages her sense of right, she is always thoroughly kind in expression. I think this trait of carefulness for the feelings of others a gift from her mother, who had a nature exceedingly genial and kind. It is indeed a blessed thing for our country that such a woman had the training of our President's wife."

Dear reader, perhaps that little girl of yours is yet to be the hostess of the nation. Will you not give her just as good advantages for the discipline of her mind as you afford her brothers, and for her heart a daily exhibition of the faith that works by love?

> So shall she make the humblest station high.
> So shall she 'mong the highest take her seat
> And find herself at home.

Two years at the Ohio Wesleyan University were followed by several years of study in the Cincinnati Wesleyan Female College, of which Rev. Mr. and Mrs. P. B. Wilbur had the management. Many of the noblest women of the West, foremost in missionary, temperance, and other Christian work, were graduated here. Under the influence of these gifted educators and their successors, the daughters of Ohio have matured characters full of the benignant strength which discipline of mind can only give when Christ in the heart tempers and mellows the clear light it has imparted. One of these students, a life-long friend of Mrs. Hayes, and foremost among the women philanthropists of our day, writes as follows:

"Lucy Webb was a first-class student. I was a member of the same class in botany and other studies with her, and I have reason to recall my feeling of mingled annoyance and admiration, as our teacher, Miss De Forest, would turn from us older girls to Miss Webb, who sat at the head of the class, and get from her a clear analysis of the flower under discussion, or the correct transposition of some involved line of poetry. Somewhat of this accuracy was doubtless due to the fact that she had been trained in the severe drill of the O. W. University. She remained in the Ladies' College of Cincinnati until she completed its course of study."

While yet in her teens, she met Rutherford B. Hayes, who, after his graduation at Kenyon College, Ohio, had opened a law office in Cincinnati. He writes of her:

"My friend Jones has introduced me to many of our city belles, but I do not see any who make me forget the natural gaiety and attractiveness of Miss Lucy."

One of her friends gives these interesting items:

"It was my good fortune to be a guest at the small and unpretentious wedding of Lucy Webb, in 1852. The only attendant of the young pair was a beautiful child of eight years, the daughter of the bridegroom's only sister. A few days ago, this same child, now the wife of a distinguished citizen of Columbus, O., sat beside her aunt, Mrs. Hayes, acting once more as her attendant, and looking down from the gallery on the sublimely simple ceremonies of the inauguration of R. B. Hayes as President of these United States. It has been a marriage of almost ideal happiness, and to overstate the devotion of Mrs. Hayes to her home, her husband, and her children, would be almost impossible. The heroism she displayed in sharing her husband's army life has been the theme of many an admiring newspaper reporter. There are some incidents connected with this chapter in her history which would enhance its beauty and impressiveness, but they are too sacred for our pen."

Her characteristics are perhaps sufficiently indicated in the foregoing statements. "Bright loveliness and devotion to principle" are given as the chief. What might have been positive and almost angular in another, is so tempered by sweetness and gaiety of spirit, that she is the most influential of all persons with her husband. "His heart doth safely trust in her."

Mrs. Hayes has been from childhood an earnest Christian, a member of the Methodist Church. Her expressions of sympathy for the suffering and her constant benefactions to the poor, are not offered through the accepted public channels, but rather so quietly that, prominent as her social position has long been, they are almost lost to the public gaze. Her unostentatious habits are well known to our people already. Since the Republic was founded, its shoddy element has never received a more substantial rebuke than from the simple costume, gentle home life, and quiet manners of this model "Lady of the White House."

To dress "as becometh women professing godliness,"

yet not so as to attract special attention, is the endeavor
of a larger number of thoughtful ladies to-day than in any
previous age, and the women of the church are fortunate
in having such a leader as Mrs. Hayes.   Notice the quiet
good taste of her costume, the simple, natural dressing of
the hair, the modestly covered throat, and fair, un-
punctured ears of this noble Christian matron—this
" Cornelia," whose " jewels " are the three bright boys
and sweet young girl who call her mother.

HER TEMPERANCE RECORD.

To us this is a subject of peculiar interest, and especial
effort has been made to get at " the truth, the whole
truth, and nothing but the truth."   Although she never,
so far as has been learned, participated in the crusade
work, she sympathized heartily with those who did so,
and was at least a nominal member of the Executive
Committee of the League in Fremont, Ohio.   An officer
of that society writes : " Occasionally her noble face
brightened our meetings with prayer.   General Hayes
gave us the use of his hall for our temperance mass
meetings and daily prayer meetings.   I have attended
receptions at his residence after his election as Governor,
and never was a drop of anything stronger than coffee
offered to his guests.   The temperance women of America
may congratulate themselves on having a Christian
woman, true as steel, in the White House, and as such
she is certainly entitled to our confidence, and I should
deprecate any course on our part that savored of dictation
or distrust."

Mrs. Hayes has been the most eloquent of temperance
lecturers to those about her, by reason of her total abstinence from the products of the vineyard, the brewery, the
still, and yet she never " speaks in public."   Her home
life is most lovely, her children are models of noble

behavior, her charities are unobtrusive and unfailing as the dew.

For the last two years Mrs. Hayes has been associated with her friend Mrs. Dr. John Davis, also Mrs. Dr. Rust, Mrs. A. R. Clark, and other leading ladies of Cincinnati and elsewhere, in the Woman's Home Missionary Society of the M. E. Church, of which she has accepted the Presidency. It will coöperate cordially with the W. C. T. U. in temperance work among the ignorant and ungospelled masses of the South, and on the far frontier.

Two years after the great crusade we began the new century with a temperance man from the Crusade State as President, and an earnest Christian temperance woman for the hostess of the White House.

In this we trace a "justice" both "poetic," and, what is vastly better, providential.

THE HAYES TESTIMONIAL COMMISSION.

This was formed on the suggestion of Rev. Frederick Merrick, a well-known professor in Ohio Wesleyan University. Dr. Merrick privately addressed letters to temperance leaders, suggesting a temperance memorial of the noble course pursued by Mrs. Hayes in banishing from the White House all intoxicating liquors as a drink. The plan met with earnest approval and a " commission" was appointed, in which by Dr. Merrick's request and that of the W. C. T. U. of Delaware, O., I accepted the "laboring oar." But for the coöperation of Miss Esther Pugh I could not have discharged the duties of this arduous position, in addition to those already assumed. In the interest of the movement, thousands of documents were sent out and addresses delivered in all the leading cities. Our local unions did most of the "honest, hard work," the Good Templars showing the same fraternal and helpful spirit they have uniformly manifested toward us. It was decided that the memorial should take the form of a portrait of Mrs. Hayes, to be presented to the nation through the incoming President. David Huntington, of New York, President of the National Academy of Design, was chosen as the artist. An elegant frame was carved, under the superintendence of Ben. Pitman, by pupils of the Cincinnati Art School, and presented by ladies of that city, and a photo-gravure of the picture executed by Barrie, of Philadelphia. It is hoped that this representation of the painting may be sold so extensively as to lay the foundation of a fund for the free distribution of temperance literature. All the work done by the commission was a free gift, and whatever income may be realized for the fund will be applied to the purpose named.

PRESENTATION OF THE PORTRAIT AT THE WHITE HOUSE.

On the 7th of March, 1881, while Washington was in splendid spirits and gala attire, our commission was represented there by its executive committee and other leading ladies of our society. Mrs. Clara L. Roach, President of our auxiliary in the District of Columbia, with her capable coadjutors, had made all needed preparations for us. Mrs. Senator Blair and her noble husband had not spared pains to help; Miss Caroline Ransom, the gifted artist, had rendered invaluable service; and Rev. Dr. Lanahan, from the first our wise and genial counsellor, was untiring in his efforts on our behalf.

Some of us were in the brilliant Senate Chamber on Inauguration Day. Most of us heard President Garfield's inaugural, and all witnessed the unrivalled pageant of the streets. On the afternoon of that day President Hayes and Mrs. Hayes, with their sons, came privately to see the picture. Most of our committee being present, Mrs. Hayes warmly greeted her old friends, Dr. and Mrs. Merrick, and spoke kindly to each of us, saying, in her simple, friendly fashion: "I have done nothing worthy of all this, and I do not know how to thank you for your kindness."

In the evening, at Lincoln Hall, public exercises were held, and, in the presence of an immense audience, the picture was unveiled by Dr. Merrick. It is ten feet in height and seven in width, the frame, with its monogram, clusters of grapes, and symbolic leaves and flowers, being a casket worthy of the jewel it enshrines. Mrs. Hayes, plainly but richly dressed in velvet and lace, stands in the foreground of a pleasing landscape, the only reminder of the picture's *motif* being a bas-relief upon a pedestal, representing a symbolic figure of Temperance leaning upon an urn, whence flows good, old-fashioned cold water, "sparkling and bright in its liquid light." Banked with rare flowers, the great picture was the center of a stage adorned by the W. C. T. U. of Washington with plants and vines, until the ladies seated behind the bright footlights, seemed in the midst of a brilliant parterre, to which the rarest charm was added by a magnificent basket of flowers sent from the conservatories of the White House by Mrs. President Garfield. Only a synopsis can be furnished of the addresses made on that occasion, and my own is given first only because its "official" character renders this the decorous order.

ADDRESS.

Before we can at all estimate the significance, to the Temperance Cause, of her example whom we are here to honor, we must turn away from the victories already gained and contemplate the mountains of difficulty that loom up ahead of our advancing hosts. For there are three mighty realms of influence, which the Temperance Reform, based as it is on science, experience, and the golden rule, has hardly yet invaded. The world of the fine arts, of romance, and of fashion still sneer at our total abstinence "Daniel come to judgment," and deny him a place in their stately halls and at their festal boards. From the days of Homer and Virgil to those of Tennyson and Longfellow, the poets have been singing, in tuneful cadences, the praise of wine.

From Praxiteles to Powers, the sculptors have delighted to idealize the coarse features of Bacchus, and those types of female beauty which correlate with his. From the antique frescoes of Pompeii, through gorgeous pictures of the Italian, Dutch, French, and Spanish schools, down to those of Meissonier and Bougereau, the choicest pigments of the painter have been lavished to furnish forth convivial feasts, and throw a halo around the orgies of the satyr and the merry-making of the priest.

Music, too, has always been the alluring Circe of the wine cup, whose captivating charm in classic days lent a fascination not its own to the triumphal procession of staggering bacchanals, and drinking songs are to-day the favorites of those college glee clubs, successors to the antique choruses, which help to demoralize young manhood in the bewildered years of the second and third decades. But what shall be said of the wizard pen of the romancer, with its boundless sweep through time and space? Alas, with what borrowed livery of the imagination has it not disguised the dangers of the moderate drinker, and bedecked the brutal pleasures of the debauchee! Heroes have been men mighty to drink wine, and heroines have found their prototype in Hebe, cup-bearer to the gods. From the sensuous pages of the Greek romancers, through mediæval tale and legend, the reeling pages of Fielding, the chivalric pageantry of Scott, the splendid society drama of Thackeray, and the matchless character panoramas of Dickens, down to our own society novelists; in all the witching volumes over which the beaming eyes of youth have lingered, the high lights of convivial enjoyment have been brought out in most vivid word painting, and its black shadows as studiously concealed. Now, be it remembered, that the poet, the artist, and the novelist, mighty interpreters of nature and the soul, will always maintain their empire over the human heart so long as it is a willing captive to the love of beauty, and the beauty of love. So that until we win an assured place for the Temperance Reform in these supremely influential realms of thought and expression, our success cannot be considered permanent. Until Genius, with her starry eyes, shall be gently persuaded to lay her choicest trophies at the feet of Temperance, there will remain for us much territory to be possessed. But be it ours to form a solemn covenant and one never to be broken, with the high priests of the æsthetic and emotional, so that the most romantic Reform in Christendom, the most poetic, ideal, and generous shall be fitly celebrated by sculptor's chisel, artist's brush, and novelist's enchanting pen. The beautiful portrait soon to be displayed, painted by the noblest master of his art in all the land, is the *avant-courier* of many a trophy which our cause is yet to win.

But the question will be asked, How is this reciprocity to be

achieved? The answer is not far to seek.   One other question yields
it: What is that other realm, even more potent in its influence than
that of the fine arts or the romancer?   Who build the libraries, the
picture galleries, the academies of music?   Who have the leisure and
resources to cultivate that fine discrimination which alone satisfies the
exigent demands of the artistic temperament?   Who but that class,
small, yet most potent, which by wealth, position, culture—one or all
of these — is called the "fashionable class," because its example
becomes the law of the social world?   That which is fashioned is shaped
or moulded, and the shaping, moulding power of the fashionable
class has abundant illustration in this audience and everywhere.   A
queen wore high-heeled shoes to conceal the shortness of her stature,
when lo, for women tall and short there went forth a dispensation of
high heels.   A prince had a wry neck and put on standing collars,
when behold, standing collars became the rule for all men everywhere.   A lady of the court decided that the abnormal frontal con-
figuration of her cerebrum would be best concealed by bangs, and
you, young ladies, know how that "bang" has reverberated throughout
Christendom !

Now, key to concert pitch the significance of facts like these; lift it
above the paltry, evanescent fashion of an hour to the level of a
fashion having such moral significance as sets the joy-bells ringing in
the hearts of hopeless mothers and unhappy wives.   Think what is
meant to that total abstinence cause, which seeks God's glory
through man's conformity to the indwelling law of a clear brain and
steady hand, when the first lady of the Republic, instead of cherishing
intoxicating liquors in their immemorial place of honor as the emblem
of hospitality and kindness and good-will, banished them from cellar,
side-board, and table, as the enemies of her home and of the guests to
whom she would do honor!

"From the days of Alexander the Drunk to the present, wine has
freely flowed in the houses inhabited by the world's rulers.   Lucy
Webb Hayes has stopped that flow in one."   The keynote of social
observances is set high up in the octave of society.   "Where Mc-
Gregor sits is head of the table."   The first question in fashionable
life is not "What ought I to do ?" but, "What will Mrs. Grundy
say about it ?"   "It is not for kings, O Lemuel, it is not for kings
to drink wine," had been for ages the reproving voice of inspiration, and those to whom it spoke had turned a deaf ear to its
counsel and squandered their priceless opportunities for good, so that
it was left for a Christian Queen of American Society to be the first
who should not only hear but heed this voice of God.

What arithmetic can calculate the sum total of homes restored,
hopes brightened, temptations routed, brains clear, that would have

been clouded, eyes bright that would have been blood-shot or tear-stained, but for this one woman's brave, thoughtful, loving deed! It has been like a beam in darkness, a torch held up in the gloom, "a light in the window for thee, brother," a beacon flaming grandly out on the most dangerous headland of the Republic's coast, and it shall grow and gather light and mount up to the zenith like another sun, shedding its genial rays into the darkest heart and most desolate home. It is for this we honor, and shall always love her, the gentle lady of the White House, who deserves the grateful homage of this Nation more than many a hero in whose honor statues have been carved, odes written, and pæns sung. It is for this that many loving hands have wrought in the Testimonial Commission, and millions of loving hearts will perpetually enshrine her memory. What shall be the decision of our new President and his wife we cannot tell, but we can wait and pray. By nature, he belongs to the people of church and home and philanthropic guild; we know he has a great, kind heart, and his gentle wife has sent us, on this happy evening, these beautiful flowers, in token of her interest and good will. God bless and guide them both!

The chief aim of our temperance workers in this day, is to cause an arrest of thought concerning the reasonableness of total abstinence, in the minds of the intelligent and well disposed. There are many ways of doing this, but none, perhaps, more effective in our practical age than the argument from experience and observation. The guest at a dinner whence the hostess had banished wine was met by logic of this sort, when he petulantly murmured in the ear of his next neighbor, "At this rate it won't be long till these fanatics will announce that we must dispense with mustard on our roast beef." Whereupon the answer was: "If taking too much mustard on roast beef had saddled this country with taxes, disrupted its homes, dishonored its manhood, agonized its women and children, emptied its churches, and crowded its jails and poor-houses to overflowing, I think I would be willing to take my roast beef without the mustard to the end of time." Analogous to this line of thought is that which seven years of honest hard work have impressed upon the temperance women of America. Going out with the Gospel life-boat, these Grace Darlings of Christ's Church have rescued the wrecks of manhood just as they were sinking beneath the seething flood of intemperance; but faster than they could pull these out of the swift tide others came floating down, until at last the women resolved to go higher up stream seeking the cause of this ·awful waste of human life, when, behold, they found two bridges upon which endless processions of people were crossing. One was of solid masonry, so strong that the heaviest railroad train or a caravan of elephants could hardly cause a vibration of its mighty arches, which rested on the massive piers of science, and the golden rule. Across the entrance was carved this motto, *Abstain from fleshly lusts which war against the soul.* Behold the healthful happy throng upon the grand teetotal bridge! Remember they are at a premium with life insurance companies, and in time of pestilence they are of all classes most likely to escape; remember too, that from their ranks the successful arctic and tropical explorers have been taken, also the champion athletes of every kind. Watch where they move, the early pioneers, Billy J. Clark and Lebbeus Armstrong, the doctor of medicine and the doctor of divinity arm in arm. See Lyman Beecher and Justin Edwards, side by side; Pierpont the poet and Delevan the man of wealth; gentle Father Matthew and his army of followers, John Hawkins and his Baltimore comrades, with the Washingtonians behind them, Sons of Temperance and Good Templars, with their brotherly mottoes and bright regalia; the Catholic Total Abstinence Society; Neal Dow, and John B. Gough, the first saying "total abstinence for the individual and total prohibition for the State," the other ruefully declaring, "I could no more drink moderately than you could fire off a gun moderately." Look where fall into line Francis Murphy, with "malice toward none, and charity for all," his blue ribbon army following, and Dr. Reynolds, Knight of the Red Ribbon, with the manhood of Michigan behind him, "Daring to do right." See the long procession of the W. C. T. U. with the badge of white and its favorite motto, "For God and home and native land." Proud are all these to serve as guard of honor to Lucy Webb Hayes, who moves forward with the step of a queen, saying, "Why should not America set its own fashions and develop its own individuality? Why should Europe furnish our social precedents? They have standing armies; we do not imitate them; they have crowns, we do not wear them!"

> "Now I beheld with eyes serene
> The very pulse of the machine!
> A being breathing thoughtful breath,
> A traveler between life or death,
> A perfect woman nobly planned
> To warn, to comfort and command,
> A creature not too bright or good,
> For human-nature's daily food,
> And yet a spirit, still and bright,
> With something of an angel's light."

But look again, the Church moves forward; the Bishops of York, Exeter, and Gloucester, Canon Farrar and Canon Wilberforce, side by side with five thousand of the leading clergy of the Church of England, true to the glorious motto of "*Noblesse oblige.*"

Here follows the Methodist Church, with Bishop Simpson at its
head, the Society of Friends, Spurgeon and Moody, Theodore Cuyler,
and William E. Dodge, Edward Everett Hale and Dr. Miner, with the
flower of all the clergy from both sides of the sea. And next march
those noble leaders in the State, who, amid the jeers and cavils of the
majority, have borne and labored and had patience, Sir Wilfrid Lawson, temperance chief in England's Parliament, and our own noble
Senator, Henry W. Blair, the Temperance leader of the American
Congress, God bless him.

Behind them march Justice Strong and Secretary Windom, Senators Dawes and Logan, with a goodly following in Congress. Next
come Governor St. John, of Kansas, the hero of the Constitutional
Amendment, and Governor Plaisted, of Maine, with the red ribbon in
his button-hole; then the Governors of Massachusetts and of Georgia,
with a procession of their peers in rank, while countless myriads follow from all classes of our rich and varied civilization, both North and
South, and behind them all comes the quick tread of childish feet, as
the Sunday-school and Band of Hope send their recruits, carrying bright
banners, on which gleam the talismanic words, *Tremble, King Alcohol,
we shall grow up!* Thank God for the total abstinence bridge, so safe
and solid, and for those who walk thereon for their own and others' sake!

But stretching across the dark and swollen river of intemperance is
another bridge, rocking and rickety, standing on the outworn piles of
custom, precedent, and self-indulgence, with "Moderation" carved
upon its entrance, and about half-way across, one long, swaying
narrow plank, where, with great circumspection, and a very level
head, some balance themselves successfully, as did Blondin at Niagara.
Great and motley is the throng that sets out upon this bridge, unmindful of warning voices in the air calling, *Be not deceived, God is not
mocked, whatsoever a man soweth, that shall he also reap! Wine is a
mocker! At the last it biteth like a serpent and stingeth like an adder.*
The ignorant, the sensual, and base are here, with the trade-mark of
the drink demon burnt into their cheeks; the young and rash are here,
and, strange to say, in the great army march thousands of the gifted
and the good, whose eyes are holden by the tight cords of antiquated
but relentless social usage. Ministers march here with Bible under
arm, ear-marked with the proof-text of their special pleading, and
unmindful of the spirit of His philosophy and life, who to a benighted
age declared, "I have many things to say, but ye cannot bear them
now." Many walk carefully the narrow plank, and with a fortunate
heredity, and an exceptionally balanced organization, cross in safety
and beckon to the deluded throng behind them, who sway to right
and left, and tumble headlong into the surging flood. Men of most
brain grow dizzy first, because strong drink darts to the brain as a
panther leaps upon a deer. Hence, when men boast of how much

liquor they can drink without being overcome, they unwittingly reveal their close relationship to evolutionary ancestors! Listen to Byron's dirge, one of the most illustrious of the brilliant geniuses who have fallen from Moderation Bridge:

> "My days are in the yellow leaf,
> The flower and fruit of love are gone,
> The worm, the canker, and the grief
> Are mine alone."

Listen to Robert Burns:

> "Then gently scan your brother man,
> Still gentler sister woman;
> Though they may gang a kennin' wrang,
> To step aside is human,"

And then he steps aside, to rise no more.

Listen to Edgar Poe, crying out in his remorse:

> "Take thy beak from out my heart,
> And thy form from off my door!"
> Quoth the raven—"Nevermore!"

Listen to the tortured moan of Charles Lamb, of Richard Brinsley Sheridan, of Webster, of Tom Marshall, of poor Dick Yates, and the pitiful procession of poets, wits, and orators who have made the awful plunge from Dr. Crosby's bridge. Remember that the tendency of yesterday becomes the habit of to-day and the bondage of to-morrow. Remember the testimony of that officer of justice, who said: "I never yet in my lifetime of experience sent a total abstainer to the poor-house or the jail." Remember, all who have fallen into the dark river of intemperance have fallen from Moderation Bridge, none from the other. Remember, if there were no drunkard on earth to-day and moderate drinking should continue, there would be plenty of them to-morrow. Look once more at the procession headed by half a million drunkards dropping into the tide, a million moderate drinkers, two millions of occasional, fashionable drinkers, and behind them all the boys and young men of our land—and then, as you shall face the record in eternity, I call on you to choose on which bridge you will cross, as a brother of humanity, a patriot, a Christian!"

To Dr. Merrick the thought of this work, now approaching its culmination, was first given, and his was the pleasant office of displaying to the eager throng the artist's work. He spoke as follows:

DR. MERRICK'S ADDRESS.

It is the declaration of Him whose every utterance is truth, and whose are the kingdoms of this world, that "righteousness exalteth a nation, but sin is a reproach to any people;" that "it is not for kings to drink wine, nor princes strong drink, lest they drink, and forget the law, and pervert judgment." The same high authority declares

11

drunkenness to be a sin, and because it is a sin, and the destruction of all man's highest interests, pronounces a solemn woe upon him who gives his neighbor drink.

Drunkenness, though confined to no age or people, is eminently the reproach of our modern civilization. The evil is wide-spread and deep-rooted. It is the vice of no particular class. It is found in the palace of royalty, as well as in the hovel of the peasant; in halls of legislation and seats of learning, as well as in the marts of trade and the guilds of industry. It pervades every department of society. Culture, social standing, and political position furnishing but slight power to resist its solicitations, while the wreck and ruin which follow in its path defy description. The very earth groans under the tread of this monster vice. That it is destructive of individual welfare, of domestic peace and social order; that it is the most prolific source of pauperism and crime; that it demands an enormous waste of the public resources, and heavily burdens the people with needless taxation, thus retarding human progress and greatly depressing the standard of civilization, is unquestionable.

Modern science in unveiling this mystery of iniquity, shows these results of the use of intoxicating beverages to be inevitable. She not only confirms the teaching of Revelation, that "wine is a mocker, and strong drink raging," but explains that from the action of alcohol upon the human organism, it must be so. It follows from a law as inexorable as fate. How to check, and finally to eradicate this great evil, is becoming one of the vital questions of the age; one worthy the serious attention of statesmen, as well as of philanthropists.

Though not my purpose now to attempt a portrayal of the evils of intemperance, or to discuss methods of reform, I may be allowed to say that the vice is many-sided, and that one of its most salient points is social custom. The social glass is undoubtedly the most frequent initial step to drunkenness. Plato recognizes the fact. Lord Brougham quotes his remarks approvingly, and finds their illustration in English society. John Bright, for this reason, urges the higher classes to banish the intoxicating cup from their tables. Luther styled this custom the "sauf teufel" of Germany. Bismarck has taken up the watchword, and is sounding it through the Fatherland. Leading statesmen of France, as Guizot, Thiers, and Jules Simon, with many others, have not only seen and lamented the evil of social drinking, but have set the example of abstinence.

Undoubtedly, whatever is done to render unfashionable the wine cup at social gatherings, tends greatly to diminish the amount of drunkenness. Many appreciating this fact, have ceased to treat their guests to intoxicating beverages. But no other instance of this has occurred so marked, and influential for good, as that of her, who for the past four years has been the honored mistress of the White House.

The moial courage, the exquisite tact, the inimitable grace with which this change was effected, command our highest admiration. While cheerfully recognizing, and heartily commending what others have done in encouragement of this most desirable reform, we must be allowed to say, in the words of the ancient prophetess, "Many daughters have done virtuously, but thou excellest them all."

Appreciating its moral grandeur, and recognizing the beneficial results that have followed, and which must continue to follow this act, the friends of temperance and good order throughout the country, irrespective of party affiliations, have caused to be executed a memorial painting as their testimonial to the noble example thus furnished in the exclusion of intoxicating drinks from the table of the Executive Mansion for the past four years.

I esteem it a high honor to be permitted, in this distinguished presence, to unveil a portrait of her whom the people delight thus to honor—late the mistress of the Presidential Mansion—Mrs. Lucy Hayes. *Eccam!*

With his closing words Dr. Merrick drew aside the screen and gave the lovely picture to the view of an admiring audience, which testified its pleasure by continued applause. Both eye and ear were charmed ; for to afford opportunity to enjoy the sight, music filled the interval. Mrs. Woodbridge's name, as President of Ohio W. C. T. U., was next on the programme, and although not fully recovered from recent illness, she had come to Washington to fill her appointment, but her suffering returned with such intensity that she was obliged to leave the platform, to the very great disappointment of her many friends.

LETTERS.

Mrs. Alford, Corresponding Secretary of the Committee, read extracts from the large number of letters received, expressive of full endorsement of the movement, and of regret at inability to be present at this time so fraught with interest. Rev. Dr. Cuyler, Felix R. Brunot, Mrs. E. J. Thompson, Mrs. Elizabeth Thompson, Neal Dow, Dr. Holland, John G. Whittier, General Hancock, Mrs. E. G. Hibben, President Woolsey, Mrs. Livermore, Gov. Littlefield, Mrs. Dr. McCabe, Mr. Huntington, the artist, and Mrs. M. A. Marshall, sent messages of regret.

Bishop Jaggar of the Episcopal, and Bishop Simpson of the M. E. Church, Hon. Wm. E. Dodge, and many others had already written, expressing entire sympathy and hearty unity with the movement.

Mrs. Fanny Barnes, of New York, now spoke a few graceful and forcible words in behalf of the young ladies of the country, after which Mrs. Judith Ellen Foster was introduced.

MRS. FOSTER'S ADDRESS.

In no way can we estimate more clearly the civilization of any age or time than in the study of the laws of that age, or time, or people, for law is the crystallization of ideas, and the embodiment of sentiment. Through the whole Justinian code, in the Magna Charta, and bill of rights in the Declaration of Independence, in the Constitution of the United States, in the constitutions and statutes of the various States, in the ordinances of our cities, in the petty regulations of our school districts do we see this illustrated. It is so under despotism. Law is the crystallization of the despot's thought or will. It is so under all forms of aristocracy. Law there is the embodiment of the sentiment of a few or part of the people. Particularly true is this of our American civilization, of our age and time, for here every man makes his direct impress upon the law. I wish every woman did. Then do you ask, dear friends, why I am here to speak of the department of temperance work that I represent—the legislative ? Because I know that any example like this will help to give us righteous law. Because I know that when the women of America, and the men of America shall think and feel as this noble woman thought and felt, the laws on our statute books will be a terror to evil doers and praise to them that do well; and thus, dear friends, representing as I do the department of legislation of the Woman's National Christian Temperance Union, I rejoice to-night to know that sometime the will of that brain shall be crystallized into law; and thus I appeal to you, dear, good women, if you honor her and her example, make it yours; men, if you honor her example, make it yours, and then by and by it shall be the voice of the law. We have said much of woman's work, but, gentlemen, our interests and yours are one; what helps you helps us, and what helps us helps you. I remember, as I stand here to-night, that it was the hand of a man that painted this beautiful picture. But I remember also that a day or two ago I stood in the studio of a lady of our city, and I beheld a woman* painting the glorious picture of a glorious man—General Thomas, the hero of many a battle. I said: 'That is all right; you paint us and we will paint you.'

Dear friends, I come from the West, where the Mississippi rolls down to the Gulf, and as I look over this audience, I see men from my own State; see others from brave, grand Kansas, that not only helped to free the slaves, but has been the first in the sisterhood of States to put a protest against the rum traffic into its organic law.

There are men here, too, whose homes are where the Golden Gate opens upon the beautiful Pacific. If I were to bring a garland to-night from the homes of these, it would be of grain, such as is grown upon our prairies that roll and roll and laugh out loud in streams of joy, so glad they are the soil is free—of flowers, also, that grew upon our prairies, not so delicate, perhaps, as those greenhouse tints, but of richer hues and deeper green, and I should have it tied by a ribbon of gold and silver taken from our mountains, wherein is hid the wealth of nations—and then, having laid it before this queen, I would pray that dews distilled from our rivers might fall softly upon it and keep it ever fresh.

I cannot do the work which comes to me to-night, unless I give you one last appeal. A great English statesman has said: "It is the business of civil law to make it hard to do wrong and easy to do right." The woman we are here to honor has made it easy to do right and hard to do wrong; and thus in her own dear self she has accomplished that which is the end and aim of all legislation, is it not? But, dear friends, we want every one of you to put his sentiment where it shall be as wide as the possible limit of his influence. Men, we come to you to-night as women, and we ask of you legislation concerning this terrible traffic that is the enemy of us all. We want you to put away the liquor traffic by law—we cannot do that; we can reign in the parlor; we can reign in the home, but the parlor and the home are set over against the saloon; we want you to put away the saloon; we want you to be as brave in your work as she has been in hers; we know this means a good deal for some of you; you will excuse me if I say to you that in my acquaintance with men that are assembled together to make the laws, a great many who seemed ready to do great things somehow lacked the courage to do so. When I am about to talk to an audience in Massachusetts, I speak about the Legislature of New York. In New York I speak about the Legislature of Massachusetts. But here I am in Washington. Who shall I talk about? You have come from everywhere. Can I talk about the Legislature of Iowa? I would not, if I could, slander my own State. I have met in the Legislature of Iowa three classes of men. The first great,

---

* Miss Ransom.

grand men—men who have clear intellectual convictions; men who grasp the situation and take it in, who have conscience behind their intellects to press them to do a thing if they see it is right to be done. Magnificent men they are; as Holland has said: "Men whom the lusts of office could not kill, whom the spoils of office could not buy; men who had influence and a will; men who had honor and who would not lie; men who could stand and face a demagogue and damn his treacherous villainies without winking." But of this class there are not enough to carry any measure.

There is another class of men—clean, well shaven, wearing good clothes, and very courteous in manner. They smiled, they spoke kindly, and took our hands in friendly greeting when we pleaded for total abstinence and its blessings and righteous laws. They looked kindly and said: "Why, dear women, you're all right; of course you are." So we left them, thinking we had their votes; but we didn't always have them. We noticed, when counting over the list afterwards, that some were absent and some voted against us. I think I have found the solution of this trouble. I have noticed that those men were constructed in such a manner that they could not help it. They swayed to and fro like a pendulum, first this way and then the other, and it happened that they swayed the other way when the vote was counted. This class illustrates that principle in mechanics known as the universal joint. I will tell you, ladies, what that is. It is a ball in a socket, shaped so as to go every way; sometimes so, sometimes so. It don't make any difference; it will go either way. It is very useful, you see—it prevents friction in a great many places. Now these men must have, somewhere about the base of their spine, a universal joint. As I said before, I don't think these gentlemen are to blame. It is the way they are put up. So they go and go in every direction.

But we must have the votes of these men, because they count so many. We must have them on our side, if we are to have righteous law. How shall we get these votes? When mechanics do not want the universal joint to turn they set it, and then it stays. If we can set these men it is all right—if you can, somehow or other, prop them up so that they will stay up, they are all right. How shall they be set? Reinforce such men with their poor, weak will—reinforce them by such an example as this (pointing to the picture). Women, set them right by your example in the parlor; men, set them right by your example in the store, in the shop, in the political caucus, in the bank, on the farm—everywhere set them, and they will do very well.

Then, again, there is another class of men. They are few—thank God, very few. They are bad men—men who drink liquor, and love it; men who "grovel in the soil and feed on garbage." What shall we do with such men? They don't know anything about the prayers of women. We can only hold over them a club. What shall the club be? Your will, men, backed by your vote. Let such men know they cannot occupy positions of honor, positions of trust, unless they are right on moral questions. Gentlemen, by the teachings of our Christianity, by the sweet influences that come from the home, by our prayers—by all these things we may succor and encourage and hold up the weak. But you must hold over the others the club of your vote.

And now, dear friends, I leave my message with you. I am constrained to say this. I know I am standing to-day in the nation's capital. I know I am surrounded by the representatives of the greatest and most glorious nation that the sun shines on, and I love its flag as I do nothing else save the cross of Christ; but I do want to say to you, old men, whose heads are white—you who occupy positions of trust in the gift of the people—some of you drink liquor; the people only *tolerate* you because of your years of service. Young men, don't *you* expect anything from the American people unless you are sober! When these men, whose heads are white, have passed away, there will be a better sentiment than there is now. When the tempter smiles upon you as you move among your acquaintances in society, see that you yield not. We are sorry *for them.* But you, young men, know better. By and by, if women (did I say *if?* I am speaking prophecy to-night)—*when* we occupy positions in the Government—when we women shall not only plead, but hold the club—when we can do that there will be no hope for you if you use intoxicating drink. You had better begin to make your record now. It won't do to wait until that time; then it will be too late.

THE FLOWERS FROM MRS. GARFIELD.

To Rev. Mr. Power, the pastor of President Garfield's Church, was committed a beautiful part of the evening's service—the presentation of Mrs. Garfield's basket of flowers to the president of the Commission. His few sentences were especially felicitous, and my off-hand reply was so well received by the audience that its closing sentences are given *: "As we have prayed for Lucy, so we will pray for Lucretia: God bless James A. Garfield and Lucretia, his wife!"

---

* The next day I was invited to lunch at the White House, and President Garfield told me those words "had won his heart."

With the benediction by Rev. Mr. Power, the evening services closed upon a delighted audience. But all this was only preliminary to

THE CEREMONY AT THE EXECUTIVE MANSION.

Previous to the inauguration I had written President Garfield, asking him to name a date when he could receive the portrait. The following is the General's reply:

MENTOR, OHIO, February 21, 1881.

DEAR MISS WILLARD:—Yours of the 16th inst. came duly to hand. I shall be glad to consult your convenience in the matter to which your letter refers, but it is impossible for me at this date to fix a time for receiving you and your friends. It will be better for you to send word to me—say on the 5th of March, when a definite arrangement can be made.   Very truly yours,

J. A. GARFIELD.

After the arrival of the Commission in Washington, the following correspondence between the Commission and the President took place:

WASHINGTON, D. C., March 5, 1881.

TO THE PRESIDENT:—The Executive Committee of the Commission on a Temperance Testimonial, from the people to Mrs. President Hayes, desires to present her portrait, painted by Huntington for the Commission, to you personally as the nation's representative, at the earliest practicable date. We are instructed to request that this testimonial may be placed in the east room of the White House, where it will be at all times easy of access to the public.

The Commission awaits the pleasure of the President.

FRANCES E. WILLARD, President,   C. CORNELIA ALFORD, Cor. Sec'y,
FREDERICK MERRICK,   ESTHER PUGH, Treasurer,
MARY A. WOODBRIDGE,   M. B. O'DONNELL.

EXECUTIVE MANSION, ⎰
WASHINGTON, March 5, 1881. ⎱

DEAR MADAM:—The President directs me to acknowledge the receipt, through the kindness of Mr. Jones, of your note of this morning, and also desires me to ascertain the probable number of persons who will attend at the presentation. It is very desirable, if not imperatively necessary, that the number be as small as possible.

Upon the receipt of this information the President will send you the day and hour when it will be most practicable for him to receive the portrait.

Awaiting your answer, I am,

Very respectfully,

J. STANLEY BROWN, Sec.

J. Stanley Brown, Private Secretary to President:

DEAR SIR:—Please convey to the President our thanks for his prompt reply and kind consideration. We will not invite more than twenty-five or thirty, and fewer if he expresses that preference. As the President is busy, we venture to suggest Tuesday, March 8th, at 10 A. M., if agreeable to him, as the portrait will be at Lincoln Hall until after the public exercises on Monday evening, the 7th.

Respectfully,

FRANCES E. WILLARD, President of Commission.

EXECUTIVE MANSION, WASHINGTON, March 5, 1881.

MISS WILLARD:—The President desires me to inform you that the time (March 8th) named in your note of this morning, is entirely satisfactory to him.

Very respectfully,

J. STANLEY BROWN.

In accordance with this arrangement, the portrait was conveyed to the Executive Mansion, Tuesday morning, March 8th, and hung on the east wall of the east room, near the picture of Martha Washington. At ten o'clock the members of the Commission, with a few invited guests—among them Mrs. Senator Blair and Miss C. L. Ransom, the artist, and intimate friend of Mrs. Garfield —Mrs. Chase, of Pennsylvania; Mrs. Foster, Mrs. Barnes, Mrs. Merrick, Rev. Dr. Lanahan and wife, several members of Washington W. C. T. U., and a few other ladies and gentlemen—assembled in front of the picture, and soon President and Mrs. Garfield, accompanied by Private Secretary Brown and Mrs. Gen. Sheldon, entered the room. As the President and party advanced, Miss Ransom led me forward and introduced me to the President (with whom I had already a pleasant acquaintance). Both then advanced until we stood directly before the picture, and with much inward trepidation I addressed my noble friend as follows:

MR. PRESIDENT—We are here to present to the nation, through its honored chief, a temperance testimonial from the men and women, high and low, rich and poor, fortunate and unfortunate, who have loved her whose pictured presence is now before us, because they felt that she was the defender of their homes ; because amid the fogs of a time-worn social conservatism she held steadily aloft the torch of an example safe, gentle, and benignant. We stand in the presence of one whose utterances and character are known to all the nation. I do not forget how in the tumult and strife of a great polit- ical convention James A. Garfield of Ohio said, "Remember it is in the home where the sovereign citizen has his wife and children gath- ered around him that God prepares the verdict of the American peo- ple." I do not forget that he reminded the women of Cleveland when they came to Mentor with their congratulations, that in every army there are three classes: the scouts, who go ahead; the soldiers who do the fighting; and, within all, the home guards, and that he said, "God bless the women, they are America's home guards." I do not forget that in his inaugural he reminded us by the sacred words, "A little child shall lead them," that the tenderness and sweetness of childhood had a place in his thought in that supreme hour; and so standing here I feel very much at home, as do we all, in this kind and brotherly presence. Mr. President, whom do we represent ? We are a part of your constituency, and we represent a great deal of earnest hard work done in the name of God, and home, and native land. We represent a volume of prayer rising like incense to God from the very first hour that we knew the burden which had been laid upon you; and always have we sought a blessing also from on high upon her who is the mother of your sons and of your sweet young daughter, and upon her who bore and cherished you. We represent that num- berless throng who have a right to be heard in this presence because of all that they have suffered. We cannot speak to you of the graves of the living and the graves of the dead that have strewn our pathway, because of the cup that tempts only to destroy. Our principles and our endeavors are the inevitable outcome of the philosophy of our century. Well is it understood by the scholar President! For one dominant purpose runs through all our modern civilization. Science spells it out slowly from the writing in the rocks, from scattered monuments and fossil languages and pronounces it the Unity of Man. Statesmanship discovers that the woes of one nation are the misfortune of all, and so frames treaties and forms alliances of mutual defence and service in the name of the Solidarity of Man, but Christianity per- ceiving the higher significance of all these studies and their practical results, prays, pleads, and labors for the Universal Brotherhood of Man. Among the applications of this great underlying principle none is gaining ground more rapidly than the practice of a free and voluntary total abstinence, for our own and others sake, from those alcoholic drinks which have alienated more hearts, dissolved more homes, poisoned the air with more cruel words, and moved kind hands to more hateful deeds than any other agency outside of Pandemonium. "Where is thy brother?" is to-day the central question in that larger home which we call social life, answered by a thousand kindly charities, but most significantly answered, as we believe, by the great army of total abstainers, which in the present military exigency is calling all up and down the land for volunteers. We are here to leave in your care the picture which symbolizes so much of hope and glad expectation for the future. We are here because it is women who have given the choicest hostages to fortune. Beyond the arms that shield them long the boys go forth and come not back again, and the mother heart prays that society may hedge them round about with loving safeguards and restraints; and fervent is our hope that a steady signal light may shine forth for them from the conspicuous windows of the Presidential Mansion. As members of the Church of Christ, we appeal to you to help hasten the time when all men's weal shall be each man's care, and we pray God's blessing upon you, upon your wife, and upon those that cluster around you in your home. Well has the laureate said concerning the "good time coming," which the triumph of the temperance cause shall help us to usher in:

> "Ring out old shapes of foul disease,
> Ring out the narrowing lust of gold,
> Ring out the thousand wars of old,
> Ring in the thousand years of peace.

> "Ring out a slowly dying cause,
> And ancient forms of party strife,
> Ring in the nobler modes of strife,
> With sweeter manners, purer laws.

> "Ring in the valiant man and free,
> The larger heart. the kindlier hand,
> Ring out the darkness of the land,
> Ring in the Christ that is to be."

THE PRESIDENT'S REPLY.

Miss Willard, ladies and gentlemen: The very appropriate gift to the Executive Mansion which you have brought, the portrait of its late mistress, I gladly accept. It shall take its place beside the portraits of the other noble women who have graced this house. She is my friend. Nothing I can say will be equal to my high appreciation of the character of the lady whose picture is now added to the treasures of this place. She is noble; the friend of all good people. Her portrait will take, and I hope will always hold in this house an hon-

ored place. I have observed the significance which you have given
to this portrait from the standpoint you occupy, and in connection
with that work in which you are engaged. First, I approve most
heartily what you have said in reference to the freedom of individual
judgment and action symbolized in this portrait. There are several
sovereignties in this country. First, a sovereignty of the American
people ; then the sovereignty nearest to us all—that sovereignty of the
family, the absolute right of each family to control its affairs in
accordance with the conscience and convictions of duty of the heads
of the family. In the picture before us that is bravely symbolized.
I have no doubt the American people will always tenderly regard this
household sovereignty, and however households may differ in their
views and convictions, I believe that those differences will be
respected. Each household, by following its own convictions and
holding itself responsible to God, will, I think, be respected by the
American people. What you have said concerning these evils of
intemperance meets my most hearty concurrence. I have been in my
way, and in accordance with my own convictions, an earnest advocate of temperance, not in so narrow a sense as some, but in a very
definite and practical sense. These convictions are deep, and will be
maintained. Whether I shall be able to meet the views of all people
in regard to all the phases of that question remains to be seen. But
I shall do what I can to abate the great evils of intemperance. I
shall be glad to have this picture upon these walls, and shall be glad
to remember your kind expressions to me and my family, and in your
efforts to better mankind by your work I hope you will be guided by
wisdom, and that you will achieve a worthy success. Thanking you
for this meeting and greeting, I bid you good morning.

The party were then introduced to President and Mrs.
Garfield, and spent a few moments in pleasant conversa-
tion. Mrs. Woodbridge, on behalf of the National W. C.
T. U., presented the resolution adopted at the Boston
Convention, reading as follows :

"We heartily endorse the movement, and make it our own, which
proposes a suitable testimonial to Mrs. Lucy W. Hayes, the honored
wife of our Chief Magistrate, whose brave stand for total abstinence
at the White House has been so successful, and who has thus presented a noble example for imitation; and we recommend that the
Woman's National Christian Temperance Union, before adjourning,
appoint a suitable committee of ladies to visit her successor as soon as
possible after the Presidential election, to urge, with gentle and courteous entreaty, that the good work begun by Mrs. Hayes may not be
interrupted on her retirement to private life."

The company went through the conservatory, and Miss Ransom, ever watchful to promote the pleasure of all, arranged for a reception by the elder Mrs. Garfield, and each one enjoyed a handshake and friendly word with "Grandma."

PRAYER MEETING.

[Miss Pugh gives the following account.]

"It was announced that the committee and friends of the Commission would adjourn to "Temple Cafe" for a prayer-meeting. And here, in a few moments, about fifty gathered, to commit the words and work of the day to God, and to ask his blessing upon our President and his household. The meeting was a pentecostal season, wherein we sat together in heavenly places in Christ Jesus, great liberty being given in prayer and praise, the Holy Spirit brooding over all, melting all into unity before God. It seemed almost impossible to close this precious season, and when we finally parted it was with hearts filled with thanksgiving for the presence and power under which we had met."

THROUGH THE EYE TO THE HEART.

The saloon-keepers understand this new proverb,— "Through the eye to the heart." "King Gambrinus," in garb of green and red and purple, flourishing aloft his foaming mug of beer, and bestriding a huge cask of the same refining beverage, sits above the doors of all leading dram-shops. In Kansas, just after the prohibition law went into force, I saw a picture displayed in the empty windows of the closed saloons, which was artfully contrived to arouse the dormant appetite of every drinking man who looked sorrowfully toward the scene of his former exploits. A generous glass of ale, brimming with beaded foam, was done in colors carefully laid on, and this tempting but now impossible draught was surrounded by separate hands, all the fingers of each one being represented in most ardent, expectant attitudes of grasping, clutching, and clawing all in vain, to reach the coveted but unattainable glass. The tobacconist, with similar wit and shrewdness, attracts attention to his demoralizing wares by placing before his door a statuesque Indian maiden, who offers a bunch of artificial cigars, while to get the real ones, of which she sets the foolish young man thinking, he must go inside. But our temperance reformers have been inexplicably slow to appreciate, and still slower to apply the principle illustrated on every hand by their opponents. Patriotism is silently taught in every home by pictured faces of our nation's heroes looking down upon us from the walls. Religion has its noble object-lessons in engravings from great masters, but temperance, pure and lovely handmaid of them both, is left without a witness even in the dwellings of our standard-bearers. Not a dozen times in my nine years' temperance sojourn in almost forty States, have I found a temperance picture even in a temperance home. Dear friends, can we not have an "arousement" on this subject? Do we not need an "arrest of thought" here, as really as those for whom we labor need that same "arrest" on the total-abstinence question? Are we not strangely blind to the silent, sure, and permeating influence of that which passes "through the eye to the heart"? Nay, more, as women, should we not manifest more strongly our appreciation of the first national engraving, secured through woman's influence, of a woman's face, of which the annals of our history make mention? And such a woman! So strong, yet gentle; so true to her possibilities of help to ignorant, tempted, and sorrowful humanity.

What has not been wrought of pure and healthful influence for the total-abstinence movement by thirty years of "The Old Oaken Bucket" engraving on the walls of a thousand homes? And what may we not expect of beneficent sentiment to be educated and enforced by "line upon line and precept upon precept," not in abstract formula, but incarnated in a presence so noble, and enforced by a character so earnest and attractive as that of Lucy Webb

Hayes? "Biography is history teaching by example," and that lesson can in no other way be made so vivid as by keeping that example before the radiant eyes of youth in home and school-room and public institution. Right well have many of the temperance societies wrought for the Hayes portrait testimonial. Grateful and glad ought we to be that in the White House hangs a frame of majestic proportions, the finest ever executed in America, carved by women's skilled fingers in the Cincinnati Academy of Design, and paid for by the gifts of women, headed by Mrs. A. R. Clark, of that city, and that inside this frame is a noble, full-length painting of Mrs. Hayes, by Daniel Huntington, the finest artist in America. But if this national picture in its high place teaches perpetually its glorious lesson to the traveling public, why shall not Barrie's beautiful photo-gravure (30 × 20 in size) teach the same lesson to the great, blessed democracy of those who stay at home, especially to our young folks in their impressible and clear-cut days? Should we not, then, order the photo-gravure as a birthday, Christmas anniversary, or every-day present for son, daughter, pastor, teacher, physician, or representative in Congress, as the case may be? Remember, this is no private speculation, but a national enterprise, beginning and ending with "We, the people of these United States," (and for this once it means not only men, but we women, too!) Our brothers have helped us, though, as they always do and always will when we are in dead earnest. The I. O. G. T. and S. of T. have sent out special circulars urging their auxiliaries to secure this work of noble sentiment as well as art. Remember, too, that all the money beyond actual cost of the engraving will be used to buy and circulate temperance literature, thus directly advancing our cause.

LUCY HAYES TEA-PARTIES.

This method of blending social recreation with work for the cause is becoming so popular with our girls, and so many reports have come to us of successful enterprises of this kind, that we give a few brief notices. Such a tea-party was held in the town hall at Brattleboro', Vermont. A fine collection of antiquities was got together, among them teaspoons 130 years old, and crockery which once graced the table of King James of Scotland, supposed to be at least 300 years old. "Hayes mottoes," in red, white, and blue, ornamented the hall. The personations were good; speeches and singing enlivened the occasion, and the receipts were most encouraging.

Another Lucy Hayes tea-party, of which a full account has been sent us, was held at Port Chester, N. Y., on February 22d.

Another of these enjoyable affairs took place at Greenwich, Washington county, N. Y. The dresses were bright and picturesque; the supper — served in old-fashioned china, and cooked after the manner of " ye olden time " was excellent.

Still another was given at Poughkeepsie, several hundred citizens being present. The exercises were much the same as usual in such cases. One little girl recited a poem from OUR UNION, and a young lady personated its editor, and sold many copies of the " Lucy Hayes " number. George and Martha Washington were the life of the evening.

THE MOST BRILLIANT OF THE SEASON.

A " Lucy Hayes Reception " was given by the Boston Y. W. C. T. U., in Odd Fellows Hall. About three hundred persons were present. The entertainment consisted of music, dramatic recitations, and refreshments. Many of the regular and honorary members of the Union were dressed in costume, representing distinguished characters

of the olden time—General and Mrs. Washington, Governor
and Mrs. Bradford, Governor and Mrs. Winthrop, John
Alden and Priscilla, Roger Williams and his wife, etc., etc.
Mrs.˙ Hayes was personated by a lady who looked the
part to perfection, and aroused a suspicion among the
more unsophisticated that the Union had induced the real
Mrs. Hayes to grace the reception. The costumes were
beautiful and striking, and made the hall look like a
flower garden. Pledge books were circulated, and an
opportunity was afforded to all to inscribe their names.
The Union secured a number of new members, and a substantial addition to its treasury. Part of the proceeds will
be devoted to the Lucy Hayes memorial fund, and the
remainder to the work of the Y. W. C. T. U.

IMPRESSIONS OF THE GARFIELDS.

I first met General Garfield in 1876, when we went to
Washington with the "Home Protection Petition." Some
of our committee had sent their cards to him in the
House of Representatives, and he came out hurriedly into
the ante-room, evidently much preoccupied, and while
they presented our plans to him, I stood at a little distance "to take him in," for his name had attracted me
years before, and I believed him to be the most complete
embodiment of American ideas and Christian statesmanship the country had seen for many a day. He remained
but a moment, listening gravely to what was said, and
promising to give it due consideration. Pleading an im-
pending vote in the House, which he must not miss, he
bowed with courteous dignity and disappeared. As I photo-
graphed for memory's magic gallery that tall, well-knit,
and robust form, soldierly bearing, and strong, regnant
countenance, in which " the manhood of strength and gentleness " was mirrored, I thought: This is the victorious
Norseman of old, with his giant strength, his eyes blue as

a Scandinavian fiord, and complexion clear as the sky of the midnight sun, but heart mellowed by the light that fell upon the hills of Galilee.

In 1878, taking the palace car at Elmira, New York, one afternoon, young Dr. Adele Gleason bade me good-bye, and left the train after it had begun to move. Anxiously I followed her to the door, and, returning when she was landed, saw a tall man whose chair was just ahead of mine, leaning out of the window, then turning to ask me hurriedly " if that young lady was safe " ? I did not look up so far as his face, hence did not recognize him; but, replying that she was, began to write and read, as is my custom, in the only study I have known for years—the great, swift, roaring train, to whose rhythm one's thoughts keep time. After a while I noticed that my little nugget of a traveling bag, packed to suffocation with books and papers, was out-ranked by the huge and handsome portmanteau which the tall man opened, and that from under his great, soft, felt hat he was peering into the books, magazines, and manuscripts which formed a large part of his outfit.

"That's James A. Garfield," I said to myself when I had noted him more carefully, for I had just been reading his great speech on hard money, delivered the night before at Rochester. Busily he read on, and I could not help seeing—even if I had wished to—that the *Princeton Review* and "Milman's History of the Jews" were among his current studies. Later on, when the New York dailies reached us, he bought them all, with that desire to "hear both sides" which has given such splendid equipoise to his character, and, turning to me, he frankly said he "heard the young lady ask me when I was to speak next, wondered whether I was as tired of it as his campaign was tiring him"—at the same time offering me the *Tribune.* I replied that " I never made acquaintances upon the cars, but believed this was General Garfield, of whom my friend, Mrs. Woodbridge, of Ohio, had often spoken." "The same," he said; whereupon I told my name, address, and employment. We shook hands cordially, and from then until I got off at Paterson, N. J., we talked on. I think the General's conversation that day would fill a good-sized book, and I have often characterized the range of subjects by saying that "he treated of everything from protoplasm to Omnipotence." So rapid was his thought, so clear and forcible the stream of his utterance, so considerate and kindly his criticism, so varied and available his information, that I learned more about him, and profited more largely by his knowledge than it would be in the power of most persons I have met to reveal and teach in half a lifetime. He talked of books, science, and invention, — of great characters, and foreign travel.

He told me of his life—nearly everything that I have since seen in books; of his religious history; that in his church all men are preachers, and the Bible the only creed; of his school and college days, and of Mark Hopkins, and Miss Almeda Booth, the former, president of Williams College when he went there, and the latter preceptress at Hiram, and a woman, (much older than himself and long since dead,) for whom he seems to have felt the deepest reverence. He talked of the Credit Mobilier, and other legislative scandals. After telling how deeply he was wounded by seeing his name, for the first time after so many years of public life, associated with imputations of dishonor, he felt that God said to him in the depths of his soul: "*You* know that you meant to do right, and *I* know it—that is enough." After which he never worried about the matter any more. Among other things, we talked of temperance, and he said strong drink was never a snare to him—he had better uses for his faculties and

for his time. "Now and then, on a public occasion, or
the drinking of a toast," he said he tasted wine. I begged
him to think how significant the gesture of his hand
would be (and, to my mind, more eloquent than any gesture employed in a great speech,) as it waived aside the
cup that tempts so many to their ruin. He listened
kindly, but was not convinced. He talked of the South,
and its great men, its generous sympathies and bright
outlook for the future, and most of all he dwelt upon
Lamar, of Mississippi, with a brother's fondness. As I
went my way, the thought that stayed longest with me
concerning this big-hearted, big-brained man's career, was
this: *He is foreordained to be our President!* I never
saw him again until he walked sturdily into the Senate
chamber on Inauguration day, and as soon as he was
seated on President Hayes's right hand, looked smilingly
up to the gallery where his mother, his wife and children
sat, and bowed to them. An hour later, he stood on the
steps of the Capitol and pronounced his inaugural with a
forcefulness of utterance which carried the words to my
ear far away, and at the close, amid the hurrahs of the
acres of human beings around him, stooped to kiss his
noble mother and faithful wife. On the next Friday the
President received our memorial portrait of Mrs. Hayes,
and on the next a note from Mrs. Garfield invited Miss
Ransom, the artist, to bring me to the White House to
lunch.

I hardly know how to do justice to the impression made
upon my mind by Mrs. Garfield. "Pure, womanly," expresses it, if one had been so fortunately trained that the
"sweet reasonableness" of a strong mind, tempered by
the "gentleness of Christ," go into the definition of that
royal word, "womanly." Looking across the wide lunch
table at his wife, the President said to me: "I can hardly
believe, as I see her sitting there, that she who has taught

Latin to my boys, was learning it of me a score of years ago"; and again: "Don't blame the dear little woman yonder if all your hopes are not fulfilled"; and again, when I said we temperance women wished he would read Canon Farrar and Dr. Richardson, he replied: "Whatever you send me I will carefully read; only, if you want me to be sure to get it, mail it to my wife." Then, laughingly, he said: "When I replied to you ladies, the day the Hayes portrait came, you may have deemed me unsatisfactory; but I thought I would rather take the part of 'I-go-not-sir-and-went,' than 'I-go-sir-and-went-not'"; and he added,—"You will respect my convictions, I am confident, whatever the result." I told him we certainly would, do so, but how the gentle words of Mrs. Garfield cheered me when she said: "I hope I shall not disappoint your expectations." So, with thoughtful, friendly words the time sped on, and I could but feel, looking upon the delicate, responsive face of the wife, noting the noble son's quiet attention to his mother, and the whole-hearted ways of Mollie Garfield and the boys, that here, if I had ever seen one, was the typical American home. How little did President Garfield dream that day, as he told me of his mother's anxiety lest harm might come to him, and added "I suppose a man in my position is an attractive target to a crank," that a few weeks later the whole nation would be thrilled by the terrible story of a snake in the eagle's nest!

SOCIETY WORK OF YOUNG WOMEN.

From the beginning of our work, young women have held an honored place in the W. C. T. U. It was a dear Ohio girl who selected for her mother the first scripture ever read in a saloon, the 146th Psalm, now historic in our annals. In Cincinnati was another, a charming girl, who always took the arm of her grandmother when the long, solemn procession marched from the church to the rum-shop, singing " Rock of ages, cleft for me," and who, when challenged by the words, " I will sign if you will," uttered by a drunken workman, who owed the roof over his head to her father's clemency, put her fair autograph upon the pledge she had opened on a saloon table, wet with the drippings of potations upon which her visit had blessedly intruded. We also recall the brave Arkansas girl who, when a saloon-keeper raised his pistol, and dared the praying women's band to cross his threshold, sprang lightly to his side, singing " Never be afraid to work for Jesus," and laid her gentle hand upon his weapon.

Let it be thoughtfully remembered by young women, and by the mothers to whom they look for counsel, that home, if it is to be the sacred shrine that we would have it, demands not only a priestess but a *priest* to keep its altars pure and bright. As Mrs. Lathrop often says " There must be honor for honor, purity for purity, total abstinence for total abstinence."

To all, with equal force, comes the voice of God declar-ing that " to be carnally-minded is death, but to be spiritually-minded is life and peace."

Clearly, then, young women must require of men whom they admit to their society and to their homes, a purity of personal life such as they have not in the past required. But, on the other hand, it is their duty to do all in their power to make this nobler habit of life less difficult of attainment by offsetting the temptations of the saloon (be it the grimy grog-shop, the gilded "restaurant," or costly "bil-liard hall ") by the attractions of the temperance reading-room and literary or musical reunion. Undertakings of this character may, with propriety, engage the efforts of young women, and have been successfully carried on in many places since the great temperance awakening.

In their own social circle they can do still more by

scattering all about them the light of a pure example, and of gently uttered argument in favor of total abstinence as the only personal security. The autograph pledge-book upon the parlor table would be in itself an influence for good of incalculable value. It would call attention to the subject, occasion argument, and result often in the confirmation of good principles or the conviction of bad ones.

Recently in Cleveland, the work of the Young Women's Christian Temperance Unions was clearly outlined in the following brief address by Miss Anna Gordon:

Our good friend Mrs. Ingham has urged me to take the witness stand to-night and testify to the work that young women are doing in the temperance reform. It is now more than five years since my own heart was specially enlisted in this branch of Christian endeavor, and nothing has ever given me so much happiness as to see the young women of our land rallying to the call of the W. C. T. U. In every State of the North, and in nearly all the Southern States, young women are organized in separate societies, have taken the total abstinence pledge, donned the white ribbon, and dedicated their fresh young energies to the cause of "God, and home, and native land." Their work may be properly divided under three heads. First, influence in society; second, self-education on all questions pertaining to the temperance reform; and third, teaching the children. We begin by forming a society which is really a social club with total abstinence as its basis. Young gentlemen are invited to join as honorary members. Thus we secure their names to our pledge in a delicate way which does not offend their pride, and gradually they become interested in temperance work by association with their young lady friends, who are actively engaged in it.

I recently attended a fortnightly reception given by one of the young women's societies of Baltimore. It was, in fact, an evening party, to which all came in their best attire, and there were as many young gentlemen present as ladies. Upon a signal from the presiding officer of the evening (an honorary member, by the way), a hush came over the happy group, and a significance was given the entertainment soon to follow, by an impressive reading of the Scripture lesson, beginning "Put on, therefore, the whole armor of God."

Then came the programme prepared for the occasion, consisting of a well-written essay, two or three select readings, good music, promenading, and refreshments, the young men taking an equal part in the exercises, and evincing just as much interest as the young ladies. The open pledge book on the centre table gave an opportunity for new names to be added, and who can tell what a shelter from temptation and safeguard from the formation of bad habits that society may prove to those who are so much more tempted than young women are by false social usages, which this society will help to render obsolete ? Thus it will be seen that the central thought of our work is to add a noble moral significance to social gatherings and entertainments of young people, so that, as I have heard many a sweet girl say, "We may have our pleasant, social evenings all the same, and yet be doing good to somebody." Who can estimate how much or how far-reaching is this "good ?" What homes it brightens even now, what mothers' hearts it renders glad, what wayward lives it helps to chasten, and in the future what joy in other homes, not formed as yet, shall linger as its blessed sequel !

But while the social side of this work is its most important feature, the Y. W. C. T. U. branches out in varied forms of active usefulness.

Its regular meetings are made interesting and profitable by topical study of scientific temperance, by debates, and occasionally a literary or musical programme, after business is laid aside.

Bands of Hope for children, and night schools for boys, are often conducted by our young ladies, and many other lines of work, suggested by the needs of different localities, are successfully pursued. I was glad to see that the Young Women's Temperance League of Cleveland had arranged for a special course of lectures on the chemistry of alcohol and its effects, and that they were enterprising enough to have the excellent one given recently, well reported for the press. In Rochester, N. Y., the young women go to the public schools, by permission of the Board of Education, and give lessons to the children on the scientific aspects of the temperance question. In many cities, the kitchen garden, so successful in Cleveland, which teaches the household arts to girls, is a charming feature of our work. Dear young ladies of this audience, let me urge upon your thought an interest in this temperance work. It will help to teach you, as it has helped to teach me, the secret of a happy life.

If you are in doubt as to what you are capable of doing, let me leave with you my favorite motto: "Get thy spindle and thy distaff ready, and God will give thee flax."

MRS. FRANCES J. BARNES,

National Superintendent of Young Women's C. T. U.

There is a lovely Quaker home in Skaneateles, N. Y., where temperance workers are always welcome. A lady "who has the Gospel in her looks" presides over this

"Weary Women's Rest." "Saint Letitia" we call her, as we smooth her soft, bright silver hair, and she looks up with deprecation in those kind eyes; for Quakers don't believe in titled saints, though their "Society" has furnished more real ones than any other of the same dimensions since time began. A well-to-do merchant, C. W. Allis by name, is joint partner in this establishment, and "Daughter Fanny" is the joy and pride of both. It is hard to write with judicial calmness of a friend so dear. She was not known to me until her bright girlhood and school days were over, and as Mrs. Fanny J. Barnes, the wife of a young lawyer, she came to Chicago from New York in 1875. I was holding a meeting in the lecture-room of the Clark Street Church, and had observed a stylish-looking young lady seated beside my good Quaker friend, Mrs. Isabella Jones. "I wonder what she came for," was in my mind, for temperance was not what it has since grown to be in fashionable circles. What was my delight when this sweet-faced lady came forward with Mrs. Jones, and declared her readiness to "do anything she could to help." So frankly was this said, and so truly has my "younger sister" (as I have often called her) lived up to those words that, on the instant, she grew dear to me. In those days of our novitiate, how pleasantly we wrought, "true yoke fellows," with never a jar or a difference from then till now. Fanny—I must call her so, even if she is a "National Superintendent"—used to come over from her elegant home at the Sherman House to my dingy office in the Y. M. C. A., and there we planned our small campaigns; but how huge they seemed to us then! We helped to carry on that blessed "three-o'clock gospel temperance meeting" in Lower Farwell Hall, where so many men have found Christ in the eight years of its steady work. We held afternoon and evening meetings in church parlors; we

12

spoke at the Newsboys' Home; we received temperance
calls on New Year's Day; we climbed together up the
stairs of printing offices, and swung aloft in the dizzying
"elevator" to editorial sanctums; we went to Springfield,
and spoke in the stately Hall of Representatives for
"Home Protection." Not for some years did my gentle
friend differentiate into her chosen work for girls, by
which she is now known wherever the W. C. T. U. has
gained a foothold. In her New York home, with such
grand friends as Mrs. Margaret Bottome, Mrs. Mary Lowe
Dickinson, and that true-hearted "Lady Bountiful," Mrs.
James Talcott, Mrs. Barnes is steadily building up the
different departments of a model Y. W. C. T. U. Mrs.
F. W. Evans is her Secretary and staunch ally. There
is no prettier sight in bewildering New York than the
charming home of Mrs. Barnes, in whose manifold and
bright mosaic her own identity seems tangled, where she
sits with quiet young Mrs. Evans, "planning the National
work." "The Boys' Loyal Temperance Legion" is a
great success, and parlors are soon to be opened for the
Y. W. C. T. U. But in that mighty Babel the laborers
are few, and I have letters half droll and half pathetic,
from my gentle friend. In one of them she said: "Think
pitifully of me — prayerfully too --- for in this roaring
Gotham I am the veriest, futile atom of temperance dust."

Mrs. Barnes has the choice endowment of a sunny,
loving spirit, a versatile mind, a piquant style, and happy
gifts of speech and pen. She might be a poet if she only
had time; of this her "Easter Lilies" is sufficient proof.
At the Louisville National Convention (1882) she gave
her annual report in a delightful fashion. Coming before
the great audience with an exquisite basket of flowers,
and gracefully "suiting the action to the word," she gave
a "floral report" of the young women's work, representing the different localities by flowers indigenous to them
or whose language was appropriate.

From every word and deed of Mrs. Barnes shines forth
the gentleness of the true Christian lady. Her work as
an ambassador of Christ is but begun.

ANNA A. GORDON.

On a dim February day in 1877, Berkeley Street Congregational Church, Boston, was crowded with women.
They had come over from the great Tabernacle meeting,
held every forenoon by Mr. Moody, and were now to have,
as was the daily custom during the three months of that
marvelous revival, a noon meeting of their own.

The lady who was to lead found herself in a trying
position, for the organist was late. Turning to the
audience, she called for a volunteer musician. There
was an ominous silence—a craning of necks to see if
anybody would come forward—but no response. The
dilemma became painful, and the request was renewed in
terms of entreaty. "Was this music-famed Boston, and
yet not a lady—not a young lady—even would come forward for His dear sake, in whose name we were met, to
lead us in a hymn of praise?" A moment's pause ensued,
and then along the aisle, with quiet step, came a slight
figure in the garb of mourning. A winsome, spiritual
face smiled deprecatingly into that of the leader, and a
gentle voice said simply: "I will try."

This was sweet Anna Gordon's "first appearance on
any stage," but from that day she has been quietly going forward in the work of the W. C. T. U., with whose varied
methods she is as familiar as any person living, and which
she has served without money and without official honors,
in a spirit so gentle, unselfish, and meek as to win for her
a place in every heart.

It is worth while to look below the surface in a life so
unique and a character so rounded.

Anna Adams Gordon was born in Boston, christened

by Rev. Nehemiah Adams, for one of whose daughters she was named, and became a member of the Congregational Church in Auburndale, a Boston suburb, at the age of twelve. A lovelier Christian home cannot be found than that from which she had the rare fortune to derive both "nature and nurture." Her father, James M. Gordon, was for ten years Treasurer of the American Board of Commissioners for Foreign Missions, and among his seven children no one inherits so much of his strong yet strangely gentle individuality. Her mother is the incarnation of unselfish character. Both have rare vocal gifts, and the morning hymn at family worship, led by the parents, with their four daughters and three sons taking the different parts, has lifted many a tired soul almost to the gates of paradise. In later years, after Anna became my faithful friend and invaluable Secretary, how many times has the music at this fireside rested me as neither psalm nor sermon could! For these were Christians, every one, and sang, not with the understanding only, but the Spirit. As I went out from the sweet shelter of their home, how often have they chanted, as is their custom on the morning of a guest's departure, the 121st psalm ("The Lord shall bless thy going out and thy coming in from this time forth, even forever more")! In such an atmosphere was trained the oldest child, now Alice Gordon Gulick, the well-known missionary to Spain, who, equally with her husband, carries on the church and school at San Sebastian. In such a home lived Mary, the second daughter with her sweet gift of song, whose death, two years ago, removed one of the loveliest spirits that ever passed from earth to heaven. What wonder that of the five children now living one is in the foreign, and one (Prof. Henry Gordon, of Trinidad, Colorado), in the home missionary field, a third (Anna) in the temperance work, while Miss Bessie Gordon—the peer of any in beauty of character—stays at home, that her parents may not be lonely, and is the center of the Young Women's work of Auburndale, and a second brother, amid the temptations of a young business man at the South, holds firm to his religious principles, of which total abstinence is one.

Mount Holyoke, that glorious monument of glorious Mary Lyon, was the schooling place of these earnest women workers, and carried forward the development so auspiciously begun by their inheritance and home environment.

But the depths of the young soul whose history we would depict were never stirred until sorrow troubled the pool. She had gone quietly along the pleasant path of life, studious of books and music, observant of the splendid object lesson afforded by her native city, thoughtful when the noble men and women who were so often guests in her home had told of the world's sin and sorrow. She was tender in heart, so that she needed not the lovely lesson of Cowper's lines,

> "Never to blend thy pleasure or thy pride
> With sorrow of the meanest thing that feels."

She had a love of nature so acute that when a little child of three years old, she was coming home from church in early spring, she broke away from her mother's guiding hand to run in at an open gate and kneel beside a bed of violets, the first she had ever seen in bloom; while she threw her little arms around the wee, shy posies, and cried out, almost with tears, "O, mamma, I didn't know that!"

She had spent a year abroad, chiefly in Spain, and would, perhaps, have been a missionary but for the "home ache" for her parents and her native land. But the eternal stars outshine only when it is dark enough. Her blithe young spirit had up to this time dwelt at ease. Rowing her adventurous boat along the classic Charles, or skating merrily over its frozen surface; the life of sleighing par-

ties, picnics, and Christmas festivities,—no hand had cast
the plummet line of a great purpose into her deepest
heart.   Less than a month before we met in the dim
church of Berkeley street, Anna had seen the light die
out forever from eyes she dearly loved; her noble brother
Arthur, a gifted, heavenly-minded boy of eighteen, her life-
long comrade, had suddenly died.   She had never before
seen death, and it was terrible.   Closing his eyes with
her own firm, tender touch, she knelt beside the bed, and
in such heart-break as the soul knows but once, dedicated
her life to Christ in the service of humanity.   Everything was different after that.   She saw what life is for.
She knew it could not be to her a summer holiday.   Timid
by nature, and conservative in training, her first hope was
that, with her passionate love of music, it might be her
vocation to inspire and lift up human hearts through the
medium of the organ.   But there was other work for her.
She had never heard a woman speak yet her prejudices
were not difficult to overcome.   Soon we were steadfast
friends.   She played for me all through the Boston meetings, and in Park Street church stood tremulously before
the audience, and for the first time publicly witnessed for
Christ in language.

One day I placed in Anna's hand a bundle of letters,
containing invitations for me to speak through the New
England States.   " Please answer these," I said, " making
out a trip for me at your discretion."   This was another
of the " new departures," all of which she has taken so
quietly.   Ten days later she brought me a neat little book
with the trip admirably arranged, every train carefully
marked, the name of every place of entertainment indicated ; in short, the whole trip so minutely planned that
I went through it like an express package labeled " with
care."   From that time this clear-brained, quick-witted
girl has been my secretary, traveling with me in nearly

every State and Territory of the nation, an "organized Providence" superintending every detail of my life and work. But she has been far more than this. The famous Home Protection campaign of Illinois, by which in nine weeks we secured 180,000 signatures, and festooned the Hall of Representatives at Springfield with a petition one-fifth of a mile long, was more largely Anna Gordon's work than that of any other, though until now this had not been avowed. The three trips South were chiefly planned by her. Indeed, she is so superior to any one I have ever known in arranging a lecture trip that, after a month's experience with a well known lyceum bureau, during which I was exploited over the country with as little regard to comfort as if I had been an alligator, I returned to Miss Gordon's fostering care with inexpressible relief and gratitude. But in the young women's work her place is second to none. She often speaks in public, and always with acceptance ; she organizes with a skill and method which her "senior partner" vainly emulates ; and writes letters, "between times," with the quiet persistency of a perpetual motion. Sometimes I look up from the steady grind of work "on the cars" and see "far-away thoughts" in the little woman's face, when, lo ! a few minutes later, she places a sweet bit of verses in my hand ; sometimes gay, but often full of pathos. These she never permits to see the light, though I have surreptitiously confiscated one or two wee manuscripts for our paper. My purpose in giving these details of this young woman's life work is two-fold. I know she has thousands of friends who will enjoy and be helped by them ; but, more than that, I see in fancy the faces of the bright girls I love, in homes all over this broad land, bending over the pages where this record of a gracious young life is made, and I pray that some sweet sense of the power to "go and do likewise" may stir their gentle spirits as they read.

THE YOUNG WOMEN AT SCHOOL.

One evening, in 1878, the W. C. T. U. held a meeting in the great Lecture Hall of Michigan University, at Ann Arbor. It was my part to speak of young women's influence. A message was handed me, when I had finished, to this effect: " The lady students of the university are coming forward to put their names upon the pledge roll and receive the red ribbon. They do this as a sacred duty, in the interest of their brother students, and earnestly request that there may be no applause." Knowing the uproarious customs of collegians, I feared the petition had been made in vain, for the galleries were filled with young men. But no; in perfect silence those brave girls moved forward down the aisle, and in silence registered their names, and took the badge of the Reform Club. Professor Olney, whose mathematical works are so well known, and who is one of the noblest temperance men in all the land, was chairman of the meeting. When the young ladies had resumed their seats, Robert Frazer, a gifted lawyer, reformed man, and alumnus of the university, asked permission to speak. He said:

" Mr. Chairman: I have always been conservative on the question of women's higher education and wider work. To the extent of my power I opposed their admission to the privileges of my alma mater. But to-night I've had a change of heart, and I say, God forgive me, and God bless them! They'll save us men if we give them half a chance. And now, boys, you've been gentlemen and respected the wish of these young ladies. But I say we've had a glimpse of the moral sublime, and here goes for three cheers for the girls that signed the pledge. *Hip-hip-hurrah!* "

Wellesley College, that palatial school founded by Henry F. Durant of Boston, and presided over by gifted

Miss Alice Freeman, Ph. D., has a thriving Y. W. C. T. U. of one hundred members and furnishes a course of lectures in the interest of temperance, besides conducting a Band of Hope in a manufacturing village near by. Its president is a young lady in her senior year. Alleghany College, Meadville, Pa., has also a model society among its lady students, and invited Hon. Neal Dow to give an address upon "Commencement Day." The good accomplished by these associations is beyond computation. They furnish "society" in the best and noblest sense. Their pleasures are such as do not "perish in the using."

THE KITCHEN GARDEN.

The "newest thing" in Y. W. C. T. U. work is the "kitchen garden." Miss Mary McClees of Yonkers, N. Y., is at the head of this department in the National Union, and is most successful in her work, having organized in Baltimore, Louisville, and elsewhere. The general plan is to teach by object lessons the complete duty of a housekeeper, keeping time to the movements of bed-making, table-setting, sweeping, etc., by music and songs that teach just how to do these things properly. Each girl has a doll's bed completely fitted out, and makes it, to music, in the most approved style; the rhymes sung helping to fix firmly in the mind the very best rules for exercising the art. Breakfast and dinner are prepared and served—in fancy's eye, as to the food—but with table, cloth, napkins, and crockery complete. Sweeping and dusting are carried out to perfection, also tending the door, going to market, and many other exercises. Interspersed with these lessons can be temperance songs and lessons, *ad libitum*, and the giving out of temperance books and stories. Mrs. F. R. Tuttle is superintendent of this work in Cleveland, and to see her teaching these girls to make a graceful bow is a picture, indeed

—the model being so full of womanly attractiveness. A lady recently came to Miss Minnie Gillette of that city, at the close of her charming kitchen garden exhibition, and said she would like to engage one of the class as a servant—which is precisely what the temperance ladies hope may result from the general introduction of this work, to the great advantage of both mistress and maid.

This branch of work enlists fashionable young ladies who would not be likely to interest themselves in more direct temperance methods, but who in this way learn to understand the relation of good food and good housekeeping to habits of sobriety. Beginning with the kitchen garden, they are quite likely to take all the degrees of temperance work in the natural evolution of their knowledge and experience.

SENSIBLE GIRLS.

A number of Maine girls have formed a protective union, and adopted a series of resolutions for their government. The following extract from the constitution and by-laws gives a very fair idea of the nature, aims, and objects of the society: " That we will receive the attention of no self-styled young gentleman who has not learned some business or engaged in some steady employment; for it is apprehended that after the bird is caught it may starve in the cage. That we will promise marriage to no young man who is in the habit of tippling or using tobacco, for we are assured that his wife will come to want and his children go barefooted. That we will marry no young man if he is not a patron of his neighborhood newspaper, for it is not only a strong evidence of his want of intelligence, but that he will prove too stingy to provide for his family, to educate his children, or encourage institutions of learning in his community."

AN APPEAL TO MEMBERS OF THE W. C. T. U. WHO ARE
GOING ABROAD.

Dear sisters,— Your loyalty to the " Muster Roll
Pledge " of the great total abstinence army is about to
be tested on the field. Perhaps the captain will ask you
to take wine with him at the very first dinner " on board."
Unquestionably the good physician will prescribe champagne as the specific for sea sickness. Absolutely a
chorus of " more experienced " travelers beyond the sea,
will warn you against the danger of drinking water, far
more than they would against the danger of drinking
drams. But your sisters are persuaded that we shall
hear better things of you. Like a lovely girl to whom one
of us said good-bye this morning, wishing her " bon
voyage," and saying, " Be loyal—don't touch wine;" you
will answer, " Trust me—I will not forget."

In carrying out this noble resolution, you may be
fortified by facts like these: Mr. Thomas Cook, the most
persistent of tourists, says that in his lifetime of voyag-
ing, including trips around the world, he has been a strict
teetotaller, and with the happiest results.

Bishops of the Methodist Church who travel in Asia
and Africa, as well as Europe, have told me concurrent
experience in exactly the same line ; also ministers representing many denominations have corroborated this
testimony.

Some of our own members joined parties last summer,
in which they were the only total abstainers, and by
parity of reasoning, the only ones who escaped the harmful effects against which their companions vainly attempted
to provide.

Boiled water or milk can always be had, and will
always be far safer than any stimulating drink. May
you, dear friends, exhibit the courage of your convictions

as you journey, and come back to us with pledge un-
tarnished and health restored, or unimpaired, is the earnest prayer of your sister and friend.

"THE W. T. U. WILL RECEIVE."

So far as I can learn, the first announcement of this
kind on record, was made in the Chicago papers a few
days before the New Year in 1875.   A dozen of our
leading ladies spent the day at headquarters in the
Y. M. C. A.   We had nearly a hundred calls, many signers
to the pledge, and some brief prayer meeting scenes, which
my heart recalls with fervent gratitude.   The announcement that follows we made to our unions at large in
1877 :

"The first New Year's Day of America's second
century is just at hand.   How may we fitly signalize it,
as workers in a reform which means as much more to
our country's future than civil service or currency reforms, as home means more than bank or office ?   In the
long past, women with Circean blandishments have done
what other women, gentle and loving, have ignorantly
imitated, and by means of both, the New Year festival
has been too often a reminder of bacchanalian feasts.   But
in the land we love, civilization's choicest flower, the world's
hope, and scene of Christ's most blessed triumphs, it shall
not be so any more.   There is a ' right about face' in the
attitude of public sentiment.   Banished from presidential
receptions, governors' banquets, and social reunions, 'the
wine cup in the jeweled hand' is rapidly becoming a relic
of the past.   The appeals sent forth by so many of our
unions in these two years succeeding the Crusade, have
not been useless.   Let us repeat them through the local
press this year, in every town where our organization
exists, and make them specially emphatic; and whenever
practicable, let us do more than this.   Last year, in

many places, the ladies' temperance headquarters were adorned with evergreens and mottoes, in some instances made attractive by 'refreshments,' and here a committee appointed for the purpose received the calls of gentlemen interested in the cause, and of those also who wished on that auspicious day to 'turn over a new leaf.' Many a poor fellow would screw his courage to the sticking point of signing the pledge under the impetus of Christian sympathy thus expressed, who otherwise might fail. We do not speak at random, but testify of what we have seen in the office of our union at Chicago, where we have spent the two most delightful 'New Years' of our lives—as much sweeter than the ceremonious 'occasions' of other days, as it is sweeter to minister of heavenly things than to be ministered unto of earthly things. Shall it not be then that along with other 'social events pertaining to the season,' we shall see in many a newspaper the significant announcement, 'The W. C. T. Union will receive.' (By the way, an adorned 'mite box,' with appropriate inscription, might give a secondary meaning to the words, which friends of temperance would doubtless heed!)"

NOBLER THEMES.

Doubtless it is well that our temperance women think but little of the incalculable advantage of the movement to themselves. Among unsympathetic outsiders, however, no observation is more frequent than that "The W. C. T. Unions are accomplishing good things for women, even if they are not doing much for temperance." For ourselves we prefer that concerning woman's kingdom, which, we are persuaded, is closely related to the kingdom of Heaven, it should also be truly said, "It cometh not by observation."

The "Human Question," including in it the woman question, as a circle includes an arc, is the objective point we aim at; for the "Everybody Chorus" is to our ears the most inspiring music this side the hallelujah chorus of Heaven. We want no solo of bass or soprano—we want no Paganini twanging one string, even though his art were magical. Give us the orchestra! But all the same, we are thankful to note the rapid development of our members in power and clearness of mental grasp, vigor of expression, business ability, knowledge of parliamentary usage, and many other particulars which tend toward that personality which is the glory of the home as of the State. For as it is the study of a florist to differentiate and perfect the undeveloped into the individualized plant, so in God's glorious human garden there is no work so significant to the well-being of all, as the fullest evolution of each into his best—*her* best. Beyond all who have ever lived, Christ was the prophet and the priest of *individuality*. In Sparta the person existed but for the State; in a Christian civilization, all offices and ordinances find their *raison d'etre* in the person, and justify their being only in so far as they develop and ennoble him—and her. But in turn, this is for the sake of the whole. In no particular have we been more impressed with this growth of our Christian workers, than in their themes of conversation. Truly "their speech bewrayeth them." They learn to look beyond home's four walls, and take an interest in the larger home of social and governmental life. The widening march of our society is quite correctly indicated by the increasing number of women who read the newspapers and can tell you what the legislature is doing! When two of our members meet, they condense their observations on the weather, the servant girl, and the family ailments, that they may discuss the new plan of district work and the conduct of City Council and State Legislature. The opinions of Canon Farrar and Dr. Richardson are as familiar to them as were the views held by Mrs. A. concerning Mrs. B.'s milliner, in the days of our grandmothers. God's great gift of speech never willingly but often ignorantly abused by women, was never turned to nobler uses than in the seven years past. But there remaineth much territory to be possessed. The solitude of the masculine intellect must be still further invaded. We could mention a home of beauty and thrift, whose hospitable board is surrounded by lovely daughters and noble sons, and whose head is a man of rare and gifted nature, and yet, so thoroughly has "small talk in the family," that relic of oriental habitude, permeated the modes of expression even in this Christian home, that the table talk is a dreary waste of platitudes. Interested in every great cause, conversant with all the philanthropic movements of the day, and ready to bear a generous part therein, these Christian people content themselves on intellectual husks, when there is bread enough to spare. The different dishes and their flavor; the history and mystery of the day's doings in the kitchen and among the pets; the false reports of "Old Probs," these, with impossible conundrums and puns, altogether unpardonably fill up the hour.

Emerson says, "We invariably descend to meet," an observation, the subtilty of which is illustrated by a million tea-tables even at this hour. Let us hope, however, that this statement is historic only, and not prophetic. For, behold! in the sitting-room or on the piazza, the gentlemen of the household referred to, adjourned from tea, begin with one accord to talk of themes more level to their intellectual status. Affairs of church and State, the leading editorial in a great metropolitan daily, Cook's lectures, Crosby's sermon, Gladstone's land bill, Garfield's Southern policy, all these come to the surface, and in discussing them how quick their utterance, how intelligent their analysis. Meanwhile the sisterhood go their way, and if they think their thoughts concerning these discrepancies between household gossip and post-prandial conversation, no looker-on in Venice is the wiser for their lucubrations. Brethren and sisters, these things ought not so to be, and to help unify the thought and talk of home, our W. C. T. U. is one of the grandest institutions that has been invented up to date.

"ALL FOR TEMPERANCE."

So far as possible, this should be our motto and our rallying cry. Let us claim everything that is good, whether it be great or small, as ours by affinity and adoption. The other day, at Newark, N. J., in the Temperance Convention of Essex County, we had a fresh illustration of what I mean. Noble men and true had called the meeting; that devoted Newark W. C. T. U. was out in force, with the Christian Reform Club its "Guard of Honor." Rev. Dr. L. H. Dunn was in the chair. We were in thorough working humor—you could see the spirit beaming in each face. Dr. Dunn came forward at the close of a speech, and said, "Sing 'Auld Lang Syne.'" Now, it is a blessed tune, and full of sweetness and tender memories; but we could by no means tolerate its bacchanalian allusions. Think of an audience of zealous temperance campaigners declaring,

> "We'll tak' a right good Willy waught,"

Or—

> "We'll tak' a cup o' kindness yet,
> For auld lang syne."

But in these days, when temperance claims all good things for its own, our genial chairman readily found a a way out of the difficulty by the following amendment: "Sing, 'Am I a soldier of the Cross?' to the tune of 'Auld Lang Syne.'" These words cut the Gordian knot, and if ever hearts and voices joined with "a right good will," it was in the last verse:

> " Thy saints, in all this glorious war,
>   Shall conquer though they die;
> *They see the triumph from afar,*
>   *By faith they bring it nigh.*"

Since then the following beautiful version of "Auld Lang Syne" has come to light. It is destined to replace the words which embalm social customs from which our more kindly and enlightened age is fast emerging. So the good work goes on, and shall deepen and extend until poetry, music, and romance—last of all citadels to yield— become strongholds of total abstinence sentiment as now, alas! they are of the sentimentalism which looks with toleration upon inebriety.

The New Old Lang Syne.

" It singeth low in every heart,
   We hear it, each and all,
 A song for those who answer not,
   However we may call.

" They throng the silence of the breast,
   We see them as before,
 The brave, the kind, the true, the sweet,
   Who walk with us no more.

" 'Tis hard to take life's burden up,
   When these have laid it down,
 They sweetened every joy of life,
   They softened every frown.

" But O, 'tis good to think of them,
   When we are troubled sore;
 The brave, the kind, the true, the sweet,
   Who walk with us no more.

" More friendly seems the great Unknown,
   Since they have entered there;
 To follow them were not so hard,
   However they may fare.

" They cannot be where God is not,
   On any sea or shore;
 What e'er betides, Thy Love abides,
   Our God forever more."

MISS ESTHER PUGH,

Treasurer of National W. C. T. U.

Two of our workers were talking about epitaphs. Said
No. One: " Of all others yet penned, I would prefer to merit
these words upon my tombstone, ' She was dependable.' "
At this her comrade answered : " Whether you or I merit
so much may be an open question ; but I'll tell you who
does, and that's our ' watch-dog of the treasury,'—Esther
Pugh."

This is high, ante-funeral-oration praise, but we are
safe in putting it on record. One look into our Esther's
face, with its broad forehead arching above those solemn
brows and steadfast eyes, would settle that question in
the most doubtful mind. Like many another woman of
forceful life, " she is her father over again," the resemblance in features being no stronger than in character.
He was a man of iron mould and spotless reputation—a
Quaker of the Quakers, long the publisher of a leading
Cincinnati daily paper, and well reported for what a good
pastor of mine used to call " common religion," or Christianity applied to business dealings and other every-day
affairs.

The mother was all sweetness and loveliness in character, and was idolized by her strong-natured husband
and daughter. Miss Pugh was a leader at the dawn of
the Crusade ; indeed the Quakers have such sensible,
primitive views about " following the Master," that it did
not seem an unheard-of stepping out to them to " go tell "
the gospel story to those who, of all others, were least
likely to come and hear it inside the Lord's especial
courts.

Waynesboro, Ohio, was the scene of exploits that have
been often recounted in the annals of " the great
uprising," and which Miss Pugh narrates with exceeding
vivacity, having been foremost in that band.

MISS ESTHER PUGH.

It was in strict accordance with spiritual dynamic laws that, from those days to these, Esther Pugh has been closely identified with the W. C. T. U. She had the brain, the heart, and, best of all, the *will* to do this work. At first an officer in the Cincinnati Union, then in the State, and now for years in the National, she knows our W. C. T. U. by heart, and its friendships, work, and inspirations have been her solace in many recent sorrows—for father, mother, and the sheltering home conserved by their presence, all have passed away in these last years.

Esther Pugh is a woman for difficult emergencies. Some of us know how she has " stood in the gap" when any but a veteran would have beat a retreat. As editor and publisher of *Our Union*, she has faced duties at once irksome and difficult, but always with a fortitude little less than heroic. As the responsible, though not the actual head of the " Hayes Commission," she had thrust upon her the burden of grave decisions and heavy financial obligations, which she assumed without fee or reward, and carried with a skill and faithfulness worthy of all praise. But as Treasurer of the National W. C. T. U. she has earned the right to our profoundest gratitude. The forlorn hope of an empty exchequer occupies a position to the last degree unenviable, and, alas, too often thankless. If the facts could be known concerning her letters, circulars, interviews, and appeals for money to pay the actual current expenses of printing, postage, rent, etc., at our New York office; if the picture of our Treasurer, kneeling in prayer, with the unpaid bills before her and sometimes with tears upon her cheeks, could come to the knowledge of the good people who " believe in temperance," Esther Pugh's relation to our great and growing work would not be so difficult as it has been up to this day.

But I must not sketch my friend in lines too somber, for despite her trying rôle as custodian of an empty treasury, she is a woman of most cheerful spirit, sees the droll as well as the serious side of every situation, and brightens her letters, as she always does her conversation, with rare sallies of wit and pleasantry.

MRS. J. ELLEN FOSTER.

CHAPTER XX.

THE W. C. T. U. IN THE GOVERNMENT.

Mrs. Judith Ellen Foster—A Boston girl, a lawyer, an orator—Her work part and parcel of the W. C. T. U.—As wife, mother, and Christian—Philosophy of the W. C. T. U. in the Government—The Keithsburg election, or the "Women who dared"—The story of Rockford—Home protection in Arkansas—A practical application—Observations *en route*—The famous law—Extract from Fourth of July address—Local option—Plan for local campaign—How not to do it—How it has been done—Temperance tabernacles—History of Illinois' great petition—About petitions—Days of prayer—Copy of the petition—Home protection hymn—Mrs. Pellucid at the Capitol —A specimen Legislature—Valedictory thoughts—Temperance tonic —Yankee home protection catechism—A heart-sorrow in an unprotected home—The dragon's council hall—Home guards of Illinois— How one little woman saved the day in Kansas—Election day in Iowa—Incidents of the campaign—A Southern incident—Childhood's part in the victory.

MRS. JUDITH ELLEN FOSTER, OF IOWA.

A SKETCH of our Superintendent of the Legislative Department fitly opens the chapter on our work "in the Government."

"Blood will tell" is a pithy proverb, and one well illustrated in our "Temperance Portia's" vigorous brain, firm hand, and generous heart. Her father, Rev. Jotham Horton, was a typical son of New England, born in Boston in 1789; her mother, a native of Duxbury, on Cape Cod, was a descendent of General Warren, of Revolutionary fame. Under the preaching of Bishop Hedding her father was converted, and began to preach in the Methodist Church before he was twenty-one years of age. When convicted of sin he was also convicted of the duty

(321)

and beauty of total abstinence, and, when he pledged to the church his soldiership under the Captain of our salvation, he pledged himself never to touch intoxicating liquors. This was long before he ever heard of a temperance organization outside the Nazarites and Rechabites, so highly recommended in the Bible. For four years he worked in his father's blacksmith shop, and when the men drank rum " between the heats " he drank water, notwithstanding the derisive laugh of his comrades. They perished ignobly, but he endured, becoming one of New England's most successful preachers, foremost in all reforms; dowered with " the hate of hate, the scorn of scorn, the love of love," and in his gifted daughter still breathes and speaks his lofty and indomitable spirit. Terrible in denunciation and strong in argument, he hated sin, loved righteousness, and was a redoubtable soldier of Christ. Mrs. Foster's mother was a quite different type, the daughter of a sea-captain, reared in the quiet of a New England farm, she never met the world till called to stand beside this fiery champion of the cross. Beautiful in face and form and graceful in manner, she was the ideal complement of her husband. When Judith (for I can but call her thus, believing that the Iowa liquor traffic shall yet turn out to be her Holofernes,) was not quite seven years old, she lost this lovely mother. Born at Lowell, Mass., November 3, 1840, motherless at seven, and an orphan at twelve years of age, Judith Ellen's short life had already comprehended the most significant vicissitudes, when her oldest sister, Mrs. Charles Pierce, wife of a wealthy business man of Boston, received the young girl into her home and directed her education, first in the public schools of Boston, then at Charlestown Female Seminary, and last at the Genesee Wesleyan Seminary, Lima, N. Y. Her musical education was carried on in Boston, under the best teachers. After leaving school she taught briefly, but at twenty years of age (1860) she was married to a promising young merchant of the city.

Concerning this painful episode in her history, the following facts are furnished by a friend: "This union, desired and approved by mutual friends, promised naught but joy and blessedness; but clouds soon gathered, and after years of poverty and toil and wanderings to and fro, and vain attempts to cover up and bear the shame that came because she bore his name, nothing was left of this sad marriage but two children for her to love and rear. In the home of a brother she put on widow's weeds, sadder far than those that come at death."

Having secured a divorce, she was married to Hon. E. C. Foster, who is a prominent lawyer and politician of Iowa, a life-long temperance man, and earnest, working Christian.

She read law first for his entertainment, and afterwards, by his suggestion and under his supervision, she pursued a systematic course of legal study, with, however, no thought of admission to the bar. She read, with her babies about her, and instead of amusing herself with fashion plates or fiction, such learned tomes as Blackstone and Kent, Bishop and Story. She never had an ambition for public speaking or public life. Although reared in the Methodist church, she had never, until about the time of the crusade, heard a woman preach or lecture, but when that trumpet blast resounded, she, in common with her sisters, responded to the call, and lifted up her voice in protest against the iniquity of the drink traffic. Her acceptance with the people just at the time when she had completed her legal studies, seemed a providential indication, and her husband said: "If you can talk before an audience, you could before a court or jury"; and he insisted upon her being examined for admission to the

bar. Prior to this time she had prepared pleadings and
written arguments for the courts; but without formal
admission she could not personally appear. She was
examined, admitted, and took the oath to "support the
constitution and the laws." This triumph won the approbation of friends and the increased hatred of the liquor
party, who knew that it meant not only warfare upon the
temperance platform, but in the legal forum also. The
night of the day on which she was admitted to practice
saw her home in Clinton, Iowa, in flames. There was
little doubt that the fire was kindled by two liquor-sellers
whom Mr. Foster had prosecuted, and who had just
returned from the county jail. Mrs. Foster was the first
woman admitted to practice in the State supreme court.
She has recently defended a woman under sentence of
death, and after a ten days' trial, in which our lady lawyer made the closing argument, the verdict of the jury
was modified to imprisonment for life. Mrs. Foster
enjoys the absolute confidence and support of her husband
in her legal and temperance work. He was its instigator,
and more than any other rejoices in it.

Mrs. Foster has lost two little girls. Two sons remain,
one of whom is a student in the Northwestern University,
at Evanston, Ill., and another often accompanies his
mother in her work. In her own home Mrs. Foster is
universally honored, and for her beloved Iowa she has
grandly wrought from the beginning until now, when,
more by her exertions than those of any other individual,
the constitutional amendment has been ratified by the
people. Mrs. Foster's life, since the crusade of 1874, is
part and parcel of the W. C. T. U. She has never been
absent from one of our national conventions, and her
quick brain, ready and pointed utterance, and rare knowledge of parliamentary forms, have added incalculably to
the success of these great meetings. There is not a State

at the North in which our cause is not to-day more powerful than it would have been but for her logic and her
eloquence. Whether making her famous two hours' argument for the constitutional amendment, as she did night
after night for successive months in the Northwest, writing a treatise on that great subject, as she has lately done,
or following the intricacies of debate in a convention and
conducting a prayer-meeting between the sessions, whether
leading the music of an out-door meeting, answering Dr.
Crosby at Tremont Temple, Boston, pleading for woman's
ballot in Iowa, or for prohibition in Washington; whether
playing with her boys at home, reading Plato in the cars,
preaching the gospel from a dry-goods box on the street
corner of her own town, or speaking in the great tabernacle at Chautauqua, Mrs. Foster is always witty, wise, and
kind, and thorough mistress of the situation. Her husband's heart doth safely trust in her, and her boys glory
in a mother who can not only say with Cornelia, of Rome,
" These are my jewels," but whose great heart reaches
out to restore to the rifled casket of many another woman's
home, whence strong drink has stolen them, these gems
of priceless cost. Best of all, she loves the Lord Jesus
Christ, and above her chief joy desires and labors to build
up His kingdom on the earth.

PHILOSOPHY OF THE W. C. T. U. IN THE GOVERNMENT.

When a ray of light starts forth from the Sun of Righteousness, men may not limit its flight nor prescribe its
influence. When the fisherman, in "Arabian Nights,"
broke the strange kettle, and the genie emerged and " expanded its pinions in nebulous bars," it was a waste of
words to order the apparition back into the limits which,
once for all, it had escaped. When the Woman's Christian Temperance Union began its evolution, the law of
spiritual force predicted its expansion till, in the fullness

13

of time, its leaven should leaven the whole lump. What if, in fifty days, the crusade by its prayers and persuasions routed the liquor traffic, " horse, foot, and dragoons," out of two hundred and fifty towns and villages? Did they not spring up again like so many Canada thistles? What if, on three hundred and sixty-four days in the year, women wrought patiently to build defences around their homes with their moral suasion weapons, did not the voters carry them away as with a flood upon election day, intrenching the triumphant dram-shop behind the sheltering ægis of the commonwealth? What wonder, then, that by the most natural gradations; by growth rather than by a forcing process; " by evolution rather than by revolution," as Joseph Cook so aptly puts it, the W. C. T. U., passing through the stages of petition work, local-option work, and constitutional-prohibition-amendment work, have come to the conviction that women must have the ballot as a " home protection" weapon?

The long, slow marches of the years; the logic of events, and the argument of defeat in our warfare against the dram-shop; the strange discovery that the Ten Commandments and the Sermon on the Mount are voted up, or voted down, upon election day; the reiterated lesson in temperance arithmetic that, in spite of home, and church, and school; in spite of Y. M. C. A., and W. C. T. U., WHEN VOTERS MEET VOTERS, THE SIDE ALWAYS WINS THAT HAS MOST VOTES — all these have led us up to our conclusion. The men of the liquor traffic have themselves contributed not a little to our schooling. In their official organs, secret circulars to political aspirants, and by the mightier eloquence of votes paid for with very hard cash, they have united in the declaration (here given in their own words): "Woman's ballot will be the death knell of the liquor traffic!"

On the other hand, when our simple-minded temperance

women have gone to reputable men of affairs with the question: "Why is the sale of strong drink protected by law in our commonwealth?" the answer has invariably been: "Because the public sentiment seems to require it."

But we slowly learned to follow up that question with another far more significant, "*Whose* public sentiment; that of the church?" Oh, no; two-thirds of the church are women, and well do they understand that Christ's cause has no enemy so bitter and redoubtable as the traffic in strong drink.

"Whose public sentiment; that of the home?" Oh, no; the home guards have learned by pitiful experience that home—the shrine for the sake of which all that is pure and good on earth exists—has no enemy so subtle as the dram-shop.

"Whose public sentiment?" Why, that of men who make and sell the poisonous beverages; men who drink them, and other men dependent for patronage in business, professional life, and for political preferment on those who drink and sell.

These classes, as the outcome of deliberate choice, based upon selfish motives, saddle the liquor traffic on our communities, year after year. But all the while they were outraging the "public sentiment" lodged in the brain, heart, and conscience of the women in their homes!

Moreover, the class thus unrepresented in the most important decision that local government involves, is not committed to the liquor interest by any of the motives out of which the choices grew whose outcome was the license ballot in the fateful box. They are not entangled with business interests or partnerships; they have, as a rule, no connection with professional life; no aspirations for political preferment. By nature, and by the circumstances of their lives, they would bring to this decision a set of motives altogether new, and of resultant choices alto-

gether different. By not utilizing this " public sentiment '
at the point where a conviction can pass into a vote, and
a heart-break into a law, we temperance women became
convinced that good men conspicuously exhibited their
lack of the serpent-like wisdom which is as authoritatively
enjoined on Christian soldiers as is the dove-like harm-
lessness.

But while convinced that woman's ballot, for purposes
of home protection, must be the outcome of the temperance reform in its governmental phase, our W. C. T. U.
everywhere falls in with the prevailing sentiment as to its
legal work. In the South there is no effort to introduce
the " home protection movement," as this work for the
ballot is called. In Kansas and Iowa the women worked
hard for prohibition, and were proud and grateful that
the votes of men secured a boon so blessed. In Pennsylvania and Michigan they are " the power behind the
throne," in the present efforts towards the same end.
But all the same, their eyes have been opened to see that
(as a gifted one has said) " while prohibition is the nail,
woman's ballot is the hammer that must drive it home."
For while the issue is to a great extent non-partisan during the period of legislating for the prohibitory amendment itself, it must at once cease to be so when the
executive officers who alone give its provisions force are
to be chosen. For example, when in each locality the
magistrate, the sheriff, the constable are to be chosen,
then the liquor interest will rally its forces under one
party banner, and the temperance forces under another.
Precisely here comes in the " dead pull" in tugging
prohibition up the Hill Difficulty ; precisely here the votes
of women will turn the scale for temperance. Is this
doubted ?

THE KEITHSBURG ELECTION ; OR "THE WOMEN WHO DARED."

" The things which are impossible with men are possible with God."
" All things are possible to him that believeth."

The following letter wàs written by Miss Lois Smith of Rhode Island, in reply to the query, " What about the Keithsburg election ?"

MONMOUTH, Ill., April, 1880.

MY DEAR FRIEND—To begin at the beginning: While attending a district convention at Bushnell, Ill., last week, I became acquainted with the fact that the Town Board of Keithsburg, Ill., had recently passed a "Home Protection Ordinance" (and that unanimously), and that women over eighteen years of age, residing in the town, were by its provisions invited to vote "for license" or "against license," on Monday, the 5th day of April, 1880. The Keithsburg W. C. T. U., through a committee of twelve ladies, had explained the ordinance, and read the invitation to vote to every woman in the town (the work of this canvassing committee told on election day, I assure you). Now, thought I, "seeing is believing" it is said, and so I at once resolved that "Naomi" and I would be there to see. We accordingly made our way to Monmouth, stopped for the night at the hospitable residence of Mr. and Mrs. Kirkpatrick, and next morning, in company with Mrs. M. L. Wells of Springfield, and Mrs. E. G. Hibben of Peoria (the newly-elected successor of Frances E. Willard), President of Illinois W. C. T. U., we set off for "the seat of war." Keithsburg is a town of about fifteen hundred inhabitants, in Mercer county, Illinois, on the Mississippi river, "beautiful for situation," and but for the unenviable fact of being the only " license " corporation in the county, would be a thriving little town. Upon our arrival at Keithsburg we were received at the depot by Mrs. Slocum, the energetic President of the W. C. T. U., with a carriage and horses, and speedily transferred to her own and other homes of Keithsburg.

PRELIMINARY MEETING.

At half-past three o'clock P. M. we met the ladies of the W. C. T. U., and some of the citizens, in the Presbyterian Church for conference. The meeting was held at the close of the preparatory sermon previous to the Sacrament of the Lord's Supper. I sat in amazed meditation and reflected. Here we are, holding this meeting, and talking about the voting of women, in immediate connection with this especial religious service, in a Presbyterian meeting house ! Shade of the Puritans ! How this world is moving on ! The meeting was opened with prayer by Lois L. Smith; Mrs. Hibben and Mrs. Wells addressed the ladies present, and Messrs. Pepper and Taliaferro answered the questions concerning the ordinance, etc., closing with prayer by Cassie L. Smith.

There was a temperance mass meeting held in the evening, addressed by Mr. Pepper, at the M. E. Church.

SABBATH.

The use of the M. E. Church was kindly given, and meetings held in the forenoon and evening. At eleven A. M. Mrs. Hibben read the Scripture lessons, and prayer was offered by Cassie L. Smith. The following telegram from Miss Frances E. Willard was read: "Eager eyes are watching you from a thousand darkened homes. God help you to be brave and true!" Lois L. Smith spoke as God gave her utterance, from Ephesians 6: 12, 13, "For we wrestle not against flesh and blood," endeavoring to show the true nature of the liquor traffic (*i. e.*, actuated by Satanic power), and the means to be used for its overthrow, viz.: a holy, consecrated Church, using such weapons as God has ordained.

At half-past two P. M. a Children's Meeting was held in the Presbyterian Church, conducted by Cassie L. Smith.

At half-past four P. M. Mr. I. M. Kirkpatrick of Monmouth, whose interest in the occasion was such that he had procured a substitute for an engagement that he had made to speak in a neighboring town on that day, in order that he might be present at the Keithsburg election, spoke with apparently Methodistic fire and fervor at the most public street corners, using a lumber wagon for a pulpit, after the fashion of pioneer Methodist preachers.

The evening meeting was addressed by Mrs. Hibben and Mrs. Wells. The singing during the day and at nearly all the subsequent meetings was led by a grand choir of young women, of whom there are a goodly number in the Keithsburg W. C. T. U., which is but four months organized, and numbers seventy members. Their singing contributed much to the interest and success of the meeting.

ELECTION DAY.

Monday at seven A. M., a prayer-meeting of rare spiritual power was led by Mrs. Hibben, who opened the meeting by announcing the hymns, "Where He leads we will follow," and "Triumph by-and-bye." Reading 121st Psalm and 124th Psalm. Requests for prayer: for the salvation of six men with whom I talked yesterday; for four young ladies who are undecided; for Keithsburg W. C. T. U., and for the young men and young women of Keithsburg. This request was made by Mrs. Taliaferro, and accompanied by a tearful exhortation for many loved ones. Mrs. Hibben led in prayer for these requests, and was evidently helped with the divine unction while she prayed. Singing: "I will sing of my Redeemer," followed by the reading of Dean Trench's poem on prayer, "Lord what a change within us one short hour." Prayer by Cassie L. Smith for following requests: for the men of Keithsburg who are wavering; for young men, about whom there is a special whisky influence; for little boys of Keithsburg. Also prayer by Mrs. Wells. Singing: "Hallelujah, 'tis done." Mrs. Hibben then read a letter from a reformed man, a German, and formerly an infidel. Other prayers and requests. Singing: "I need Thee every hour." Miss Cassie L. Smith then asked the question: "Who will be on the Lord's side?" and nearly every person present arose, among them a number who were not professing Christians; then Lois L. Smith led in a prayer of consecration, "while heaven came down our souls to greet, and glory crowned the mercy seat." "Blest be the tie that binds" was then sung, and the first company of women, forty-seven in number, proceeded quietly to the place for voting. It was my rare good fortune to take on my arm an aged Presbyterian lady, of Southern birth and education, who could hardly tell how such strange things had come about, but was nevertheless not behind in her duty on this important day, and also to attend Baby Slocum in his phæton while his papa and mamma went together to deposit their ballots. During the day the Keithsburg band volunteered their services, "because it was the first time the women ever voted, you know."

The election proceeded very quietly, and all hands agreed there never was such an election day. Several men who had always voted "for license," came with their wives and voted "against license." One man who had always voted the whisky ticket said: "I could stand everything but the woman's prayers. I shall vote no license." He was present at the seven A. M. prayer-meeting. Young Mr. Taliaferro said that, so far as he could learn, all the young men who voted for the first time, voted the "anti-license ticket" for town board as well as "against license."

At five P. M. of election day. One hundred and fifty-four women have voted up to this time. One lady said, "I have lived to see my prayers answered. My son and three daughters have voted together against whisky." Banners are out with "Bad luck to whisky," and "Down with License." The band is playing and the enthusiasm rises. Temperance ahead. Men who have formerly voted whisky are running their teams to gather up votes for "temperance." Much to our regret Mrs. Hibben was obliged to leave on the afternoon train for Chicago. "God bless you women," she said, as the omnibus in which we accompanied her to the depot passed the voting place where the women were hard at work.

EVENING OF ELECTION DAY.

Meeting at the M. E. Church at half-past seven P. M. The singers were on hand, and sang with inspiration, although many of them had been working hard all day, and were very weary.

Lois L. Smith read Psalms 81 and 82. (I didn't dare read "Then sang Deborah," until the election returns were announced, although I had two places in my Bible opened, awaiting developments.)

Cassie L. Smith led the expectant congregation in prayer. The choir sang again, and just then the messenger came with the election returns, and our hearts swelled unutterably full of thanksgiving to the prayer-answering God as the announcement was made, "No license in Keithsburg! A clean sweep for temperance!" The figures were slightly incorrect. The following is the official statement kindly furnished to me by the clerk. (Three women were among the judges and clerks of the election):

Anti-license for Town Board, - - - - -	517
For license, - - - - - - - -	451

(These tickets were of course only voted by men.)

ON THE QUESTION OF LICENSE OR NO LICENSE.

Women voting against license, - - - - -	159
Men, - - - - - - - - -	98
Men for license, - - - - - - -	1

Not one woman for license. The intense enthusiasm of the hour is impossible to describe. The choir sang "Hurrah! hurrah!" and "Glory, Hallelujah!" After the excitement had measurably subsided, Mrs. Wells, who had been announced as the speaker for the evening, began her address, but she was soon interrupted by the band, who came at once on their reception of the joyful news, to serenade "the women."

Mrs. President Slocum immediately invited them to take seats in the church, and for two hours the people rejoiced greatly with songs and speech making. Several men signed the pledge—one, the son of an invalid mother, for whom many prayers had been offered. 'Twas a wonderful day! The answers to prayer were so marked that we were constrained to say, as one after another the requests that were made at the early morning prayer meeting were fulfilled: "Give unto the Lord the glory due unto His name." A deep undercurrent of spiritual power pervaded the community, and I was reminded of the saying of good Esther Pugh, as she tells of the days when the crusade began, "Our chief thought was, God is here." God was there, at Keithsburg. I paused at one time on the street and looked down its length toward the river, and I wished I could photograph the whole. Young men and maidens, old men, women and children, all working for the right, and not a few faithful women were endeavoring to win souls for Christ along the highway.   There is now a demand for revival work that seems to be so imperative that it is difficult to deny, but our engagements are fixed.   It is impossible to remain.   It was an eventful day, but the end is not yet.   "So may all thy enemies perish, O Lord."

THE STORY OF ROCKFORD.

Illinois has hardly another town so beautiful for situa-tion as Rockford, on the rolling river beloved by some of us from childhood's sacred days.   The crusade took a deep hold here, and Mrs. Henry lived out the pages of her well-known book, "The Pledge and Cross," in the real work of Rockford W. C. T. U.   Here have "borne and labored and had patience," those elect ladies, Mrs. Backus, Mrs. Wilkins, and Mrs. Melancthon Starr, with their worthy coadjutors.   Conservative by nature and by prac-tice, this W. C. T. U. was reluctant to fall into line when the White Ribbon Regiment of Illinois, moved gently to the front and planted firmly "once for all" its Home Protection Banner.   Twelve towns of the Prairie State permitted women to vote on the question of license, and in them all the "Home Guards" fulfilled the predictions of their friends by outlawing the liquor traffic.   As year after year passed on, and our Rockford sisters learned by what they suffered from the mighty power by which the sovereign citizen throws around the dram-shop the guarantees and safeguards of the State, they took a solemn resolution.   In pursuance thereof, a petition was carried to the city council (T. B. Wilkins, the hus-band of Mrs. Wilkins, being mayor) asking, that since by the laws of Illinois, the question of licensing dram-shops is left discretionary with the local authorities, they should pass an ordinance under which they should be pledged to grant no licenses, if by popular vote of men and women over twenty-one years of age, the majority should declare against license. Such an ordinance was adopted, and the spring campaign was entered upon with energy, the ladies canvassing the city with their petitions, and going to the polls two thousand strong. Now, be it remembered that Rockford is a manufacturing town, with a large foreign population, but that notwithstanding this, hundreds of poor women and foreign women put on their best Sunday attire and marched in the procession that day to drop in their *no license* ballots, while but two women (and they homeless and debased) voted in favor of continuing dram-shops among the institutions of a town in which mothers were to rear their children.

Mrs. Wilkins wrote me as follows:

Manufacturers, ministers, merchants, doctors, lawyers—all classes, indeed—came with their wives to the polls, with as much good feeling and dignity as they would manifest in going to church. Young women came alone or in pairs. We had a quiet, pleasant day—no disturbances or need of police in the whole city. Even our enemies confessed in the papers next day that their prophecies concerning that election, viz., that the best women would not vote, and we should have disorder at the polls, had failed.

But note the sequel. While women, under the special ordinance, were voting on the " non-partisan " question of "license or no license," the liquor interest had its party ticket in the field, and, though good men wrought valiantly, there was not enough who " stood up to be counted " to make a majority; consequently a license board was elected, the ordinance under which the women voted was at once repealed, and dram shops flourished like the green bay tree.

Note also that if the women, too, had been permitted to vote for the officers themselves, as well as on the abstract question of license (that is, for the enforcer as well as the enforcement Act), the majority would have been overwhelming for prohibition. An ounce of fact is worth a ton of theory.

"HOME PROTECTION" IN ARKANSAS.

We met in the Hall of Representatives at Little Rock, where, in 1880, through the efforts of temperance men and women, a law was passed by which, within three miles of a church or school-house, the sale of intoxicating liquors could be prohibited by the will of the majority of the *men and women*, expressed in the form of their signatures to a petition. Delegates to this grand jubilee were present from all parts of the State, the majority being ministers, lawyers, and editors, those three mighty factors in the problem of public sentiment. Unlike most of our Northern States, Arkansas boasts a judiciary wherein almost every member is a friend of this law by which the people actually rule.

These dignified gentlemen were out in force, and their opinions had great weight with the audiences which for three days and evenings assembled in the historic hall. My notes of several leading addresses will best reproduce the impression which has so renewed my strength as a temperance advocate.

Rev. H. R. Withers, a pioneer preacher and editor, spoke somewhat as follows:

Nearly forty years ago Dr. R. L. Dodge, a young medical missionary from Vermont, was sent out by the American Board of Foreign Missions to help evangelize the Creek Indians. He rode two thousand miles on horseback, from Danville, Pa., to Fort Gibson. Ten years later he established the first temperance paper ever known in the then wild State of Arkansas. He had a heart as big as the wilderness around him and true as the stars that lighted his pathway through the forest. Pure and clear, but small and almost unheeded, he sent forth his clarion voice for prohibition. Yonder he sits, God bless him, full of years and honors, the noblest Roman of them all! Are we not glad he has lived to see this day? Look over the map of our beloved State, where we and our wives have so long labored and

had patience, trace the line from Fort Smith to Little Rock and all
along the Iron Mountain Road, look over the counties, and from
three-fourths of them you will find the liquor traffic routed, horse,
foot, and dragoons. Women did it! We men put the weapon of law
in their hands, and they have wielded it like true daughters of the
Church, the State, the home! We welcome you to the first temperance
jubilee that Arkansas has ever known, because never before had the
sovereign people an opportunity to assert its conviction and to avenge
its heartache.

The next speech was by Col. Porter Grace, a leading
lawyer, and I will sum up in my report what I heard him
say in public and in private on this question. Learning
that he was the member of the committee which reported
to the Legislature the wishes of the temperance people
for this bill, I was desirous to know his motive. This
was his testimony :

In my career as a lawyer I have prosecuted or defended one hundred
and thirty men for homicide in my part of the State. Fully nine-
tenths of all my cases at court have been directly traceable to the
liquor traffic. I have seen women suffer so much that I determined
to befriend them, if I could. Two facts stood out in bold relief as the
result of my experience: first, intoxicating drinks are at the bottom
of crime; second, the women, as a class, not only do not drink, but
are set against the habit. Then came the question: "What can be
done to protect the homes?" Our Legislature had not got up, nor
down, nor around (just as you please to call it) to the idea of the full
ballot for women. So, as I could not put that in their hands, I
resolved to do my level best to give them the vote by signature. We
asked for this law, and secured it by a large majority. Be it said to
the everlasting credit of women withal that, as a class, without regard
to color, they stood for the right when we gave them the power.

I learned that the Woman's Christian Temperance
Union in fourteen counties sent in petitions to the Legislature, and that first called the attention of Col. Grace
and his committee to the immediate demand on the part
of the people for this measure. Senator Mitchell, who
was the chief champion in the Senate, said :

I was always opposed to the ballot for women; but they have so
nobly vindicated their right to it in our State, and by their quiet and

divine action have done so much more to increase the sum of human welfare here than any single force has ever before done, that I am prepared to use my influence to invest them with full sovereignty *pro bono publico.*

Hon. H. M. McVeagh, one of the most gifted lawyers in the State, said:

I come from Osceola, in the northwest county of our State. A few years ago we were given up to drink. I have often heard Judge ——, who sits there at my left, discharge the jury because they were too drunk to serve. I have seen members of the grand jury, when a murder case was being tried, fall asleep because of drunkenness, and start up when nudged by a lawyer, and say: "What—case—we—a-tryin' now?" Then the only code was that you must be able to hold more than the other fellow. That was where your gifts and prowess came in. Arkansas had no use for a man who didn't drink. My friend, the judge, will corroborate this statement. There was a young man in our county who achieved the position of sheriff when only twenty-two years old. He was a graduate of Mississippi University, and worth $40,000 in his own right. He was the handsomest man in the State, and married a beautiful young woman. From taking an occasional glass, he went down in five years so that he spent one-half of his time in jail for stealing the wherewithal to buy liquor, and the other half whipping his mother and his wife. After several times trying to kill himself, he died suddenly, a common drunkard and pauper. Yes, we were given to drink; but I want you just to imagine the change, when, to say nothing of our closed-out saloons, a river steamboat stopping at our wharf shuts up its bar! One of our drinkers went on board but yesterday and tried to get a glass. "No," said the captain, "I have no mind to be shut up in Osceola jail." Imagine the change when our marshal says: "You might as well abolish my office. For one month I have had no cases of drunken and disorderly conduct, and not a single arrest save one for thieving." You may imagine the change when a mean-spirited business man in our community said to an old resident: "You can't keep up your town. No arrests, no fines. You can't even keep your sidewalks in repair." And some farmers, standing by, laughed their contempt for the speech, and one of them said to the rest: "What a pity it is, boys, that a lot of us can't be jerked up by the marshal, carried out to court, and sawed up into the right length for sidewalks."

I want you to remember that no outsider came to help us. We've had no "movement" and no excitement. Our political leaders have stood aloof; but the law had sharpened a weapon for us. The majesty of the people registered their decree according to the motto, prophetic

as it now seems, of our dear old State: "*Regnat populos.*" Arkansas
is religious. Go out into our backwoods, and you will find a Bible in
the house and bowed heads around the table, asking God's blessing on
the daily bread. "The people of the rural dee-stricts," as they are
sometimes called, can be trusted to take their own destiny in their
hands, only you must let them all come to the front in solid phalanx
against their foe. For law is merely public sentiment organized. The
Supreme Court has declared our law constitutional; so, the other day,
when a saloon-keeper lost his case in the District Court, somebody
asked him if he was going to appeal it, and he answered, with an oath:
"What use would it be, when the Supreme Court has turned itself
into one big Murphy meeting? "

Rev. Dr. Winfield, one of the most gifted men in the
Methodist Church, South, made the closing speech of the
evening. He spoke with exceeding pathos, saying:

I have cast in my lot with Arkansas and worn out my life in her
service. I have a right to complain of the stinging injustice done me
by the laws that tempt my boy to ruin, so that it is a positive danger
for him to pass along these streets of Little Rock. And I claim for
my home at the capital the protection already given to other towns,
so that the provisions of this law may extend to a city of the first
class.

Dr. Winfield's wife is President of the W. C. T. U. of
the capital, and Dr. Dodge's of the State. The most
important question before the Convention was whether,
at the next session of the Legislature, the temperance
people should try for a constitutional amendment or to
extend the present law to the largest towns. It is noteworthy that, notwithstanding the prevailing enthusiasm
for constitutional prohibition, the unanimous advice of the
judges present—than whom I never saw a body of more
intelligent, whole-hearted temperance men—was to adhere
to the present form, but to enlarge its scope. This was,
after full discussion, acceded to by a unanimous vote.
The argument of the saloon-keepers, made by their lawyer
before the Supreme Court, has in it matter for reflection
by those who consider the weapon of law a "carnal one"
in woman's hands, even though it prove "mighty for the

pulling down of strongholds." I quote from the printed "brief" furnished me by Col. Wittick, one of the leading lawyers of the State :

None but male persons of sound mind can vote; but their rights are destroyed, and the idiot, alien, and *females* step in and usurp their rights in popular government. Since females, idiots, and aliens cannot vote, they should not be permitted to accomplish the same purpose by signing a petition; for the signature of an adult to a petition is the substance of a ballot in taking the popular sense of the community. It merely changes the form, and is identical in effect.

May God hasten the day when all good people who oppose this "Home Protection Movement" shall see that they have allies whom they can but detest, and when this most Christian method of temperance work shall become universal in this Christian land.

A PRACTICAL APPLICATION OF THE ARKANSAS LAW.

With this keen threshing instrument of a "Home Protection" law in hand, let us look in upon the little town of Ball Knob, Ark. The population is made up of men engaged in quarrying for a railroad, and the saloon-traps catch these poor, undeveloped souls as they emerge from the paymaster's car, which comes along the track once a week, and divert their wages from supplying the flour-barrel at home to supplying the till of the dram-shop. Merchants have been obliged to "garnishee" the earnings of these men in the interests of the hungry wife and children at home, as the only means of preventing the disruption of their families. But members of the Women's Christian Temperance Union started out one bright morning, on a preconcerted signal, and quietly canvassing the town, secured the names of a majority of the people to a petition against the leeches that were gorging themselves on the blood of industry and famishing the homes of the poor. Within twenty-four hours the liquor-dealers had "folded their tents like the Arab, and as silently stolen away," leaving women's hearts full of a strange new joy. They had not even known, so ignorant were they, that any such door of escape had been opened to them by this benignant law. Some of them could not write their own names, but gratefully made the sign of the cross. O blessed cross! symbol beloved of that Christ who lifts woman up out of her degradation, and places her feet upon the beautiful mountains of privilege and hope.

This illustration is but one among scores that might be cited, the total influence of which has been to shut up the saloons in three-fourths of the counties of Arkansas. So will it always be when our Christianity becomes so practical that *the united force of all good men and women* can be brought to bear against the liquor traffic *at the point where conviction can be correlated with law.*

OBSERVATIONS EN ROUTE.

(From a Letter Home.)

Winter of 1882: It is a gala day for all good people in Arkansas. . Little Opportune and I are on the train, taking a ten hours' ride from the capital to the border of Indian Territory, where, in the wickedest town of the State, we are to hold four temperance meetings to-morrow (Sabbath), and to get a foothold for our dearly beloved Women's Christian Temperance Union. On the train men are talking of nothing else save this local option law, which has recently gone into effect, and by the provisions of which women as well as men have the vote by signature on the question of licensing saloons. It is, in effect, the very same law for which we worked so hard in Illinois. As a prominent lawyer just said to me on the cars, "We have been so cursed in Arkansas by drink, the homes and the women have been so oppressed, that when, in response to the petitions of the Women's Christian Temperance Union, and the hard work of Colonel Grace, J. L. Palmer,

and others, the last Legislature said to our people, ' *Up,
and at 'em !*' you may be sure we didn't stand on ceremony. The women have displayed a loyalty and earnestness beyond all praise, and in three-fourths of our counties
prohibition is the law. We are fortunate in having the
press and the lawyers almost solid on our side, as well as
the ministers, and so we get thorough enforcement."

As we fly along on the train from town to town, it is
a strange and blessed sight to see every saloon—and
there are always so many in sight from the depot—her-
metically sealed, the lonesomest looking places I have
ever beheld outside the glimpse I had in Egypt of the
Desert of Sahara. A good minister seated behind me—
the Rev. Mr. Boone—has just shown me his elegant gold-
headed cane, given him by the temperance people of
Morrillton in return for his hard work in getting up the
death-dealing petition that closed out the liquor traffic
there. Perhaps their appreciation was enhanced by the
fact that, as the good man was leaving their town when
his work was ended, a venomous saloon-keeper came to
the depot and spat in his face. Having done this, the
miserable fellow took out his pistol and said, " Come on ;
I'm ready." " Oh, no," replied the good-natured-looking
minister, " I should be no match for you in the use of the
weapons you have chosen."

Just now we passed a town at which the temperance
man pointed triumphantly, saying, " They had a blind
tiger here " (meaning the secret sale of grog), " but the
good folks closed him out yesterday to the tune of $500
and costs."

The machinery of the law is superb. No " remon-
strance " or counter petition is permitted. The simple
question, " Do we want dram-shops ? " is answered by the
signatures of men and women, and that settles the matter—not for a year only, but " once for all." In not a

single case where the vote has been taken, has it favored the abomination of desolation. The outrages upon the home have been borne so long that "wrath has been treasured up against the day of wrath." Too often the "drug-store nuisance" succeeds that of the saloon, and prescriptions at so much apiece fly thick as autumn leaves from the hands of recreant members of the medical fraternity. Not so here. Each doctor makes public affidavit, under pains and penalties, that only in cases of extreme necessity will he so prescribe. The only people aside from saloon-keepers who have, so far as I can learn, antagonized the law, are the "Hard-shell Baptists." They have joined in the hue and cry that "alcohol is a good creature of God," and angrily declared that women had better stay inside their own proper sphere, and let politics alone.

General Erwin, of Des Arc, and his earnest-hearted wife, gave me a most interesting account of their work in that remote but wide-awake community. It seems they have a Woman's Christian Temperance Union of fifty members; a flourishing Juvenile Society, which has carefully studied Dr. Sewall's "Stomach Plates," and Julia Colman's "Catechism." They have thus built up a solid and intelligent sentiment, and when the law declared that women might have power equal to men in the decision of this great home question, thus for the first time in the history of their town expressing the actual public sentiment in a concrete form on the question of the dramshops, there was no question as to the result. Mrs. Erwin took her horse and buggy and went in one direction, her husband rode on horseback in another, and obtained the decision of "We, the people of Des Arc," and within twenty-four hours the death-knell of the saloons was sounded.

This is only a specimen case. In Forrest City the

Woman's Christian Temperance Union quietly and secretly districted the town, went out to their work in the morning, and before sundown announced that they had the majority upon their books.

Among all the delegates, though many had far better education, none was endowed with a nobler manliness than General Erwin, " born and reared in Prairie County, and proud to be a native of redeemed Arkansas," as he told us; a brave officer on the Confederate side during the late unpleasantry, but hearty in his expressions of delight at "the co-operation of the two sections in this home protection work." He was for twenty years a moderate drinker; and spent his money freely in treating at the bar. One day he heard the saloon men boasting of the patronage he· brought. " Bless my heart!" said he; " these fellows aint agoin' to make a spring-board o' me to ruin no more likely young men." So he signed the pledge. He also and at once gave up tobacco. It was a great encouragement to hear the earnest words of this great, generous-hearted man, who came into our women's meeting to report for his wife, who was too timid. " She's a major hand with her pen," he said, looking proudly at the dark, earnest face of his wife; " beats me all hollow at that; but I have to do the talking for the family." " We had some trouble to get our most conservative women started out in this petition work," he added; " but we jest collected 'em up, and my wife, she prayed and I argued, and they got to see that it was ' for God and home and native land' they was a-workin', and that they was a military company in the great Union army of the Woman's Christian Temperance Union, that belongs to the South as much as to the North, and so you see it just knocked the pins out from under their little timidity, and the women saved the day."

So shall it be ere long all over this great country, when

the " human question " comes squarely to the front, and the unit of our race, formed from the fractions man and woman, adds united strength to the Prohibition vote in the name of humanity and God. The Woman's Christian Temperance Unions have borne themselves most nobly in this great uprising—the like of which has not been seen since the crusade of 1874. Having been the first to petition for the law, they have quietly districted the towns, and gathered in the priceless signatures, thus for the first time in the history of this wild Western State, having expressed the *real* public sentiment, and made the power of the church actively felt as a force which can overmaster the saloon.

THE FAMOUS " HOME PROTECTION " LAW OF THE STATE OF ARKANSAS. APPROVED MARCH 21, 1881.

Let me earnestly commend to the careful attention of all our workers the following statute, declared by the best attorneys of Arkansas (when it shall extend to cities of the first and second class) to be superior to any measure yet enacted. Their reason is that while *in effect strictly prohibitory*, it rests upon the widest basis of active public sentiment, and furnishes the simplest machinery for enforcement. The italics are my own.

Be it enacted by the General Assembly of the State of Arkansas :

SECTION 1. That whenever the adult inhabitants residing within three (3) miles of any school-house, academy, college, university, or other institution of learning, or of any church house in this State, shall desire to prohibit the sale or giving away of any vinous, spirituous, or intoxicating liquors of any kind, or any compound or preparation thereof commonly called *tonics* or *bitters*, and a majority of such inhabitants shall petition the county court of the county wherein such institution of learning or church house is situated, praying that the sale or giving away of the intoxicating liquors enumerated in the premises be prohibited within three (3) miles of any such institution of learning or church house; whereupon said county court, being satisfied that a majority of such inhabitants have signed such petition, shall make an order in accordance with the prayer thereof, and *thereafter* it shall be unlawful for any person to vend or give away any spirituous or intoxicating liquors within the limits aforesaid; *Provided,* that this act shall not affect persons who may have already obtained a license to sell spirituous liquors in any locality wherein this act shall be put in force, until such license shall expire; *and, provided further,* that nothing in this act shall be construed as affecting or repealing any special law now in force prohibiting the sale or giving away of spirituous or intoxicating liquors in any particular locality.

SEC. 2. *For the purposes of this act, females as well as males are competent subscribers to the petition herein provided for.*

SEC. 3. That this act shall not be construed as prohibiting the use of wine for sacramental purposes, or to prevent the prescribing and furnishing of alcoholic stimulants by a regular practicing physician *to the sick under his charge,* when he may deem the same *necessary;* but before such physician shall be authorized to so prescribe and furnish such alcoholic stimulants, in order to protect himself from the penalty of this act he shall file in the office of the county clerk of the county in which he resides, an affidavit which shall be in the following form, to wit:

I, ———, do solemnly swear (or affirm) that I am a regular practicing physician, and that I will not prescribe or furnish any vinous or alcoholic stimulants to any one, except it be, in my judgment, *a necessity in the treatment of the disease* with which he shall be *at the time afflicted.*

SEC. 4. *Be it further enacted,* That the provisions of this act shall not apply to cities of the first and second classes, in which a regular police force is maintained.

SEC. 5. That any person violating the provisions of this act shall be deemed guilty of a misdemeanor, and upon conviction either in the circuit court or before any justice of the peace, shall be fined in any sum not less than twenty-five dollars, nor more than one hundred dollars.

SEC. 6. That all laws in conflict with the provisions of this act be and hereby are repealed, and this act take effect and be in force from and after its passage.

"HOME PROTECTION."

(Extract from Fourth of July Address at "The Independent's" Celebration, 1879.)

KING MAJORITY.

Once more will the time-honored declaration be made to-day by a thousand Fourth of July orators, that "the Americans are a free people." But I insist that we are governed by the most powerful king whose iron rule ever determined the policy, moulded the institutions, or controlled the destinies of a great nation.

So pervasive is his influence that it penetrates to the most obscure and distant hamlet with the same readiness, and there wields the same potency as in his empire's capital; nay (with reverence be it said), he is like Deity in that his actual presence is co-extensive with his vast domain. Our legislatures are his playthings, our congressmen his puppets, and our honored President the child of his adoption. We do not often call him by his name, this potentate of million hands and myriad voices; but, to my thinking, nothing is to-day so vital to America as that we become better acquainted with our ruler. Let me then present to your thought his Majestic Highness, KING MAJORITY, Sovereign Ruler of these United States.

KING ALCOHOL.

Permit me now to introduce a different character, who comes to the court of King Majority as chief ambassador from the empire of his Satanic Majesty. Behold! I show you the skeleton at our patriotic banquet. It has a skull with straightened forehead and sickening smile; but bedecked with wreaths of vine, clusters of grape, and heads of golden grain—King Alcohol, present at court in radiant disguise. With a foaming beer-mug at his lips, he drinks the health of King Majority; and placing at his feet a chest of gold labeled "Internal Revenue," he desireth conditions of peace.

THE QUESTION.

Behold in these two figures the bewildering danger and the ineffable hope of the Republic! How can we rouse the stolid giant, King Majority? How light in those sleepy eyes the fires of a holy and relentless purpose? How nerve once more, with the resistless force that smote African slavery to death, the mighty sinews of the Republic's sleeping king?

AN ANSWER.

How? Only by "sweet reasonableness;" only by ceaseless persuasion; only by noble examples; only by honest hard work, based upon fervent and effectual prayer.

Human heads and hearts are much alike. I remember that the great Temperance Crusade of 1874 found me with a beer keg in my cellar, a fatal haziness in my opinions, and a blighting indifference to the temperance reform upon my will. But how did its intense pathos melt my heart; how did its mighty logic tune the lax cords of opinion to concert pitch; how did its miracle of prayer bring thousands to their knees, crying, "Lord, what wouldst thou have me to do?" For myself, I could never be the same after that. As a woman, a patriot, a Christian, my heart is fixed in deathless enmity to all that can intoxicate. The same influences which so transformed one brain and heart, are steadily at work to-day in a thousand quiet ways.

The sober second thought of the Woman's Temperance Crusade was organization. The voice of God called to them from the lips of his prophet: "Make a chain, for the land is full of bloody crimes and the city is full of violence." And so in every town and village we are forming these chains of light and of loving helpfulness, which we call "Women's Christian Temperance Unions." We have already twenty-three States organized, with thousands of local auxiliaries. Every day brings fresh accessions of women, translated out of the passive and into the active voice on this great question of the protection of their homes. Of the nine thousand papers published in this country, three thousand have had temperance facts and figures regularly provided by members of our societies. Temperance literature is being circulated; *Our Union*, the official organ of the Women's Temperance Society, has a large subscription list; Sabbath schools are adopting our plans of temperance instruction; and hundreds of juvenile societies are inscribing on their banners: "Tremble, King Alcohol! We shall grow up." Friendly inns and temperance reading-rooms are multiplying; gospel meetings, conducted by women, are reaching the drinking class in hundreds of communities; the Red and Blue Ribbon movements have attained magnificent proportions; and all this many-sided work is fast concentrating its influence to place the ballot in the hand of woman, and thus capture for the greatest of reforms old King Majority. Magnificent is the spectacle of these new forces now rallying to the fray. Side by side with the 500,000 men whose united energies are expended in making and selling strong drink, we are working day by day. While they brew beer we are brewing public sentiment; while they distill whisky we are distilling facts; while they rectify brandy we are rectifying political constituencies; and ere long their fuming tide of intoxicating liquor shall be met and driven back by the overwhelming flood of enlightened sentiment and divinely aroused energy.

OBJECTION.—"PROHIBITION A FAILURE."

"To be sure, King Majority gave prohibition to Maine; but prohibition doesn't prohibit," interrupts Sir Sapient, whose remark furnishes a striking illustration of the power of the human mind to resist knowledge. Just take the spyglass of observation, and behold from Kittery to Calais the gleaming refutation of your error.

Less than thirty years ago they had four hundred open hotel bars and ten miles of saloons. To-day, Dr. Hamlin of Constantinople, tells us that, coming home after forty years absence, he finds his native

State thoroughly renovated from the liquor traffic. General Neal Dow testifies that the law has absolutely driven the sale of strong drink out of all rural districts; and in the larger towns, instead of the free, open sale of former years, it is crowded into secret places, kept by the lowest class of foreigners. Ex-Governors Dingley and Perham, and Senator Blaine and Representative Fry declare that prohibition is as well enforced as the law against stealing; and even sensational journalists have not told us that thieves flourish in the Pine Tree State. Mr. Reuter of Boston, President of the National Brewers' Convention, held in St. Louis four weeks ago, says: "Formerly Maine produced nearly ten thousand barrels of beer annually; but this has fallen to *seven barrels*, in consequence of the local enforcement of prohibitory law." Surely this gentleman should be considered as good authority on this subject, as a convict is of the strength of his prison bars!

MAINE AN EXCEPTION.

But you say "Maine is different from any other State." Why so? Are not its citizens of like passions with other men? Turn your glass upon a panorama of Maine as it was in former days. See yonder stalwart workers in the harvest-field paying vigorous addresses to the little brown jug; observe its ubiquitous presence at the logging bee, the "raising," the wedding, and the funeral; see it pass from lip to lip around the fireside circle; observe the Gospel minister refreshing himself from the demijohn of his parishioner and host; and be assured that within the memory of men now living these were every day events. I have this testimony from the most honored residents of Maine, whose recitals involved the words, "all of which I saw, and part of which I was." But, as gallant Neal Dow hath it, "Maine was sown knee-deep with temperance literature before we reaped the harvest of prohibition." Let us note the evolution of this seed-planting. Land-owners found that two-thirds of their taxes resulted from the liquor traffic (largely in cost of prosecuting criminals, and taking care of lunatics and paupers); so they concluded that legalizing saloons for the sake of the revenue was penny wisdom and pound foolishness. Business men discovered that the liquor traffic is a pirate on the high seas of trade, that the more the grog-shop is patronized the fewer customers there are for flour and fuel, boots, shoes, and clothes; and so, in self-defence, they declared for prohibition. Church people found that fifteen times as much money went to the dram-shop as to the church, and that the teachings of the one more than offset those of the other with the young men of the State; so they perceived they could not conscientiously ally themselves with the liquor traffic by their votes. Those interested in education learned that enough money was swallowed in drinks that deteriorate the brain, to furnish a school-house for every fifty boys and girls, and to set over them teachers of the highest culture; and they saw it was unreasonable to defend the liquor traffic. In short, the majority came to believe that, between the upper and nether mill-stones of starving out saloons on the one hand, and voting them out on the other, they could be pounded to death; and they have so pounded them. The question of selling as a beverage the drinks which we know by centuries of demonstration will so craze men that they commit every crime, and show the subtlest cruelty to those they love the best, is not to-day in Maine an open question with either party, any more than trial by jury or imprisonment for theft. True, the people had a thirty years' war before the declaration of this blessed peace: but what are thirty years, when crowned at last by the surrender of King Alcohol to King Majority?

KEY TO THE POSITION.

"Ah! but," pursues our doubting friend, "Maine is a peculiar State, in this; it has few foreigners, with their traditions of whisky and of beer."

I grant you, there we are at disadvantage. But go with me to the Cunard wharves of Boston, and to Castle Garden of New York, and, as the long procession of emigrants steps across the gangway, you will find *three times as many men as women*. How can we offset their vote for free liquor, on Sundays and all days? Surely, the answer to this question is not far to seek. Strengthen the sinews of old King Majority, by counting in the home vote to offset that of Hamburg and of Cork, and let American customs survive by utilizing (at the point where, by the correlation of governmental forces "opinion" passes into "law") the opinion of those gentle "natives" who are the necessary and tender guardians of the home, of tempted manhood and untaught little children.

Hands which have just put aside the beer-mug, the decanter, and the greasy pack of cards are casting ballots which undermine our Sabbaths, license social crimes that shall be nameless, and open 250,000 dram-shops in the shadow of the church and public school. I solemnly call upon my countrymen to release those other hands, familiar with the pages of the Book of God, busied with sacred duties of the home and gracious deeds of charity, that they may drop in those whiter ballots, which, as God lives, alone can save the State!

THE WOMEN OF ILLINOIS.

Kind friends, I am not theorizing. I speak that I do know, and testify what I have seen. Out on the Illinois prairies we have resolved to expend on voters the work at first bestowed upon saloon-keepers. We have transferred the scene of our crusade from the dram-shop to

14

the council-room of the municipal authorities, whence the dram-shop
derives its guaranties and safeguards. Nay, more. The bitter argument of defeat led us to trace the tawny, seething, foaming tide of
beer and whisky to its source; and there we found it surging forth
from the stately capitol of Illinois, with its proud dome and flag of
stripes and stars. So we have made that capitol the centre of our
operations; and last winter, as one among the many branches of our
work, we gathered up 175,000 names of Illinois's best men and women
(80,000 being the names of voters), who asked the Legislature for a
law giving women the ballot on the temperance question. In prosecuting our canvass for these names, we sent copies of our "Home
Protection Petition" to every minister, editor, and postmaster in the
State; also to all leading temperance men and women, and to every
society and corporation from which we had anything to hope.

In this way our great State was permeated, and in most of its towns
the petition was brought before the people. The religious press was a
unit in our favor. The reform clubs of the State, with ribbons blue
and red, helped us with their usual heartiness and efficiency. And
what shall be thought of the advance in public sentiment, when (as
was often done) all the churches join on Sabbath night in a " Union
Home Protection Meeting," and ministers of all denominations (Presbyterians included) conduct the opening exercises, after which a
woman presents the religious duty of women to seek, and men to
supply the temperance ballot; and, to crown all, conservative young
ladies go up and down the aisles earnestly asking for signatures, and
the audience unite in singing:

> " Stand up, stand up for Jesus,
> Ye soldiers of the Cross;
> Lift high His royal banner,
> It must not suffer loss."

Friends, it means something for women of the churches to take this
radical position. America has developed no movement more significant for good since the first dawning of the day we celebrate.

The State of Indiana stands with us; only there the temperance
women have worked out the problem of deliverance further than we,
and asked the ballot on all questions whatsoever. They do the same
in Minnesota and in Iowa; while at the East the W. C. T. U. of grand
old Maine endorses the temperance vote, and Rhode Island sends to
Illinois resolutions of approval, while Massachusetts, under Mary A.
Livermore, has declared for home protection, and is preparing for the
fall campaign; and within a few days Ohio, the Crusade State, which
is the mother of us all, has fallen into line. The most conservative
States are Connecticut, New Jersey, Pennsylvania, and New York;
but in each of these there are many brave women who but bide their

time for this same declaration, and the whole twenty-three States already joined in the Woman's National Christian Temperance Union will ere long clasp hands in the only work which can ever fulfill the glorious prophecy of the Crusade. History tells us that on the morning of December 23d, 1873, when in Hillsboro', Ohio, the pentecostal power fell on the "praying band" which first went forth, the leading men of that rum-cursed town went out from the church where their wives and mothers had assembled, saying: "We can only leave this business with the women and the Lord." History has repeated itself this winter in our Illinois crusade. Men have placed money in our hands to carry on the Home Protection work, saying: "The women of America must solve this problem. Our business relations, our financial interests, our political affiliations and ambitions have tied our hands; but we will set yours free, that you may rid us of this awful curse."

WOULD WOMEN VOTE RIGHT?

Yet a few men and women, densely ignorant about this movement, have been heard to say: "Who knows that women would vote right?" I confess that nothing has more deeply grieved me than this question from the lips of Christian people. Have distillers, brewers, and saloon-keepers, then, more confidence in woman's sense and goodness than she has herself? They have a very practical method of exhibiting their faith. They declare war to the knife, and the knife to the hilt against the Home Protection movement. By secret circulars, by lobbyists and attorneys, by the ridicule of their newspaper organs, and threats of personal violence to such women of their families as sign our petition, they display their confidence in womankind.

The only town in Illinois which sent up a delegation of citizens openly to oppose our petition was Belleville, with its heavy liquor interest and ten thousand German to three thousand American inhabitants; and among our 204 legislators there were no other dozen men whose annoyance of the Home Protection Committee was so persistent and so petty as that of the Senator who openly declared he was there to defend the vested interests of his Peoria constituents, who in 1878 paid to the government a million dollars revenue each month on ardent spirits. Nay, verily, woman's vote is the way out of our misery and shame, " our enemies themselves being judges;" and none see this so clearly as the liquor dealers, whose alligator eye is their pocket-book, and the politicians, whose Achilles heel is their ambition. The women of the Crusade must come once more to judgment—not, as aforetime, with trembling lip and tearful eye; but reaching devout hands to grasp the weapon of power, and crying with reverent voice, "The sword of the Lord and of Gideon!"

HOW WOMEN DO VOTE.

But, after all, "seeing" is a large part of "believing" with this square-headed Yankee nation; so let us seek the testimony of experience.

In Kansas the law provides that the signatures of women shall be requisite to a petition asking for a dram-shop before that boon shall be conferred upon any given community. This arrangement wrought such mischief with the liquor dealers that they secured an amendment exempting large towns from such bondage. But in small towns and villages it has greatly interfered with the traffic, and has so educated public sentiment that prohibition can, with impunity, form the theme of a Governor's inaugural, and Kansas is on the war-path for a law hardly less stringent than that of Maine.

In Des Moines, Iowa, a few weeks since, as a test of popular opinion, the women voted on the license question; twelve declaring in favor of saloons and 800 against them. In Newton, Iowa, at an election ordered by the council, 172 men voted for license to 319 against—not two to one against it; while the women's vote stood one in favor to 394 against licensing saloons. In Kirkville, Mo., ten women favored the liquor traffic, twenty declined to declare themselves, and 500 wanted "no license." In our Illinois campaign, which resulted in 90,000 names of women who expressed their wish to vote against saloons, not one woman in ten declined to affix her name to our petition.

THE CATHOLIC CHURCH, GERMANS, ETC.

The attitude of the Catholic Church was friendly to our petition, many priests urging their people to sign. Irish women, as a rule, gave us their names, and saloon-keepers' wives often secretly did so. Scandinavians were generally enthusiastic for the petition. Germans opposed us; but the reply of one of them indicates the chivalric nature which will come to our aid when the invincible argument against beer shall be brought in contact with German brain and German conscience. He said: "If it is not the pledge, I will sign it. I cannot give up my beer; but I want to help the ladies." To be sure, German saloon-keepers were universally and bitterly antagonistic, and had much to say about "women keeping inside their proper sphere."

ARGUMENT FROM THE NATURE OF THE CASE.

But the convictions which supply me with unalterable courage and unflagging enthusiasm in the Home Protection work are not based upon any proof I have yet given. No argument is impregnable unless founded on the nature of things.

The deepest instincts and the dearest interests of those who have the power to enact a law must be enlisted for its enforcement before it will achieve success. For instance, the Fifteenth Amendment to the Constitution of the United States is going to be enforced by the ballots of the colored men who once were slaves, just so long as those men retain their reason and their color. By parity of reasoning, if you can enlist in favor of a local option or prohibition law the dearest interest of a class in the community which in all ages of wine and beer and brandy drinking has not developed (as a class) the appetite for them nor formed the habit of their use, you will have something trustworthy on which to base your law. We temperance people have looked over at the rum power very much as the soldiers of Israel did at Goliath of Gath. We have said: "He has upon his side two of the most deeply-rooted instincts of human nature—in the dealer the appetite for gain, and in the drinker the appetite for stimulants—and we have nothing adequate to match against this frightful pair."

But, looking deeper, we perceive that, as God has provided in Nature an antidote for every poison, and in the kingdom of His grace a compensation for every loss, so in human society He has ordained against King Alcohol, that worst foe of the social state, an enemy beneath whose blows he is to bite the dust. Take the instinct of self-protection (and there is none more deeply seated): What will be its action in woman when the question comes up of licensing the sale of a stimulant which nerves with dangerous strength the arm already so much stronger than her own, and which at the same so crazes the brain God meant to guide that manly arm that it strikes down the wife a man loves and the little children for whom when sober he would die? Dependent for the support of herself and little ones, and for the maintenance of her home, upon the strength which alcohol masters and the skill it renders futile, will the wife and mother cast her vote to open or to close the rum-shop door over against that home?

Then there is a second instinct, so much higher and more sacred that I would not speak of it too near the first. It is as deep, but how high it reaches up toward Heaven—the instinct of a mother's love, a wife's devotion, a sister's faithfulness, a daughter's loyalty! Friends, this love of women's hearts was given for purposes of wider blessing to poor humanity than some of us have dreamed. Before this century shall end the rays of love which shine out from woman's heart shall no longer be, as now, divergent so far as the liquor traffic is concerned; but through that magic lens, that powerful sun glass which we term the ballot, they shall all converge their power, and burn and blaze on the saloon, till it shrivels up and in lurid vapors curls away like mist under the hot gaze of sunshine. Ere long our brothers, hedged about by temptations, even as we are by safeguards, shall thus match force with force; shall set over against the dealer's avarice our timid instinct of self-protection, and match the drinker's love of liquor by our love of him. When this is done you will have doomed the rum power in America, even as you doomed the slave power when you gave the ballot to the slave.

OBJECTIONS—WOMAN'S INFLUENCE.

"But women should content themselves with educating public sentiment," says one. Nay, we can shorten the process; for we have the sentiment all educated and stored away, ready for use in brain and heart. Only give us•the opportunity to turn it to account, where in the least time it can achieve the most! Let the great guns of influence, now pointing into vacancy, be swung to the level of benignant use, and pointed on election day straight into the faces of the foe! "No; but she should train her son to vote aright," suggests another. But if she could go along with him, and thus make one vote two, should we then have a superfluous majority in a struggle intense as this one is to be? And then how unequal is her combat for the right to train her boy! Enter yonder saloon. See them gathered around their fiery or their foamy cups, according to the predominance in their veins of Celtic or of Teuton blood. What are they talking of, those sovereign citizens? The times have changed. It is no longer tariff or no tariff, resumption of specie payments, or even the behavior of our Southern brethren that occupies their thought. No. Home questions have come elbowing their way to the front. The child in the midst is also in the market-place, and they are bidding for him there, the politicians of the saloon. So skillfully will they make out the slate, so vigorously turn the crank of the machine, that, in spite of churches and temperance societies combined, the measures dear to them will triumph and measures dear to the fond mother heart will fail. Give her, at least, a fair chance to offset by her ballot the machinations which imperil her son.

WOMEN CANNOT FIGHT.

"But women cannot fight," you say, "and for every ballot cast we must tally with a bayonet." Pray tell us when the law was promulgated that we must analyze the vote at an election, and throw out the ballots of all men aged and decrepit, halt and blind? Do not let the colossal example of Judge David Davis so fill our field of vision that we cannot perceive brain, and not bulk, to be the rational basis of citizenship. Avoirdupois counts greatly among the Zulus; but it is a consideration far less weighty with the Americans than it was before the Geneva Arbitration. I venture the prediction that this Republic will prove herself the greatest fighter of the nineteenth and twentieth centuries; but her bullets will be molded into printers' type, her Gatling guns will be the pulpit and the platform, her war will be a war of words, and under the white storm of men's and women's ballots her enemies—the saloon, and the commune—shall find their only shroud.

" WOMAN'S RIGHT."

Of the right of woman to the ballot I shall say nothing. All persons of intelligence, whose prejudices have not become indurated beyond the power of logic's sledge-hammer to break them, have been convinced already. For the rest there is no cure save ne—the death cure—which comes sooner or later, and will open more eyes than it closes. Of the Republic's right to woman's ballot I might say much. Well did two leaders of public thought set forth that right when Joseph Cook declared that "woman's vote would be to the vices in our great cities what the lightning is to the oak ;" and when Richard S. Storrs said: " If women want the suffrage, they will be sure to have it; and I don't know but when it comes it will turn out to be the precious amethyst that drives drunkenness out of politics."

WOMEN DO NOT WISH TO VOTE.

"But women do not care to vote." This is the "last ditch" of the conservatives. The evolution of temperance sentiment among women hitherto conservative refutes this argument; yet I confess there are many who do not yet perceive their duty. But Jack's bean-stalk furnishes only a tame illustration of the growth of women in this direction in the years since the Crusade. Of this swift growth I have already given abundant proof. It is, in my judgment, the most solid basis of gratitude on this national anniversary.

During past years the brave women who pioneered the equal suffrage movement, and whose perceptions of justice were keen as a Damascus blade, took for their rallying cry: "Taxation without representation is tyranny." But the average woman, who has nothing to be taxed, declines to go forth to battle on that issue. Since the Crusade, plain, practical temperance people have begun appealing to this same average woman, saying: "With your vote we can close the saloons that tempt your boys to ruin;" and behold! they have transfixed with the arrow of conviction that mother's heart, and she is ready for the fray. Not rights, but duties; not her need alone, but that of her children and her country; not the "woman," but the "human" question is stirring women's hearts and breaking down their prejudice to-day. For they begin to perceive the divine fact that civilization, in proportion as it becomes Christianized, will make increasing demands upon creation's gentler half; that the Ten Commandments and the Sermon on the Mount are voted up or voted down upon election day; and that a military exigency requires the army of the Prince of Peace to call out its reserves.

LOCAL OPTION.

In the grand sweep of sentiment for constitutional amendment we must not forget the great advantages of local option as an educator, not less than as a practical measure of temperance reform.   Its usefulness has been splendidly demonstrated in Maryland and other States, and with the woman's ballot to give it a consistency efficient on the day when enforcing officers are chosen, it would be a mighty power.

But some have said that local option is an inconsistency, for no community would ever place a bill against stealing before the people for their option, and the liquor traffic is a crime as bad as stealing.   But no law was ever enacted against stealing, except as the result of an option (a free choice) in the Legislatures of State and Nation.   It was voted upon, and men voted as they chose.   The immense public sentiment in favor of such a law caused the vote to be unanimous, and this will some day be the case with prohibitory law.   Meanwhile, in States where the sentiment would not yet give us a prohibitory law (which we could only get by a local option in the locality known as the "Halls of Legislation"), let us not say to less conspicuous places—municipalities, for instance—that because the whole State *will* not they *may* not vote the legalized dram-shop out of their boundaries.   Since in a representative government we can pass no law except by leaving it open to the chances of a "local option," and since this same option is the only possible method by which we can delegate to localities under a government "of the people, by the people," power to enact in the territory nearest them, and in which they are most interested a prohibitory law, therefore, local option is a necessity *per se*, and the surest forerunner of that more general form of local option popularly known as prohibition.

PLAN FOR LOCAL CAMPAIGN "TO CARRY NO-LICENSE."

I.—HOW TO DO IT.

1. Complain all the preceding year of the utter failure of no-license, and do nothing whatever to secure its enforcement, though you voted (or worked) for it at the last election.

2. Tell (in private) what astonishing "dead letter" tokens you see every time you go down town; but never give your evidence, influence, or money to help convict the law-breakers.

3. Never speak in pulpit or prayer-meeting about the law. Treat it as a Gentile, that has no place in the courts of the Lord.

3. Let it be generally understood that the best people in town are utterly discouraged and disgusted with prohibition, and ready to return to license, " since it helps to keep up the sidewalks, at least."

5. Aroused by the straightforward arguments of an earnest temperance worker, imported by somebody three days before election, come out brighter than ever—perhaps because of this temporary eclipse—and declare that it's a shame to let the town go by default. Induce the temperance sojourner to remain. Whisper softly whenever convenient that there are to be meetings held; but don't mention the fact out loud. Light up the church dimly; gather in a couple of hundred excellent people who need no repentance; furnish no music, save as Deacon Fugue "raises" "Old Hundred" higher than the church-gable; and expect the dead community to be gal-

vanized into ghastly and imbecile motion at the eleventh
hour.

Forget that the rum party held secret caucuses while
you were asleep ; selected their candidates while you were
scolding at the law; and canvassed for votes while you
were busy getting reconverted! In brief, though you are
harmless as a dove, don't on any account allow yourself
to be wise as a serpent.

II.—HOW IT HAS BEEN DONE.

1. The W. C. T. U. co-operated with other temperance
societies and with the churches in raising a fund by private subscription and public pledges.

2. This was placed in the hands of an Executive Committee or "Home Protection Alliance," and by them
invested in securing speakers and circulating prohibition
documents. These last were given out at all public meetings, left in all stores and offices, hung up on lamp-posts,
in street-cars, and everywhere, and carried to all homes by
judicious sub-committees. Tracts in their own language
are sure to gain the attention of Germans and Scandinavians. A column of carefully selected facts and arguments
was supplied every week in the year for the weekly press
by women specially appointed, who used their scissors to
excellent purpose on the teeming columns of the temperance papers furnished them by the Executive Committee.

When, as has been computed, a million words of temperance logic can be had for the price of a drink, and the
cost of a yoke of oxen invested in such words will so
revolutionize public sentiment that local option is carried
in a whole county, where is the sense or grace in temperance people who complain that "they don't know what to
do," and are "only waiting" for work?

3. Temperance meetings were regularly held throughout the year, "to work up public sentiment." The first

six months they were held every fortnight: the next three, every week; the last two, several times a week; and the last month, every night. These meetings were handsomely placarded through the town, and thoroughly advertised in press and pulpit. The managers of a theatrical company could hardly have taken more pains to invite people to come than did this temperance committee. During the last month a band of music played every night in front of the hall where the best interests of the community were to be discussed by earnest, practical men and women, devoted to the cause. Often speakers were met at the depot by the White-ribbon Brigade and the Reform Club. All speakers were instructed to use no bitter epithets nor harsh personal allusions. Facts, logic, persuasion, embellished by narratives, brightened by wit—these were their sufficient stock in trade. Ministers of the Gospel bore a prominent part in this work, speaking from their pulpits on Sunday, and steadily lending their influence to the work. Children from the public schools recited selections, witty and sad; young men declaimed; young women read and sang. There was a place for everybody, and grandly were those places filled.

4. Two or three weeks beforehand, at a large public meeting, the people's ticket was announced, having been agreed upon by the Executive Committee, appointed at the beginning of the campaign, and consisting of a member from each church and two from each temperance society. The men chosen as municipal officers were remarkable for something besides their devotion to the temperance cause. They stood well in the community; had thoroughly practical and liberal views concerning town affairs; were thorough financiers; and hard-headed men of business could pick no flaw in their integrity. They were not the sort of nominees whom you can pick

up the evening before to "fill a gap," which will be wider
the day after election than at any previous date. They
were solid citizens, who would never have come forward
thus, save on the call of a committee which had shown
skill equal to its earnestness, and common sense no whit
behind the clear grit it had exhibited.

The candidates made brief addresses, and, from mayor
to constable, pledged themselves to a faithful execution of
the laws. Now came the seething of the caldron, which
had been heated long. The town, already districted by
the committees on circulating documents, was thoroughly
canvassed once more—this time with a petition similar to
that which follows :

"We, the undersigned, voters and women of legal age within the
corporate limits of the town of ———, do respectfully and earnestly
petition all persons who will support the following

PEOPLE'S TICKET

....
....
....
....
....
....

to affix their signatures to this paper; women's names being a promise
to use their influence in favor of the ticket, and men's names being a
promise to vote the said ticket on election day."

MEN. | WOMEN.

Thus every signature was not only a personal agree-
ment, but had also the force of a request to all other
residents of the community. This canvass was conducted
chiefly by women carefully chosen for their discretion and
their gentleness. The results of it were published in the
local papers, figures being given, but not names.

5. Election day arrived. The ladies had secured permission to decorate the engine-house with wreaths,

flowers, and patriotic mottoes. They furnished a tooth-some free lunch next door, to which everybody was invited, and where the temperance pledge was offered, and the people's ticket and a buttonhole bouquet furnished to all who would accept them. Hundreds of voters were fed and won, and scores of homes were brightened by new resolves that day; and toward night the church-bells rang out the tidings of a victory that had been earned, a success that had been organized, as all true successes are.

6. But the Executive Committee did not stop here. The headquarters were still kept open, and a secretary employed who kept a bright lookout for opportunities to strengthen the hands of the authorities in that enforcement of law which alone makes it respected and enduring.

To the W. C. T. Unions which are "waiting for work" this plan is recommended for study. Its most important suggestions may be universally applied, and its campaign lasts all the year round.

TEMPERANCE TABERNACLES.

A local habitation, a name, and an earnest, practical woman who could give her entire time to the work would quadruple the results attained by our W. C. T. Unions. Compare the work done by those equipped in this way with that of the general run of our societies, and learn once more that God has chosen in this world to work by means. In many Western towns a great, rough, one-story hall is the rallying place of our forces, and demonstrates to the enemy that which he hates to think— namely, that we have come to stay. The Temperance Tabernacle of Atlanta, Illinois, is a fine illustration. First an enthusiasm was aroused by a series of meetings conducted by a reformed man. Before that had time to subside, several clear-headed men of business invited the people to take stock in shares of $10 each in a building which should be the temperance headquarters for meetings, concerts, etc., and which could be rented as a hall to any one who would pay a fair price. This ten dollars was understood to be a gift, the "certificates of shares" —like many others supposed to be more valuable—being mere souvenirs of the transaction. A piece of ground was purchased for a nominal sum; lumber and hardware merchants furnished the material at cost rates; masons and carpenters, painters and glaziers gave their services at half price; women made handsome mottoes and decorations; and the place speedily became the favorite audience-room of all the country round. Add to this a reading-room and an office for the Secretary of the W. C. T. U., and we should have a base of operations worthy the magnitude of our endeavor. Here our Sunday Gospel-meetings would be held, the poor feeling themselves especially welcome and at home; here would be the great mass meetings of the no-license campaign, the depository for temperance literature and subscription books of our paper; here, by frequent sociables and entertainments, we could help replenish our treasury; and here perhaps, some day, as the rallying point of beneficent influence for all, might be located the ballot-box, which is always either the coffin or the throne of the saloon.

HISTORY OF THE GREAT HOME PROTECTION PETITION IN ILLINOIS.

[As a matter of history and for future comparison with other campaigns, the following is copied:]

October 10*th*, 1878.—The Annual Meeting of the Illinois Woman's Christian Temperance Union, at Monmouth, ordered the petition to be prepared, which was accordingly done by Miss Willard, assisted by W. P. Black, an attorney-at-law, of Chicago.

December 5th.—The draft prepared was accepted by the Executive Committee of the State Union.

December 12th.—The first presentation was made by Miss Willard, at Geneseo; but no great effort was made until January.

January 1st, 1879.—Less than 1,000 names had been obtained.

March 1st.—The petitions were called in for presentation, the entire canvass having occupied but about two months or nine weeks. The signatures were pasted on strong white muslin, eighteen inches wide, bound with red ribbon on one edge and blue on the other. The entire supervision of this (the first) petition and putting it together were the weighty task of Miss Anna Gordon, Miss Willard's private secretary, and the work was admirably done. Prominent business men of Chicago, chief of whom was R. J. Fowler, Esq., furnished the funds for postage, printing, and necessaries.

March 4th (Evening).—There was a reception in the Governor's rooms at the Capitol, with addresses by a number of ladies and gentlemen.

March 5th (Evening).—There was a mass meeting in the Representatives' Chamber, previously granted for that purpose. The petition was gracefully festooned around the chamber, and stirring addresses were delivered by ladies of the Presentation Committee, and by Mrs. Foster, the lady lawyer of Clinton, Iowa, who was present by invitation of the ladies and presented the legal aspects of the case. The Presentation Committee were: Miss Frances E. Willard, President of W. C. T. U. of Illinois; Mrs. T. B. Carse, President of Chicago W. C. T. U.; Mrs. L. A. Hagans, Mrs. Willis A. Barnes, Mrs. C. H. Case, Mrs. D. J. True, all of Chicago; Mrs. Prof. Fry and Mrs. A. R. Riggs, of Bloomington; Mrs. C. H. St. John, of Eureka; Mrs. M. H. Villars, of Pana; Miss Mary A. West, of

Galesburg; Mrs. E. W. Kirkpatrick, of Monmouth; Mrs. H. A. Calkins and Mrs. E. G. Hibben, of Peoria; Mrs. M. L. Wells and Mrs. R. Beach, of Springfield; and Miss Anna Gordon, of Massachusetts (Mrs. M. Wait, of Galesburg, former President State W. C. T. U., and Miss Kate Ross, of Abingdon, also members, were unable to be present).

March 6th.—Presentation of the petition to the House of Representatives, with an address by Judge Hinds, of Stephenson County. Three of the ladies—Miss Willard, Mrs. Foster, and Mrs. St. John—by invitation of the House, on the motion of Hon. Sol. Hopkins, then addressed the House, this being the first time a lady had ever spoken in an open session of the Illinois Legislature. The number of signatures to the petition was 110,000, of men over twenty-one and women over eighteen years of age, about half of these being voters.

April 9th (Evening).—Mass meeting in the Senate Chamber, with supplemental petition exhibited in like manner as above, which petition contained at least 70,000 additional names, all secured in less than four weeks. The putting together of this last petition was the work of the women of Springfield, under supervision of Miss Barnett.

April 10th.—Presentation in the Senate by Senator Taliafero. An effectual objection being made to the ladies speaking in open session, a motion for a recess of thirty minutes prevailed, and Miss Willard occupied the time in speaking on the objects of the petition. Twenty-four senators voted for the recess, and nineteen against it. Three senators left the chamber, returning at the close of the recess.

The Presentation Committee was the same as before, with the addition of the following persons: Mrs. H. A. Allyn, of Springfield; Mrs. R. Greenlee, Mrs. M. A.

Cummings, Mrs. J. B. Hobbs, and Miss Lucia Kimball,
of Chicago; Mrs. G. H. Read, of Bloomington; Mrs. H.
W. Harwood and Mrs. H. C. Cullom, of Joliet; Mrs. S.
B. Mooney, of Pana; Mrs. S. M. I. Henry, of Rockford;
and Mrs. M. A. Taliafero, of Keithsburg.*

ABOUT PETITIONS.

Persons of small thoughtfulness are wont to say, when
our petitions are not granted: "How much time and
money have been lost." But they forget the reflex influence of such work; the entire change in public sentiment
which a thorough canvass has often wrought in a locality,
and the indirect results achieved. If we mean that crowds
shall gather, there must be something for them to rally
around, and a petition to which their signatures are
sought affords this nucleus. Our Home Protection campaign in Illinois has crystalized the thoughts of the people
around the idea of a law against the liquor traffic. Sermons and speeches by the score have reached and convinced them by the thousand, and the louder voice of the
press, coming with cogent and oft-repeated arguments, has
changed the views of tens of thousands. The quiet house-
to-house canvass of an army of women who could not
speak in public has brought home to the fireside and the
wife and mother, with little time to read, reasons enforced
by practical illustrations taken from everyday life; and
thus hosts of friends for woman's temperance ballot have
been raised up where all were passive and inert before.
Of the 832 towns that voted on the question of license
while our campaign was in progress, 645 declared for no
license—a much larger number than ever before; and

* The entire number of names on the petition was 180,000. It is
now under the care of the Chicago Historical Society, and will be
brought to light once more when what it asked for is an achieved
power in Illinois.

experienced men say it was largely due to the Home Protection Petition work of the W. C. T. Unions. It has also reacted most favorably on all departments of our society, greatly extending the knowledge of our methods, multiplying our organizations, and bringing out an army of helpers of whom we had not known before.

Similar results would attend the circulation of a petition to the county or municipal authorities on any phase of our manifold cause. Let us remember that, in giving prominence to this branch of work, we are but transferring the Crusade from the saloon to the sources whence the saloon derives its guaranties and safeguards. Surely this does not change our work from sacred to secular! Surely that is a short-sighted view which says: "It was womanly to plead with saloon-keepers not to sell; but it is unwomanly to plead with law-makers not to legalize the sale and to give us power to prevent it." No wonder the Ohio Crusaders, who have spent hours in the stifling atmosphere of the saloons, do not deem it indelicate to enter airy council-rooms and stately legislative halls; and they, like the W. C. T. U. of Illinois, have enlisted for a seven years campaign, or one of fourteen years, if need be, not expecting immediate success, but going forth in the crusade spirit of dependence upon God and consecration to His service. "The letter killeth, but the spirit giveth life." Methods constantly change, but motives must have their spring in everlasting truth and righteousness.

DAYS OF PRAYER.

The "Home Protection Crusade" for woman's temperance ballot is the natural successor of the Temperance Crusade of 1873–4, and simply changes its objective point. If rightly understood and faithfully pursued, the new movement will do much toward fulfilling the sacred prophecies of its divine forerunner. Then let our work

be begun, continued, and ended in prayer. Let every
document prepared or sent out, every address delivered,
every name asked for the petition be accompanied by
breathings of the soul to God for a right spirit in ourselves and a heavenly blessing on our endeavor. Let not
the noon-hour of united prayer for our W. C. T. Unions
and their work be overlooked, and let stated days of
prayer be appointed by the officers of the State Union, at
the opening of the campaign, and on the day when the
committee present the petition to the Legislature. Evermore, as our growing hosts move forward, may our
watchword be:

> "Prayer is the Christian's vital breath—
> The Christian's native air."

COPY OF THE GREAT PETITION.

As a matter of interest and suggestion, an exact copy
of the petition is here given:

Home Protection Petition, Illinois W. C. T. U.

[Editors please publish and temperance people circulate.]

FOR GOD AND HOME AND NATIVE LAND.

[Among the many prominent religious newspapers which have
editorially endorsed this petition are the following: *Christian Union,
Independent,* and *Witness,* New York; *Northwestern Christian Advocate,
Advance, Interior, Standard,* and *Alliance,* Chicago; *The Golden Rule*
and *Zion's Herald,* Boston.]

To be returned to——, at——, by the——day of——, without fail.

[N.B.—This petition will be presented at the State Capital at the
earliest possible date in the session of the Legislature, which convenes
on the —— day of —— 187—, by the following committee: ——
Any number of copies will be sent to any address, if desired; but it is
also earnestly requested that persons interested in utilizing the influence of woman against the legalized traffic in strong drink will
have printed or written copies of the petition made and circulated
from house to house. Let them also be sent to editors, ministers,
Sunday-school and public school teachers, and to all Reform Clubs
and other temperance societies. All ministers and temperance speakers
are requested to present the petition to their audiences after a sermon,
address, or exhortation on the subject of which it treats. The following method of securing signatures in audiences is recommended:
Previous to opening the meeting, place in each pew a narrow strip of
paper, with the words "Names of men over twenty-one" written

across the top, and "Names of women over twenty-one" half way down the strip. After reading the petition, at the close of the meeting, call attention to these papers and constitute the gentleman or lady sitting in the end of each of each pew or seat nearest the aisle *a committee of one* to see that all in that seat have the opportunity to sign the slip of paper. Let one person be in attendance in each aisle with pencils to lend, and let this person gather up the slips as soon as signed. These autographs are to be sent to headquarters, to be pasted upon the petition. While the signing proceeds, such hyms as "America" or Miss Lathbury's "Home Protection Hymn" may be sung by the choir. When the largest number of signatures possible has been obtained, send the list of autograph signatures, stating plainly where they were obtained and paying postage in full, to —— ——, at Headquarters State W. C. T. U., in —— ——. Write on one side only, giving name of town and county on each list of names. Paste more paper on the petition as required. Names may be signed in pencil, and autographs only are desired.]

To the Senate and House of Representatives of the State of Illinois:

Whereas, In these years of temperance work the argument of defeat in our contest with the saloons has taught us that our efforts are merely palliative of a disease in the body politic, which can never be cured until law and moral suasion go hand in hand in our beloved State; and

Whereas, The instincts of self-protection and of apprehension for the safety of her children, her tempted loved ones, and her home, render woman the natural enemy of the saloons; therefore, your petitioners, men and women of the State of Illinois, having at heart the protection of our homes from their worst enemy, the legalized traffic in strong drink, do hereby most earnestly pray your honorable body that, by suitable legislation, it may be provided that in the State of Illinois the question of licensing at any time, in any locality, the sale of any and all intoxicating drinks shall be submitted to and determined by ballot, in which women of lawful age shall be privileged to take part, in the same manner as men, when voting on the question of license.

BACK OF THE PETITION.

[Please have this printed in local papers.]

Among the many prominent religious newspapers which have editorially endorsed this petition are the following: *Christian Union, Independent,* and *Witness,* New York; *Northwestern Christian Advocate, Advance, Interior, Standard,* and *Alliance,* Chicago; *The Golden Rule* and *Zion's Herald,* Boston.

In a recent "Monday Lecture," Rev. Joseph Cook of Boston, spoke thus:

"There stands a noble statehouse in the cornfields near Springfield, Illinois, and Lincoln's grave lies under its shadow. Above his grave a Legislature will be petitioned this winter by ladies of Illinois, to give women of legal age the right to vote in cases of local option under temperance laws. . . . In New Hampshire the line has already been broken as to the exclusion of women from participation in the settlement of questions closely touching the home. Let it be noticed that New Hampshire, a conservative New England State, has just given to women the right to vote on all questions concerning the school laws. I am not a woman suffragist. Do not applaud this platform under the mistaken idea that I am a defender of extreme positions as to woman's rights. I am meditating on that theme. But this I dare say, that one of the fragments of self-protection for women—namely, a right to vote concerning temperance laws, when the question of local option is up—I am willing to defend, and intend to defend, to the end of the chapter. Great natural justice is on the side of such a demand. Woman's interests are among the chief ones concerned; and as to family divisions, why, they come largely from temperance laxness. Woman surely has political intelligence enough to understand the difference between license and no license, especially when she has suffered under a lax execution of the temperance laws. The difference is so plain between local freedom and no local freedom to sell liquor that woman, without any great participation in the turmoil of politics, might be expected to have an intelligent vote on this subject. I know that many cultivated and refined women say they do not want women to vote, because they do not want to increase the amount of ignorant suffrage. Well, I respect the intelligence and the refinement of the ladies who make such remarks; but I believe that on most moral questions woman is likely to be more intelligent and certainly more disinterested than man. I am told by many of the best authorities that women who are opposed to female suffrage at large are usually in favor of this modified measure. I am assured that a majority of the thoughtful, cultivated women of the United States, or certainly of the Northern States, can be expected to favor this demand for a vote to be given to women in questions of local option, concerning temperance laws. If a majority of women want such a vote, Heaven grant their desire! Women would be united on this topic. Woman's vote would be to city vices depending on intemperance what the lightning is to the oak. God send us that lightning!" [Applause.]

HOME PROTECTION HYMN.

(Sung at our "Rallies" in the West.)

BY MARY A. LATHBURY.

Tune: " Arise and Shine."   *Gospel Hymns No. 2.*

O trust ye in the Lord forever!
Strong is His arm, and wide His love;
He keepeth truth, He faileth never,
Though earth, and sea, and heaven remove.

CHORUS:

Sing to the Lord ! He goes before us;
  His strength is ours, His truth shall stand
Till east and west shall join the chorus,
  "For God, and home, and native land."

Be strong, O men who bear in battle
  For us the banner and the shield,
For strong to conquer, as to suffer,
  Is He who leads you in the field.

Lift up your eyes, O women, weeping
  Beside your dead ! The dawning day
Has rent the seal of death forever,
  And angels roll the stone away.

Room for the right ! Make room before us
  For truth and righteousness to stand,
And plant the holy banner o'er us
  For God, and home, and native land.

Easter, 1879.

MRS. PELLUCID AT THE CAPITAL OF ILLINOIS.

Mrs. Pellucid* was my companion at the capitol, where
with other ladies, we spent several weeks in the endeavor
to secure legislative support for our Home Protection
measures.   One of the members, when earnestly appealed
to, replied with a rueful grimace: " Ladies, when I tell
you the leading towns in the district I represent, you will
see that I cannot do as you wish," and he rattled off such
names as " Frankfort, Hamburg, and Bremen," wished us
"the success that our earnestness merited," and bowed
himself out.

" Why—what—does—he—mean ? " inquired my lovely
conservative, in astonishment.

A committee clerk stood by, who answered, briskly :
" Why, ladies, Mr. Teutonius represents a district in
which German voters are in the majority; therefore, he
cannot support your bill."

" Why, I thought a lawmaker was to represent his own

---

* Otherwise Mrs. E. G. Hibben, a cultured Presbyterian lady of Peoria, and my
successor as President of the W. C. T. U. of Illinois.

judgment and conscience," murmured the sweet-voiced lady.

"His judgment, yes; for that tells him on which side the majority of votes in his district is located. His conscience, no; for that would often cost him his chances for a political future," answered the well-instructed youth.

"O-o-oh!" softly ejaculated Mrs. Pellucid, in the key of E flat, minor scale.

By this time Mr. Politicus entered, in response to our invitation of course, he never would have come on his own motion. After a brief conversation, he pledged himself to vote for our bill, and to make a speech in our favor. Nevertheless, if you should glance over the list we are carefully preserving and industriously circulating in Illinois, of men who voted against us, you would find his name. But he is an honest fellow in his way, and we owe it to a motion made by him that women were, for the first time in history, allowed to speak before the Legislature of Illinois. He explained his desertion of the temperance cause on this wise: "I tell you, ladies, I've got to go back on you. I'm the leader of my party in the House, and they've cracked the party whip mighty lively around my ears. The long and short of it is, I've got to represent the fellows that voted me in."

Poor Mrs. Pellucid! How appealing was her voice, as she replied: "But I am sure your better nature tells you to represent us." Mr. Politicus brought his great fist down on the table with a stalwart thump, and said: "Course it does, madam, but Lord bless you women, you can't stand by a fellow that stands by you, for you hain't got any votes." Just here a young lady of the group piped up: "Oh! but we would persuade our friends to vote for you." "Beg pardon, miss; but you couldn't do nothin' of the kind," said he. "Don't you s'pose I know the lay o' the land in my district?" The young lady now

grasped the other horn of the dilemma, saying, desper-
ately : " But we will get the temperance men in your district to vote against you if you desert us in this manner."
His rejoinder was a deplorable revelation to our simple-
minded company : " Never a bit on't, miss. The temperance men are an easy-going lot, and will vote the party
ticket anyhow. Old dog Tray's ever faithful ! We've
ignored them for years ; but they come up smilin', and
vote the Republican ticket all the same. You'll see ! "
" But won't you stand by us for God and home and native
land ! " pleaded Mrs. Pellucid, with a sweetness that would
have captured any man not already caught in the snares
of a gainsaying constituency. The worthy politician
thumped the table again, and closed the interview by saying : " You women are altogether too good to live in this
world. If you could only vote, you'd have this Legislature solid. But, since you can't, I'm bound to stand by
such a conscience as I've got, and it tells me to stick to
the fellows that voted me in. Good morning ! " And he
got speedily out of the range of those clear, sad eyes.
Mr. Readyright (an ex-Senator) came in. With all the
vehemence of his Irish nature he anathematized the
" weak-kneed temperance men." " Sure as you're living,
Politicus told you the truth," said he. " The temperance
men are the foot-ball of parties. There's none so poor to
do 'em reverence. Where are the plucky young fellows
that were here when we gave Illinois her present local
option law ? " (By the way, that law bears the name of
this valiant Senator, who is by the same token a Democrat.) " Where are they ? Out in the cold, to be sure.
Did the temperance folks remember their services and
send 'em back ? Not a bit of it. But the whisky men
didn't forget the grudge they owed 'em ; and they're on
the shelf to-day—every last man of 'em." " I tell you,"
and the wise old gentleman gesticulated wildly in his

wrath, " until you women have the power to say who shall make the laws and who enforce 'em, and to reward by re-election them that are faithful to your cause, and punish by defeat them that go back upon it, you may hang your bonnets on a very high nail, for you'll not need 'em to attend the funeral of the liquor traffic!" "Why," exclaimed one of the ladies, confusedly, " you don't mean to say that the temperance ballot is not enough, and that we must follow in the footsteps of Susan B. Anthony?" The sturdy old gentleman walked to the door, and fired this Parthian arrow back at us : " Susan could teach any one of ye your a-b-abs. This winter's defeat'll be a pay-ing investment to ye all, if ye learn that a politician is now and ever will be the drawn image, pocket edition, safety-valve, and speakin' trumpet of the folks that voted him in."

The ladies drew a long breath. "I begin to see men as trees walking," slowly murmured sweet Sister Pellucid.

" But we must bide the Lord's time," warningly uttered an old lady, who had just arrived. To her the brisk committee clerk ventured this answer: " But Senator Readyright says you'll find the Lord's time will come just about twenty-four hours after the women get their eyes open!"

A temperance member of the House is the last caller whom I will report. He spake in this wise: " Ladies, I pretend to no superior saintship. I am like other men, only I come from a district that would behead me if I did not stand by you. I have a pocket full of letters, received to-day from party leaders at home, assuring me I run no risk." At the close of three weeks of such a school as this, one of our radicals asked Mrs. Pellucid, chief of conservatives, this pointed question : " Are you still for the Home Protection vote alone, or for the ballot on all questions?" She replied in thrilling tones and

15

most explicit words : " Any temperance woman who could have shared our bitter experience here without desiring to vote on every officer, from constable to President, would be either a knave or a fool."

MAKE SELF-INTEREST OUR ALLY.

This lady reasoned that, since we are solemnly bound to be wise as serpents, we must harness self-interest to our on-moving chariot. The great majority of men who are in office desire to be re-elected, by fair means, if they can ; but to be re-elected anyhow. Only in one way can they bring this to pass and that is by securing on their side old King Majority. If we furnish them with a constituency committed to the proposition " The saloon must go," then go it will, and on the double quick. Let the city council know that women have the ballot, and will not vote for them if they license saloons, and they will soon come out for prohibition. Let the sheriff, marshal, and constable know that their tenure of office depends on their success in executing the law thus secured, and their faithfulness will leave nothing to be desired. Let the shuffling justice and the truckling judge know that a severe interpretation of the law will brighten their chances of promotion, and you will behold rigors of penalty which Neal Dow himself would wince to see.

There is also great force in the consideration that if women, not themselves eligible to office, had the power to elect or to defeat men (who will alone be eligible for a long while yet), the precise check might by this arrangement be supplied, which would keep politics from forming with the worst elements of society that unholy alliance which is to-day the grief of Christians and the despair of patriots. Belonging to no party ourselves, we might be able to lift the Sabbath, the temperance movement, and kindred moral questions out of the mire of merely partisan politics into which they have fallen. It is, at least, worth trying. Into the seething caldron, where the witch's broth is bubbling, let us cast this one ingredient more. In speaking thus I am aware that I transcend the present purpose of my constituency, and represent myself rather than " the folks that voted me in ! "

PLANS FOR THE FUTURE.

Our temperance women in the West are learning that, while the primary meetings are the most easily influenced, they are the most influential political bodies in America. Ere long the W. C. T. Unions will attend these, beginning in the smaller and more reputable communities. We are confident that nothing would be so effective in securing the attendance of the respectable voter as the presence at the primaries of "his sisters and his cousins and his aunts." To be " in at the birth" of measures vital to the well being of society seems to us, in the light of last winter's experience, a more useful investment of our influence than to be " in at the death." At Springfield we found the enemy entrenched, while in the primaries his soldiers are not yet even recruited. We intend also to open in each locality books of record ; and, by thorough canvass to secure an informal registration of all men and women —the former as to how they will, and the latter how they would (mournful potential mood !) vote on the question of permitting saloons. Every such effort helps to obliterate party lines ; or, more correctly, to mass the moral elements by which alone society coheres, against the disintegrating forces, which of themselves would drive us into chaos and old night.

New England must lead. Let not the west outstrip you in this glorious race. I appeal to the women of the east. Already New Hampshire and Massachusetts have placed in your hands the educational vote, which has a

direct bearing on the temperance question, since by its use
the mothers of this land can place on the school committees those who will make the scientific reasons for
total abstinence a regular study of the children. I beg
you, by its use, to testify your fitness and desire for the
more powerful weapon it foretells. It comes to you as
the gift of a few earnest, persistent women, who steadily
asked your legislators to bestow it, even as they will the
larger gift, if you as diligently seek it. Your undertaking will not be so gigantic as ours in Illinois, for with us
34 in the Senate and 102 in the House must first agree to
a constitutional amendment, and then the concurrence of
two-thirds of our voters must be secured. Another contrast further illustrates the favorable conditions here.
Negro suffrage at the South was forced upon wide areas
occupied by a voting population bitterly hostile to the
innovation. Here woman's vote must first be granted by
free consent of a majority of the representatives chosen
directly by those who are already citizens; and by operat-
ing over the small area of a single State at a time it would
arouse no violent upheaval of the opposition. Besides,
the large excess of women here makes this the fitting
battle-ground of a foregone victory. Women of New
England! among all the divisions of our great White
Ribbon Army you occupy the strategic position. Truly,
your valiant daughter, Illinois, earlier flung down the
gauge of the new battle; but your blood is in our veins,
your courage nerves our hearts, your practical foresight
determines our methods of work. I come from the prairies, where we are marshaling forces for a fresh attack,
and solemnly adjure you to lead us in this fight for God
and home and native land. .Still, let dear old New England take her natural place in the forefront of the battle;
and from an enemy more hateful than King George let
the descendants of our foremothers deliver Concord and

Lexington, and wield once more in Boston, with its eight miles of grog-shops, the sword of Bunker Hill! To chronicle the deeds by which your devotion shall add fresh luster to names renowned and hallowed, the Muse of History prepares her tablet and poises her impartial pen.

Friends, there is always a way out for humanity, but evermore in earth's affairs God works by means. To-day he hurls back upon us our complaining cry : "How long? O Lord! how long?" Even as he answered faint-hearted Israel, so he replies to us : What can I do for this people that I have not done? "Speak unto the children of Israel that they go forward."

> " There's a light about to beam,
> There's a fount about to stream,
> There's a warmth about to glow,
> There's a flower about to blow.
> There's a midnight blackness
>   Changing into gray;
> Men of thoughts, of votes, of action,
>   *Clear the way !*
>
> Aid that dawning tongue and pen;
> Aid it, hopes of honest men;
> Aid it paper, aid it type,
> Aid it, for the hour is ripe,
> And our earnest must not slacken into play.
> Men of thoughts, of *votes*, of action,
>   *Clear the way !*

A LOOK AT THE ILLINOIS LEGISLATURE.

(A SPECIMEN OF ALL.)

A peep from the ladies' gallery of the "Thirty-second General Assembly " of Illinois may not be amiss on this opening day of the session. Of course, it will be from a temperance point of view. The liquor men are already on hand. "Early and often," is their motto, which we shall some day be wise enough to emulate. They have a pair

of lawyers with them, and their lobbying will be contem-
poraneous with the first appearance of a Solon on the
scene. But the temperance people are also on the alert.
This afternoon we have a consultation meeting with the
local W. C. T. U.; and on the 15th we begin a series of
meetings culminating in the "Alliance Convention"
(Jan. 18 and 19), at which all temperance societies will
be represented.

The Hinds bill, by which women have a voice, through
petition, on local license questions, will be promptly presented, and a lively contest kept up, as the friends of temperance rally to the standard raised.

But I must not forget to look up from these pencilings to
the moving panorama before me. With eye and ear I
must act as your reporter. It is twenty minutes of
twelve, and the opening exercises begin at noon. In the
ladies' gallery are gathered many of our true-hearted
temperance women. Behind me, a couple of politicians
are talking. One says:

"They'll meet and sit, and what'll they do? They've
got nothing to do—that's the fact of the business. We
want no new legislation. Things are in splendid shape!"

Happy man, to be endowed with powers to squint thus
at the human race, seeing but half of it. There are a
score of women within ear-shot of him who will not rest
until the "home guards" have somewhat to say about the
home question of the dram-shop.

At my left, a veteran employee is giving to a bright
young lady scribe minute accounts of the state and standing of the members as touching the Hinds bill. "Favorable to Hinds bill." "Voted for us last time." "Bitter
against us." "A promising young man, but has been
bought by whisky votes." These are the statements
which the swift pencil, "when found, makes a note on."
In the men's gallery (ought I to say *gentle*-men's?) are

"sovereigns" in considerable numbers, with hat on head and pipe in mouth. Already the air is blue and sickening with tobacco smoke; members walking up and down, puffing in one another's faces. I am glad to say these ill-bred personages constitute less than a tenth of the 153 in the House. What forlorn mothers—or fathers—they must have had. It is interesting to note that the men who smoke almost invariably wear their hats. Selfishness and ill-breeding are twin-born. At 11.50 the members are nearly all assembled. Somebody beside me says, "A better looking collection than in '79; more fine foreheads; better clothes, and fewer red noses." Another says, "Not a dozen bald heads—mostly men of middle age." Another, "Look at the Democrats! They are on their good behavior, and well they may be. Less smoking on their side than on the Republican."

But the hour strikes, the gavel falls, Secretary of State Harlow calls the House to order, and calls on Dr. Wines to offer prayer. Almost every head is bowed, a few old men rising instead; the great hall is as quiet as a church, while slowly and tenderly fall on our ears the words first spoken by the world's elder Brother and Redeemer when he said, "After this manner therefore pray ye."

How unutterably significant, at such a time, in such a place, were the words that floated on the mild air of Judea, and into the ears of a dozen fishermen, but which, coming from lips divine, had life immortal in them. That we are partly barbarous yet, was signified by the effigy of manhood who, with feet on desk, head erect and cigar in mouth, puffed right on through the prayer. Secretary Harlow now reads his graceful valedictory, "After twenty-six years of public life," which is kindly received with applause, the roll of members is called, and certificates presented. And now the fight begins by the nomination of temporary chairman; on the Republican side,

Mr. John M. Pearson; on the Democratic, Mr. Young-blood. Of course, this is a form, for the "party that saved the Union" has eleven majority. Mr. Pearson is duly elected, conducted with much ceremony to the chair, makes a sensible speech one minute long, and the House proceeds to other uninteresting business.

The general impression is that this House is not as favorable to temperance measures as it might have been had not so many of our good people slept while the enemy sowed tares. Still, there are decided gains in some quarters, and we have a basis of hope. The election of Gen. H. H. Thomas in the Republican caucus last evening is a gain for the temperance side. The forces will soon be organized, and we can better judge of the situation. The air is full of rumors as to the "position" of our members, many preferring to maintain the character of "lookers-on in Venice" for a while. But we

> Bate not one jot of heart or hope;
> Ours is the future, grand and great,
> The safe appeal of truth to time,
> So we can wait.

VALEDICTORY THOUGHTS, 1878.

BELOVED SISTERS OF THE W. C. T. U., OF ILLINOIS: For fifteen months I have been honored by the leadership of the "women who dared." My life has witnessed no other period of equal 'length into which so much happiness has been crowded, for in no other have I been blessed with such transcendent opportunities of usefulness. Forever it remains God's universal law that the more constant, effective, and beneficent our reaction on the mass of humanity about us, the more steadfast and rational is that joy in us which this world cannot give nor take away. Profoundly then I thank you for the fulcrum and the leverage vouchsafed to me by your love and confidence, but most of all, by your intelligent and energetic coöperation.

But by your will and that of other women like you, both East and West, I am transferred to the leadership of all the States instead of one, and it is essential that my relationship to all should be that of impartial interest and endeavor; hence the dissolving of our earlier relationships by the executive committee's acceptance of my resignation.

Yet I linger in the doorway of my dear prairie home, and before turning my face eastward, send from a loving heart the benediction, God bless thee, Illinois! In long procession thy legions go marching through my memory with banner, prayer, and song—the Home Protection army of that great campaign, which was the Sumter gun of America's latest and most heroic anti-slavery war. Behold them marching in the van, those brave, true-hearted warriors of God, who from a thousand pulpits preached and prayed that woman's pleading might give place to woman's power. See the rallying clans of the reformed men, always our chivalric guard of honor, as they fall into line, with ribbons blue and red, singing "Rally round the flag, boys, rally once again." See the heavy columns of artillery, the noble legion of editors Christian and editors secular, the Gatling guns of the metropolitan press leading the grand advance! Notice the veteran corps of the old line temperance societies marching along with closed ranks and what the greatest captain of the age has called "the swing of conquest," and see filling up our broadest prairies the swift advancing lines of the grand army, the one hundred and eighty thousand men and women who signed the muster-roll of the great petition as volunteers. Here, with steps so rapid they can hardly grade them to the company's music, march the business men of Chicago, who provided the sinews of war for our campaign; the Swedes of the Nord Seit; the miners of Streator, the moral aristocracy of

Peoria, stronghold of our relentless foe, and the best blood of Springfield, where Lincoln's memory makes stern hearts kind; while southern Illinois, the "Egypt" of our misapprehension, moves forward with tens of thousands, led by kindly old Cairo, where the gallant "Club" and liberal-hearted "Union" share the honors each has earned. Next these deploy the students from our schools, young men and women with no geometrical formula for bounding anybody's "sphere," but content to let God's "Thus far and no farther," written in the nature of things, replace the crude "Thus far and no farther" which has rung from custom's pinched lips, checking woman's buoyant steps in all the ages past. The Present doffs its cap to these as they file onward, and salutes them as "burgomasters of the future."

There are ninety thousand women in this procession, the advance guard of an army which is gathering from every State, and the music of their marching feet is keyed to the tune of "Home, Sweet Home." Set for the defence of a principle, they have wrought into the granite of deeds what others have been content to "declare" in "resolutions" meagerly enforced by pitifully small "petitions," and their record is the guiding "signal" light of the countless hosts who shall come after them.

But who are these now passing up through the shining ranks of the great white-ribbon army, as the gentle soldiers gaze on them with eyes that cannot see for tears? Ah, theirs are memorable faces, theirs are names to be emblazoned on our banners and our hearts; the seventy-eight who voted for our bill, headed by Senator Taliafero and Judge Hinds, the brave Republican and Democrat who presented our petition at the capital. Forget them! Nay, not we! See where they march, brave Speaker James and Chairman Black, noble Peters of Watseka, German of the Germans, forerunner of the army that ere long shall keep their *Wacht am Rhein* for the protection of our homes ; see where they march and hear the soft " God bless you," of a hundred thousand tremulous voices as Whiting, Ford of Galva, Dysart, Neal, and Tice march by, heading the total of ninety votes we mustered in both Houses at " headquarters." Other men there were fought in the ranks of the Black Dragon, when the battle raged under the capitol's great dome ; in whose sight greed of office, of party, and of gold were stronger than God's eternal justice, and more regarded than the tears of the oppressed. Their names shall pass into a swift oblivion, but some tall shaft upon the generous soil of the first Home Protection battle ground, shall yet bear down to happier generations the names of the true and loyal knights who, even now, wear fadeless honors in memory's review.

Farewell, dauntless vice-presidents, you who have borne and labored and had patience ; noble sisters of the pen and the exchequer, wide awake general superintendent of the " ninety-and-nine " that went not astray, tireless office secretary, indomitable founder of the SIGNAL, beloved editor, who in sorrow's night hast earned the title " bravest of the brave," and manly publisher, whose royal spirit deems it an honor to help our woman's enterprise, and accepts exile from his country for the dearer love he bears our cause ; farewell, heroic presidents of the local Unions, who " hold the fort " amid the storms of defeat, the gloom of apathy ; farewell to you, unvanquished soldiers of the rank and file, whose faithful courage often puts to blush our own. God's blessing be upon you, each and all.

Step to thy rightful place, *Elizabeth, Queen of the Home Protection army in the pioneer prairie State. Trained under the guns of the enemy, Peoria sends her

---

* Mrs. Elizabeth Grier Hibben, the new president.

choicest daughter forth to a broader, but not a fiercer
battle ground. Thy gentleness hath made thee great.
The future shall bring us tidings of such victories as
shall make the Past appear the tyro that she is.

Attack the enemy in squads, this winter, with the local
ordinance and petition. Yoke last year's enthusiasm to
this year's discipline; by your success in local elections,
throw the ordinance into the courts, where the decision
can but establish its validity, and next autumn send back
to the legislature the friends who stood by us, and do
your utmost to retire those who were false or faint of
heart.

> Strike till the last armed foe expires;
> Strike for your altars and your fires;
> Strike for the freedom of your sires,
> God, home, and native land.

TEMPERANCE TONIC FOR VOTERS.

The following pledge, used by the W. C. T. U., has been
extensively circulated, the final sentence being changed
to suit the prevailing sentiment in different localities.

Copy of pledge to be written in little book and given to
women appointed for the purpose in every W. C. T. U.

I, the undersigned, a voter of ———, hereby pledge
myself, as an act of justice to the mothers, wives, and
daughters of ———, who can get no representation at
the polls except through their fathers, husbands, brothers,
and sons, that I will attend every primary meeting, caucus,
and election wherein the temperance question is directly
or indirectly involved, and that I will then and there give
my influence and vote in favor of such men and measures
as will advance the cause of the total prohibition of the
liquor traffic (or of local option) ; (or of the ballot for
women as a weapon of protection for her home from the
outrages of the liquor traffic; or the triumph of the constitutional prohibitory amendment.)

A YANKEE HOME PROTECTION CATECHISM ; OR ONE QUESTION
ANSWERED BY ANOTHER.

Question.—Is work for woman's full ballot a "side
issue" in temperance reform ?

Answer.—Do the brewers so regard it ?

Q.—Would men who never voted prohibition themselves give us women the power to do so ?

A.—Have they done so in Arkansas ?

Q.—Is not the subject of prohibition less unpopular than
that of woman's ballot ?

A.—Is the superior popularity of prohibition indicated
by the fact that four States have the suffrage amendment
now pending, and two have the prohibition, and that in
twelve States the woman's educational ballot is a part of the
State government ? Or by the fact that while neither
branch of Congress has a temperance, both have a suffrage
committee now in full blast ? Or by the further fact that,
while in the House of Representatives they would not so
much as grant a commission to investigate the results of
the liquor traffic, they have granted the woman's suffrage
committee aforesaid ?

Q.—Is not the home protection movement less popular
than it was years ago ?

A.—Do you rely for proof of this upon the fact that the
S. S. workers of Illinois, at their recent temperance meeting, and the Congregational ministers, at their annual
association, resolved to stand by the W. C. T. U., which
is thoroughly pronounced for woman's full ballot ? Or
upon the fact that our leading temperance women are
freely invited to speak in Presbyterian churches on Sabbath evenings, when their utterances about the ballot are
sure to have no uncertain sound ? Or upon the fact that
at the District Convention held this spring, our " women
of the churches," confessedly conservative, have stood up
so unanimously for the ballot, when the question was

called, that it has been declared "positively cruel" to put the negative?

Q.—Is it not easier to get prohibition than the ballot for women?

A.—Do the foregoing *facts* (not fine spun theories) point in that direction? Is it easier for a legislator to go to his whisky constituents and say, "I voted to submit a prohibition amendment," or "I voted to submit an equal franchise amendment?" Which sounds the worst in the distiller's ears? Did you know that a large element among the "liberals"—Germans and others—believe it an act of justice to let all the adult population share directly in making the laws by which they are governed? Had you heard that the editor of a leading German beer paper said to one of our workers, "I hate to have the women vote, because they will vote against beer; but I shall cast my ballot on their side because I believe in your American Declaration of Independence?"

Q.—Will not the majority of foreigners vote against temperance?

A.—Then has not temperance something to gain from letting women vote, since at least two foreign men come to us where one foreign woman comes, and the proportion of native born women to native born men is in our favor?

Q.—Did not Kansas declare for prohibition without woman's help?

A.—Is it not true that for fifteen years previous to carrying the amendment, Kansas had allowed the signature of a woman to count just as much as that of a man on license questions, thus giving to women the "vote by signature?" Did not that, according to the admission of Kansas people, help mightily in building public sentiment for prohibition? And does not Governor St. John declare they must give women the ballot that they may help to elect such officers in the large cities of Kansas as will

make the law something more than a rusty sword in a
still more rusty scabbard?

Q.—Will not the ballot come to women in due season
without the special efforts of temperance women?

A.—Is it not true, as Garfield said, that things don't
turn up in this world, but somebody must go to work and
turn them up? If the "ballot by signature" in women's
hands closed the grog shops in three-fourths of the counties of Arkansas, is it not in harmony with temperance
for the W. C. T. U. to hasten its advent to the utmost?

Q.—Have not the woman suffragists come into the
W. C. T. U. for the purpose of using its forces in the
interest of their cause?

A.—Will you please furnish a list of those who have so
entered our work? Is there a general officer of the
National W. C. T. U. who has ever been affliated with
the suffrage movement except as a W. C. T. U. worker?
Is there a State President except Mary A. Livermore and
Mary T. Lathrap (now a conservative) who ever spoke in
a suffrage meeting? Let us have facts.

Q.—Have not those W. C. T. Unions that have
included work for the ballot among their methods become
hobbyists and laid down the Gospel to take up the ballot?

A.—Which has most auxiliaries and the greatest number of temperance schools, evangelistic meetings, etc.—
the Home Protection States or the conservatives? (Look
in the annual reports of the National W. C. T. U. and
see.) Which State furnished for years the national
superintendent of the evangelistic work? (Illinois—and
a more fervent Christian worker or a more pronounced
Home Protectionist is not to be found in America than
Mrs. Henry.) Which furnishes the superintendent of the
Sunday-school work? Illinois. Of "unfermented wine at
the sacrament?" Illinois. On which side have the
veterans of the crusade ranged themselves? "By their
fruits ye shall know them."

Q.—Is not the Bible opposed to woman's ballot?

A.—Do you refer to the place where it says " male and female created he *them* and called *their* name Adam?" or to the account of Miriam and Deborah, Huldah and Esther, Anna and Elizabeth, and the Marys? or to the Apostle's declaration: " There is neither male nor female, but ye are all one in Christ Jesus?" Nay, as the outcome of our Christian civilization let us have

> " Two heads in counsel, two beside the hearth ;
> Two in the tangled business of the world;
> Two in the liberal offices of life;
> Two plummets dropped to sound the abyss of science,
> And the secrets of the mind."

A HEART-SORROW IN AN UNPROTECTED HOME.

The accompanying letter so stirred my heart when I received it that I determined to pass it along to the good and thoughtful people who will read this book, and ask them to think it over :

DEAR SISTER:—Thanking you as far as words can do it, for the kind mention you always make of me, for your tender sympathy, which has bound me to you, I will give you a picture of my life since my arrival on Saturday, and if it will help to open blind eyes, or rouse to thought one indifferent mind, use it as you will, only for my dear son's sake suppress the name.

I came home after the week's work—work I tried to do lovingly as for the Master, looking gladly toward the rest, and the welcome of home faces and sweet home voices.

My boy had reached it before me; he had been at work this week, after many months without employment. Part of his wages he left with a friend, saying " it would be safer so." He knew his weakness to withstand the tempter's lures. Then he went to make some purchases, which he intended as a pleasant surprise towards home comfort—went, as he thought, safe in his loving desire to make home bright in atonement for the many dark days he had caused there.

After a few hours he came, with unsteady feet, brain heated and bewildered; the face that God had made so fair swollen, flushed, disfigured; the beautiful eyes, that were to have watched for his mother's home coming, bloodshot and wild in their brightness. This was on Saturday night. On God's holy day he stole out, and drank again and again to quench the thirst that it but enkindles anew. To-day when the mother pleaded, when her hand would have held him back, keeping him within home's shelter, the lips she used to kiss so lovingly cursed the day that he was born, cursed the mother that gave him birth, the mother who would die to save him now, and went out again on the road that leads to death. The law has no redress for me, no restraining influence for him. He is of age, say the lawyers; the men of whom he buys liquid fire are licensed to sell it. What are we mothers to do? Shall we sit quietly down and watch the ending, the dark, dreary ending? God help us. God give us strength to put aside our timid shrinking. Let us petition—petition—until we have the right to say by our actions as well as our prayers that this slaughter of souls must cease. I must do what alone is left. If the law hedges about the rumseller because he has a voice, a tribute for the revenue, a vote that intimidates even those who wish well to the temperance cause, if he and his saloon are protected, why should not I, who, because I am a woman, need it more, have Home Protection for my helpless ones, myself, my weak and wandering boy, who but for rum's traffic would be, with his rich gifts of heart and mind, an ornament to society, a power for good in the land?

Yours,

A SUFFERER, IF NOT WHOLLY A SUFFRAGIST.

THE DRAGON'S COUNCIL HALL — A TEMPERANCE ALLEGORY.

Behold his Satanic Majesty in cabinet council assembled, with his minions and his emissaries just returned from this sin-stricken earth. Each brings the latest news concerning the endless conflict between darkness and light, ignorance and wisdom, sin and righteousness. Each gives the most carefully considered suggestions for the building up of Satan's kingdom—for the multiplication of murders, robberies, outrages, and conflagrations. "Permit the suggestion, your Majesty," says one brimstone-colored satellite, "that you will build a new distillery at Spiritsville, for at that point the church people are growing rapidly in power." "Not at all," tartly replies he of the horns and hoofs; "don't you know better than to be always showing your hand in that fashion! Do this instead: Put it into the heart of John Barleycorn, proprietor of the distillery I have already there, to subscribe a thousand dollars toward finishing the church."

The order was entered in lurid letters on the books, and Emissary No. 2 proceeded to report: "In Temperanceville they have so few saloons that the young men are rapidly getting out from under thy sway, and I humbly suggest the imperative necessity of a special order on the Stygian Manufactory for six well-instructed and experienced imps, who shall put it into the heads of six men now engaged in other business to open six saloons, as business is so lively at Cincinnati and Peoria that we can spare none of our already enlisted forces." "Tut, tut!" roared the devil; "I can beat that device, with only half trying. Send a beer-drinking pastor to Temperanceville, and let him preach in favor of the Business Men's Moderation Society, and show up the idiotic theories of those stiff-necked teetotalers." No. 3 now ventured to suggest that in Tippleton the women had opened a Sunday-afternoon meeting, and had given out that they should offer a free lunch at the polls on the approaching election day. He therefore asked for a detailed escort of fiends, who should be commanded to set fire to the Temperance Reading Rooms and drive the President of the W. C. T. U. raving distracted." "You are a callow young limb of perdition to go so clumsily about your business," roared the devil. "I won't send a special squad, for they are all employed in the saloons working up the voting lists against the next election, in the interests of the whisky governor; but do you go and put it into the head of Deacon Setbones to prove to that W. C. T. U. President that the Scriptures do plainly teach that it's a sin and shame for a woman to speak in any public place, and that the whole spirit of Christianity is set against the insane notion of a woman's undertaking to preside at an electioneering lunch down at the polls."

And now comes the last and most lugubrious-looking messenger, with this doleful story to relate: "I ask that pestilence and famine be let loose, for I am terribly alarmed for the stability of thy kingdom in the province of which Chicago (otherwise Beeropolis) is the chief city; for be it known unto your majesty there is a serious revolt among those whom thou hast kept in strict subordination, lo, these centuries! The women are rousing themselves to the cry of ' Home Protection,' studying into the structure of the Government, tracing back to their source the temptations that have so admirably succeeded in capturing boys and men for thy great armies. These frightful women, neglecting their proper sphere and the submission that has been so long their convenient characteristic, have actually dared to publish figures showing that the majority of voters are on thy side, and that thus thou dost hold thyself in power by keeping thine ambassador, King Alcohol, intrenched among the people." Here the fiendish messenger turned a sickly yellow and gasped with rage, as he concluded his awful revelation in these words: "They even ask—and many ministers, church editors, and other strong allies of Him whom thou didst tempt and crucify are asking for them—the power to vote upon all questions relating to the sale of alcoholic drinks."

O, what a scene was that! The devil quaked in every limb, his sharp knees smote together, and a howl of hellish hate and rage rang through the sulphurous air of the dark council chamber as he cried:

"Away with you, fools that you are! Talk of letting loose famine and pestilence! If things have reached this pass—if the women have discovered that the side always wins which has most votes—let me make haste. I'll send no stupid, clumsy-footed subaltern in an emergency like this! I'll steal in among those timid and silly rebels who have always hated me and sought the triumph of Him who wore the thorn-crown, and from a thousand

pulpits I'll declare that woman leaves her home on this
vile errand at the peril of society ; that you cannot carry
temperance, much less the Gospel, into politics ; and that
on the day when woman votes the home will fall in everlasting ruin, and woman turn herself into a Jezebel.
Exuent omnes.

THE HOME GUARDS OF ILLINOIS.

In his eloquent sermon at Lake Bluff, near Chicago,
Chaplain McCabe, while fully and frankly avowing his
belief in woman's vote as a means of advancing the
temperance cause, stated some difficulties.   As the Lake
Bluff Temperance Convocation was called by the W. C. T.
Union of Illinois, whose work for the temperance ballot is
well known, Miss Willard briefly replied to the points
made by the chaplain, and the following is an abstract of
her impromptu :

She said : " Our good chaplain's first objection is that " It
is unwise to enlarge the law-making power while the
law-executing power is not increased."   But the beauty of
it is that in the nature of things this can't be done.   The
persons whom you add to the law-making power (for
instance, women with the temperance ballot on the Local
Option question) are by this new prerogative translated
out of the passive and into the active voice ; they become
interested in the enforcement of law.   The chaplain
draws a humorous picture of woman's weapons, showing
how inappropriate the sewing-machine and darning-needle
would be as engines of war, but Mrs. Plum of Streator,
one of our vice-presidents, can tell you of women who,
having first changed the public sentiment of that community by years of holding meetings, circulating temperance literature, and canvassing for the Home Protection
petition, finally secured local prohibition for the first
time in the history of that mining town, and then, with

their knitting in their hands and their darning-needles, for aught I know, went over to the court and prosecuted infractions of the law.

The difficulty presented is fancied, not real, and vanishes in the light of practical experience. The Home Protection movement in Illinois did more to awaken and solidify both law-making and law-enforcing power than any movement our State has ever seen. This is the admission of our practical workers, who go from one part of the State to the other, and of the dram-shop keepers themselves. Of 832 towns that voted on the question of license in the Spring of 1879, following our campaign, 645 voted "no license," a vastly larger proportion than at any previous time. If to-day women are not the law-executing power in Illinois, where our local unions have grown at the rate of 100 a year since the Home Protection movement was inaugurated, what class in our State constitutes that power? The chaplain would have known all this, and h ₴ heart would have been cheered by it, if the great circle around which he swings in his broader orbit had not led him outside our State for the most part.

Second objection: "Would not men vote as readily for prohibition as for woman's temperance ballot, and is not that the more direct way of coming at the difficulty?"

Until it can be proved that every man who opposes or dares not vote for prohibition also opposes or dares not vote for woman's temperance ballot, this objection is but chimerical. But it can never be thus proved. On the contrary, all experience points the other way. Some men, unlike our brave Chaplain McCabe, were unwilling to go themselves to the war, but quite ready to sacrifice upon the shrine of patriotism all of their wives' relations. In like manner, men are constantly saying to us, "You women must do this work. Your hands will soon be free to undertake it. We will give money to help you on, but our business interests and political ambitions are a ball and chain to us." Others, who are not frank enough to say this, show by their actions that they think it. Besides, there is a large class who, though not awake to the value of prohibition, do earnestly believe in woman's vote. Listen to intelligent conversation upon this subject, and you will find this to be true.

Third objection: "Behind the policeman's star, which is the symbol of the majesty of law, the offender sees the executive power of force residing in the strong arm of manhood. When women are ready to carry the sabre and ride to the cavalry charge, then their law-making power will avail something tangible for temperance."

Nay, let us think a little farther as to what is behind the star on that policeman's breast. If he is in Canada or England, a woman named Queen Victoria is behind it! But, jesting aside, everywhere that humanity has risen above brute force into the realm of law, you will find Christ's philosophy prevailing. Go back along the life-path of your statesman, your legislator, who made those statutes by which the Anglo-Saxon race is lifted from brute force to the level of constitutional law, and you will find a home, a mother's training, a Christian cradle hymn, a child's sweet prayer. Put men by themselves in camp and wilderness, and how long is law their arbiter rather than the matched strength of arm with arm and blow for blow? It is pure, ennobled Christian woman-hood, with her teachings and example, that has made law possible to the Anglo-Saxon race. Reverently let it be said, behind the policeman's star gleams the Star of Bethlehem. We women of Illinois believe in force. It rules the world; it always will. Force of brain, of heart, of conscience—these are the vital powers that move the world. It was said of a great chieftain:

> "One blast upon his bugle horn
> Was worth a thousand men!"

It was said of a great general–

> " I have brought you Sheridan all the way
> From Winchester down to save the day."

We believe in force of patriotism and leadership. They will always win, and women have them in abundant measure. It was not the bayonet, but the schoolmaster, that conquered at Sedan. In Switzerland it was not brute force that triumphed, but such a spirit in the people as that of Arnold of Winkelreid, when he opened his arms to gather to his faithful breast a sheaf of Austrian spears, and fell crying " Make way for liberty!" But should it come about that woman's help was needed on the battlefield in driving back the rum power for the defence of home, there are plenty of women in this convention who would lead a regiment just as ably and successfully as they now preside over a county convention. We temperance women of America believe in One who shall yet be crowned the King of nations, as He is now the King of saints, and we are ready to do and dare and die for Him. O Christ, it is not brute force that has carried on the triumph of Thy cross since the little procession of fishermen and women started out along the hillsides of Judea! No, it has been one mightier far, for love force has won the battles by which Thy cross grows regnant day by day. Prayer force, even as the chaplain says, is mighty to the pulling down of strongholds. Prayer, from the blessed days of the Ohio crusade, has been raising a citadel around our workers, high as the hope of a saint, deep as the depths of a drunkard's despair. If prayer and womanly influence are doing so much as forces for God by indirect methods, how shall it be when that electric force is brought to bear through the battery of the ballot-box along the wires of law ?

We mean to go straight on. Illinois will never call a halt. Let other States work for a prohibitory amendment, and may God bless them, but we will experiment along another line, first making sure of a trained constituency for prohibition, and then seeking constitutional law. We shall have the womanhood of this State with us. In Keithsburg, white and black, high and low, Catholic and Protestant women made common cause when invited to register their opinion on the saloon question. We have three American women to one woman foreign born to help to offset the vote of Hamburg and of Cork. We mean to be as good-natured as sunshine, but as persistent as fate, and may God defend the right!

HOW ONE LITTLE WOMAN SAVED THE DAY.

A KANSAS INCIDENT.

Neither poet nor painter need wish a more dramatic subject than is afforded by the history of how the constitutional amendment for prohibition came to be submitted to the people of Kansas. For fifteen years that brave young State had been under a blessed process of education by means of a local option law, by which, in cities of the second class, women had an equal voice with men concerning the legal status of the dram-shop. But though this method secured to the smaller towns immunity from the saloon, it did not reach the cities, and temperance legislators were anxious for a more sweeping law. Then it was that the liquor interest, dreading a statute like that of Maine, and not expecting their proposition to be accepted, made the suggestion that no legislation should be had, but the whole matter referred to the people. Whereupon the temperance men turned their jest to earnest, and for the first time in history a resolution was adopted to submit to popular vote a constitutional amendment for the total prohibition of the liquor traffic. It is not generally known that one little woman's heart was

the pivot on which this mighty movement turned, but
nothing is more true. For while the resolution to submit
passed the Senate without special difficulty, in the House
it trembled in the balance. Public feeling was at fever
heat, debate was long and full of animation, not to say
recrimination. Temperance men and women flocked to
the capitol, and the liquor men were out in force. At
last the issue was joined at midnight, after a stormy
closing debate. The roll of ayes and noes was called,
while every ear in the vast assembly that filled galleries
and corridor was strained to catch the responses of these
men, "dressed in a little brief authority," but none the
less men of destiny to-night. Busy pencils kept the tally,
and when the voting ceased a sigh from many a temperance man's heart accompanied the words: "We've lost
our cause by just one vote!"

But look, a woman, gentle, modest, sweet, advances
from the crowd. What, is she going down that aisle,
where woman never trod before, and in among that group
of party leaders? Yea, verily, and every eye follows her
with intense interest, and the throng is strangely still as
she goes straight to her husband, takes his big hands in
her little ones, lifts her dark eyes to his face, and speaks
these thrilling words: "My darling, for my sake, for the
sake of our sweet home, for Kansas' sake and God's, I
beseech you change your vote." When lo! upon the
silence broke a man's deep voice: "Mr. Speaker, before
the clerk reads the result *I wish to change my vote from
no to aye!*" How loud rang out the cheers of men: how
fell the rain of women's tears, for love had conquered, as
it always will, at last, and the voices of the people, when
heard in Kansas, said: "Give us prohibition for home's
and children's sake." So Kansas leads the van, and one
little woman saved the day.

16

THE BATTLE IN IOWA.

The victory gained June 27th in Iowa was the culmination of a hard-fought campaign, extending over eight courageous years. As everybody knows, our great Civil War was followed by a period of apathy in the temperance reform, public opinion having been solely occupied with one absorbing issue, and our citizen soldiery returning from the field with personal habits and moral standards reduced to lower levels by their long loss of home's sweet safeguards and exposure to the life of camp and field.

In 1874 came that mighty reaction known as the Woman's Temperance Crusade, by which the peaceful weapons of prayer and persuasion drove the saloons from 250 towns in fifty days ; by which crime was diminished by nine-tenths, and attendance at church was increased 100 per cent. Although these results were largely temporary, the sober second thought of that crusade was organization, and the "Woman's Christian Temperance Union," now extended over the entire Republic, the Dominion of Canada, and the Kingdom of Great Britain, is the most effective temperance society as yet known to philanthropic annals. From the beginning this society has had a splendid growth in Iowa, and under the leadership of Mrs. Judith Ellen Foster, Mrs. M. J. Aldrich, Mrs. L. D. Carhart, Mrs. V. M. Moore, Mrs. A. M. Palmer, Mrs. M. F. Goode, Mrs. Dr. Thrall, Mrs. Florence Miller, Mrs. Thickstun, Mrs. M. J. Callanan, and others, it has wrought with an energy and patience worthy of all praise. By their invitation and help, Francis Murphy of Maine, John W. Drew of New Hampshire, I. C. Bonticon, and Capt. Linscott of Michigan, and other leaders among reformed men, wrought valiantly in years past to persuade drinking men to cease patronizing the saloons. By their efforts also Bands of Hope were organized in every town, pledged to total abstinence from strong drink, tobacco, and profanity. By their efforts reading-rooms were opened, Gospel meetings held, literature scattered, and audiences convened in every corner of the commonwealth where, with gentleness of utterance and strength of argument, moral and legal suasion (the two millstones between which intemperance is to be crushed) were presented to the intellect and conscience of the Hawkeye State. From the first these women were convinced of the reasonableness of these twin methods of attack, and never ceased to urge them upon public attention. When, in 1875, the temperance men nominated Chaplain Lozier for Governor on an independent-prohibition ticket, the conscience of the W. C. T. U. was with the movement, though the society was then too weak to make itself felt, and the brave chaplain received but 1,400 votes. When, in 1877, Hon. Elias Jessup, a State Senator, was nominated by a convention of the Temperance Alliance, and twelve thousand independent votes were cast for him, Mrs. Foster, the most gifted and influential woman in the State, took the platform on his behalf.

When, in 1879, the Republicans heard the sound in the mulberry trees, and knew that the people were preparing to assert themselves, judging the signs of these times by the fact that there was greater defection from their ranks and discontent within than had heretofore been known, they agreed, by request of the W. C. T. U., and the brave men who had worked side by side with them, to submit to the people a constitutional amendment forever prohibiting the manufacture and sale of intoxicating liquors (including ale, wine, and beer) as a drink. Mrs. Foster was the first in the State to make this public recommendation. She did so at the annual convention of the State W. C. T. U., at Burlington, in 1878, as Superintendent of the Department of Legislative Work. Mrs. Foster and her husband, E. C. Foster, Esq., are both lawyers, and had carefully studied this subject, having heard Aaron M. Powell of New York make an address upon it at the Chicago Temperance Convention in 1875, knowing also the opinions and work of the Hon. S. D. Hastings, of Wisconsin, an early champion of the constitutional method, and being conversant with the noble undertaking of Senator Henry W. Blair of New Hampshire, at Washington. To the everlasting credit of the Republican party, be it said that they acceded to the appeals made them by the people of Iowa in the form of a petition, drafted by Mrs. Foster for the W. C. T. Unions, and by them carefully circulated throughout the State. The question that followed and stirred the heart of every temperance man and woman in Iowa was now before them. Having passed this measure once, will the dominant party have courage to do so again at the next biennial session? But the party stood manfully to its pledge—placed in its platform at the next State convention precisely the resolution which the ladies asked—namely, reiterating the same form of amendment as before, and pledging its submission at a special election.

Governor Sherman, who has frankly championed the amendment, was nominated and elected with a full understanding of that fact; the Speaker of the House was chosen on that issue; the election of James H. Wilson, Iowa's grand new Senator, was another temperance victory; and by excellent majorities the Legislature again voted to submit. Mr. Clarkson, of the Des Moines *Register*, the ablest and most influential paper in the State, battled from the first for the amendment. The strong men of the State took up the war-cry; Senator Wilson's magnificent speech was scattered by thousands; James Wilson, "of Tama," was true as a canny Scotsman only can be; Aaron Kimball, a State Senator and Chairman of the Amendment Association, gave time and

money to the battle ; the best lawyers in the State took
the stump ; the pulpit was solid, a thousand sermons a
Sunday being brought to bear upon the people from texts
like these : " Woe unto him that justifieth the wicked for
a reward." " Every plant that my Heavenly Father hath
not planted shall be rooted up." Speakers were invited
from other States. Governor St. John, of Kansas, from the
glorious standpoint of victory attained, told them how
fields were won ; George W. Bain, of Kentucky, " with
malice toward none and charity for all," plead with his
matchless eloquence the sacred cause of Home *versus*
Saloon ; John B. Finch, a lawyer from Nebraska, dealt
blows of logic that resounded throughout the State ;
George Woodford, of Illinois, put a reformed man's
pathos into his powerful plea ; Mrs. S. Skelton, of Germany, the daughter of a Darmstadt professor, talked to
our German friends in the beloved language of their
fatherland ; Mrs. Fixen, of Minnesota, spoke their own
tongue to the Scandinavians ; John Sobeski, of Poland,
one of the most genial, witty, and delightful of speakers,
won all who heard him ; and " Steamboat Frank," the
converted Modoc, through a good Quaker interpreter, Ira
D. Kellogg, of Indian Territory, warned the pale faces
against the fire-water. During the month of June one
hundred speakers were constantly in the field, not to
mention local workers. Mrs. Goode rallied the children,
teaching them "The Constitutional Amendment Catechism," until they knew as much as most lawyers on that
weighty subject, and went back to reason with, as well as
to persuade, the voters in their homes. The committee
at headquarters kept up a steady cannonade with temperance literature, sending to every chairman of a county or
a township regular and frequent assignments of printed
arguments. There were statistics for the farmers,
prepared by a leading temperance woman and said to

have been one of the most helpful of campaign documents; speeches by Senator Wilson and Judith Ellen Foster, by Governor St. John and many others ; also the publications of J. N. Stearns and D. C. Cook—these went by cart-loads, paid for by the business men of Iowa. The opposition tried similar tactics. Two men, with " Rev." prefixed to their names, took the stump; also an editor or two. We will kindly drop their names into the same oblivion into which their sorry work has fallen. A pamphlet on " Personal Liberty " (said to be by Henry Clay Dean) was circulated, and manifestoes by a German Free Thinker, who was chairman of the " Anti-Amendment Association."

Letters from Kansas were sent out, claiming that there was more liquor sold than ever, and yet winding up with the assertion that all foreign immigration was driven away, because there was nothing to drink. Statements about Maine. to the effect that in illiteracy, crime, etc., the old Pine Tree State brings up the rear of the Union, caused people of intelligence to smile. Statistics, duly watered, striving to prove the teetotal failure of prohibition wherever tried, were offset by counter statements from Neal Dow and Governor St. John. Many Democrats came out in strong advocacy of the amendment, and many Republicans in bitter opposition. There was but one subject discussed on the cars, one in the stores, shops, offices, and on the pavement, and that was the amendment. Temperance workers spoke two and three times a day, and rode across the country in the dead of the night, to catch the train for next forenoon's appointment. Governor St. John spoke in Cedar Rapids at 8 A. M. to an immense audience, and at Missouri Valley Junction, from the steps of the railroad station, " every man, woman, child, and dog in town " being present, by actual count. (I have it from an " eye-witness.")

Arriving on short notice at a wayside station, and urged to speak to an impromptu audience, the present chronicler was vastly amused to hear, between the pauses of her address on " Personal Liberty," the boy of the period ringing his mother's dinner-bell, as he perambulated the streets and shouted, in his shrill falsetto: " Lecture at Blank's Hall, now—now—now. Miss ——, of Illinois ; everybody invited."

Can we ever forget such days ? Never did those sacred words, " The People," have significance so full of comfort. No " fence-mending" politicians, no wheedling demagogues, •no imperious " bosses " could prevail. " The cause " had radiated out from the quiet prayer-room into the wide, free area of a mighty State ; " the plan " had been adopted by a great party ; " the appeal " of woman's heart was to become the dictum of the sovereign citizen ; the hope of the gentle had become the purpose of the strong. What one of America's great leaders said was coming true: " The verdict of the people can always be trusted when they have had a fair chance to hear the evidence." For eight years the Commonwealth of Iowa has been studying this question ; for four years that splendid State has been one great debating club. What wonder that on the 27th of June the jury thus summed up the evidence: " In the interest of the Home, the Saloon must henceforth be an outlaw. The Lord reigneth ; let the earth rejoice."

ELECTION DAY IN IOWA.

" All of which I saw," can only be said by the Omniscient, of so great a movement as that in Iowa. One little glimpse in a single pleasant village came to me. Marion, near Cedar Rapids, is one among the fifteen hundred polling-places of the " Hawkeye State." Out of its ninety-nine counties seventy-five gave a majority of over fifty

thousand on the 27th of June for a constitutional amendment prohibiting the liquor traffic.   Marion has about
one thousand voters, of whom nine hundred cast their
ballots, and of these seven hundred were for prohibition.
As Mrs. L. H. Carhart, the earnest-hearted President of
the Woman's Christian Temperance Union, lives in
Marion, I determined to spend the " day of days " with
her, after having visited, by her invitation, twenty towns
and cities, " speaking unto the children of Israel that they
go forward," and urging upon them our temperance war-
cry, " The sword of the Lord and of Gideon."   Picture a
lovely tree-embowered village, a fair June day, a population voluntarily turned out of doors, but all so orderly
and quiet that an almost Sabbath restfulness is in the air.
Promptly at nine o'clock the deep tones of the Court
House bell summon the Sunday-school children to the
Methodist church, whence, headed by the Band of Hope,
they are to march to the park, just opposite the polls.
Soon after, the Presbyterian bell calls the women to their
all-day prayer-meeting, the voters not being invited, for
the motto is, " The home expects every man to do his
duty—at the polls."   As a matter of fact, I rang a church
bell for the first time in my life on the 27th of June, we
women having it all our own way ; pastors, deacons, and
laymen spending the entire day at the City Hall, most
of them not even going to dinner.   Toward night some of
them came by way of jubilee to tell us what a victory was
gained, the good Methodist minister and the principal of
the high school taking the lead when the closing hours
arrived.   The bell rang every hour to denote that a new
meeting was begun.   Some of our good friends said,
" Enter into thy closet and shut thy door," and inveighed
against the frequent bell, but gentle Mrs. Carhart said:
" ' With the heart man believeth unto righteousness, and
with the mouth confession is made unto salvation ; ' that

bell is the voice of the Christian people of this village confessing him ' upon whose shoulder the government shall be.' "

But while the chastened voices of their mothers sang "Rock of Ages" at the church on the corner, near the City Hall, what a din their young hopefuls were making two blocks away, at the Methodist rendezvous. Having opened the women's prayer-meeting, Mrs. Carhart's swift steps passed on to where the clamoring throng were decking themselves with badges, and dividing the spoils of flags and banners. There was a strong tendency manifest for "all to be corporals," and to indicate the fact by hoisting some insignia aloft, perceiving which, with ready tact, the ladies in attendance improvised mottoes and wreaths of evergreens, fastened to bits of lath, broomstick, or hoe-handle, and the boys' hearts were set at rest. Meekly the girls marched forth two by two, and stood upon the order of their going until carefully graded according to their height, when, with plume and banner gay, they led off to the lovely park with the boys following; such mottoes as "Please vote for the Homes of Marion," "Tremble, King Alcohol, we shall grow up," "Stand aside, gentlemen, here come the future voters," while the star-spangled banner, stuck in hat bands or borne aloft in eager little hands, made its mute but eloquent appeal. Up and down through the streets they marched, the ladies forming their guard of honor, and finally drawing up in the park, they sang in their clear, cheery tone:

" My drink is water bright, water bright, water bright,
My drink is water bright, from the crystal springs."

This was followed by :

" Get ready for the jubilee,
Hurrah! hurrah!
When this our country shall be free,
Hurrah! hurrah!

> The girls will sing, the boys will shout,
>   When alcohol is voted out,
> And we'll all be gay
>   When temperance rules our land."

These musical exhortations were applauded by the grave citizens in the great group across the way, and thus encouraged, the children sang "Keep to the Right," gave a three times three for the amendment, and retired in good order from the field.

Meanwhile, about three doors from the City Hall, a beautiful flag had been flung to the breeze, and the announcement of "W. C. T. U. Free Lunch for all" greeted the eye. Here a committee of ladies worked hard all day, and fragrant coffee sent forth its pleasant invitation on the breeze. Voters were constantly passing in and out, temperance men would enter and confidentially allow the leading ladies to peep at the "tally," which they carefully kept, and here were brought to us the telegrams from all over the State: "Day fine, voters all out, ladies all out, business suspended, prospects good"—words which we could hardly see for tears of joy and hope. The lunch-room was adorned with those pretty things that women bring from home—plants, trailing vines, brackets, pictures, and flowers; Washington, and Martha by his side, Lincoln and Garfield, our greatest and best. "Oh," said the active local president, "they call this a fast age, and so it is, but in a blessed sense fast when you come to the temperance question. Neither Washington nor Lincoln saw greater things for God and home and native land than we shall see and share in."

An old gentleman, past eighty, came in after casting his vote, and as he took us by the hand he said: "To think I have lived to see this day, and to help on its victory! Now lettest thou thy servant depart in peace, O Lord, for mine eyes have seen thy salvation." The dear old man called it "voting for the improvement," and we women thought he had stumbled on the right, if not the legal phrase. Every few minutes some temperance man would rush in with such incidents as these : " Ladies, what do you think ? Blank, the brewer, took his team and went into the country for a sick man he felt sure would stand by him. The poor fellow was hardly able to come, but he did ; and when the brewer had helped him in and offered him a ballot against the amendment, what did he do but fumble in his pocket, fetch out one of our kind that his wife had got for him, and put it in, with all the anti fellows looking blank enough." Another man went to vote, while the saloon-keeper who brought him was entangled in an argument by our minister. He voted all right, and when the saloon-keeper found it out he looked like a cat that has lost its mouse, and said : " How dare he ? Why, the fellow owes me this very minute for at least one keg of beer !" A man who has always patronized the saloons came to Dr. C. and said : " I'm about wrecked. I've paid the money into these places that belonged to my family, and ought to have gone into flour and coal; but I tell you I'm bound to strike one blow for the right, now that I've got such a grand chance."

All day ﹏ong at the polls stood the Congregational minister, with sprained and painful ankle, supporting himself by leaning on his cane, pleading good-naturedly with voters, holding men who had come to peddle anti-amendment ballots in endless argument, and lifting up his heart to God for victory. All day long the best brain and brawn of Marion were all things to all men, that by all means they might win the most. It is like the *nil-admirari* school of fossiliferous communities to speak about " keeping clear of politics," but the best men of the bravest State in the Republic do not so speak. They " go in to win," as runs their own forcible phrase, and they honor the mothers that bore, the teachers who taught, the preachers who exhorted, and the homes that are proud of them. The only man whom I saw in Marion who seemed out of tune with the " Gloria " of the day was a crumpled up, cranky, and slightly intoxicated old Englishman (no fair exponent of that splendid race), who, after we had given him lunch and when we offered him the right kind of a ballot, fired up with these words: " You're too late ; I voted 'fore I came to lunch. I'm dead set agen your law and I'll always be dead set agen it, because I'm opposed to this here *female rule!*"

There was no more " telling " work than that of the young ladies and the children. They stripped the gardens of their choicest flowers, made them up into bouquets, and gave them out to men who agreed to vote for the amendment. I saw many a man in his shirt sleeves wearing a bunch of flowers, the symbol of home's sweetness, love, and purity. I saw colored men whose whole faces were one smile of delight as fair fingers proffered them a sprig of violets and mignonette, because they said they would vote for the amendment. I saw a rough farmer in " stogy boots " carefully putting his flowers aside, " to take home for my wife," he said.

When sunset came and we knew we had the victory, and knew that the saloon-men were saying, " Now, are you folks going to jeer at us and get up a big blow-out over this thing?" it was sweet and memorable to hear the womanly voice of the president saying, in that last hour of prayer, " Let us remember the Gospel exhortation, ' Be pitiful, be courteous.' " In keeping with this spirit were the resolutions passed next day by the State W. C. T. U., " pledging the good word, good will, and patronage of the women of Iowa to those whose business has been declared illegal whenever they enter on any occupation that is beneficial to society." No wonder there was joy in the homes of Iowa. The women have been so intent upon their temperance work that, as Mrs. J. Ellen Foster said (she who, more than any other, has wrought for the glorious consummation) : " It has filled our very souls. Why, the frogs in the swamps have croaked ' 'Mendment' in my ears ; the birds in the branches have twittered ' 'Mendment ; ' the little lambs have bleated, and the mother sheep baaed, and the cows in the pastures have mooed ' 'Mendment ; ' and there is no other word in Iowa until we win."

In the winning how many hearts rejoice! Iowa sent eighty-three thousand men to fight the South, but those gentle women yonder, whom we were once taught to call implacable, prayed all day long for the success of this greatest battle ever fought by the Hawkeye State. I have their kind letters from " all along shore" of the sea-board and the Gulf, desiring me to tell the women of Iowa of their love and their prayers. From Maine to Oregon, from Charleston to Sacramento, from New Orleans to Salt Lake, the temperance women were on their knees that day. In Chicago our best pastors led the meeting of our Union at Farwell Hall, and it was a millennial ray to see in the great secular papers a tele-gram with such a heading as " Availeth much. Let us take courage."

> " God 's in his heaven;
> All 's right with the world,"

or, as Mrs. Stowe divinely puts it, " Whatever ought to happen is going to happen."

EVANSTON, ILL.

INCIDENTS OF IOWA'S CONSTITUTIONAL AMENDMENT CAMPAIGN.

German speakers addressed audiences in their native tongue. Mrs. Skeldon, daughter of a Heidelberg profes-sor, won votes by hundreds among her own people, both through her addresses and the circulation of her paper, *Der Bahnbrecher*. Scandinavian ministers stood at the polls, church directory in hand, to check off their voters and be sure they had the prohibition ballot. A conference of German ministers came out unanimously in its favor. There was no fighting; no rough behavior at the polls. The ladies went the night before and decorated the city halls, engine houses, and other places where the ballot-box was set with pictures, mottoes, evergreens, and flowers. "Please vote to protect our homes," "The father's constituency is his family," "Iowa expects every man to do his duty," "For God, and home, and native land," were some of these.

In several cities the stores, offices, etc., were closed, and the notice posted up, "Gone to work for the Amendment." "The Band of Hope" marched in the procession, singing "Home, sweet home," "Dare to do right."

> "Get ready for the jubilee,
>   Hurrah! hurrah!
> When dear Iowa shall be free,
>   Hurrah! hurrah!
> The girls shall sing, the boys shall shout,
>   When alcohol is driven out,
> And we'll all be gay
>   When temperance rules our land."

Speaking in twenty of the chief towns, I had told

A SOUTHERN INCIDENT

which had touched my heart, as related by a temperance gentleman in Texas. It was the story of a Kentuckian who after years of hard drinking had reformed, had got the flask out of his side pocket and the New Testament in there instead, and had fastened his weak and wavering will to God's will omnipotent, by belts of faith and bands of prayer. On the morning of election day his wife said to him, timidly, "John, have I been a good wife to you, and tried to make our home pleasant, and to help you in your struggle for a better life?" and he answered, "Why Sallie, if you hadn't stood by me and helped me like a saint, as you are, I'd never have won this fight. You've been God's own special providence to me from the first day I ever saw your face." And then she said, with tears in her gentle eyes, "Dear John, you know I never said a word about your politics before, but if I've been a comfort to you, do please go to-day and vote against the saloon for my sake and that of our little ones." John made no reply, but went straight out of the house and over to the polls. His old cronies called out, "Why, where have you kept yourself so long, old fellow? We've missed you and mourned you, but you've got around in the very nick o' time; the fight's pretty tough; stand up for your old friends; here's your regular regulation ballot," and they handed him one with "license" in large letters. But a temperance man stood by with earnest face and a bunch of different votes. "See here, I reckon I'll sample your lot," said John, turning to him, and receiving a clean temperance ballot. Then the reformed man held up the first that all might see, tore it into little bits and scattered it to the winds, but afterward, with heaven's own sunshine on his face, he held the temperance ballot aloft and said: "Boys, I've always joined with you before, but, by the grace of God, here goes a vote *for Sallie and the children.*" It has been a great comfort to me to hear from different parts of the State of Northern men as noble as this generous Southron, who said, as they cast in their ballots on the 27th of June, in Iowa, "Well, I do this just as John did, away down South, 'for Sallie and the children.'"

So the great cause binds us with new and tender ties, and shall yet blot Mason and Dixon's line out of the heart as well as off the map, and give us in a sense we had not known before a really re-United States, and may God speed the day !

A lovely omen was the unbroken circle of prayer in our W. C. T. Unions on Iowa's behalf. Letters are coming to me from all parts of the South, asking me to tell the ladies there of the meetings held and the earnest petitions from tender hearts that God would deliver their fair young State from the cruelty of the rum power. Let me here gratefully acknowledge these sisterly messages on behalf of those to whom they were so kindly sent.

CHILDHOOD'S PART IN IOWA'S VICTORY.

"To the children of the State, whose hearts and songs were the sunshine that never left the banner of the amendment, let no one forget the fullest measure of gratitude." This sentence is from the Iowa State *Register*, which, in circulation and influence, stands at the head of journalism in that commonwealth, and is edited by Mr. Clarkson, a noble man and brilliant writer, whose utmost strength has been exerted for the success of prohibition, and whose paper has, by unanimous consent, done more to ensure the recent victory for temperance than any other single force. Mr. Clarkson was himself a member of the Cadets of Temperance twenty years ago, and is a conspicuous illustration of results to be expected from honest, hard work among the children. Perhaps there is no parallel, in the history of a great reform, to the efforts made for temperance education among the children of Iowa for eight years past, and to the power exerted by them in securing the result by which the liquor traffic in that State was recently outlawed by a majority of over fifty thousand in seventy-five out of its ninety-nine counties.

As the genius of temperance does not belong to that class in society who "reap where they have not sown, and gather where they have not strewn," it will be instructive to study the methods by which the children have become one grand " cold-water army." In the first place, the translation of Christian women out of the passive and into the active voice on this question has had an immense influence on their little ones at home. I know of more than one mother in Iowa whose little boy would go two blocks out of his way rather than pass a saloon. The Woman's Christian Temperance Union is perhaps stronger in that State than in any other; and the table-talk, the juvenile literature that comes into the homes, indeed, the whole atmosphere, is tinged with an influence that leads toward purity in the conduct of life, and away from " fleshly lusts that war against the soul." Then, in many localities, the Woman's Christian Temperance Union has succeeded in getting the Temperance Lesson Book of Dr. Benjamin Ward Richardson, and the Alcohol and Hygiene of Miss Julia Colman, into the public schools, where the effects of strong drink on the tissues of the body and the temper of the spirit have been regularly taught. We have not yet succeeded in securing a legislative enactment by which the teaching of this branch is as obligatory as that of grammar and arithmetic, but expect to do so at the next session, petitions having been largely circulated to this end. Minnesota has the honor of being the first State to adopt such a law, and Iowa will doubtless be the second.

But the " good general," as she is called, of the juvenile temperance forces, is Mrs. M. F. Goode, a widow with children of her own, whose home is in Villesca, Iowa, but whose praise is on the lips of her great Band of Hope Army throughout the State. As Superintendent of juvenile temperance work, this lady has done more than any other in our ranks along this special line of duty. She is of just the nature most agreeable to childhood,— strong, healthful, cheery, and loving-hearted, with such motherly ways that every boy and girl turns as instinct-

ively to her as chickens to the mother hen. She has no
"holy horror" in look or tone, but has a warm hand to
lift with if anybody wants to climb, and a gift of making
the climb itself attractive. She is the sort of person who
can and does with impunity stop a crowd of boys emerging from a shooting-gallery, gathering them around her
in the street as she makes a platform of the curbstone's
edge, and calling out: "Now, my young men, I wish
every one of you that chews or smokes tobacco would just
lift up your hand." On the occasion of which I write,
among twenty boys, fifteen lifted their hands, and all
were under sixteen years of age.

Mrs. Goode has organized the Band of Hope throughout
the State, in which the reasonableness of total abstinence
is taught by lessons, experiments, and blackboard illustrations. The children's reading is largely supervised in
the interest of temperance as opposed to the Jesse James
pictorials, and the triple pledge (against intoxicating
liquors, tobacco, and swearing) intelligently made.

Added to these instrumentalities are two others of
paramount importance. The ministers of Iowa preach
against the making and the use of intoxicating liquors as
a drink, with almost concurrent testimony and power,
while the Sunday-school is earnest, clear, and systematic
in its teaching. The Quarterly Temperance Lesson and
Exercises have been generally introduced, and meet the
hearty approbation of the people. The recent Sunday-
school convention at Waterloo was a real temperance
jubilee. All our leading speakers were invited, and
among those present to whom time was given were Mrs.
J. Ellen Foster, the leading exponent of temperance reform
in the Woman's Christian Temperance Union of Iowa;
Colonel George W. Bain, the Southern orator; Mrs. M.
J. Aldrich, a Presbyterian lady of Cedar Rapids, who
gives constant and most efficient service to the cause; and
Mrs. A. M. Palmer, our State evangelist.

Let me conclude with a few incidents of the memorable day (June 27th) when the people of Iowa voted so to amend their constitution as forever to prohibit the manufacture and sale of intoxicating liquors, including wine, beer, and ale, as a drink.

Mrs. Goode had issued " Military Order No. —" to her Band of Hope ; namely, that, " at 9 A. M. they should meet at an appointed rendezvous, wearing their badges, and carrying flags and banners, and should march through the streets with a band of music at the head of their battalion, singing near the polls their cold-water songs, giving three cheers for the amendment, and returning in good order to the starting-place." These young folks were not raw recruits,—many a time had they marched before. They were not ignorant of the import of this day. " The Constitutional Amendment Catechism" had been so carefully studied at their regular meetings that little people, eight years old, knew the difference between constitutional and statutory law—and the reasons of superiority in the first. They knew the facts and figures —having them illustrated by diagrams and pictures. " How much grain is used in our breweries ? " " What is Iowa's annual drink bill ? " " What proportion of our taxes, crime, pauperism, lunacy, comes of strong drink in our State ? "

These and a score of such subjects had been thoroughly set forth in the Socratic method, and few voters were better informed than these boys and girls. They had also been urged to repeat all this at home, and to plead with fathers and brothers to vote aright. With a woman's tact, Mrs. Goode had told them that at present the theory of our government is that the father represents "the people" in his home, and that is why we say " we, the people of Iowa," will vote on these great public questions and decide them. So she urged the children to get papa to take the census in his own home, and go to the polls to represent not himself only, but his constituency.

It is well known in Iowa that the children did a vast amount of delightful and most effective electioneering at their own home hearths; and on the final day barefooted urchins went timidly up to well-dressed business men, and said, " Please, sir, won't you vote for my mother and me ?— my father is a drunkard." Little boys marched up and down through the crowd of voters with banners wreathed in evergreen, whereon, in fleecy white letters, cut from cotton batting, were the words, " Please vote for the home," or " Tremble, King Alcohol, we shall grow up," or " Our guns are ballots, our bullets are ideas." Little girls went out two by two, with baskets heaped with button-hole bouquets, and while, at a little distance, fond motherly eyes watched their proceedings, they said to voters : " Won't you put in a ballot, sir, for the amendment ? " And if they said they had, or would, the little fingers handed up a dewy bunch of flowers. I gained new hope for poor humanity as I saw rough men carefully pinning childhood's sweet gift of " posies " on their checked shirts; Germans and Swedes fastening a sprig of mignonette in their old hat-bands ; and colored men, with gleaming ivories, tying a full-blown rose to the only button left upon a threadbare coat, and saying, " Yes, honey, dis chile is fur de 'men'ment every time."

In one of the river towns the mayor brought in a bloated German beer-drinker to vote the " whisky ticket," when the German's children, fresh from the Band of Hope procession, hurried forward, the little girl throwing her arms around her father's neck, and saying, with tears, " Papa, please vote for us at home," and the boy, who was a cripple, taking him by the hand, with the same plea. " Ach, mein Gott, dis vas too much ! " exclaimed the German, breaking away from the man who had

counted on him, and going up to the ballot-box with the
vote his little daughter gave him, while she held one
hand, and the lame boy hobbled on the other side as
guardian.   Not an eye that looked upon the group could
see it clearly because of tears.   "A touch of nature
makes the whole world kin."

Truly "a little child shall lead them."   Truly that
little child is " the fortress of the future," standing away
out on the frontier of time.   Let us furnish the fortress
with provisions, weapons, ammunition ; and eager hearts
shall "hold the fort" when we grow weary.   God bless

" The little soldiers newly mustered in."

CHAPTER XXI.

MRS. MARY A. LIVERMORE,

Our Chief Speaker, and President of the Massachusetts W. C. T. U.

Seen from afar—Personal reminiscences—A racy sketch of her Melrose home—Sermon on Immortality—Incidents of early years—Religious character—Her coadjutors—Elizabeth Stuart Phelps' Letter to Massachusetts W. C. T. U.

IN the seclusion of Evanston, our idyllic suburban village, we read much during the later years of the war, about Mrs. Livermore and her great-hearted associate, Mrs. A. H. Hodge of Chicago. As the projectors of those mammoth "sanitary fairs," which were a national astonishment, these ladies loomed like colossal figures in the imagination of one obscure school teacher, who would have deemed it the height of impertinence to seek acquaintance with women so distinguished. Their Amazonian courage seemed to be equaled only by their motherly tenderness. Now canvassing the great Northwest for hospital supplies; then conducting a fair which yielded one hundred thousand dollars as a net profit to the sanitary commission, and anon watching over the wounded in hospitals and on the field, those women were heroines to be gazed on from afar, but also loved and prayed for as one's "very own." Years after, during my residence abroad, mother wrote a letter full of enthusiasm relative to a "woman's convention" she had just attended in Chicago, in which occurred these words: "Mrs. Mary A. Livermore, who presided throughout the session, is a queen among women. Of stately presence, deep, melodious voice, and most womanly nature, she was head and shoulders above every

(418)

MRS. MARY A. LIVERMORE.

other person present. Would not such a woman adorn the U. S. Senate? Yea, verily, far beyond most of the men who get themselves elected to that august body, and I fervently hope she may live to take the seat for which nature has certainly ordained her." As my mother is to me "final authority" upon a theme like that, I was more than ever an admirer of Mary A. Livermore. On my return home I found that Mrs. Hodge had become a resident of Evanston. I soon enjoyed the rare pleasure of being associated with her in the work of our new college for ladies. We planned the "Woman's Fourth of July," a mammoth celebration, at which ten thousand people were amused and fed, the entire proceeds going to the new educational enterprise to which we were devoted. In our frequent meetings, how often Mrs. Hodge spoke to us of her gifted associate, and in reply to my fusilade of questions—for nothing on this planet attracts me like a noble, *grandiose* woman—I learned more of Mrs. Livermore than the numerous, eagerly-scanned biographies had ever taught. As Mrs. Hodge waxed eloquent over her choice theme, some of us used to say, "It takes one gifted woman adequately to describe another." How she dwelt upon the "reserve power" of her friend—that surest mark of a great nature; the subtle keenness of perception; the fertility of resource; the intrepidity of execution! I learned that Mrs. Livermore was as gifted as though not industrious, and as industrious as though not gifted. "Often, when we were at the front after a battle," said Mrs. Hodge, "and I had gone to my bed in utter exhaustion after a day's nursing, I would hear the pen of that indomitable woman scratching away into the night or unto the dawn. Articles for her husband's paper in Chicago, appeals to the people for supplies, letters to the anxious friends of wounded soldiers,—these she would toss off at electric speed, resuming her hospital work betimes, next day."

I was newly reminded of these words when the press
circulated a touching incident which recently occurred in
a Michigan town where Mrs. Livermore lectured.   A
woman from the country, who had taken a long ride over
rough roads to hear her, came timidly forward at the
close, and carefully producing a thin, gold ring, gave it to
the famous lecturer, saying : " Do you remember writing
out the dying message of a soldier to his wife, and by his
wish, sending this ring?" Mrs. Livermore was obliged
to confess that she had written so many such letters she
could not remember this specific case, upon which the
aged woman explained, with tears, that the soldier's
widow was her only child, who, dying, had charged her
mother to give back this ring to Mrs. Livermore if she
ever had the opportunity.

It was to Mrs. Hodge we were indebted for the long-
coveted pleasure of hearing Mrs. Livermore at Evanston.
She came and gave us a lecture for the benefit of our new
enterprise, in which her generous heart was deeply interested.   The church was packed, the scene historic, as the
two foremost women of the war sat side by side, the
senior a Presbyterian of conservative training and theology, the junior a liberal in her views (perhaps the
intellectual rebound of an adventurous spirit from a Baptist deacon's training), but both too intellectual and
royal-hearted to permit divergent " views " to alienate
them in their philanthropic deeds.

" What shall we do with our daughters?" was the
theme.   Happy was the aspiring girl (and our college
was out in force) who heard its invulnerable logic, its
tender pathos, and its ringing eloquence.   What would I
not have given to be this woman's auditor when I, like
them, was in my teens!   The admiration and love then
kindled in my breast and heart for Mrs. Livermore have
been perennial.   Never have I had more inspiring talks

with gifted persons than with " our Temperance Great
Heart," as I like to call her, at Melrose, Mass., or the
Twin Mountain House, where I have been her guest. To
write out some account of these to me memorable occasions, especially to describe that genial, loving fireside
circle in her heart's-ease of a home, was on my mind
when the following racy sketch by Virginia F. Townsend,
the talented author, came in my way. Every temperance
woman in the land will read it with keen pleasure. It is
called

A NIGHT AT THE HOME OF MARY A. LIVERMORE.

"'Melrose!' shouted the conductor. I was out on the
platform in a moment, with the rest of the human pack-
ages, staring curiously up and down the quaint old town,
which strikes one at first sight as comfortably taking its
ease and the world at large in a peaceful, Rip-Van-Winkle
sort of atmosphere. Melrose, however, is only seven
miles from Boston, and, despite the air of serene respectability with which it confronts a stranger, must come in
for its share in the seasoning of Attic salt, and, no doubt,
get to the heart of it, is well tinctured with heresies and
radicalism. It was the late afternoon of one of those
June days Lowell sings about so felicitously, when I made
my way through the shadows of the pleasant, dreamy old
street to the home across whose threshold I was now to
pass for the first time. A soft, poetic sunshine was on
leaves and flowers; there were hushes of winds among
locusts and maples, and the sweet twitter of robins
through the stillness when I found myself at the house
where I was to pass the night. A quiet, unpretending
New England home stood before me, finished up in
browns, even to the blinds, a veranda across the front,
and June roses in a very glee and riot of blossoming—the
extreme simplicity of the whole in fine harmony with the

17

old town and the shadowy street, even though the presiding divinity here was the strong, earnest, intent soul of Mary A. Livermore. I may as well say at this point that, measured by hours and interviews, we were almost strangers to each other. A brief meeting or two, a letter sent me when the heart of the writer was at white heat with the work and the glory of the Chicago Sanitary Fair, comprised our personal acquaintance; yet, despite this fact, I was certain that hostess and guest would meet to-night not as strangers do. If one does not feel at home with the first glance at the house, one is certain to the moment he is across the threshold.

"The parlor which received me was a place to dream in for a day, with pictures, and engravings, and pretty brackets that gave color, and grace, and a certain artistic effect to the whole room, while that subtle charm of a real home atmosphere brooded over all. I had expected to find in Mrs. Livermore a good housekeeper; indeed, come to think of it, I never knew a literary woman, in the highest sense of that word, who did not prove herself in her own home a capable domestic ' manager '; and having been in more than one of these homes I am, despite the traditional blue stocking, entitled to speak *ex-cathedra* on this matter. My own room, too, when I went into it, proved the very 'pink essence' of order and comfort, with pictures and brackets again, and delicate little artistic touches everywhere. I sat down by the window, too content for any thing but watching the sunshine in the cherry and locust trees outside, and waited, but not long. There was a rap at the door—no soft, appealing flutter of fingers, but prompt, strong, decisive—and, getting up, I confronted Mrs. Livermore. She was a tall, dignified, matronly presence, an earnest, intent, attractive face, with a smile that comes suddenly and breaks up the gravity with a sweet archness, a voice full of a clear, ringing helpfulness and decision, and the more you see of her the more you grow into a sense of her reserve force and her wonderful magnetic power, and comprehend what a shrewd physician meant when he said: 'The Lord made you up, Mrs. Livermore, to do a big job of work in this world.' 'I should have come to you at once,' she said, with her cordial warmth of speech and manner, 'but my husband's congregation at Hingham gave us a reception yesterday, and this morning I was obliged to take the six o'clock train into Boston to see to the getting out of the paper, so, when I learned you were coming, I primed myself with a couple of hours' sleep.' We took our supper alone together that night. A silver goblet stood by my plate, and when I had taken my first draught Mrs. Livermore remarked: 'That goblet was given me by the soldiers at the Chicago Sanitary Fair.' Perhaps I was unusually thirsty that night; at any rate, it seemed to me as I drained the goblet that no water had ever tasted so sweet. The silver was simple enough, with its chasing and Latin inscriptions, but it spoke to me of weary journeys through days and nights in 'mud-spankers,' over the wide, lonely plains of the Northwest; of burdens under which a strong man might well have faltered, always with calm, unflinching courage; of wounded men in dreary hospitals starting at the sound of the clear, helpful voice, and glancing up with tearful joy as that woman's shadow fell into their pain and loneliness.

"Before we had finished our supper Mr. Livermore entered—a fine-looking, rather portly gentleman, who evidently has a relish for a joke and a profound faith in looking on the bright side of things. He reminded me of some jolly English squire, who would enjoy riding to cover in the dew and sunshine of an autumn morning, and spurring on horse and hound to the chase with the bravest, but he is in reality the pastor of a Universalist church at Hingham. 'We exchange works sometimes,' said his wife, with a laugh. 'When there is a high pressure of business on me he obligingly spares me the trouble of writing an editorial, and, in turn, I occasionally preach for him.' Despite the appalling fact that his wife is an editor, a lecturer, an occasional preacher, and a leader in the Woman's Rights Movement, nobody, seeing them half an hour together, could doubt that the Hingham pastor was a proud and a happy husband.

"After supper we went over the house, and Mrs. Livermore took me into her sanctum, a quiet little nook, and as orderly as Sir Walter Scott's library at Abbotsford. From the back windows the idyl of Mrs. Livermore's home burst suddenly upon me in the shape of 'Crystal Lake,' a delicious little sheet of water on whose shores her house stands. It was just at sunset, and the winds were out, and there was a very dazzle of silver waves along the banks as I first caught sight of the little lake between its low-lying shores. Here, too, lay a dainty little row-boat, just fitted for the fairy stream it was to navigate.

"But the cream of the evening was yet to come. At last we· were quietly settled down in Mrs. Livermore's own room for the 'talk' we had been so long promising ourselves. It was a talk which, following no law, glanced all over Mrs. Livermore's life. The stately matron was again a child, with Copp's Hill Cemetery for her playground, and without a fear of the quiet sleepers under her riotous sport. She drew herself a wild, impetuous, overflowing 'tom-boy' of a girl, brimming with fun and mischief; the strong, native, vital forces in her bringing her forever to grief, yet never permanently checked; the champion always of the poor and friendless; and a strange, underlying sadness getting sometimes to the surface through all the boisterous mirth and mischief. This woman was evidently cut out on a grand pattern from the beginning. The royal Hebrew's injunction of ' not sparing the rod ' was faithfully observed in the training of the eager, intense, tumultuous New England girl. She was sent supperless to bed; she was defrauded of that crowning treasure and delight of childhood, Saturday afternoon; she was scolded at and urged; and she cried herself sick, or would if any such thing had been possible to the fibre that went to the making of the stout, robust little figure, and wished she was dead, and then broke the cords which held her a prisoner in the chair, and, mounting that, made it serve for a pulpit and preached to the walls, warning sinners to 'flee from the wrath to come,' while father and mother would stand listening outside in amused bewilderment at the child's passionate eloquence. Sometimes, too, the old Baptist deacon would look mournfully at his daughter, and say: ' If you had only been a boy, Mary, what a preacher in that case you would have made! I would certainly have educated you for the ministry, and what a world of good you might have done!' But it never so much as entered the Boston deacon's heart that this strange, impulsive, fiery little soul, whose sex he so keenly deplored, had her own work to do in the world, and would yet hold vast masses breathless under the power of her logic, the magic charm of her eloquence. But the years went on, and the Boston deacon's daughter grew into girlhood and womanhood, with her marvelous energy, with her keen, alert mind, with her hungry greed of knowledge, with her swift scorn of sophistries, but with the warm, generous heart, a little steadied with the gathering years, as swift and helpful now as in those old days when it danced in Copp's burying-ground, and was the champion of all the poor, neglected children.

"' When we were married,' said Mrs. Livermore, with

that humor whose current plays and sparkles through all the earnestness of her talk, ' our capital consisted of books. I did all my own work. I cut and made my husband's coats and pants. There is no kind of house work with which I am not familiar. I defy anybody to rival me in that line. My drawers, my closets, my whole house are always free for inspection.'

"It is marvelous, when you come to think of it, the amount of mental and physical strain which this woman manages to undergo. There is the constant wear and tear of nerve and brain. For three weeks at a time, during the lecture season, she assures me she has not slept on a bed, except such poor substitutes of one as lounges on cars and steamboats afford. Even during the summer her engagements are so numerous that the evening I passed with her was the solitary one she could command for the ensuing month. She was to speak in a few days in Clifton, N. Y., and to lecture before the graduating class of the divinity school in Canton, this being the first time in the history of American institutions that such an honor has been awarded to a woman. Add to this her constant reading, her duties as chief editress of the *Woman's Journal*, the letters that must be answered, the ocean of manuscripts that must be waded through. One cannot help sympathizing with the sentiment of the distich which she quoted to me as a sample of the avalanche of rhyme which poured down on the *Woman's Journal:*

> "Art thou not tired, my dear M. A. L.,
> Working forever, so hard and so well ?"

' There were actually four pages in this key,' she said. Of course no woman could bear all this physical and mental strain without the foundation of an admirable physique. With few exceptions, she has always enjoyed splendid health. The stamina of her Puritan grandmother seems to have been bequeathed unweakened to

Mary A. Livermore. Then, there are the constant claims on her time and charity. As an instance in point, one year she found homes for thirty-three children, worse than orphans.

"'I never in my life,' she said, 'turned anybody away who came to me for help. I never willfully wronged a human being.' How few of us could in our inmost souls say these words!

"Amid our talk there shine two sentences of my hostess which have come back to me so often and which seem two such clear crystals of truth that I cannot choose but write them here. One was, 'A Divine discontent must pursue all human lives;' and the other, 'Life is lonely to every soul.'

"But the pleasantest hours have an end, and we were on the flood-tide of our talk, and Mrs. Livermore wore the look of an inspired sybil, and the hours were wearing toward midnight, when the Hingham pastor, with his pleasant face and his air of the English squire, broke in upon us, saying, quietly, that to-morrow would demand too heavy a toil for the night's lost sleep, and he must send us to bed. I entreated him to furnish us some cordial that would hold us awake and alert for the precious hours of that one night, but it was evident that his pharmacy yielded no such inspiring draught, and his wife—I must tell the honest truth here—seemed disposed to 'obey' him with as much meekness and alacrity as though she regarded that obnoxious verb a binding part of the marriage covenant—as though she had never stood upon a platform, or preached from a pulpit, or gone down bravely to the hospitals and bound the quivering limbs of poor, wounded soldiers, or held a cooling draught to their fevered lips—nay, even as though the woman whom Boston long ago gave to Chicago, and whom Chicago, after the grand work of the Sanitary Fair was accomplished, gave back in the prime of her womanhood and the ripeness of her intellect to Boston, had never waved the banner and raised the war-cry of the *Woman's Journal*."

Since Mrs. Townsend's sketch was written, Mrs. Livermore has ceased to edit this foremost paper of the woman's movement, and concentrates her powers on lyceum lecturing and the temperance reform, preaching frequently on Sabbath nights in the pulpits of almost all denominations. I shall never forget a sermon on "Immortality" delivered by her in Chicago. It had the motherhood of God in it, no less than His Fatherly character, and seemed to me to supply the "missing link" which I had always felt rather than known in the discourses of men. None but a mother—and one as true and tender as Mrs. Livermore has always been—could have talked as she did about the love of God.

Some facts of her early life must be referred to before I close. Mary Ashton Rice (her maiden name) was born in Boston, Dec. 19, 1821, and at fourteen years of age, graduated with high honors from Hancock school, taking the Franklin medal. She at once entered the Charlestown Female Seminary, a Baptist institution; remained there three years as teacher and pupil, being advanced to the position of instructor in Latin, Italian, and French. She also acquired enough Greek to render her eligible to enter Harvard University, and she actually went with a few daring young schoolmates like herself to President Quincy, then at the head of that conservative institution, and sought admission. It seemed hardly possible for the good man to regard their intention as serious, and to say they got no countenance whatever is a feeble image of their discomfiture.

The childhood of Mary Livermore was no humdrum affair, but quite as remarkable in its way as her later history. She always had a great heart. The family was in moderate circumstances, and she was so anxious to be a helper rather than a burden that she went privately to a shop and took some shirts to make at six cents apiece. Her mother, finding this out, wept at this proof of her little girl's devotion. "The platform spirit was in her earlier than this," writes one who furnished me these items, "for she would go into the shed, set up blocks of wood for an audience, and then orate to her heart's content, getting so earnest, almost to tears, over her theme, which was often drawn from "Fox's Book of Martyrs," of which her father was a diligent expounder. So strong an impression did this book make upon her childish imagination that "playing martyr" was among her favorite pastimes, and in that character she even burned in the old-fashioned fire-place a handsome doll given by her grandmother. At the age of ten she was so gifted in composition that her teacher, Master Field of Hancock school, couldn't believe she wrote the essays whose authorship she claimed, and to test the matter she was shut up in a recitation room with paper and pencil only, and upon the theme assigned to her—"Self-government"! she wrote a composition so remarkable that all doubts vanished, and she was thenceforth taken into special favor."

It would be a study of absorbing interest to trace the religious history of this earnest-hearted woman. No passage in her many-sided life is more characteristic or suggestive. But this is not the place for that delineation. Mrs. E. R. Hanson of Chicago, in her attractive book, "Our Woman Workers," published at the office of *The Star and Covenant,* has given this history in full. Happily we have emerged upon an era when the theory of Christian life is by all thoughtful people held in abeyance to the Christian life itself. Measured by this standard, every true heart must pay glad homage to the character and deeds of Mary A. Livermore. Grand leadership invariably develops a royal "following," and the W. C. T. U. of Massachusetts is an emphatic illustration of this rule. We have no abler women than those who are grouped around this noble leader, and to recount their work would be pleasant indeed. But their chief has " made history " at such a rate herself, that space is lacking for the notes I had designed of Mrs. L. B. Barrett, her schoolmate and life-long friend, Mrs. P. S. J. Talbot, the devoted " member for Malden," Mrs. Rev. Dr. Gordon, the model President of Boston W. C. T. U., Mrs. Fenno Tudor, that wealthy woman with a wealthy heart, Miss Elizabeth S. Tobey, who leads the work of the young women, Mrs. Emily McLaughlin, and Mrs. Mary G. C. Leavitt, the gifted lecturers, and many of their earnest-hearted sisters. I am confident these loyal workers will applaud my decision to curtail these personal notices, that I may enrich my book with the matchless letter of Elizabeth Stuart Phelps, written for their last annual meeting:

CONDITIONS OF TEMPERANCE WORK.

Ladies of the Christian Temperance Union:

You have asked me for an address which I am disabled from giving; for an address which I am not in health to write. Yet I find it difficult to pass by with silence your kind recognition of my sympathy with the cause for which you are "toiling" so "terribly."

Those wisest of words, of one of the wisest of men, never return to me with more force than when I am brought to bay before these moral ferocities of society such as it is your privilege and your pain to combat. We must "toil" as "terribly" to save a soul, as to discover a star,—to purify a village, as to win a continent. Most of us, at the outset of life and labor, have to learn, perhaps, that philanthropic effort is not intellectual ease. "A scholar," it has been well said, "is the result of the abnegation, of the sacrifice, of generations." Let me remind you that it takes no less of precedent and of cost to make a reformer. The mushrooms of our little kindly impulses sprout up every day and in any nature. The aloe of the great moral martyr demands its century to blossom in. What ancestries of pure blood, humane culture, religious sensitiveness, go to his creation! The successful philanthropist is never an accident. Heredity and circumstances hem him in, and urge him on to his inevitable sequence. The consistent, unfaltering life of balanced usefulness is as much a consequence of ordered causes as fame, or the gallows. Such a life is not a thing that comes by wishing. Mere zeal can never make a power of a good intention. It is a drawn game, perhaps, yet, in the history of the world, which works the deepest mischief, head without heart, or heart without head? Good works mean, above all else, good thoughts. Humanity is nothing if it is not common sense. Benevolence without wisdom becomes maleficence. These are old saws which every kind of effort in social progress must resharpen for use, but there are few directions in which we are forced to hack away with them so often, or so hard, as in this one work of reforming the laws, which make it almost impossible for men to live sober, and of dealing properly with the man when he is drunk.

I have little knowledge to offer you but that of a limited invalid experience in the great effort which needs the health, the heart, and the hope of the country to urge it on. You are veterans in a cause where I am but a raw and disabled recruit. Yet if on the battle-field you would pause to hear a whisper from the hospital, I can only give you the one thing that the work itself has given to me:

It is not so much a work of the emotions as it has been superficially supposed—and often practically proved—to be. It is more a work of reflection than we are forewarned to consider it. We have made our share of mistakes in this point of the compass. Our praying bands at street corners, and State-houses draped with petitions, and vicious men spoiled by lavish womanly tenderness, have had their dramatic, but their pitiable aspects. Now we are coming to the undramatic, the unemotional, the dogged hard work without brilliant effects. Perhaps now we must learn that hardest of tasks—how to hope without the excitement of electric returns.

Nothing impresses me so much about this reform as the eternity of it. It goes on, and goes on, in our individual experience, like Carlyle's "everlasting No," perhaps like the golden ring of love itself, wherein there seems no beginning and no ending to our joy.

This I have learned—that there is no end. There can be no end to our education, to our mistakes, to our strain of muscle and strength of nerve, to our courage that must break up and out like trodden flame, to our patience that should sleep like the deepest depth of mid-ocean, or the bluest height of mid-heaven, behind and below all the little bluster that goes to make up the storms of progress.

It takes a good many drops of the heart's blood to save one drunkard, but it takes as many brain-cells. It calls for the fire of a soldier, but the repose of a saint. We must be men in daring, but women in devotion—girls in enthusiasm, but aged in discretion—dizzy with fervor, but poised with wisdom. Like all else in life, it is an infinitely more complex thing than we know till we have tried it, to handle the great forces of tempted human souls.

If, dear friends, when all is done, each woman of you has but restored one diseased nature, has only helped, by the weight of one individuality, to the creation of that public sentiment which will some day make it almost as disreputable to tolerate drunkenness as to get drunk, is it worth while ?

It seems to me that the answer to this question, whereon the law and prophets of the matter hang, rests altogether with our individual selves. There is a cheap and easy way of disposing of such moral problems, as if, forsooth, the force of any one creature successfully expended on any one other must be of necessity good politico-spiritual economy. This is not true. It does not follow that it is always worth while to do every good deed that presents itself to us. The value of our efforts depends quite as much upon the results to ourselves as upon the effect on those for whom we sacrifice ourselves.

Are *we* the better, nobler, richer in nature, larger in grace, for the reform or philanthropy which we have selected to be the outlet of our restless nerve, or our compressed consecration? We have a right to ask ourselves this question. The drunkard is not the only soul to be considered. The delicate woman who has the variousness and sweetness of all human uses and pleasures open to her choice—she who commands the welcome and the warmth of so many a social value—she too shall be estimated as a factor in this sum. Sometimes she too must ask herself, in very honesty, the question which lookers-on, in easy phrasing, ask her,—*Is she wasted?*

Women of this Union ! banded together to go down into the dens and slums and horrors, thence to lead out woe and shame and vice— *Are you wasted?* You, who turn from your children's evening prayer to lead a "reformed man" safely home past the fifteen grog-shops he must pass before he can reach *his* children's waiting faces—and then back again to kiss your own babies in their sleep—are *you* wasted?

Wasted? Nay, then, you are saved at spiritual usury. Wasted? Nay, for it is your own fault if you do not treble your own value by this work. I have no fears, and speak with no uncertain sound, on this one point, at least. Whatever individual mistake may do with it, the work of saving tempted men and women from this one form of ruin *can* be made the source of the deepest growth in womanly character, and the sweetest blessedness of womanly content.

If you are wasted in the "passion for people who are pelted;" if you are wasted in lifting the miserable out of the mud; then He was wasted who saved Magdalene and Matthew. Then Gethsemane was a waste, so also was Calvary. Then life itself is a waste, and the high value of humanity a pitiful deceit. Praying God to speed and guide you, I am,   Sincerely your friend,
                                           ELIZABETH STUART PHELPS.

MRS. C. B BUELL.

CHAPTER XXII.

CAROLINE BROWN BUELL,

Corresponding Secretary National W. C. T. U.

The universal Brown family—A vigorous ancestry—An itinerant preacher's home—The War tragedy—Her brother's helper—Hears the Crusade tocsin—A noble life—That Saratoga Convention.

THOMAS HUGHES opens his well-known story of English school life, " Tom Brown's School Days at Rugby," with an amusing and graphic characterization of the universal Brown family, who, he says, " for centuries, in their quiet, dogged, home-spun way, have been subduing the earth in most English counties and leaving their mark in American forests and Australian uplands, * * * * getting hard knocks and hard work in plenty, which was on the whole what they looked for, and the best thing for them; and little praise or pudding, which indeed they, and most of us, are better without."

The subject of this brief and very imperfect sketch is an honorable offshoot and fair sample of a respectable branch of the prolific Brown family. Her paternal ancestry was early transplanted from Old to New England, where both history and tradition agree that they grappled manfully with the labors, hardships, and dangers of pioneer life in the then howling wilderness, now known as New Hampshire. These sturdy, square-headed, broad-shouldered, God-fearing Englishmen reared their long-lived progeny who, in due time, grew up to make good citizens and sterling patriots; and when the fulness of the time was come in a later generation, Caroline's grandfather became a rampant rebel, and

(437)

shouldering his gun, marched to Bunker's Hill, and
helped to "fire the shot heard round the world." His
wife, too, was of like vigorous stock—not like the puny,
dainty, spindling girls of this period, reared only in hot-
house luxury; but she was a hearty, healthy Yankee
woman, who nurtured her little family of fifteen boys and
girls, born in the parental likeness, and yet found time to
read so largely that far and near it was a marvel, as it
was in the case of Goldsmith's village schoolmaster, "that
one small head could carry all she knew." Withal, she
was a politician who was able to hold her own in an
argument, and "even when vanquished she could argue
still." Both she and her husband lived to a good and
ripe old age, as did their fathers and mothers before
them, and they died near a hundred years old, full of
honors.

The pioneer spirit also possessed the maternal ancestry,
which was imported into New England in the earliest
period of its history, in the little "Mayflower," and colon-
ized finally in Connecticut.

Sprung from such robust stock, Caroline Brown first
saw the light in the old Bay State, being the only daughter
of an itinerant Methodist minister; and so, lest the
history and traditions of the Brown family should be
rudely broken, she had her early experiences of life amid
the hard knocks and diversified trials that constitute the
sunshine and shadow of a Methodist itinerant's family
life. Thus, unused to enervating surroundings, and forced
to struggle with adverse circumstances and conditions,
she grew to early womanhood with a sound physical constitution and a gradually developed, vigorous mental
character. Burning with desire for larger intellectual
culture, she embraced every means afforded her to that
end, and supplemented the discipline of trial and the
tuition of experience with earnest study and diligent

reading as opportunity offered, both in and outside the
regular curriculum of school life. In such a school, by
such severe discipline, were developed the traits which
have made her so wise a counsellor and so judicious an
adviser.

She had arrived at the blush and beauty of maidenhood
when the grand event occurred that changed the tenor of
thousands of lives, and hers was not to be the exception.
The great civil war broke out; the life of the nation was
imperiled; the call was made for men to come and stand
in the imminent deadly breach. Frederick W. H. Buell,
a noble, manly, brave, pure-hearted, and patriotic young
man, of Connecticut nativity, was among those who
responded. The day before he left home for the camp he
claimed his bride, and she was left alone. Thenceforward,
the story runs, as in so many narratives of those sad
days—thank God! they are only a dream now—the
dreadful nightmare of a dreary night of sorrow and
death! With intensest interest she followed, day by day,
the movements of the regiment with which he marched,
and not he alone, for one of her brothers marched with
him, and later her grey-haired father, as the chaplain of
the regiment; for husband, three brothers, and father—
all the male members of the family—were enrolled in the
army or navy, and she and her mother were left alone
as the "Home Guard" through those eventful years.
Sometimes she lost sight, for a while, of the regiment,
while the awful tempest of war swept over it, and her
loved ones were lost in the smoke and dust of the battle,
as at Cold Harbor, or Drury's Bluff, and then the cloud
would lift for a little while, and the straining eyes would
be relieved, while peace and sunshine for a brief space
would fall on the battle-torn banners. So the awful
tragedy of the war went on; the struggle was almost
over, and hearts "weary with waiting for the war to

cease" began to take courage, because the end seemed so near; till, on a winter night, early in a new year, without one word of warning, for the young lieutenant was well when she last heard,

"Home they brought her warrior dead."

So the great grief of her life came to that young and untried heart. It was a lightning-stroke from a clear sky —sharp, swift, decisive, terrible! But Caroline Buell had early learned to trust in God. She did not rebel, neither did she despair, but until he grew to man's estate, her noble boy was her first care, as he has always been the solace of the loving heart that said in its hour of greatest grief, "Sweet my child, I live for thee."

Thus, years passed on—they had little of history in them—till called by the death of her eldest brother's wife to give her aid and comfort to the bereaved family, she hastened to take the care of his motherless children. Here she spent more than three years of earnest and unselfish labor, leaving on the hearts of those she cared for impressions for good that will never be erased. It was here she was found when, in 1876, she was chosen to be the Corresponding Secretary of the W. C. T. U. of Connecticut, which had been organized in some measure the preceding year. She entered at once heartily into the work devolved upon her, and gave to the organization the benefit of her great natural executive ability, so that speedily the Woman's Christian Temperance work in Connecticut was put into orderly and effective shape.* Annually, since that period, Mrs. Buell has been honored by re-election to the Corresponding Secretary's position, though she would have gladly chosen to decline it.

---

* It was in her first year as Corresponding Secretary of the Connecticut Union that she devised the plan of quarterly returns, that has been since very largely adopted all over the country by the various State Unions.

In 1880 the National W. C. T. U., at its session in Boston, elected Mrs. Buell, very unexpectedly to herself, to be Corresponding Secretary of that body. She entered at once upon her work, and by her pen and upon the platform has abounded in labors in behalf of the cause and the organization. The difficult duties of the position she has so efficiently discharged that she has been twice re-elected by nearly unanimous votes.

In person Mrs. Buell is about medium height and size; graceful in form and carriage, easy in address, of fine personal presence; fair, open countenance, keen, dark eyes, and hair now silvering prematurely. Upon the platform, as a speaker before an audience, she is always self-poised, self-unconscious, earnest, and impressive. In her mental characteristics she does honor to the stock from whence she sprung, for she has the "quiet, dogged, homespun" perseverance which Thomas Hughes assigns to her family—the getting-hold-of and never-letting-go disposition of mind that that will "fight it out on this line, if it takes all summer."

Mrs. Buell is a woman of singularly gentle nature and quiet manners, combined with altogether exceptional force of character. Unselfish to a fault and altogether free from personal ambition, the hearts of her friends do safely trust in her, and no woman in our ranks is more devoutly loyal to God and home and native land.

THAT SARATOGA CONVENTION, OR MEN, WOMEN, AND TEMPERANCE.

Time, June 21 and 22, 1881; place, the big, handsome Methodist church at Saratoga; people, many of the representative temperance men and women of America, to the number of 400, with a spicy sprinkling of Canada thrown in. "Sir, we had good talk," said old Sam Johnson, after an evening with the wits and wisdoms of Lon-

don. "Good talk" it was that crowded full those two
delightful days—the echo of grand triumphs and the
bugle blast of victories yet to be. The quick, incisive
brain that planned it all was J. N. Stearns. The clear-
headed, available men, ready for every good word and
work, were J. L. Bradley (husband of our Nellie H.
Bradley) and C. H. Meade, of Buffalo, N. Y. The men
of wise and thunderous speech were Judge Black, of Lan-
caster, Pa., and Rev. Dr. Peck, of Brooklyn. Dr. S. J.
Gordon, of Boston, the "Temperance Hercules" of that
city, was our mellow-voiced president, so tolerant in
spirit that he shared that honor with two of the vice-
presidents, selecting impartially from the ranks of Adam
and Eve as well, the latter piece of poetic justice never
having been previously awarded.

Joshua L. Bailey, the Quaker gentleman of Philadelphia and prince of coffee-house founders, who feeds
twenty thousand a day on the best fare at the least rates
of any man in America, was first vice-president, and a
first-class presiding officer. Our gentle Eliza Thompson,
all the way from Hillsboro, Ohio, was the second, and her
bright, crisp speeches enlivened the proceedings not a
little. Age is said to contribute to garrulity, but there is
not a woman in our ranks who can make a point so
briefly and at the same time so well as this same Crusade mother of us all. Forty-five years before this date
she attended the first temperance convention ever held in
Saratoga, being then a merry girl and coming with her
father, Governor Allan Trimble, of Ohio. As she entered
the dining-room of the hotel where the first committee
meeting was held, and saw a few men, but no woman
present, she said to her father : "I can't go in alone,"
when he replied : "Never be afraid to stand alone in a
good cause, my child."

Little did she think that, a long lifetime later, she was

to prove so true to this exhortation by leading the van of the Crusade. The foregoing is her first speech at the last convention, only the application was made by us delegates. On the platform, beside Brother Stearns, sat the Corresponding Secretary of our National W. C. T. U., Mrs. C. B. Buell, and beside her Mrs. L. D. Douglass, of Meadville, Pa., Assistant Lady Secretary; and there was another gentleman, C. K. Sambling, from noble old Oberlin, Ohio, queen of total abstinence towns.

Dr. Eaton, pastor of the church, welcomed the delegates in royal fashion, and Mother Stewart replied in her best vein. " Our Temperance Portia," Mrs. Judith Ellen Foster (I tell her she is Judith, and the liquor traffic in Iowa is to be her Holofernes) read an admirable paper on her favorite theme of " Constitutional Amendment." This is, as a " third-party " delegate remarked, *sotto voce* (the " current craze "), all allusions to it being received with enthusiasm and adopted without dissent. A grand thought it is, and one which, within twenty-five years, will be brought out in every State.

But without woman's ballot it will never universally " materialize," and this is distinctly perceived by many in our ranks. Aside from this " common consent " theme, the two most vital subjects seemed to be an organized ballot for temperance men and the effort to secure that death-dealing little weapon, the ballot bullet, for women. The first was long and earnestly debated, and advanced opinion is clearly shown in the fact that Judge Black's resolution was unanimously carried. This is as follows :

WHEREAS, The Beer Brewers' Association, and kindred liquor dealers' organizations, during a score of years past have declared the traffic in intoxicating drink to be a legitimate part of American commerce, entitled to and demanding for it the protection of law and the fostering care of the State and National Governments, denying the right to prohibit or restrict the same, have yearly avowed their purpose to vote for no man who favored legislation in the interests of temperance, and constantly have used their political franchise for the continuation of their trade; in the past have received the countenance of political parties in support of the positions and selfish interests thus assumed, securing through such aid the rescinding of constitutional enactments and the repeal, modification, or impairment in efficiency of acts of Congress and of the State restrictive of their business, and by many and other influences have secured the election of friends and the defeat of supposed opponents. Having thus deliberately resolved and acted by the consent and co-operation of the party press leaders, they have forced the liquor question into National and State politics, making their traffic an issue in State and municipal elections, and in their interest largely secured the administration of government law. Therefore

Resolved, That the interests of the public peace and welfare, the defence of personal liberty, the safety and protection of home, with faithfulness to avowed convictions, demand from the friends of temperance, good government, and free institutions the acceptance of this field of contest and their gage of battle, and this convention declares it to be the duty of every temperance voter to cast his ballot at every election only for such candidates for public office as may be relied upon on this liquor question to use official power and place for securing the enactment and due execution of law for the prohibition of the manufacture, sale, or importation of alcoholic liquors for drinking uses. That an organized ballot, whether under the name of Prohibition Party, or for securing and maintaining amendment of the National and State Constitutions, or general or local prohibition, or the restraint of the liquor trade in view of the platform declarations of present parties, against the prohibition of such trade, and of the machinations and organizations of the brewing, distilling, and liquor-selling interests for political ends, has become a present and imperative necessity in order to purify our politics and legislation, and save our free institutions from the blight of the God-defying and virtue-despising liquor business. That adhesion to party allied with liquor manufacturers and sellers is to give aid and comfort to the enemy, and is treason to temperance. Prayer and the ballot should be as inseparable as faith and works.

Resolved, That we recommend the immediate organization in every election district of all voters favorable to the prohibition of the liquor traffic, and pledged to support only such candidates as will accept and promote the constitutional and statutory prohibition of the liquor traffic.

Resolved, That the hearty participation of woman in the organization and work for temperance is received and acknowledged thankfully, as a boon from a beneficent God, and we claim and shall persistently demand for her legal power to aid and defend her home and children from the curse of rum as fully as she now holds her equal, created social and religious privileges and duties with man, and equal duties and responsibilities demand equal power and liberty.

George Vibbert of Massachusetts, gifted and nobly loyal defender of the prohibition party (which was founded by Judge Black), insisted that its name should be inserted, but the grand old judge, in an admirable speech, said : " The *principle* is in the resolution which I drafted, I don't care for the name. I am called James Black, but if you changed it to John Smith I should be the same man. The *idea* is what I'm after." And to his "idea" the convention certainly acceded. As for the "Home Guards," they are "third party" almost to a woman. As one said to me, " I wouldn't give a penny for the difference between Republican beer and Democratic whisky," and another, "I'll have nothing to do with either party, for both are held together by barrel hoops," and a third party whispered, as the fiery Vibbert made his telling points, "I know just what his line of argument will be, I've had it in the top of my head, and the bottom of my heart, lo, these many days."

Our dauntless Mrs. T. B. Carse, founder of *The Signal* and President of the Chicago W. C. T. U., related the experience of the recent Chicago campaign, and declared to the committee on resolutions that if they had survived such an experience they would never again question the imperative need of the " organized temperance ballot" with a vertebrate candidate behind it. Rev. Dr. D. C. Babcock, one of the best minds in the convention, read an excellent essay, in which he advises the effort first to secure satisfactory nominations from some existing party, and when they fail to furnish them, then the coming out independently. This position was taken by Mrs. Foster and other able advocates, and finally represented the majority, though there was a tremendous ground swell for a party, be it first, second, or third, wherein dwelleth the righteousness of a steady, uncompromising front to the foe, and I confess my convictions lead me there, with the "old guard," the anti-slavery party of the new war, the independents who are determined to know nothing among you but the extermination of the rum power, and to crystallize around this changeless purpose a new departure in politics. To this complexion it must come at last—and *why not now?* No speaker made a more delightful impression than my beloved "Deborah"—Mrs. Gov. Wallace of Indiana. By special invitation she "spoke her mind," but, with her rare good sense, she spoke it briefly. Men, she said, had conquered the forces of nature. She thanked them for the inventions which had freed woman's hands from slavery to the spinning-wheel, the loom, the needle, that they might busy themselves with the moral and spiritual problems of the child's training, the home's development, the State's purification. Her strong, gentle, motherly words were applauded to the echo by the noble, brotherly men of that incomparable convention, and we women could have cried for joy. Indeed I have never in any previous assembly seen a truly Christian republic so admirably forecast as here. Down to the smallest and up to the highest particular, womanhood was recognized as a help so meet for manhood that its place was by his side, not at his feet, and those gentlemen were so thoroughly civilized that they gloried in the facts for which we were so proudly grateful. When our noble-hearted president was escorted to the chair, General Wagner, Judge Black, and Dr. Babcock laughingly stood back to let the two ladies of the committee of five conduct the ceremony, and giving an arm to each, the president mounted the platform amid applause. It was so all the way through, and on the second day a dignified Presbyterian doctor of divinity, from Philadelphia, made an off-hand speech (received with a storm of hand clapping), in which he said " He was thoroughly converted. He hadn't a word to say and never should have again against a woman doing anything in this world that she pleased. If any man would deprive the women in this convention of the ballot, he wasn't worthy to be set with the dogs of the flock. The cerebrum of woman would never be questioned as to its size or quality again by the gentlemen who were so fortunate as to attend this nineteenth century convention. The question was not whether women needed the vote, it was how in the world this government had got along at all without their casting it."

The resolution on this question, drawn by Judge Black, after admirable discussion by that Bayard of our cause, A. M. Powell of New York, Rev. Mr. Montgomery, the whole-souled Irish minister of Connecticut, George Vibbert, and others in favor, and by Mrs. Wittenmyer against (who was called out, and spoke earnestly and well), was carried with but twelve dissenting votes, and only one of these was from a woman. Hon. Felix R. Brunot, of Pittsburgh, made a droll explanation of his negative vote, saying that while he could make a good speech against woman's ballot, he could make a much better one in favor, and he wanted to quote a Scripture often overlooked in citing authorities on the affirmative side, and that was from Acts in these words, " *Let her drive!*" He said, however, that he was opposed to the resolution not on its merits, but because he thought it would retard the prohibition movement.

Mrs. Mary H. Hunt made a brief, clear speech on the scientific aspects of total abstinence, and Mrs. Mary C. Johnson spoke in a very happy vein of the willingness of conservative women like herself, taught by the severe

reverses of past years along the line of prohibition, to use
the ballot when we have it in our hands, " although we
do not clamor for it."

But the charm of those two days beguiles me into the
prolixity I have condemned. It would be pleasant to
write at length of Rev. Dr. Peck's splendid speech, in
which he came out for the first time in favor of " the
organized ballot," and of John B. Gough's magnificent
utterances, among others this, " While I can speak against
this awful crime, I'll speak; when I can't do that, I'll
whisper; and when that fails me, *I'll just make motions*—
they say I'm good at that!"

I want also to mention the great satisfaction felt in the
selection of such a superb committee on resolutions, with
Rev. A. G. Lawson of Brooklyn at its head, one of the
noblest Romans of them all.

Brief speeches were made by Mrs. Leavitt of Boston,
Mrs. Washington of New Jersey, late of Iowa; Miss
Esther Pugh; Miss Colman, our indomitable superintendent of temperance literature; Professor Foster, who
strongly represented the Canada delegation headed by
Sir Leonard Tilley, and many others. New England was
well represented by Mrs. L. B. Barrett, Mrs. Dr. Gordon,
Miss Wendell, Charles Hovey, Eugene Clapp, and others.
The South had but few delegates, but the leader of the
Southern delegation, Hon. Mr. Daniels, Local Option
champion of Maryland, was a host in himself. The only
colored man was from New Jersey. His unique excuse
for going beyond time, "If I say it all now, you won't
have to hear me again," brought down the house.

The tobacco question was vigorously handled, and no
resolution was more applauded than the one denouncing
the vile weed. The Hayes memorial was heartily endorsed.

Surely this convention took its place upon the picket

line of progress. Best of all, it did so in the name of
Christ. Earnest and devout were these men and women
all. Prayer-meetings in the morning; noon hour observed
on Tuesday, by dear Mother Hill's request; the Bible
insisted on as "the only permanent temperance document"—these are the signs of that power by which God's
militant host shall surely conquer, and His Son shall
reign "whose right it is."

CHAPTER XXIII.

THE following address is the first I ever gave on the theme dear to my heart. It came to me in its entirety, as to the name and argument, while alone on my knees one Sabbath in the capital of the Crusade State, as I lifted my heart to God, crying, "What wouldst thou have me to do"? This was in May of the centennial year. At that time I was corresponding secretary of the National W. C. T. U., and was making a trip through the State under the direction of Mrs. Dr. L. D. McCabe, then president of the Ohio W. C. T. U. I at once wrote my superior officer, Mrs. Wittenmyer, asking permission to give this address at our projected centennial temperance meeting in the Academy of Music, Philadelphia. She declined, and I went to Chautauqua, where by invitation of my good friend, Dr. John H. Vincent, I was to speak. There I met that brave champion of Home Protection, Rev. Dr. Theodore L. Flood, who several years later debated this question in the great auditorium there, and won not only his cause but the gratitude of women everywhere. Dr. Flood urged me to give my new speech then and there, none of our W. C. T. U. having at that time publicly taken a position so decided. Going to Dr. Vincent I frankly stated the case; but, while he pleasantly said, "Our platform is free to those whom we invite," I felt his preference so strongly that I refrained from speaking out my deepest thought. Going on to Old Orchard Beach, where Francis Murphy was the presiding genius, I asked again if I might bring on my pet heresy. "O, yes, speak right on till you're understood," replied that tolerant soul, in his rich brogue, although he did not then agree with the views I felt constrained to declare. And so in the fragrant air of Maine's dear "piney woods," with the great free ocean's salt spray to invigorate lungs and soul, I first avowed the faith that was within me. There is something wonderfully novel and inspiring in the outlook of a pioneer along fresh lines of reform work. All around, my good friends looked so much surprised — and some of them so sorry!

The Woman's Congress at St. George's Hall gave me my next Home Protection audience, and there I felt at home. This was no new gospel to Maria Mitchell, president of that society, nor to Elizabeth Churchill, who grasped my hand with a sister's warmth and cheered me on to the fray. And the fray came. In Newark, N. J., we held our third annual meeting (or "Convention"), of the National W. C. T. U., and by this time my soul had come to " woe is me if I declare not this gospel." Welcome or not, the words must come. In a great, crowded church, with smiles on some faces and frowns on others, I came forward. Our gifted Mary Lathrop had told a war story in one of her addresses, about a colored man who saw a boat bearing down upon the skiff drawn up to shore in which he and three white men were concealed. If he could only push off instantly they would be saved, but to show himself was fatal. But he did not hesitate; calling out, " Somebody's got to be killed, and it might as well be me," he launched the boat and fell with a bullet in his heart. In that difficult hour this story came to me, and as I told it some of my good friends wept at the thought of ostracism which, from that day to this, has been its sequel — not as a rule, but a painful exception. When I had finished the argument, a lady from New York, gray-haired and dignified, who was presiding, said to the audience:

"The National W. C. T. U. is not responsible for the utterances of this evening. We have no mind to trail our skirts in the mire of politics." She doubtless felt it her duty so to speak, and I had no thought of blame, only regret. As we left the church, one of our chief women said: "You might have been a leader in our national councils, but you have deliberately chosen to be only a scout."

THE ADDRESS.

The rum power looms like a Chimborazo among the mountains of difficulty over which our native land must climb to reach the future of our dreams. The problem of the rum power's overthrow may well engage our thoughts as women and as patriots. To-night I ask you to consider it in the light of a truth which Frederick Douglass has embodied in these words: "We can in the long run trust all the knowledge in the community to take care of all the ignorance of the community, and all of its virtue to take care of all of its vice." The difficulty in the application of this principle lies in the fact that vice is always in the active, virtue often in the passive. Vice is aggressive. It deals swift, sure blows, delights in keen-edged weapons, and prefers a hand-to-hand conflict, while virtue instinctively fights its unsavory antagonist at arm's length; its great guns are unwieldy and slow to swing into range.

Vice is the tiger, with keen eyes, alert ears, and cat-like tread, while virtue is the slow-paced, complacent, easy-going elephant, whose greatest danger lies in its ponderous weight and consciousness of power. So the great question narrows down to one of two(?) methods. It is not, when we look carefully into the conditions of the problem, How shall we develop more virtue in the community to offset the tropical growth of vice by which we find ourselves environed? but rather, How the tremendous force we have may best be brought to bear, how we may unlimber the huge cannon now pointing into vacancy, and direct their full charge at short range upon our nimble, wily, vigilant foe?

As bearing upon a consideration of that question, I lay down this proposition: All pure and Christian sentiment concerning any line of conduct which vitally affects humanity will, sooner or later, crystallize into law. But the keystone of law can only be firm and secure when it is held in place by the arch of that keystone, which is public sentiment.

I make another statement not so often reiterated, but just as true, viz.: The more thoroughly you can enlist in favor of your law the

natural instincts of those who have the power to make that law, and
to select the officers who shall enforce it, the more securely stands the
law. And still another: First among the powerful and controlling
instincts in our nature stands that of self-preservation, and next after
this, if it does not claim superior rank, comes that of a mother's love.
You can count upon that every time; it is sure and resistless as the
tides of the sea, for it is founded in the changeless nature given to her
from God.

Now that the stronghold of the rum power lies in the fact that it
has upon its side two deeply rooted appetites, namely: in the dealer,
the appetite for gain, and in the drinker, the appetite for stimulants.
We have dolorously said in times gone by that on the human plane
we have nothing adequate to match against this frightful pair. But
let us think more carefully, and we shall find that, as in nature, God
has given us an antidote to every poison, and in grace a compensation
for every loss; so in human society he has prepared against alcohol,
that worst foe of the social state, an enemy under whose weapons it is
to bite the dust.

Think of it! There is a class in every one of our communities—in
many of them far the most numerous class—which (I speak not vaunt-
ingly; I but name it as a fact) has not in all the centuries of wine, beer,
and brandy-drinking developed, as a class, an appetite for alcohol, but
whose instincts, on the contrary, set so strongly against intoxicants
that if the liquor traffic were dependent on their patronage alone, it
would collapse this night as though all the nitro-glycerine of Hell Gate
reef had exploded under it.

There is a class whose instinct of self-preservation must forever be
opposed to a stimulant which nerves, with dangerous strength, arms
already so much stronger than their own, and so maddens the brain
God meant to guide those arms, that they strike down the wives men
love, and the little children for whom, when sober, they would die.
The wife, largely dependent for the support of herself and little ones
upon the brain which strong drink paralyzes, the arm it masters, and
the skill it renders futile, will, in the nature of the case, prove herself
unfriendly to the actual or potential source of so much misery. But
besides this primal instinct of self-preservation, we have, in the same
class of which I speak, another far more high and sacred—I mean the
instinct of a mother's love, a wife's devotion, a sister's faithfulness, a
daughter's loyalty. And now I ask you to consider earnestly the fact
that none of these blessed rays of light and power from woman's
heart, are as yet brought to bear upon the rum-shop at the focus of
power. They are, I know, the sweet and pleasant sunshine of our
homes; they are the beams which light the larger home of social life
and send their gentle radiance out even into the great and busy world.

But I know, and as the knowledge has grown clearer, my heart was thrilled with gratitude and hope too deep for words, that in a republic all these now divergent beams of light can, through that magic lens, that powerful sun-glass which we name the ballot, be made to converge upon the rum-shop in a blaze of light that shall reveal its full abominations, and a white flame of heat which, like a pitiless moxa, shall burn this cancerous excrescence from America's fair form. Yes, for there is nothing in the universe so sure, so strong, as love; and love shall do all this—the love of maid for sweetheart, wife for husband, of a sister for her brother, of a mother for her son. And I call upon you who are here to-day, good men and brave—you who have welcomed us to other fields in the great fight of the angel against the dragon in society —I call upon you thus to match force with force, to set over against the liquor-dealer's avarice our instinct of self-preservation; and to match the drinker's love of liquor with our love of him! When you can centre all this power in that small bit of paper which falls

" As silently as snow-flakes fall upon the sod,
But executes a freeman's will as lightnings do the will of God,"

the rum power will be as much doomed as was the slave power when you gave the ballot to the slaves.

In our argument it has been claimed that by the changeless instincts of her nature and through the most sacred relationships of which that nature has been rendered capable, God has indicated woman, who is the born conservator of home, to be the Nemesis of home's arch enemy, King Alcohol. And further, that in a republic, this power of hers may be most effectively exercised by giving her a voice in the decision by which the rum-shop door shall be opened or closed beside her home.

This position is strongly supported by evidence. About the year 1850 petitions were extensively circulated in Cincinnati (later the fiercest battle ground of the woman's crusade), asking that the liquor traffic be put under the ban of law. Bishop Simpson—one of the noblest and most discerning minds of his century—was deeply interested in this movement. It was decided to ask for the names of women as well as those of men, and it was found that the former signed the petition more readily and in much larger numbers than the latter. Another fact was ascertained which rebuts the hackneyed assertion that women of the lower class will not be on the temperance side in this great war. For it was found—as might, indeed, have been most reasonably predicted—that the ignorant, the poor (many of them wives, mothers, and daughters of intemperate men), were among the most eager to sign the petition.

MANY A HAND WAS TAKEN FROM THE WASH-TUB

to hold the pencil and affix the signature of women of this class, and many another, which could only make the sign of the cross, did that with tears, and a hearty "God bless you." "That was a wonderful lesson to me," said the good Bishop, and he has always believed since then that God will give our enemy into our hands by giving to us an ally still more powerful, woman with the ballot against rum-shops in our land. It has been said so often that the very frequency of reiteration has in some minds induced belief that women of the better class will never consent to declare themselves at the polls. But tens of thousands from the most tenderly-sheltered homes have gone day after day to the saloons, and have spent hour after hour upon their sanded floors, and in their reeking air—places in which not the worst politician would dare to locate the ballot box of freemen—though they but stay a moment at the window, slip in their votes, and go their way.

Nothing worse can ever happen to women at the polls than has been endured by the hour on the part of conservative women of the churches in this land, as they, in scores of towns, have plead with rough, half-drunken men to vote the temperance tickets they have handed them, and which, with vastly more of propriety and fitness they might have dropped into the box themselves. They could have done this in a moment, and returned to their homes, instead of spending the whole day in the often futile endeavor to beg from men like these the votes which should preserve their homes from the whisky serpent's breath for one uncertain year. I spent last May in Ohio, traveling constantly, and seeking on every side to learn the views of the noble women of the Crusade. They put their opinions in words like these: "We believe that as God led us into this work by way of the saloons,

HE WILL LEAD US OUT BY WAY OF THE BALLOT.

We have never prayed more earnestly over the one than we will over the other. One was the Wilderness, the other is the Promised Land."

A Presbyterian lady, rigidly conservative, said: "For my part, I never wanted to vote until our gentlemen passed a prohibition ordinance so as to get us to stop visiting saloons, and a month later repealed it and chose a saloon-keeper for mayor."

Said a grand-daughter of Jonathan Edwards, a woman with no toleration toward the Suffrage Movement, a woman crowned with the glory of gray hairs—a central figure in her native town—

AND AS SHE SPOKE THE COURAGE AND FAITH OF THE PURITANS
THRILLED HER VOICE—

"If, with the ballot in our hands, we can, as I firmly believe, put down this awful traffic, I am ready to lead the women of my town to the polls, as I have often led them to the rum shops."

We must not forget that for every woman who joins the Temperance Unions now springing up all through the land, there are at least a score who sympathize but do not join. Home influence and cares prevent them, ignorance of our aims and methods, lack of consecration to Christian work—a thousand reasons, sufficient in their estimation, though not in ours, hold them away from us. And yet they have this Temperance cause warmly at heart; the logic of events has shown them that there is but one side on which a woman may safely stand in this great battle, and on that side they would indubitably range themselves in the quick, decisive battle of election day, nor would they give their voice a second time in favor of the man who had once betrayed his pledge to enforce the most stringent law for the protection of their homes. There are many noble women, too, who, though they do not think as do the Temperance Unions about the deep things of religion, and are not as yet decided in their total abstinence sentiments, nor ready for the blessed work of prayer, are nevertheless decided in their views of Woman Suffrage, and ready to vote a Temperance ticket side by side with us. And there are the drunkard's wife and daughters, who from very shame will not come with us, or who dare not, yet who could freely vote with us upon this question; for the folded ballot tells no tales.

Among other cumulative proofs in this argument from experience, let us consider, briefly, the attitude of the Catholic Church toward the Temperance Reform. It is friendly, at least. Father Matthew's spirit lives to-day in many a faithful parish priest. In our procession on the Centennial Fourth of July, the banners of Catholic Total Abstinence Societies were often the only reminders that the Republic has any temperance people within its borders, as they were the only offset to brewers' wagons and distillers' casks, while among the monuments of our cause, by which this memorable year is signalized, their fountain in Fairmount Park—standing in the midst of eighty drinking places licensed by our Government—is chief. Catholic women would vote with Protestant women upon this issue for the protection of their homes.

Again, among the sixty thousand churches of America, with their eight million members, two-thirds are women. Thus, only one-third of this trustworthy and thoughtful class has any voice in the laws by which, between the church and the public school, the rum shop nestles in this Christian land. Surely all this must change before the Government shall be upon His shoulders "Who shall one day reign King of nations as He now reigns King of saints."

Furthermore, four-fifths of the teachers in this land are women, whose thoughtful judgment, expressed with the authority of which I speak, would greatly help forward the victory of our cause. And, finally, by those who fear the effect of the foreign element in our country, let it be remembered that we have sixty native for every one woman who is foreign born, for it is men who emigrate in largest number to our shores.

When all these facts (and many more that might be added) are marshaled into line, how illogical it seems for good men to harangue us as they do about our "duty to educate public sentiment to the level of better law," and their exhortations to American mothers to "train their sons to vote aright." As said Mrs. Governor Wallace, of Indiana—until the Crusade an opponent of the franchise — " What a bitter sarcasm you utter, gentlemen, to us who have the public sentiment of which you speak, all burning in our hearts, and yet are not permitted to turn it to account."

Let us, then, each one of us, offer our earnest prayer to God, and speak our honest word to man in favor of this added weapon in woman's hands, remembering that every petition in the ear of God, and every utterance in the ears of men, swells the dimensions of that resistless tide of influence which shall yet float within our reach all that we ask or need. Dear Christian women who have crusaded in the rum shops, I urge that you begin crusading in halls of legislation, in primary meetings, and the offices of excise commissioners. Roll in your petitions, burnish your arguments, multiply your prayers. Go to the voters in your town—procure the official list and see them one by one—and get them pledged to a local ordinance requiring the votes of men and women before a license can be issued to open rum-shop doors beside your homes; go to the Legislature with the same; remember this may be just as really Christian work as praying in saloons was in those other glorious days. Let us not limit God, whose modes of operation are so infinitely varied in nature and in grace. I believe in the correlation of spiritual forces, and that the heat which melted hearts to tenderness in the Crusade is soon to be the light which shall reveal our opportunity and duty as the Republic's daughters.

Longer ago than I shall tell, my father returned one night to the far-off Wisconsin home where I was reared; and, sitting by my mother's chair, with a child's attentive ear, I listened to their words. He told us of the news that day had brought about Neal Dow and the great fight for prohibition down in Maine, and then he said: " I wonder if poor, rum-cursed Wisconsin will ever get a law like that?" And mother rocked a while in silence in the dear old chair I love, and then she gently said:

"YES, JOSIAH, THERE'LL BE SUCH A LAW ALL OVER THE LAND SOME DAY, WHEN WOMEN VOTE."

My father had never heard her say so much before. He was a great conservative; so he looked tremendously astonished, and replied, in his keen, sarcastic voice: "And pray how will you arrange it so that women shall vote?" Mother's chair went to and fro a little faster for a minute, and then, looking not into his face, but into the flickering flames of the grate, she slowly answered: "Well, I say to you, as the apostle Paul said to his jailor, ' You have put us into prison, we being Romans, and you must come and take us out."

That was a seed-thought in a girl's brain and heart. Years passed on, in which nothing more was said upon this dangerous theme. My brother grew to manhood, and soon after he was twenty-one years old he went with his father to vote. Standing by the window, a girl of sixteen years, a girl of simple, homely fancies, not at all strong-minded, and altogether ignorant of the world, I looked out as they drove away, my father and my brother, and as I looked I felt a strange ache in my heart, and tears sprang to my eyes. Turning to my sister Mary, who stood beside me, I saw that the dear little innocent seemed wonderfully sober, too. I said: "Don't you wish we could go with them when we are old enough? Don't we love our country just as well as they do?" and her little frightened voice piped out: "Yes, of course we ought. Don't I know that? but you mustn't tell a soul—not mother, even; we should be called strong-minded."

In all the years since then I have kept these things, and many others like them, and pondered them in my heart; but two years of struggle in this temperance reform have shown me, as they have ten thousand other women, so clearly and so impressively, my duty, that

I HAVE PASSED THE RUBICON OF SILENCE,

and am ready for any battle that shall be involved in this honest declaration of the faith that is within me. "Fight behind masked batteries a little longer," whisper good friends and true. So I have been fighting hitherto; but it is a style of warfare altogether foreign to my temperament and mode of life. Reared on the prairies, I seemed pre-determined to join the cavalry forces in this great spiritual war, and I must tilt a free lance henceforth on the splendid battle-field of this reform; where the earth shall soon be shaken by the onset of contending hosts; where legions of valiant soldiers are deploying; where to the grand encounter marches to-day a great army, gentle of mein and mild of utterance, but with hearts for any fate; where there are trumpets and bugles calling strong souls onward to a victory which Heaven might envy, and

"Where, behind the dim Unknown,
Standeth God within the shadow,
Keeping watch above His own."

I thought that women ought to have the ballot as I paid the hard-earned taxes upon my mother's cottage home—but I never said as much—somehow the motive did not command my heart. For my own sake, I had not courage, but I have for thy sake, dear native land, for thy necessity is as much greater than mine as thy transcendant hope is greater than the personal interest of thy humble child. For love of you, heart-broken wives, whose tremulous lips have blessed me; for love of you, sweet mothers, who, in the cradle's shadow, kneel this night beside your infant sons, and you, sorrowful little children, who listen at this hour, with faces strangely old, for him whose footsteps frighten you; for love of you have I thus spoken.

Ah, it is women who have given the costliest hostages to fortune. Out into the battle of life they have sent their best beloved, with fearful odds against them, with snares that men have legalized and set for them on every hand. Beyond the arms that held them long, their boys have gone forever. Oh! by the danger they have dared; by the hours of patient watching over beds where helpless children lay; by the incense of ten thousand prayers wafted from their gentle lips to Heaven, I charge you give them power to protect, along life's treacherous highway, those whom they have so loved. Let it no longer be that they must sit back among the shadows, hopelessly mourning over their strong staff broken, and their beautiful rod; but when the sons they love shall go forth to life's battle, still let their mothers walk beside them, sweet and serious, and clad in the garments of power.

CHAPTER XXIV.

WOMEN'S BRIGHT WORDS.

Priscilla Shrewdly and Charlotte Cheeryble — One woman's experi-
ence—Our letter bag—From a Pennsylvania girl—From an Illinois
working man—From a Michigan lady—From a Missouri lady—
From Rockford, Ills.—From a reformed man in Philadelphia—
From a New York lady—The temperance house that Jack built—
One day in a temperance woman's life—From a New England girl's
letter—Concerning the word "Christian"—From Senator and Mrs.
Blair.

MRS. A.: "Nobody need grumble to me about "third
party" as though it was something dreadful. I'd
like to know if Illinois isn't governed by one to-day. A
"third party" that is throttling the best life of our communities, and its name is "whiskyite."

Strange that a truth so simple should be so hard to
discover by the average mind! Second, Mrs. B———, a
gray-haired leader, with a most quizzical smile, was
speaking of the hubbub caused at Springfield by the "local
election," because the temperancers wanted to put a living-
issue ticket before the people. She said: "You ought to have
seen our voters. They reminded me of nothing so much
as our old hens when the sun was eclipsed. For both hens
and voters were 'struck of a heap.' They didn't know
whether to go to roost as they did at night, or to get
under the shed as they did when it rained. But they
seemed to feel that something had to be done right
straight away, so they took to whirling round and round
like a parcel of crazy Janes, and nobody could guess where
they would fetch up at last. A terror of great darkness
was upon 'em, and more than that we shall never cer-

(460)

tainly know till the secrets of the artful dodger's heart
shall be revealed." Mrs. C. to the (un) common council
of (in) harmonious workers at Bloomington: "Gentlemen, it is of no use to expect me to give up my views on
the subject of the woman's ballot as the road to prohibition—for, like Josiah Allen's wife, 'I'm up on my cast-
iron principles, and nothing on this earth can change
me.'" All of which items were refreshing to "a chiel
amang ye takin' notes," and now she prints 'em.

TESTIMONY FROM THE OTHER SIDE; (GIVEN BY A W. C. T. U. WOMAN.)

A year ago last winter, when the W. C. T. U. was
laboring at Springfield for the passage of the Hinds bill,
a gentleman was journeying in the central part of the
State, and in crossing the river on the ice, stopped on an
island in the only habitation there, to get warm. The
house proved to be a saloon. Presently a man came in
for his grog. As he raised the glass he said: "I wish to
God there was none of this stuff ever made." "O, don't
wish dat," said the Dutchman at the bar, "Dat time come
soon enough." "No," returned the drinker, "It'll never
come—this miserable whisky'll always be manufactured."
"You tink so? Nein, I tell you nein. Wat dem vimmens doing at Springfield? Dem vimmens down dere
now. Den dey'll vote. Den vere'll de beer and whisky
be?" Echo answers, "Where?"

PRISCILLA SHREWDLY AND CHARLOTTE CHEERYBLE; OR, BEHIND THE SCENES.

Two of our beloved "temperance women" were sitting
up "to talk the meeting over." For Plumpton had
enjoyed the sensation of a mass meeting in the interest of
the reform dear to their hearts. Moreover, to-morrow
was the day set for the annual election of officers in the

W. C. T. U., whose varied fortunes they had watched
since the crusade that swept them into the temperance
work. With such an achievement just behind, and such
a crisis just before them, it wasn't to be supposed that
they could quietly lie down to dreams.

Mrs. Cheeryble was the hostess, and welcomed Miss
Shrewdly to the easiest chair in her snug sitting-room,
brought her a dish of hot oyster soup and the fleece-lined
slippers in which her guest delighted. Then, having
ensconced her own plump figure in the low rocking-chair
on the other side of the fireplace, she uttered a single
syllable, but one whose inimitable inflection " spoke volumes " of cuteness and curiosity. " Well ? "

Miss Shrewdly was not the woman to hesitate about
taking the initiative. Her opinions were to be had " on
call " by any who wanted them; nay, they were often
forthcoming without even that small provocation.

" Well, did you say ? " was her sprightly rejoinder.
" It may do for you, perhaps, to use that word in connection with such proceedings as were had in Smith's hall to-
night, but then you're the easiest soul that ever sat still
and saw other people inaugurate and carry to a triumphant conclusion the *failure* they are foreordained to make
but never to suspect."

" Why, I thought our president did better than usual;
she hasn't studied ' Roberts's Rules of Order ' in vain,"
was the kindly reply. " I really enjoy seeing such women
come to the front."

" I should think you did," replied her guest, " and I
agree with your husband, who I wish were here to stand
by me in the argument, that the mistake of your life,
Charlotte Cheeryble, is that you take such a rose-colored
view of people and their possibilities; you seem to see in
them what nobody else does, and what certainly never
comes to the surface. Then you lack backbone; you're

as roly-poly in your policy as in your figure, and, if you'll pardon the allusion — here we are, thirty good and true women of the W. C. T. U.; we all like you and can work harmoniously with you as our leader; when you say that you'll leave the Union by the door, the minute sectarianism enters by the window, somebody moves we table the resolution excluding Universalists; when you tell us it's a shame for us to withhold our dues from the National Union, even Misses Prune and Prism open their lips in smiles and their pocketbooks in greenbacks—"

"BEWARE, OH, PURITAN MAIDEN, PRISCILLA,"

interrupted the hostess with a smile like a small sunrise, "your logic is sadly at fault. The indictment accuses me of being an invertebrate, of the species known in science as roly-poly. The evidence acquits me by recounting deeds of prowess worthy of the Iron Duke."

"Not a bit of it, queen of the sophists," retorted Priscilla Shrewdly, putting aside the soup plate she had emptied, and addressing herself actively to the case in hand, "birds that can sing and won't sing are the naughtiest of all, and women who can cause things to come to pass, who are born leaders and yet won't lead, but will allow themselves to be set aside, as you do, and bring disgrace upon us by allowing an empty-headed, pushing woman like"—

"No harshness, my high-toned friend," quickly interrupted her hostess. "Remember the second word in the name we bear — Woman's *Christian* Temperance Union."

"You're right—you're always right," and Priscilla came over to her friend's side of the hearth and grasped her hand. "Nevertheless," and Miss Shrewdly stood before Mrs. Cheeryble gesticulating with less of grace than vigor, "nevertheless, I will say that in such a meeting as we had to-night, with a great crowd, grand gospel singing, and rousing speeches by reformed men, Mrs.

Blank's manner of presiding was a regular wet blanket—there!" and the flush on her cheeks was hardly less brilliant than the light in her eyes. "Nay, more," and now her friend saw that it was useless to protest, for Priscilla had reached the point known in such phenomena as "dangerous," "I hold that it ought not to be possible for such an exhibition to be made before the eyes of all Plumpton. We women are, in a sense, on trial. While the public is willing to let us make the attempt, it is keen-eyed to note the failure. Ours will be a lost cause in Plumpton if this sort of thing continues. I can see her now, standing before that magnificent audience, and (don't interrupt me; I won't speak as harshly as I feel and the facts warrant) mumbling the Crusade Psalm. O, what a psalm it is, and how you would have read it! So she dulled the keen edge of their interest, and even the reformed men couldn't sharpen it with all their force and fire. Then, nobody could hear hardly anything she said, save when she said she 'wan't a-goin' to close without takin' a collection for these poor fellows'; whereat the audience filed out, and the "fellows" took on an apoplectic hue. No, Charlotte,"—and now the speaker renewed the attack by a full-arm gesture right in the face of her mild-mannered opponent—"I believe in the survival of the fittest, and if you don't see fit to take the presidency at to-morrow's election, I think I shall have some sort of fit myself. One thing is *sure*, I won't be reëlected treasurer if you don't take the presidency!"

"Has the lady done? Has she completely done?" inquired the gentle matron, taking Priscilla's hand and leading her back to the easy chair whence she had been borne upon the whirlwind of her emotions. "That oyster soup must surely have been medicated. Another time I shall give you milk to restore you after the reading of your report. Why, Silly, for you merit the nickname, though you've caught me with guile, your speech is a regular electioneering tirade, a campaign document committed to memory. Where's your 'slate?' Have you the ticket all ready, and nothing for the Union to do but just say 'aye,' a sort of human equivalent to the 'bah' of so many sheep? No, mademoiselle. You reminded me that the people are on the lookout to see how we women steer our boats in the rapids of public life. I will remind you, in turn, that if an inefficient presiding officer is a snag in the stream, an office-seeking membership is a bottomless whirlpool. Have we then read the history of men's failures in vain? Can we think of nothing better than to bring a rapier rather than a bludgeon with which to do the same deed? It is your dream that by the suffrages of women the end shall come to our long and dreary contest. Sometimes I share the hope. But I should pray that the time might never come, if I thought that on the larger stage of national politics women would be guilty of the meanness we sometimes see displayed in our smallest temperance meetings. Be assured I will never countenance anybody, even you, in coming to me with harsh words of another, or getting me to aid and abet your 'pipe-laying,' as the politicians call it, for myself as her successor."

This was rather strong meat for the discerning Priscilla. " I guess I'll go home," she said, looking down piteously at the pretty slippers with a curled up kitten embroidered on each toe. " Charlotte, you're too harsh " —Miss Shrewdly's nether lip began to quiver—" I know I've spoken plainly, but I've told the truth, and you are well aware of it. Come now, do *you* think Mrs. Blank a good presiding officer ? "

" Well," said Mrs. Cheeryble, once more, this time with the falling inflection, " I have made up my mind to tell *her*—not the Union—that before another meeting I'd like to go over to the church with her, and listen while we practice speaking, so as to be heard in every part of it. I will also suggest a little more care for the feelings of others in alluding to the object of the collection. Mrs. Blank is a true and noble woman, one of our best workers and most earnest Christians. This was her first public meeting, and she was somewhat embarrassed. I believe she is capable of doing admirably, however, with practice."

"And now, in conclusion," with these words the gentle lady took Priscilla's hand once more, "I knew from the staccato way your head moved about after the meeting, that you were afflicted with an attack of ' caucus,' and determined to help you through to the best of my ability."

Priscilla smiled—what else had she to do ?—and, taking her friend's bright face, " fair, fat, and forty," in her slim hands, inquired :

"And how does Judge Cheeryble propose to have candidates chosen and business conducted on this foot-stool, anyway ?"

"Roly-poly as I am, I expect to have considerable influence in choosing ours," she archly replied, "and, in a word, my 'policy,' as you call it, may be outlined thus— A fair, full trial to all, and, on my part, by God's grace, obedience to the blessed precept, ' Whosoever will be great among you, let him be your minister, and whosoever will be chief among you, let him be your servant,' and that we ponder more these wondrous words of Christ : ' I am among you as him that serveth.'"

ONE WOMAN'S W. C. T. U. EXPERIENCE.

[This came to me from a leading worker whose name I am not at liberty to give.]

No arguments changed me, and I am happy to say not one person in all the convention opened her lips individually to me in regard to Home Protection. I had thought I had consecrated myself to the Lord, to work for Him both in the Church and in temperance work; I thought I was willing to use any weapon for truth, justice, and virtue that He might place in my hand. But when I came into convention the conviction kept forcing itself upon me that I was not wholly consecrated to His service; I was not willing to do anything and everything for Him. There was that fearful ballot—woman " unsexing herself," etc., etc., according to Dr. Bushnell, whose arguments you know, and of which every letter I have hitherto endorsed. The question came to me, and with it the conviction that the women who stood before me, and whose words I heard, were consecrated women—not ambitious seekers of power. I had never been thrown with our workers before; I had seen very little in the narrow limits of my horizon, and the prejudices of old made me feel unjustly, no doubt, that all advocates of suffrage were party aspirants and grumblers, who were shrieking over the wrongs of women. God had been so good to me, I did not think that women had such a hard time after all; nor, in fact, do I now. But here were these gentle temperance women, wholly and solely working for the freedom of our land from the tyranny of rum. I felt I was not doing all I could to help. I simply laid my heart bare before my God and asked Him to make me willing to do His will—to gather up my prejudices as a bundle, and lay them aside. They did not vanish like mist before sunshine; they remained tangible and tough, but I laid them aside. I do not array them before me any more, and I feel so much lighter in my heart and conscience.

This is the story of my conversion. It came to me after nights of waking and weeping, for I felt the dear Lord was preparing me for something, and when the hour of trial came He did not want me to be burdened with that bundle. In Methodist parlance, my way grows brighter and brighter. This is for you. It would sound very strange and far-fetched to many ears, even absurd, that a woman should be morally and religiously converted to Home Protection. I feel I was actually converted by the Lord's Spirit, and led to a deeper feeling, if not deeper knowledge, of the truth.

OUR LETTER BAG.

Writing and receiving ten thousand letters and postals a year, most of this and my newspaper work being done on the cars, I have had glimpses into so many hearts and homes that it seems selfish to keep such riches all to myself. A few specimen sentences are here given in this "open letter" of a book.

FROM A PENNSYLVANIA GIRL OF FOURTEEN.

"I saw in the paper that you would send word how to form a juvenile society to anybody that asked you, and I thought may be I could do good in that way. Our town is in a dreadful state; it seems as if whisky almost ran along the streets, and the boys and young men almost all drink. Yesterday I saw a boy of fifteen lying under a rail fence, dead drunk. If we could have a temperance society that was real interesting, so they would like to come, I thought it might do good, and I will help along all I can, if you will tell me how."

FROM AN ILLINOIS WORKING MAN.

"You spoke about a catechism that was to be used in the children's temperance societies, to show them the evil of strong drink. I would like to buy one, to use in my own family, so my boys will know better than to form the habit, for it's ignorance that's the matter with a great many people that become drinking men."

FROM A MICHIGAN LADY.

We are bound to have the temperance cause brought up in every ministerial gathering, in every Sunday-school convention, at every camp meeting, and to 'keep it before the people' just so far as our influence permits. It's grand to be in a work where the more it is talked about the better you are pleased."

FROM A LADY IN HANNIBAL, MO.

" After our defeats we were, for awhile, lulled into our old poppy-dreams again, when somebody's good genius started a pair of us off to St. Louis to the Woman's State Convention, and that roused us for a new endeavor. My life is a busy one. I've two juvenile voters, dear little fellows, to train 'for the right side,' but my spare time I pledge to direct work in the temperance cause. A good friend and co-laborer has promised to assist me in taking charge of a weekly column in one, and perhaps two, of our papers. Our Union meets every Thursday P. M. We hope soon to have a Sabbath P. M. service, when all good temperance Christians may unite to worship, and to hold it in a part of the city where worldly men do congregate.

" Is not the report of the National Brewers' Association encouraging to us? Even our own Missouri, which we have so lamented over as being at the very rear of the marching hosts, reports that 38 out of 130 breweries have "shut up shop " within a year. Well, it's a grand age in which to have a part, and by God's grace I will not be wholly unworthy of its matchless opportunities of good."

FROM ROCKFORD, ILLINOIS.

Our Fourth of July celebration produced an excellent impression on the public mind. No cannon, no sky-rocket, no broken thumbs, but three hundred boys, in simple uniform of black pants, white shirts, drab caps, and red, white, and blue ribbons, headed by a reformed and Christian colonel, and followed by a hundred sweet girls in white dresses and white sashes, singing cold water songs. The speech of young Captain Wellington was excellent, setting forth that their weapons were spiritual, and their war one of ideas and against the old Goliath of rum. This idea of military music and drill combined, with hurrahing for the pledge, and teaching the common sense of total abstinence, is going to win the boys of our land as nothing else can.

FROM A PRINTER.

I don't want you to think I will take your counsel as a tedious lecture. I am not so great a coward as to shrink from good advice which I know I ought to follow. I see in the many illustrations which are constantly before me, of the printers who have been ruined by whisky, and yet who still retained many brilliant qualities, that the only way for one of my trade is to make a pledge *and keep it*, for there is no class so constantly thrown in the way of temptation, by the very character of their work. I know, and you can imagine how hard it is, about one o'clock at night, when a man is exhausted and sleepy from over-work, and he hears, while dreaming over the manuscript on his case, " Come, have something to brighten you up!" to refuse that which will stimulate him to complete his task. Strong drink possesses a fascination which the strongest find hard to resist, and under which the noblest minds are reduced to commit the basest actions. If I was philosophical, I would regulate my actions by previous examples, but as I am not—"

FROM A REFORMED MAN IN PHILADELPHIA.

I am holding firmly to my pledge, by God's help, and write to you ladies to ask your prayers, and to encourage you. In returning from Chicago, for the first time in years, I found I could travel without staying myself up by drink. Every afternoon, at three o'clock, I get down my " Gospel Songs," and my wife plays the melodeon, and we sing the hymns I have heard there. My wife wants me to thank you that she has her husband back again, and we both pray God to keep us true to Him. I shall go to the Ladies' Temperance Prayer-Meeting here. What a blessed thing it is that a man can now find such a haven of rest in almost every city or village in our land.

Dear friends, who have read these echoes of the greatest battle now being fought on earth, will you not buckle on your armor and join the gentle host that is daily increasing in numbers and in courage, and marching on to certain victory in the name of the Captain of our salvation, who is the " Prince of Peace."

WHO WILL TAKE OUR PLACES?

Here are some sweet, warm words from a gifted and very influential lady at the East. I wish I might write *who* for the general encouragement, but hardly feel free to do that. The letter is from Ocean Grove, N. Y., and here are a few sentences:

I have taken several steps within a week—and some *inward bounds* besides! At a young people's meeting the other morning I told them my experience. Mrs. Foster of Iowa had spoken, and had said she knew the time was before her when she would be tired. She was speaking especially to the young ladies. Colonel Bain followed, addressing the young men. I was then called on to speak by the leader of the meeting, and I told them of our friendship since last winter when you were in New York city, and how I then signed the pledge and joined the W. C. T. U. Also of how I reproached myself in the presence of the women in that city who had worked so hard and grown so tired. I then called on all the ladies, young and old, who would join me, to pledge ourselves that we would come up to the help of yourself and Mrs. Foster, and turning to her asked if it wouldn't rest her a little if she could see a new band of workers coming to the front? The tears were on her cheek as her reply. Then I asked Colonel Bain, that royal man, if he would like to have the young men do the same? You may know how he answered. And last of all I asked for the vote—the brave, fresh volunteers—and it would have cheered your heart to see the young men and women who rose. They were lovely, cultivated girls, and our boys here on vacation from their colleges. We are coming—do not be discouraged! The great wave hardly touches our New York shore, but it is coming. We are on the watch. March forward—the imperial reinforcements will yet arrive!

Undaunted as are the women of the West, " Strong in the strength that God supplies through His eternal Son," it is nevertheless like a " Dinna ye hear the slogan?" to know how true their hearts are beating away toward the rising sun! God bless us every one!

THE TEMPERANCE " HOUSE THAT JACK BUILT."

Our temperance women have a marvelous versatility. Witness the following droll bit of rhyme and reason from Mrs. E. E. Orendorff of Delavan, Illinois, President of the local W. C. T. U. My bright friend sends me her impromptu, with the following explanation:

" How our town expenses can be kept up without license money seems to puzzle many. Improvements to be made, sidewalks built, repairs attended to, and the treasury low. They shake their heads and point to the income to be derived from licensing the liquor traffic. Sixteen years ago there were no sidewalks in Delavan. A little west of the main street the ladies had a long, low building, erected of rough boards, in which were held exhibitions, concerts, etc., for the purpose of raising money for a sidewalk.

" One of the songs they sang ran as follows:

> For the right and the might and the truth shall be,
> And come what there may to stand in the way,
> That day the world shall see.

"Their efforts were successful; they drove nails and sawed boards, and Delavan had a sidewalk. Now when the nails start up and I view the broken places, I tremble lest our people may think license necessary to keep up repairs, and up and down, see-saw, through my brain—after the manner of the " House that Jack Built "—go these words:

> This is the town of Delavan;
> Once there were women that built a walk
> In this town of Delavan.

> Now here are men that talk and talk,
> Though once there were women who built a walk
> In this town of Delavan.

> There are the sidewalks broken and worn,
> And here is the Town Board all forlorn,
> And there are the men that talk and talk,
> Though once there were women who built a walk
> In this town of Delavan.

> The treasury's bare of silvery chink,
> And the lovers of alcohol bound to drink,
> And here is the Town Board all forlorn,
> And there are the sidewalks broken and torn,
> And here are the men that talk and talk,
> Though there were women that built a walk
> In this town of Delavan.

> But list! a voice! Don't lessen your joys!
> And sidewalks I'll build if you'll give me your boys—
> For the treasury's bare of silvery chink,
> And the lovers of whisky are bound to drink,
> And here is the Town Board all forlorn,
> And there are the sidewalks broken and torn,
> And there are the men that talk and talk,
> Although there were women that built a walk
> In this town of Delavan.

But look at the women,—just look at them rise,
They know 'tis old Satan in friendliest guise,
And the gay and the staid, the aged and fair,
All come to the rescue with work and with prayer,
And they'll give all their joys and glittering toys,
They'll give all their time, *but they won't give their boys.*
Though the treasury's bare of silvery chink,
And lovers of alcohol bound to drink,
And though the Town Board is all forlorn,
And though the sidewalk 's broken and worn,
Yet there are men that can work and talk,
And women here that can build a walk,
In this town of Delavan."

ONE DAY IN A TEMPERANCE WOMAN'S EXPERIENCE.

There is not a better worker in Christendom than the one who wrote me this letter. She is a State President, and has led her hosts to a victory, grand as that which Miriam sang.

"I certainly believe and act the 'do-everything policy' about as much as anyone I know, in more ways than in temperance work. You would laugh to know how often I change my employment; sometimes copying from poll-books, writing letters, dress-making, plain sewing, when my husband is away, acting chore-boy, raking door-yard, soliciting for temperance work, holding a temperance social in my house, and at last extremity, instead of oysters must have a chicken pie—so prepare the chickens and make five chicken pies in the afternoon, stopping to answer calls, receive donations, answer questions; in the evening, play hostess, wait on table, etc., etc., and withal think, think, think."

FROM A NEW ENGLAND GIRL'S LETTER.

"Sunday doesn't satisfy me any more when I have to hear the Rev. Mr. ——'s abstract disquisitions on some Scripture passage, in place of a sermon which might electrify into action every dormant soul in his congregation. How long must this continue? 'Oh, wad some power!' Well, I'm ready to shout for joy and sing praises to the Lord when I think of the Y. W. C. T. U. fairly set agoing at last in this good town. The influence it will have in quickening the consciences of these indifferent people; the reflex influence on the girls themselves; the talk it will create on a subject discussed so little heretofore—all this is beyond human measurement. It's a wonderful thing to be brought thus out of one's little round of personal cares and interests; and I'm sure we girls little dream of all that's going to come of it, and of the effect upon our characters in all the future. And to think that the most conservative girl in the Episcopal church has been made our President!"

19

CONCERNING THE WORD "CHRISTIAN."

Frequent letters have this query, and I publish my reply to one, which is equally suited to all:

"Is it best in this rationalistic community to hold firmly to our principles as implied in our name—"Woman's *Christian* Temperance Union?"

Answer—God forbid that we should boast save in the Cross of Christ. Nail that signal to the mast. "By this sign conquer." "If I forget thee, O Jerusalem, let my right hand forget her cunning, and my tongue cleave to the roof of my mouth." Hoist your flag and let the people rally around it. Bring the regiment up to the colors. No compromise prospers; no "expediency" will stand the test of time. Truth is magnetic—do not be afraid. The cross attracts—the multitude will gravitate toward it like the tides to the sun.

FROM SENATOR AND MRS. BLAIR.

U. S. SENATE CHAMBER, WASHINGTON.

My Dear Mrs. Buell—I found on my desk in the Senate this morning an exquisite basket of flowers, presented by the Woman's Christian Temperance Union.

I can think of nothing so like them in beauty and sweetness as those who gave them to me, while the immortal natures of the givers supply all that is wanting in the fading hues and dying perfumes of these selectest treasures of the gardens of earth.

Please accept my sincerest thanks, and convey to those who have thus delicately manifested this personal regard, and more than full appreciation of whatever slight service I may have rendered the great cause of "God and Home and Native Land," these acknowledgments of my appreciation of their confidence and regard.

I am, Dear Madame,

Very Respectfully,

Your Obedient Servant,

HENRY W. BLAIR.

MRS. BUELL, Corresponding Secretary of W. C. T. U.

WASHINGTON, D. C., October 31, 1881.

Mrs. Chapin, and the Ladies of the South :

Saturday evening the cheers and hearty good will of the ladies melted my heart.

Ten minutes later I would have given much to speak what I now write, but I am not one of those who can be satisfactorily surprised. Let me now say to you that I was deeply touched by your gift of flowers, because of the kindliness which I know prompted its bestowal.

No one could appreciate the gracious sentiment of those roses more than I did. They stand for affection. Let them be "for a sign" "between thee and me," and " between thy people and my people."

The love of woman has always been a great factor in affairs, civil as well as religious, and between us, whose swords have severed and wounded, it is eminently fitting that this strong compelling force should unite and heal.

Come and see us. What you did for Miss Willard in the South shall be done for you in the North. If you think us cold and stern, look on us in our homes. You will find that in the crevices of our rough ledges the hare-bells grow, and all along our highways bloom the forget-me-nots.

Sincerely yours,

E. N. BLAIR.

October 14, 1881.

CHAPTER XXV.

MRS. ZERELDA G. WALLACE, OF INDIANA.

Our Temperance Deborah—Her place—A Character—Incident—The Newspaper—A Bible Student—Home life—Her Temperance Baptism—Figures in "Ben Hur"—A Christian.

IN his essay on Friendship, Emerson uses the following language: "A new friend is a great hope—a sea to swim in; but soon we find its shores; it was only a pond after all."

Experience has, doubtless, enforced the truth of the great thinker's statement in repeated instances for all of us, but surely our grand Zerelda Wallace furnishes to those who are so happy as to call her "friend" a striking contrast to his illustration.

By the resources of her mind, the stores of her memory, the treasures of her judgment, the power of her conscience, aud the magnanimity of her heart, she reminds us of the line, "Still there's more to follow," and verifies her title to the epithet often applied to her, "The noblest Roman of them all." As illustrations of her character, take a few instances from the National Conventions of the W. C. T. U., at four of whose sessions she has been not only a presence, but a power.

In 1874, when in Cleveland the crusade clans rallied to the slogan of "organization," and we met for the first time, gathering to the call from eighteen different States, I remember whispering to a friend as Mrs. Wallace came forward to speak, "Who is that senatorial and motherly-looking lady?"

As she stood before us, in her exceeding simplicity of

(476)

MRS. Z. G. WALLACE.

dress, manner, and utterance, I did not dream she had presided at many a gubernatorial levee, graced the *salons* of Washington, and "brought up" gifted General Lew Wallace, now our Minister to Turkey, and what is more, the author of "Ben Hur." But there was something in that benignant face, that rich alto voice, those earnest words, and that solemnly-brandished silver spectacle-case, which made a more profound impression on my mind than any other of all the noble personalities in the Convention.

Although Mrs. Wallace had been nominated Chairman of the Committee on Resolutions, it seemed to us that Mother Stewart, as more closely identified with the Crusade, should occupy that position, and I therefore moved the substitution of Mother Stewart's name, which was effected by a large majority. Immediately after, I went to Mrs. Wallace, and the first words I ever addressed to her were words of explanation and apology. Grasping my hand warmly, she said : " When you know me better, my friend, you will discover that in this sacred cause I have lost sight of all personal considerations." Magnanimous heart! How many times since then, in the clash of preferences, have you proved true to that high declaration! What a victory will it be for us all as professed followers of Him "who was meek and lowly in heart," when, in our wide domain of National, State, and local societies, we can say as honestly as was then said, "*I have lost sight of personal considerations in this sacred cause.*" At the next National Convention (Cincinnati, 1875), our "Temperance Deborah" stood up all alone and sounded the first note for Home Protection. Having prayed much over her "Resolution," and written it with great care, she came before the Convention, in St. Paul's M. E. Church, and presented the first resolution asking woman's ballot on the temperance question. This was adopted, without debate, by an almost unanimous vote.

It is a matter of unique interest to know the history of a character at once so judicial and so womanly as our "Temperance Deborah." My heart rejoices in the fact that Mrs. Wallace is a Southerner. Looking, as I do, with eager and expectant eyes to the women of the South, where I have invested so much work, it is an augury of good to hail in one of our noble leaders a daughter of that sunny land. Kentucky is her native State, and her father was Dr. Saunders, a prominent physician there. She was the youngest of five daughters, and, unlike many narrow souls, her father taught his daughters as he had himself been taught, and talked with them of all great questions, religious, political, and scientific. You may select women thus broadly and blessedly trained by many signs infallible.

Among these a temperance traveler has learned to include the reading of the daily newspaper. Whatever daughter of Eve contrives, under the new dispensation of Trial by Newspaper, to suppress her interest in the human race to that degree which renders the morning paper an unattractive object must, indeed, have early been indoctrinated with the superstition that " women have no business with matters and things outside the house." If one must judge by the fraction of women who read newspapers on the cars, and in their homes as well, the generous training which enables Mrs. Wallace to say, with the poet Terence, "I am human, and whatever touches humanity touches me," is small indeed.

But the Bible was the foundation of all her education and culture. At the age of twelve she had committed it to memory as far as the book of Chronicles, and its truths had been heeded so honestly that at fourteen years of age she joined the " Christian " Church. At nineteen she became the second wife of David Wallace of Indianapolis, whose three sons she reared, besides six children of her own; and she has put aside the public duties crowding upon her now that she might be a mother to a quartette of grand-children bequeathed to her care by their parents' death.

She has earned the right to repudiate with dignity the aspersions of those who say that an interest in public affairs mars the gentleness of womanhood, and to declare that, having cradled three generations in her arms, she thinks her home record may well pass muster. Here let me quote from a brilliant sketch of Mrs. Wallace, recently published in a leading journal of the West:

"By virtue of her social position and rare mental qualities, Mrs. Wallace might have been what is known as a 'leader' in social circles; but that kind of glory was not to her taste. She cared for society only as she found in it men and women of grand ideas and splendid purpose. Her husband was a man of fine literary culture, and together they enjoyed every new book, every speech or sermon, and every newspaper that came in their way. She tells how delightful were their evenings at home, when the babies were put to bed, and she sat with her foot on the rocker of the cradle and listened to Mr. Wallace as he read the latest political speech or newest book, which they discussed with the zest of professional critics. Everything Governor Wallace wrote, speech, essay, or argument, was submitted to her for criticism or approval. Though she knew nothing of equity, he complimented her by saying that her unerring sense of justice at once lighted upon any defect or discrepancy in jurisprudence, while her fine literary taste was invaluable in regard to rhetorical symmetry. As her stepsons grew older she read law with them, and is to-day better educated in the science of jurisprudence than any woman not a professional lawyer."

Mrs. Wallace has been a widow twenty-two years. She

was left with a home but no income, and thus many years of her widowhood were spent in providing means for her children's support and education.

The story of how she was aroused to a sense of responsibility as an individual factor in society, as a citizen, is this: About nine years ago, when the temperance question was agitated with remarkable vigor, a meeting was called in its interest at one of the churches, to which Mrs. Wallace went. Though deeply interested in the exercises, when she was appointed on a committee she made several ineffectual attempts to rise and beg that she be excused from duty, so great was her dread of publicity. A little later she listened to an eloquent lecture on the evils of intemperance from Mr. Curry, at Fort Wayne, and then for the first time felt that it was her imperative duty to do what she could to check the devastating vice. One day afterward a lady was visiting her, and they talked together on this subject with all the earnestness and interest of zealots. At last her friend said, "Mrs. Wallace, if you would consent to go before our next meeting at Masonic Hall, and talk exactly as you talk to me, I believe it would do good." She was prevailed on to consent to appear, though she trembled at the very thought of the trial it would be to her, and was upheld only by an unfaltering sense of duty. She hurriedly wrote out her speech, and in excess of fear stood before her audience. " But," said she, "the moment I began to speak all terror left me, and the devotion I felt for my theme gave me an almost superhuman confidence."

She did not become a woman suffragist until about five years ago. Her convictions came with the suddenness of electricity, and through a humiliation and a scourge, as most higher developments do come. She was appointed by the temperance women to speak before the Legislature against the repeal of the Baxter temperance law. Before this her contact and association with men had been of such a fortunate nature as to lead her to suppose that she had only to prove to them, singly or in bodies, that a cause was just and right in order to have them support it with all their souls. The appointed day came, and in company with a hundred or more women, she went to the legislative halls to address the " august body." For the first time in her life, she says, she was made to feel ashamed of being a woman. As soon as she entered she discerned the spirit of the " honorable body." Nudges, leers, and even winks, went significantly around the membership. Most of them could scarcely conceal their contempt for women in general, and temperance women in particular. Mrs. Wallace's quick acumen read the minds of the law-makers at once, and she suffered an all but mortal humiliation. She had prepared her speech in the full belief that it was to be delivered to thoughtful, intelligent, well-bred gentlemen. It opened with a modest disclaimer of any wish to usurp man's " rightful place " in government or to be " mixed in the issues of politics," and begged that the assembly would consider the cause she presented as being specially a woman's cause, etc. She laughs in good-natured scorn at her lack of knowledge when she talks of that occasion, and says: " I am happy to say that it is the last time I ever gave voice to such opinions." The " honorable body" heard her through in a bored sort of way, the shoulder-shrugging and contemptuous leering being kept up mildly throughout. The general air and hinted language of the " honorable body" was to the effect that they would let " the ladies, God bless 'em," talk ; it would be an affliction, but they would submit to it in a gallant spirit. When Mrs. Wallace sat down, a Marion County representative, a senator, arose and said something to the effect that representatives could not always vote as they would like to, or as conscience dictated. They were not there to represent their own convictions, but to represent their constituency, and his constituency wanted liquor license; therefore he should vote liquor license. "Instantly," says Mrs. Wallace, "there flashed into my mind the question: 'Why am I not one of this constituency which Marion County's representatives must vote to please?'" After adjournment Mrs. Wallace shook hands with the senator, and said to him: "You are against our cause, but I am still grateful to you, because you have made me a woman-suffragist. You have proved to me how trifling a cipher an unfranchised person is in the eyes of a Legislature." From that day to this she has made it a part of her religion to labor for the removal of woman's political disabilities, and to establish a distinct idea in the public mind of the rights of the race without regard to sex or color.

A deep sense of individual responsibility alone actuates her in her public work. For all women who are unjustly discriminated against in law and life she feels an unutterable sympathy—a yearning to give them the helping hand which, in drafting the Constitution, the founders of the Republic failed to remember.

She is one of the few women who do not fall behind the times. She will be interesting and capable of teaching the thinking people as long as she lives, because she will always be well versed in the thought of the age. She takes a newspaper on every leading phase of thought, and critically reads them all. She regards the decent and dignified press as the great educator."

Mrs. Wallace has been from the beginning of our work Indiana's best beloved and most influential leader. The noblest and best political men in that State are her friends and allies. She might have made a name that would have lived in history. A man of equal ability would have been entitled to lead a party or to organize a cabinet.

But she has, instead, built her character and principles into the W. C. T. U. of Indiana, of which she is president; and let us hope to see them reflected in the nature and work of her children and grandchildren, who may well call her blessed.

To those who have read that marvelous book, "Ben Hur," by her step-son, Gen. Lew Wallace—upon the margin of whose credentials as minister to Turkey President Garfield wrote the name of that famous Christian romance —the following incident will illustrate the home qualities of Mrs. Wallace as a panegyric would fail to do. The first time they met after the book was printed, the author asked his step-mother for her opinion, when she replied: "O, my son, it is a non-such of a story; but how did you ever invent that magnificent character, the Mother?" "Why, you dear simple heart," he answered, with a kiss; "how could you fail to know that the original of that picture is your own blessed self?"

The well-worn Bible which lies upon the table beside her couch, and is the book read earliest, latest, longest of all books, explains alike her character and her career. Well would it be if all the generous-hearted and liberal-minded women who, in this astonishing age, lead the van in working out the deliverance of their sex from traditional hindrances to the best development, could sum up their "views" in words like these of Mrs. Wallace:

"The broader my views grow, and the more knowledge of the philosophy of human life I gain, the stronger is my faith in the Bible, and the firmer is my belief that ' *The fear of the Lord is the beginning of wisdom.*'"

Mrs. Wallace has a noble band of coadjutors, and the Indiana W. C. T. U. has no superior in the breadth and earnestness of its work. A dozen names rush to the point of my pen, the characterization of whose work would be a labor of love to me. But space is wanting, and I regretfully pass on.

CHAPTER XXVI.

"PERSONAL LIBERTY."

"The Open Secret."

THE main points of the following were made in my Iowa addresses during the constitutional amendment campaign:

ADDRESS.

KIND FRIENDS: The stereoscopic view is most complete because it presents the same object under two angles of vision. By plain analogy prohibition, like other moral issues, gains in clearness and perspective when we bring to bear upon it the different but united vision of manhood and of womanhood. Fitting is it, then, that Governor St. John should be succeeded on the platform by J. Ellen Foster, and representatives of your voters' Temperance Alliance by those of our W. C. T. U.

There is, moreover, historic and poetic, as well as scientific justice in a woman's plea for prohibition. Not long ago I sat beside Neal Dow, in his Portland home, and learned from him that thirty years ago in that very room came a broken-hearted wife, once the schoolmate of his own, beseeching him to bring her drunken husband from a saloon, the name of which she gave. General Dow went at once to the proprietor, stated the case, made a plea on behalf of the sorrowful housewife, and was ordered out of the saloon, the keeper saying, "There's my license on the wall; this man is one of my best customers; I'll not offend him."

General Dow then asked: "Do you mean that you will go right on selling whisky to him?" and received this reply: "I shall sell to him just as long as he can pay for his drinks."

General Dow left the saloon with these words: "The people of the State of Maine will see how long you'll go on selling." For then and there was born in his soul the purpose of a deadly contest with the liquor traffic through prohibitory law.

Remember, then, dear friends, that I am speaking on behalf of homes no less bereft, and women no less desolate than those whose misery touched the compassionate heart and moved the mighty will of him whose name stands peerless upon history's page as the father of prohibitory law.

(486)

The psalm of life was set by our Creator to the key-note of "happiness." The very word betokens this. Happiness is made up of that which happens, and these haps have been in the sum total so much more pleasurable than painful that we call them happiness. Out under the pleasant sky we listen to nature's cheerful testimony and find that disease and casualty form the exceptions, but health and soundness are the rule. Man is slowly learning the significance of nature's harmony and joy. Our own age, more than any other, has evolved the fact that the philosophy and formula of God's world is summed up in the words "according to law." Not the smallest infraction from the benignant law of "their being's end and aim" seems to be willfully made, through all the joyous ranks from the firefly in the grass to the sun in the sky.

But here is man himself, the eager student of all these laws and their attendant harmonies; man, with the mystical, magical brain which can contain God's thoughts and photograph a universe on the sensitive plates of memory; man, with his head lifted toward the stars, and in his eyes a light which never shone on sea or shore; who, with clear brain and steady pulse, was meant to be the calmest, the most joyous, the most fortunate of all, but who has sold himself a slave to misery, disease, and death by trampling on the kindly law written in his members by his heavenly Father.

Here is man's brain, with its fine and delicate mechanism, by which the body is controlled as Theodore Thomas controls an orchestra, as the engineer controls his train, or the operator his line of telegraph. Given so much clear thought, and you will get so much clear action; given so much disordered thought, and you will get so much disordered action. No law of mathematics is less variable; no statement of geometry more axiomatic. Consider this thinking machine, in its snug, round box on the top of the head. Thirty years of scientific study have yielded us some priceless certainties concerning it. In an idiot this brain weighs about twelve; in a good level head about fifty, and in a "philosopher" about sixty ounces. In composition, it bears a resemblance to the white of an egg; and into its innumerable convolutions are dipped the ends of the great system of nerves which form the telegraphic network of the body, and it is traversed by one-sixth of the entire circulation. Quiet and healthful is the ripple of the nerve vibrations which center in the brain, when the blood pumped into its delicate network is calm and healthful in its flow, and rational messages go from it then to every portion of the body's intricate machinery. But man, in his ignorance of all these laws, has been accustomed to go forth into the fragrant fields and shady vineyards, and, with the brook at which he, like all other animals, was meant to slake his thirst, tinkling its disregarded invitation in his ears, he has gathered the kindly grains and fruits of the earth provided for his food, and by soaking, bruising, and boiling them has got for himself a set of mixtures and decoctions known as "intoxicating"—which literally means, according to the dictionary's rough truthfulness, "poisoning beverages." Now the attractive ingredient of all these drinks is alcohol, of which brandy, rum, whisky, and gin contain, in varying proportions, from fifty-four to eighty-eight per cent.; wine from eight or nine to twenty-five per cent.; ale and beer from one to ten per cent. The effects of these drinks are shown by the law of Massachusetts, which, though not a temperance State, defines as "intoxicating" all beverages containing three per cent. of alcohol. But it is the changless law of alcohol, when brought in contact with vital tissues, that, though by the liquid quality of the beverages in which it is mixed it seems to appease, it really creates thirst. It does this by absorbing the fluids of the body, notably of the brain, because in the brain, as has been shown, there is so much fluid to absorb. Hence, the more brain a man has, the less liquor he can stand up under, and the less brain the more impervious he is to the assaults of alcohol, which helps to explain why the epoch of our revolutionary ancestors may have been less darkened by drunkenness than our own. The alcohol in drinks acts in exact proportion to the quantity imbibed upon the albuminous matter of the brain precisely as fire acts upon water, lapping it up with a fierce and insatiable thirst, which still, like the horse-leech's daughter, keeps crying "Give!" until its hot lips have sucked out the last particle with which they came in contact. For it cannot be too strongly stated that the affinity of alcohol for moisture is like a feverish and consuming passion, and the blistered nose, burnt brain, and parboiled stomach of the man who makes a business of drinking are nature's perpetual object-lessons to illustrate that alcohol is the redoubtable enemy of an organism made up, as the human body is, of seven in every eight parts water. It should also be said that the tendency of the appetite for alcoholic drinks is toward self-perpetuation, so that the life of the drinker is likely to be comprised in two periods, in the first of which he could leave off drinking if he would, and in the second he would do so if he could. For it has been truly said that alcoholic beverages are the only ones on God's footstool which have no power of self-limitation. One glass says two, two say three, and so on, and this because the more this liquid-absorbing ingredient is swallowed the dryer one literally becomes. "All the physiologists who oppose the temperance reform do not touch the Gibraltar of that argument."

But the statement that an appetite for alcoholic drinks is inherent with mankind has been so often made that its very reiteration has given it the semblance of truth. The appetite may be well nigh as universal as savagery and sin, but that fact should be our strongest incentive to lift men to a higher plane of knowledge and enjoyment. With just as much reasonableness might it be said that the appetite for tobacco is universal among Americans, because in the years since its discovery and Sir Walter Raleigh's bad example that habit has been so generally acquired. Moreover, one-half the human race, its gentler half, has never found either of these tastes "inherent" to itself. But, on the other hand, we find that the men of greatest physical achievement have not belonged to the drinking class. Lieut. Schwatka and his companions on their sledge journey of three thousand miles in the arctic zone; Hanlan, the champion oarsman; successful travelers, pedestrians, jockeys, and pugilists are all witnesses of incontestible authority in support of this fact. Nor is it irrelevant to instance the health and strength of the huge vertebrate animals, whose general structure is analogous to man's, but which are water-drinkers, every one.

If, then, a great curse afflicts our race; if science shows that the tendency of occasional indulgence in alcoholic beverages is toward their habitual use, rather than away from it; if the appetite is no more inherent than other evil appetites which civilization must wage war upon—what lines of remedy naturally suggest themselves whereby man may be restored to the normal condition of happiness which comes only through obedience to God's laws, as wrought into our constitution?

1. Suppose that, with a knowledge of all these facts, a being, wise and good, should come from loftier regions and alight upon our poor old planet earth. Is it not probable that—as the celestial visitant observed that by keeping out of the fire we avoid being burned—it would occur to him that, in like manner, by keeping the products of the wine-press, the brewery, the still outside of our lips, we tempted mortals might avoid the pitiful consequences which sooner or later are likely to prove the sequel to their use? Thousands have seen and followed this straight, sure pathway to personal security and beneficent example; they are among the wisest and kindest of our race; they are at a premium with the life insurance companies. Other thousands sneer at the simplicity of the expedient, or murmur at the fancied hardships, and we must good-naturedly assail them with the Gatling gun of press, platform, and pulpit, and keep up our cannonading at eye-gate and ear-gate until the arguments which have convinced us shall do their work on them.

Our German friends will not be easily convinced, because the considerations urged are comparatively new to them, but a people so intelligent and kindly will finally be among the mere trophies of a reform which has for its motto: "Come, let us reason together."

Their own great chemist, Baron Liebig, says that "there is more nutriment in as much flour as can be held on the point of a table-knife than in nine quarts of the best Bavarian beer." Their own Martin Luther. characterized the brewing business as of the devil; their own Bismarck declares it is the great demoralizing power of the German Empire, and at the last session of the Reichstag their own Minister of Finance proposed a tax upon it because of its deteriorating influence on the health, morals, and manners of the people.

PRO AND CON.

It is true that at the sixth brewers' congress, in St. Louis, a medical pamphlet on the virtues of beer was ordered printed, and this remarkable statement was made: "It ought to come before the public, not as an issue of the brewers, but of well-known and distinguished physicians." It is also true that such an issue was forthcoming, in which the theories of "inherent appetite," and that "beer is food," were advocated by distinguished names, supposed by the unsuspecting public to be perfectly disinterested in their utterances. But, per contra, take the following from Sir Henry Thompson and Mr. Darwin. (The speaker here read the unqualified statements of the gentlemen referred to, that even fermented liquors were very deleterious to health, and continued.) When such scientific instruction as the foregoing is furnished in our public schools, and with the dignity of the State to emphasize it, we shall not see the boys of our country baited with beer, and led onward into the coarse habits which deteriorate the tissues of the body and the temper of the soul.

But, in general terms, the question now before the people's jury in the State of Iowa is this: Ought a civilized nation to legalize and derive revenue from the sale of alcoholic compounds to be used as beverages, when it has been proved by centuries of awful demonstration that such use results in untold misery and ruin? Ought an intelligent nation to protect a traffic which sets two schools of ignorance and vice over against each public school house in the land? Ought a home-loving nation to tolerate an institution which is the arch foe of woman's peace and childhood's purity? Ought a Christian nation to foster the saloon system, which empties churches, scoffs at the law of Christ, and can succeed only in the proportion that His gospel fails?

Twenty years from this time it will seem as unaccountable that, on this subject, there should be a difference of opinion among good men, as it does now that twenty years ago men just as good took texts from the New Testament, from which to prove African slavery divine. But at the present stage of public enlightenment it will be urged, not among the ignorant alone, but also as the honest opinion of intelligent and estimable men, that a law prohibiting the liquor traffic is "a dangerous infringement of personal liberty."

Let us seek the meaning of this current phrase.

The poet Cowper represents Robinson Crusoe in these familiar lines:

> I am monarch of all I survey,
> My right there is none to dispute,
> From the centre all round to the sea,
> I am lord of the fowl and the brute.

But when Crûsoe saw upon the sandy shore of his desolate island a foot-print not his own, that very moment he was no longer monarch and no longer lord. From that moment his personal liberty was divided by two; from that moment self-hood (that pitiful pivot on which so many windmills turn), had to take cognizance of *otherhood.* Ever after that, "I" (that tall telegraph pole of a pronoun) had to take note of *y-o-u*, with its pathetic echo of "*I owe you.*" Or, to put the matter somewhat differently: Out on his island Robinson could reach forth his nimble fingers and gather whatever seemed to him good for food, and nobody was there to interfere. But suppose him transferred to this capital city of Iowa, and practicing the same light-fingered method in your grocery store, good citizen, or at your pantry shelf, dear lady! What a catastrophe would then occur! Out on his island he could appropriate what he liked for clothing, but let him try the same method in your tailoring establishment, my friend—it wouldn't work at all. Out on his island he had the freedom of the place, and might shout hello at the top of his lungs, but just let him try it on in this audience! Why, I have scores of brothers present, not known to me by name, who would take the intruder by the collar and march him down this aisle upon the double quick. This very audience, by its kindly attention and courteous quiet, is a splendid object lesson to illustrate my point, that a citizen's liberty is relative, not absolute, and I am confident you will accept the definition I would now offer you, viz.: That all law, from the days of Justinian's code down to your own Iowa amendment that is to be, is but a drawing of the circuit of one person's liberty just so large around and far across as is consistent with the number of circles to be drawn within a given space. Take this audience again--it is an illustration perfectly in point. Within these four walls the circles must be small, for there is only so much space, and there are so many circles to be drawn. You have all resigned the abstract right of unrestricted locomotion and vocal utterance. Your personal liberties are very much abridged thereby, but there is the given space, the four walls of this auditorium, and here the many circles to be drawn; the elbow room is thus defined with accuracy almost mathematical.

It is just so in the wide but crowded realm of civilization. Centuries of the gentle teaching of Christ's gospel are requisite to clarify the intellectual vision, so that we can dwell together in this good and pleasant estate of brotherly kindness, and mould our laws so that they shall illustrate Gladstone's motto, "The State should make it as easy as possible for everybody to do right." Three classes are outside the charmed circle of our civilization—the idiot, the savage, and the child. The first has no brain to be impressed by such considerations as I have tried to urge, hence he cannot form one in our social compact, but we provide for him the conditions suited to his imbecile condition.

The savage has the freedom, but at the same time submits to the privations of "all out doors," and yet unless he is the very "last of the Mohicans," he observes certain unwritten laws of brotherhood, dividing his venison steak and his buffalo robe with a needy comrade. "Baby is King" has passed into a proverb. He pulls your hair or doubles up his tiny fist, and thrusts the same into your eye. But let anybody else try it, and how soon you will develop that unconscious but clear-cut theory of a restricted liberty in the benignant basis of which you live and move and have your being. Behold with what persistence the enginery of civilization takes that little child in hand to teach it what are the dimensions of the home circle of personal liberty.

Before he can speak he has learned to divide; to keep the peace; to fold his little hands while papa asks the blessing. The little angular fragment of human character, under the attrition of home life, grows smooth and symmetrical, as the pebbles on the shore of my own Lake Michigan are rounded and polished by the untiring waves. Then after a while the mother hands her child over to the school. Having taught 2,000 pupils in my time, I know how our work supplements that of the home. "You must not be tardy, little man." "Why?" "Because the rest of us can't wait for you." And so on with respect to silence, order, and good lessons. Then comes the church to teach the reasonableness of all these inroads upon personal liberty that they are based upon the golden rule, and that "what is good for the hive is good for the bee." Now, if these three agencies have done their work well, a man's personal liberty will never be, consciously to him, restricted by law. Its crude requirements will sweep far outside the circle of his cultured and brotherly conduct of life. Christianity, and the institutions growing out of it, were meant to work this very transformation.

I am happy to address an audience, most, if not all, of whose members doubtless look upon the laws of the land (prohibitory and all) as I do. For I was so fortunate in my mother, my teachers, and my pastors, that law is a kind brother to me, and that alone. Its clutches I have never felt—shall never feel. It is the law that gives my mother the title deed to her quiet home at Evanston; it is the law that hedges her daily path and mine with a thousand guarantees and safeguards. It is the law which says, even to the snorting iron horse that bears me safely over uncounted thousands of swift miles, "Thus far shalt thou go and no further." But "no man feels the halter draw with good opinion of the law," and it comes as a stern schoolmaster and a remorseless avenger to those who, failing to have or to heed the lessons of home, school, and church, project their ignorant and lawless individuality across the wide sweep of its sharp, relentless circle, to their wounding and their hurt.

With this clear understanding we turn now to Robinson Crusoe and other solitary souls like him, inviting them to enter the civilized, the social, the human family, and sit down by its broad and cheerful hearth. We say to them: "You shall share with us in the long result of time. All that art yields and all that nature can decree shall be poured like a libation at your feet. You must give up many things, but you shall gain a thousand fold for all that you relinquish. Conquest over the forces of nature, instead of slavery to them, shall be given you by our clear-eyed men of science and the magic wand of our inventors. For you our philosophers shall ponder, travelers explore, and poets sing; for you our artisans put forth the manly energies of the strong arm or skillful hand. The very viands on your table, the very garments on your back, shall be the product of splendid prowess and tireless energy of thousands, who have

> Ransacked the ages,
> Spoiled the climes

for you. Come in with us and we will do you good. But remember there are two parties to this contract. Meum and Tuum are both involved; hence the swift question *what will you do* for this great and generous firm of We, Us & Company? What shall your relation be to that magnificent everybody who knows so much more than anybody? Ah, that's the question. There comes in the crucial test of what you are. For civilization has her enemies—implacable vindictives—and chief among them the drink habit and the liquor traffic. What attitude will you take toward them? Shall your example be like a torch held up in the gloom? 'A light in the window for thee, brother.' Will you, of your own free and voluntary choice, enact a prohibitory law for one in the legislature of your intellect, declare it constitutional in the supreme court of your judgment, and enforce it by the executive of your own benignant will? That is what we come to urge upon your conscience along the lines of moral suasion."

"But no," you say, "I will eat, drink, wear, speak, just what I please." Nay, friend, you cannot speak what you please. It will be easy for you to utter words so blasphemous or so unfit for ears polite that you will trench on the sharp circle of the law. It will be easy for you to appear among us in such garb that we shall hand you over to the courts.

Edmund Burke says that when man enters the civil out of the solitary state, he relinquishes the very first of personal liberties upon the threshold. What is that? The liberty to defend himself—he must resign his case to judge and jury. If at the outset he gives up so much, surely (while we may only plead with him not to patronize the products of the vineyard, the brewery, the still) we may require him to earn his living by honest sweat of brow or brain—not to absorb it like a leech out of the body politic, giving no quid pro quo. And so we come with the question, "What business do you intend to follow? In your contract with society it is important to have an answer to this question before we let you in." "I shall start a gambling house." "O, no, you won't, my friend; the principle of gambling is a principle of getting something for nothing, and would be utterly subversive of society." "Well, then; I will have a shop to sell vile literature." "O, no, you won't; we shall interfere with your personal liberty just at that point in the sacred interest of childhood and of home."

"I will set up a tannery, a slaughter-house, a powder-mill alongside of your houses." "No you will not; for we will declare them a nuisance on the instant.

"You may not even build a house of such material as you happen to prefer. We legislate on all these matters in the interest of the majority."

"Well, then; I will start an opium den."

"No; we will have an ordinance against that whenever you attempt such an atrocity. We are not so ignorant as you suppose. There is a history about opium. Taken in small quantities it seems to do no harm at first, and exceptionally strong constitutions bear up under its curse for a long period. But it is a poison, and the law of poisons is its law, viz.: The tendency of yesterday becomes the habit of to-day and the bondage of to-morrow. It makes maniacs out of some men, and its tendency is that way in the case of all, either directly or by transmission to their children. What legislation can do to root out your shop it will, and it is much to make an outlaw and an Ishmaelite out of any man's method of getting gain."

"But if you are so hard on me, I will start a saloon instead."

"No you will not, my friend; and for the self-same reason that we will not tolerate the traffic in opium—poison gathered from poppies— we will not let you sell the alcohol poison distilled from fruits and grains. The opening of your saloon would be the opening of Pandora's box. It would light the incendiary's torch, impel the random bullet and the pernicious knife stroke, and descend in heaviest blows on the gentlest and most innocent among us. Fifty per cent. of the insanity comes of strong drink; seventy-five per cent. of the crimes have their inspiration in the dram-shop; eighty per cent. of our paupers and ninety per cent. of our worthless youths emerge from drunkard's homes. The personal liberty the dealer really seeks is his own liberty to enslave a class. His practice proves too much against his theory. In proportion as the slavery of the drink appetite enchains his patrons are his own receipts increased. Ours is a country where each man is supposed to be king over one—that one himself—but when the integers in the problem of free government are systematically converted into ciphers by the effects of strong drink and the education of the saloon, then is the danger widespread and appalling. The home, too, has its rights which the saloon is bound to respect.

"The child in the midst is also in the market place, and the men who deal in alcoholic stimulants are swift to bid for him. We propose to stop this auctioneering for the best beloved of tender mothers' hearts. The protection of society must be withdrawn from the saloon, and its sheltering ægis thrown around the home. The enlightened influence of society must be condensed and brought to bear through the electric battery of the ballot-box along the tingling wires of law. With all kindly regard for our German population, we propose to level up and not down, to go forward and not back, and to lend a hand to those who mourn over their strong staff broken, and their beautiful rod.

"Listening to crude arguments for 'personal liberty,' heard everywhere in Iowa, from the lips of the ignorant, the thoughtless, and the base, we remember the infinite pathos of Madame Roland's words, that noblest of patriots and martyrs in the lawless days of the French Revolution. Condemned to death by those who knew her love and loyalty to France, she trod the scaffold with firm steps, and said as her last words, 'O, Liberty! what crimes are committed in thy sacred name.'"

SOME QUERIES ANSWERED.

Aside from the foregoing argument concerning personal liberty, Miss Willard's address contained answers to queries constantly made by press and people. These were considered under the title, "Amendment Question Box," and are here answered in condensed form:

Question. The Iowa amendment, which is to be submitted to our voters on the 27th of June declares that "no person shall manufacture for sale, sell, or keep for sale as a beverage, any intoxicating liquors whatever, including ale, wine, and beer," and requires the legislature to prescribe regulations of enforcements and penalties for violation. Now, then, is not this contrary to the constitution of the United States?

Answer. All persons of fair intelligence (with the exception of

Senator Voorhees of Indiana) know that Judge Taney and Judge Grier, of the United States Supreme Court, long ago rendered decisions explicitly declaring that prohibitory law is in no wise contrary to the letter or to the spirit of the national constitution.

OHIO AND IOWA COMPARED.

Q. What is the difference between the constitution of Ohio and that proposed for Iowa?

A. That of Ohio says no saloon shall ever be licensed to sell liquor, but it does not say that liquor shall not be sold. That of Iowa (if amended) will prohibit both sale and manufacture. The former is negative; the latter positive. Ohio says: "The State declines to receive revenue from the liquor business," but fails to say, "The business shall not be carried on."

Iowa says to manufacturer and dealer, "Close out your saloon, or we will close you out." And yet Governor Foster of Ohio, and the Chicago *Tribune*, and the anti-amendment papers of Iowa delight to confuse the minds of the people as to their difference, although it is as great as the difference between black and white, imbecility and action, something and nothing, life and death.

WHY NOT A STATUTE?

Q. But we object to putting the police power of the State into the constitution. Why not let it go in a statute instead?

A. The constitution enunciates principles; the statute provides for carrying them into practical effect. The principle of anti-slavery was imbedded in the fourteenth and fifteenth amendments of the national constitution; the statutes carried that principle into effect. In like manner the pending amendment in Iowa declares a great principle, places it beyond the fluctuations of politics, and empowers the legislature to render it efficient by statutory law. But aside from all other arguments, the people being sovereign, being themselves the original source of power, may put into their constitution whatsoever they please.

CAN IT BE ENFORCED?

Q. But if we find it so difficult to enforce our present law, what reason have we to think the new one would work any better?

A. In the first place, a new, stronger, and more direct expression of the people's will (for the present statute was from the legislature only) would give great additional force to the execution of law. In the next place, the present law opens the door for perjury, as every body knows who has tried to enforce it. The wine and beer clause makes it almost a dead letter, just as the liquor dealers, who went to such pains to secure it, knew would be the case. For it is a historical fact that the only towns in Iowa where the present law is not a dead letter, are those where (as in Grinnell) the people have, by local ordinance, prohibited the sale of ale, wine, and beer, as well as the distilled drinks. As things are now, saloons are a legal institution, and to prove just what kind of intoxicating liquors are sold inside them, whether beer or brandy, whisky or wine, is well nigh impossible. Under the amendment, the very existence of a saloon, the very presence of its outfit and paraphernalia would be prima facie evidence of violated law. Now, if a man has a saloon, the presumption is that he sells only wine and beer; then, if he had a saloon or any symptoms of one, the presumption is that he is violating law.

DOES PROHIBITION PROHIBIT?

Q. "Ah, but," we hear on every side, "prohibition doesn't prohibit." How is that?

A. The temperance people do not claim that prohibition is perfectly carried out, any more than other laws. They admit that after its adoption in any State it will require a long time to secure its complete enforcement in large cities; but history shows that it is immediately effective in villages and towns, and gradually becomes so in cities, its force being educational and always beneficial. Aside from individual statistical testimony, there are three ways in which the fact that prohibition is not a failure can be proved. First, by the positive statement of those who are enemies to prohibition. Henry Reuter, at one time President of the Brewers' Association, admits that "unfriendly legislation has driven the brewing business from Maine;" and no one denies that distilleries are banished from the favored precincts of that State. At the National Liquor Dealers' League, recently held at Chicago, the following declaration was made by Peter Lieber, a well-known brewer of Indianapolis. Upon being elected temporary Chairman, he made a speech of acknowledgment, in the course of which he said: "Gentlemen, the history of prohibition is a history of success." But actions speak louder than words, and the actions of liquor dealers from Maine to California prove that they detest and dread this law. They combine against it everywhere, and we know that men do not compass sea and land to make one proselyte in a State Legislature or municipal council unless their business suffers from the law they so remorsely fight. Besides, it is a plain principle of political economy that no business ever yet succeeded better because the law was against it. Again, the opponents of prohibition prove too much when they say in one breath that beer-loving foreigners are leaving Kansas, and in another that there was never so much liquor sold and drank there as under prohibition. Finally, no law is self-executing. The officers and people may be a failure, but not the law;

for a law is never a failure, save when its principle is *wrong*. But we turn the tables on our objector with this question:

If prohibition does not prohibit,

DOES LICENSE "REGULATE?"

Let Chicago answer, with her three thousand licensed and three hundred unlicensed dram-shops open on the Sabbath day; with her drunken boys and abandoned girls thronging these haunts of infamy; with her drunkards freely obtaining liquor enough to keep flourishing the crop of arrests for criminal assault; with her jails crowded by murderers, her vile "concert" saloons in violation of an ordinance which declares a penalty for every exhibition of the kind; with her horrid scenes at the police courts, where drunken men and women are sent to the bridewell and the jail, but no indictment found against the saloon-keepers who, in open violation of law, sold them the liquor that sent them there, and who will do so again as soon as they can get them back into their clutches. Chicago, with her municipal authorities and executive officers solemnly sworn to enforce the license law, is a suggestive commentary upon the comparative excellences of license and prohibitory laws; and remember Chicago is but a type of every town and city in the land.

"But let us discriminate between the sale of whisky and of beer," is the specific offered by some well-meaning people. The Duke of Wellington was of this number, and thought he had won a greater victory than Waterloo when he secured the passage of the "beer act" in the British Parliament. For thirty-nine years this remained in full force, and meanwhile England sank deeper and deeper in drunkenness. The Convocation of Canterbury, a department of the English Church which has ecclesiastical supervision over fourteen millions of persons, then instituted a careful inquiry into the results of this same beer act. Let me give you the summing up of the testimony taken from the lips of thousands of witnesses, not themselves temperance people either, but for the most part public officers of the law:

"This ale and beer act, though introduced for the avowed purpose of repressing intemperance by counteracting the temptation to excessive drinking of ardent spirits, has been abundantly proved not only to have failed of its benevolent purpose, but to have served, throughout the country, to multiply and intensify the very evils it was intended to remove."

If ever history learned a costly lesson that she might teach it to posterity, it was this one, which America ignores to-day.

But the evils of beer legislation must not, in this connection, be overlooked. We live in a Republic where each man counts one in every decision by which public opinion crystalizes into law. The brewers are fast becoming dictators to those in power. I quote Mr. Schade, the editor of their organ at Washington:

"No, gentlemen, first personal and then political liberty. First beer, then politics. If we want to succeed, we must do it at the ballot-box."

I quote Mr. Clausen, president of the tenth Brewers' Congress:

"Unity is necessary, and we must form an organization which not only controls a capital of $200,000,000, but which also commands thousands of votes. By our efforts the former minority in the Assembly of New York State was changed to a majority of twenty in our favor."

It is as dangerous to the Republic to be governed by an oligarchy of beer-brewing and beer-drinking citizens as by a single wicked tyrant. Yet our cities are rapidly being thus governed, and no one can read the Congressional record and see the steady concessions to the brewing interest without being aware that beer is already the determining factor in our politics. Before this blear-eyed, foamy-mouthed monster Legislatures bow the knee, municipal authorities grovel in the dust, crying: "Great is Gambrinus of the Teutonians." When a million blurred and muddled ballots are cast into the box on election day, the Goddess of Liberty may well veil her face in shame.

WHY NOT HIGH LICENSE.

Q. But would not high license work as well and be a more practicable measure, at the same time adding to the public revenue?

A. In the first place, the principle is wrong, and, in the next place, the increased tax to pay the cost of taking care of the results of the liquor traffic (crime, pauperism, etc.) render the method penny wise and pound foolish. Besides, high license saddles the saloon system upon the community, renders it impossible to prove up cases of violated law, and surrounds the dram-shop with an air of attractiveness and respectability in the last degree dangerous to young men.

OUTLAWING DISTILLERS.

Q. But do we not break faith with the manufacturers by outlawing their business, heretofore legal?

A. No more than we do when any other kind of business is condemned by law. This is a risk to be taken by liquor dealers at the outset, as they very well know. Of course this condemnation always involves loss, but we may be measurably consoled in this case by contemplating the enormous gains of the past—"the eight-cent profit on a ten cent drink," by which saloon-keepers have enjoyed a higher interest on their investment than any other class of men. In general terms, all

20

progress, all inventions, bear heavily for a while upon a class. But public policy must be considered, and *pro bono publico* and survival of the fittest must prevail. The question, therefore, resolves itself into this: Shall we let those people engaged in the liquor traffic suffer, or shall we leave defenceless the people's homes?

HOW ABOUT DRUGGISTS?

Q. But is not this simply a method of transferring sales of drink from saloon-keepers to druggists?

A. To some extent this will be true, but you have now to contend against the double evil, for these two institutions stand side by side. Under the amendment you will simplify the problem and know just whom you are fighting. In Arkansas they have hedged the druggists about by requiring a sworn pledge from every physician, under heavy penalty, that he will not furnish a prescription to those not actually ill, and they also keep a list of all prescriptions open to public inspection and render the druggist who violates the law liable to fine and imprisonment.

IS THIS TIME PREMATURE?

Q. But has the time arrived for such a sweeping measure? Is not this action premature?

A. Let this be answered by the fact that two separate Legislatures, at intervals covering four years, representative bodies coming directly from the people and supposed to know the wishes of their constituents (yea, verily, and the political results to themselves) have by large majorities placed the amendment squarely before the people. Besides, as Senator Wilson so pithily puts it, "If there is doubt remaining as to whether this is the time, we propose to set it at rest on the 27th of June."

IS IT A SUMPTUARY LAW?

Q. But is not this a sumptuary law?

A. In no sense of that much misunderstood term. Sumptuary laws flourished in the days of ancient Rome, and at certain oppressive periods of English history, and aimed to regulate personal and household expenses in such a way that more money would pass into the treasury of the State. How often a dinner party could be given, of how many courses it could consist, and how many guests might be invited at a time—these were matters regulated by law. Now, the brewers even, will not maintain that it is a sumptuary law by which saloons are closed upon election day, for this is done as a measure of public safety, no man's personal habits being thereby legislated against. But if the public conscience becomes sufficiently enlightened to perceive that the saloons are a danger not only upon election, but every other day, and, thus perceiving, extends the provisions of the law. is it sumptuary in the last case any more than in the first? By parity of reasoning it is not. Sumptuary law regulates personal habits, prohibition assails a harmful business; sumptuary law interferes with the drinker, prohibition with the seller; the first is oppressive, the second legitimate.

WHAT SHALL BE DONE WITH BUYERS.

Q. But ought not the drunkard to bear his part of the blame, and does not this kind of legislation unjustly discriminate against the seller?

A. These things ought ye to have done, and not have left the other undone. Doubtless the drinker ought to have been dealt with as to the results of his crime, and he can be by the statutes. Let us not then throw away so good a tool as the amendment because it is not perfect. As a general principle you can deal with a barrel of whisky in the shop of the seller more readily than in the flask or stomach of the consumer.

THE QUESTION OF HEALTH.

Q. But after all, is it not true that alcoholic stimulants, taken in moderation, are good for people's health?

A. No; because men of the greatest physical endurance do not belong to the drinking class, as is proved by the statistics of life-insurance companies, by the death-rate in cases of pestilence and sunstroke, also by the record of successful explorers, pedestrians, oarsmen, etc. The same fact is also proven from the changeless tendency of the appetite for alcoholic drinks toward self-perpetuation, so that one glass says two, two call for three, and so on. "All the physiologists living cannot touch the Gibraltar of this argument." Science, experience, and the golden rule unite to answer this last question with the most emphatic negative. But, let it be remembered, this amendment limits no man as to what he shall drink. Do not let us confound things that are different. Shall the liquor traffic be legalized? The amendment answers no! May we all take for our motto the words of Christ: "Every plant that my Heavenly Father hath not planted shall be rooted up."

Friends, there is always a way out for humanity. Progress never calls a halt, but beats her drums and waves her banners far up the heights where courageous voices shout "Excelsior." When Sir Wilfred Lawson's local option resolution was adopted in Parliament last spring, *The London Times* made a comment which has in it the explosive force of nitro-glycerine, for it declared that "this measure would never succeed until woman had the ballot."

The day will come, and is not distant, when to offset the vote of Cork and Hamburg, the "home vote" will be counted in, not out.

This expectation is based on the fact that the thoughtful classes in the community are already committed to the movement that State after State is steadily enlarging the scope of woman's power; that in four-fifths of the Woman' Christian Temperance Unions the movement has been formally indorsed, and that press and pulpit are ranging themselves in favor of the change.

Dear ladies, let us be of good courage. The gentlemen of this audience will not decline to represent us at the polls. Constitutional prohibition will be secured in this generous, wide-awake "Hawkeye State," through manhood suffrage. But when, on the issue of enforcement the question becomes partisan, as assuredly it must, Barak will call Deborah to his side in the Prohibition party of the future, and humanity's full voice will then be heard giving everywhere a temperance majority "*For God and Home and Native Land.*"

> " Somewhere beneath the vaulted sky,
> Or underneath the slumbering sod,
> Wrath broods its thunders ere they fly,
> Pale Justice steels her toughening rod;
> When wealth and power have had their hour,
> *Comes for the weak the hour of God.*"

THE OPEN SECRET.

Here follows a fair sample of revelations coming to me continually as a temperance worker. This is from a former schoolmate—the gayest and one of the most gifted in our college. She is writing of her husband:

—, Michigan.

"Last Sunday, for the first time, I was obliged to have help, Ned was so bad. I had not slept for three successive nights. Every evening I had hunted him up and brought him home, but he would slip away about four o'clock in the morning. I had been to the saloons and begged them not to sell him liquor. One man denied that he kept it, swore at me, and ordered me out of his place. O, my friend, *where has God gone?* He certainly has forsaken this town of —. Three gentlemen staid with Ned all day Sunday and Sunday night and Monday. He is so penitent when it is over, and promises never to touch strong drink again. Sometimes it will be several months before he does, and then some one, perhaps a prominent man, *and one who knows his weakness*, will invite him to take a drink, and with one glass he loses all control. I have humiliated myself again and again by being pleasant to men I despised, just that I might influence them to let Ned alone, and then, perhaps, have failed. I have been in saloons full of quarrelsome men, late at night and all alone, to persuade my husband to come home. I have questioned lawyers to know if I can not prevent liquor dealers from selling to him. They always shake their heads. The trouble is they are *afraid* to do anything about it. The liquor dealers control our lawyers, some of our ministers, and all our public schools. Why, we have a forty thousand dollar school-house built from the taxes on our saloons. I could not get a single newspaper to publish that little announcement you sent me of a W. C. T. U. Convention. I took it to a pastor and asked him to use his influence to get it in, but he shook his head and said " it was of no use to try." Poor Ned! He is such a grand, good fellow when he is sober that only the welfare of my boys would make me wish to leave him, and that not always, but sometimes. It is such a relief to talk straight out of my tired heart. I have repressed my feelings and shut up my troubles so long that I am in great danger of changing into an icy-hearted woman—who used to be so merry. Dear friend of better days, please do not forget to pray for me, for my faith does not grow stronger."

CHAPTER XXVII.

THE MODOCS OF THE LAVA BEDS IN THE INDIAN TERRITORY.

A Quaker conquest—Miss Willard among the Modocs.

OCEAN GROVE, N. J., August, 1881.

FIGURE to yourself three scenes: The first is in the lava beds of Oregon. Here the fierce, wild Modoc Indians are scalping General Canby and the Rev. Dr. Thomas, while Colonel Meacham is left upon the field for dead,—and all this comes to pass under a flag of truce. In the desperate fight squaws redden their hands in the white men's blood, for so desperate is the struggle that women's hearts become as hard as those of life-long warriors. News of the slaughter is quickly carried along telegraphic wires, and throughout the civilized world the name of "Modoc" becomes the synonym of savage cruelty.

The second scene transports us to the simple Quaker home of Asa and Emeline Tuttle, of the Quapaw agency, Indian Territory. He is a Quaker preacher from the State of Maine, and she a teacher from the State of Indiana, and to both there came, many years since, "a deep concern" for their red brethren, insomuch that they dedicated their lives to each other and also to that Indian peace policy, which was the happiest Presidential thought of General Grant. Beloved by her Indian pupils, and delighted with the work in which she and her husband have been so grandly useful, Emeline Tuttle, from the

(504)

day on which she learns of the horrid Modoc fight, sighs for new worlds to conquer!

With an earnestness which becomes like a fire in the bones, she covets these heathen for her inheritance, and these uttermost parts of the earth for her possession. Often in the twilight she goes away alone into a little grove and prays with a fervor that would frighten her did she not feel it "borne in upon her soul," as the Quakers say, and in the night she wakes, with tears of joy upon her face from dreams in which the Modocs have indeed been given her to teach. So praying, trusting, and meanwhile teaching her Indian school, the days "go on, go on."

Nearly a year passes, when behold, one autumn afternoon a shabby railroad train rolls along the prairie, and from some creaking old cars are literally dumped, almost at Mrs. Tuttle's feet, the horrible, marauding Modocs of the Lava Beds. They are in paint, and blankets, and tattooing, with rings in their noses and (pardon, ladies) in their ears also. Unkempt, uncleanly, huddled together in squatting attitude, with untaught hands, brains cobwebbed by superstition, and bodies diseased by strong drink; without habits of industry, instincts of home, and knowledge of Christianity; this band of savages is turned over to Brother Asa and Sister Emeline to see what the New Testament and the total abstinence pledge can do for them.

Seven years or thereabouts have flown, and on Saturday evening, the 23d of May last, it was my fortune to be landed in the Modoc settlement, to spend a few days with Mrs. Tuttle, now vice-president for the Indian Territory of our National W. C. T. U. And this is the last scene of the "dissolving view" of sloughed-off barbarism—the dawn of a new manhood in Christ Jesus. Driving along the fragrant prairie we passed farm after farm belonging

to different members of the tribe.   Under the guidance
of a kind Quaker farmer fences were building and crops
being planted, while on every hand comfortable log-houses
were to be seen.   In a neat white cottage, I found my
Quaker friends, and in great peace and quietness slept
the sleep of the weary that night in a community where
the hands that used to clasp scalping-knives had grown
familiar with plough-handles, and the voices that yelled
the lava beds' war-whoop now sang the Moody hymns.

The next day was the Sabbath, and trooping from every
side came the swarthy-faced men, women, and children of
this strange race.   In a pretty building, seated with Hol-
brook's furniture, and answering the double purpose of
church and school, we gathered for morning service.   It
had been decorated in honor of my visit, and the motto
of our W. C. T. U. was arched in evergreen letters behind
the simple pulpit: " For God, and home, and native land."
The Sunday-school lesson for that day—which the Modocs
studied in common with all other Christians!—was
" Answers to Prayer," and after a scripture recitation, in
which all the younger ones participated with remarkable
clearness of English, I was asked to tell them once more
the story of the temperance crusade—the greatest prayer
movement of the nineteenth century.   They had heard it
often from Mrs. Tuttle's lips, but listened with all the
more appreciation on that account.   The Indian "Ugh,"
of which we hear so much, was frequently employed, and
when I had finished that thrilling and pathetic story of
" The Women who Dared," those Indians, with their tall
heads, swart faces, and beaming, dark eyes, sang " Rock
of Ages " (our crusade hymn), as I have seldom heard it
sung in church or prayer-meeting.

The invitation was then given for any to speak.   Colonel
D. R. Dyer of Illinois, agent of this reservation, and an
earnest temperance man, spoke of his determination to

enforce in his domain the prohibitory law with which the
entire Territory is blessed. Asa Tuttle recounted the
splendid growth of public sentiment among the Modocs,
until now every man, woman, and child wears the ribbon
and belongs to the Woman's Christian Temperance Union,
and most of them are members of the Society of Friends.
The Indians then stood forward one by one to speak, an
exercise of which, by the way, they highly approve. With
inimitable reverence "Scar-Face Charlie," "Long George,"
"Steamboat Frank," and others pointed to the great gilt-
edged Bible as the book that makes the white man what
he is, and with impressive gravity to the bottles of alcohol
I had just used in an experiment, as the "fire-water"
which has reduced the Indian to degradation.

Princess Mary, sister to Captain Jack, was present;
also his two wives, comely-faced women, but with no
oratorical ambitions. Steamboat Frank's wife spoke with
more freedom and eloquence than any other person, and
the Modocs recognize her as decidedly superior to her
husband, albeit he is the "preacher" of the tribe. The
perfect equality of men and women in the Lord's house
has, of course, been thoroughly set forth by these
enlightened Quakers, and is thoroughly accepted by the
Indians, abhorrent as would have been the thought seven
years ago. A Cherokee lady named Mrs. Arnold, the
post-mistress at Vinita, I. T., had accompanied me to the
Modoc settlement, and it was indeed suggestive to see in
her the fruit of generations of Christian training, as she
came gently forward, saying, "I am so glad, dear friends,
that you have embraced temperance and the gospel, for
they have redeemed our Cherokee nation; and we are
proud of our Indian blood, and are doing all we can to
make the Cherokee name respected, even as you will
make the name of Modoc noble and honorable."

And now four little Modoc girls came forth, with

bright, handsome faces, roguish looks, and in their hands a pretty bead basket, trimmed with gay ribbons. In perfect English and musical unison they thanked me for my visit (Hiawatha fashion, " Since you come far to see us"), and said that as "poor little Modoc girls, they hadn't much to give, but had made this little basket to remind me of them when I was far away," concluding with the sweet Bible benediction, " The Lord bless thee and keep thee; the Lord make His face to shine upon thee and be gracious unto thee; the Lord lift up His countenance upon thee and give thee peace." Well, when those fresh young voices ceased, it was very quiet in the little church, for I tried in vain to speak, and we all cried together. Somehow it was so blessed and so wonderful—the change in these " Modocs of the lava beds," and the dear gospel temperance cause which brought us face to face had renewed so many ruined lives of those who sat about me, that "I wished in vain that my tongue might utter the thoughts which arose in me." But after awhile I told them that though I had been welcomed by noble people in nearly forty States and Territories for the temperance union's sake, by Governor St. John of Kansas, and Governor Colquitt of Georgia, in words most brotherly, and though I had talked with the Great Chief at the White House, I had never, until these little Modoc girls spoke kindly to me, been so deeply touched by human words that I had vainly tried to make reply.

In conclusion: intelligent men and women in the Indian Territory desire me to urge two considerations upon our people at home. *First:* The importance of *trade schools.* Head, heart, and *hand* must all be educated, if we would bind the Indians to us in a covenant never to be broken. It is a proverb that " no Indian can build a bridge." So little of our Yankee skill have they by heredity or rearing, that for this reason we should make all the more strenuous efforts for their development in this respect. Many a youth and maiden (especially the latter) have returned to their tribes after years of schooling, and by reason of their inability to show any practical results of their efforts, have become the butt of ridicule, and have been forced by their friends to resume their blanket, paint, and moccasins. But let them return skilled in some useful art, and they will "hold their own" and lead others to desire similar acquirements, greatly advancing their tribes in the outward forms of civilization.

Second: The advantages of having the schools in the territory. The reflex influence of the faculty and institution on surrounding Indian communities would be strong and beneficent. Students would suffer less in health and heart than they do by this virtual exile from home and country; would also be less liable to the alienations from their people which now ensue. A favorite project is a university for the Five Nations, at their capital, Telequah, with a board of trustees selected from the tribes, and the Indian commissioner at the head.

Third: There as here, the prohibitory law does not enforce itself. Without vigilant efforts on the part of the agents, it is but a rusty sword in a still more rusty scabbard. Under perfidious Commissioner Hayt (whose entire wits were absorbed in fraudulent attempts to make money out of his office) the prohibitory law was largely a dead letter in towns and villages. But since the advent of Commissioner Hiram Price of Iowa, a thorough, active temperance man, there is a vigorous tension of the reins, with a marked approval on the part of all save those who "feel the halter draw."

In Colonel Dyer's reservation (the "Quapaw") there has, however, been strict enforcement for years, and no better object teaching on the merits of prohibition can be desired than is here furnished. Fourteen mounted Indians in Uncle Sam's uniform strike terror to the hearts of men with big box, little box, carpet-sack, or bundle, suspected of containing the products of vineyard, brewery, or still. Missionaries come and go at pleasure, travelers camp out minus escort or weapons; ladies drive their spirited horses hither and yon with none to molest them or make them afraid. We must revise our ignorant fancies of Indian Territory by the fact that it abounds in churches, school-houses, and homes, but is minus bar-rooms and grog-shops. God speed the day when Massachusetts may have a record equally encouraging.

CHAPTER XXVIII.

MRS. L. M. N. STEVENS OF MAINE.—MRS. F. A. BENT,
WITH HER GOLDEN CORNET.

NOTWITHSTANDING her earnest plea to be left out of this veracious chronicle, "Mrs. Stevens of Maine" is a figure too central for such treatment. Her native pines are a true symbol of the rectitude and wholesomeness that individualize the character of this brave and womanly coadjutor of Neal Dow in the later temperance work of Maine. As president of the State W. C. T. U., and recording secretary of our national society, Mrs. Stevens has been conspicuous in much of the most thorough work we have inaugurated. As she said to a friend, "When I heard about the Ohio crusade, I thought, 'That means me, too!' I joined the army then and there, and have marched right along ever since." For seven years she has conducted meetings in her own city, and all kinds of temperance work are as familiar to her as knitting stockings was to her grandmother. She has a generous and well-to-do husband, glad and proud of his wife's work, and one lovely child—her "sunbeam," a bright girl of fifteen, who already writes debates on prohibition and the ballot for woman as a "Home Protection" weapon. Mrs. Stevens is of fragile physique, and her health was delicate until the temperance work welcomed her to a life largely spent in the open air. The streets of Portland have not a sight more familiar, and surely none more welcome to all save evil-doers, than Mrs. Stevens in her phæton rapidly driving her spirited horse from police station to Friendly Inn; from Erring Woman's Refuge to the sher-

(511)

iff's office. The round of her duties for the day would be far more thrilling than the *dilettante* society novelist knows how to imagine, much less depict. Histories full of the real heart-throb, and the romance of actual misery are poured into her ears as she kneels to pray beside some newly-arrested woman at the jail. Betrayer and betrayed sometimes accept her gentle arbitration; friendless boys from country homes owe to her the open door into a better way of life; drunkards consecrate themselves to Christ in her meetings; time-serving officials dread her evidence at court; saloon-keepers hate the keen scrutiny of her fearless investigation. She often says to the devoted women associated with her: " When I enlisted in the W. C. T. U. warfare, it was for life, and when the day is darkest my courage is the best." In a letter to one of them, she refers to her religious experience in words so characteristic that we borrow them:

" I was but twelve years old when my only brother died, and the expression of the minister who said, ' He died like a Christian and a philosopher,' lodged in my childish head. From that time the problem of a religious life came to be mixed in with mathematical and other problems. My invalid mother was a Baptist, my scholarly father was a Universalist, and to me there were things unreasonable and things beautiful in both beliefs. But the thing most beautiful of all was the love of Christ, and so when I came to a place where it seemed to me I needed a church home, I could but choose it where the creed to which I must subscribe did not limit His love and power, but asserted it to be strong enough somehow and somewhere to restore all souls to holiness and happiness. So you see, my religious ' confession of faith' is not thrilling at all, like most of our dear women's, but to me it is *meaning-full*, and I am happy."

Mrs. Stevens, though disagreeing with the majority of

MRS. M. A. BENT, WITH HER CORNET.

our W. C. T. U. in her theory of the future, is in perfect unity with us as to methods and plans, and joins us in the sacrament of sacred deeds.

MRS. F. A. BENT, OF PORTLAND,

the charming cornetist of our National W. C. T. U. Conventions, is a niece of Mrs. Stevens, the wife of a young business man of Portland, who is himself a fine amateur musician. Playfully taking his instrument one day, his wife found she could make music, too, and henceforth, encouraged by his generous aid, the gifted little woman has been going on with her study of this inspiring instrument under the best Boston teachers, and now she is glad to lay her gifts and acquisitions on the altar of the temperance reform.

The pretty, slight figure with the golden cornet has been for years one of the pleasant features of the national meeting. In Louisville a leading pastor playfully said, " Mrs. Bent, you at least can blow your own horn," whereupon the bright little woman replied, " O, no, sir; you mistake; I am only blowing Maine's prohibition bugle, and I expect to do so until the echoes fly from all the States."

In the Mammoth Cave excursion of our delegates, the golden cornet enlivened the long ride, and sent old "Coronation" sounding through the wierd " Star Chamber " in a fashion not easy to forget.

The muster roll of Maine is too ample for my book. Miss Mary Crosby and Mrs. Crossman of Bangor, Mrs. Hunt of Augusta, and Mrs. George S. Hunt of Portland, are among the leaders.

CHAPTER XXIX.

LIFE AND WORK OF JULIA COLMAN,*

Superintendent of the Literature Department of the National W. C. T. U.

THIS well-known temperance worker came of mingled Puritan and Huguenot blood. The Colman family from England settled in Wethersfield, Conn., in 1634. About the year 1800 her grandfather's family moved "away out west" to Northampton, Montgomery County (now Fulton County), New York, which was her native village. Her mother, Livia Spier, was of Welsh ancestry, who came to Boston eight generations since.

Her father, Rev. Henry R. Colman, a clergyman of the M. E. Church, after several years itinerancy in the Troy Conference, went in 1840 to Wisconsin as missionary to the Oneida Indians, and settled near Green Bay. Here the child Julia took lessons in self-denying labor, and, in her juvenile efforts to communicate with these untaught children of the forest, laid the foundation of that simplicity and directness of style for which her writings are noted, and which constitute both the charm and success of her extended literary productions. There were no schools in that then wild region which she could attend, but the lack was supplied by careful home teaching, and the privation only excited her youthful energies to greater exertion. In true Yankee-girl fashion, she early commenced teaching in Calumet and Fond-du-lac Counties, "living in the parlor"—as boarding around from family to family was there termed—and industriously continuing her own studies as she could. During

---

*This sketch was furnished by Mrs. Helen E. Brown of New York.

this period she commenced the study of botany, analyzing and classifying over three hundred specimens before having the aid of any teacher. This was a rare achievement, strikingly indicating, and at the same time helping to develop the faculty for accurate observation with which nature had endowed her, and training her into those habits of careful research which have since proved so useful in other departments.

When Lawrence University, at Appleton, opened its doors for students, Miss Colman was in the first classes. She remained there for nearly two years, and then spent two years at Cazenovia Seminary, New York, under Rev. Dr. Bannister, graduating in the first class in the collegiate or five years' course. Her specialties were the languages and moral science, with unusual aptitude in physiology and chemistry.

After a year or two longer in teaching, she deliberately chose literary pursuits, accepting a position in the editorial office of the Methodist Sunday-school Union and Tract Society, where she remained over thirteen years, as librarian and assistant to Drs. Kidder, Wise, and Vincent, making acquaintance with editorial, publishing, and benevolent society work, which has been of the greatest value to her in her present position. During a portion of this time she assisted in editing the *Sunday-School Advocate*, which then had a circulation of nearly 400,000, and where her articles, signed "Aunt Julia," attracted much attention.

Here she commenced a crusade against tobacco by inducing the boys to form local "Anti-Tobacco Leagues," to learn about tobacco, and to work against it, especially by distributing anti-tobacco literature. She provided them with a manual and other requisites, and over one hundred such leagues were formed in different parts of the country. They were ephemeral, as boys' societies necessarily are, but they aimed in the right direction, and doubtless did something towards checking a great and growing evil. It was, at all events, a foreshadowing of future work.

Translations from the French and German of articles for the *National Magazine* and letters for the *Christian Advocate*, the preparation of a number of small books for the children on natural history, anti-slavery, and temperance, were among the literary labors of that period; while benevolent efforts in the large Sunday-school of Greene Street church, where for five years she was lady superintendent, constituted her outside work. These constant and pressing demands, however, finally proved too much for her health, and she relinquished a portion of them for a series of studies in medicine and physiology. Through these she found her way into restored health, which has continued almost unbroken to the present time. She was also providentially led in this way into an acquaintance with the medical and scientific aspects of the temperance question. Are not the Lord's ways as far above ours as the heavens are higher than the earth? Thus it is that He chooses one and another, develops, adapts, and ordains them that they may go and bring forth fruit, and that their fruit may remain.

Previous to this, the subject of our sketch had been, like most others, largely unmoved by the needs of temperance. She saw and deplored the great evil of intemperance; but, like those around her in the Church of God, she sat with folded hands, because she could see no effective method of checking it. The question had never come to her practically, either in her own person or among her kindred; but now, in the course of these later studies, her eyes were opened. She was taught of God to see the immense responsibility of the medical profession in the use, and especially in the moral support given by them to the use, of alcoholic liquors.

She immediately began to study and write on the question, and, not finding sufficient access to the public through the press at her command, she prepared a lecture on "Alcohol our Enemy," which, after a good deal of earnest effort and patient waiting, she was permitted to deliver. It was in March, 1868, before a crowded house in the church of which she was then a member, in the presence and with the assistance of her pastor and other influential friends, the lecture was given, and was subsequently repeated many times in other places.

Finding her time and interest engrossed in this topic of temperance and in the kindred subject of food and diet, she, in the autumn of 1867, severed her long connection with the Methodist Publishing House, where, however pleasant it might be, there was little chance (being a woman) of advancement. She then gave two courses of lectures on "Food" in the Dixon Institute, Brooklyn, N. Y., wrote a long series of articles on that subject for the *Ladies' Repository*, and still more for the *Rural New Yorker*, for *Home and Health, Science of Health*, etc., etc., besides temperance articles for the National Temperance Publishing House, and for the *Youth's Temperance Visitor* in Maine. Through the latter she was led incidentally to a long series of engagements to lecture in that State on temperance. This gave her the much-desired opportunity of studying the temperance problem upon that soil, and learning the conditions which led to its wonderful advancement and success there. During the winter and spring of 1870 and 1871 she filled nearly one hundred engagements, speaking sometimes before Methodist conferences and sometimes before teachers' institutes, where she faithfully advocated temperance teaching in the day-school, sounding the first notes on that topic.

She finally concluded, however, that she could reach a greater number by the pen, if exclusively devoted to this subject, and thus more effectively promote a cause in which her interest was becoming more and more engrossed. She wished also to take a course of lectures in medicine, which she preferred to do at different colleges, that she might learn the various ideas about the uses of alcohol in medicine. She gave especial attention during this period of study to the chemical course. This broken method did not favor her taking a diploma, which, however, was offered her. But she declined the honor, as she did not propose to practice, and did not care to flourish a medical title. She also paid much attention to the chemistry and preparation of food, making investigations in several health institutions, and subsequently published no less than seventy-five consecutive articles on this subject in the *Monthly Science of Health* and *Phrenological Journal.*

It was while carrying out some of these engagements, so that she could not give her personal attention to the cause, that the remarkable temperance crusade swept over the land. But when, in the summer of 1875, she retired to an inland country town for needed rest, taking with her for preparation the "Twenty Tracts on Temperance"—now twenty-five—issued by the Methodist Book Concern, she engaged actively in the new temperance work. She helped to start in that town a local Temperance Union, and became Superintendent of the first so-called "Temperance School." In this she used the catechism on alcohol, which she had written and published three years before, and worked out the method afterwards developed in her "Lessons from Nature," published in *Our Union* in 1877, and more fully in the *Juvenile Temperance Manual.* Accounts of this school in the papers and elsewhere attracted attention, and at the National Convention of the W. C. T. U., in Newark, in 1876, Miss Colman was elected to edit one page of

" Our Union " for the children, preparing lessons explana-
tory of the catechism. She was also made Chairman of
a " Leaflet Committee," which was the starting point of
the present extended and constantly extending literature
work, of which she has been for six years the indefatigable
and eminently successful Superintendent.

Her work in this department aims to devise effective
measures for the distribution of temperance literature,
favoring special topics to harmonize with other lines of
work, and more particularly the accurate knowledge of
the nature and effects of intoxicants as indispensable to
getting rid of them. This is to be followed with tract
after tract, and then courses of readings on each topic, as
" Readings on Beer," already issued. These are designed
for the local unions, to be accompanied by the distribution
of the tracts and hand-bills, one kind at a time. These will
lead to the study of books which will become a part of a
loan and reference library, and which may be made available and effective by the efforts of the members of the
unions.

Miss Colman aims not so much to produce new publications as to utilize the best of what are published. What
is lacking she supplies, as in the Union Leaflets (71),
especially adapted to the various needs of the woman's
work ; the Beer Series of Handbills (57) ; the Gospel
Series (30), etc. A large share of her attention has been
devoted to the work for children. For this she has
written the " Catechism on Alcohol," " Juvenile Temperance Manual," " The Temperance School," and adapted a
variety of tracts, leaflets, chromo, and hymn cards, making a complete system of requisites. More recently she
has written " Alcohol and Hygiene," a school text-book,
intended to precede Richardson's " Temperance Lesson
Book" in the graded schools. This has been well received. She has also commenced a series of " Leaflets

for Young People," suited for distribution with others in schools and colleges, meeting a felt want in the work.

In a similar manner she has classified a great variety of the best tracts, handbills, and leaflets into sets, according to their character, so that it is easy to procure specimens of tracts for definite uses; and her directions are so simple and clear that the work of tract distribution is becoming both pleasant and effective.

She has also suggested and planned the dime collection system to supply the wants of her department, as churches provide for their tract work, by their tract collections. This plan was adopted by the National Convention at Boston in 1880. But it does not provide for her personal expenses, which she supplies mostly by her contributions to the press outside of her department labors, or by editorial work like that she bestowed upon the "Young People's Comrade." Thus she can say, like Paul, while preaching by voice and pen the gospel of temperance: "These hands have ministered unto my necessities," "that we might not be chargeable to any of you."

Surely the Lord, who sees "the end from the beginning," the Master Workman, the Divine Husbandman, knows where and how to find workers for his work, and work for his workers; and we can but stand aside and admire his adaptations. He has by nature endowed, by education fitted, by discipline cultured, and by grace made willing this his disciple, and has brought her to the place where her peculiar talents and gifts may have free and ample exercise.

And he has also opened and prepared the field. Just when his trained and obedient servant stood ready, asking "Lord, what wilt thou have me to do?" came the crisis in the great temperance reform when the printed word was needed to be scattered, as the sower sows the seed, upon the ploughed ground; seed that is to grow, we " know not how," but which will surely, by the grace of God, germinate and bear fruit abundantly to his glory. Miss Colman is, emphatically, our seed-sower; and we garland her name with the precious words of inspiration, " BLESSED are ye that sow beside all waters," and " In due season ye shall reap if ye faint not."

CHAPTER XXX.

OUR JOURNALISTS.

Mrs. Sarah K. Bolton—Miss Margaret E. Winslow—"Crowned"—
Mrs. Mary Bannister Willard—"John Brant's wife, who was not a
Crusader,"—A sketch.

MRS. SARAH K. BOLTON.

MRS. BOLTON of Cleveland, Ohio, is a woman of
special gifts and culture as a journalist. She has
the rare art of putting much in little space; is one of the
best informed women in America, and has, withal,
unbounded pride and faith in women, sparing no pains to
bring them out and help them up. She was one of the
original crusaders, and by voice and pen has stood by that
great movement from the first, has written its history, and
also put it in the form of an attractive narrative entitled
"The Present Problem," and set forth our work in most
influential quarters on both sides of the sea. As a
member of the editorial staff of the Boston *Congregationalist* Mrs. Bolton did us excellent service, and earlier,
as assistant corresponding secretary of the National
W. C. T. U., she kept articles, paragraphs, and enlight-
ening excerpts before the public which did more toward
setting our new methods before the people than any single
agency has ever compassed up to this time. After spending some years abroad with her husband and only child
in study and travel, Mrs. Bolton has recently returned to
Cleveland, where she is actively aiding her philanthropic
husband, ·Charles E. Bolton, Esq., in a most successful
enterprise for reaching the masses with first-class lectures

(524)

MRS. SARAH K. BOLTON.

and reading matter. There is material for study in this new departure, by which a counter attraction to saloon tastes and comradeship is offered in the city where, of all others, the crusade attained most permanent success. Mrs. Bolton is in her early prime, and if she lives, her record will be second to few if any of our "twentieth century women" of the W. C. T. U.

MISS MARGARET E. WINSLOW, EDITOR OF "OUR UNION."

Mrs. Willing, Mrs. Bent, Miss Winslow, and Miss Pugh —these are the names of the faithful quartette whose thankless task it has been to edit *Our Union.* All of them are women of brains and energy, and each did better in her place than we had any right or reason to expect. We set before them the impossible task of making a fifty-cent monthly paper sufficiently fresh, varied, and attractive to suit the tastes of a great constituency whose standard had been set by the choicest religious weeklies and costliest monthly magazines. Making "bricks without straw" would be as a bagatelle in the comparison. That our editors did so well is a marvel, and we who criticised so freely merit the retribution invoked by one of them in a moment of impatience: "I wish you had to take my place for just one month." But even this anathema was tempered with mercy, for she might have said "one year."

Among our journalistic martyrs, already promoted to apotheosis in the firmament of every well regulated W. C. T. U. memory, Margaret Elizabeth Winslow is chief, for she filled the position at two separate times, and during the longest period of any. Miss Winslow is, like our leaders generally, well descended. She was born of Puritan antecedents, in New York city, and has spent most of her life in Brooklyn, and Saugerties on the Hudson. She was educated partly at the Abbot Institution in New York, and partly at Packer Institute, of which she is a graduate,

21

and in which for twelve years she was a teacher. The last year of her stay she held the position of composition teacher, and had charge of the Art Department of Pictures, Coins, etc. At the age of nineteen she united with the Episcopal church, of which she has remained a loyal member. She spent 1869–70 in Europe studying and traveling in England, France, Italy, and Germany. She became acquainted with many foreign Protestants, and on coming home was made one of Mr. Albert Woodruff's "Foreign S. S. Association" (Italian Committee), and still fills that position.

Eight years ago Miss Winslow began writing for the press, and still has articles in the N. Y. *Observer*, N. Y. *Evangelist, Independent, Christian Union, Churchman, Christian at Work, Christian Advocate, Christian Register, S. S. Times, St. Nicholas*, etc. She is the author of five or six story books of pure spirit and style, published by the National Temperance Society, American S. S. Union, etc.

Miss Winslow signed the pledge and wrote temperance compositions when but eight years old. At fifteen, she declined to come into the parlor on New Year's Day if wine was offered, and carried her point.

The crusade in Ohio roused her interest and enthusiasm. A friend said, "Are you going to kneel on the pavements before liquor saloons?" "By no means," she replied, "I am a lady." Dr. Dio Lewis came to Brooklyn fresh from the great awakening in Ohio. The Packer Institute teacher attended several temperance prayer-meetings, and was present at the one (March 17th, 1874) at which the first Brooklyn W. C. T. U. was organized. Desiring to attend the daily meetings which followed, she persuaded the editor of the *New York Witness* to accept reports, and every day for fourteen weeks went directly from school to the Y. M. C. A. in Brooklyn, where these meetings were held. Here was uttered her first public testimony for Christ. One evening Miss W. went with fifteen ladies to a prayer meeting in a liquor saloon. In a letter to one of her friends she thus graphically describes the scene:

"I shall never forget that sight. Before us was a barricade of tables smeared with deadly-looking rings. From the walls large pictures looked down upon us, such pictures as I had never seen before. The room was thronged with men and boys, and the hall whose door was open behind us, with women and girls of the lowest description. The front room was separated by a screen, over and between the interstices of which gleamed curious eyes and grimy hands. The meeting began; there was singing and prayer, the ladies spoke, one after another, in the old prayer-meeting fashion, with shut eyes, trembling and tear-choked voices. The audience became disorderly. Boys tripped each other up, girls tittered, and a drunken man in the middle made faces, to the great distress of a sweet little girl of seven, who accompanied him. The leader of the meeting whispered to me, "Can't you say something?" "I,—" was my exclamation, drawing myself up, "I speak in meeting; I, an Episcopal lady?" "Why did you come then?" she asked, sadly. And I thought, "Why did I come, indeed? was it from curiosity only? I profess to hold in my hand and heart the one divine remedy for all the crime and misery in this world, part of which is now before me, and conventionality shut my lips from offering it as I felt I could!"

In an instant I was on my feet. I felt as though invisible hands lifted me there. I was conscious that those hundreds of eyes were all fastened upon me; there was a dead silence, and I found myself not talking temperance, but painting a word picture of the crucified Christ. Sixteen of the saloon habitues present that night were, as we had reason to hope, converted during the following week. This was my ordination."

From that time Miss W. spoke at temperance gatherings, missions, prisons, etc., in Brooklyn and elsewhere. She also took part in Mr. Moody's work in Brooklyn, and later in New York. Later on she went to Florida, but was present at the National W. C. T. U. Convention held in Newark, 1876; was chosen editor of *Our Union*. She declined re-appointment to the position for a principle—because she objected to the Home Protection movement. Becoming somewhat less conservative, she accepted this position again in 1880, and retained it until the paper was united with *The Signal* in 1883.

It was a burst of inspiration from Miss Winslow, relative to its simplicity and purity, which at the Chicago Convention determined us to wear the white ribbon as a badge rather than the red, white, and blue which was strongly urged by many.

Our friend's poetic gift is perhaps her best. The poem on Garfield is among the very best evoked by that pathetic theme, and the one " To Mrs. Hayes " is beautiful. Miss Winslow's exceptional talents and culture, with her great native refinement of character, render her an honored and admired member of our great fraternity.

CROWNED.

(MRS. LUCY WEBB HAYES.)

Not the fair chaplet of her girlhood hours,
The mingled rose and lily-bloom of flowers;
Not the bright coronal that crowns the bride,
The matron comeliness, the mother pride;
Nay, not the artist wreath she well may win
Of bays, like those that crowned the proud Corinne,
Is woman's best adornment.
                    She may claim
Her coronation at the hands of fame
Or love, and men will worship; but the crown
Before whose radiance earth and heaven bow down,
Inspiring poets and seraphic lays,
And drawing from the Master's lips high praise,

Is hers who for the righteous cause and good,
In her great Leader's name, did what she could.
And so, "elected lady," as to-day
Our loving reverence at thy feet we lay,
And in our nation's mansion-house of pride
Place thee and our lands' mother side by side.
We build no monument of soulless stone,
Engrave no tales of glittering triumphs won,
But bid the witchery of thy holy eyes
Speak forth the soul in God's own wisdom wise
To do, and strong to dare for man and right,
And thus assert the woman's purest might.
Upon thy brow we place no crown of flowers,
No jeweled diadem in gift is ours,
But glowing canvas and rich carving mean
That our act crowns thee womanhood's fair queen;
That loves bold daring, woman's highest praise,
Circles its aureole round our Lucy Hayes;
That by the soul who does as she has done,
The noblest crown of woman will be won.

MARGARET E. WINSLOW.

MRS. MARY BANNISTER WILLARD,

Editor of *The Union Signal* (organ of the National W. C. T. U.)

In March, 1858, I first met this endowed and distinctive woman, who was then my sister Mary's class-mate in the Northwestern Female College at Evanston—now a department of the University. She was known to me at first as the eldest daughter of Rev. Dr. Henry Bannister, for for many years Principal of Cazenovia Seminary, New York (which was her birthplace), and Professor of Hebrew in Garrett Biblical Institute at Evanston, the western theological school of the Methodist church. She was known to me when months passed by as a student to whom, by native gifts and life-long scholarly surroundings, intellectual work was a source of unfailing delight, and supremacy in the recitation room was a foregone conclusion. Some of us took high rank in special branches, but "Mary Bannister" shone conspicuous in Greek and algebra alike. Rhetoric and chemistry, debate and essay-writing seemed to be " all one " (and " all won " also, I sometimes ruefully thought) to that clear, intent, and many-sided brain. But she was not ambitious, and plumed herself so little on her achievements that her very modesty would have made her a universal favorite, had she not, in addition to it, possessed the gift of comrade-ship beyond almost any person whom I have met. Withal, she was, though of marked poetic temperament, and devoted to music, the most practical young woman in the college. It was a proverb among " us girls " " that little Mary Bannister can make any article of food known to a civilized *cuisine*, and every article of her wardrobe from hat to shoe." Some minds are opaque; some, like a mirror, reflect the passing scene; others, like a magnet, draw to themselves after their kind. The friend I am describing is of this last variety ; what she acquires she retains, and having been attracted only to the noblest realms of thought, she might well say, were she not too unassuming even to think the poet's words:

"My mind to me a kingdom is."

Intent upon a useful life, she taught for one year after completing the classical course of study, spending some months at the South, but at the close of that period she married my only brother, Oliver A. Willard, and until his death, nearly sixteen years later, found in her home and children—of whom four remain to her—labors and cares which to her loyal heart meant the putting aside of the " career " to which by nature and training she was exceptionally called.

Among the many noble traits of my brother, there is none which I remember with more pleasure than the pride he always manifested in his wife's gifts. He was passion-ately fond of books, had a choice library, and delighted in high themes of conversation.

So the home life of this young pair rose at once above the commonplace level at which so many men, even of culture, are content to remain in household converse. Together they read their favorite authors, with constant notes, queries, and commentary ; together they talked of every plan and purpose they had formed. When my brother became an editor, it was to his wife that he turned for criticism as well as praise. She was cognizant of all his literary work, and, as years passed on, wrote not a little for the columns of his paper, *The Chicago Evening Mail* (later *The Evening Post*). When his death occurred, in 1878, after an illness of less than three days, it was her heroic thought to undertake the herculean task of carrying on the paper. Surely a spirit so indomitable was never enshrined in form so fragile. I could but think, and would have deemed myself indeed disloyal had I refused to stand beside my life-long friend and sister in a breach so "imminent and deadly." But the long-gathering financial storm soon broke upon us and upon the friends who had been so true and helpful. My sister then, after an interval of office work, became editor of *The Signal*, now consolidated with *Our Union*. In these three years of her widest opportunity she has abundantly demonstrated her ability as a journalist, and gained a grand constituency of friends and coadjutors. She has also developed exceptional ability as a speaker and organizer, few women in Illinois having more influence in our State councils. The summer of 1881 she spent abroad, combining temperance observations with those of a tourist, and by her addresses since her return giving us at the West more information concerning our British temperance cousins than we have acquired from any other source.

She is a woman of abounding spirituality, whose intuitions of Christ, conscience, and immortality, supplemented by life-long Bible study, anchor her firmly in a broad, deep, living faith, which no outward circumstance of bereavement or disaster has in the least degree disturbed.

In her cosy Evanston home she maintains a delightful Christian hospitality, and the picture to which, of all others, my eyes most fondly turn is that of the twin cottages (of which my mother's "Rest Cottage" is one), where the tranquil-hearted grandmother, the true and tender daughter-in-law, and the bright children, busy with their studies, share "the dearest spot on earth" to them and me.

JOHN BRANT'S WIFE—WHO WAS NOT A CRUSADER.

I close this sketch with a charming temperance picture by our editor, Mary Bannister Willard.

She was only an ordinary woman who bore no great part in the society of the brisk little Indiana town in which she lived, felt no great burden of soul for the various reforms, and heard, or least heeded, no call to religious and secular crusades. Her duty, John Brant's wife always said, began and ended at home; and well it might, if she thoroughly fulfilled it, since in the seven or eight years of her life with John, four little children had called her mother. Called her so still, each at the rate of seventy-seven times per diem, and the clamor of their voices scarcely ever left her ear. If she went out of an afternoon to a social tea, it was still there; very much, she said, in a quaint sort of a way, as once when she was driving away from a camp-meeting—the echoes of the prayer and praise seemed all lodged in the crown of her Shaker bonnet, and she carried them all the way home.

One can readily see that such a woman, with such preoccupations, would not be found in the van of the temperance crusade. John himself, too, was of the rank and

file, led sometimes, but never leader—a master mechanic
who kept good faith with his employers, and was consequently in a thrifty way, and never out of work. A good
family man, too, who kept things snug and trim at home
in the house and yard, looked after the marketing and the
children's shoes with an attention that your professional
man often fails to devote to such ignoble things.

In a general way, both these honest people were living
religious lives, going regularly to a little church where
they heard a plain gospel discoursed in simple speech,
having cast their lots in with this rather primitive people
on a Sunday when the elder "opened the pale." All this,
however, was not to them at all inconsistent with John's
flask of ale put up daily in the tin pail which carried his
luncheon. If, indeed, any thought had been bestowed
upon it, it was only that economy and thrift demanded
that the ale should be drawn at home from the five gallon
cask that cost very little, rather than taken by the glass
at the saloon nearest his work, at five cents a glass.
John's wife said it "heartened him amazingly; not that
he had a taste for liquor—it was simply like a new backbone in the middle of the day ; it helped him to do his
afternoon work better, and so to earn his daily bread."

When the New Dispensation of Temperance was fairly
inaugurated, however, new ideas began to creep in under
Mrs. John's thinking cap. They wedged themselves into
her roughly crystalized consciousness, sank down and
lodged deep in her soul. It was many days before she
ventured to speak of them to John, and when she did it
was met with such coarseness of rebuff as might have
filled her with encouragement if she had only been more
of a philosopher—showing that the arrow had entered
his soul also. Things went on as usual for days, only
that the pangs grew severer each morning that his wife
filled his canteen. She did it under a sort of protest
these days, but soon the siege began.

First it was—" John, shan't I fill the flask with coffee
to-day ? " The next day—" John, *mayn't* I fill the flask,"
etc.; the next—" *Please*, John, *let* me fill," etc. John
Brant was not wholly unmoved when his wife said
" please." There was enough of the love of their courting
days left in him to give her a kiss and bravely succumb.
At night he said, " Your coffee is as good coffee, Mary, as
man ever drank, but it didn't go to the right spot to-day.
'Twasn't hot, you know."

The next morning, however, he accepted the coffee-
filled can without a word, which meek submission was the
sorest trial Mary had yet had to bear. It almost ended
the crusade. A few hours after, she went down into the
woodhouse to see Mike, the wood sawyer, and get a few
lengths of the solid hickory cut a little smaller for the
dining-room stove.

Strange to say, Mike wasn't there. Strange, for only a
moment before she had heard the whirr of his saw distinctly. She came back to her work ; soon the music of
the saw began again, but an unexpected interruption
delayed her going down for the second time. When at
last she was ready to go, there was no Mike again. He
came rushing up the street, however, wiping his lips with
an old bandana, and into the woodhouse as cheery and
heartsome as few men feel after working five or six
hours.

" I'd jest stipped round the corner, mem, faylin the
nade of a wee dhrop. Sich a goneness come to the pit o'
me stummick along of this old saw and this hickory
wood, mem. An' thin it's the dyspepsy, I'm thinkin',
that gives me no joiy o' me food savin' for a glass of
whisky now and thin. It hairtens me up, loike, an' it's
not so mony bits o' comfort a poor mon loike me has, I
kin till ye, mem."

" Heartens him up"—just the words she had used

about John's ale; but then this was whisky. Did everything drift that way? Would nothing else answer as
well? The coffee didn't answer John as well, for it
wasn't hot. She might try Mike with hot coffee, seeing
he was right here, handy.

"Mike," said she, "if you won't go to Downie's any
more to-day for whisky, every time you feel that goneness,
come up into the kitchen and I'll give you a cup of hot,
strong coffee. See, now, if that won't do just as well."

"Och, mem, an' whin did ye jine wid those perrayin'
wimmen? Shure, an' it's all along o' thim."

"No, Mike, it's only an experiment. John's trying it
too, only, poor fellow, he don't get his coffee hot, as you
will."

"The Virgin kape ye, mem. I'll come intil yer experiment shure, though me rheumatics is that bad, mem, it's
hopin' I'll git up thim stairs," and Mike's eyes rolled
desparingly at the short flight of steps to the warm
kitchen.

Mike's rheumatics did not stand in the way of his coming once, twice, three times during the next three hours,
and each time the cup was ready, steaming hot and well
creamed. And Mrs. John could really scarcely see that
the smack of his lips and the flourish of the old bandana
were not as hearty and grateful as after the "wee dhrop"
at Downie's.

"I've got my idea—I am going on *my crusade*," she
cried so suddenly and vehemently that the little twelve-
year-old "help"—Biddy Mahan—started alarmed. The
idea was infectious, however. It crept slowly into Biddy's
head, and after leaving her in charge of the children and
the coffee dispensary, Mrs. John found her young lieutenant hanging surprisingly on to her skirts and mutter-
ing, "Would ye mind steppin' round to mother's, Mrs.
Brant, to see if she's a bit comfortable loike, and jist to

find out how me fayther is doin'—the prayin' women got
a hold on him the other day, and mother 'n me sort o'
hopes it'll last him."

Mrs. Brant went straight to Downie's, thinking as she
went, " How can it last them when there's nothing to take
the place of whisky ? "

She marched up to the bar, her courage undaunted by
the straggling customers on the outskirts and two or three
loafing inside. They moved aside to let her pass without
a jeering word, for John Brant's wife was not a crusader,
but a keeper-at-home—a woman they, in their rough way
respected. " Mr. Downie (her voice was clear and her
tone so respectful—who had called him aught but Old
Downie or Jack before ?) I've never been here before.
I'm not one of the crusading women. God forgive me
that I haven't been ! but I've come to tell you that I'm
going to run opposition to you unless you come on to my
side. I'm going to keep saloon in my own house, and sell
hot coffee at three cents a cup, and a nice fresh roll,
buttered with the best butter I can make, for one cent
more ; or (here was the pivot on which turned destinies
so high, so grandly high that Providence took the burden
off little Mrs. John's shoulders and poised it on the
Almighty Arm) you may have my idea, the good will and
all, turn out your whisky and sell my coffee and buttered
rolls instead—for I'll make 'em for you ; then I'll know
these poor fellows are getting the worth of their money."

Sec how Providence undertook for her, and then tell
me the age of miracles is past ! The poor, blear-eyed,
trembling creatures that Jack Downie had been killing
inch by inch all these years straightened up into men,
gave one triumphant yell as the demon, exorcised by
unseen forces, left their poor decaying bodies, and out into
the miserable little street that Mrs. John had hardly ever
so much as entered before—it was so miserable—rolled

the one old whisky barrel that constituted Downie's stock in trade. Trade had been getting duller and duller, and even the glass bottles and decanters that followed were not so full as common; but Bond street seemed cleaner than ever before, though sprinkled smartly with glass splinters and whisky. Mrs. Brant stood, like many another who has invoked Omnipotence to his aid, utterly stunned at the results.

"B—bless me," said Peter Hayney, changing his cursing to blessing at a comrade's nudge, "I'm that busted, I believe if anybody had a pledge here now I'd sign it."

Who should bring out the desired pledge but Old Downey himself. "The wimmun stuck it at me this mornin'," he apologized; and there, sure enough, closely folded inside the rum-sellers, lay the drunkard's pledge—quite suggestive of the fitness of things, and in sweetest accord. On the rolling surface of the empty barrel Jack Downie steadied his hand and wrote his name to the first. The barrel was tilting, and so were the signatures; here and there over the paper the scrawls meandered up and down, but there were ten names deciphered on the drunkard's pledge that night, and one of them Biddy Mahan nearly blotted out with tears.

"I must really get back now," said plain, ordinary Mrs. Brant; "John and the babies will soon be needing me."

Just then Biddy's pleading "look after fayther," came to her remembrance. She darted back, forgetting for a minute. "It's all right, I guess," she said to herself, returning, "he's *looked after.*"

To crusaders at large.—Moral : Nature abhors a vacuum. "Goneness at the pit o' the stummick" is a factor in the problem of the crusade. Can you eliminate it by any better than Mrs. Brant's way ?

CHAPTER XXXI.

OUR SOUTHERN ALLIES.

Mrs. Sallie F. Chapin of S. C.—Sketch of her life—Address at Washington—Mrs. Georgia Hulse McLeod of Md.—Mrs. J. C. Johnson of Tenn.—Mrs. J. L. Lyons of Fla.—Mrs. W. C. Sibley of Ga.—Miss Fanny Griffin of Ala.—Other representative Southern ladies—Mrs. Judge Merrick of New Orleans—Address at Saratoga on my Southern trip—Texas and temperance.

"THE SUNNY SOUTH."

WITHIN three years three temperance trips have been made to the South, of which some account will be made later on. Never was welcome more cordial or coöperation more hearty vouchsafed to strangers in a strange land. Never in the North has a deeper interest been shown or have larger results been achieved in the same space of time. Among the noble women "to the manor born" who will ever stand as pioneers of the W. C. T. U. in the South are those whose life history is briefly outlined in this chapter.

MRS. SALLIE F. CHAPIN OF CHARLESTON,

stands at the head of our Southern work as superintendent. By intellect, culture, and influence this lady may justly be called "representative." There is hardly a distinguished South Carolinian of her epoch with whom she has not been acquainted. W. Gilmore Sims, the novelist, was a fireside friend; the pen with which the ordinance of secession was signed, was given to Mrs. Chapin by her gifted brother, a leader in the movement. Her well-known novel, "Fitzhugh St. Clair, the rebel boy of

MRS. SALLIE F. CHAPIN.

South Carolina" (published by Claxton, Remsen & Co., Philadelphia), is dedicated to the children of the Southern Confederacy, and devoted to a statement of the causes of the war from a Southern point of view. "With all its phases she was familiar. Living in a besieged city, where the crashing of shells was heard from morning till night, almost in sight of bloody battlefields, her efforts in the hospital of Charleston and vicinity were constantly demanded and freely made."

As a writer and conversationalist, Mrs. Chapin has been compared to that brilliant daughter of the North, Gail Hamilton, a Southern gentleman having said, " Personal friends of these two ladies find them congenial spirits in boldness of thought and independence of utterance, though in politics far apart as the poles. Both are intense believers in womanhood—the one being acknowledged as the ablest literary champion of woman's rights, while the other is equally forcible and possibly more eloquent on woman's wrongs." Wherever Mrs. Chapin travels at the North—and she has made repeated visits in the interest of the W. C. T. U.—she rouses the enthusiasm of the people by her noble presence and bearing, refreshing humor, and great-hearted sympathy. Her speech in Washington at the National Convention was an event. Foundry church never held so delighted an audience. Entirely unaccustomed to public speaking, Mrs. Chapin seems born for the platform, to which she transfers all the graces of the drawing-room. At the Chicago Convention (August 23, 1882), where the independent temperance party was launched under the new name of "Prohibition Home Protection Party," Mrs. Chapin was made a member of the executive committee, and since then has popularized the movement wherever she has spoken in the South. In common with many others, she believes it to be the key to the position for a really reunited States.

In a letter to one of her associates, Mrs. Chapin thus naively replies to questions concerning her past life:

"Like the old knife-grinder, dear friend, 'I have no history.' My maternal ancestry were Huguenots, who came to this country in 1685, after the revocation of the Edict of Nantes. Two of my great-grandfathers, Vigneron and Tousager, were revolutionary officers, and were both killed.

My maiden name was Moore. My grandfather Moore was one of the inevitable three brothers who always "came over." He settled in Charleston; the others in New York, and Kentucky. He was a man of large means, so that my father, although an itinerant Methodist preacher, was not dependent on the church for the education of his children. We lived in our own house, and were attended by servants who had always been in the family.

I was born in Charleston, but a great fire having burned our home and all that was in it, together with other houses belonging to my father, we removed to the upper part of the State. My father's property was all uninsured, for at that time many of our ministers thought it as absolutely wrong to insure as some of them now think it is for women to speak for Christ. The world moves—thank God for it.

I was raised and educated in Cokesbury, Abbeville county, then celebrated for having the best educational advantages in this State.

From a school-girl I have been a literary scribbler. My first newspaper effort was made in reply to an article which we school-girls did not altogether endorse, written by one who is now the learned and distinguished judge of Florida. He was at the "vine-and-oak" age, and made the vines altogether too twiney to "suit our tastes; so I pointedly set forth my views," and I am afraid I will have to take him in hand again, for by the *Advocate* I see he is still worried lest the women of the nineteenth century will overleap the bounds prescribed by Paul for our brawling Corinthian sisters, ages ago. He forgets that it would be just as sensible for us in this country and age to go to foot-washing (which is equally commanded), as to carry out this other rule, specifically made for that particular time and people. Paul lays down the grand principle that " there is neither male nor female in Christ Jesus " ; but we do not often hear him quoted as making a declaration so grand. But if not, why not? Let the conservatives reply! To attend one W. C. T. U. convention and hear some of our women speak, would put these obsolete ideas about woman on the platform to everlasting flight from all sensible brains.

I married young, and had one of the most devoted husbands God ever gave to a woman. We were both fond of society, and entertained largely.

Mr. Chapin was one of the founders of the Y. M. C. A. of Charleston, and was its chief officer for years. This brought to our knowledge a great many strangers, and during the winter months we were seldom without a house full of Northern friends. The remembrance of these delightful years often comes to me as a haunting memory of the " dead that return not." My mother and father both died during the war ; the latter dying in the pulpit at a union camp-meeting, while on his knees in prayer. He was laid out in the altar, with his head pillowed on the Bible and hymn-book. My brother had been killed " at the head of his brigade, in the thickest of the fight," the dispatch said, and that broke my father's heart. My brother was a lawyer and an editor. My father had superintended the closing up of his law office and packed away his books the day before he died, and it is supposed it was too great a trial for him. I have written enough to make half a dozen books if it was collected, but I have published only one book—Fitzhugh St. Clair, the Rebel Boy of South Carolina. I was president of our Soldiers' Relief Society during the war, and worked day and night in hospitals and with my needle. We lost (as almost every one did) a great deal by the war, and then after it, for three successive years, my husband lost by the caterpillar his cotton crop. These repeated troubles proved too much for him and caused his death by congestion of the brain. I was so prostrated and paralyzed by the suddenness of the shock that I did not leave my house for a year. Life had become an intolerable burden, and but for the temperance work, I am sure I should ere this have been in my grave. This work has, unsought for and unplanned for, been put into my hands by God so manifestly, that I dare not doubt it; and whenever I grow discouraged, something occurs to assure me that, imperfect and feeble as my efforts are, God blesses them, and " the Master has need of *even me.*"

Mrs. Chapin is a great-hearted woman, as is proved by her attitude on the " Home Protection " question. Reared a conservative, she was approached on her visit north by some good ladies, who deplored the liberal spirit of our National W. C. T. U. toward such States as desired to work along this line, and was urged to take a stand against this policy. " Why should I ?" answered Mrs. Chapin, in her spirited but pleasant way, " Why should I insist that the whole army keep step to the slowest foot in the last battalion ? If those brave women of the West find the ballot helpful to their work, let them seek it by all means—we of the South shall not object; we can't and be consistent, for we believe in State rights, don't you know. To be sure this branch of work would never do for us—nothing would hinder our work more at the present juncture of affairs, but why can't we *live and let live ?*" But Mrs Chapin is her own best interpreter, and I close this sketch of one dear as a sister to me, with her own bright words and original poem, given at our Washington meeting in 1881:

RESPONSE ON BEHALF OF THE SOUTH (WASHINGTON, D. C., 1881) TO ADDRESSES OF WELCOME.

BY MRS. SALLIE F. CHAPIN.

I thank you, Miss President, for the kind and cordial greeting you have given my section in this, the nerve center of the nation.

It is said by those who understand atmospheric and ærial phenomena, that, at a certain height in the air, all sounds are as one, and they are all set to the key of C. I think the same phenomena must be produced by coming to the Convention of the W. N. C. T. U., for here I have found

> No North, no South, no alien name,
> Firm in one cause we stand;
> Hearts melted in the sacred flame
> For God and native land.

Ruskin says that when the women of Christendom resolve that war shall cease, it will cease. I see before me to-night earnest, consecrated women representing every State in the Union; and from the shores of that broad ocean whose surging billows dash and break against the sea wall of my native city, to where the Golden Gate lets out into the broad Pacific, all are here, brought together by the threatening of a common peril, and all deeply, earnestly resolved that this war against our homes and dear ones *shall cease.*

All have come. They have brought their best thoughts and richest experiences to cast them into the common stock, and we have come from the South. We are in Washington, so I suppose we must be asking for a place; I believe everybody who comes here does that! We have not come to ask for a place from Congress or the Presi-

dent at the Capitol; we will ask our own peerless
president. We want a place. We have come for it and
you will have to find out what that place is. I think as
platform orators we will not be a success, and the
departments seem to be all filled. Mistress Livermore,
whose title to Queen of the Platform I have never heard
disputed, will tell you that the thousands of emigrants
who are landing at Castle Garden every week will not,
without prohibition, be able to determine who shall make
the laws and govern this grand nation. Mrs. Foster, our
gifted lawyer, the chronometer by which we set our legal
opinions, will tell you that although the rum-seller has the
image and superscription of Cæsar upon his credentials,
chartered wrongs and legalized crimes are not different
from other abuses. Mrs. Hunt has the "Key to the
Situation." She has let in rays of light upon our
ignorance, and our schoolboys now know what alcohol is,
and our rum-sellers will soon know it, or she will tell
them if they want to know. And the rest of the ladies
are all equally good in their line, so there really seems to
be no vacancy for us on the platform. But we want a
place. We have come for a place.

At Montauk light-house a Douglass lamp illuminates the
water for miles around. This lamp has six wicks, one
within another. When I was there this Summer we asked
the keeper if it would burn with five. He said ' Yes, but
it burned better with six." We have come to make the
sixth wick. I don't think we can add one scintilla to
your bright galaxy, for we have no crusade victories to
report. We are a mighty quiet people down there where
I come from. We are afraid to have our voices heard.
You don't know how much afraid of it I am. But I came
at Miss Willard's request. She had all things her own
way down South, as a stranger last Winter, and here she
just queens it right royally over us all. She has said that

I must respond to this address. We have come to be the sixth wick. Well, here we are. What are you going to do with us?

Dr. Hepworth said that when he was in Europe he was told by all means to see the stained glass windows of the Milan Cathedral, they are so very beautiful. He sought the spot, he said, and looked at the windows. There was the cathedral and there the windows; the conditions, too, were all met, for the sun was shining on them, but he saw nothing to admire; he went on the other side of the street and looked up, and was disgusted, and made a note to that effect in his note book. He walked off and met his wife and told her how much disappointed he was; the windows were so terribly overrated. She proposed that they should return. They did so. When they reached the place he started to cross the street again. She said to him, "Why, what are you going to do?" "Cross over here." "Why, go inside, go inside," she said. He went inside; and oh, such radiance of glory as those broken rays made as they fell upon the tesselated pavement—a whole heaven of rainbows. And so we Southrons want to come inside! That is what we have come here to do.

I have been North this summer; I have attended a great many of these temperance meetings, and your love has been to my darkened life what I did not suppose could ever come there again, and I wanted my Southern sisters to come and know you as I know you, and then I knew they would love you as I do, with all my heart.

"No North, no South." We have a South, and we have a problem at the South. Temperance at the South is a peculiar thing. You know a cloud coming between the sun and us causes the mercury to sink in the thermometer. Well, last summer, week after week, accompanied by Bishop Stevens of the Episcopal Church, we went to the colored churches, and we got thousands of names signed to a petition for prohibition, and we thought everything was going on well. The colored people are naturally religious. They were so before the war. Their recreations were religious; their plantation melodies full of hallelujahs, and they would have been so yet if it had not been for the sediment that settled down among us after the war. Now they are demoralized; taught by bar-room teachings they speak flippantly of sacred things, and they say they want whisky and more of it.

A minister of the Gospel told me that he heard, only a few weeks ago, a corner shop rum-seller say to a Western distiller, that the barrel of whisky he had bought from him, doctored, had turned out twelve barrels of whisky for the colored people that he had bought it for. Now, what kind of liquor do you suppose that was? And that is the kind of liquor that is being sold to these newly enfranchised people, and they are drinking it!

Do you call them free? Ah, they are in far more abject slavery than we ever held them in. You have done only half of your duty. You have got to have prohibition, *prohibition!* Instead of worshiping their God they worship their party. I tell you it is time for honest people to come out from parties; they have had their day. Slavery is dead, forever dead. It is not among the current issues of the day any longer, and although I cannot truthfully say I think it was exactly fair for us who had nothing to do with bringing it here to have to bear all the expense of getting it away, we would not have those people put into slavery again, not upon any consideration. To Christian owners they were a responsibility greater than children. Who is responsible for them now? They have been alienated from us. *Who* is responsible? They are the wards of the nation. What is the nation doing for them? Licensing bad men to sell them burning, fiery poison; that is what it is doing, and it should not boast of enfranchising them until it banishes the saloons which overwhelm them in a bondage far more terrible. The nation ought to take care of them as it does of the Indian and the soldier. Before the war it was an offence punished by law to sell liquor to a slave; then you never saw a slave drunk; now the best of them get drunk, and the religious among them deplore it deeply. It is the duty of the nation to give us prohibition, that is it! We could work together in a prohibition movement.

In this new platform, which we of the South have come to help you build, we should have an educational qualification. What do these men that landed at Castle Garden a few weeks ago—whisky, beer-drinking Irish and Germans, and their wives not much better than they— what do they know about using the ballot? The idea that they are the men that are in five years to make our laws is a disgrace, and we will never, never have a Christian country again until we put an educational plank in our platform. We need it, we ought to have it.

But I am not here to talk politics. I only came to ask for a place and to speak for my people. I wanted to come inside. I wanted you to know us. We do not know one another, that is the trouble.

A few years ago, when the yellow fever raged in Charleston, one who had been an officer in the Federal army and fought bravely during the whole war, and at its close came South and went into business, took the fever. I went to see him. He wasn't a very near neighbor of mine, but, as he was sick and a stranger, I thought I would stretch the etiquette of the occasion. A lady said to me the other day the Southern people made neighbors four and five squares off. When I called on him he was very glad to see me; but I saw him signaling to his wife, and she turned his picture with the epaulets on the shoulder to the wall. I never felt so badly in all my life; that I, who had professed religion from a child, that I could be thought to have a resentful feeling toward that man because he fought as God gave him the right to fight— according to his light—even as we did! I told him to turn out his picture from the wall, I wanted to see it; I believed in a man fighting for his colors. Magnanimity is the greatest virtue, I believe, in the world, and I tried to cultivate it then and there!

When I was in Canada this summer, I saw a monument raised by England that pleased me—a monument built to Wolf and Montcalm—and upon it was the inscription: " We give them a common tomb, and posterity will give them a common history." But, then, our own President, the other day, did something that was beautifully courteous when he had the British flag saluted. It was the flag of the Queen, the royal woman who stretched out her hand across the water to the widow of a man not born in the purple. It was a beautiful courtesy; it was right, the newspapers to the contrary notwithstanding, although I also go with the papers; that is, whenever they think as I do I go right with them! But I thought that President Arthur did just the right thing in that when he ordered the British flag saluted, and said it was not so much a want of bravery as it was that the British were outnumbered one hundred years ago.

> "You have careful thoughts for the stranger,
>   Kind words for the sometime guest;
>   But for your own, the bitter tone,
>   Though you love your own the best."

There is a brave nation nearer to you than England. Did you ever tell *them* they were outnumbered? Your children will, but those who would feel it will then be dead and gone. Speak those words. It will grapple them to you with hooks of steel. Speak to them as did our president, who, as she went from home to home, carried all hearts captive, and you know we don't approve of women speaking down there. Oh, say kind words; it is so much better than bitter ones, and

> " Angels look downward from the skies
> Upon no holier ground,
> Than where defeated valor lies,
> By generous foemen crowned."

We have come for a place. That is what brought us here. We knew this was the place to come—Washington. Everybody wants a place here. We are not going to ask President Arthur for it. We would not be prepared to fill it if he was to give it to us. That is not what I want. We are not voters down where I came from. If peace comes to this country it will come through the women, and we have come for this place *inside of your hearts*. We want you inside of ours. Down at the South we are quick to resent, but easy to forgive. Didn't we vote for your man who had fought against us, every one us! We were better to him than you were! And we gave allegiance to the man you elected, and when the assassin struck him it went to the heart of everybody at the South : they forgot their own private sorrows to think of the sorrows right here. If you knew us' better you would love us more.

Now we have come. Here we are. We have come for a place. We want you to give it to us right in your hearts—right in your hearts. I used to be the staunchest Democrat, and I think a great deal of Hancock yet; but Mr. Arthur did beautifully the other day at Yorktown— he really did! I like him. I have given my allegiance to Mr. Arthur. I really have, though I am not going to ask him for a place !

I want you to hear how we women mean to build a platform.

22

Then let us build what men in vain
    Have sought to rear these hundred years,
And failed in throes of heart and brain,
    And torture deep and blood and tears;
A platform broad as all the land,
    Where North and South and East and West,
In grand and' high accord may stand,
    Arm linked with arm and breast with breast.

Where Maine may bring her plank of pine
    To mortice with palmetto beam,
And round the stately elm entwine
    Vines from the bayou's turbid stream;
White stanchions set in granite rock
    From old New Hampshire's bosom brought,
Will stand all storms nor heed their shock,
    With Alabama iron wrought.

Where Mississippi hand to hand
    With Minnesota asks to be,
Seeking redemption for our land,
    Struggling to set the nation free;
And Florida from out her groves
    Of tropic fruit and towering palm,
Stands with brave Kansas whom she loves,
    And joins her in the inspiring psalm.
Where all the old and grand thirteen
    Who broke, as one, the tyrants' sway,
May with their sister States be seen
    Engaged again in deadliest fray.

Yes, women, build; for be ye sure
    Ye build far better than you know;
And that your building will endure
    Till time itself will be no more.
Ye hold alone the place sublime;
    No claims of section, creed, or pride,
Nor thought of color, class, or clime
    Your love-embattled ranks divide.
Deep unto deep with answering cry,
    Atlantic and Pacific pleads,
Hold, women, to your purpose high,
    And prove your faith by words and deeds!

The cruel gulf by carnage made
  Is bridged for aye by mortal blood,
And where our slaughtered chief was laid
  The arch of peace there spans the flood.
With every sound of discord stilled,
  High on that glorious arch we stand,
With one resolve each heart is filled,
  To strike for home and native land.

Late Yorktown's doubly sacred sod
  Saw foes as friends again arrayed,
So for our cause, for home, for God
  Be our white banners high displayed!

GEORGIA HULSE M'LEOD.

Mrs. McLeod, daughter of Dr. Isaac Hulse, of the United States Navy, was born near Barrancas, Florida, at the naval hospital, of which her father was then surgeon. She very early evinced a taste for literature and a predilection for poetry, in which she was encouraged by Mrs. Lydia H. Sigourney, of Connecticut, and Dr. Thompson, historian, of Long Island, her father's friend. In her childhood she mingled much in French society, the naval officers of French men-of-war being frequent guests of her father when in port; and, in order to complete her French education, she was sent to a convent school, taught by native Parisians, where she remained some years.

In her early girlhood she contributed to several periodicals, under various *noms de plume*. Before completing her school education, she wrote "Sunbeams and Shadows" and "Aunt Minnie's Portfolio," published by Messrs. Appleton & Co., New York, and afterwards republished by Routledge & Co., London, under the title of "Gertrude and Eulalie."

In 1853 she was married to the Rev. Alexander W. McLeod, D. D., a well-known theological writer and editor of the official organ of the Wesleyan Methodists of the lower provinces. Her later works are "Ivy Leaves," published in Halifax, Nova Scotia, followed by "Thine and Mine," published by Messrs. Derby & Jackson, and "Sea Drifts," by Carter & Brothers, New York. She has in preparation a work entitled "Unprotected Homes," a prohibition story.

"Her writings," says an able critic, "evince steady growth and culture, marked by fine sensibility and high-toned morality." Mrs. McLeod is widely known and loved for her pure womanliness and exalted piety, as well as for her gifts of mind. For many years she was principal of the "Southern Literary Institute for Young Ladies," located in Baltimore, which became one of the most popular and successful educational institutions in the South, her pupils, scattered through the different Southern States, to this day holding her in veneration and affection. On account of ill health, at the earnest solicitation of her friends, she reluctantly gave up the school; and on the organization of the Woman's Christian Temperance Union of Maryland she was unanimously elected Corresponding Secretary, a position she still holds.

For eighteen years it was her privilege to correspond with Henry W. Longfellow, who took much interest in her and her works, and of her fugitive poems coming under his notice, and which he pronounced good, were "Under the Sea," "The Old Tower," "Exiled," "Tribute Leaf," *in memoriam* of Charles Green, Esq., Savannah, Ga.; the last being characterized by him as "a poem of exquisite pathos."

Mrs. McLeod, being an advocate for State rights, warmly espoused the cause of her section in the late war. Her love for her sunny South land has grown with the years, and the organization of Woman's Christian Temperance Unions in every Southern State has brought to her the joy of an answered prayer.

MRS. J. C. JOHNSON

is a Presbyterian lady of Memphis, Tenn., and has been a
leading pioneer, having come into the work when Mrs.
Wittenmyer and Mrs. Denman of New Jersey, went
South on an organizing trip in 1876.   Mrs. Johnson was
associated with Mrs. Jefferson Davis in the Woman's
Christian Association of Memphis, and maintains also a
home for women desiring to reform.   She and her noble
husband entered heartily into our work, and she has been
for years President of the W. C. T. U. of Tennessee.

MRS. REV. DR. J. L. LYONS,

of Jacksonville, Fla., has been our leader in that State
for many years.   Formerly a missionary in Syria, Mrs.
L. "takes naturally" to active service for Christ, and,
with the earnest ladies associated with her, has made our
society a felt force, sending petitions (local option) to
the Legislature, the effect of which was plainly visible at
Tallahassee on my recent visit.

MRS. W. C. SIBLEY,

President of W. C. T. U. of Georgia, is a Southern leader,
the daughter of the distinguished Judge Thomas, of
Columbus, Ga., and the wife of W. C. Sibley, President of
Sibley Cotton Mills, with one exception the largest manufactory in the South.   From her elegant home, where she
is surrounded by seven charming sons and daughters,
Mrs. Sibley goes forth with her kind husband's hearty
endorsement, speaking (Presbyterian though she is) to
her Christian sisters, "that they go forward."   I shall
never forget her words when, without previous consultation, she was elected President of the local W. C. T. U.
of aristocratic old Augusta.   She came forward at the
close of the meeting held in Rev. Mr. La Prade's church
one Sabbath afternoon, and said, as she took my hand

warmly: "I am surprised that the lot should have fallen
on me; but, since it has, I promise you I will try to use
this sacred office solely in the interest of the homes of
our beautiful city." Nor shall I forget how this sweet-
natured lady stood before a great audience at the W. C.
T. U. Convention of Atlanta, all unused to public speaking as she is, and gently said: "Dear friends, I am
grateful that so many are here; but I tell you truly if
there were not another to stand between the dram-shops
of Georgia and its homes, so dearly do I love this temperance cause, *I would stand there all alone.*"

MISS FANNIE GRIFFIN,

of Montgomery, Ala., is one of the most gifted young
women I have met North or South. She it was who said
to me on my first visit, in 1880: "The war was terrible,
but had its compensations. It developed individuality—
it gave many of us to ourselves in a deeper, wider consciousness of power. It set me at work, and I am thankful for it. A bee is worth more than a butterfly, no
matter how prosaic the one and poetic the other." It
was she also who said: "I am not 'reconstructed,' please
take notice! I was just as loyal to my highest beliefs as
you were to yours. Always you were taught to spell
Nation with a capital N, and I to spell Alabama with a
capital A. It was my best beloved land; it was my
Nation. What could I do but follow its fortunes in victory
or defeat? But let that pass. I can clasp hands with
you warmly in this new warfare. Let us be friends."
And so we are "for always." I spent a delightful evening with Miss Griffin and gifted Will Hayne—only child of
the poet and his lovely wife—in the home of Captain Bush,
of Montgomery. Miss Follansbee, principal of the leading
ladies' school of that exclusive city, was President also of
the "Chautauqua Circle," which met at Captain Bush's,

"round the evening lamp." We had good talk—well
worth reporting—but I give from its full quiver only this
Parthian arrow fired by Miss Griffin at a gentleman who
"didn't altogether believe in women's speaking":

"No doubt, sir, you have moulded and rounded the
pretty little tea-cup that represents our 'sphere;' but you
forget that the great reservoir of the nineteenth century
is pouring in its wealth of knowledge and of opportunity;
the poor little limits are quite drowned out; the fragile
cup is broken; there is no help for it. Now, since the
pouring-in process cannot cease, is there anything to do
but to *enlarge the sphere?*"

I can give no idea of the vivacity and electric force
with which Miss Griffin speaks. She is the lady principal of the public schools in Montgomery; is up and at her
books by 6 A. M., studies French, German, literature, history, etc., and is my "temperance stand-by" in the capital city of Alabama, aided by the true-hearted women I
have named, and several of their friends. Time would
fail me to map out the galaxy of our new allies in the
South. Who that saw it can forget the group of southern
delegates at the Louisville convention. Even as they
crowded that broad platform, the space around me as I
write these lines is peopled with the gracious and winsome presences of those who, by reason of our blessed
work, have become sisters beloved to me and all of us.
How their kind faces beam on me. There are Mrs. Francis Crook and Mrs. Summerfield Baldwin of Baltimore,
and the score of other women that cheery Mrs. Dr.
Thomas leads, Mrs. Judge Cochrane of Virginia, and her
associates; Mrs. John Staples of North Carolina, and the
the true hearts at Raleigh; Mrs. Bishop Wightman, Mrs.
Harley Walters, and their coadjutors of the Palmetto
State, Mrs. Shropshire, my beloved friend in Rome, Ga.,
with loyal Miss Missouri H. Stokes, gentle Mrs. Witter of

Atlanta, capable Mrs. Webb of Savannah, and Mrs. Alice
Cobb of Macon, who has a gift at causing things to come
to pass; there too is Mrs. Judge Horton of Mobile, Ala.,
Mrs. Gen. Stewart of Oxford, Miss., Mrs. Samuel Watson
of Memphis, Mrs. Col. G. W. Bain "of ours" in Kentucky, Mrs. Dr. Dodge, President of Arkansas W. C. T.
U., with noble Mrs. Winfield, Mrs. Sample, and Mrs.
Erwin "of Des Arc;" there is dear young Texas with its
sixteen towns, where the seed of the W. C. T. U. was
sown in joy one year ago, where Mrs. Senator Maxey
stands at the head; Mesdames Johnson and Hathaway,
Preston and Acheson, Underhill; but how the names and
faces throng! It were idle to attempt a "muster roll"
so endless. Among our Southern allies

MRS. JUDGE MERRICK OF NEW ORLEANS,

shall be the rare theme of a closing sketch. In reply to
my note asking for data, this beloved comrade in arms
wrote me as follows:

"The life of a woman who has staid at home all her
life, and been pleasantly shaded by a distinguished husband, offers poor material to the biographer."

Mrs. Merrick's case is, however, an exception to this
rule, by reason of her rare antecedents, training, and
character. As a lady whom she had benefited once said
of her: "Why I was so outspoken with Mrs. Merrick I
cannot tell, unless because I felt that in her I had found
a woman whose great heart could sympathize and help
not only her own immediate circle, but the whole of
womankind."

Captain David Thomas, the father of Mrs. Merrick,
belonged to an old South Carolina family, and was born
in the "Edgefield District." He was a commissioned
officer under Gen. Jackson, who was his special friend,
and he served in the war of 1812. President Longstreet

MRS. CAROLINE E. MERRICK.

(author of the famous "Georgia Scenes") was another
friend, and delivered an eloquent eulogy on Captain
Thomas at the commencement exercises of Centenary
College, Jackson, La., of whose Board of Trustees the
captain was an influential member. He was a stoical,
philosophical man, and could be thoroughly depended
upon as friend or enemy. Although he had a fine vein
of humor, which his daughter inherits, he was stern and
rigid in his notions of family government. His children
were under no circumstances allowed to spend a night
from home, nor to make the smallest visit unaccompanied
by aunt or mother. He was a conscientious, consistent
Christian man, universally respected and beloved, and
possessing common sense enough to amount to positive
genius. This is his gifted daughter's testimony.

Caroline Elizabeth Merrick was born at Cottage Hall,
parish of East Feliciana, La., on the 24th of November,
1825. Her mother died when she was seven years old.
The father said, "a step-mother is far better than none,"
so he soon gave one to his four little girls and two boys.
They lived on a plantation, five miles from Jackson, but
the professors in the well-known college located there,
which is the Alma Mater of some of the South's most
celebrated men, were frequent visitors, and their learned
conversation and discussions around the fireside could but
cultivate in the bright, attentive little girl a love of books
and noble themes.

In a private letter, Mrs. Merrick thus writes with
generous enthusiasm of her stepmother:

"I owed most of all to my father's third wife (I was
the seventh child of the second), whose name was Susan
Brewer, and who was for ten years associated with that
eminent teacher and divine, Rev. Dr. Wilbur Fisk, as
preceptress of Wilbraham Seminary. Two years later she
came to Tuscaloosa, Alabama, where she had the highest

reputation as an educator, being called by Dr. Fisk 'the pioneer in the cause of woman's education in the South,' for, in addition to her own work, she brought no less than sixty northern ladies of the highest character to us as teachers. She had a high reputation as a writer, and after my father's death, spent two years abroad visiting nearly every capital of Europe and the East, and publishing her observations in book form. After her marriage she devoted herself entirely to her step-children, training us in the most careful and methodical manner. She was a great and gifted woman. Her eloquence in prayer, her love of learning, and her power in conversation were unrivaled. Every one who met her was forced to recognize her gifts, and in nearly the above words, I had an inscription made upon the monument she raised to her parents in Wilbraham, Mass., her native village, where she lies buried."

This lady was the maternal aunt of Edwin T. Merrick, who is a cousin of our honored Rev. Dr. Frederick Merrick of Delaware, O. (projector of the Hayes memorial portrait). It was from this fact that the young people became acquainted, when E. T. Merrick, a rising young lawyer, came to the South, and in 1840 our Caroline became his wife. They lived in Clinton, La., fifteen years, where three of her children were born. In 1855 her husband was elected Chief Justice of the State, and they removed to New Orleans, where their home has been ever since, except the four years of the war, during which they lived at Myrtle Grove plantation. Mrs. Merrick sometimes refers to her exciting war experiences, for Myrtle Grove was alternately within the Federal and Confederate lines, yet she thinks upon that period now as the happiest epoch of her life, notwithstanding many privations and trials. Every faculty of her mind was in lively exercise, for she was thrown entirely upon her own resources, and the very dangers and uncertainties of the times enhanced the value of whatever good or happiness which presented itself. Then while her mother heart went out in trembling anxiety for her young son who had left college to join the army in Virginia, she found comfort in her baby boy and his lovely sisters, who were her constant companions. In her husband's long absences on his official duties, Mrs. Merrick carried on the plantation, supplied the stores, often making hazardous voyages for this purpose on river and bayou; cared for the wounded of both armies, and wrote sketches in dialect fresh from the lips of her faithful servitors, not a whit inferior to those by "Uncle Remus." These, it is hoped, will some day see the light. Mrs. Merrick is that rare, unique, refreshing specimen of humanity, "a character." Neither wealth, culture, nor social *prestige* have been able to deprive her of this crowning charm—a strong, irrepressible individuality. For instance, as secretary of St. Ann's Charitable Asylum, she submitted to her husband, in his capacity of legal adviser, a will, witnessed by the officers of that institution (all of them ladies), in which a sum of money was bequeathed for its use. "Why, my dear," said the Judge, "that document is not worth the paper on which it is written. Women cannot be witnesses of wills in Louisiana!" and he showed her the statute where the "incapables" are enumerated as "insane, idiotic, felons, and—women," and the capables designated as "all males above the age of sixteen years." At this Mrs. Merrick's righteous indignation was stirred. She set out with a petition for the removal of these and all other legal disabilities of women (for she has a thorough fashion of doing well what she thinks it worth while to set about at all), and though she had never spoken above that low, velvety "parlor voice" for which she is distinguished, she went before the Constitutional Convention of her native State and made a rousing speech in defence of her position. This was on June 16, 1879. Be it remembered that in this she had the hearty sympathy of her noble husband and high-minded children. " Go, by all means," said the Judge, when she asked his consent, " you have always desired to do something for your own sex—and here is your opportunity."

Two other brave women spoke with Mrs. Merrick, one representing the reformatory forces of New Orleans (Mrs. Saxon), the other standing for women in professional life (Dr. ———), but the friendly legislators (for there were some) said Mrs. Merrick must represent the potent voice of society. As a result of these addresses, the Constitution declares women eligible to all school offices in the State, which is the prophetic crumb of the surely preparing loaf.

One day Mrs. Merrick playfully remarked to the President of a " female college " (for that is still the name throughout the South) that " she marvelled greatly to see that women were never invited to address the ' sweet girl graduates,' and wondered what a senior class of young men would think, should a lady presume to discourse to them of their duty and destiny ; " whereat the sensible president urged her to come and talk to his fair girls. She did so, nothing loth, and the address is described as inimitably witty and wise. At its close she turned to the lords of creation present and said, with her handsome face beaming with drollery : " And now a few words to the gentlemen, God bless them ! We wouldn't forget them for the world. Are they not the delight of our hearts and the sunshine of our homes ? " The noble lords saw how adroitly she had turned the tables of their own " from time immemorial " regulation speeches upon them, and her peroration " brought down the house."

It was this speech of hers that made us acquainted, for

I read an account of it and said in my heart: "That is the lady who can make the W. C. T. U. a success, even in the volatile city of the Mardi Gras." So I wrote Rev. D. L. Mitchell, Secretary of the Y. M. C. A. (an organization which has been the kindest of older brothers to our W. C. T. U.), and inquired if he thought her influence could be enlisted. Subsequently I learned that the gracious purpose to help me had already been born in her heart, not because she was specially interested in my mission, but for the equally good reason that she liked to help women, and as a southern lady, she desired to show me kindness. I shall never forget her first letter, written in January, 1882, perfumed with rare flowers from her garden, nor the reception awaiting Anna Gordon and me as we arrived after a weary ride from Houston, Texas, and beheld awaiting us before the wide open doors of a beautiful home this queenly lady, who clasped us in her arms, saying: "Welcome to my home and heart, and remember all that I have is yours." Wise in her generation, Mrs. Merrick said: "First of all, the keynote of society must be set at concert pitch. I am going to give you a reception." How thoughtfully and lovingly she planned it all, decorating her parlors, banking up the mantels with flowers, and adorning the walls with beautiful vines. What an air of the higher social converse she imparted by choice music and classic Shakspearian scene, and how delightful was the company she gathered, of men and women well known in New Orleans society, literature, and art.

But the flower-wreathed punch bowl held only lemonade, and the elegant table offered nothing stronger than "the cup that cheers but not inebriates." For Mrs. Merrick had signed the pledge since our arrival, and joined our W. C. T. U. A few days later, with great reluctance, yet gently obedient to a call she couldn't disregard, she

became president of our work in the city and the State.
Soon after, an elegant banquet was given to John Mc-
Cullough, the great actor, at the residence of Mrs. Merrick's son-in-law. Wine was freely offered, but she
turned her glasses right side up—or upside down. Her
friends looked on in amazement as she explained with
gentle grace that she had "joined the noble army of the
W. C. T. U." And so she gave a temperance lecture in
a circle not often penetrated by a white ribbon soldier,
God bless her true heart! There are no brighter, better
women anywhere than Mrs. Merrick's coadjutors. Mrs.
Bishop Parker is Corresponding Secretary for New Orleans, and I never see her without recalling Dinah
Mulock's words, "Douglas, Douglas, tender and true."
Her husband, one of the most influential bishops of the
South, stands by her in this "new departure," and a more
loyal heart was seldom wedded to a stronger brain. Mrs.
Dr. Lyon, wife of a leading physician of the city, is also
Mrs. Merrick's true yoke-fellow in every good word and
work. Mrs. Dr. Lendrum, wife of a chief Baptist pastor,
Miss Anna Prophet, a prophet indeed, with her lovely
gifts of brain and heart, Misses Brewer, Lyon, Mitchell,
dear Mrs. Harp, the "charter member" who never was
discouraged, all these are representatives of the strong
and varied forces at work in the Crescent City for our
cause. There never was a convention more illustrative
of the religious spirit of our work than that presided over
recently by Mrs. Merrick, opened with an extempore
prayer by an Episcopal minister, and enlivened by the
inspired impromptus of Christian women who never speak
in public. As Mrs. Merrick said, "It was prayer-meeting,
love-feast, and church sociable combined." Whoever
fears the effect of a "woman's convention" upon anything but sin, would have been thoroughly disabused of
his (or her) anxiety by witnessing the gentle strength of

those who were "brought out" by the first assembly of the sort ever held in New Orleans. We had a charming report from the W. C. T. U. at Baton Rouge by a Catholic lady ; a thrilling appeal for work among the Germans, from the wife of the leading Lutheran minister, a song of praise from a faithful teacher among the colored people, sandwiched between Mrs. Judge Merrick's beautiful address and Mrs. Judge Parker's melodiously read "Report." As the former has said, "There is always a strong cohering influence in high aims directed toward benignant ends," and this memorable convention was a beautiful commentary upon that sentiment.

I have been reluctant to dwell upon the sorrows so bravely borne by my beloved friend in the loss of her beautiful and gifted daughter Laura, who died of yellow fever in 1878, and Clara, whom she lost in September, 1882. Both had been belles in New Orleans society, both were married, and both left young and lovely children. As so many others have said, so this deep, motherly heart, well nigh broken, testified: "This temperance work has come to me like a beam of heavenly sunshine in the great darkness of my grief."

AN ADDRESS DELIVERED AT THE NATIONAL TEMPERANCE CONVENTION, SARATOGA SPRINGS, N. Y., JUNE 21, 1881.

In the spring of 1863 two great armies were encamped on either side of the Rappahannock River, one dressed in blue and the other in grey. As twilight fell the bands of music on the Union side began to play the martial music, "The Star Spangled Banner" and "Rally Round the Flag," and that challenge of music was taken up by those upon the other side, and they responded with "The Bonnie Blue Flag" and "Away Down South in Dixie." It was borne in upon the soul of a single soldier in one of those bands of music to begin a sweeter and more tender air, and slowly as he played it they joined in a sort of chorus of all the instruments upon the Union side, until finally a great and mighty chorus swelled up and down our army—" Home, Sweet Home." When they had finished there was no challenge yonder, for every Confederate band had taken up that lovely air, so attuned to all that is holiest and dearest, and one great chorus of the two great hosts went up to God; and when they had finished, from the boys in grey came a challenge, " Three cheers for home!" and as they went resounding through the skies from both sides of the river " something upon the soldiers' cheeks washed off the stains of powder."

Dear friends, I am proud to belong to an army which makes kindred those who have stood in arms against each other. I am glad to come from the sunny South, my own dear South as I can say to-night, after three months of journeying and of working in its principal cities and towns, during which the whole fourteen Southern States were visited, and to bring back good tidings of great joy which shall be for all us people. My forerunner in all that work was a secessionist of the secessionists, Mrs. Georgia McLeod, whose son gave a right arm in the Confederate service, and who herself had to have the English flag above her door to prevent her being sent off to Fortress Monroe. But she is reconstructed now, and she has just as warm a heart beating for the temperance cause as I have; and as our hands were clasped in sisterly friendship we thanked God with tears that there was one cause which brought us into such sweet harmony.

And so we started with our faces to the South. A letter came to us from Richmond, and it said: " This is a bootless errand; it will be a most disastrous failure, for there are three great disadvantages under which you will labor—to go there as a woman, a Northern woman, and a Northern temperance woman." Far be it from thy servant to draw conclusions, but we found out afterward that that discouraging letter was written by a Northern man in the Custom-house! The doors of the Methodist Church South were opened; a Quaker sat in the chancel; the people gathered; we were welcomed warmly and cordially. A convention was held in North Carolina, at which Mrs. McLeod was present, where Governor Jarvis had not only the flag of North Carolina, but the Stars and Stripes waving beside it. He came out and said he was not afraid to stand by the temperance people. It was the winning issue, because it was a live issue.

It was Banquo's ghost that would not down for any politician, and he meant to be on the right side. In that convention at Raleigh, composed of five hundred delegates, half were colored men. The prejudices against color gave way at the eloquent utterances of some of the speakers, and as former masters waved their hats, the temperance women thanked God that the color-line was broken at last by the Southerners themselves. So let us take new heart and hope as our cause branches out.

Going on to South Carolina, in a great church crowded with the intelligent and thoughtful, a number of pastors being present, I was gently led forward to speak. By whom? By Colonel Stevens, whose battery fired first on Sumter's flag, but who is transformed into Bishop Stevens of the Episcopal Church, and who is one of the most ardent temperance men in all the South. He had no difficulty with me nor I with him, though I was Northern to the very heart's core. My hostess in Charleston was Sallie F. Chapin, who wrote a secession novel, and was at the head of the sanitary commission in the rebel army of that State. She was so thorough in her rebellion that when one of our officers said, "I must have your military map," she went into her inner room, reduced it to fragments, took it to the Union officer, and said, "Officer, there's your map." That woman, so thoroughgoing in her secession, is now glad that the slaves are free. I never met one with whom I had more heartfelt sympathy. Though she was invited to Saratoga and Long Branch last summer, she still stayed in Charleston and wrought for her temperance boys, whose glory is that Mrs. Chapin is their leader. Let us be encouraged, as these grand women are coming up to the help of the Lord against the mighty, by weaving strong bands of sympathy that are stretching across what we used to call the bloody chasm. Something happened to us in the South which is not often seen in the North, and that was to have an Episcopal Church opened to us to form a temperance society. Something else happened in Georgia, and that was to have a judge of a court preside at our meeting. He said to me, " As you have not time to organize a Woman's Christian Temperance Union, I pledge my hand you shall find one when you come along next winter," and he has sent me the names of the society.

Governor Colquitt, in Georgia, stood forth in his own church on Sunday night and welcomed us with warm and brotherly words. The Methodist Southerners are more devout than those at the North, and yet on Sunday night they applauded the sentiment that the North and the South would be united on the temperance reform.

Going on to Florida, with its sunshine and its beautiful skies, we found that the Woman's Union had introduced a petition to the Legislature for a local option law, and had quite a good showing for a State which had not much experience in that line, and the minority vote which a prohibitory law received last winter in many of the Southern States was so strong that it would prove a Waterloo to the majority to get many such votes in the North.

Passing on to Alabama, I met a beautiful girl, a

thorough Southerner, who became a teacher in the college at Montgomery. " The war was a grand thing," she said, " for it taught us the beauty and desirability of earning our own bread and of being self-dependent. You of the North were taught to spell nation with a big N; I was taught to spell Alabama with a big A." She is ready now to spell temperance as we do. Rev. Dr. Vedder, a distinguished preacher in Charleston, tried to describe to them the meaning of the four cabalistic letters which stand for the name of our woman's society. This bright-minded man came forward and said: " It has puzzled me to know what the ladies mean by W. C. T. U. I have been thinking it over lately, and I have come to the conclusion that it means about this—that if all the temperance people are united, if the women form a society and the men do their duty at the polls, the four letters will pretty soon come to mean, ' We Come to Unite;'" and said he, " if the temperance people make common cause, it won't be long until the rum power will know that they also mean ' We Come to Upset.' Is not that just what we have come for ?" I thought to myself " We Northerners will have to be very bright and wide-awake to keep ahead of the Southerners at that rate," and my heart rejoiced in the great, potential fact of fraternity between once severed sections of our great Republic—the helping to weave that cloth-of-gold web which shall tangle in its meshes all our hearts, and give us once for all a really " Re-United States." What a marvel of God's providence is this, in our many-sided work ! The small, sweet courtesies of life, in which our Southern friends so charmingly excel, will blossom richly when engrafted upon a Northern stem, and the practicality of our colder clime will mingle with the grace of their sunny land, to form as beautiful a combination as the world has ever seen. It is impossible for any one who has not worked among them to do justice to the mingled sweetness and fervor of the Southern women when enlisted for our cause, while the enthusiasm and courage of men in high position there—judges, governors, senators—may well provoke to emulation our Northern patriots of corresponding grade. But in all these inspiring considerations, there is nothing so significant, to my own thought, as the renewed and boundless triumph of Christ's church, and the uplifting of half a race to the level of equal participation in the government. These two great " Government movements must go forward side by side. The government can never be upon His shoulder " until the Deborahs and Miriams, the Hannahs, Elizabeths, and Marys of His church shall exercise not only their present indirect, but their *direct* vital and energetic influence upon the decisions through which law is formulated and the *enforcer* is chosen behind the law as its executive. Let us be patient while we toil, for

> "The heavenly forces with us side!
> The stars are watching at their post."

A LETTER FROM THE SOUTH—TEXAS AND TEMPERANCE.

Texas is stirring up. The ministers and lawyers are taking a hand at this temperance reform, and I predict the philanthropic future of this great State—thirty-five times as large as Massachusetts—will keep pace with its material progress. They have a local option law, and I learn the following facts from Rev. Mr. Young, a whole-souled worker in Paris, Texas:

Rockwall County has had prohibition four years. At the end of the second, the doors of the jail, like the gates of Gospel grace, stood open night and day. This year they have empaneled no jury, and have no cases to try.

Grimes County, with 600 freedmen to vote and 125 whites, carried prohibition. Score a long credit mark for the colored race.

Oak Grove County had but one man in it who voted against prohibition, and he was a foreigner, and has since moved away, to the relief of the community.

Joe, a workingman of Denison, Texas, used to drink right along, and spent the lion's share of his wages in that way. A few months ago he left Texas, and worked for ninety days in Parsons, Kansas. When he came home he began to fix up his house, to paper, paint, and beautify. His family physician happening in, said: "Why, Joe, you've got handsomer paper on your walls than I have; what's changed the looks of things so around here?"

"O, I went up to Parsons, Kansas, where they have prohibition," the man replied, "saved $100 clear cash on my drink bill, and gave it to my wife."

In Paris (La Mar County) the W. C. T. U. has the credit from the gentlemen of leading the campaign, where a grand success has been won. They, too, have organized a colored W. C. T. U. Mrs. Mary S. Hathaway, their Secretary, a Mississippi lady of fine education and great intellectual gifts, is, to my mind, "come unto the kingdom for such a time as this."

Concerning results at Paris, the mayor makes affidavit that while, during a period of three months and ten days while the sale of drink was licensed, there were one hundred and thirty-five cases on his docket, of which eighty-four were for drunkenness, there were, during the same period under prohibition the year following (October 22, 1881, to January 31, 1882) only thirty-eight cases, of which twenty-three were for drunkenness. This shows that not only the total number of cases, but the cases of drunkenness, fell off almost seventy-five per cent.; and no other reason can be assigned than the prohibition of the sale of liquor.

The minds of good people are also being stirred up to

"clear ideas" concerning enforcement of law. For instance, a business man and a judge, here in Dallas, were discussing the all-absorbing theme, last evening, at a dinner where I was among the guests.

Said the business man : "We temperance people have been too much in a hurry for a certain form of prohibition — the more strict the better — and have not watched as carefully as we should the *machinery of enforcement.* But that is where the saloon men fix their scrutiny. They don't care how much law we have, so that it is non-effective. Indeed some of them are almost ready to say with the Old Bourbon member of the Maine Legislature : 'I'm for the law, if you want it so bad, but I'm dead set *agin its* enforcement.' Too often our statute, on which we bestow so much pains, is like a suspension bridge with no railroad track laid down by which we may get any good of it."

"Yes," said the judge, "we make a fatal failure just there. For instance, we let these fellows appeal their cases when we ought to give the minor courts final jurisdiction in the matter. So they drag along from month to month, and the temperance people get discouraged. Then the liquor advocates publish figures about the great increase of cases, the courts being clogged, etc., and the thoughtless read these figures just as they did those of Senator Beck, of Kentucky. You know he claimed the jails of Maine are just as full as those of his own paradise of whisky and murderers, but he omitted to state that while Kentucky fills its prisons with blood—criminals crazed and cruel by reason of drink—Maine crowds hers with saloon-keepers who try to violate the prohibitory law!"

"Yes," replied the business man, "and how blind our industrial classes are to facts like these. A policeman here gets one dollar for every drunkard he arrests. So they keep it up in a lively manner, and we boast that few such unsightly objects are seen upon our streets. But what are the facts? The saloon-keeper gets paid by the man whom he makes drunk, and oftentimes is in league with the police to make as many men drunk as possible (at so much per head) and then have them arrested by the police, who divide the fines with the saloon-keeper, so he gets two prices for every man made drunk, and at the same time, by keeping these 'finished specimens' of his work out of sight, deceives people into saying: 'This is a remarkably temperate town—how few intoxicated men one sees.' They play this game constantly on the colored men—year in and year out. But where does that dollar fine come from? O, from the pockets of our industrial class—our men of business who have accumulated property that can be taxed. The grog-shops dance and we meekly pay the piper; we beat the bush—they catch the bird! What a set of fools we have been anyhow!"

It is to this "arrest of thought" on the part of "We, Us, and Company," all up and down the land, that I look for the downfall of the most outrageous system of oppression that ever a deluded people permitted to be fastened upon upon it like a leech and an abomination.

I heard a Southern lady say recently: "When as a member of the W. C. T. U. I had to go out to the wood-pile and persuade the colored man there to vote for pro-hibition, I had a thought that never came to me before, and I went in and said to my husband: 'I have got to the place now that I want to vote myself,' and he answered heartily: '*I wish you could, Maria!*'"

Thus the world moves! Upon this question, however, I say nothing to these friends. My work is to take the sentiment as I find it, and crystalize as much of it as possible into organic form. The woman's ballot is not a living issue in the South outside of Arkansas, and even there I do not think it best to agitate it. Two or three evenings ago we had an immense meeting in the Opera House at Denison, in the interest of local prohibition. The Episcopal minister was on the platform with us, as earnest as any one present. The ladies presided over the meeting, and the pastors conducted the devotional exercises. Next morning I attended the Presbyterian church with my hostess (a church, by the way, with forty-five women and nine men, yet in which none of the sisters take part). Before me sat a dear, bright little woman— an officer of the W. C. T. U. She turned and whispered playfully:

"I made my contribution to the temperance cause by taking care of five little babes, so that their mothers might go to your meeting at the Opera House!"

To "a heart at leisure from itself to soothe and sympathize," how many ways there are to contribute to the great golden-rule cause of temperance!

I must not close without telling you that Anna Gordon speaks in all my day meetings, is a great favorite with them, and at Sherman, where five hundred went away after the Court House was filled, they called for an "overflow meeting, and "a speech by Miss Gordon"—so good an impression had she made on Sabbath afternoon. But the demure little maiden was not present, and so escaped the trying ordeal.

We are both well and happy, and more than glad we came. From the north we hear nothing—seeing only the local papers, save with rare exceptions. But we are sure the W. C. T. U. is alive and flourishing. Do not for a moment imagine that we expect to reach that place of which a Kentucky hard-shell preacher spoke when he prayed that "A blessing might rest upon all places where the foot of man hath never trod, and which the eye of God hath never seen." Never were we in the midst of a livelier or more cosmopolitan population, and Texas is yet to head the column of the States in moral power, as she does to-day in enterprise and territory.

As I extend my observations, meet the noble workers of different States, study the varying methods, and march onward with the great temperance army, there is one thought more frequent than any other, one question which constantly recurs : *Who am I that any part should be given me in this magnificent work of God?* Nothing in all my life's experience has so helped me to an understanding of passages like these : "They must have clean hands who bear the vessels of the Lord!" "What carefulness this wrought in you ; what clearing of yourselves." "Who is sufficient for these things ?"

Verily "they builded better than they knew," the grand old veterans who laid, in love to God and hope for many, the foundations of this noblest of reforms. Its reflex influence upon our own aims and purposes in life is good beyond all computation. We have indeed given hostages to fortune ; we cannot forget, in the high calling wherewith we are called, that glorious old motto, "*noblesse oblige.*"

So transcendent is the significance of this reform, that the time is not distant when those who are now but "lookers-on in Venice" will forget that it was not inaugurated by themselves alone.

23

CHAPTER XXXII.

GLIMPSES OF THE WOMEN AT WORK.

Miss Elizabeth W. Greenwood—Miss F. Jennie Duty of Ohio, the Minister at Large—Mrs. J. K. Barney of Rhode Island, the Prisoner's Friend—Mrs. Henrietta Skelton, the German Lecturer—Mrs. Elizabeth L. Comstock, the Quaker Philanthropist—One husband's birthday gift.

ELIZABETH W. GREENWOOD.

MISS ELISABETH WARD GREENWOOD was born in Brooklyn, N. Y., in 1850. Living on the Brooklyn Heights, she had every inducement which health and society could offer to lead a fashionable and selfish life, but at the age of fourteen "a strange power, which men feel but never see," crept into the secret chambers of her heart, and commenced the quiet work of chiseling her soul into the image of her Lord and Saviour, and from that time she was filled with an absorbing ambition to embody her highest ideal of intellectual Christian womanhood.

The earlier years of her life were entirely devoted to severe study. Of these years Dr. Charles E. West, President of the Brooklyn Heights Seminary, writes: "Never was pupil more diligent in study and more successful in attaining knowledge." After graduating, in 1869, she took a post-graduate course, and then spent some time in her Alma Mater as a teacher of the higher branches, and in giving weekly lectures in the Senior and Junior departments. Then came years of continued study and literary pursuits.

As the temperance enthusiasm spread from Ohio east-

(580)

MISS ELIZABETH W. GREENWOOD.

ward, Miss Greenwood became deeply interested in the movement in her own city, and soon found in its variety of work an arena for her versatility of talent. Beginning in the W. C. T. U., and many of the churches of Brooklyn, her work has extended to nearly all the conservative churches of our large cities and towns in the East; while she has been equally at home in its jails, asylums, factories, and saloons.

With a clear voice, a logical mind, and a rich fund of illustration, with ease and grace of manner, and an indescribable magnetism, she removes all prejudice against woman's work, and delights all who listen, even to little children. Though so deeply interested in the varied departments of the temperance work, Miss Greenwood's heart is especially drawn to the exposition of the word of God. In her rural summer home among the hills of Berkshire, whither she goes for rest, she has given Bible expositions to large and intelligent audiences on the Sabbath, and there as elsewhere they have been most helpful. As National Superintendent of Juvenile Work, State Superintendent of Scientific Instruction, President of the Brooklyn Woman's Christian Temperance Union on the Hill, and the Juvenile Union, in frequent work abroad as a lecturer and evangelist, and in the supply each Sabbath evening of a pulpit in her own city, her hands and heart are full of work for the Master.

These doors of service have been opened by Providence, without human effort, and her steady success has been owing not only to her varied ability, but to a deep and increasing consciousness that without the spirit of God her words will be in vain. This consecration gives an earnestness which is truest eloquence, and adds to her character its greatest charm.

MISS F. JENNIE DUTY.

The Ohio temperance work would in no sense be fully represented, were not something said of Miss F. Jennie Duty. A young lady of superior mental endowments, most attractive in face and manner, of good family, she has won for herself not only the devotion of the poor, but the honor of the whole city. For two years she was identified with the Ohio Female College at Cincinnati, and later principal of Wheeling Female College, but she gave up this work to devote herself entirely to temperance. From the earliest days of the crusade she has been untiring, both in the city and State work. Her executive ability has been unsurpassed, while her devotion to the work, and power, especially in saving souls, is rarely equaled. Largely through her instrumentality nine meetings are held weekly at Central Place Friendly Inn, and her Bible addresses are listened to with delight by large audiences. A "Temperance Union Church" has been formed with simple articles of faith, believing in God the Father, Jesus Christ the Son, and in the Holy Spirit, in the Bible as the word of God, in salvation only by the Saviour, in the judgment and resurrection. Every person who assents to these articles of belief, takes the total abstinence pledge. Several hundreds are members of this church, of which Miss Duty is the required leader. She is chairman of the Inn work in the national organization, and has given much thought to this branch of labor. She is also the Superintendent of a large Sunday-school at the Inn. In the effort for constitutional prohibition in the State, she has been a leading spirit. Her energy, good judgment, and fearless devotion to right made her co-workers justly proud of her, while her devotion to her parents, and the assistance rendered to her dear, aged father in his business, emphasize the tender womanliness which is the crowning charm of her character. Mrs. J.

MRS. J. K. BARNEY.

S. Prother, the President of the League, a most efficient woman, Mrs. E. H. Adams, the Secretary, an able writer and thinker, Mrs. Charles Wheeler, a devoted and noble woman, deserve especial mention.

MRS. J. K. BARNEY OF PROVIDENCE, R. I.

Our gentle Mrs. Barney is the daughter of Dr. John A. Hammond, a physician, and was born in Massachusetts. When but thirteen years of age she was a regular contributor to several public journals. Her strongest early proclivity was for the work of foreign missions, although in those days very few women were sent out. Ill health and the strong opposition of friends prevented the fulfillment of this purpose, and in 1854 she was married to Josiah K. Barney of Providence, R. I., where her home has since been, with the exception of several years on the Pacific Coast. Immediately after the organization of the Woman's Foreign Missionary Society of the M. E. Church, she made her first attempts at public speaking in its interests, and has always been closely identified with its work. Previous to this time, however, she had become greatly interested in prison and jail work, and was one of the founders of the Prisoners' Aid Society of R. I. Mrs. Barney was among the earliest workers in the W. C. T. U. of Rhode Island, was chosen its President in its first year, and has filled the office ever since with great acceptance. It is but justice to say that no woman in the State wields an equal influence or possesses the confidence of all classes of people to an equal degree.

The devotion of the W. C. T. U. of "Little Rhody" to their accomplished leader is conclusive proof of *her* devotion to the work.

But Mrs. Barney is best known to us as National Superintendent of Prison, Jail, Police, and Almshouse Visitation. The following extracts from her last annual report are of great interest:

" We recommend for the coming year the continuance of efforts to secure the appointment of police matrons in all cities. The agitation of this question, if not resulting immediately in all desired, will lead to greater care and lessen existing abuses. It frequently occurs that young women are arrested on suspicion; afterwards proved innocent. They feel disgraced and disheartened, and the next step down is an easy one. Women are taken to the stations who for the time being are wholly irresponsible and utterly regardless of all the proprieties of life. Sick, filthy, and with their clothing torn from them in such a manner that common decency demands for them womanly care and protection. Let us see to it that it is supplied as soon as possible.

We should also continue, with increased earnestness, the efforts to secure the appointment of matrons in all prisons and jails where women are committed. It will usually be found that women, after serving their time in jails and houses of correction, seem less amenable to good influences. Girls and young women, arrested for petty offences, are exposed in these places to the influence of those convicted for felony, and who are called dissolute and abandoned characters. A matron could guard against many of these evils, and inspire in the hearts of some of them a desire for a better life.

It is a standing rebuke to our civilization that women are arrested and given into the hands of men to be searched and cared for, tried by men, sentenced by men, and committed to our various institutions for months— and even years—where only men officials have access to them, and where in sickness, or direst need, no womanly help or visitation is vouchsafed them. In Washington, where, upon an average, fifteen women per day are committed, such a state of things exists.

The demand should be persistently made for the com-

plete separation of the sexes, and for the classification of
prisoners, separating juvenile from older criminals. The
old jails of our land are a standing reproach to us as an
enlightened people.

The almshouse work has received increased attention
this year. Hundreds of these inmates who were living in
more than pagan darkness, have heard the story of Jesus'
love and have caught the first gleam of hope which they
have known for weary years.

One of the most pitiful sights found in these places is
the *pauper child*. Many of them illegitimate offspring of
imbecile mothers, they inherit a fearful proclivity to vice
and crime from their vicious and pauperised parentage,
and they are environed with such conditions that the
chances of their escape from utter degradation seem hopeless. Something must be done to save them and it must
be done quickly.

These points so briefly touched, and many others closely
connected with them, and which will be obvious to a
thoughtful mind, should be thoroughly investigated. Let
light in upon these abuses through the press and the
public will demand their removal. So much has already
been accomplished that it gives us a glimpse of what
might be expected if the work could be thoroughly taken
up in each State.

'Let the sighing of the prisoner come before thee,' and
'the blessing of those ready to perish be upon thee.'

Number of States reporting officially or otherwise, 35."

Aside from her work in prisons, where her presence is
as the coming of light into gloom, Mrs. Barney's labors
as an evangelist have been very acceptable, her sermons
being spoken of in terms of high commendation by pastors,
and her services sought by nearly all denominations. The
public duties of our friend have never eclipsed her home
life, and the conscientious fulfillment of her duties as a

wife and mother is a marked and gracious feature in her character. But her wide sympathies take in the homeless, and her sweet ministries have won for her, beyond any other in our ranks, the title of "The Prisoner's Friend."

MRS. H. SKELTON,

Our German Superintendent.

Practically this important department began with the discovery by Mrs. Lathrap of Mrs. H. Skelton, then a Canadian worker just beginning, but now well known throughout our borders. Elsewhere in this volume her work is mentioned with that of her co-laborers. In a pleasant volume recently written by Mrs. Skelton, entitled "The Christmas Tree," she presents much of her home life. She was born in Gissen, Germany, where her father was three years connected with the University. He was then called to Darmstadt, and later as a professor to Heidelberg, where he died when Henriette was but fifteen. Soon after her mother died, and the children removed to Canada, where, later on, the daughter married Mr. Skelton, who was for many years traffic superintendent of the Northern Railroad. He died ten years ago, leaving his wife with one son, a fine young man, living in Toronto. Thus the gifted brain and warm heart of Mrs. Skelton were liberated for blessed service in carrying the temperance gospel to her own people in our land, speaking to them in their own tongue wherein they were born. In this work she has been most successful, for the German mind, beyond almost any other, is approachable upon the plane of "Come, let us reason together."

Der Bahnbrecher is a temperance paper founded by Mrs. Skelton, and now conducted by Professor Adolph Schmitz of Chicago; and with Mrs. Skelton we have Mrs. Emma Obenauer, and Mrs. H. W. Harris, all of whom are building up our work with commendable earnestness and skill.

MRS. ELIZABETH COMSTOCK.

ELIZABETH L. COMSTOCK.

The scene is laid in England. The time is half a century ago. We enter, in imagination, a quiet Quaker home. The father and mother are seated near a lady visitor, whose face and stately figure are enhanced by manners which combine the elegance of society with the sweetness of a saint. Upon a cushion beside this wonderful lady a little girl is kneeling, her bright, observant eyes fixed on the eloquent face of her mother's guest, who is speaking in a voice as rich as her face is beautiful. Let us, too, listen with the rest.

" I met an old friend to-day, as I was going to my dear prisoners at Newgate," thus the lady speaks, "and she declared it was a mystery that I, who had known the rarest pleasures of the gay world, I, a daughter of the Gurneys, should be content to spend my time with outcasts and with thieves. But I told her that God had revealed to me so plainly what life is for, that I could no longer be deceived by the allurements of the world. I told her that I never knew real happiness until, in my dear Master's name, I learned to go about doing good."

As she said this, Elizabeth Fry, once the elegant woman of society, now the Quaker preacher and " prison angel," bent down and laid her gentle hand on the head of the little girl, her namesake, with the words, " Remember what I tell thee, dear Elizabeth: to be Christ's messenger to those who know him not, that is the happiest life." Elizabeth L. Comstock, whose kind face looks out upon us from this page, has shown by her whole life that England's foremost woman philanthropist did not speak these words to her in vain. The blessed compensations of the Gospel have a pleasant illustration in the influences which gave direction to these two women's lives. Good William Savery, a preacher in the Society of Friends, went from America to England on a religious mission.

There in the Friends' meeting-house at Norwich, Elizabeth
Gurney formed one of his congregation, and his discourse
made such an impression upon her that she changed her
mode of life to that prescribed by the most rigid and
orthodox of his sect.   The change was consummated by
her marriage with Joseph Fry, who was a "Plain Friend."
A few years later she joined the ministry, and thenceforward devoted herself to works of the purest piety and
benevolence.   Owing to her unwearied exertions, important reforms were effected in the prison systems, not
only of Great Britain, but also of France and Germany,
and she spent nearly forty years laboring among the poor
and criminal.   But the wave of benignant influence to
which her life may be compared, was started by an
American, who, not as a mere tourist or adventurer, but
in the name of God and for His glory, went to the dear
Motherland.   In turn, Elizabeth Fry's life and words
inspired her gentle namesake, who came to our snores,
and whose philanthropic career has made her name a
household word in ten thousand American homes.   During our late war, Elizabeth Comstock spent her time in
camps and hospitals, and talked of the love and mercy of
our Heavenly Father, and of the dear names of mother
and home to our hundred and ninety-five thousand sick
and wounded soldiers.   In the last twenty years she has
devoted most of her time to the visitation of prisons, hospitals, poor-houses, and various benevolent and reformatory institutions.   She has visited prisoners on both sides
of the Atlantic.   Of these, a hundred and twenty-two
thousand were in criminal prisons, and thirty thousand
were prisoners of war.   Besides these, eighty-five thousand inmates of poor-houses have heard from her lips of

> " The home for the homeless prepared in the skies,
> The rest for the soul that on Jesus relies,
> The joy in believing, the hope, and the stay
> That this world can not give nor this world take away."

Thus she carried out her avowed purpose in life: "To bear our Father's messages of love and mercy to the largest household on earth—the household of affliction." These experiences have thoroughly aroused her to the importance of laboring in the temperance cause, for she expressly says in her public addresses that she "has found upon investigation and inquiry that seventy-five per cent. of those confined in State prisons, county jails, and city Bridewells are there (directly or indirectly) through intemperance. In alms-houses the percentage is still larger."

The Woman's Temperance Crusade began during a visit to her native land, and she rendered signal service to the ladies in England in gospel temperance work, having held over three hundred meetings, chiefly in the large cities and towns. But our own country has shared liberally in the temperance work of this beloved bearer of good tidings.

Accompanied by our dear Mrs. Thompson of Hillsboro', Ohio, she went east by invitation of the enterprising Brooklyn Woman's Temperance Union, and the two addressed large audiences in many of the principal churches of that city, rousing the interest of the fortunate class—so difficult to reach, yet so important to secure. Mrs. Comstock has also held Gospel temperance meetings in many of our large cities and towns, both east and west, besides speaking at our northern conventions of men and women. Her home is in Rollin, Michigan, where she resides with her husband and daughter. Ill health has alone prevented her from active co-operation in the "Red Ribbon Movement," which, within a year, under the leadership of Dr. Reynolds, has brought Michigan into the foremost rank as a temperance State. God bless Elizabeth Comstock, and may the sinful and the sorrowing long be comforted by her tender invitations to the Lamb of God, who taketh away the sin of the world.

EVANSTON, August 7, 1877.

ONE HUSBAND'S BIRTHDAY GIFT.

Some rich men give their wives a set of diamonds on their birthday. These gleam on the breast or hang in the ears, *a la sauvage*, exciting envy as they flash their cold splendors, and doing no mortal one atom of good. R. G. Peters, of Manistee, is a rich man, but not one of that great class whose lavish personal and home expenditures utter the daily prayer, which a wag has thus expressed in words: "O Lord, bless me and my wife, my son John and his wife, us four and no more." The birthday gift of this successful lumber merchant to his gentle wife Evelyn, was a home for the W. C. T. U. of Manistee (of which she is President), and it cost him twenty-five thousand dollars. Yesterday Mrs. Henry, Anna Gordon, and I participated in the dedication services of this beautiful place, all the places on the long and varied programme being filled by women and children (saving and excepting the benedictions).

The building is a gem—Milwaukee brick, slate roof, five chimneys, picturesque sky line, frescoed walls, amphitheatre shape; chairs for twelve hundred persons; "temperance school" rooms; library; dining-room for two hundred, with table linen, crockery, and silver; kitchen furnace, and everything according to the most recent improvements. "W. C. T. U." in gilt letters greets the eye from the handsome gable, from the elegantly painted drop curtains, and from the flower-adorned front of the stage. "For God and Home and Native Land," in sky blue letters of hope, beams from the gallery front: flags of all nations hang along the circle of the upper tier of eats, while David C. Cook's bright colored pledge roll is conspicuous below. The scene on Sunday afternoon, when a hundred children sat on the platform, surrounded by blooming plants, and three hundred more faced them in the centre of the " Union Hall " (for that is the " christened name "), while Mrs. Peters, with her happy face, called off the parts, and the older people looked on contentedly, was a most lovely sequel of the crusade. Our dear Mrs. Henry certainly merits " special mention " for her part in all these preparations, of which her own gifted brain and heart have been the inspiration. She it was who started the free kindergarten and temperance school, who wrote the two beautiful dedication hymns, and whose responsive reading of Solomon's dedication service of the temple, and whose tender, motherly prayers in offering this womanly gift of a Temperance Hall to God, were the most impressive and blessed part of the services. She had trained the choir of a hundred children to sing the hymn she had written for their meeting, and to " suit the action to the words." As their little hands went gradually up and up and up, to symbolize the words, they constantly repeated "Rise, temple, rise," to a sweet, swinging air, there was hardly a dry eye in the house. If I were a minister, I would rather hear those pure young voices chant the dedication hymn of my church than all the prima donnas in christendom. Listen to the song :

> Brick and stone and timber fair,
> Rise, temple, rise;
> Upward through the sunny air
> Rise, temple, rise.
>
> Walls so grand and doors so wide,
> Rise, temple, rise;
> We are coming side by side,
> Rise, temple, rise.
>
> Little eyes have watched you grow,
> Rise, temple, rise;
> You were built for us, you know,
> Rise, temple, rise.

You were built for temperance, too,
  Rise, temple, rise;
All things good and pure and true,
  Rise, temple, rise.

Chorus:

Rise, temple, rise,
Rise, temple, rise,
Rise, temple, rise.

Then after prayer, Mrs. Peters read the First Psalm, then a beautiful pledge-song was sung, and Mrs. Henry made a speech; then after I tried to transfer to the walls four temperance pictures, which they could see with their eyes shut, the hymn, " My Country, 'Tis of Thee," was sung with great unction by the youthful choir carefully trained to all this by an accomplished vocalist. It seemed a "fair play, turn-about" when their voices rang out on "Our mother's God, to Thee, Author of Liberty."

Mrs. Stancel, the Secretary of the society, then surprised Mrs. Peters by presenting to her the large flower-stand that had been a chief feature of the ornamentation, being filled full of bouquets brought by the children. The gracious, gentle mistress of ceremonies responded in a few earnest words, while bright tears of joy sparkled in her eyes.

Directly after this meeting, our modest Anna Gordon held a private session with the girls of Manistee, concerning which I learned that it was of deep spiritual power, and resulted in most valuable accessions to the membership.

At night the hall was packed again, and Mrs. J. F. Nuttall, a lovely singer ("with the spirit" not less than "with the understanding") gave us "Nearer, my God, to Thee" to that tender, pathetic tune of "Robin Adair." I tried to illustrate the history, aims, and methods of our beloved W. C. T. U., especially enforcing the work of prevention and transformation (juvenile and evangelistic), and at the close our clear-voiced chorus sang, "O, prodigal child, come home."

The churches were closed, and all the leading pastors were with us on the platform. Letters of appreciation were read from President (on behalf of Mrs.) R. B. Hayes, Neal Dow, Mary A. Woodbridge, Esther Pugh, Mrs. Stevens of Maine, etc.

Dear sisters, everywhere, let us go and do likewise. There is but one R. G. Peters, but there are many noble men and women who will gladly help us to a "local habitation" for the W. C. T. U. We might rather use the name coined by the Quaker lady, who encouraged a timid sister to pray in a public place by saying, "Where the temperance women meet, there is the 'Lord's parlor.'" It looked just like such a parlor—that restful, homelike "Union Hall," with its pleasant circles of thoughtful people at the dedication services upon the Sabbath day.

CHAPTER XXXIII.

THE CANADIAN LEADERS.

Mrs. Letitia Youmans, the Lecturer—Mrs. D. B. Chisholm, President
of Ontario W. C. T. U., etc.

THE briefest possible definition of our Canadian sister
is found in Paul's sententious words, " much, every
way." Whether we consider her ample avoirdupois or
the remarkable breadth of her views, the warmth of her
heart or the weight of her arguments, the strength of her
convictions or the many-sided brilliancy of her wit, the
vigor of her common sense or the wide extent of her
influence, Mrs. Youmans is a woman altogether remarkable.
Like most natures which unite so many royal qualities,
and whose kindness and simplicity are, after all, their
crowning charm, Mrs. Youmans is a combination in her
ancestry and her experience of widely varying elements.
Her father, John Creighton, was an Irishman, her mother
was a Yankee, and she herself was born and reared in
Canada. She had the advantage of a close companionship
with nature, having been brought up on her father's farm
near Coburg, where she was born in 1827. Dr. Van
Norman, now a well-known educator in New York city,
was her earliest teacher, and from his school, the " Burlington Academy," at Hamilton, she graduated with high
honor, at the age of twenty years. Here Letitia Creighton
remained two years as a teacher. "From her early days
[says a Canada paper] she manifested in a remarkable
degree what have since become the most prominent traits
of her character, namely: an intense desire for knowledge,
an almost unlimited capacity for hard, intellectual toil, an

(598)

MRS. LETITIA YOUMANS.

unwavering determination to devote herself to the realization of a high ideal of life, and an intense sympathy with sorrowing and suffering humanity. The practical view she took of whatever most interested her, prevented this sympathy from being dissipated into mere sensibility, and made her an earnest and active promoter of whatever had for its object the amelioration of the condition of others. While at the Academy she was not more distinguished among her schoolmates for hard work and rapid progress than for her zeal in enlarging the school library, in projecting and sustaining a literary periodical for the improvement of herself and fellow-students, and in setting on foot and maintaining in operation schemes of active benevolence."

At one of the Old Orchard Temperance Camp Meetings, Mrs. Youmans told us that a speech made by Neal Dow in her home at Picton, thirty years ago, convinced her that the liquor traffic is " the gigantic crime of crimes," and that right reason, enlightened conscience, and wise statesmanship, all demand its prohibition.

Though always sympathizing with the temperance cause, as with every form of philanthropy, the day of Mrs. Youmans' active public labors was long postponed. She was married at the age of twenty-three, and from that time lived quietly in Picton, Province of Ontario, until the trumpet call of the " Women's Temperance Crusade " woke in her heart the deepest echo it had ever known. She had already organized a Band of Hope, numbering hundreds of the children of her neighborhood, and the first autumn after the memorable crusade year (1874), Mrs. Youmans, unheralded and uncredentialed, appeared in Trinity M. E. Church, Cincinnati, at the first anniversary meeting of the W. N. C. T. Union. She modestly stated that she had " come to learn," but was courteously invited to address an evening mass meeting, and her powerful voice rang out for the first time over the historic battle-ground of the new and mighty war. Her American sisters were electrified. What a magazine of power was here, and what an explosion it would cause among the conservatives of the Dominion! From that time to this the name of Mrs. Youmans has been beloved and honored in "the States" even as it had already been "in her ain countree," and at nearly all the great summer meetings she has been our invited guest, always accompanied by her husband, a dignified and genial gentleman, who is very proud of her.*

Her cheery greetings and unfailing *bonhommie* have greatly helped to strengthen the ties between the two sides of the line, and her favorite prediction about "the women tying together across Lake Erie, the Union Jack and Stars and Stripes with ribbons that are total abstinence badges, while the Yankee eagle soars above and the British lion crouches beneath," never fails to "bring down the house."

Mrs. Youmans was for years President of W. C. T. U. of Ontario, and by her great gifts as a speaker, and her remarkable energy and effective work, has done more than any other one to make the W. C. T. U. known in Canada. Talented, earnest, and consecrated women have rallied to her side, and an amount of solid achievement might already be reported sufficient to transcend the limits of a sketch like this. The great advance of the temperance movement in the county of Prince Edward, the triumph of the Scott Act (prohibitory), the address before a convention of members of Parliament in Montreal, all these are matters of well-known history in Canada. Clear and logical as are all of her appeals, Mrs. Youmans is never so effective as on her favorite theme of "Home Protection," though she declines to give to those

---

* Mr. Youmans has lately died.

words, dear to our Illinoisans, the broader significance they have acquired upon the prairies. Her addresses, founded on the books of Esther and Nehemiah, are among the most forcible appeals ever uttered for prohibitory law. All honor to brave Letitia Youmans, and may "the ripe, round mellow years" of her life's benignant afternoon be crowded full of trophies for the Master whom she loves.

It would be pleasant to write of other Canadian leaders, for the terms of our temperance "Reciprocity Treaty" are such that we are well acquainted. Mrs. D. B. Chisholm of Hamilton, is the admirable successor of Mrs. Youmans as President. Mrs. Tilton of Ottawa (a lady of great influence at the capital), is President. Dr. Jennie K. Trout, a noble-hearted Scotchwoman of Toronto, is one of the clearest heads, and Miss Minnie Phelps of St. Catharines, among the most progressive of the workers. The Neal Dow of Canada is Professor George E. Foster, who resigned his position in the University of New Brunswick to take the field for temperance reform, and is now a member of Parliament. He has always been a staunch friend of our W. C. T. U.

CHAPTER XXXIV.

THE CHILDREN.

Miss Lathbury's poem—Boy's Temperance speech—How to reach the children.

[NOTE.—Miss Lathbury, founder of the Chautauqua "Look-up Legion," author of books, poems, etc., "our special artist" to the W. C. T. U.]

" BY THIS WE CONQUER."

(Inscribed to our "Bands of Hope.")

Hark! in the air a song,
    With an undertone below
Like the marching of a mighty throng;
    What coming host hath so
Sent Hope a-singing through the land,
    Her wings with light aglow?

The children are a-field!
    They march to meet their King;
Each bears a standard and a shield,
    And each an offering;
And all the air is ringing with
    The songs of faith they sing.

What shield is this they bear?
    What standard doth the Lord
Uplift beside the waters, where—
    According to His Word—
The fierce incoming floods are stayed,
    The breath of Heaven stirred?

A lifted cross I see,
    And, in a sacred sign,
The flag, in holy unity,
    Enfolds its form divine;
And from its floating blue the stars
    Forever shine and shine.

MARY A. LATHBURY.

(604)

THE FUTURE LEGISLATOR.

EVERYBODY'S WAR.

[Dear mothers and teachers, can you not use this when a young hopeful comes to you with the ever-recurring question: "Where shall I find a piece to speak at school?" I prepared it with the said irrepressible "in my mind's eye, Horatio!"]

I wonder how many of these young folks know that there is a great war going on in this city, on the west side, north side, south side—going on all over the State from end to end, and all through the land of the Star-Spangled Banner from Maine to Florida, and Massachusetts to California? Haven't you heard the rattle of muskets, booming of cannon, beating of drums? No? Well, pray, where do you keep your ears?

Haven't you seen any barracks, arsenals, fortresses, fortifications? Where do you keep your eyes?

Why, this very night you're in one of the forts belonging to our side—that is, the loyal troops. I've seen bullets and bombshells shot out of this pulpit that have given no small fright to the enemy and no small courage to my heart when times looked dark. I want you to be duly impressed with the fact that there *is* a war. We call it an irrepressible conflict and a fight against spiritual darkness in high places. The captain on our side is He of whom you often sing:

"Oh! surely the Captain may depend on me,
Though but an armor-bearer I may be."

The Lord of Hosts is His name. The captain on the other side is described in these lines from another of your hymns:

"See the mighty host advancing, Satan leading on."

The recruiting-offices of our side are the church, the Sunday-school, the home; while those of the enemy are breweries, distilleries, and grog-shops. To join our army you sign the muster-roll called "The Total-Abstinence Iron-Clad;" to join theirs you clink beer-mugs and brandy-glasses and hurrah for blear-eyed old King Gambrinus. The uniform of the enemy's soldiers is an old coat out at the elbows and a shocking bad hat, and their badge a fiery red nose; while we have transferred the red to a ribbon in the button-hole. Our soldiers are well but plainly dressed, and the girls and women among them wear a pretty knot of white ribbon. The weapons of the enemy are a shillalah or a doubled-up, pin-cushiony fist; they aim straight at the brain or at the heart. Our weapons aim there, too, only for the first we have keen thoughts, and for the last tender, pleading, and eloquent pathos. The soldiers on the other side are bewildered, untaught youth, ignorant men, and vicious dotards; on our side the smallest boy or girl is up to regulation height, gray hairs exempt nobody, you can't hire a substitute if you would, and when you come to think it over you really don't want to if you could. Best of all, ours is an army in which your mothers, gentle and soft-voiced and very much afraid of guns and gunpowder, can yet keep step with the sturdy and the strong, keeping time to the company's music as they march calmly forward in the name of "God, and home, and native land." Now, my youthful hearers, are *you* enlisted soldiers? Have you "pledged perpetual hate to all that can intoxicate," from cider to champagne? If not, why not? Come, we want you to bear aloft a banner in your firm, young hands, and to inscribe upon it: "*Tremble, King Alcohol! we shall grow up!*"

HOW TO REACH THE CHILDREN — HOW TO REACH THEM IN THE PUBLIC SCHOOLS — THE COLD WATER BOYS AND SISTERS OF THE REGIMENT.

Two of the temperance societies in Massachusetts have tried to introduce temperance work into the public schools.

A circular was sent out, setting forth the fact that intemperance is one of the deadliest foes to the country; that total abstinence is the only effective example, and speakers were sent to present these and other facts to the young people. This has been done with marked success in a State requiring prohibition, at least on its statute book. Seventy per cent. of the young people (at least sixty or seventy thousand) signed the total abstinence pledge. Prizes were offered to schools of a higher grade for essays showing the evils and cure of intemperance. Ninety schools accepted the offer, and five thousand children competed for the prizes. Thus they were set to ransacking libraries—there was an incalculable amount of reading done by those children—and when the essays were decided upon, a crowd of men and women said: "We must go and see how these young, intellectual gladiators fight!"

The year before I left the Northwestern University in Evanston I commenced the work in my own classes, and I set them to work debating on the question. Some of the most rousing debates I ever heard were presented there.

We have a juvenile work in connection with our Woman's Temperance Union. We make the children officers or corporals. We make a good share of them vice-presidents, responsible for good order. Vice-presidents Nos. 1, 2, 3 provide entertainments, and so on. When they have public meetings, fathers and mothers, brothers and sisters come to look on. We all know there is a certain magnetism about the children that makes us all interested in what they do, so we lay burdens and duties on them, and give them honors, while older people guide the helm.

I will tell you what I have seen at Rockford, Ill., my adopted State. We met in a large town hall and organized a company. It is a good plan to have town-hall meetings for children in a good cause. This came about in this wise : Two or three boys going home from Sunday-school said :

"Why not have a society of our own?"

"First rate; let's; and what shall be our pledge?"

"We do pledge ourselves to abstain from all intoxicating liquors, from cider, and tobacco."

There was a good deal of talking over cider; the boys agonized over the tobacco question, and their mothers prayed with them, and finally they thought they could give it up. The ladies heard about it, and they put an advertisement in the Rockford papers : "Any boys who want to fight against rum and sin, meet the temperance ladies in the town hall on such a day." This caused a rally among the boys. We proposed to them to enlist under this their own original pledge : "We do solemnly promise to abstain from the use of all intoxicating liquors, and from cider as a beverage ; also from the use of tobacco in any form, and to do all in our power to promote the temperance cause." We met those who agreed to sign (three hundred strong they were) in the large hall, and, with the help of a military officer who was also a reformed man, we organized three companies, A, B, and C, with the regular company officers. They have badges of ribbon about three inches wide, a different color for each company. The first has green, printed thus : "Cold Water Boys, Company A."

Children like to march, hop, skip, and jump. They like gymnastics, and thus we organize. They are learning the regular military drill. Each company has an appropriate banner; they are full of enthusiasm, and are enlisting recruits. On Decoration Day they were out in full force. They were drawn up in the public square, and Mrs. Henry came forward and administered the pledge to them as they stood with hats in their left hands, and right hands lifted in solemn gesture of assent. Then they gave three cheers for the pledge and marched out. There is nothing dangerous in these military arrangements. We are organizing the girls into "Sisters of the Regiment" to help the Cold Water Army in its campaign against the rum power, somewhat as the Sanitary and Christian Commission Societies were to the army.

We see the saloon-keeper's boys marching side by side with the temperance man's boys; and when those boys hurrah, they hurrah for the pledge.

24

CHAPTER XXXV.

HOW TO ORGANIZE A W. C. T. U.

How ought a Local W. C. T. U. to conduct a Public Meeting?

I. THE PRELIMINARIES.

THESE are of two kinds: First, Notices to the public. Second, Opening exercises.

Your notices should be printed in all the local papers at least one week beforehand, and sent to each pulpit on the Sabbath previous. The following form is recommended:

To the ladies of ———

The National W. C. T. U. has twenty-five auxiliaries, and is the largest and most influential society ever composed and conducted exclusively by women. It has nearly three thousand local auxiliaries and hundreds of juvenile organizations. It is a lineal descendant of the great temperance crusade of 1873–4, and is a union of women from all denominations, for the purpose of educating the young, forming a better public sentiment, reforming the drinking classes, transforming by the power of Divine grace those who are enslaved by alcohol, and removing the dram-shop from our streets by law.

Mrs. ——— of ———, duly authorized by ——— W. C. T. U. to undertake this work, will speak in ——— on ——— at ——— o'clock on the history, aims, and methods of this society. All ladies are earnestly requested to attend. The presence of pastors is respectfully invited.

On the same slip put the following:

ATTENTION, BOYS AND GIRLS!

You have a friend who would like very much to meet and talk with you at ———— on ———— at ——— o'clock. She will show you some interesting experiments, blackboard exercises and charts. Please come, and we will try to organize a Band of Hope. Yours for clear heads and true hearts. Mrs. ————

This should be sent to Sunday-schools and public schools as well as to pulpit and press. It is a false—let us rather say an ignorant—delicacy which hesitates to give full information through all legitimate channels, of the time, place, and object of any attempt to build up Christ's kingdom by benefiting the race for which he died.

But our workers have gone hundreds of miles to form a local union only to find a single stray line in the corner of one newspaper as the only notice given, or a brief mention at a rainy Sunday morning service their only herald. Not thus does the enemy permit his opportunities to go by default.

Second, The opening exercises. Let these be informal, but full of earnestness. Many a time have I seen the devotional spirit frozen out by the mechanical air of the leader, added to the slow process of hunting up and distributing hymn books, waiting for the organ key to be sent for; persuading some reluctant musician to come forward, and so on to the doleful climax of failure. Suppose you just omit all that—come forward at once with some pleasant allusion to a familiar hymn as " one of the special favorites in our work," strike up yourself, or have some one ready to do so without loss of time. As to Scriptural selections, I could spend a whole day exhibiting the choice cabinet of jewels in delightful variety and marvelous adaptation to our needs, which the past years of study have disclosed. As I listen to our women, East and West, in local meetings and conventions, I am impressed by none of their beautiful gifts so much as that they are indeed workmen who need not be ashamed, rightly dividing the Word of God. From Mrs. Leavitt of Cincinnati, with her "Saloon Keeper's Psalm (the tenth), to Mrs. Carhart of Iowa, reading Miriam's Song at the jubilee in June; whether it be Sanballat, Gideon's Band, Deborah and Barak, Queen Esther, Joel (second chapter), or the Prodigal Son, and Good Samaritan, our workers have proved themselves mighty in the Scriptures ever since those wondrous school days when they learned to read their Bibles in the grog-shops of the land. Their "Crusade Psalm" (the 146th) is unrivaled for expository use. It is capable of being wrought into a delightful evening's "Bible Reading," but this must be greatly abridged in your opening exercises. Suppose you study its ten verses for the purpose of finding our bugle call, our key word, exhortation, basis, complete plan of work, prophecy, and philosophy, and song of jubilee—for all of these and vastly more are there!

If a pastor is present ask him to offer prayer.

II. THE ORGANIZATION.

And now, with preliminaries arranged, the spirit of praise and prayer evoked, a secretary *pro tem.* appointed to keep the important record of "first things," and a group of women gathered around you in home or church parlor, what are you to say and do that they shall love our cause and work with us?

First, Don't take too much for granted. Don't think because these are women of general intelligence and Christian experience they are also clear in their respective minds as to the history, mystery, and methods of the W. C. T. U. On that subject you had better take it for granted they are outside barbarians. At least I was of this description when the crusade of 1874 struck the classic suburb of Evanston. Fancy the ignorance of one who had never, that she knew of, seen a saloon, and yet had lived for nearly twenty years within a few miles of Chicago. Imagine the illiteracy that had never once laid eyes upon a temperance paper nor heard the name of J. N. Stearns. Conceive of the crudity that led me in my sober senses to make a bee line to Boston, that I might learn of Dr. Dio Lewis the whole duty of a W. C. T. U. woman, and for the same reason to Portland that I might sit at the feet of Neal Dow.

But all this is hardly more absurd than the revelation of failure (after I thought myself a veteran in our ranks) made to me the most unwittingly by a dear old lady down in Delaware, who, after I had talked an hour by the clock on the " Aims and Methods of the W. C. T. U." said in a droll soliloquy, as she scrawled her name upon my membership card : " I'm sure I don't know what she wants us to do, but I reckon it's a good deal in temperance work as it is in goin' to prayer meetin' of a dark night—I can't see but a step to a time, but when I've taken one step, why I'm there and the lantern's there too, and we just go along to the next. So if the Lord has got temperance work for me to do he'll give me light to do it by." Learn then, dear temperance workers, that in this day of specialists you are safe in assuming that your group of good women have minds as vacant as a thimble, and about as much expanded on the scope and working and laws of the W. C. T. U. Their interest is general, not specific ; they have come on purpose to find out what it is your business (not theirs) to know. Therefore, take nothing for granted save that each of them is fitted out with brain and heart and conscience on which you are to act by knowledge, sympathy, conviction.

Second, Don't assume the role of Sir Oracle. Teach without seeming to do so. Carefully skip around all such "hard words" as "Take notice," "I call your attention," "Do you understand?" and on no account conclude a sentence with that irritating grammatical nondescript "See?" Put yourself in the attitude of a learner along with the rest. Thus your style will be suggestive and winsome rather than authoritative and disagreeable. I shall never forget Bishop Warren's opening words to a room full of young people in a southern school. He stood before them with a face wise, kindly, and benignant, and gently called them "Fellow students."

Third, Don't despise the day of small things. You have no reason to be discouraged because your audience is small. I have organized seventy women into a weak society and seven into a strong one. Well do I recall a winter afternoon in 1870, when, complying with an invitation previously given by my first Bible class teacher (of auld lang syne), Mrs. Governor Beveridge, as we call her now, half a score women of Evanston went to a missionary meeting in that lady's parlor. Its object was to organize a Woman's Foreign Missionary Society, and though I had traveled in several Oriental countries, and as a tourist seen something of evangelistic work there, I found myself rudimentary in knowledge beside one who had made the subject a specialty and brought Mrs. Willing's thoroughness of grasp to the theme of woman's martyrology in lands unsunned by Christ. Less than a dozen names were that day enrolled to form our local auxiliary. A dozen years have passed, and through the influence—direct and indirect—of this society, nearly forty young people have gone out from Evanston to the foreign field, to say nothing of thousands of dollars gathered and dispensed through its treasury.

Fourth, Don't fail thoroughly to premeditate your "impromptus." The Holy Spirit seems better pleased to inspire the process of reflection and composition than to atone for what Miss Ophelia called "shiftlessness," by an eleventh hour inspiration. We want no scattering fire in our public utterances, but the sober second thought of your brightest and most studious hours. As a general outline speech I would offer the following:

1. Very brief allusion to the origin and progress of temperance movements, with earnest acknowledgment of what has been done by the Church, the Washingtonian movement, Good Templars, Catholic Total Abstinence Society, etc.

2. Brief and pictorial (not abstract) account of the Woman's Crusade.

3. Organization as its sequel—origin of National W. C. T. U., at Chautauqua in 1874.

4. Growth of the Society in the United States, in Canada, England, and elsewhere, evolution of its work, number and variety of its departments; notwithstanding this general uniformity, the National like a photograph of imperial size; the State a cabinet, the local a *carte de visite*.

5. Why we have superintendents instead of committees to insure individual responsibility. Illustrate by blackboard with our departments written out.

6. Reasons why women should join us. I have often given these in anecdotal form, telling just what women, old and young, grave and gay, had said to me about the convictions resulting from their own observation and experience which had led them into temperance work.

7. Appeal from considerations embodied in our motto 1. For God; 2. For home; 3. For native land.

This address, mixed with the Word of God and prayer, both in its preparation and recital, should be followed by a humble petition for His blessing.

Fifth, Don't fail to suit the action to the word. Ask for a motion to organize, stating it in due form and requesting any lady who has the matter at heart to make it. Get a second to the motion and make a few incidental remarks about the importance of that etiquette of assemblies which we call parliamentary usage. Recommend them to buy Roberts' Rules of Order, and learn a little of it at each meeting. When it comes to a vote after the parliamentary interval for remarks, mention that you are tired of your own voice and anxious to hear theirs, adding in your clearest tones, "All in favor of that motion will please to say aye," and let your final word be in the most decided sense a rising circumflex. You will be surprised to see the readiness with which you can thus call out the voices of the timid, partly out of good nature and partly because their musical perceptions lead them to put a climax to your incomplete inflection by their own. Do not go through the dumb show of " the lifted hand," nor the imbecility of " manifest it by the usual sign " (when there are several signs), but call out that most inspiring response, the human voice divine. Remember too, that thus you educate women out of the silence which has stifled their beautiful gifts so long. Next follows the form of constitution for local auxiliaries, which should be gone over rapidly, reading only the important points, and remarking that this is the form usually adopted and subject to revision at their regular meetings. (Mrs. Buell, our National Corresponding Secretary, at 53 Bible House, New York, furnishes the best.) After a *viva voce* vote on this, read with emphasis our pledge. It includes total abstinence from wine, beer, and cider as a beverage. Explain about the annual membership fee of fifty cents ; exhibit *Our Union-Signal*, stating price, and send out ladies previously appointed to solicit memberships and subscribers.

This moment is the crucial test. To it everything has pointed—failing to secure its objects you will fail indeed. But just at this point we are too often unpardonably heedless. What would be said of the angler whose awkwardness at the critical moment should frighten away the fish he was about to impale? Or the farmer who should forget his scythe when going to the hay-field? But how often have we seen such a stale, flat, and unprofitable half hour succeed the aforementioned address, that it seemed as though a premium was put upon a general stampede of the auditors. " Has any one a pencil to take names?" is a question equally pregnant and imbecile, while vandal hands have made a raid upon stray hymn-books, and their fly-leaves have been ruthlessly confiscated to take the place of the enrolling tablets, conspicuous for their absence. The best way is for the leader of the meeting to keep up a running fire of pleasant explanation or of reply to questions invited by her from the pews. Among the questions which her clear-cut preliminary statements should anticipate are: " Must we pay the membership fee when we give our names?" (No, not unless it is convenient.) " Can young ladies join?" (Most gladly.) " Does this mean all kinds of cider?" (It does.) " Then I cannot join." Well, you can at least attend the regular meetings of the union to follow this, in which the cider leaflets will be discussed, and become an associate if not a regular member (only the latter are eligible to office). It should be explicitly stated that by our new basis of organization, adopted at Washington, we are entitled in the National Convention (beside our State officers) to one delegate for each five hundred members, and as we desire for a large representation, we are anxious to enroll the names of all women who are sufficiently intelligent and devoted friends of temperance to take the pledge and pay the fee, even though they are unable to do any work or to meet with us regularly. The use to be made of the fee should be distinctly stated. Draw a fifty-cent coin on the blackboard—or make a drawing of the same—and have it hung up. Divide it into equal parts, representing that one of these remains to be used in the local work, the other going to the State treasury to extend the organization, save that one-fifth of it is taken out and sent to the National W. C. T. U. to carry on its work. Explain that the National has never had a salaried officer until within three years, and now but pays the current expenses of its Corresponding Secretary at the headquarters, 53 Bible House. Bring forward *Our Union-Signal* and solicit subscribers to the national organ; speak of the Hayes memorial portrait and exhibit the ten cent a share cards by which children so readily raise the five dollars requisite to secure a copy of the same. Give references to the National Temperance Publishing House, 58 Reade Street, New York, and D. C. Cook, Chicago, by no means forgetting our own literature department, conducted by Miss Colman, at 76 Bible House, New York. Distribute the Annual Leaflet of the National W. C. T. U., which has all needed information as to who and where are our superintendents of departments. If there is a piece of fine music prepared, or if you have an interesting speaker present besides yourself, it will be well to mention that attraction as a counter-inducement to those inclined to go.

But all these exercises, from your first bow to your closing *Benedicite*, must be marked *staccato*, and must be made brief and crisp, or your group of guests (for such, do not forget, they are) will file out and hie itself away. The change from one exercise to another, if effected with sufficient ingenuity to avoid jumbling, will help to hold your audience, but most will depend upon your compliance with the suggestion—

Sixth, Don't fail to keep your wit, wisdom, and patience well to the front. Somebody will come to you then and there will be *sotto voce* gossip, with legends and histories of societies previously organized and now fossiliferous, or the prayer-meeting killer of the neighborhood will stray in and begin his sanguinary work upon your feeble banking of a society; or Miss Contretemps, of the contrary part, will state her objections to the pledge, or Madame Pharisee feel called upon to explain that she never was cursed with this demon in her own home and therefore can not, etc., etc., drowsily oblivious of the statement you—should—have made, that ninety per cent. of our members share the exemption which she, with small good taste, parades. Now is the time to prove what manner of spirit you are of. Does your courage rise with danger? Are you fertile in resource? You are being tested now as they test steam engine boilers. The force is applied— the tension noted—and the strong, well wrought metal holds its own, but the thin, flaw-eaten, gives way in its weakest part. Are you master of the situation? "He that ruleth his spirit is better than he who taketh a city." Now is your chance for *mastery*. Many of these annoyances may be prevented by circulating the question papers before the meeting opens and asking that any query, comment, or criticism be written and placed in the question-box, to be circulated before the meeting is closed. This gathering up of questions, as well as the circulation of the various documents I have mentioned, should be attended to by the Secretary *pro tem.*—to be appointed at the opening of the meeting.

Seventh, Don't be precipitate in choice of standard bearers. In this choice will be involved the success or failure of your entire movement. You are trying to launch a life-boat, but if the captain be near-sighted and the mate a blunderer, your craft will swamp before it gets beyond the breakers. The worst of it is that you are at the mercy of the raw hands who must select these officers from their own newly-enlisted crew. In this choice the element of deliberation is important, for while you will be often urged to select the officers then and there, "for fear we cannot get the women together again," my experience is that in the long run we get better results by a careful canvass of the pros and cons. Too often when we try to finish up the business of electing at first meeting, we discover, later on, that the finish was an extinguisher. From a recent confidential letter I make this extract:

A W. C. T. U. was recently organized in our village and there isn't a quarrel in the neighborhood that was not represented on our board of officers.

As you will naturally conclude, I do not expect the liquor traffic in that locality need stand in special fear of said society. This was away down east, but a remark made to me on the frontier has in it equal food for reflection. It was from a new worker, and was so simply said, and with so much of large-eyed wonder "for the cause," that if not so tragic I would have deemed it vastly comical: "Why, do you know, that until our new President was elected I did not know that anybody could be an officer at all and yet be such a poor one!"

Alas for the applications of this utterance, which all of us have seen! Now, while we cannot hope to avoid these calamities in the present partially developed condition of woman's work; while it is doubtless true that girls now acquiring the systematic training of our public schools and colleges will make the more efficient officers of our future work, it is nevertheless possible for us to secure, in a majority of instances, excellent services from the good women of the present. But here, as always, the preliminary part of the recipe is: "First catch your hare," and I

am confident a choice specimen will be caught by appointing (by previous consultation) such a committee on
nomination as will represent the different churches and
social circles, and adjourning to a day not distant when
said committee shall report. It should also include,
among its duties, the preparation of a plan of work for
the society, and the organizer should furnish it with a
model from our State or National minutes, with a leaflet
of the National containing our list of superintendents of
departments. In appointing the list of Vice-Presidents,
insist on one from each denomination, including Catholics,
Jews, etc., and appoint one "at large" to represent the
great and kindly outside fraternity which has this cause
at heart. Insist on a Superintendent of Temperance
Literature, who shall also be Librarian of your Loan
Library and agent for our journalistic organ. Make these
Superintendents members of your Executive Committee—
which should meet weekly, while the W. C. T. U. meets
monthly and has a religious, literary, and business
programme. Fix the government of both meetings at
five—so that the exceeding deference which causes our
good women to lose so much time rather than "act
without the prescribed number," may not endanger their
results of work. Wear the white ribbon yourself, and
urge all to do the same. Close your meeting by singing
"Blest be the Tie that Binds."

I have suggested that you follow this meeting at once
by another for the children. This is of paramount
importance for its own sake; also to conciliate public
sentiment and give your new society that *sine qua non* of
its existence, to say nothing of its success—something
to do.

HOW OUGHT A LOCAL W. C. T. U. TO CONDUCT A PUBLIC MEETING?

Not on the hap-hazard method, which too often prevails in our temperance meetings. It is found in those of men, notwithstanding fifty years experience, and naturally enough, but most unfortunately, in those of women also. " Who shall preside?" " What shall we sing?" " Who shall take the collection?" Questions like these asked under fire of the eyes in the audience, might do for children, but are pitiable from " grown folks."

Not on the " cut and dried " method, where the President reads every word she says, and if her sight is blurred, or her spectacles are mislaid, finds herself all out at sea. " Mrs. — —, Secretary of—no—Treasurer. of the Woman's Association, no—the Female National—no—National Female—no—the W. C. T. U." That comes of " losing your mind." Put somebody to the fore who don't lose hers (or his).

The common sense method is the right one.

1. Plan matters thoroughly beforehand. Rehearse if necessary—you do this for a wedding, and we shall never wed the W. C. T. U. to the people's heart until we conduct our meetings without hitch or flaw. Keep the machinery out of sight. Let everything be natural, but let it be clear-cut, systematic, " ship shape." For instance:

1. Advertise well, insist on an opportunity for Sunday announcements from the pulpits and schools. Don't make the blunder of ignoring the children. They can be instructed, grounded, confirmed, and this is the place to do it in. Some speaker may miss the old folks, but if he has any skill at all in taking aim, he will be sure to hit the youngsters. Childhood is the fortress of the future— furnish it with rations and with weapons, and it will hold the fort when we are mustered out.

2. Don't be afraid to hold your meetings in a church,

you may warm up a cold one; enlist their apathetic but well-meaning minister, elder, or deacon; touch the conscience of a drowsy layman or woman. The church is a good place in which to do good work.

3. Don't let your music go by default. You discount your speaker one-half at the start by this culpable neglect. Reformers are a sympathetic, natural, poetic sort of folk. Besides, don't forget that a hymn with the gospel ring in the united voices that sing it; a solo from some sweet woman's heart and voice, or from that of some good and true man, a chorus lifting the audience to concert pitch, will utterly transform your audience as to its receptivity, its support, its mental elevation. The poor, tired talker goes into the church hoping for a benediction from psalm, and prayer, and song. If you have no method, no music, no amenity, it will all be taken patiently, turned to account as a means of discipline by the disappointed speaker, but you will lose, and lose immeasurably, in the results you had hoped to witness, and (gently be it uttered) you deserve to. But that is not the point. What signify speakers, W. C. T. U., or audience, in such a calculation? They are mere ciphers, but there looms up the great, pure, loving, divine "cause"—and that "Cause" is but another name for Christ, with tender and sorrowful eyes, saying, "Could ye not watch" (could ye not sing, plan, work) "with Me one hour?"

"Seeking to save, not willing that any should perish." "Every plant that my Father hath not planted shall be rooted up"—these are our watchwords—this our basis of operations, and yet we gather the people and then spoil the result—because of our ignominious neglect. Singers, have you no duty here? How are you investing your sweet and beautiful gifts? Do you build them into the cause of temperance, or are you, too, "wounding the Lord in the house of His friends?"

4. Make the place fair and gracious with flowers. See the saloon windows decked with vines and potted plants. Notice the desecration of the *arbor vitae*—that noblest of evergreens—to be a mere sign-post for bloated, beery, old King Gambrinus. Shall we not claim the tender and ennobling ministry of God's thought in plant life and flower language for these meetings, held in His name and for the good of His dear, benighted children? I would have also the flag of my country always before my eyes when I speak in her sacred name, but though the request is regularly made, it is complied with on an average once a year.

5. Let the President of the W. C. T. U. preside and go forward, quietly to her duty, as a matter of course. Provide seats in pulpit and chancel for the pastors, and ask them to participate in the opening exercises, on call of the President. We desire to treat him with special courtesy; we need their help; we shall almost inavariably have it if we are considerate and wise. Do not have long opening exercises—there is so much " more to follow." The remark is often made (often by the minister, I am sorry to say), " We will omit Bible reading." No, we will not. This, of all others, is not the o'clock o' the century for Christians to leave the keystone out of the arch, or for W. C. T. U. women to adjourn the " Home Book " lesson. On the other hand, let the reading be brief and appropriate to the occasion.

The 10th ("Saloon Keeper's") psalm; the 147th ("Crusade") psalm; the parable of the Good Samaritan, " Prodigal Son," or the song of Barak and Deborah (*i. e.*, its main features), all are just to the point. Indeed I wish our temperance papers would publish "outlines" for these headings, with hymns attached. Let the President distinctly designate the number of verses to be sung, and let the choir abide this decision (which it generally does not—making up in length as a general rule what it lacks in strength of melody and spirit).

6. Immediately on the conclusion of the address take your collection. Wait for a hymn at this juncture and your audience will file out. Now comes the crucial test of your "level headedness," dear manager. Choose, with all the wisdom of the united society, the man (or woman, and the latter usually succeeds best), who shall attend to this part of your religious exercises. Who in your town has "a gift" for showing to the people the sacred side of this dedication of their substance to the Lord? Who can, while doing this, interest and perhaps, later on, harmlessly amuse and "hold the people?" That is the man for you (or the woman—usually the last). Give to this blessed genius a list of those who are to take the collection, and just where they are to begin (make a draft on your best soldiers of rank and file in the W. C. T. U.), and let them go forth promptly.

Let the collection baskets be ready beforehand in front of the pulpit. An audience very properly criticises those who bungle with it. An audience is the guest of the W. C. T. U. for the time, and everything should be made just as lovely and pleasant for this guest as possible. Don't keep it waiting for your incoherent whispered consultations; don't let it feel uncomfortable by reason of your own lack of poise and mastership. Rehearse, practice, become perfect. A well-appointed meeting is a work of art. Treat your audience as carefully and charmingly as you would a guest in your own home. I am always sure you will do beautifully by me; treat your audience as well. It will take thought, planning, courage that comes of consecration and prayer. In asking the collection, set forth clearly the objects of your society. It helps to familiarize the public with them. Public intelligence as to your aims and good will, as to your motives, forms a large share of your capital stock for the cause. Be definite; business men like that. But to this end you need not make a scape-goat of your poor lecturer, drag him (or her) to the front and expatiate on the "needs of the hour" in a bold and literal sense. You may state in general terms that a temperance meeting does not "happen"—it is not a sort of spontaneous, fungus growth, but comes as the result of definite aims and engagements. Also, if you choose, mention that our workers and officers in all temperance societies (without exception, almost) are unsalaried, and must meet current expenses with current receipts, and that a part of the regular work of the W. C. T. U. is to hold these meetings for the education of public sentiment. If the children were taught to bring a nickel or a penny to every temperance meeting, and to earn it as well, the temperance education they are receiving would be far more symmetrical. A few weeks ago a dear little four-year-old girl came up the aisle to me with five cents, saying she earned it for the temperance meeting. I thought it the very choicest nickel I had ever seen.

7. But now, while the collection proceeds, let all work to secure membership in your society. Send out eight or ten or twelve ladies with our "Enrolling Tablets"—half of them going to the rear of the church, half to the front, and meeting in the middle of the house. Perhaps your lecturer will read the pledge for you and try to entertain the audience during this effort. If you carefully work up this matter you will be constantly adding to the pledged population of your town ("gentlemen as honorary members," you know); and also augmenting your financial resources at "fifty cents apiece." Besides, by the present arrangement, we have no representation in national (and soon shall only have in State) councils, save on the basis of our paid-up memberships.

Now then, we approach the close. Let the President cordially thank the audience for its presence and attention; for the memberships and collection. If she can put in a kind remembrance of the children and their good behavior, it will not be lost. Also thank the choir. Then have a good, full-chested doxology, and then the benediction.

Postscript.—Don't forget the following items either: To entertain your speaker in a quiet home (with a fire in the room always, in winter). Not to expect much socially, in the way of calls, invitations to tea, etc.; for if you do, your already over-worked talking machine will have so little vitality left that you will be punished by a sleepy speech at night. One of the most distinguished lecturers in this country always says, when invited to meet callers or go out to a meal: "You, my dear friends, love the cause—so do I. You shall take your choice. I will put myself into colloquial talking or into the evening lecture,—just which you think is best. I cannot do you any credit in both of these roles!" Dear friends, remember this, the best rule is: "Enter into one house and there abide." Finally: report your lectures,—not in the way of compliment, but give your best points to the editors. Get your quickest, brightest members to do this for all the papers of your town. Thus you mould public sentiment in the great class that does not move, and therefore must be moved upon; that will not hear with its ears, but will with its eyes, if you put the thoughts before them in the pages of their local paper. Utilize the public meeting by distributing temperance literature at the close, and advertising National and State Temperance papers. Yet again: When you introduce your speaker, give the full name, the official status (if he has one), and where he "hails from." It does a stranger good to be announced as from somewhere in particular.

Positively, last time: Don't be tardy in beginning. Imitate Moody in this,—be on the minute. Enter from rear of church whenever feasible. Rise yourself, and ask the audience to do so, during singing. It deadens a meeting to have everybody sit stolidly through the music. The foregoing suggestions grow out of evils that I have seen under the sun, and are respectfully submitted.

"BUT, AFTER ALL, WHAT CAN I DO?"

Many a Christian woman, earnest and true, will lay down the book I have written on purpose for them with this question in her heart. May I suggest some of the answers which have come to my own mind, first reminding my readers that they need not neglect home's sacred ministries for any other? Take the time, rather, that has been given to things that were unnecessary, to superfluous sewing, calling, visiting, reading, resting, reverie, and this alone for this "Home Missionary Work."

1. Dear sister in Christ Jesus, you can kneel before God and ask him to show you what he would have you to do. You can also ask his daily blessing on the field, and on the workers there.

2. You can begin in your own home in the lullaby song, the twilight story, the family pledge, with "line upon line and precept upon precept," to train your sons and daughters to be total abstainers.

3. You can prepare the way for consistent precepts by a perfect example, abstaining scrupulously yourself, not only from even partaking of or offering the beverage, but the *medicinal use* and *culinary* use of intoxicating drinks; and you can study to prepare food that shall be so wholesome that it will not "lie like lead" upon the stomach, which often craves a drink to "wash down" an ill-cooked meal.

4. You can study to make your own home so attract-

ive, by reason of its cleanliness, its simple yet attractive adornings, its books, music, and games, and, above all, by its sweet, Christian atmosphere, that its attractions for your sons will not be outmatched by those of the saloon.

5. You can organize your Sunday-school class into a temperance society, getting each member to sign the pledge, and by prayer and personal influence securing the conversion of each; for, after all, as a reformed man said, with shaking voice and tearful eyes, " If I'm to stand, ladies, it's got to be the Lord behind the pledge! "

6. You can personally pray for and appeal to any intemperate man of your own acquaintance; visit the homes of inebriates to lend them " the helping hand," if needed, to pray with and for them, and to use your influence for their restoration to manhood.

7. You can go to the prison in your vicinity, visit the inmates, talk with them of Christ, pray with them, leave little books and papers full of blessed lessons, and get them to sign the pledge.

8. You can circulate Brother Randolph's temperance papers and publications. A dollar bill will secure you a good many papers and tracts.

9. You can go quietly, with the loving spirit of Christ in your heart, and gentle words on your lips, to the home of the saloon-keeper, and talk with his wife and family, and put some temperance publications in their hands.

10. You can, with one or two lady friends, go to any saloon in your neighborhood, and talk and pray with its keeper, and those who frequent its bar, taking your pledge-book, and seeking signatures.

11. But you can never do these things at all, in any effective and true sense, until your own heart is full of Christ's love and consecrated fully to his service, and unless your practical, good Samaritan help goes hand in hand with your prayer and faith.

But, per contra, if you begin this day simply and honestly to do any of these things, or any other true and womanly thing in this cause which your own heart suggests, how you will "grow in grace!" How your own deepest nature will be lighted up by God's own smile! How sweetly you will learn what Christ can become to the soul that goes gently and lovingly upon his errands!

Dear Christian sister who reads these lines, you are one of the "living epistles" by which this critical age is deciding how it will answer the question, "What think ye of Christ?" You are a leaf out of the world's Bible. It "wants facts." In God's name, give it the shining fact of your loving, helpful life "hid with Christ in God."

APPENDIX.

Constitution and Plan of Work for a local W. C. T. U.
Plan of Work of 1874.   Plan of Work for 1883.

[It is hoped that many pastors and Christian women who read this book may be interested to form a local society. All needed information has been already given except the following forms.]

TO PASTORS AND TEMPERANCE PEOPLE.

CONSTITUTION FOR A LOCAL W. C. T. U.

ARTICLE I.—NAME.

This society shall be called the Woman's Christian Temperance Union of ———, auxiliary to the W. C. T. U. of ——— state and of the United States.

ARTICLE II.—OBJECT.

The object of this Union shall be to educate public sentiment up to the level of total abstinence, to train the young, reform and save the inebriate, and hasten the time when the dram-shops shall be banished from the streets by law.

ARTICLE III.—MEMBERSHIP.

Any lady may become a member of this Union by signing the pledge of total abstinence from all intoxicating liquors (including wine, beer, and cider) as a beverage, and paying fifty cents a year into the treasury of the Society. Any gentleman may become an honorary member by signing the same pledge and paying fifty cents annually (or one dollar as may be decided by the new union).

ARTICLE IV.—OFFICERS.

The officers shall be a president, vice-president from each church, corresponding secretary, recording secretary, treasurer, and librarian, who together with the various superintendents of departments shall constitute an executive committee to plan and lead the work.

(633)

ARTICLE V.—DUTIES OF OFFICERS.

The president shall preside at all meetings and give general directions for the work of the society;. the vice-presidents shall preside in turn in the absence of the president, and use their influence to secure members in their respective churches. The corresponding secretary shall conduct all correspondence with lecturers, state and national officers and superintendents, and shall report annually to the corresponding secretary of the state, give a full account of all that has been attempted and accomplished, with a history of the society from the beginning. The recording secretary shall notify the public through the press and pulpit of all meetings, and keep a full record of the same. She shall also furnish each vice-president with a small blankbook, having Article III (membership) written therein, so that each church may be carefully canvassed for names. The treasurer shall personally collect the membership fees as promptly as possible, shall have the care of all money raised by the society, and shall pay out the same upon the president's order, countersigned by the recording secretary. The librarian shall have charge of all books, charts, leaflets, and handbills belonging to the society, lending them or giving them away according to the wishes of the society, and shall superintend the putting up of hooks or tin boxes in the depots and other public places, and keep them supplied with literature, also superintending the distribution of the same in public meetings. She shall be agent of *Our Union* (the official organ of our societies), and may call for a committee on literature to aid her if she desires, of which committee she shall be chairman. She will also circulate the " class papers " of David C. Cook, of Chicago, according to his plan, through the post-office.

ARTICLE VI.—SUPERINTENDENTS OF DEPARTMENTS.

There shall be the following superintendents of departments: On forming juvenile societies. On Sunday-school work, to secure a Bible temperance lesson once each quarter, also to introduce temperance books into the Sunday-school libraries and papers into the Sunday-schools. On introducing Miss Julia Colman's " Alcohol and Hygiene " and Dr. Richard's " Temperance Lesson Book " into all public and private schools. On selecting extracts from temperance books and papers, to be published regularly in the columns of the press, also to specially report the work of the W. C. T. U., local and national, for the press. On holding public meetings, at least once a month, also gospel temperance meetings on the Sabbath day, at hours that are not in conflict with church services. These meetings to be provided with good music and addresses by such gentlemen or ladies as the Union may be able to secure. On inducing the churches to hold Union temperance prayer-meetings at stated intervals. On social entertainments, such as lawn parties and temperance receptions, at which the pledge is to be offered—this committee to be composed of young ladies. On temperance reading room,—this committee is discretionary. On finance—to be composed of both ladies and gentlemen.

ARTICLE VII.—MEETINGS.

The meetings of the executive committee shall be held weekly, and those of the Union once a month, at which time a programme shall be provided, by which, after the devotional exercises and business, there shall be a brief address, essay, debate, recitation, or reading from some temperance book. This programme to be arranged by the executive committee.

ARTICLE VIII.—ANNIVERSARY.

The Annual Meeting shall be held on the anniversary of the organization of the Union, at which time reports shall be made by officers, superintendents and standing committees; an address is also to be provided and an effort made to secure members for the society, and subscribers for *Our Union*.

ARTICLE IX.—AMENDMENTS.

This constitution may be altered or amended, at any regular meeting, by a two-thirds vote of the members present.

ORDER OF EXERCISES FOR MEETINGS OF EXECUTIVE COMMITTEE.

I. Devotional exercises.

II. Minutes of previous meeting.

III. Reports from each officer, viz. :

1. President—General outlook.

2. Each vice-president—From her own church, number of members gained and what the church is doing.

3. Report of letters written and received by corresponding secretary.

4. Report of money received and expended by treasurer.

5. Report of superintendent of juvenile work.

6. Report of superintendent of temperance literature.

7. Report of superintendent of Sunday-school work.

8. Report of superintendent of securing space for temperance items in local press.

9. Report of superintendent of scientific temperance instruction in public and private schools.

10. Report of superintendent of public meetings.

11. Report of superintendent of social entertainments.

12. Report of superintendent of temperance reading room (or restaurant).

13. Report of finance committee.

IV. Consideration of new business.

V. Closing hymn or prayer.

The order of exercises for the regular monthly meeting of the W. C. T. U. is just the same, except that the president shall provide for an essay, reading, recitation, music, or something special, for the edification of members. Miss Coleman's "Beer Series," Eli Johnson's "Drinks, and how they make them," best extracts from temperance speeches and papers, short addresses from pastors, physicians, ladies, —all will be of great service.

Parliamentary usage may be studied. (Get "Roberts' Rules of of Order," S. C. Griggs & Co., Chicago.) The "Duties of Women,"* by Frances Power Cobbe, may be read and discussed, and in many ways the W. C. T. U. may be made not only a philanthropic but also an intellectual circle.

LIST OF PUBLICATIONS FOR SUPERINTENDENTS OF DEPARTMENTS.

Juvenile work; Sunday-school work; scientific instructions; temperance literature; legislative work; young women's work; relation of intemperance to labor and capital; influencing the press; evangelistic work; friendly inns, restaurants, etc.; prison and police station work; unfermented wine at the Lord's Table; Drawing-room meetings; work among the Germans; hygiene; securing day of prayer in week of prayer; work among colored people; work among railroad employes; presenting our cause before influential bodies; on introduction of the Hayes' Testimonial into schools, etc.; unfortunate women; relative statistics; State and county fairs.

The foregoing list is intended to exhibit the many lines of work entered upon by the National W. C. T. U., and may prove suggestive and helpful to the local societies.

Send for all needed literature to the National Temperance Publishing Society, New York, and Revolution Temperance Publishing House, Chicago.

"LOOK ON THIS PICTURE, THEN ON THAT."

The plan of work given below was submitted to the first National W. C. T. U. Convention at Cleveland, in 1874. To show the growth of nine years' work, it is followed by our plan for 1883.

PLAN OF WORK.

I.—OF ORGANIZATION.

Since organization is the sun-glass which brings to a focus scattered influence and effort, we urge the formation of a Woman's Temperance Union in every State, city, town, and village. We will furnish a

---

*For this book send 25 cts. to GEO. H. ELLIS, Publisher, Boston.

Constitution for auxiliaries, with all needed information, to any lady applying to corresponding secretary.

II.—OF MAKING PUBLIC SENTIMENT.

The evolution of temperance ideas in this order : the people are informed, convinced, convicted, pledged. With these facts in view we urge:

First.—Frequent temperance mass meetings.

Second. The careful circulation of temperance literature in the peoples' homes and in saloons.

Third.—Teaching the children in Sabbath-Schools and public schools, the ethics, chemistry, physiology, and hygiene of total abstinence.

Fourth.—Offering prizes in these schools for essays on different aspects of the subject.

Fifth.—Placing a copy of the engraving known as " The Railroad to Ruin," and similar pictures, on the walls of every school-room.

Sixth.—Organizing temperance glee clubs of young people to sing temperance doctrines into the people's hearts as well as heads.

Seventh.—Seeking permission to edit a column in the interest of temperance in every newspaper in the land, and in all possible ways enlisting the press in this reform.

Eighth.—Endeavoring to secure for pastors everywhere frequent temperance sermons, and special services in connection with the weekly prayer-meeting and the Sabbath-School at stated intervals, if they be only quarterly.

Ninth.—Preserving facts connected with the general subject, and with our work, in temperance scrap-books, to be placed in the hands of a special officer appointed for this purpose.

III.—OF JUVENILE TEMPERANCE SOCIETIES.

Catholicism's wisest words are these: Give us the first ten years of the children's lives, and you may have the rest.

In our judgment, one of the great hopes of the ultimate triumph of Temperance Reform lies in the thorough training of the youth of the land in such principles and practices of temperance as will show them the fatal dangers of drinking and criminal guilt of selling liquors; and to end, we earnestly entreat the friends of the cause, and especially the pastors of churches and superintendents of Sabbath-schools throughout the State, to take immediate measures in their respective cities and towns for the formation and perpetual continuance of temperance societies, to be composed of the children and youth.

IV.—OF THE PLEDGE.

If nobody would drink, then nobody would sell.

First.—We urge the circulation of the total abstinence pledge as fast and as far as facilities permit, life signatures being sought, but names being taken for any length of time, however brief.

Second.—We have a special pledge for women, involving the instruction and pledging of themselves, their children, and as far as possible their households; banishing alcohol in all its forms from the sideboard and the kitchen, enjoining quiet, persistent work for temperance in their own social circles.

Third.—We earnestly recommend ladies to get permission to place a pledge-book in every church and Sabbath-school room, where it shall be kept perpetually open in a convenient place, indicated by a motto placed above it. Also that each member of our unions keep an autograph pledge-book on her parlor table, and carry one in her pocket.

V.—OF SACRAMENTAL WINE.

We do not see that the passage, "Woe unto him that putteth the bottle to his neighbor's lips" has in it any "saving clause" for the communion table. We know that many who have thought their appetite completely overcome by months of abstinence have fallen by the odor and the taste of the cup at the Lord's table.

We strongly recommend our unions everywhere, to appoint a committee of ladies in each church who shall try to enlist the pastor and church officials in offering only unfermented wine at the communion table.

VI.—OF THE ANTI-TREAT LEAGUE.

"Come, let's take something together," has been to thousands the key-note of destruction. We are laboring for the organization of a league which shall enroll as members those who, though not ready to sign the pledge, are willing to refrain from "putting the bottle to their neighbor's lips" by pledging their honor that they will neither "be treated" nor "treat."

VII.—OF TEMPERANCE COFFEE ROOMS.

If we would have men forsake saloons, we must invite them to a better place, where they can find shelter, and food, and company. We would open small, neat coffee-rooms, with reading-rooms attached, which the ladies might supply with books and papers from their own homes, and by solicited friends. When practicable, there should also be Friendly Inns, connected with which there might be provided for those willing to compensate by their labor for their food and lodging, a manufacturing shop, comprising many trades.

VIII.—HOME FOR INEBRIATE WOMEN.

These should be established in the cities,—our unions soliciting aid from the State and municipal governments, and from the general public for this purpose.

IX.—THE REFORMED MEN'S CLUBS,

recently projected in New England, will be powerful auxiliaries in our work, and we urge the Women's Unions to help establish them in every community.

X.—A BUREAU OF INFORMATION.

Already, by means of correspondence, our choice of unions has been a medium of communication between parents and their absent sons, by means of which the former in their homes have lent a helping hand to the latter amid their temptations. We suggest careful attention to this important branch of our beneficent task.

XI.—COUNTER ATTRACTIONS OF HOME.

Much has been said about our negligence in rendering our homes attractive and our cuisine appetizing, and not always without reason. We therefore recommend that in our unions essays on the science and art of making home outwardly wholesome and attractive be read, books on that subject circulated, and all possible effort made to secure a more scientific attention to the products of the kitchen and a higher æsthetic standard for the parlor.

XII.—HOME MISSIONARY WORK.

Private visitation of those who drink and those who sell we contemplate still further, our aim being to go in a spirit of prayerful and helpful kindness.

XIII.—GOSPEL TEMPERANCE MEETINGS.

We recommend our unions to hold these meetings in the streets, billiard-halls, and churches, making them protracted if the interest warrant it; offering the Gospel cure for intemperance; going through the audience to get persons to come forward and sign it, to the tune of "Jesus, lover of my soul," investing the act with all the solemnity and enthusiasm of a religious service.

XIV.—FOUNTAINS.

We urge our unions everywhere to signalize the coming hundreth birth-day of America by erecting in every village, and town, and city fountains of water, inscribed with such mottoes as shall show what sort of drink the women of America believe in, and as shall be a sermon in their persuasiveness to our fathers, brothers, and sons.

XV.—OF MONEY.

Our cause cannot forego the sinews of war, be it peaceable or profane. We must have money. Our financial plan asks each member to give a cent a week toward the temperance cause, and we urge this feature as one of great importance. Let us say that all needed information under any or all of the preceding heads will be gladly furnished on application with stamp to our corresponding secretary.

XVI.—TRYSTING TIME WITH GOD.

Our work came forth to us from God. The miracle of the Crusade was wrought by prayer. Let us women of America, and of all lands, dedicate the evening twilight hour to prayerful thoughts about this greatest of all reforms. Wherever we are let us lift up our hearts, whether alone or in company, in the closet or on the street, and ask God's blessing on the temperance work and on those whom it would help. Let us form the habit of keeping sacredly at heart some moments of this hour as our trysting time with God.

CONCLUSION.

Dear sisters, we have laid before you the plan of the long campaign. Will you work with us? We wage our peaceful war in loving expectation of that day "when all men's weal shall be each man's care," when "nothing shall hurt or destroy in all my holy mountain," saith the Lord; and in our day we may live to see America, beloved mother of thrice grateful daughters, set at liberty, full and complete, from foamy King Gambrinus and fiery old King Alcohol.

Plan of Work of the National W. C. T. U. for 1883,

SHOWING THE AIMS, METHODS, AND BOUNDARIES OF THE DEPARTMENTS OF WORK, WITH A LIST OF NATIONAL SUPERINTENDENTS, AND THEIR SECRETARIES AND STANDING COMMITTEES.

NOTE 1. No Superintendent of a National Department fulfills her official obligation unless she steadily labors to secure in each State and Territory a Superintendent with whom she is in constant co-operation for the objects herein set forth, and each State Superintendent is in duty bound to secure, so far as practicable, the appointment of a local Superintendent in each W. C. T. U.

2. For all needed information and documents relative to these departments address their respective superintendents.

3. In the order of evolution, the departments of work are embraced under the following general classification: I. Preventive.

II. Educational; III. Evangelistic; IV. Social; V. Legal, to which
is added, VI. The Department of Organization.
Total number of departments, 28; committees, 2.

I. PREVENTIVE.

1. HEREDITY.

Supt.—MARY WEEKS BURNETT, M. D., Room 1, Central Hall, Chicago, Ill.

This department aims to enlighten the members of the W. C. T. U.
by wise and careful words concerning the relation of prenatal influences and natal inheritance to the appetite for intoxicating drinks.
Its methods are the circulation of books and leaflets, addresses by
lady physicians before the local unions, and meetings for women in
connection with District, State, and National Conventions.

2. HYGIENE.

Supt.—MRS. DR. J. H. KELLOGG, Sanitarium, Battle Creek, Mich.

Aims to extend the reverent study of God's health decalogue, with
a view to returning sanity in our methods of daily living. The study
of the laws of health, including their relation to food, dress, cleanliness, exercise, ventilation, and the entire physical conduct of life are
among the methods; also a department of hygiene in the *Union-Signal*
(our official organ), and instruction in the art of *home-making* as super-
added to "Housekeeping."

II. EDUCATIONAL.

1. SCIENTIFIC INSTRUCTION.

Supt.—MRS. MARY H. HUNT, Hyde Park, Mass.
Secretary.—MRS. C. C. ALFORD, 315 Monroe street, Brooklyn, N. Y.

Aims to introduce such text-books in chemistry, physiology, and
hygiene as inculcate the scientific importance of total abstinence into
the curriculum of all schools, seminaries, and colleges, but especially
into all normal and public schools, and to secure such legislation,
local and State, as shall make the study and teaching of the laws of
health, with special reference to the effects of stimulants upon the
human system, obligatory throughout the entire system of public
education.

2. SUNDAY-SCHOOL WORK.

Supt.—MISS LUCIA E. F. KIMBALL, 644 W. Monroe street, Chicago.

Aims to teach the same habits and principles as the foregoing, but
strictly from a Bible point of view, and by means of exercises and
lessons regularly prepared by established Sunday-school publications,
and taught on a quarterly Sabbath dedicated to this purpose.

3. JUVENILE WORK.

Supt.—Miss NELLIE H. BAYLEY, 78 Lincoln avenue, Chicago, Ill.

This department aims to instruct boys and girls in the reasonableness and duty of total abstinence from alcoholic stimulants, tobacco, and profanity, by a regular course of study, scientific, ethical, and governmental, systematically taught in juvenile temperance unions, bands of hope, or, with the military feature added, in cadets of temperance. Prizes are also offered for the best essays and debates, our engraving of the Mrs. Hayes' Memorial Portrait being adapted to this use. Entertainments, exhibitions, etc., are given, through which public sentiment is moulded and money made for the society. Prohibition and Home Protection principles may also be here illustrated and impressed.

4. TEMPERANCE LITERATURE.

Supt.—Miss JULIA COLMAN, 76 Bible House, New York.

Aims to prepare and circulate books, papers, leaflets, etc., for the general education of public sentiment, but especially for topical study in all the departments of W. C. T. U. work, that our local meetings may be made interesting and profitable, and our members thoroughly educated in all branches of Temperance Reform.

Miss Colman keeps on hand every variety of temperance literature.

5. INFLUENCING THE PRESS.

Supt.—Mrs. CAROLINE B. BUELL, 53 Bible House, New York.

Aims to keep the press, both religious and secular, thoroughly informed concerning the movements of the W. C. T. U., by means of a weekly bulletin from headquarters, also to set forth wisely and steadily the history, aims, and methods of our work, securing editorials and editorial paragraphs helpful to the education of public sentiment in favor of every department of our work, particular attention being paid to the metropolitan press in the twelve large cities, also to the associated press and co-operative newspapers, a superintendent to be secured in each State and a special correspondent in each large city; capital cities to receive special attention during political campaigns and sessions of the Legislature.

6. CONFERENCE WITH ECCLESIASTICAL, S. S., EDUCATIONAL, MEDICAL, AND OTHER ASSOCIATIONS.

Supt.—Mrs. EMILY McLAUGHLIN, 4 Story street, So. Boston, Mass.

Aims to secure the presentation of our work before all the societies above mentioned, and any others of suitable character, in towns, counties, districts, States, and the nation, and that the W. C. T. U. may be known and appreciated in influential quarters. The method is to endeavor through members of these associations to secure the passage of a resolution approving our work, and committing the associations themselves to do all in their power in their respective fields to advance the cause of total abstinence and prohibition.

7. RELATIVE STATISTICS.

Supt.—Mrs. FRANCES CROOK, cor. Madison avenue and Townsend street, Baltimore, Md.

Aims to make the people more intelligent regarding the waste, pauperism, and crime resulting from the liquor traffic, by gathering the latest statistics, properly classifying and placing them before the people in leaflets and through the press. These will be of service to our speakers and writers, and should come before the public in every possible way. A chart exhibiting relative statistics to the eye by means of lines and colors would be of service.

Tobacco statistics might be very properly included with the foregoing.

8. TRAINING SCHOOLS.

Supt.—Mrs. S. M. I. HENRY, Evanstown, Ill.

Aims to furnish careful systematic instruction by skilled specialists in all departments teaching our work, not only the theory, but the practice; the former by means of a course of study and reading, to be pursued at home, upon which written examination will be based, and the latter by conducting "model" meetings of a local, juvenile, and Y. W. C. T. U., a model Sunday-school temperance lesson, model Gospel institutes, conventions, etc. In this school, organizers, corresponding secretaries, superintendents of departments, etc., will be trained and certificates of proficiency awarded. At first this will be a summer training school, but it is hoped that eventually it may become permanent, and attract hundreds of earnest women who desire to enter on a Christian vocation.

III. EVANGELISTIC.

1. EVANGELISTIC.

Supt.—Mrs. H. W. SMITH, 4653 Germantown avenue, Philadelphia, Pa.

Aims to increase the interest of our society in Bible study, especially with reference to the exposition of temperance principles, by regularly furnishing them with lesson leaflets for use in local meetings, and to carry the Gospel cure to the drinking classes by holding evangelistic services in reading-rooms, depots, theatres, etc.; also by inviting pastors to preach upon the temperance question, securing a *union* temperance prayer-meeting of the churches once a quarter, on the regular prayer-meeting night; enlisting the people to build temperance tabernacles for the masses, and holding Gospel temperance institutes for the training of women in methods of conducting evangelistic services.

2. EVANGELISTIC WORK AMONG THE GERMANS.

Supt.—MRS. EMMA OBENAUER, 157 La Salle street, Chicago, Ill.

Aims to bring our work before the Germans, on the religious plane, and by the same methods enumerated under the superintendency of evangelistic work so far as may be practicable.

3. PRISONS AND POLICE STATIONS.

Supt.—MRS. J. K. BARNEY, Providence, R. I.

Aims to carry Gospel Temperance to men and women in prisons, jails, and alms houses, to co-operate in the work of Prisoners' Aid Associations; to aid in establishing women's reformatory prisons and Industrial Homes for the criminal class; to secure the appointment of women on State boards of charities; and the maintenance of matrons in all prisons and police stations where women are arrested or imprisoned. The Gospel and police matron work is directly related to the W. C. T. U., and carried on by personal visitation, by letter and literature. The other branches are co-operative with outside organizations, and involve letters and petitions to influence legislatures and corporations. In this way, philanthropic work on a grand scale may be instigated and inspired by our societies.

4. WORK AMONG INTEMPERATE WOMEN.

Supt.—MRS. GEO. S. HUNT, Portland, Me.

Aims to establish under State patronage and by private beneficence, Christian temperance homes for the drinking class among women, in two departments, one for those who can pay for treatment, another for those who cannot; also to circulate appropriate literature through the post-office and by personal visitation, in homes cursed by the intemperance of women.

5. WORK AMONG R. R. EMPLOYÉS.

Supt.—MISS JENNIE E. SMITH, Mountain Lake Park, Md.
MISS ADELAIDE SHERMAN, Secretary.

Aims to carry the Gospel and temperance pledge to R. R. employés, and to organize among them Gospel and temperance clubs, or "R. R. Unions."

6. SOLDIERS AND SAILORS.

Supt.—MRS. S. A. McCLEES, Yonkers, N. Y.

Aims to reach the army and navy with Gospel temperance, also the pledge and temperance literature, through co-operation with commanders and chaplains, by correspondents, articles in papers read by soldiers and sailors, and personal visitation. The methods of Miss Agnes Weston, of England, will be largely followed in this work.

7. TO SECURE THE USE OF THE UNFERMENTED JUICE OF THE GRAPE AT THE LORD'S TABLE.

Supt.—MISS MARY ALLEN WEST, Galesburg, Ill.

Aims to convince all good people that the pure juice of the grape should be substituted for wine at the Lord's table, in deference to the golden rule and the Pauline doctrine of regard for the weaker brother. Circulation of literature and appeals to ministerial assemblies are the methods employed.

8. SECURING DAY OF PRAYER IN WEEK OF PRAYER.

Supt.—MRS. ELLEN M. WATSON, 112 Smithfield St., Pittsburg, Pa.

Aims to secure by petitions from ecclesiastical and philanthropic bodies to the alliance, by articles in the secular and religious press and by private correspondence, in the annual programme of the Evangelical Alliance, a day of prayer in the week of prayer, to be devoted to the temperance reform.

IV. SOCIAL.

1. YOUNG WOMEN'S TEMPERANCE WORK.

Supt.—MRS. FRANCES J. BARNES, 73 East Fifty-fourth street, New York. MRS. F. S. EVANS, Secretary, 71 East Fifty-fourth street, New York.

Aims to enlist young women to form separate societies ("Y. W. C. T. Unions") for the purpose of making total abstinence a fashionable social custom, to the end that young men may be held to a higher standard of personal habits, and thus shielded from contamination, by a power analogous to that which has effectually restrained their sisters; also to teach young women the scientific and ethic reasons for total abstinence and prohibition, and to develop a new army of trained temperance workers, to whom the care of the children's work may be at once entrusted, and who will eventually replace the veterans of the W. C. T. U.

The methods are first, a social club (the Y. W. C. T. U. itself) in which young gentlemen become honorary members by signing the pledge and paying the membership fee of 50 cents per year; private and public entertainments; a systematic course of reading, and work in bands of hope; night schools for boys, reading-rooms, kitchen gardens, etc., etc.

2.   PARLOR MEETINGS.

Supt.—Mrs. Margaret Bottome, 117 East 17th street, New York.

Aims to reach the conservative class who do not attend public temperance meetings.   Invitations are sent as to a reception, and brief devotional exercises are followed by a bible talk, or practical temperance subjects are treated, and objections replied to in conversational style; literature may be given out at the close, or the autograph pledge book circulated.   Sometimes gentlemen come in at the conclusion of these exercises, and refreshments are served.

3.   KITCHEN GARDEN.

Chairman of Committee.—Miss Mary C. McClees, 141 Warburton street, Yonkers, N. Y.   Miss Hallie Quigley, Louisville, Ky.   Mrs. A. C. Robinson, Baltimore, Md.

Aims to enlist the efforts of young ladies in teaching by object lessons the household art to poor girls; with a view to ameliorating the conduct of life in their homes, present and future, and preparing them to earn their own living as skilled servants.   Specific temperance instruction may be incorporated with these lessons.

4.   FLOWER MISSION.

Supt.—Miss Jennie Casseday, 216 East Chestnut street, Louisville, Ky.

Aims to graft our work upon this beautiful philanthropy.   Bouquets to be tied with white ribbon and a scripture verse or selection to be attached, relative to temperance, our literature to be circulated to accompany flowers, and the total abstinence pledge offered at appropriate times.   Also an effort made to induce all ladies engaged in this department to meet for topical study according to the course prepared by our corresponding secretary.

5.   STATE AND COUNTY FAIRS.

Supt.—Mrs. Mary A. Leavitt, Vernon, Ind.

Aims to bring temperance ideas and practices in contact with the people at these and other great holiday gatherings by means of a booth (suitably designated by mottoes and pictures and other decorations) where temperance drinks are sold and literature circulated; also to secure if possible favorable reference to the subject in public addresses, made either by those appointed by authorities of the fair, or if this is impracticable, presentation of the subject by our own speakers.   This department protests against the sale of intoxicants on holiday occasions, and makes systematic effort to secure the enactment and enforcement of laws to this end.

6. RELATION OF TEMPERANCE TO CAPITAL AND LABOR.

Supt.—Mrs. M. C. Nobles, Atlantic Highlands, New Jersey.

Aims to induce employers to require total abstinence in employees, to extend the discrimination in favor of abstinent habits to every branch of insurance risks, to induce all organizations of working men to introduce the same discrimination into their societies, etc. The methods are circular letters, personal appeals, articles for the press, and efforts to secure editorial co-operation.

V. LEGAL.

1. LEGISLATION AND PETITIONS.

Supt.—Mrs. J. Ellen Foster, Clinton, Iowa.

Aims to secure prohibition by constitutional and statutory law in every State and Territory, and to secure a prohibitory amendment to the National Constitution. Methods are varied as the manifold work of the W. C. T. U. All roads lead to Rome, and every purpose and plan point to the consummation defined under this all-embracing "aim." Specifically, petitions to legislative bodies, systematic efforts to enforce existing law, and a course of study and reading for local unions are included under this department.

2. FRANCHISE.

Supt.—Mrs. M. G. C. Leavitt, 115 Warren ave., Boston, Mass.

To aid those States that desire to utilize for temperance purposes the school ballot, if already conferred, or to secure in whole or in part the ballot for women as a weapon of protection to their homes from the liquor traffic and its attendant evils. Methods—Circular letters, with instructions, forms of petition, etc.; distribution and sale of appropriate literature; articles to the press; correspondence and public addresses.

(N. B. —Neither this nor any other department of work is obligatory upon any Union, local or State.)

VI. DEPARTMENT OF ORGANIZATION.

1. SOUTHERN WORK.

Supt.—Mrs. Sallie F. Chapin, Charleston, S. C.

Aims to secure a thorough systematic organization of all the Southern States upon a basis of paid memberships in each local W. C. T. U. (at 50 cents a year), and the introduction, as rapidly as possible, of all our departments of work in each State and local W. C. T. U.

The work among colored people in the South contemplates the organization of separate W. C. T. Unions, local and State.

2. WORK AMONG GERMANS.

Supt.—Mrs. HENRIETTA SKELTON, Lake Bluff, Ill.

Aims at organizing our society among the German population to such a degree as may be practicable; introducing Sunday-school temperance lessons and other literature, and giving addresses in their own language; circulating *Der Bahnbrecher*, published at Chicago, and edited by Prof. A. Schmitz (organ of the German Total Abstinence Association), and co-operating with that Society so far as in our power. Send to A. F. Hofer, McGregor, Iowa, for German leaflets.

3. WORK AMONG THE SCANDINAVIANS.

Supt.—Mrs. N. H. HARRIS, Lake Bluff, Ill.

Aims and methods the same as the German work.

4. WORK AMONG THE COLORED PEOPLE OF THE NORTH.

Supt.—Mrs. CHAS. KINNEY, Port Huron, Mich.

Aims and methods identical with those described under work among the colored people South.

Religion in America
Series II

An Arno Press Collection

Adler, Felix. **Creed and Deed:** A Series of Discourses. New York, 1877.

Alexander, Archibald. **Evidences of the Authenticity, Inspiration, and Canonical Authority of the Holy Scriptures.** Philadelphia, 1836.

Allen, Joseph Henry. **Our Liberal Movement in Theology:** Chiefly as Shown in Recollections of the History of Unitarianism in New England. 3rd edition. Boston, 1892.

American Temperance Society. **Permanent Temperance Documents of the American Temperance Society.** Boston, 1835.

American Tract Society. **The American Tract Society Documents, 1824-1925.** New York, 1972.

Bacon, Leonard. **The Genesis of the New England Churches.** New York, 1874.

Bartlett, S[amuel] C. **Historical Sketches of the Missions of the American Board.** New York, 1972.

Beecher, Lyman. **Lyman Beecher and the Reform of Society:** Four Sermons, 1804-1828. New York, 1972.

[Bishop, Isabella Lucy Bird.] **The Aspects of Religion in the United States of America.** London, 1859.

Bowden, James. **The History of the Society of Friends in America.** London, 1850, 1854. Two volumes in one.

Briggs, Charles Augustus. **Inaugural Address and Defense,** 1891-1893. New York, 1972.

Colwell, Stephen. **The Position of Christianity in the United States,** in Its Relations with Our Political Institutions, and Specially with Reference to Religious Instruction in the Public Schools. Philadelphia, 1854.

Dalcho, Frederick. **An Historical Account of the Protestant Episcopal Church, in South-Carolina,** from the First Settlement of the Province, to the War of the Revolution. Charleston, 1820.

Elliott, Walter. **The Life of Father Hecker.** New York, 1891.

Gibbons, James Cardinal. **A Retrospect of Fifty Years.** Baltimore, 1916. Two volumes in one.

Hammond, L[ily] H[ardy]. **Race and the South:** Two Studies, 1914-1922. New York, 1972.

Hayden, A[mos] S. **Early History of the Disciples in the Western Reserve, Ohio;** With Biographical Sketches of the Principal Agents in their Religious Movement. Cincinnati, 1875.

Hinke, William J., editor. **Life and Letters of the Rev. John Philip Boehm:** Founder of the Reformed Church in Pennsylvania, 1683-1749. Philadelphia, 1916.

Hopkins, Samuel. **A Treatise on the Millennium.** Boston, 1793.

Kallen, Horace M. **Judaism at Bay:** Essays Toward the Adjustment of Judaism to Modernity. New York, 1932.

Kreider, Harry Julius. **Lutheranism in Colonial New York.** New York, 1942.

Loughborough, J. N. **The Great Second Advent Movement:** Its Rise and Progress. Washington, 1905.

M'Clure, David and Elijah Parish. **Memoirs of the Rev. Eleazar Wheelock, D.D.** Newburyport, 1811.

McKinney, Richard I. **Religion in Higher Education Among Negroes.** New Haven, 1945.

Mayhew, Jonathan. **Observations on the Charter and Conduct of the Society for the Propagation of the Gospel in Foreign Parts;** Designed to Shew Their Non-conformity to Each Other. Boston, 1763.

Mott, John R. **The Evangelization of the World in this Generation.** New York, 1900.

Payne, Bishop Daniel A. **Sermons and Addresses,** 1853-1891. New York, 1972.

Phillips, C[harles] H. **The History of the Colored Methodist Episcopal Church in America:** Comprising Its Organization, Subsequent Development, and Present Status. Jackson, Tenn., 1898.

Reverend Elhanan Winchester: Biography and Letters. New York, 1972.

Riggs, Stephen R. **Tah-Koo Wah-Kan; Or, the Gospel Among the Dakotas.** Boston, 1869.

Rogers, Elder John. **The Biography of Eld. Barton Warren Stone, Written by Himself:** With Additions and Reflections. Cincinnati, 1847.

Booth-Tucker, Frederick. **The Salvation Army in America:** Selected Reports, 1899-1903. New York, 1972.

Satolli, Francis Archbishop. **Loyalty to Church and State.** Baltimore, 1895.

Schaff, Philip. **Church and State in the United States** or the American Idea of Religious Liberty and its Practical Effects with Official Documents. New York and London, 1888. (Reprinted from *Papers of the American Historical Association,* Vol. II, No. 4.)

Smith, Horace Wemyss. **Life and Correspondence of the Rev. William Smith, D.D.** Philadelphia, 1879, 1880. Two volumes in one.

Spalding, M[artin] J. **Sketches of the Early Catholic Missions of Kentucky;** From Their Commencement in 1787 to the Jubilee of 1826-7. Louisville, 1844.

Steiner, Bernard C., editor. **Rev. Thomas Bray:** His Life and Selected Works Relating to Maryland. Baltimore, 1901. (Reprinted from *Maryland Historical Society Fund Publication,* No. 37.)

To Win the West: Missionary Viewpoints, 1814-1815. New York, 1972.

Wayland, Francis and H. L. Wayland. **A Memoir of the Life and Labors of Francis Wayland, D.D., LL.D.** New York, 1867. Two volumes in one.

Willard, Frances E. **Woman and Temperance:** Or, the Work and Workers of the Woman's Christian Temperance Union. Hartford, 1883.